MULTICULTURALISM, CRIME, AND CRIMINAL JUSTICE

MULTICULTURALISM, CRIME, AND CRIMINAL JUSTICE

Robert McNamara

Ronald Burns

NEW YORK   OXFORD
OXFORD UNIVERSITY PRESS

Oxford University Press is a department of the University of Oxford. It furthers the University's objective of excellence in research, scholarship, and education by publishing worldwide. Oxford is a registered trademark of Oxford University Press in the UK and certain other countries.

Published in the United States of America by Oxford University Press
198 Madison Avenue, New York, NY 10016, United States of America.

For titles covered by Section 112 of the US Higher Education Opportunity Act, please visit www.oup.com/us/he for the latest information about pricing and alternate formats.

Library of Congress Cataloging-in-Publication Data

Names: McNamara, Robert Hartmann, author. | Burns, Ronald G., 1968- author.
Title: Multiculturalism, crime, and criminal justice / Robert McNamara,
   Ronald Burns.
Description: New York, NY : Oxford University Press, 2018.
Identifiers: LCCN 2017013361 (print) | LCCN 2017016858 (ebook) | ISBN
   9780190642686 (ebook) | ISBN 9780190642631 (pbk) | ISBN 9780190642693
   (looseleaf)
Subjects: LCSH: Discrimination in criminal justice administration—United
   States. | Criminal justice, Administration of—United States. |
   Multiculturalism—United States.
Classification: LCC HV9950 (ebook) | LCC HV9950 .M427 2018 (print) | DDC
   364.30973—dc23
LC record available at https://lccn.loc.gov/2017013361

Printing number: 9 8 7 6 5 4

Printed by Webcom, Canada.

DEDICATION

To Carey, who sees no color; and to Connor, whom I hope
follows in his mother's footsteps.

To Lisa, Ryan, Lily, and all others who make the world a better place.

BRIEF CONTENTS

CONTENTS

PREFACE

The creation of this work stemmed from the absence of a thorough work on diversity, multiculturalism, crime, and justice. Many developments and incidents in relation to the topics have prompted us to develop a book that comprehensively addresses the issues in a reader-friendly manner. Consider, for instance, the incidents and developments in the last several years, and how justice-based practices have impacted police-community relations and perceptions of justice. Some of these events are startling reminders of the fragility of human life and the delicate nature of the relationships we form with others. In thinking about these issues, which are discussed in each chapter, we note that there is increasingly more evidence and research being done on the disproportionality within the justice process and why it occurs. Unfortunately, much of the evidence is mixed or inconclusive and the answers to why discrimination occurs, and how it impacts our society, continue to elude researchers, policy makers, and practitioners. Questions still remain about whether the system is biased against minorities, whether offenders tend to come primarily from minority groups, or whether they are so heavily represented in crime statistics due to greater attention given to certain neighborhoods by the police, which leads to more arrests.

We hope that this text contributes to the multiculturalism narrative, particularly as it relates to crime and justice. The significance of this book is evidenced by events such as the recent episodes of White officers shooting Black men, and the subsequent backlashes, including the killing of police officers, some of whom, ironically, were protecting protestors at a demonstration against the excessive use of force by police officers. Other events, such as the debate about whether transgender people should be allowed to use the bathroom of their choice, have also had an impact on public policy and the public's perception of race, gender, discrimination, and other issues. Race, ethnicity, crime, and discrimination were also central topics of discussion in one of the most sensational presidential campaigns in recent memory, with two controversial and polarizing candidates, along with allegations of impropriety and insensitivity launched at each party and candidate by both sides. All of these events shape and define this country's understanding of diversity and multiculturalism and their economic, social, and political impacts on its members.

This book focuses on marginalized groups and expands understanding of multiculturalism to the entire criminal justice field. Particularly, the work addresses how different groups are impacted by law enforcement, the courts, and correctional agencies, including discussion of the unique problems and issues each group faces. Most significant for this book is coverage of how multiculturalism affects officials within the criminal justice system. Thus, the chapters include coverage of the unique problems members of minority groups face as individuals who work within the system.

The book provides a comprehensive view of multiculturalism as well as the problems stemming from it in relation to all dimensions of the system. It is a valuable tool for professors teaching a wide array of courses, but even those who strictly use it for courses on diversity and multiculturalism will find it a compelling and comprehensive resource for their students. Perhaps equally important, the book, while empirically accurate and balanced in its presentation of various issues, is written in a style that is easy for students to understand, and instructors will find it helpful for generating classroom discussion.

Within the discussion of the experiences of the various groups, some of the most controversial and celebrated topics within criminal justice are explored. Examples include the impact of police shootings upon minority communities, disparities in sentencing for African Americans, drug trafficking and Hispanics, hate crimes against gays and lesbians, and gang problems and human trafficking among Asian Americans. In addition, attention is given to the cultural and social biases found in the processing of offenders, as well as the host of internal problems faced by different employees within the criminal justice system.

The book is divided into three logically organized parts that would likely be the outline for a course on this topic. Part I of the book deals with developing an understanding of the difficulty in defining multiculturalism, race, and ethnicity. These topics are critical to laying the foundation of the problems various groups face in American society. There is also discussion of the structure and process of group dynamics, the various ways people communicate and develop ideas, and the ways in which this leads to a perception of different groups and cultures. We also address how these tendencies translate into problems for disenfranchised groups.

Part II of the book addresses cultural specifics in the criminal justice system. It consists of several chapters that include a description of cultural groups that are most likely to experience problems within the criminal justice system. These include African Americans, Hispanic/Latinos, Asian American, Native Americans, women, the LGBT community, the elderly, and juveniles. The problems each group experience are discussed in each of these chapters, for instance as they relate to profiling, sentencing disparities, jurisdictional issues, child trafficking, misuse of powers, hate crimes, health concerns (e.g., for elderly inmates), sexual harassment, and immigration issues.

Part III of the book addresses the means by which multiculturalism affects criminal justice personnel in particular and the system as a whole, preparing for and addressing multiculturalism through policies and training, and the future of multiculturalism in the criminal justice system. With chapters on police, courts, and corrections, the book addresses key components of problems internal to the criminal justice system. This is true not only of the particular problems certain groups might face, but also how and in what ways do criminal justice personnel interact with other cultural groups. In this section we also address responses to diversity and multiculturalism with particular concern for training and policies. A final chapter offers a look to the future of multiculturalism, crime, and criminal justice, which provides a suitable concluding chapter of the book.

Throughout the book, a comprehensive assessment of the issues and problems for each group or topic are presented, with an eye toward a balanced description of the material. This approach is useful for instructors who wish to explore individual topics in more depth and generate lively discussion. Thus, rather than simply being an historical account of each group or simply a collection of characteristics of them, the problems and issues come alive in the context of a discussion, which allows students to grasp the underlying factors that contribute to the problems.

The book has many strengths not found in similar works focused on multiculturalism, diversity, and criminal justice. To begin, it offers a thorough grounding in the foundational chapters about the nature of social interaction, group dynamics, and communication. This foundation provides context for the remaining chapters, which focus on a variety of different groups and their involvement in crime and the criminal justice system. Second, carefully constructed boxed inserts conveying important issues and incidents alert students to how these themes recur. These boxed inserts provide short examples of the issues in the chapter, and are accompanied by critical thinking questions.

Further, boxed inserts of "You Make the Call" provide examples of dilemmas as they relate to multiculturalism. These real life scenarios challenge students to appreciate the complexity and difficulty of decisions that are made regarding multiculturalism in the criminal justice system. The organization of the book also sets it apart from many other books, as it is divided into three logically organized sections. In Part 2, in particular, our work differs from others in the sense that we devote entire chapters to particular groups with regard to crime and criminal justice. Particularly, we focus closely on African Americans, Hispanic Americans, Asian Americans, Native Americans, women, the gay community, the elderly, and juveniles. Other books comment on these groups, however our directed focus on each sets this work apart.

Finally, both authors have published scholarly works addressing issues pertaining to multiculturalism and crime/justice, and are familiar with the historical and recent research literature in the area. As such, recent, relevant research is shared throughout the text.

Each chapter has learning objectives, a list of key terms, key terms in bold type, discussion questions, and suggestions for further reading. There is also a complete list of references, a companion website that acts as a student study guide with chapter outlines, study questions, and update features, and an instructor's guide and test bank to assist professors in the design and implementation of the course. Also, PowerPoint slides and transparencies have been developed for each chapter.

One merely needs to consider recent events around the country (perhaps most notably in Ferguson, Baltimore, New York, and Chicago) to recognize the significance of multiculturalism and diversity as they relate to crime and the criminal justice system. This book addresses these and many other issues, while enlightening readers regarding three very important areas: diversity, multiculturalism, and criminal justice.

Many social issues currently challenge our society, however some pose more obstacles than others. This book covers key aspects of important contributors to many of society's concerns, and does so in a manner that brings the issues to life. We hope you enjoy reading it, and that it encourages you to give due consideration to how injustices occur, what can be done to prevent them, and how each one of us can continue to make the world a better place.

ACKNOWLEDGMENTS

A project of this magnitude cannot be accomplished without a substantial amount of assistance. While authors often get all the credit, success usually comes from those behind the scenes making things happen for them. This is true in our cases, where we had many people picking up the slack while we were distracted and encouraging us to work harder. From a professional standpoint, we cannot express enough gratitude to Steve Helba, Larissa Albright, and Frank Mortimer from Oxford University Press for their support, encouragement, and belief in both the project and in us. We also owe our families a debt of gratitude for their patience and understanding while completing this project. Families of academics often bear a considerable cost that is often overlooked and it is something we wish to acknowledge and we would like to express our thanks for the gift of being able to pursue our passions. We would also like to thank the following reviewers for their input: Scott Chenault, University of Central Missouri; Addrain Conyers, Marist College; Charles Crawford, Western Michigan University; Nicole Doctor, Ivy Tech Community College; B. C. Franson, Southwest Minnesota State University; Robert Haywood, Ivy Tech Community College; Kelly Howard, Kean University; Karen McElrath, Fayetteville State University; Tim Turner, Anderson University.

ABOUT THE AUTHORS

Robert Hartmann McNamara is currently a professor of criminal justice at the Citadel. He is the former associate provost and dean of the graduate college at the Citadel and the former founding associate dean of evening undergraduate studies at the Citadel and founding director of the 2 + 2 program in criminal justice. He is the author of twenty-five books, including: *Juvenile Delinquency: Bridging Theory to Practice; Problem Children: Special Populations in Delinquency; Multiculturalism in the Criminal Justice System; Homelessness in America*, 3 vols.; *The Lost Population: Status Offenders in America; In My Father's Hands; Boundary Dwellers: The Lives of Homeless Women in Transitional Housing; A New Look at American Society; Perspectives on Social Problems; Understanding Contemporary Social Problems; Crossing the Line: Interracial Couples in the South; Crime Displacement: The Other Side of Prevention; The Times Square Hustler: Male Prostitution in New York City; Sex, Scams, and Street Life: The Sociology of New York City's Times Square; Beating the Odds: Crime, Poverty, and Life in the Inner City; Police and Policing; The Urban Landscape: Selected Readings*; and *Social Gerontology*. Dr. McNamara has also served as a senior research fellow for the National Strategy Information Center, the Policy Lab, the Police Executive Research Forum, in Washington, DC, and the Pacific Institute for Research and Evaluation in Baltimore, Maryland.

Dr. McNamara has also published numerous articles on a variety of topics and has been a consultant for state, federal, and private agencies on topics such as AIDS, drug abuse, urban redevelopment, homelessness, policing, gangs, and healthcare. He also worked with the Regional Community Policing Institute at Eastern Kentucky University to study school safety in eight high schools across the state. He also worked with the Mexican government and the National Strategy Information Center to develop an anti-corruption curriculum in their public schools. In 2015, Dr. McNamara was a fellow at the American Council on Education as part of the Emerging Leaders program, and was a fellow at the Executive Leadership Academy at the American Leadership Institute in Washington, DC. He has extensive leadership training and has worked with a number of institutions in higher education on a variety of issues. Dr. McNamara holds a PhD in sociology from Yale University.

Ronald Burns is department chair and professor of criminal justice at Texas Christian University (TCU). He has published over seventy-five articles in areas such as multiculturalism in the criminal justice system, the criminal justice system, policing, and white-collar crime. He is the author, coauthor, or editor of eight books, including *Multiculturalism in the Criminal Justice System*; *Environmental Law, Crime and Justice* (2nd edition); *Federal Law Enforcement*; *Policing: A Modular Approach*; *Critical Issues in Criminal Justice*; *The Criminal Justice System*; *Environmental Crime: A Sourcebook*, and *Policing and Violence*. Dr. Burns graduated from Florida State University in 1997 and has been at TCU ever since.

PART I

AN INTRODUCTION TO MULTICULTURALISM

CHAPTER 1

INTRODUCTION

CHAPTER OBJECTIVES

After reading this chapter, you should be able to:

- Define the issues surrounding race and ethnicity in the United States
- Define concepts such as race, ethnicity, minority groups, multiculturalism, prejudice, and discrimination as they are used in the social science literature
- Contrast the debate of whether or not multiculturalism is a valuable idea in American society
- Understand how race and ethnicity play a role in the criminal justice system

- In February 2015, at the University of Missouri, in response to the way the president addressed matters relating to race and discrimination against students, a graduate student went on a hunger strike and at least thirty Black football players refused to play for the team unless the president resigned or was fired. A few days later, President Tom Wolf stepped down.
- In June 2015, in Charleston, South Carolina, Dylann Roof, a twenty-one-year-old student, entered the Emanuel African Methodist Episcopal Church and opened fire on a group of parishioners who were part of a Bible study group. He killed nine people and injured several others. Roof allegedly singled out victims "because of their race and in order to interfere with their exercise of their religion."
- In July 2014, Aniya "Ray Ray" Parker, a transgender woman of color was shot in the head and killed as she was fleeing from three men who had confronted her on a sidewalk in Hollywood. Los Angeles Police Department officers immediately told news reporters at the scene that this tragic incident appeared to be a "robbery gone bad." Within hours, local media ran headlines of a transgender person killed in a "botched robbery." The police, they reported, were not considering this a hate crime but simply a random "robbery gone sideways."

- In July 2016, Alton Sterling, a Black man, was shot and killed during an altercation with Baton Rouge police officers. Protesters took to the streets nationwide after video surfaced of his fatal encounter. The next day a video of the fatal police shooting of another Black man in Minnesota, Philando Castile, went viral.
- Also in July 2016, three police officers were killed and three other were wounded in an ambush in Baton Rouge, Louisiana, by a former marine who was angry with the police for the recent shooting of Sterling and Castile.
- In Dallas, Texas, five police officers were killed in an ambush by a gunman with alleged ties to the Black Lives Matter movement. Like the situation in Baton Rouge, these officers were killed in response to incidents involving officer shootings of Black men around the country.

Incidents such as these suggest that the United States has a long history of tension between different groups, particularly as they relate to race, ethnicity, sexual orientation, and religion. While many refer to America as a **melting pot**, or a society that blends together a variety of backgrounds and cultures into a cohesive whole, this is actually a misnomer. While there is a great deal of diversity in the United States, there is also considerable intergroup conflict. According to the U.S. Census Bureau, there are approximately 322 million people living in America, many of whom come from a host of different backgrounds.[1] This diversity is one of the defining features of American culture, and, at the same time, presents one of its more difficult and enduring problems.

On one hand, living in a society where everyone is the same has advantages. For instance, in small **homogeneous societies**, people tend to know each other more intimately, they tend to see the world the same way, making disagreements less common, and the sense of conformity and treatment of others is more equitable. People in societies such as this tend to be figuratively "on the same page" with regard to social life. People also feel more connected to the larger society.

The downside to living in such a place, however, is that change happens slowly, if at all.

Life in small towns can be characterized as having a strong sense of social cohesion and collective conscience.

As life becomes more diverse, such as in major cities, there are different ideas about what is appropriate and acceptable. This can sometimes lead to disagreements about elements of social life.

Additionally, people can be too intimately involved in each other's day to day lives, making privacy difficult. Ask anyone who lives in a small town: one of the things they like the most, and, at the same time, the least, about living there is that they are known by most people. In general, social control is easier to achieve in small towns because there is general agreement about what is right or wrong, good or bad, legal or illegal. It is what sociologist Émile Durkheim called the **collective conscience**.[2] In other words, the morality of a society is stronger because there is greater consensus on the meaning and importance of social life.

In contrast, in **heterogeneous societies**, people come from a wide range of backgrounds and experiences. They may come from other countries, participate in cultures with different attitudes, values, norms, and belief systems, and there tends to be a lower degree of consensus on how people should meet their social responsibilities. In other words, the people living in diverse societies tend to have different ideas about how the world works as well as their place in it. In Durkheim's terms, the collective conscience tends to be weaker since there is a lack of consensus as well as a generally lower degree of connectedness to the larger group.[3]

This also means that people tend to think of social relationships in a different way. Instead of building trust and intimacy, people tend to interact based on what the people around them can offer in meeting their individual needs. It is this distinction that surrounds much of the efforts relating to community policing. How does the government or the police department generate a sense of community in places where little collective conscience exists? How can police officers bring people together in a neighborhood to solve problems in the spirit of cooperation?

Living in a diverse society also means that some groups are going to acquire more economic, social, and political power than others. In fact, that is often how groups distinguish themselves: by their ownership or control of scarce resources. How does living in a diverse society create problems for groups that do not have much power? How are they treated? What are the consequences for being placed in a less powerful status? Much of these discussions relate to criminal justice in that differences in crime statistics, sentencing practices, the use of police discretion, and the overall treatment of minority group members are all symptoms of larger issues. While this book does not attempt to solve the problems of the unequal treatment of some groups, it does explore how some groups are treated when they come to the attention of the criminal justice system. This book also examines what it is like to be a member of a minority group and work within the system itself.

Prior to any discussion of how some groups are treated with regard to crime and criminal justice, a number of terms must be defined. In research methodology, this is called **operationalization**. In simple terms, it refers to the way concepts are defined. For example, when people talk about minority groups, they might have different ideas about what that really means. Some might think in terms of numerical size (e.g., the fewest number of redheads in a group of people) or they might use political influence (e.g., they do not have a lot of political power so they are not able to change policy or laws regulating certain behaviors). In the next few sections, we will spend some time defining our terms to ensure that readers understand what we mean by them.

RACE

Race has a variety of meanings, which can make its discussion confusing and difficult. In fact, probably the only thing about race that is clear is that people are confused about the proper use of the term. If one looked at the definition of race in biology textbooks, they would likely find that race has a precise meaning. It would say something like, "a biological race is a genetically isolated group characterized by a high degree of inbreeding that leads to distinctive gene frequencies. This distinctiveness is made most apparent by the presence of inherited physical characteristics that differentiate members of a group from others."[4] What does that mean? It means that, essentially, you can see the differences between people from different races.

However, it is very difficult to consider race in a strictly biological sense. Given that people have migrated over a wide range of geographic areas for hundreds of years, pure genetic types have not existed for some time, if ever. Think about it for a minute. Are there mutually exclusive races? Can you really tell where one race begins and another race ends? If so, on what basis is that difference identified? It is not as though a person can take a blood test to determine their race; such measures do not work with any real accuracy. Given interbreeding of races over the sweep of history, where, for example, many African Americans are light-skinned and a large number of Whites have African American ancestry, is it even possible to tell where to draw the line between races?

As an illustration, several years ago, Reverend Al Sharpton, a Black community activist who has spent his career exposing racism and the mistreatment of African Americans, was discovered to be related to former U.S. senator Strom Thurmond, a conservative Republican from South Carolina who spent a good part of his career maintaining the White-dominated status quo in the South.[5] This ironic familial tie serves as an example of the difficulty in separating races.

Though race is not a useful biological category, it is clear there are certain groups with similar traits. What is important is that race becomes significant, not because it matters in a biological sense, but because society has constructed it in such a way to symbolize certain attitudes, values, and beliefs about members who possess those physical traits. Race matters, in other words, because society has made it matter. This is sometimes referred to as the **social construction of race**. Every culture must determine which physical features are used to define membership in certain races (Americans typically use skin color) and also determine which attitudes and values are associated with a particular

Al Sharpton, one of the more controversial figures in American society, actually has a historical linkage to a prominent and ultra conservative Southern White family.

race. Simply put, people attach significance to the concept of race and consider it a real and important way to categorize people. As long as people believe that differences in certain physical traits are meaningful, they will act on those beliefs, which influence how they see and interact with others. Unfortunately, in doing so, people often rely on stereotypes to determine the behavior patterns of certain groups.

Another problem with using the term race is that it often suggests a type of homogeneity among the different races. When Americans talk about "Blacks" in the United States, they typically think of African Americans, or those whose ancestry dates back to American slavery. However, there are a host of differences between Jamaicans, Haitians, and even immigrants from various parts of Africa, which have little in common with African Americans. Similarly, another example might be to use the term "Whites" as if all are part of the same cultural group. There are significant differences between Polish Americans and Jewish Americans as well as Irish Americans and Italian Americans, yet we often do not see those differences when using those labels.[6]

ETHNICITY

In its most simplistic form, an ethnic group is a collection of individuals and organizations identified by national origin, cultural distinctiveness, racial characteristics or religious affiliation. This gets a bit tricky since most textbooks define ethnicity as being a distinction based on cultural heritage and racial groups based on physical features. However, because of the problems and disagreement on its scientific validity, many social scientists have avoided using the term "race" and instead use "ethnic group" to describe those groups commonly defined as racial. In the United States, African Americans, Chinese Americans, and Native Americans all have the elements of ethnic groups: a unique culture and in some cases even physical territory. But at the same time most members of these groups are physically differently from Americans of European origin. Calling these groups ethnic seems reasonable because there are always consistent and significant cultural traits that set them apart from other groups.[7]

MINORITY GROUPS

This seems simple enough, right? The group with the fewest members. But minority status is not necessarily the result of being outnumbered. In the social sciences, a minority group is defined as a subordinate group whose members have significantly less control or power over their own lives than the members of the dominant group. While numerical size may be important and related, the issue is really one of power.[8]

In one sense, the idea of minority groups seems fair to people. After all, this is a democracy and the majority rules. The subordination of a minority, however, is more than its inability to rule over society. A member of a minority group experiences fewer opportunities for education, wealth, and success that go beyond any personal shortcoming they may have. In other words a minority group does not share in proportion to its numbers what a given society defines as valuable.[9]

Moreover, being numerically superior does not guarantee power, control over its destiny, or majority status. For example, think of the Republic of South Africa during the apartheid regime. During that era, the majority of people in South Africa were Black, but under the apartheid system of government, Blacks did not have any significant control over their lives. In terms of making sense of minority groups, the following are important characteristics to consider.

DISTINGUISHING PHYSICAL OR CULTURAL TRAITS

Each society has its own arbitrary standard for determining which characteristics are most important in determining if a person belongs to a minority group. Examples might include skin color (as in the case of African Americans in the United States) or fluency in a certain language (as in the case of Hispanics/Latinos).

UNEQUAL TREATMENT BY THOSE IN POWER

As mentioned, minorities experience unequal treatment and have less power over their lives than members of a dominant group. Social inequality may be created or maintained in a variety of ways including prejudice, discrimination, and/or segregation. In extreme

During apartheid, Blacks in South Africa, who constituted a majority of the
population, had little control over their own lives.

cases, the dominant group attempts to eliminate minorities completely, what is sometimes
referred to as **extermination**.

INVOLUNTARY MEMBERSHIP

Membership into a minority group is not voluntary. Often this involuntary membership is
not changeable either. This is particularly true in American society, where skin color and
other physical features often identify a minority.

SOLIDARITY OF MEMBERS

Perhaps due to the mistreatment or denial of equality, minority members are very conscious of their status. They also tend to be more sympathetic to other similarly stigmatized groups. This can explain some of the relationships minority groups form with
each other (e.g., women as a discriminated group and the gay community). At the same
time, minority groups can also be hostile towards each other. An example might be
some of the tension between African Americans and Hispanics, who, because of their
unequal treatment, feel a sense of competition for power, however little it might be.
Thus, there is a sense of exclusivity to most groups, but particularly those that have been
mistreated or denied equal status in society. Because of their position in society, there
is a need for affiliation.

In prisons for example, inmates often segregate themselves by ethnicity. For example, let's say that a White male inmate is new to the prison but does not wish to join the Aryan Brotherhood gang (the noted White supremacist prison gang), preferring to remain on his own. The norm of gang solidarity is so strong that members from every gang in the prison will attempt to victimize that inmate until he makes the decision to join a particular gang. If the inmate does join the Aryan Brotherhood, his contact with African American or Hispanic gangs will be limited because they are perceived as a threat to him. However, all gang members in the prison, regardless of race, generally oppose the correctional staff and the administration. In this example, being a member of a group not only increases the cohesion between members and demonstrates the tension between the groups, it also identifies the commonality of the groups as they come together against a common adversary.

IN-GROUP MARRIAGE

As a general rule, most people marry people a lot like themselves in terms of religious background, educational levels, occupational levels, and ethnicity. A member of a dominant group is often unwilling to join a supposedly inferior minority by marrying one of its members. Moreover, the group's sense of solidarity encourages marriages within the group and discourages out-group marriages.[10] This is why for so many years interracial marriage, particularly when Blacks married Whites, was considered unacceptable to many Americans.[11] This has since changed and interracial marriage is far more common today than in the past, but at one time there were laws that prohibited Blacks from marrying Whites.[12]

TYPES OF MINORITY GROUPS

In making the distinction between different types of minority groups, there is an immediate problem: what are the boundaries between the criteria? While race as a concept is defined by the physical distinctions between one group of people and another, there are instances where physical features are insufficient. For example, Hispanics/Latinos have some clearly defined physical features, but they are generally considered an ethnic group rather than a racial one. Similarly, Jews would normally be categorized as a religious group, but because their culture is such an essential component to their identity, experts tend to classify them as an ethnic group. This is why, as mentioned earlier, using the term ethnicity seems more reasonable. However, the thing to remember is that this distinction is used as a general way of categorizing minorities and should not be taken as definitive and complete.

RACIAL GROUPS

This term is reserved for those minorities who are classified according to obvious physical differences. The crucial words are obvious and physical. What is obvious? Hair color? Earlobe shape? As mentioned, each society defines that which is considered obvious. In the United States, skin color is perhaps the main characteristic in determining the difference between one race and another. In the United States, minority races include Blacks, Native Americans, and Asian Americans.

ETHNIC GROUPS

Minority groups who are designated by their ethnicity are distinguished from the dominant group on the basis of cultural differences such as language, attitudes toward marriage, food habits, and so on. Ethnic groups are set apart from others because of their national origin or distinctive cultural patterns. Ethnic groups in the United States include a grouping that we refer to collectively as *Hispanics* or *Latinos*. While there are distinguishing physical features that might cause someone to consider this group a racial category, because language and heritage is such a fundamental part of the Hispanic and Latino experience, they are classified as an ethnic group instead. This includes Puerto Ricans, Cubans, Mexicans, and other Latin Americans in the United States. European ethnic groups include: Irish, German, Polish, Norwegian, and Italian, among others.

RELIGIOUS GROUPS

The third basis for minority status is association with a religion other than the dominant faith. As mentioned, Jews are excluded from this category and placed among ethnic groups because in their case, culture is a more important defining trait than religious ideology. Jews share a cultural tradition that goes beyond theology. In this sense, it is appropriate to view them as an ethnic group rather than as members of a religious faith.

GENDER GROUPS

The final attribute that divides dominant and subordinate groups is gender: males are the social majority and females, although more numerous, are relegated to the position of social minority. Women are a minority even though they do not exhibit all the characteristics outlined earlier. For instance, women encounter prejudice and discrimination and are physically visible. Group membership is involuntary and women who are members of racial and ethnic minorities face special challenges to achieving equality. They suffer from a form of double jeopardy because they belong to two separate minority groups: a racial or ethnic group plus a subordinate gender group.[13]

CREATING SUBORDINATE GROUPS

You might be wondering how this all happens. How did society get to a point where there are all these groups and some of them are mistreated? You may be also wondering why such groups might stay in this country, given the way they have been treated. These are good questions and some of the answer is found in how some minority groups came to this country in the first place. There are really three situations that are likely to lead to the construction of a minority group: migration, annexation, and colonialism.

MIGRATION

Migration is the general term to describe any transfer of population. There are really two types of migration, where people come into a country. **Voluntary migration** consists of those people who immigrate to a new country willingly looking for a better life.

Upon arrival however, they often find themselves in the position of social minority. The immigrant is often set apart from the dominant group by cultural or physical traits or religious affiliation.

Although many may come to the new country voluntarily, the choice to leave the home country is often due to a lack of options. Wars, political unrest, or economic disasters in native countries (such as the potato crop failure in Ireland and Germany of the 1840s,) are often the catalyst behind migration. In contrast, **involuntary migration** occurs, for instance, when individuals have been brought into a new land as slaves.

ANNEXATION

There are times when countries will attach land as part of a war or conquest. An example would be the treaty that ended the Mexican-American war in 1848, which gave the United States California, Utah, Nevada, most of New Mexico, and parts of Arizona, Wyoming, and Colorado. When annexation occurs, the dominant group usually makes a considerable effort to force a change in the attitudes, values, and beliefs of the minority groups.

COLONIALISM

This is the most frequent way for one group of people to dominate another. Colonialism is the cultural, political, economic, and social domination of a people by a foreign power for an extended period of time. Unlike annexation, it does not involve actual incorporation into the dominant people's nation. Relations between the colonial nation and the colonized people are similar to those between a dominant group and exploited subordinate groups. The colonial subjects are generally limited to menial jobs, and the profits from their labor and from natural resources benefit members of the ruling class. Interestingly, while most of the countries that were colonies prior to World War I have achieved political independence, many of them could not develop their own industries and technology. As a result, they remained dependent on their dominators long after they separated from them politically. This dependence and domination is known as **neocolonialism**.[14]

THE CONSEQUENCES OF SUBORDINATE GROUP STATUS

What consequences do members feel as being a part of a minority group? Essentially there are six outcomes for minority groups: extermination, expulsion, secession, segregation, fusion, assimilation.

Extermination is the most extreme way of dealing with a subordinate group. Today the term **genocide** is used to describe the deliberate, systematic killing of an entire people or nation. While it has been associated with Nazi Germany, other forms of ethnic cleansing have occurred in other parts of the world. **Expulsion** is another extreme consequence of being a minority group. As will be discussed in the chapter on Native Americans, essentially, the U.S. government drove many tribes out of their tribal land and forced them to live in uninhabitable locations. This created problems with the physical health of many Native Americans that actually resulted in the death of many members of this group, which might be considered a form of extermination.[15]

Secession is another strategy, whereby minority groups sometimes want to depart from their country or at least have an opportunity to create their own society. For example, Pakistan was created in 1947 when India was partitioned. The predominantly Muslim areas in the north became Pakistan, making India predominantly Hindu.

Segregation of minority groups usually occurs when the other strategies are not possible or effective. This usually occurs when the dominant group is forced to coexist with the minority group. However, the way the problem is addressed is to simply limit contact between the dominant group and minority members. In the United States the extent of racial isolation at one time was significant, especially between Whites and African Americans. An analysis of the 2010 census showed that neighborhood segregation is still problematic despite increases in diversity in the United States. This is especially true in the largest United States cities over the past twenty years. African Americans remain concentrated in segregated neighborhoods and immigrants still settle into particular neighborhoods where others like them are located.[16] This pattern is not limited to impoverished inner-cities: they include all-Black middle class or affluent suburban neighborhoods as well.

Even when minority groups attempt to assimilate, there can be an unequal access to opportunities for success.

Moreover, residential segregation exists for other minorities, such as Hispanics and Asian Americans, but the trend is usually less profound than that for African Americans.[17]

Cultural fusion is the goal of multiculturalism, where minority and majority groups come together to form an entirely new group. An example of cultural fusion occurred during the first part of the twentieth century, where the public believed that the United States was a cultural melting pot. The public became convinced that America should meld all of its unique cultures into one unifying ideology. This, people said, would eliminate racism, bigotry, discrimination and inter-group conflict. However, as mentioned, despite the use of the term in popular culture, it is a mistake to think of the United States as an ethnic mixing bowl. While there are superficial signs of fusion, more significant trends indicate that Americans may think little of the contribution of subordinate groups.[18]

Finally, **assimilation** is the process by which the subordinate group takes on the characteristics of the dominant group and is eventually accepted as part of that group. In the United States assimilation is difficult because the group must give up their cultural traditions to become a part of a different and often condescending culture. Members of minority groups often discover that even when these changes are made, the dominant culture still casts them in a secondary position. The result leaves the minority member in a position of marginality: they do not belong to either the dominant culture nor are they accepted completely by their native one.[19]

PREJUDICE AND DISCRIMINATION

Prejudice and discrimination are closely intertwined, so much so that people are likely to view them as the same thing. In reality they are quite distinct. **Prejudice** is a negative attitude toward certain people based solely on their membership in a particular group. Individuals are "prejudged" on the basis of whatever undesirable characteristic the whole group is assumed to have. **Discrimination** refers to behavior, particularly the unequal treatment of people, because they are members of a particular group.[20]

The relationship between prejudice and discrimination is complex. Although they are likely to go together, as Robert K. Merton demonstrated in the following typology, sometimes they do not. In fact, there are four different ways or permutations, that people may combine prejudice and discrimination. The **unprejudiced non-discriminator** is the most desirable from the point of view of American political and social values. This individual accepts other racial or ethnic groups both in belief and practice. They embrace the idea of difference, of cultural diversity as a healthy concept, and do not try to impose their own cultural and social ideas on to others. The **prejudiced discriminator** has negative feelings toward a particular group or groups and translates these sentiments into unequal and negative treatment of people in that group. Examples might include members of the Neo-Nazi party or members of the Ku Klux Klan. White supremacists in general typically have strong attitudes against Blacks and other minority groups, and they advocate segregated schools and neighborhoods.

These two types are relatively easy to understand. One is a person who accepts all people as they are, without any judgment, while the other is a person who discriminates against others. Hate groups are smaller in size but intense in their feelings towards anyone other than people like themselves. More subtle forms of discrimination and prejudice emerge with the latter two linkages. For instance, the **prejudiced non-discriminator** is the type of person who might be called a closet bigot; someone who is prejudiced against members of some groups but does not translate these attitudes into discriminatory practices. A landlord, for example may be prejudiced against Asian Americans yet still rent apartments to them because of laws forbidding housing discrimination.

Perhaps the most difficult to grasp is the **unprejudiced discriminator**. A person in this category treats members of some groups unequally not because they have any personal animosity towards them but because it is simply advantageous to do so.[21] In the 1970s, for example, it was common for real estate agents to engage in "steering" of minority clients. Steering involves efforts to convince minorities to buy homes in predominantly minority neighborhoods as homeowners in all-White communities feared a decline in property values if African Americans moved in. Since real estate agents wanted return business from affluent Whites who would likely buy more property in the future, agents tried to avoid showing homes in some neighborhoods or highlight the advantages to a minority couple of living in a more mixed community.[22]

While Merton's typology helps to gain a better sense of the relationship between prejudice and discrimination, what it does not account for is what is referred to as **institutional discrimination**, which is the type of discrimination built into the structure of society. This is dangerous because it is the type of mistreatment of certain groups whereby the people engaging in the behavior do not realize they are doing it. In fact, people who engage in institutional discrimination might even think that they are treating everyone fairly.

For example, at one time in the United States many police departments and fire departments had height and weight requirements for their candidates. Because they treated all potential candidates similarly, civil service commissions felt that they did not discriminate against any particular group. However, what we now know is that the criteria were biased. Obviously, women, Hispanics, Asians, and others were being systematically excluded from those jobs even though there was no legitimate reason for doing so. Institutional discrimination is dangerous because it can be deceptive and give the appearance that everyone is treated fairly. As a result of lawsuits, many police and fire departments were required to remove any criteria that were not clearly related to the performance of duty.[23]

RACISM

What about racism? This is perhaps one of the most commonly used terms in the discussion of minority groups and is the basis for a great deal of social policy in this country with regard to their treatment. **Racism** is the belief that people are divided into distinct hereditary groups that are innately different in their behavior and abilities.[24] Such a definition also means that groups can be ranked as superior or inferior on the basis of those abilities and behavior. The presumed superiority of some groups is used to legitimate the unequal distribution of resources as well as the mistreatment of groups thought to be inferior to others. Because these traits are innate, a misguided conclusion that is drawn by some people is that since the traits are unchangeable, those at the top are given their position by some sort of natural selection process. In other words, those that have power "deserve" it while those who are not successful are used as examples of the group's inferiority.

ENVIRONMENTAL RACISM

A chemical manufacturing company wishes to relocate its new factory in your small town. You initially think of the social and economic benefits that will accompany the relocation, including better schools and more jobs. However, the chemical waste produced by the company may have detrimental impacts on your community, including harmful impacts on the river in which you and your children swim and the water you drink. You begin to realize that you cannot enjoy the social and economic benefits without your health. Your initial optimism wanes, and you and your neighbors protest against the relocation of the company. The company offers financial incentives for all residents if permission to relocate is granted. Most of your neighbors have little money, and eventually cease protesting and support the relocation.

Historically, the United States and most other countries have shown considerable neglect of environmental protection. Recent societal concerns regarding global warming have drawn attention to protecting the environment. Part of the neglect of the environment involved the under-regulation of environmental waste sites. Perhaps the most famous incident of environmental neglect is Love Canal, in Niagara Falls, New York, where extensive dumping of hazardous waste led to numerous health problems among residents in the area.

The location of hazardous waste sites has been controversial. Unfortunately for many minorities and lower-class citizens, hazardous waste sites have historically been placed in their neighborhoods. With limited financial and political power, poor minorities have disproportionately been the target of what is called **environmental racism**. This involves the under-regulation of environmental laws, and the disproportionate placement of hazardous materials in minority neighborhoods. Similarly, **environmental justice** refers to attempts to treat all groups, regardless of race, ethnicity, or income equally with regard to environmental protection and laws. Efforts toward environmental justice also include meaningful involvement on behalf of individuals who are potentially or currently affected by environmental harms.

The environmental justice movement began in the 1960s during the civil rights movement, however, it wasn't until the 1990s that the federal government took substantial action to correct injustices. The Office of Environmental Equity within the U.S. Environmental Protection Agency (EPA) was created in 1992. In 1994 the name was changed to the Office of Environmental Justice. The federal government, specifically the EPA, has made notable progress in correcting environmental injustices, however, there is still concern among researchers that the least powerful groups in society continue to be the target of harmful environmental under-regulation.

While inherently **ethnocentric**—the tendency to judge other cultures by the standards of one's own, thinking the latter is superior[25]—racist thought is not confined only to those groups where the physical and social abilities are distinct, as is the case with the differences between Whites and Blacks in the United States. Rather, racist beliefs are those that describe any behavior that justifies superiority or attributes hatefulness or exploitation to hereditary traits. In this way, racism is not confined only to racial groups, but to any ethnic group. Racism can pertain to Italian Americans, French Canadians, Jewish Americans or Polish Americans just as easily as it can apply to African Americans or Asian Americans. In light of this, some experts have called for omitting the term racism for the same reasons that the term race is too vague. Rather, these experts contend the use of the term **ethnicism** is more appropriate because racism applies to all types of ethnic groups.[26]

WHERE DOES MULTICULTURALISM FIT INTO THE DISCUSSION?

At this point you may be confused about all the terms that define certain groups and you may be wondering how it all relates to the differences in arrests, sentences, and other aspects of the criminal justice process. You may even be wondering why we cannot seem to just get along. You might even wonder why we should be thinking about multiculturalism and why people in America have trouble living here. After all, people from different cultures should be able to simply adapt to our standards and culture, right? Is multiculturalism bad since it means there is no one standard to follow or is it a good thing to hear and be exposed to different perspectives on the same issues? After all, the world is a pretty boring place if everyone thinks, believes, and acts the same way. These are great questions and we will try to contrast this debate, although it is part of a much larger discussion. The remainder of this book highlights the issues stemming from the treatment of certain groups and how it impacts not only crime and criminal justice, but the time, energy and resources dedicated to dealing with them. Thus, it is in everyone's interest to at least know what the problems are, how extensively they affect people, and the predictions for the future. We hope that by the end of this text, you will have a greater understanding of the issues.

IS MULTICULTURALISM IN AMERICA A GOOD THING?

While some experts argue that cultural diversity enhances the social harmony that exists in society, other experts contend that the diversity serves not as a uniting point for Americans, but is the source of racial tension and conflict. One of the challenges we face in America is the tendency to engage in ethnocentrism—Americans tend to believe that their culture is far superior to all others in the world. Americans also tend to be ethnocentric within their own borders as well in comparing one group to another.

On one hand, ethnocentrism can be a unifying mechanism, as was the case in the September 11, 2001, terrorist attacks against the United States. As a result, most Americans united against the terrorists and a strong sense of compassion and cohesion was created

As seen after the attacks on September 11, 2001, when threatened, the majority group often targets all members of a group instead of the individuals responsible.

in the United States. However, at the same time, the September 11 attacks also created problems when many Americans began to believe that anyone who was from the Middle East (or even looked like they were from there) suddenly became suspected of being a terrorist. It is interesting to note that prior to 9/11, racial profiling of African Americans by police officers was one of the most controversial topics in criminal justice. However, after the attacks, the profiling of people of Middle Eastern descent appeared to be acceptable to many Americans.

Thus, the discussion of the value of **multiculturalism**, which can be defined in many ways, but includes the embracing of cultural diversity, a willingness to coexist with people from different backgrounds and cultures, and the celebration of difference, centers on whether or not it divides a society or unifies it.

Multiculturalism Divides People

In many countries, such as the United States, there exists a strong national identity or national character. This means that as Americans, people can identify with being part of the larger collectivity. While there are people from many different backgrounds and preferences, there remains a unifying theme that unites them. It is similar to baseball fans: people may support different teams and/or players, but they are all united by the love of the game. However, some people feel that as a society grows more diverse, that national character or identity loses its influence over people. This is especially true for people who are already afraid that the country's character is being diluted for the sake of diversity and individualism.

Critics of multiculturalism argue that when a society becomes more heterogeneous, cultural standards, the very essence that gives a country its character and identity, begin to fall. They argue that in the interest of protecting the different backgrounds and abilities of its members, educational standards are reduced, resulting in a decline in talent and innovative thinking. Opponents to multiculturalism also argue that this threatens the economic and political viability of the United States, as mediocrity becomes the norm rather than demanding excellence from everyone. Only when minority groups are taught to accept and validate the majority culture can any type of success be achieved. This is particularly important as the discussion turns to language, one of the most important components to a country's culture.[27] In sum, opponents of multiculturalism argue that the celebration of cultural differences does little to foster a sense of cultural identity; leads to the reduction of important educational, economic, and political standards of accountability; and weakens the overall collective conscience or morality of a society.

Multiculturalism Fosters Discrimination

A second and related area that critics of multiculturalism point to is that discrimination between groups is more likely. As multiculturalism celebrates differences in backgrounds and experiences, it also segregates people into categories or groups. While the intended goal, of course, is to strengthen and validate minority groups and their values, attitudes, and belief systems, the result is that making distinctions between groups may hasten hatred rather than promoting appreciation of the differences between groups. At the very least, it creates a climate where inequality and discrimination based on membership in those groups are more likely. Opponents to multiculturalism argue that if society attempts to reduce discrimination, prejudice and inequality, it comes not by celebrating the differences but by galvanizing around the similarities.

Related to this is the problem of **reverse discrimination**. As societies attempt to remedy past mistakes in the treatment of minority groups, one solution is to have current members provide some sort of restitution or compensation for deeds of the past. This form of payback can easily create a climate of tension rather than of restoration. An example of such practices includes programs like **affirmative action**, which were designed to remedy the historical mistreatment of some groups by providing various types of preferential treatment. While the current practice of affirmative action is not what was originally intended, the result has led some people to feel they are being punished for something over which they had no control. In effect, they are being asked to remedy the behaviors of their ancestors and this breeds hostility rather than harmony and equality towards minority members.

Related to this is the fact that multiculturalism also creates a climate in which minority groups can adopt a victim mentality. This means that as society calls for more equity and the fair distribution of economic, social, and political power, some minority group members may use that as a justification for failing to meet their responsibilities. An example might be that an individual or group might contend that the reason they have not found adequate employment is due to the legacy of slavery when, in fact, it is a result of their unwillingness to look for jobs. Such an attitude can cause even the most ardent defender of past injustices to feel they are now being exploited.

Multiculturalism Prevents Equality

A third argument against multiculturalism is that it places too heavy an emphasis on the differences between groups rather than their similarities. This discourages assimilation by minority groups and encourages them to remain isolated from the larger society. This isolation can result in people being less willing or able to get along with people from other ethnic, racial, or religious backgrounds. As this isolationism increases, it leads certain groups to feel as though they need less from the larger society in terms of skills, talents, education, and opportunities. As a result, members do not pursue these opportunities and remain locked into certain professions or jobs and do not become upwardly mobile. This creates not only an ethnic distinction between minority groups and others, it also promotes class distinctions. This is significant because there are many experts who argue that social class, not race or ethnicity, is the key to achieving social, economic, and political equality.[28]

The Value of Multiculturalism

The preceding discussion can easily be taken out of context to mean that everyone should think, look, and act like everyone else, lest society go into a cultural tailspin. Of course, there are challenges to living in a culturally diverse society, but this is a far cry from saying that unless we limit differences, we are doomed to a culture without an identity.

The other side of the debate about multiculturalism is that it creates a climate in which difference is not something to fear or reject—it actually promotes innovative thinking. America is and continues to be a culturally diverse society. This leaves us with only a few options: to remove everyone who does not think, look, and act like the majority, which is unrealistic and socially dangerous (e.g., who gets to decide?) or we can find a way to use people's different backgrounds and talents towards something positive and useful. While it can be tempting to sit around and complain about what is bad about diversity, it serves little constructive purpose. Rather, the more productive way appears to be to accept that it exists and find ways to use it to society's advantage.

In reality, there are many experts who believe that America's national identity is the composition of a collection of regional and local cultures. What makes America unique, they say, is that while there may be something of a national identity, it is made up of so many different backgrounds and cultural preferences that to section out certain parts would be virtually impossible. Perhaps more importantly, cultural diversity is central to the tenets of living in a democratic society. How can people claim to be free if they are constrained in terms of what they think and believe simply because it is different from the majority? Further, there is a historic precedent in this country for tolerating ethnic diversity. While we also have a history of the mistreatment of certain groups, we have, at least in theory, always accepted people from different cultures.

In its purest form, the arguments in favor of multiculturalism center on integration and social cohesion. While it is true that many Americans, especially those living in large American cities, can feel isolated and lacking in a sense of community, who do not know their neighbors and feel disconnected in general, one of the things that binds people together is their commonality. One of those strands might be religion while another could be ethnicity. Ethnic ancestry is said by some experts to give minorities a feeling of community—making ethnic identities a method by which a national identity can occur. Thus, not only does ethnic group membership help the individual to psychologically feel more connected to his or her larger community, it can bind them into a larger sense of what some call "peoplehood." For example, a person with an Italian background might feel better connected to their neighbors if they lived near a neighborhood comprised mostly of Italian Americans, such as the Little Italy enclave in New York City. By being better integrated at a local level, the person might also begin to affiliate with other groups, such as the local Catholic Church, which further expands his or her circle and sense of identity. The person then begins to consider their place in the larger society as a New Yorker or more generally as an American, which further stimulates their integration to the larger society. The process begins, however, at the micro level, where the person uses their cultural heritage as a starting point to affiliate with others and to begin to feel as though their place in the world matters.[29]

In the end, the process of multiculturalism has a host of implications for society. While at extremes it can become problematic, in this age of globalization, where every country is connected politically, socially, and economically to every other one, society in general will continue to diversify. This can be healthy growth, where Americans learn to celebrate differences and to evaluate others not on their differences but on their commonality, or we can fear change and differences and compartmentalize their lives because they feel threatened by some groups. The misuse of power or the tendency to exploit or take advantage of others begins with an initial perception of other groups. Many times impressions of people are based on small bits of information or on stereotypes of what is known about members of particular groups.

In the next chapter we will discuss group dynamics and how we interpret people's behavior, which influences our interactions with them. As we will see, and as the subsequent chapters on the treatment of other minority groups in the criminal justice system show, often our initial perceptions lead us to believe certain groups have attitudes, values, and beliefs regardless of whether any evidence exists to verify that perception. Unfortunately, when such perceptions translate into social policy, judicial and police practices, or in how juries decide the facts of a case, the consequences are significant and can even be life-threatening for minorities.

For those students interested in criminology or the study of the causes of crime, many of the theories can be used to not only explain why a particular person engages in unlawful acts, but the theories can also be used to understand the way minority groups are treated. That is, some theories argue that because they are exploited or denied opportunities to achieve success, some minority groups engage in criminal acts either to achieve some level of success (e.g., strain or disorganization theories) or out of frustration for the way they have been identified by others (e.g. labeling theory).

Other theories offer insight into the way people's perceptions influence their lack of understanding of cultural differences (e.g., cultural conflict theory) or that the person rejected mainstream society and made a poor choice when they decided to commit a crime (e.g., Hirschi and Gottfredson's general theory of crime). Still other explanations for the involvement of minorities in the criminal justice system may be due to the perceptions of minorities by participants in the system, such as the police, judges, or even the public when they serve as jurors. Thus, our goal in this text is not to contend that criminals are not responsible because they were oppressed or mistreated over the sweep of history, or by saying that the criminal justice system is hopelessly racist. Rather, we believe that there are a host of factors that explain the trends in crime data, including racism and social history, that get us closer to understanding the interplay between crime, minorities, and criminal justice.

Do minorities get arrested because they commit more crimes? Maybe, but it could also be due to the fact that the police spend more time looking for criminals, and minorities fit the profile officers have been trained to identify. Do African Americans get different sentences for similar crimes as Whites? In some cases, but the reasons for that may not simply be that judges are racist and intentionally hand out tougher sentences because they do not like African Americans. Human behavior is very complex and the reasons why people act as they do is difficult to determine. Unlike other scientific disciplines, where the laws regulating the universe have been discovered, social behavior remains a mystery in many ways. What is known is that a variety of factors play into a person's decision to engage in certain acts and some of these factors have historical, economic, political, and social influences. As the next chapter describes, one of the most important factors in understanding social behavior is found in the way people communicate with each other. As you will see, interaction often consists of symbolic cues that must be interpreted correctly in order for communication to be effective. However, a crucial component of that process is an understanding of the meaning of those cues and gestures. Misunderstandings, miscommunications, and preconceived ideas about what a person means, are not only the basis of poor relationships, they are at the heart of problems such as discrimination, racism, and the mistreatment of certain groups.

One final important point is needed. Americans live in an information-saturated age. Scholars, reporters, practitioners, and the general public are much more educated about issues and problems than any time in our history. As a result, they increasingly demand "proof" or "data" to support claims of a practice, a trend, the effectiveness of a particular strategy, or to justify a change in resource allocation. Consequently, researchers have spent a great deal of time studying the criminal justice system and the problems contained within it.

However, as you will see in some of the chapters, we use the most current data available to describe trends and patterns, but in some cases, the research is limited or dated. It may come as some surprise to students to learn that there are times when the information on a particular topic is sparse or has not been updated in recent years. This is particularly true with some government publications. However, know that we have reviewed the literature and what we offer is based on what is currently known.

SUMMARY

The issue of race and ethnicity in the United States remains an important factor in understanding social interaction, relationships, and the fabric of American culture. While many people like to think that issues such as racism, discrimination, and prejudice are a thing of the past, there is ample evidence to suggest that these problems remain a critical component of social life. It is also the case that many people misunderstand or misuse certain terms when discussing race-related issues. This chapter outlined the way social scientists operationalize terms such as prejudice, discrimination, minority groups, racism, race, and ethnicity. It also attempted to explain how minority groups are created, how and why they are mistreated, and the debate about the value of multiculturalism in American society. On one hand, some experts believe that too diverse a society dilutes its national identity and the social cohesion that comes from people seeing the world similarly. On the other hand, multiculturalism celebrates people from different backgrounds and offers insight into human nature as well as how groups can coexist peacefully and equitably. For students of criminal justice, the treatment of minority groups is central to understanding criminal behavior and how the administration of justice affects people without power. Many of the theories to explain crime can be used in part to describe the motivation of some offenders, but they also are framed in light of criminals' minority status. Thus, any discussion of crime in American society must contain some attention to the way certain groups are treated by the dominant culture.

YOU MAKE THE CALL

Imagine you are on vacation for the first time to a foreign country. You are sitting in a restaurant with your partner trying to figure out the menu when another customer comes in to the dining area, loudly complaining about why the menu is not in English and why so many things are different from American culture. The restaurant server looks at you and asks if you know this person...probably because they are American as well. How do you respond to the server, knowing that your answer might impact the quality of the service and the food you receive?

Do you: Offer insight into the nature of ethnocentrism, prejudice and discrimination? Or do you plead ignorance and say you don't know the person at all? Or do you confront the other patron and remind him that his behavior impacts you as well? What are the possible consequences of each possibility?

KEY TERMS

affirmative action
assimilation
collective conscience
cultural fusion
discrimination
environmental justice
environmental racism
ethnicism
ethnocentric
expulsion
extermination
genocide
heterogeneous societies
homogeneous societies
institutional discrimination
involuntary migration

melting pot
multiculturalism
neocolonialism
operationalization
prejudice
prejudiced discriminator
prejudiced non-discriminator
racism
reverse discrimination
secession
segregation
social construction of race
unprejudiced discriminator
unprejudiced non-discriminator
voluntary migration

DISCUSSION QUESTIONS

1. What role does diversity play in the strength of the collective conscience or morality of a society?
2. Why is it so difficult to identify examples of institutional discrimination? If rules apply to everyone, shouldn't that be enough to prevent unfair treatment? Can you give examples of institutional discrimination?
3. Are Americans inherently ethnocentric? Do Americans always believe their culture is better than everyone else's? Why or why not?
4. Is multiculturalism really a bad thing, as some experts have suggested? Does it really dilute the "American identity?" Why or why not?

FOR FURTHER READING

Duneier, M. *Ghetto: The Invention of a Place, the History of an Idea.* New York: Farrar, Straus, and Giroux, 2016.
Durkheim, E. *The Division of Labor in Society.* New York: The Free Press, 1893.
West, C. *Race Matters.* Boston, MA: Harvard University Press, 2000.
Wilson, W. J. *When Work Disappears.* Chicago, IL: University of Chicago Press, 1997.

NOTES

1. Robert Schlesinger, "The Size of the U.S. and the World in 2016," *US News*, January 5, 2016, available at http://www.usnews.com/opinion/blogs/robert-schlesinger/articles/2016-01-05/us-population-in-2016-according-to-census-estimates-322-762-018

2. D. Jary and J. Jary, *Collins Dictionary of Sociology* (New York: Harper Collins, 1991), 93.

3. Ibid.

4. J. Scott and G. Marshall, *A Dictionary of Sociology*, 3rd edition (New York: Oxford University Press, 2005). Available online at http://www.oxfordreference.com/view/10.1093/acref/9780199553008.001.0001/acref-9780199553008-e-1859?rskey=BVTpmt&result=1859

5. R. Shulman, "Sharpton's Ancestor Was Owned by Thurmond's" *Washington Post*, February 26, 2007, A01.

6. Scott and Marshall, *Dictionary of Sociology.*

7. Ibid.

8. Ibid.

9. Ibid.

10. Ibid.

11. See for instance, R. McNamara, M. Tempenis, M. and B. Walton, *Crossing the Line: Interracial Couples in the South* (Westport, CT: Praeger, 1999).

12. Ibid.

13. Ibid.

14. Scott and Marshall, *Dictionary of Sociology.*

15. Ibid.

16. Jeff Nesbit, "Study of Census Data Finds a Segregated America, Especially for Blacks," *US News*, July 24, 2012, available at http://www.usnews.com/news/blogs/at-the-edge/2012/07/24/study-of-census-data-finds-a-segregated-america-especially-for-blacks

17. Scott and Marshall, *A Dictionary of Sociology.*

18. Ibid.

19. Ibid.

20. Ibid.

21. R. K. Merton, "Discrimination and the American Creed," in Robert MacIver (ed.) *Discrimination and National Welfare* (New York: Harper and Row, 1949), 99–126.

22. CivilRights.Org staff, *Report: Racial Steering into Segregated Neighborhoods Most Prevalent Form of Housing Discrimination*, April 7, 2006, available at http://www.civilrights.org/fairhousing/laws/report-racial-steering-into-segregated-neighborhoods-most-prevalent-form-of-housing-discrimination-1.html and accessed July 25, 2007.

23. See for instance *Smith v. City of East Cleveland*, 363 F. Supp. 1131 (N.D. Ohio 1973).

24. Scott and Marshall, *Dictionary of Sociology.*

25. Ibid.

26. Ibid.

27. Ibid.

28. W. J. Wilson, *When Work Disappears* (Chicago: University of Chicago Press, 1997). See also W. J. Wilson, *The Declining Significance of Race* (Chicago: University of Chicago Press, 2012).

29. Tepperman and Blain, *Think Twice.*

CHAPTER 2

GROUP DYNAMICS, COMMUNICATION AND SOCIAL INTERACTION

CHAPTER OBJECTIVES

After reading this chapter, you should be able to:

- Recognize Erving Goffman's contribution to our understanding of social interaction
- Understand what constitutes a group
- Understand the basics of communication and the communication process
- Discuss the significance of verbal and nonverbal communication in the criminal justice system
- Identify the potential outcomes of minority versus nonminority interactions

Part of the problem with discrimination, prejudice, racism, and other forms of mistreatment of people is a result of a poor or limited understanding of the values, attitudes, and beliefs of the members of different groups. Limited or no contact with various groups can lead to stereotypical ideas about the motives, beliefs, and behaviors of these groups. Conversely, if the interaction that takes place between different groups tends to be negative, this can lead to problems in understanding behavior. Recall that in the first chapter we mentioned that a great deal of social interaction is ambiguous: We do not always know what people are thinking or intending; all we see is their behavior. This means that the lens with which we filter those actions becomes critical to how we understand and respond to their behavior.

An important thing to remember is how people present themselves when they act. Most of the time we are trying to convey a symbolic message with our words, facial expressions, and body language. However, there are a host of instances when what we want to convey and how that is interpreted is incongruent or misunderstood. While we can easily understand the problems that occur when groups from different cultures interact, we should note that all of us have trouble at times interacting with each other, even those we know. Many conflicts originate from the failure to effectively communicate, or misinterpretation of communication. For instance, consider a time when you texted or emailed someone who misinterpreted the meaning of your message. You may have meant one thing, but the receiver interpreted your message in another way. Certainly, many misinterpreted messages do not end in conflict, but there are times when they do. We begin this chapter with recognition of the work of Erving Goffman, who undoubtedly changed the way we recognize and understand human interaction. His work helps us to understand the interactions between the criminal justice system and those who enter the system.

ERVING GOFFMAN AND THE NATURE OF SOCIAL INTERACTION

In trying to explain the nature of social interaction, Erving Goffman, in his classic book *The Presentation of Self in Everyday Life*, tried to shed light on the nature of social interaction, particularly in a group setting. In order to maintain a stable self-image, people perform for their social audiences. As a result of this interest in performance Goffman focused on **dramaturgy**, or a view of social life as a series of dramatic performances like those performed on stage.[1]

Goffman assumed that when individuals interact, they want to present a certain sense of self that will be accepted by others. However, even as they present that self, actors are aware that members of the audience can disturb their performance. For that reason, actors need to control the audience, especially those elements that might be disruptive. They hope that the sense of self they present will cause the audience to voluntarily act as the actors intend. Goffman characterizes this central interest as *impression management*, which involves techniques that actors use to maintain certain impressions in the face of problems they are likely to encounter and methods they use to cope with the problems.

Following this analogy, Goffman spoke of a "front stage," as compared to a "backstage." The front stage is that part of the performance that generally functions in rather fixed and general ways to define the situation for those who observe the performance. Several key components of the front stage include the **setting**, which refers to the physical scene that ordinarily must be there if the actors are to perform. Without a setting the actors usually cannot perform. For instance, a correctional officer requires a prison, just like an ice skater needs ice. **Personal fronts** consist of those items of equipment that the audience identifies with the performers and expects them to carry into the setting. For instance, a police officer is expected to wear a uniform and carry weapons, much as a surgeon is expected to dress in a medical gown and have certain instruments. Pertinent to one's personal front are appearance and manner. **Appearance** includes those items that tell us the performer's social status (e.g., the police officer's uniform). **Manner** tells the audience what sort of role the performer expects to play in the situation (e.g., physical mannerisms, demeanor). A brusque manner and a meek manner may indicate quite different kinds of performances. In general, we expect appearances and manner to be consistent.

Goffman's most interesting insights lie in the domain of the interaction. He argued that because people generally try to present an idealized picture of themselves in their front stage performances, they inevitably feel that they must hide things in their performance. Accordingly, Goffman also discussed a "backstage," which is usually adjacent to the front stage, but it is also cut off from it. Performers expect that no members of their front audience will appear in the back. For instance, roll call in a police department is often conducted behind the scenes, away from the public. The information shared during roll call is typically reserved for police officers and consists of brief training periods and briefings on issues such as crime problems and community concerns. Officers tend to view roll call as "their time" away from the public, where they can speak freely with each other and not have to be concerned about members of the general public being privy to the discussion. The backstage involves several processes, including:

1. **Concealing secret pleasures**, which includes activities engaged in prior to the performance or in past lives that are incompatible with their performance. For instance, a judge may wish to prevent others from knowing that he uses recreational drugs.
2. **Concealing errors** that have been made in the preparation of the performance as well as steps that have been taken to correct these errors. For example, a police officer may seek to hide the fact that he or she wrongfully stopped someone.
3. **Showing only the end product** and concealing the process of producing them. Officers may wrongfully stop someone, but justify the stop upon finding illegal drugs.[2]

Goffman also argued that the audiences themselves may try to cope with the falsity so as not to shatter their idealized image of the actor. This reveals the interactional character of all performances. A successful performance depends on the involvement of all parties. Actors also try to make sure that all parts of any performance blend together. In some cases, a single flaw can disrupt a performance. However, performances vary in the amount of consistency required. For instance, a slip by a priest on a sacred occasion would be very disruptive but a taxi driver making a wrong turn would not damage his or her overall performance.

Goffman's discussion of how individuals present themselves is related to recent discussions of explicit and implicit biases in the criminal justice system. **Explicit bias** refers to the beliefs or attitudes an individual maintains at a conscious level. The actions associated with this type of bias are apparent to the individuals and the audience, for instance when a correctional officer uses a racially derogatory term toward an African American inmate. **Implicit bias** involves less overt cognitive processes that shape attitudes and stereotypes while operating at a below-conscious level. The individual is not consciously aware of their biased behavior, but it exists, for instance when police assume that some individuals, based primarily on their race or ethnicity, are more likely to commit crime.

IMPRESSION MANAGEMENT

Goffman closed *Presentation of Self in Everyday Life* with some additional insights on the art of impression management (IM). In general, IM is oriented to guarding against a series of unexpected actions, such as unintended gestures, inopportune intrusions, as well as intended actions such as making a scene. Goffman was interested in the various methods of dealing with such problems. Two important components of IM are dramaturgical discipline and dramaturgical circumspection. **Dramaturgical discipline** is defined as concise preparation of the performance. This includes such things as having the presence of mind to avoid slips, maintaining self-control, and managing facial expressions and the tone of voice of one's performance. Related to this is **dramaturgical circumspection**, which involves the logistical planning involved in carrying out the performance. Examples include planning for emergencies, making only brief appearances (which limits the potential for mistakes and errors), and preventing audiences access to private information (which might be used to discredit the performance in some way).[3]

One of Goffman's most interesting books is *Stigma: Notes on the Management of Spoiled Identity*. He was interested in the gap between what a person ought to be, or what he calls their "virtual social identity," and what a person actually is: their "actual social identity." Anyone who has a gap between these two identities is stigmatized. The book focuses on the dramaturgical interaction between stigmatized people and "normals."[4] The nature of that interaction depends on which of the two types of stigma an individual possesses. In the case of **discredited stigma** the actor assumes that the differences are known by the audience members or are evident to them. An example would be a paraplegic or someone who has lost a limb. Here the dramaturgical problem is how to hide the fact of the obvious stigma and demonstrate that the person is just like everyone else. The IM techniques here are called "covering." This is often accomplished by "proving" the person can do everything a normal person can do. In the case of someone confined to a wheelchair, the person may go to great lengths to demonstrate their independence.

A discreditable stigma is one in which the differences are neither known by audience members nor perceivable by them. An example might be a gay man trying to hide his lifestyle in a heterosexual environment. This is often referred to as "passing," as in passing oneself off as something they are not. For someone with a discredited stigma, the basic dramaturgical problem is managing tension produced by the fact that people know of the problem. A problem for someone with a discreditable stigma is managing information so that the problem remains unknown to the audience. For instance, historically it was difficult for gay police officers to reveal their lifestyle preference to other officers. It was, and in some cases remains, feared that other officers wouldn't be accepting. In recent years, however, officers have increasingly shared their preferences with other officers, and the stigma his dissipated.

Goffman devotes much of *Stigma* to people with obvious, often grotesque stigmas. However, as the book unfolds, one begins to realize that Goffman is really saying that we are all stigmatized at one time or another or in one setting or another. His examples include Jews "passing" in a predominantly Christian community, the obese person in a group of people of normal weight, and the individual who has lied about his past and must be constantly sure that the audience does not learn of his history.

The significance of Goffman's work is found in the nature of social interaction. We spend a great deal of time trying to present ourselves in a much more favorable light, and we tend to evaluate people on the basis of how *they* present themselves. It should be obvious, then, that many of our interactions are not smooth or successful because we are using very little information with which to determine who someone really is. It is also the case that we make mistakes that can have serious consequences for some individuals.[5]

SOCIAL INTERACTION AND THE CRIMINAL JUSTICE SYSTEM

In light of Goffman's account of social interaction, consider the following scenario as it relates to the criminal justice system:

> *A young African American man is escorted into a courtroom for his initial appearance, dressed in state-issued attire (i.e., prison garb). Handcuffed and shackled, the young man appears before a judge who informs him of his rights and the charges against him. The young man discouragingly listens with his head down, staring at the ground as the judge reads the charges. The judge begins to get frustrated by the suspect's seeming disinterest in the proceedings and suggests that the individual "look the court in the eye." The young man grudgingly lifts his head and looks at the agitated judge. "Your disinterest in this case reflects your apparent disinterest in the law," says the judge. He adds: "I've read you your rights and informed you of the charges against you. I suggest you take things seriously or you'll find yourself spending a good portion of your life in state prison."*

This account of one man's experience in a courtroom exemplifies the power of verbal and nonverbal communication in today's criminal justice system. Let's deconstruct this situation to identify the presumptions made by the two participants. Let's begin with the presence of a young African-American male in the courtroom. Author Jeffrey Reiman discussed how, despite the more severe harms resultant from white-collar offenders, society recognizes young, urban, poor, African American males as the "typical criminal." Reiman notes that the image of the typical criminal, who instills fear in most law-abiding Americans, is created and perpetuated by government practices (e.g., focusing on street crime) and media and government reports suggesting that this group commits an unreasonable amount of crime.[6] The individual entering the court in our scenario undoubtedly fits the mold of the "typical criminal."

The individual in our scenario enters the court handcuffed and shackled in state-issued attire. This look, fitting for a dangerous individual who could violently react in a moment's notice, is ascribed to an individual who is legally "innocent until proven guilty." Remove yourself from this situation and consider walking around the general public, for instance in a mall, dressed as the young man in our example. What impressions would the public have of you? Would they recognize you as "innocent?" On the other hand, do we want allegedly violent individuals to remain unconstrained in a stressful environment such as the courtroom? Needless to say, the appearance of many who enter our courts suggests they are indeed guilty as opposed to "innocent until proven guilty."

We could also question the accuracy of the judge's belief that the suspect was disinterested in the case, and ultimately the law, simply because he was not making eye contact with the judge. The significance of multicultural studies is evident in this particular exchange, as it is possible that the suspect was showing the judge respect by not looking him in the eye. It is considered rude in some cultures (e.g., in many Asian cultures) to look someone in the eyes and some cultures consider it respectful to maintain limited eye contact. Americans, however, view eye contact as a sign of respect. For instance, Americans maintain almost three times as much eye contact as Japanese persons.[7] The judge was clearly speculating and engaging in an ethnocentric manner when commenting on the motives behind the suspect's behavior.

Ethnocentrism involves believing that one's culture or group is superior to others.[8] The judge seemingly interpreted the suspect's behavior according to personal cultural beliefs, which is not uncommon. Sociologist Robert Young suggests, "Precisely because everyday patterns of behavior are culture specific, culture serves the function of binding us to those who share our culture and alienating us from those who do not." He adds, "Those who are part of the same culture will tend to behave in similar ways and have tastes and preferences similar to each other and at the same time different from those of different cultural backgrounds."[9]

The situation in our scenario could be interpreted differently from the perspective of the judge. For instance, the judge is likely familiar with nonverbal communication given the amount of time judges spend interacting with various individuals in a courtroom. It is possible that judges can, with accuracy, recognize the differences between cultural practices and disinterest. It is also possible for judges to misinterpret actions. Further, should we expect the judge to understand all cultures and respond to each, or should the judge expect all who enter the courtroom to conform to the culture the judge finds most appealing? To do so requires the judge (and all criminal justice practitioners) to familiarize themselves with, and accept, the many cultural backgrounds entering our criminal justice system. While we hope that we can reach complete understanding and acceptance of cultural differences, the limitations of human behavior regularly enter into criminal justice practices and lead to differential treatment of various group members. Recognizing and responding to the expectation of one cultural community often leads us to violate the expectations of another.[10] Finding common ground can be difficult.

The American public's perception of the criminal population is biased toward African Americans.

The same challenges and opportunities for misinterpretation, or miscommunication, discussed in our scenario could easily be applied to all facets of criminal justice. We could easily replace the courtroom scenario with a police officer reacting notably punitively upon encountering a group of young adults who don't speak English. Or a prison officer who fails to respect the rights of prisoners by disrupting the privacy of those who wish to pray several times a day. To understand our criminal justice system we must recognize that the system is composed of individuals who act within specific guidelines established by individuals.

As the United States has become increasingly diverse, criminal justice agencies have made many efforts to help employees understand and properly respond to cultural differences. For instance, recruits in the New York City police academy are provided a manual titled "Policing a Multicultural Society," which provides tips for recruits who will graduate and work in New York, a very diverse city. The manual provides various communication tips that assist officers dealing with diverse groups. For instance, it notes that police should not assume that Arab immigrants speaking loudly are arguing, given that Arabs generally do speak loudly, and failing to make eye contact with an officer is not a sign of disrespect, for instance as immigrants from rural Mexico generally avoid making eye contact with authority figures. Further the manual instructs officers who are interacting with Latin American and Asian immigrant groups to direct their questions to the head of the household if possible, and that Arab-Americans are offering a gesture of courtesy when they immediately get out of their car upon being pulled over.[11]

THE CRIMINAL JUSTICE "SYSTEM"?

The compilation of practices that involve identifying and responding to crime and delinquency is often termed a "system." Some argue that our criminal justice system is indeed a true system in its current form, although it may not be a fine-tuned one. In other words, our system does something . . . maybe not the most effective thing, but something. Others would suggest it is a finely-tuned system. Some suggest it is not a system at all. In light of accepted definitions of the term "system," which includes mention of terms such as "correlation," "coordination," and "orderly," our system of justice looks nothing like a system. Our decentralized practices of dispensing criminal justice often result in uncorrelated, uncoordinated practices at local, county, state, and federal levels. While there is greater cooperation and correlation among the levels of criminal justice practices today than there has ever been, much work remains before we could safely call ours a true system.

On paper our system of justice seems well-designed and well-planned (Table 2-1 depicts the steps of the criminal justice system). One merely needs to examine the recorded steps of the criminal justice system to see that protocol is in place for those accused and convicted of breaking the law. Simply using the term "system" conjures images of a smoothly-working entity that encounters problematic situations on rare occasions and maintains proper corrective actions for mishaps. One typically thinks of material objects as systems (e.g., an automobile or an air conditioning unit), which typically function in a more mechanical, predictable manner than does an abstract system composed of individuals. The fact that our system of criminal justice is decentralized and composed of human interactions provides several challenges for those who believe it is truly a system.

Table 2.1 What is the sequence of events in the criminal justice system?

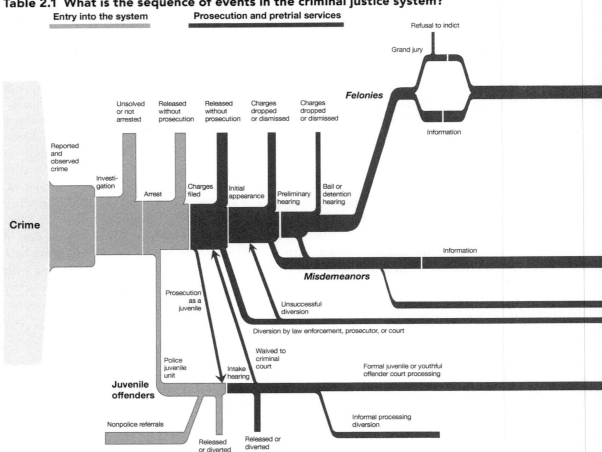

Note: This chart gives a simplified view of caseflow through the criminal justice system. Procedures vary among jurisdictions. The weights of the lines are not intended to show actual size of caseloads.

Source: Adapted from *The challenge of crime in a free society*. President's Commission on Law Enforcement and Administration of Justice, 1967. This revision, a result of the Symposium on the 30th Anniversary of the President's Commission, was prepared by the Bureau of Justice Statistics in 1997.

The effectiveness of the system, despite how fluid it looks on paper, is influenced by human practices. Humans participate on both sides of the law in the criminal justice system. Accordingly, the system is vulnerable to limitations and/or problems associated with human behavior. To clarify, it is often asked whether or not the criminal justice system is racist or biased. The answer, clear and simple is "no." The system, *as diagrammed*, does not have arrows pointing one way for minorities and another way for nonminorities. The system does not formally treat groups differently. However, humans create laws that are then enforced by police officers and interpreted by courtroom personnel and enforced again by corrections personnel. Individuals influence how justice is determined

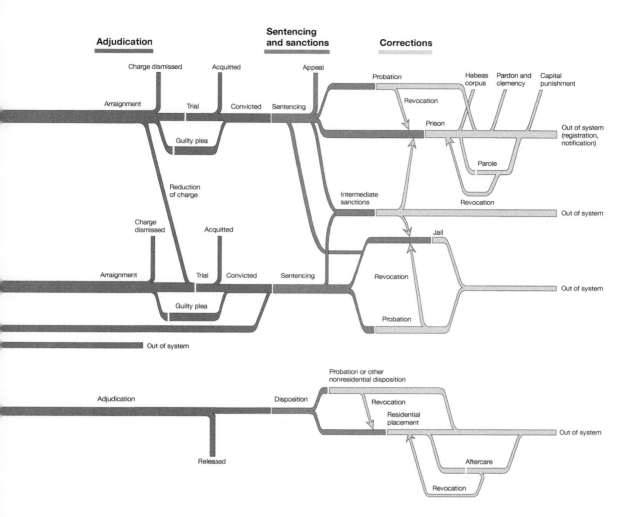

throughout these and related processes. The system is not biased. Some individuals impacting the system are biased. Fortunately, their impact is not as strong as it once was because one could make a strong argument that today's criminal justice system is more culturally-sensitive than at any time in history.

Biases in criminal justice hamper the effectiveness of the system and can result in injustices. Injustices have been abundant in the criminal justice system, as evidenced in the U.S. Supreme Court's landmark decision in the 1972 case *Furman v. Georgia*.[12] In *Furman*, the Court ruled that the death penalty, as it was being administered, constituted cruel and unusual punishment and was in violation of the Eighth and Fourteenth amendments. The majority of justices ruled that the procedures used at that time in applying the death penalty were arbitrary and unfair. The Court didn't rule that death as punishment in and of itself was unfair; instead the Court found problems with the manners in which the penalty was being applied. Thirty-eight states introduced new capital punishment statutes following *Furman*. As evidenced, the criminal justice system often takes steps to correct injustices. Other examples of corrective actions include the introduction of truth-in-sentencing laws, mandatory-minimum sentencing practices, and the use of sentencing guidelines. Nevertheless, the introduction of these actions demonstrates that the system occasionally needs corrective action given the differential treatment of groups, although some have questioned the fairness involved in each of these "corrective" approaches and sentencing practices in general.[13] Criminal justice policies have both direct and indirect impacts on the daily lives of ethnic and racial groups.[14]

Just how do humans *prevent* the criminal justice system from truly operating as a system? One primary obstacle in producing a bias-free criminal justice system involves understanding the varied cultural backgrounds of those entering and working in the system. How does the multicultural society in which we live impact simple, everyday exchanges between individuals, specifically within the criminal justice system? This remainder of this chapter addresses these questions by specifically focusing on three critical topics: "groups," "communication," and "social interaction." Comprehension of this material helps set the stage for the discussions in the chapters that follow. These issues clearly relate to one another and help to explain how the criminal justice system is not necessarily a smooth-functioning system, per se, as much as it is a behemoth entity filled with justice-seeking personnel, the accused, and the convicted. This chapter helps readers understand how and why multiculturalism is one of the most controversial issues within criminal justice.

GROUPS

We all belong to groups. Whether it's your family, your close network of friends, a church group, an athletic group, or some other group, we all associate with other individuals in varying contexts. Participants in the criminal justice system are not different. We categorize into groups those who engage in criminal justice, whether it is police officers, prosecutors, prison wardens, and the like. Yet, what specifically, constitutes a group and what factors influence group behavior? Are the students who sit in the back of the classroom considered a group? Are the three individuals communicating with each other as they walk out of a department store a group?

WHAT CONSTITUTES A GROUP?

Prominent among the varied definitions of groups include references to group size, whether or not there exists interdependence of members, group identity, the group goals, and group structure.[15]

Sociologists William Hickey and colleagues noted that **social groups** have two or more people who interact in patterned ways, "have a feeling of unity, and share interests and expectations."[16] Other researchers suggest that groups must have three members. For instance, Professor Joann Keyton notes that a group must have, at minimum, three members, for these primary reasons: 1) providing the opportunity for members to establish coalitions in which two members side against the third, 2) enabling the opportunity for

Cross-cultural relations have improved as the United States has become more diverse.

hidden communication to take place, and 3) determining how roles are assigned.[17] Regardless of the minimum size, the maximum size of a group is dependent on the context of the group. For instance, athletic teams are limited to a set number of participants, while some groups (e.g., pro-environmental groups) seek all the support they can muster. The appropriate size of a group is largely determined by the group's ability to achieve its goals.[18]

Interdependence of members is also vital to establishing a group. Members of a group must rely on group or individual actions for the group to accomplish its task(s). Individuals join groups primarily to enjoy the company of others and accomplish tasks they could not do alone. Group members rely on one another for direction, support, and interaction. Groups must also include an identity through which members identify themselves. Group members who identify with one another and the group's goals accept the values and norms of the group, which subsequently increases the motivations and abilities of group members to interact and proceed effectively.

The final characteristics central to the definition of groups are group goals and group structure. As the name suggests, **group goals** are agreed-upon tasks or activities that the group seeks to complete or accomplish. Goals are varied in nature (e.g., short-term vs. long-term; financial vs. nonfinancial) and not all members of the group have to appreciate the goal. However, there must be a shared understanding of the goal and group members must perceive it as being worthwhile.[19] Groups must also involve structure, which can be informal (e.g., classmates) or formal (e.g., a police department). **Group structure**, which is largely determined by group roles, typically evolves in accord with, or from group norms and rules.[20] The structure is vulnerable to change as norms, goals, and other factors impacting the group change. Table 2-2 summarizes the characteristics of a group.

Table 2.2 Characteristics of Groups

Group Size
Interdependence of Members
Group Identity
Group Goal
Group Structure

As noted, groups come in all sizes and shapes and there is some subjectivity in determining a group. Often, we hear of group member counts, which are sometimes used to gauge support for a particular group and its goal(s). However, simple counts do not suggest that all who are counted are active members of the group. Subjectivity enters when one makes determinations of group membership, for instance, through members paying dues, active participation, or being listed on a current roster.

Subgroups often emerge as groups become larger and group goals become distorted. Subgroups, or factions of group members that exist within the larger group, sometimes emerge and maintain the possibility of breaking off from the larger group to form an independent group. The existence of subgroups can both help and hinder the larger group as goals are sometimes more easily achieved when individuals work together with limited input and interference. Subgroups, however, may ultimately detach from the larger group, for instance, if they believe their identity or goals differ significantly from the larger group or problems may occur if the subgroup is not receptive to direction from the larger group.

GROUPS IN THE CRIMINAL JUSTICE SYSTEM

Given the elements necessary for the existence of a group, what groups exist within the criminal justice system? To be sure, there are many groups existing at various levels working toward different goals. For starters, we could loosely identify the nearly 2.5 million individuals working in our nation's justice system as a group that has the ultimate goal of ensuring justice.[21] We could also recognize each component of the criminal justice system as a group (i.e., police, courts, and corrections), and further identify groups as we observe different levels of justice (e.g., local, state, and federal). We could take it further to group individuals working particular beats, in particular courtrooms, or in specific cell blocks.

An example of a group within the criminal justice system is the **courtroom workgroup**, which is recognized as a group of individuals who work on a regular basis in a courtroom setting. The familiarity of courtroom personnel contributes to the local legal culture in the sense that there's a shared understanding of norms, practices, and expectations among courtroom practitioners. The courtroom workgroup emerges as individuals (including judges, prosecutors, and defense attorneys), working within a jurisdiction, come to understand and anticipate particular behaviors from other members of the workgroup. For instance, those regularly acting within a courtroom typically have a clear understanding of the **"going rate,"** or the penalties one can expect to be associated with particular offenses. A defense attorney can share with his or her client information culled from previous interactions with other members of the workgroup. In turn, suspects have an understanding of what to expect upon entering the courtroom. Among other things, the familiarity among members of the courtroom workgroup helps plea bargain negotiations, which is typical of proceedings in the courtroom for instance as the large majority of criminal court cases, ranging from roughly 85 to 95 percent, are resolved via plea bargaining, as opposed to criminal trials.

Recognition of suspects as members of particular groups undoubtedly affects criminal justice practices, as identified in the criminal justice research literature and throughout this book. While suspects in general do not meet the criteria of the definition of a group, primarily due to the lack of cohesiveness or organization of suspects, they undoubtedly belong to some group (e.g., based on affiliation with a gang membership or a culture-based group) and are typically pre-judged and treated in various manners.

COMMUNICATION

Communication is at the core of human interaction. It guides, conveys, directs, suggests, and so on. Effective communication is vital to the effective functioning of any group, and has saved more than one police and correctional officer's life. Communication is perhaps the most important, yet often overlooked, aspect of the criminal justice system. Take, for instance, a police officer who bases his/her decision to draw and shoot their firearm based on interpersonal communication. Consider the prison officer who interprets an inmate's behavior as unruly and proceeds to forcefully remove the inmate from his cell. With regard to parole, author/editor Marsha Bailey suggests, "In dealing with Hispanic offenders, parole officers should be direct and to the point when instructing, and should expect to see more reaction from parolees" as "Hispanics generally are more immediate and vocal in communication; sometimes the dialogue sounds more intimidating than it really is."[22] Miscommunication is the basis for some interpersonal conflict and the cause for some criminal injustice, which explains, for instance, why 91 percent of state and local law enforcement training academies include communications among their major subject areas of instruction. The median number of hours of training at the academies was 15.[23]

Communication comes in two forms: verbal and nonverbal. Verbal communication consists of the words we speak. Nonverbal communication entails all nonvocal acts that convey a message. The judge at the beginning of this chapter based his assumptions of the suspect upon nonverbal cues, and offered his input via verbal communication. The visible power differential in the courtroom, for example, with the judge dressed in a robe and sitting above the courtroom actors, is also a form of nonverbal communication (e.g., the judge expects respect).

THE COMMUNICATION PROCESS

To understand the impact of communication in the criminal justice system one could deconstruct the communication process. Deconstructing verbal communication provides a starting point for understanding nonverbal communication. Understanding verbal communication begins with the thought process of the individual sending the verbal message (the sender). At the most basic level, the sender interprets or analyzes a situation and generates thoughts. Part of the interpretation and analyses involves determining what message the sender wishes to transmit and how he or she wishes to send it. There is a filter involved as we all sometimes think about saying things, yet refrain from doing so. Some of us have a more restrictive or porous filter than others, which explains why some folks are quiet, others speak their mind, and why some are constantly putting their foot in their mouth.

Once the message is created in the sender's mind, the individual targets others (receivers) whom he or she wishes to hear the message. It sometimes occurs that we wish to convey a message to some individuals present, yet exclude others from the message, which is why we sometimes whisper or speak coyly. Upon locating proper targets, the sender conveys the message via some channel, typically either verbally or in writing. Failing to properly organize thoughts has prompted many misunderstandings and controversies. Aside from the spoken words, the pitch and tone of one's verbal message certainly influences verbal communication.

Receivers encode the message through receiving, interpreting, and analyzing the message. Proper listening is key to verbal communication. Although the act of hearing is physical in nature, listening is a mental exercise. Effective listeners often maintain the ability to lead the conversation. Many people, however, are not effective listeners, and the proliferation of distractions, in the form of electronic devices (e.g., cell phones), for instance, has hampered communication.[24]

Upon hearing and listening to the message, receivers generate a response regarding how they received, interpreted, and understood the message. For instance, the message could generate a series of verbal and nonverbal reactions, including a return message, smile, frown, punch, and/or gunshot. The communication process continues until one or all participants find a suitable point for conclusion. Of particular importance in this exchange are one's ability to generate thoughts into words or actions (including the filtering process) and the ability of others to receive, interpret, and adequately respond to the message. Former president Ronald Reagan was deemed the "Great Communicator" for his ability to inspire many with his words and actions. Table 2-3 depicts the communication process.

Of particular concern with regard to any form of communication is the message being sent. Mostly, the communication process succeeds and receivers understand the sender's message. The message, however, may generate a reaction, or series of reactions. For instance, **hate speech** includes communication that attacks individuals or groups on the basis of specific attributes, such as race, ethnicity, gender, sexual orientation, religion, or

Table 2.3 The Communication Process

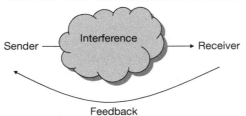

Effective communication requires messages to be sent effectively, and listeners to be receptive of the message.

disability. Such communication can be in the form of speech, conduct, writing, gestures, or displays directed against specific groups. Some cities and colleges in the United States have adopted policies that ban hate speech, however such acts have generated claims that the bans violate the First Amendment protections with regard to the freedom of speech.

NONVERBAL COMMUNICATION

Nonverbal communication also involves reception, interpretation, and reaction. One merely needs to view commercial advertising to understand the power of nonverbal communication and symbolic cues. Advertisements including vehicles driving in idealistic environments or individuals drinking beer on an exotic island suggest to consumers that purchase of a particular product will enable them to live such lifestyles. Much research and consideration goes into commercial advertising, so at some point during the advertising development phase a marketing group determined that nonverbal cues such as a hammock and a beach would entice consumers to drink their beer.

Nonverbal cues such as clothing, body posture, eye contact, and physical aggression are significant forms of communication that generate and dictate much action within the criminal justice system. Nonverbal communication begins with the nonverbal message transmitted by a sender, which can be in the form of body movements, facial expressions, and gestures. The message is then received and interpreted by the receiver, who evaluates the message and sender and reacts. Similar to verbal communication, the message being sent isn't always the message received.

Interpretation and analyses of nonverbal communication pose particular obstacles due to the greater amount of subjectivity involved, especially since a message isn't being directly conveyed like verbal exchanges. This obstacle is evident in the earlier passage when the judge interprets the suspect's behavior of failing to make eye contact as a sign of disrespect. The significance of nonverbal cues is also recognized in police departments that use a force continuum to guide officer decision-making when encountering potentially violent situations. The **continuum of force** is a concept that guides officer behavior with respect to use of force. Officers are expected to consider the continuum of force in their attempts to adequately interpret and respond to suspect behavior. For instance, officers are legally permitted to use deadly force only when they perceive suspects as posing deadly threats to the officer and/or others. The perception aspect of the laws surrounding deadly force involves officers interpreting nonverbal (and sometimes verbal) cues. Failure to react accordingly could result in death(s), civil and criminal litigation, and the officer's dismissal from the force.

Of particular importance in any discussion of communication are kinesics, vocalics, and proxemics.[25] **Kinesics** refers to body language, including gestures, facial expressions, eye behavior, and body movements. **Vocalics**, or paralanguage, refers to vocal characteristics such as inflection, tone, accent, rate, pitch, volume, and vocal interrupters. **Proxemics** refers to the space between the communicator and his/her audience. The actions within the criminal justice system take place at all levels of space. For instance, police officers are sometimes required to physically detain suspects through invasion of the individual's intimate space, while communications between prison officers and prisoners may occur within personal space. Judges sitting in a courtroom typically conduct business from a public distance. The varying levels of acceptable or expected interaction amongst cultures sometimes leads to misunderstandings and perhaps violence.

THE CONFEDERATE FLAG AND ITS MEANING

In June 2015, a White gunman killed nine people in a Black church in Charleston, South Carolina. The gunman, Dylann Roof, was captured and faced thirty-three federal hate crime charges and, among other charges, nine counts of murder by the State of South Carolina. He received the death penalty for his actions, and became the first federal hate crime defendant to receive capital punishment. The mass murder reignited arguments that South Carolina should no longer fly the Confederate flag over its State Capitol building. Following his arrest, photos of Roof appeared depicting him wrapped in a Confederate flag accompanied by a hate-filled account with his racist comments. He appeared in other photos displaying the flag.

The debate over displaying the Confederate flag has continued for decades. Some feel it is a symbol of free speech, provides recognition of the soldiers who fought for the Confederacy, and it is a proud sign of Southern heritage. They argue that displaying the flag is their right under the First Amendment. Others feel it is a symbol of White supremacy, hate, racial intolerance, and slavery. The flag means different things to different people, and has generated controversy throughout the

United States for some time. In July 2015, the Confederate flag was removed from the South Carolina State Capitol. Politicians felt pressure from many groups, and decided that the removal of the flag would help with recovery efforts from the tragedy in Charleston.

The debate over displaying the flag continues, however, as South Carolina was certainly not the only state having to address the issue, and flying the flag over the State Capitol was not the only case. For example, on the same day as the Charleston shooting, the U.S. Supreme Court ruled that Texas did not violate the First Amendment by refusing to create specialty license plates displaying the flag.[26] At the time, the flag appeared on license plates in several southern states, however the Court's ruling allows the states to ban the plates. Further, some states (e.g., Alabama, Georgia, Arkansas, Florida) have images or symbols on their flags that reflect the Confederacy. Mississippi's state flag actually features the Confederate emblem. Debates over the meaning of the Confederate flag and the Constitutionality of portraying it will continue, as the flags mean different things to different people and highlight the importance of symbolism in everyday life.

OBSTACLES AFFECTING COMMUNICATION

Many obstacles or hurdles exist in the communication process, as effective communication involves an expectation that all parties clearly understand each other. One must bear in mind that we often use words, which are human creations, to convey a message and rely on the perception of others to correctly interpret the message. The meanings of words exist in people, not in the actual spoken words.[27]

Perception refers to the act of becoming aware or apprehending something via the senses. As such, word selection is vital to effective communication as there is an assumption that all receivers have the same interpretation of the word. For instance, individuals, specifically suspects, are sometimes deemed "dangerous" or "threatening." Such a classification generally prompts a rapid, punitive response; yet, we must ask several questions before we act too rashly. For instance, we must ask, "How are they dangerous?" and "To whom are they dangerous or threatening?" For example, there was a great sense of insecurity in the United States following the terrorist attacks of September 11, 2001. In response, the criteria for perceptions of "dangerous" and "threatening" differed following the attacks, and it is argued that a substantial number of individuals were inaccurately deemed "dangerous." Ethnic profiling has become increasingly recognized in the United States since the attacks.[28]

Prominent among the hurdles involved in communication is the fact that the human body is limited in its intake capacity, and interference can certainly play a role in miscommunication. The limited capacity of the human brain prevents us from fully ingesting and interpreting all societal cues.[29] Physical challenges such as color-blindness, deafness, blindness, and speaking with a thick accent also restrict successful communication.

Of particular significance to criminal justice is the expectations that conveyed messages will be received and interpreted in the proper context. The multicultural society in which we live poses significant challenges given the numerous languages spoken and the varied values, beliefs, and expectations associated with the grouping and interactions of individuals from various cultures. The ability to speak a second (or third) language is becoming increasingly important for criminal justice professionals, particularly since language is a primary identifying feature of a culture.[30] Table 2-4 depicts results from the U.S. Census Bureau's survey of the languages spoken in U.S. households.

Table 2.4 Language Spoken at Home in the United States, 2010–2014.

Subject	Total
Population age 5 years and older	294,133,373
Speak only English	79.1%
Speak a language other than English	20.9%
Spanish	13.0%
Other Indo-European languages	3.7%
Asian and Pacific Island languages	3.3%
Other languages	.9%

Source: U.S. Census Bureau, 2010–2014 American Community Survey 5-Year Estimates

Table 2.5 Top 10 Most Spoken Languages in the World

Language	Total speakers
Chinese	1,380 million
English	850 million
Spanish	500 million
Arabic	490 million
Hindi	380 million
Bengali	271 million
Russian	260 million
Portuguese	250 million
French	220 million
Malay	220 million

Source: ABCNewspoint.com, "Top 10 Most Spoken and Most Popular Languages in the World," 2015. Accessed online at: http://www.abcnewspoint.com/top-10-most-spoken-and-most-popular-languages-in-the-world/

The limitations inherent in communication are sometimes addressed through restating, or re-emphasizing the message, as we often hear senders state, "Let me clarify . . . ," or "Put simply . . . ," or "For example. . . ." Understanding how individuals react to miscommunication and how to resolve miscommunication should be of utmost importance to criminal justice practitioners and scholars. Understanding our reactions to miscommunication is perhaps as important as recognizing the reasons why we mis-communicate.

DIFFERENTIAL TREATMENT AND SYMBOLISM

The criminal justice literature is filled with studies examining differential treatment of groups based on symbolic cues. **Symbols**, or items used to represent something else, are evident throughout the criminal justice system. For instance, the police officer's badge, the judge's gown, and the scales of justice are but a few of the many symbols used by criminal justice personnel to represent something else. The use of symbols, of course, requires that all who encounter the symbol understand what it is being symbolized.

Criminal justice personnel not only display symbols, they interpret them as well. Two well-documented examples of symbolism influencing police discretion include the concept of "symbolic assailants" and, more recently, racial profiling. Years ago scholar Jerome Skolnick used the term **symbolic assailant** to refer to particular individuals, as perceived by police officers, who appear as potential sources of violence or as enemies to be reckoned with. Skolnick described symbolic assailants as "persons who use gesture, language, and attire that the policeman has come to recognize as a prelude to violence."[31]

Racial profiling, also discussed elsewhere in this book, is among the hot topics in policing and society in general. **Racial profiling**, which involves recognizing individuals as suspects based merely upon race, has existed in society since groups of different backgrounds interacted. The relatively short history of the United States is rife with

Racial profiling occurs in many contexts and has drawn much public attention in recent years. Some view it as an effective yet illegal tool for law enforcement, while others cite the discrimination inherent in its use.

accounts of racial profiling, not the least of which involves the Anglo settlers confronting Native Americans prior to and following the Revolutionary War. It has only recently been the topic of much discussion from a research and policy standpoint, particularly in light of accounts of African American motorists being targeted by law enforcement and the differential treatment of those of Middle-Eastern descent following the terrorist attacks of September 11, 2001.[32] Racial profiling exemplifies how images and stereotypes of various racial, cultural, and ethnic groups influence formal social control efforts.[33]

Racial profiling is not always targeted toward minority groups and is not always based on race. Police officers often note that crime detection is sometimes an advanced version of the children's game "Which One of These Things is Not Like the Other." Specifically, officers identify individuals or objects that don't "fit" within the context of the situation. Examples include expensive automobiles in low income areas, a minority suspect loitering in a predominantly nonminority neighborhood, or a nonminority loitering in a predominantly minority neighborhood. In other words, officers use symbolic cues to base their actions. Proponents of racial profiling argue that categorizing individuals based on appearance is necessary for solid police work, while opponents argue that appearance alone should not dictate perceptions of one's behavior.

This base-level account of verbal and nonverbal communication is elaborated upon in the communications studies literature. We've only scratched the surface of the intricate nature of interpersonal communication in an understanding of how individuals communicate, how communications can become distorted, and the significance of miscommunication.

SOCIAL INTERACTION AND MULTICULTURALISM

Social interaction is the process through which individuals act and react in relation to other individuals. Volumes have been written on the complex nature of social interaction, and we can be sure that many more works are forthcoming. Our discussion of social interaction is restricted to the dynamics and complexities involving human interaction in a multicultural society, with particular emphasis on the criminal justice system.

A primary challenge of a multicultural society involves group members' ability to effectively coexist. To understand social interaction in a multicultural society requires recognition of what constitutes culture. Historically, a White, male, European world-view has defined and controlled the majority culture in the United States.[34] However, the world is becoming increasingly diverse as society grows and national borders continuously open. Sociologist John Macionis stated that "Multiculturalism represents a sharp change from the past, when our society downplayed cultural diversity and defined itself primarily in terms of well-off European and especially English immigrants."[35]

Social interaction is regulated by norms that are primarily determined by our culture. However, people act out norms in various means. Cultural norms provide guidance for our behavior. **Culture** refers to the learned beliefs, values, norms, behaviors, and material goods that collectively constitute a people's manner of life. Culture shapes what we do and shapes our personalities.[36] It is often categorized into two categories: material and nonmaterial. **Material culture** consists of objects that are real to the senses (e.g., a baton, handcuffs, a judge's gavel). **Nonmaterial culture** is largely composed of our shared beliefs and values, and the social expectations individuals have for one another. Because nonmaterial culture is not able to be seen, it is particularly problematic when cultures interact.[37]

Despite the conflicts that develop, people in the United States take great pride in its status as a "melting pot," in which individuals from all cultures are welcome and expected to contribute to the greater good. In turn, the United States is a notably diverse and heterogeneous society consisting of individuals from many different backgrounds and cultures. The extensive diversity in the United States continues to increase. Annually, roughly 1 million people from other countries come to the United States. In contrast, historic isolation has made Japan the most monocultural of all high-income nations. Intense immigration has contributed to the United States becoming the most multicultural of all high-income countries. A century ago most immigrants to the United States hailed from Europe, but today most immigrants arrive from Asia and Latin America.

STATUS AND ROLES

Understanding social interaction requires recognition of both status and role. **Status** involves the social position maintained by an individual. **Role** refers to the behavior that is expected of an individual who maintains a particular status. Status is part of our everyday behavior and helps dictate our relationship with those whom we interact. We each hold a status set which entails the different statuses we maintain at a given time. Statuses are subject to change over time. For instance, one could be a student, a correctional officer, and a father. The multiple statuses that we maintain at a given time dictate the roles we play in everyday life. We could play the role of judge, jury member, probation officer, or therapist. Roles refer to the actions or activities that constitute one's status.

We sometimes encounter role conflict. For instance, consider the dilemma of the police officer who is hanging out at a bar with a group of friends. The officer notices that one guy in the group may be unfit (i.e., too drunk) to drive home, even though he says he's "fine" and the others in the group see no problem letting him drive. The officer is faced with role conflict in that he took an oath to serve and protect, yet he wants to remain "one of the guys," not the "police officer friend" in the group. How should the officer handle this situation?

Statuses and roles are noticeably evident in the criminal justice system. For example, the prison officer expects, based on their status, to be treated with respect by inmates. Inmates often expect the same treatment, however, their status as "offenders" leaves them in a position to receive limited respect. There are clear hierarchies in many criminal justice agencies that specifically designate one's status in the system.

SOCIALLY CONSTRUCTING REALITY

Some researchers argue that individuals don't understand society in a truly objective manner. Instead, it is argued that people mentally construct ideas about phenomena and thus create a reality, in what is recognized as the **social construction of reality**.[38] Through interacting with one another we creatively mold a reality that could vary according to the interpretations of participants. Social interaction involves complex negotiations of reality. Most of us can agree about what occurs in everyday life; however we may all have different perceptions of what happens. Such differences, particularly as they exist in the criminal justice system and with regard to various cultures, could lead to significant miscommunication and uncomfortable interactions.

It is often argued that issues are socially constructed with particular ideologies in mind. For instance, the war on drugs has disproportionately impacted young, minority males, leading some researchers to question the identified intentions of the war. More generally, one could argue that society's preoccupation with street crime, as opposed to white collar crime, stems from the status and power differentials of the groups primarily involved in each type of crime. Street crime arrests typically involve lower-class minority males, while white collar crimes are recognized as predominantly involving wealthy non-minorities. Some argue that the constructed images of the "typical criminal" and the "war on (street) crime" enable the more powerful in society to maintain status quo with regard to the discrepancy in power.

Sports-talk radio provides an example of competing constructions of the world. Consider, for example, discussions of college football rankings. Put simply, college football rankings are highly subjective. The manner by which teams are evaluated and ranked is highly suspect, at times political, and sometimes responsible for schools earning or losing millions of dollars. To say that one team should be ranked higher than another (higher meaning better), when in fact the teams have not played each other or a common opponent leads to much discussion and argument. Sports-radio hosts and their guests debate how the teams should be ranked, all the while sharing their constructed reality that often differs from the reality created by others.

Subjectivity is inherent in communication, and in a multicultural society subjectivity becomes critical in human interaction. Consciously or subconsciously, we all incorporate subjectivity during social interaction. Sometimes, unfortunately, the subjectivity involves characteristics that hamper the coexistence of various groups and acceptance of others. Social interaction is grounded in the belief that messages conveyed will be interpreted in the manner intended. We know, however, that social interaction is often clouded by mis-hearings, mis-speaks, misinterpretations, and various other misunderstandings.[39]

SUMMARY

The significance of cultural diversity in the criminal justice system is evidenced in a Bureau of Justice Statistics report which noted that 95 percent of state and local law enforcement training academies offer training in cultural diversity and human relations, while 78 percent train cadets with regard to hate/bias crimes.[40] The median number of hours for cultural diversity training was 12, while the median number of hours devoted to hate/bias crimes was 3. The need for more effective interaction with the various cultural groups entering the criminal justice system is well-documented. Many solutions have been offered in response, including promotion of multiculturalism in criminal justice education.

Researcher William Calathes argues that "Criminal justice education has missed much by promulgating a 'melting pot' philosophy. Our students think in terms of White mono-culturalism, the assumption that we all belong to one system, which is that of White Anglo-Europeans."[41] The changing nature of society encourages greater recognition of multiculturalism in criminal justice curriculums, as today's criminal justice students are tomorrow's justice professionals.

At any stage during the suspect-turned-offender's journey through the criminal justice system, he or she could very easily encounter someone who doesn't view society in the same manner as he or she does. For instance, cultural differences may result in a jury rendering an unfavorable verdict based on preferences or prejudices. The opportunity for mis-communication increases as the number of contacts throughout case processing increases. In turn, there's a greater chance of misunderstanding and misguided behaviors because the suspect/offender encountered a greater number of individuals. An overriding goal of the criminal justice system, then, should be to eliminate, or at least reduce, the likelihood of injustices occurring from improper personal interactions.

Addressing cultural differences as they exist throughout the system is a vital first step toward addressing the issue, as evidenced for example, in the training provided correctional officers at the New Mexico Corrections Training Academy. The Academy requires cadets to recognize and practice facial expressions, posture, positioning, and distance. Such training, which is not restricted to the New Mexico Corrections Training Academy, helps cadets understand various aspects of nonverbal communication.[42]

The criminal justice system is, by nature, supported by human interaction. Consider the various contexts of human interaction found at all steps involved in criminal case processing. To begin, a crime is committed and someone contacts the authorities. The police investigate primarily through interviewing witnesses and suspects. An arrest may ultimately be made, and the suspect is turned over to the courts where he or she will interact with judges, prosecutors, defense attorneys, and possibly jurors. If convicted, the offender is turned over to the supervision of some correctional group and will encounter many different situations involving individuals from various backgrounds.

The manner in which social interaction takes place in the criminal justice system is influenced by the technological revolution society is currently experiencing. For instance, computers eliminate much of the busywork previously associated with running background checks on individuals and vehicles. The need to communicate with a dispatcher is reduced as mobile computer units are found in many police cars. In corrections, global positional satellite monitoring (GPS) is used to track some offenders serving their penalties in the community. For instance, in June 2006, South Carolina governor Mark Sanford signed a bill that mandates GPS monitoring for sex offenders convicted of certain offenses. This form of electronic monitoring will likely increase in the criminal justice system, as the number of face-to-face contacts required as part of probation and paroles plans are likely reduced. Email has significantly changed the manner in which many of us interact, as it is easier for many of us to send an email as opposed to making a phone call or personally visiting our target recipient. In the end, understanding and comprehending technology-based communications is becoming increasingly important.

YOU MAKE THE CALL

SYMBOLISM AND POLICING

Consider the following scenario. Debate the pros and cons of all options and decide what you would do.

You're a rookie police officer teamed with an experienced officer on patrol. You're both White males on patrol in a predominantly Asian neighborhood. Racial tensions between the police and the residents were enhanced last week when a White officer was accused of using excessive force on a young Asian suspect. As you patrol, you and your partner notice a young Asian male wearing a shirt that states "I hate pigs" and has a picture of a gun pointing at a police officer. You let it roll off your back, as you've been trained to do. Your partner, however, tells you to pull over. He suggests the "punk needs to show a little respect." Your partner approaches the Asian youth and tells him to get into the car. The youth complies and your partner tells you to drive off. While driving around, your partner threatens to violently beat the youth and make sure that nobody knows about it. You're taken aback by what's going on,

as you expected more from your colleague. The youth is crying, fearful for his life. He says his older brother made him wear the shirt. After awhile, your partner tells you to pull over and let the youth out. He's about two miles from where you picked him up, and is left to find a ride home. While pulling away, the officer tells the boy that if anything is said of this encounter, the officer will follow through on his threats.

Questions

1. Should our laws regarding freedom of expression permit individuals to wear hate-based, threatening clothing?
2. What type of social interaction and nonverbal communication instigated this incident?
3. Should you and your fellow officer have responded at all to the symbolism found on the youth's shirt?
4. What steps should you have taken to address this troubling situation? How would your actions have impacted your role and status as a police officer?

KEY TERMS

appearance	courtroom workgroup
concealing errors	culture
concealing secret pleasures	discredited stigma
continuum of force	dramaturgical circumspection

dramaturgical discipline
dramaturgy
ethnocentrism
explicit bias
going rate
group goals
group structure
hate speech
implicit bias
kinesics
manner
material culture
nonmaterial culture
perception

personal front
proxemics
racial profiling
role
setting
showing only the end product
social construction of reality
social groups
social interaction
status
symbolic assailant
symbols
vocalics

DISCUSSION QUESTIONS

1. Discuss how those who enter the courtroom as "innocent until proven guilty" may not be recognized as such.
2. Identify and discuss the five characteristics of a group. Would you consider the members of a football team a group? Why or why not?
3. How is assimilation different from multiculturalism? Do you believe multiculturalism is more prominent within society than assimilation? Why or why not?
4. Describe the verbal communication process and note how miscommunication occurs.
5. Describe the similarities between the "typical criminal" and the "symbolic assailant." Do you believe it is effective police practice for officers to identify individuals as threats based on demographic profiles? Do you believe it is fair for officers to do so?

FOR FURTHER READING

Beauchamp, S. R., and S. J. Baran. *Introduction to Human Communication: Perception, Meaning, and Identity.* New York: Oxford University Press, 2015.

Berger, Peter L., and Thomas Luckmann. *The Social Construction of Reality: A Treatise in the Sociology of Knowledge.* New York: Penguin Books, 1991.

Goffman, E. *The Presentation of Self in Everyday Life.* New York: Doubleday, 1959.

Reiman, J., and P. Leighton. *The Rich Get Richer and the Poor Get Prison: Ideology, Class, and Criminal Justice.* 10th ed. Boston, MA: Allyn and Bacon, 2013.

Rothwell, J. D. *In the Company of Others.* 5th ed. New York: Oxford University Press, 2016.

NOTES

1. E. Goffman, *The Presentation of Self in Everyday Life* (New York: Doubleday, 1959).
2. Ibid.
3. Ibid.
4. E. Goffman, *Stigma: Notes on the Management of Spoiled Identity* (Englewood Cliffs, NJ: Prentice-Hall, 1963).

5. Ibid.

6. J. Reiman and P. Leighton, *The Rich Get Richer and the Poor Get Prison: Ideology, Class, and Criminal Justice*, 10th ed. (Boston, MA: Allyn and Bacon, 2013).

7. John L. Graham and Yoshihiro Sano, *Smart Bargaining: Doing Business with the Japanese* (Cambridge, MA: Ballinger, 1984).

8. Robert L. Young, *Understanding Misunderstandings: A Practical Guide to More Successful Human Interaction* (Austin, TX: University of Texas Press, 1999), 122.

9. Ibid, 102.

10. Ibid, 103.

11. J. Goldstein, "Little-Known Guide Helps Police Navigate a Diverse City," *New York Times*, June 10, 2013. Accessed online at: http://www.nytimes.com/2013/06/11/nyregion/a-not-for-tourists-guide-to-navigating-a-multicultural-city.html?_r=0

12. *Furman v. Georgia*, 408 U.S. 238 (1972).

13. See, for example, Charles Crawford, Ted Chiricos, and Gary Kleck, "Race, Racial Threat, and Sentencing of Habitual Offenders," *Criminology* 36, no. 3 (1998): 481–511.

14. Nancy Rodriquez, "The Nexus Between Race and Ethnicity and Criminal Justice Policy," in *Images of Color, Images of Crime: Readings*, 3rd ed. (Los Angeles, CA: Roxbury, 2006), 249.

15. Joann Keyton, *Communicating in Groups: Building Relationships for Group Effectiveness*, 3rd ed. (New York: Oxford University Press, 2006), 4, 5.

16. W. E. Thompson, J. V. Hickey, and M. L. Thompson, *Society in Focus: An Introduction to Sociology*, 8th ed., Lanham, MD: Rowman & Littlefield, 2016), 143.

17. Keyton, *Communicating in Groups*, 5.

18. Ibid, 7.

19. Ibid, 10.

20. Ibid, 10, 11, 13.

21. D. W. Neubauer and H. F. Fradella, *America's Courts and the Criminal Justice System*, 12th ed. (Boston, MA: Cengage, 2017), 7.

22. Marsha Bailey, "Georgia Parole Officers Confront Language and Cultural Barriers." *Corrections Today* (December 1991): 118, 121.

23. B. A. Reaves, *State and Local Law Enforcement Training Academies, 2013*. U.S. Department of Justice, Bureau of Justice Statistics, 2016, NCJ 249784, 5.

24. B. Sullivan and H. Thompson, *The Plateau Effect: Getting from Stuck to Success* (New York: Dutton, 2013).

25. Keyton, *Communicating in Groups*.

26. *Walker v. Texas Division, Sons of Confederate Veterans*. (2015). 576 U.S.

27. Ronald D. Hunter, Thomas Barker and Pamela D. Mayhall, *Police-Community Relations and the Administration of Justice*, 7th ed. (Upper Saddle River, NJ: Prentice Hall, 2008).

28. D. Johnson, D. Brazier, K. Forrest, C. Ketelhut, D. Mason, and M. Mitchell, "Attitudes Toward the Use of Racial/Ethnic Profiling to Prevent Crime and Terrorism." *Criminal Justice Policy Review* 22, no. 4 (2011): 422–27.

29. C. Ray Jeffery, *Criminology: An Interdisciplinary Approach* (Englewood Cliffs, NJ: Prentice Hall, 1990).

30. Gary Cesarz and Joyce Madrid-Bustos, "Taking a Multicultural World View in Today's Corrections Facilities," *Corrections Today* 53, no. 7 (December 1991), 68–71.

31. Jerome H. Skolnick, *Justice Without Trial: Law Enforcement in a Democratic Society*, 4th ed. (New Orleands, LA: Quid Pro, 2011).

32. See e.g., Richard Lundman and Robert L. Kaufman, "Driving While Black: Effects of Race, Ethnicity, and Gender on Citizen Self-Reports on Traffic Stops and Police Actions," *Criminology* 41, no. 1 (2003): 195–220.

33. Rodriguez, "The Nexus Between Race and Ethnicity."

34. Linda S. Miller and Karen M. Hess, *The Police in the Community: Strategies for the 21st Century,* 3rd ed. (Belmont, CA: Wadsworth, 2002).

35. J. J. Macionis, *Sociology,* 15th ed. (Upper Saddle River, NJ: Pearson, 2014), 48.

36. Thompson, et al., *Society in Focus.*

37. Young, *Understanding Misunderstandings,* 101.

38. Peter L. Berger and Thomas Luckmann, *The Social Construction of Reality: A Treatise in the Sociology of Knowledge* (New York: Anchor, 1966).

39. Young, *Understanding Misunderstandings.*

40. Reaves, *State and Local Law Enforcement Training Academies.*

41. William Calathes, "The Case for a Multicultural Approach to Teaching Criminal Justice," *Journal of Criminal Justice Education* 5, no. 1 (1994): 1.

42. Cesarz and Madrid-Bustos, "Taking a Multicultural World View."

PART II

CULTURAL SPECIFICS IN THE CRIMINAL JUSTICE SYSTEM

CHAPTER 3

AFRICAN AMERICANS AND THE CRIMINAL JUSTICE SYSTEM

CHAPTER OBJECTIVES

After reading this chapter, you should be able to:

- Identify the role slavery and Reconstruction played in the history of the African American experience in this country
- Understand the current state of African Americans, particularly the rise of the Black middle class
- Describe the ways in which African Americans perceive the police
- Understand the overrepresentation of African Americans in the criminal justice system, including arrests, use of force, deadly force, sentencing, and the death penalty

The African American experience in the United States is perhaps best understood by examining their present position in American culture as well as the historical context in which this diverse group of people came to this country. While many experts recognize the varying degrees of difference among Hispanic or Latino Americans, the diversity of African Americans is often overlooked. This is particularly true as many African Americans have transcended social class, educational, and political boundaries. This chapter will explore the presence of African Americans in the social, political, and economic development of the United States as well as offer insight into how and in what ways they become involved in the criminal justice system.

HISTORICAL BACKGROUND

There is little disagreement among historians, sociologists, and anthropologists about the fact that African Americans played a significant role in the development of the United States. Black people accompanied the first explorers to this country in the early 1600s, and a Black man was among the first to die in the American Revolution.[1] In fact, over 5,000 Blacks fought in the American Revolution and over 200,000 fought during the Civil War.[2] In the 1960s, the mistreatment of African Americans resulted in numerous riots and other violent episodes in many cities across America.[3] However, the most significant event in American history as it relates to the African American experience was slavery.

SLAVERY

The significance of slavery in the United States is argued by many experts to be the basis for most of the racism, discrimination, and prejudice experienced by African Americans today. Thus, slavery was not simply a single tragic event in the development of a country; rather slavery has been an essential part of this country's social, political, and economic fabric for nearly four hundred years. In fact, for nearly half of America's history, slavery was not only tolerated, but was legally protected by the Constitution and the United States Supreme Court.[4] As slavery developed in colonial America, **slave codes**, or laws regulating slave behavior, were created to clarify the position of slaves. Because they were legal, binding, and carried the support of the law, slave codes controlled and determined all aspects of the lives of enslaved Africans, including how slaves were to think, act, and believe.[5]

In an effort to quell potential uprisings by slaves, owners often used religion as a tool to foster compliance. While African religions were forbidden, slave owners introduced slaves to a distorted version of Christianity that taught complete obedience to one's master and to Whites in general led to salvation and eternal happiness. To do otherwise (such as questioning slavery) would be to question God's will, resulting in everlasting damnation.[6] While clearly designed by slave owners to gain compliance and to reduce conflict, religion served another valuable purpose. Nightly prayer meetings and singing gave slaves a sense of unity and made their lives more bearable.[7]

THE POST-SLAVERY ERA

For a generation after the American Revolution, restrictions on slaves increased as Southerners accepted slavery as a permanent feature of the economic and social landscape. In order to appease the South, writers of the Constitution legitimized slavery's existence by allowing a slave to be counted as three-fifths of a person in determining representation in the House of Representatives.[8] **Abolitionists** contended that slavery was morally objectionable, and slaves made the problem worse by not participating in protests. Many Southern states responded to this passive acceptance of slavery by enacting **fugitive slave acts**, which required slaves who had escaped, even to a free state, to be returned to their owners.[9]

In 1863, the **Emancipation Proclamation** was signed; however, the proclamation freed slaves only in the Confederacy. Two years later abolition became a reality when the 13th Amendment abolished slavery nationwide.[10] From 1867 to 1877, a period known as **Reconstruction**, a new social, political, and economic portrait of the South was created. Because the federal government recognized that Southern states would not likely comply with the parameters of Reconstruction, The **Reconstruction Act of 1867** was passed to require compliance. According to the act, each Southern state was controlled by a military governor until a new state constitution could be written.[11] This meant that

Blacks were segregated in all aspects of life and this was the law of the land as late as 1896 and beyond.

until each state created a constitution that recognized Blacks as equal, the federal government would retain control over that state. Added to the problems of Reconstruction was the resistance Blacks felt from Whites after Reconstruction ended. Evidence of this resistance was found in the **Jim Crow** era. Jim Crow was a slave who entertained people through song and dance. White performers imitated him in singing and dancing style, and some used makeup to look like Jim Crow. The term Jim Crow eventually became a label for the social, political, and legal separation of Whites and Blacks in all aspects of society.[12]

By the end of the nineteenth century, with the legalization of segregation, discrimination against Blacks became more evident. In 1896, the U.S. Supreme Court ruled in *Plessy v. Ferguson* that state laws requiring separate but equal accommodations, such as drinking fountains or restrooms, for Blacks were a reasonable use of state government power.[13] In 1898, the Supreme Court ruled in *Williams v. Mississippi* that the use of poll taxes, literacy tests, and residential requirements were constitutional. Clearly these measures were used to discourage Blacks from voting, but even these measures did not prevent voting completely.[14] The South created a one-party system, which excluded Blacks from voting. This was considered constitutional because the party was defined as a private organization free to define its own membership.[15]

In response to the way they were treated in the South, many Blacks— nearly one million between 1914 and 1920—moved to the North in the hope of a better life.[16] However, those who thought life would be better in the North were met with a similar form of discrimination and prejudice by Whites, which led to the **Civil Rights Movement**, which began in the 1960s.

THE CIVIL RIGHTS MOVEMENT

Perhaps in the hopes of achieving equality or at least some level of respect from Whites, over one million Blacks served in the military during World War II.[17] However, Blacks soon found that discrimination also existed in the military. Training for Blacks was minimal, troops were separated by color, and most of the tasks given to Blacks were menial.[18] After the war ended, there were many opportunities for jobs due to the growth of a number of industries. As a result, many people moved to the cities for work, causing schools to become overcrowded and housing to become limited. As problems stemming from congestion escalated, the courts decided cases related to segregation issues, arguably the most important of which focused on the education of Black children.

The Civil Rights Movement was essentially the culmination of many attempts by African Americans to secure equality following World War II. Several U.S. Supreme Court decisions during this period suggested a shift in thinking away from tolerating racial inequalities. The White primary and one-party system in the South was finally challenged and declared unconstitutional in the 1944 case of *Smith v. Allwright*. However, many states simply passed laws that used other measures to frustrate African American voters.[19] One such measure was **restrictive covenants**, a private contract between neighborhood property owners, which stipulated that property could not be sold or rented to certain minority groups, thus ensuring minorities could not live in the area. In 1948, in *Shelly v. Kraemer*, the Supreme Court ruled that such covenants were unconstitutional.

While there were demonstrations and lawsuits since 1942, perhaps the most noted event for the start of the Civil Rights Movement was the 1954 U.S. Supreme Court's

The Civil Rights Movement was one of the most significant events in the history of this country and was an attempt to secure equal protections under the law for African Americans.

decision in *Brown v. Board of Education*. However, the *Brown v. Board of Education* case was not the only attack on White supremacy. There are many examples of rebellion by African Americans as early as 1942, but by 1954, unequal treatment for African Americans was a common feature of the social landscape.[20]

For the majority of Black children, public education meant attending segregated schools. Some school districts assigned children to school by race rather than by neighborhood, which is the practice that was challenged in the *Brown* case. Seven-year-old Linda Brown was not permitted to enroll in the grade school four blocks from her home in Topeka, Kansas. The policy of the local school board dictated that she attend the Black school almost two miles from her home. The NAACP Legal Defense Fund filed a lawsuit on behalf of Linda and twelve other Black children.

The NAACP argued that the 14th Amendment should rule out segregation in public schools. Thurgood Marshall argued the case for the NAACP, and he went on to become a member of the United States Supreme Court.[21] The issue for the NAACP was simply that Blacks should be allowed to go to school with Whites. Given their conditions, funding, and size, all-Black schools could never be equal to all-White schools. The result was that Black children were denied the protections of the due process clause of the Fourteenth Amendment.[22]

The reaction to the *Brown* decision to desegregate public schools "with all deliberate speed," was angry and swift. Some state legislators in the South called for the impeachment of all the Supreme Court justices, others petitioned Congress to declare the 14th Amendment unconstitutional, and some cities even closed schools rather than comply with the ruling. In Little Rock, Arkansas, the governor enlisted the National Guard to prevent Black students from entering previously all-White high schools.[23]

The most enduring resistance to *Brown* was found in the formation of White Citizens' Councils. Founded in Mississippi, these councils spread throughout the South and claimed as many as half a million members. The groups began opening private all-White **Freedom Schools** that enrolled an estimated 300,000 White children by 1970. All of this effort was done with the sole intent of evading the *Brown* decision.[24]

In 1962, school desegregation took another fascinating turn when Mississippi National Guardsmen and federal authorities clashed over the admission of James Meredith, who was the first African American admitted to the University of Mississippi. A year later, Governor George Wallace "stood in the schoolhouse door" to block two Blacks from enrolling in the University of Alabama. In response to such outlandish opposition to federal law, President Kennedy federalized the Alabama National Guard in order to guarantee that the students would be admitted to campus.[25]

CIVIL DISOBEDIENCE

On December 1, 1955, Martin Luther King Jr. began his campaign of civil disobedience after the famous Rosa Parks episode. In 1955, in Montgomery, Alabama, Parks refused to comply with a bus driver's demand to give up her seat in the "colored" section of a public bus because the "White" section was already full of passengers. This led to Parks's arrest.[26]

In response, King and his followers boycotted the bus system in Montgomery, Alabama. The bus boycott was the first of many instances in which nonviolent direct action was employed as a means of obtaining rights for Blacks. While the *Brown* decision may have awakened America to the level and scope of racial injustice experienced by African Americans, the Montgomery boycott marked a significant shift away from the historic reliance on the NAACP court battles and focused on concrete action to effect social change.[27] Under King's leadership, civil disobedience gained a measure of acceptability among some prominent Whites. King hoped that by emphasizing nonviolence, southern Blacks would express their hostility to racism and undercut any violent reactions by Whites.

MARTIN LUTHER KING JR. AND THE RIOTS

In 1963, President Kennedy submitted legislation to Congress to secure voting rights and broaden government protection of African Americans' civil rights. In August 1964, more than 200,000 people participated in the March on Washington for Jobs and Freedom, which is considered the high point of the civil rights movement. It was at this march that King delivered his famous "I Have a Dream" speech.[28]

In January 1964, the 24th Amendment to the U.S. Constitution was ratified, outlawing the poll tax that had prevented Blacks from voting. The enactment of the **Civil Rights Act**, which provided equal rights to African Americans was hailed as a major victory and provided the illusion of equality.[29] The **Voting Rights Act** was also passed, which encouraged Blacks about their role in the political process. However, the significance of this event was overshadowed by violence in the Watts section of Los Angeles.[30] In the worst riot since 1943, the Watts riot in L.A. in 1965 was shocking in its intensity and left thirty-four people dead. Many Americans believed that racial harmony had been addressed through the passing of federal legislation, however, the events in Watts were a marker of the tension felt all over the country.[31]

In fact, many scholars point to the series of riots that devastated certain cities across America as the end of the Civil Rights Movement. Between 1965 and 1967, major riots were witnessed in Cleveland, Newark, and Detroit. A presidential commission on the causes of violence estimated that, for 1967 alone, there were 257 civil disorders in 173 cities, killing 87 and injuring 2,500, leading to 19,000 arrests. In April 1968, after the assassination of Martin Luther King Jr., more cities witnessed violence.[32]

THE RISE OF BLACK POWER

In 1966, following the passage of the Voting Rights Act, James Meredith marched from Memphis to Jackson, Mississippi, in an effort to encourage fellow Blacks to vote.[33] During the march, Stokely Carmichael, an activist, proclaimed to a cheering Black crowd "What we need is Black power!" By advocating **Black Power**, Carmichael encouraged Blacks to create new institutions and emulate the political path followed by many European immigrant groups such as the Italians and the Irish, in previous generations. Prominent Black leaders opposed the concept because they feared that Whites would retaliate even more violently than before. While the Civil Rights Movement tried to end segregation, it was fairly evident that White society was not interested in equality in any meaningful sense. In contrast, Black Power contended that the only way for African Americans to ever gain a political, economic, or social influence was to be more assertive.[34]

THE NATION OF ISLAM AND BLACK IDENTITY

Few recent social movements have gained as much attention and reaction as **Black nationalism**, the philosophy that encourages Blacks to see themselves as Blacks first rather than as Americans. An important part of this movement for the individual is a transformation that leads Blacks to control their own destiny and to resist any attempts to continue their own subordination.

As mentioned, Southern slave owners encouraged and often required their slaves to attend church and to embrace a distorted version of Christianity. Black Nationalism, as a general rule, rejects this ideology. An example of Black Nationalism is found in the **Nation of Islam**, which became known as the Black Muslims, and has attracted a large number of followers. The Muslim religion was first introduced to Black America in 1930 by W. Fard Muhammad in Detroit, Michigan.[35]

Under the leadership of Elijah Muhammad, W. Fard Muhammad's successor, the Black Muslims became a well known and controversial organization. Malcolm X became the most powerful voice of this group in the 1960s.[36] In 1977, a Muslim sect led by Louis Farrakhan broke with the current leadership of the Nation of Islam and created his own group, adopting the more orthodox ideals of Elijah Muhammad such as Black moral superiority.[37]

AFRICAN AMERICANS TODAY: THE RISE OF THE BLACK MIDDLE CLASS

Some critics of African American history have attacked the generalizations of African American families arguing that historians overemphasize the poorest segment of the Black community. Instead, many scholars focus on the growth of the **Black middle class** as a testimony to the success many African Americans have achieved in overcoming a legacy of racism. However, this description of African Americans today would be equally inaccurate. Rather, a true understanding of the African American experience must include a balanced view of both the success and failure of this group to achieve some semblance of the American Dream.[38]

A clearly defined Black middle-class has emerged. According to the most recent census, nearly one-third of African Americans earned more than the median income for Whites. Yet many African Americans are more likely than Whites to be first generation middle-class, who depend on two or more sources of income and live precariously close to the lower class.[39]

In 2005, in testimony before the U.S. Commission on Civil Rights, David Besharov, a research fellow at the Enterprise Institute, a think tank in Washington, DC, argued that since 1980, while the absolute numbers have increased, the Black middle class has hardly grown as a percentage of African Americans. As evidence, Besharov points to data on median family income for Whites and Blacks. He found that between 1980 and 2003, the percentage of Black households with incomes greater than the 1980 median income of all American households increased by one-third, from about 29 percent to about 40 percent. However, at the same time, White incomes have increased, leaving the gap about the same. Thus, while there are an increasing number of African Americans who might fit into the middle-class category, the number of Whites who are also in that category has also increased. The reason for this continued stagnation has a great deal to do with the lack of educational progress for many African Americans.[40]

As some scholars have pointed out, the migration of the middle-class Blacks out of the ghetto in the 1970s and 1980s left a vacuum. Middle-class Blacks may still care about the problems of the poor, but they are no longer present as role models. As social class becomes more salient in the lives of African American families, particularly those that have gained some measure of economic and even political success, the relationship of social class, race, and poverty becomes important.[41]

Social scientists have long recognized the importance of class. It is a difficult concept to define, as many disagree on the boundaries of where one class category begins and another ends, not to mention the problems of determining a sufficient number of class categories. However, few experts argue that social class is not an important variable in the discussion of issues such as poverty, employment, healthcare, housing, and criminal justice.[42]

While the size of the Black middle class has grown, so has the size of the White middle class. Despite the fact that some Blacks have done well by any societal standard, there still remains a large number who feel the effects of discrimination despite their success.

The complexity of relative influence of race and class was apparent in the controversy surrounding William Julius Wilson's (1978) *The Declining Significance of Race.* Pointing to the increasing influence of African Americans, Wilson concluded that class has become more important than race in determining life chances or opportunities for Blacks' success in the modern world. His conclusions suggest that programs must be developed to confront class issues rather than ethnic and racial discrimination. Wilson argues that the legacy of discrimination is still alive, as reflected in the disproportionate number of Blacks who are poor, less educated, and who live in inadequate housing. However, he contends that the evidence shows that many segments of the African American population are able to effectively compete with segments of the White population.[43]

THE BLACK LIVES MATTER MOVEMENT

The relationship between race and crime, particularly for African Americans, is often seen in comments made by policy makers and political figures. Recently, the group Black Lives Matter has been at the center of a great deal of controversy surrounding the shooting of police officers. According to their website, the Black Lives Matter organization is not a group, but a movement. They state:

BlackLivesMatter was created in 2012 after Trayvon Martin's murderer, George Zimmerman, was acquitted for his crime, and dead seventeen-year old Trayvon was posthumously placed on trial for his own murder. Rooted in the experiences of Black people in this country who actively resist our dehumanization, #BlackLivesMatter is a call to action and a response to the virulent anti-Black racism that permeates our society. Black Lives Matter is a unique contribution that goes beyond extrajudicial killings of Black people by police and vigilantes.[44]

The website goes on to say that they are not a Black Nationalism movement as much as they focus their attention on the disenfranchisement of all Blacks—including those with an LGBT focus and the elderly—and the structures of society that attempt to continue to oppress Blacks. The website offers further commentary:

It goes beyond the narrow nationalism that can be prevalent within Black communities, which merely call on Black people to love Black, live Black and buy Black, keeping straight Black men in the front of the movement while our sisters, queer and trans, and disabled folk take up roles in the background or not at all.

Black Lives Matter affirms the lives of Black queer and trans folks, disabled folks, Black undocumented folks, folks with records, women and all Black lives along the gender spectrum. It centers those that have been marginalized within Black liberation movements. It is a tactic to (re)build the Black liberation movement.

What Does #BlackLivesMatter Mean?

When we say Black Lives Matter, we are broadening the conversation around state violence to include all of the ways in which Black people are intentionally left powerless at the hands of the state. We are talking about the ways in which Black lives are deprived of our basic human rights and dignity.[45]

Interestingly, unlike the Civil Rights Movement of the 1960s, the Black Lives Matter movement does not have a single leader and has instead opted to have many organizers and activists shape its direction and cause. The rationale is that, should a leader leave, as in the case of the assassination of Martin Luther King Jr., which left the Civil Rights Movement without a direction or long term commitment, the same fate could befall the Black Lives Matter movement as well. As Fredrick Harris of *Dissent Magazine* points out:

They are rejecting the charismatic leadership model that has dominated Black politics . . . and for good reason. . . . This older model is associated with Martin Luther King. . . . Black Lives Matter activists today recognize that granting decision-making power to an individual . . . poses a risk to the durability of a movement—charismatic leaders can therefore weaken them, even lead to their collapse.[46]

Another distinction between the Black Lives Matter movement and the Civil Rights Movement of the 1960s involves the use of social media. In a previous era, the ability to message a broad audience was limited given the technology of the time.

(continued)

(continued)

Today, with the advent of Facebook, Twitter, Snapchat, and Instagram, the Black Lives Matter advocates can instantaneously broadcast their message worldwide, thereby engaging a much wider audience of potential supporters.

Critics of the movement argue that this is an inflammatory group that gives attention only to certain types of lives. Others claim that they promote violence against society and the police, as evidenced by the assassination of police officers in Dallas, Texas. In response to the creation of Black Lives Matter, other groups have been created, such as the "All Lives Matter" effort or the "Blue Lives Matter" in response to the murder of police officers, often by African Americans, some of whom claim affiliation and association with the Black Lives Matter group.

It is also important to note that not all African Americans embrace the Black Lives Matter movement. According to a 2016 poll from the Pew Research Center, about 12 percent of African Americans oppose the movement (with about 5 percent strongly in opposition to it) and about 20 percent of African American adults think it will be effective. Young White adults are more enthusiastic about the movement than older Whites, suggesting that perhaps a Millennial interest is involved in the effort. While there may continue to be debate about what the goals of the organization might be, there can be little doubt that the Black Lives Matter group will remain a part of the multicultural narrative, particularly as it relates to the involvement of African Americans in the criminal justice system.

THE HISTORICAL TREATMENT OF AFRICAN AMERICANS IN THE CRIMINAL JUSTICE SYSTEM

Any discussion of the African American experience in this country is incomplete without including what some experts have referred to as a byproduct of the legacy of slavery. That so many African Americans are under the supervision of the criminal justice system, with many others touched by its extensively long hand, illustrates the social position of African Americans in the United States.

In his book, *No Equal Justice: Race and Class in the American Criminal Justice System*, David Cole (1999) argues that historically, African Americans were mistreated by the criminal justice process. This exploitation begins with the ratification of the U.S. Constitution in 1788, where, prior to the ratification of the Constitution, women could not vote and enslaved Africans counted as three-fifths of a person and had no fundamental rights of citizenship. Prior to the ratification of the U.S. Constitution, slavery had a two-hundred-year history in the colonies. The institution of slavery simultaneously was built on the tenet that Africans brought to America "had no rights which the White man was bound to respect," as articulated by the U.S. Supreme Court in the landmark case of *Dred Scott v. Sandford* in 1857 (60 U.S. 393;1857).

The ratification of the Thirteenth, Fourteenth, and Fifteenth Amendments and Reconstruction, which was purported to offer a glimmer of hope for equality and citizenship, led many African Americans to believe that equality was within their grasp. However, violence by groups such as the Ku Klux Klan kept most African Americans away from the polls.[47] Cole makes an interesting argument concerning the way the Thirteenth Amendment was written to increase the likelihood that African Americans would continue to be legally exploited despite the abolition of slavery. He states that as a legal loophole, the Thirteenth Amendment provided for the continued enslavement of individuals based on their status as a *criminal offender*.[48]

Cole also points out that during the Jim Crow Era of the late nineteenth century, African Americans were convicted of crimes at a much higher rate than Whites. As evidence of this, Cole points to statistics from Georgia, where, in 1908, Black prisoners outnumbered White prisoners 10 to 1 and the majority of the Black prisoners were convicted of nonviolent property crimes.[49]

Other scholars raise similar concerns about decisions by the U.S. Supreme Court.[50] Two of the most well-known Supreme Court decisions on criminal justice do not in practice protect African Americans. In 1963 in the case of *Gideon v. Wainwright* (372 U.S. 335; 1963), the Court held that states must provide a lawyer at state expense to all defendants charged with a serious crime who cannot afford to hire one. Three years later, in *Miranda v. Arizona* (384 U.S. 436; 1966), the Court required the police to provide poor suspects with an attorney at state expense and to inform all suspects of their rights before questioning them in custody.

Some experts argue that in these landmark decisions, the Court sought to ameliorate societal inequalities that undermined the criminal justice system's promise of equality. As the Court stated in *Miranda*, "[w]hile authorities are not required to relieve the accused of his poverty, they have the obligation not to take advantage of indigence in the administration of justice."[51] These decisions were decided by the Supreme Court under Chief Justice Earl Warren, at a time when the Court was solidly liberal and strongly committed to racial and economic equality. It is also argued that at virtually every juncture since *Gideon* and *Miranda*, the Supreme Court has undercut the principle of equality reflected in those decisions.[52]

These same scholars contend that *Gideon* is a symbol of equality unrealized in practice; poor defendants are entitled to the assistance of counsel at trial, but the Supreme Court has failed to demand that the assistance be meaningful. Cole says, "Lawyers who have slept through testimony or appeared in court drunk have nonetheless been deemed to have provided their indigent clients 'effective assistance of counsel.'"[53] These experts argue that today's Court has so diluted *Miranda* that the decision has had little effect on actual police interrogation practices.[54]

More generally, the problems of exploitation and inequality in the criminal justice system are driven by the need to balance two fundamental and competing interests: the protection of Constitutional rights and the protection of law-abiding citizens from crime. For example, without a Constitutional requirement that police have probable cause and a warrant before they conduct searches, police officers would be far more effective in rooting out and stopping crime. Without jury trials, criminal justice administration would be much more efficient. But without these safeguards, we would live in a police state, with no meaningful privacy protection. Absent jury trials, the community would have little check on overzealous prosecutors.[55]

Much of the public and academic debate about criminal justice focuses on where we should draw the line between law enforcement interests and Constitutional protections. Liberals and conservatives agree, at least in principle, that the line should be drawn in the same place for everyone. However, some experts suggest that there appears to be an inconsistency when and where that line is drawn which results in an unfair burden placed on African Americans.[56]

AFRICAN AMERICANS AND THE CRIMINAL JUSTICE SYSTEM TODAY

THE POLICE

Perhaps the most controversial interaction that African Americans have with the criminal justice system relates to the police. Much has been said and written about police-minority relations, the use of force by police officers against African Americans, and **racial profiling**. As described below, there are a number of sensational cases in which the police have mistreated members of minority groups. There also appears to be a long record of such activity involving African Americans. The following accounts are illustrative:

FERGUSON, MISSOURI. On August 9, 2014, a police officer was on patrol and encountered eighteen-year-old Michael Brown and a friend walking down a street. An altercation ensued between Officer Wilson and Brown, who at the time was standing at the window of the vehicle. Officer Wilson fired two shots from inside the vehicle, one likely grazing Brown's thumb, and the other missing him. Brown then ran away and Officer Wilson pursued him on foot. Brown stopped and turned toward Officer Wilson, who also stopped. Brown then moved toward Officer Wilson, who fired several shots, fatally wounding Brown. According to county prosecutor, Brown suffered at least seven gunshot wounds. His body lay in the street for four hours before it was removed. Wilson fired a total of twelve times, though investigators were unclear exactly how many struck Brown. Riots lasted for days in the city of Ferguson after Brown's death, as members of the African American community felt the actions of Officer Wilson were unjustified.

In November, a St. Louis County grand jury and the U.S. Justice Department failed to find enough evidence to bring charges against Officer Wilson. The panel of jurors was composed of twelve citizens: six White men, three White women, one African American man, and two African American women. Much of the evidence from witnesses was contradictory. Some of it had supported Officer Wilson's version of events. Other witness statements had appeared to support the account of Dorian Johnson, Brown's friend who was with him when he died. St. Louis County prosecutor Robert McCulloch did not recommend any charges against Officer Wilson to the jury. This caused anger in Ferguson and around the U.S. as critics said it showed an unwillingness to prosecute.[57]

BALTIMORE, MARYLAND. On April 12, 2015, Freddie Gray, a twenty-five-year-old male, was arrested by the Baltimore Police Department for allegedly possessing what was said to be an illegal switchblade. Gray was put into a police van; while in transit to the police station, he became unresponsive and fell into a coma. Gray was taken to a trauma center where he died four days later. In the video shot by a bystander, Gray shouts in pain as he is dragged into a police van. While being handled by police, the video shows that Gray's leg appears injured. From the scene where he was arrested to the police station, Gray suffered a neck and spinal injury. When taken to the trauma center, Gray was treated for three fractured vertebrae and a crushed larynx (voice box). The doctors at the trauma center said that Gray's injuries were sustained by someone who was in a car accident. Just like in Ferguson, riots ensued and lasted for days. Gray's death was ruled a homicide and six officers had legal charges brought against them for second degree murder (Caesar Goodson,

Garrett Miller, Edward Nero, William Porter, Brian Rice, and Alicia White). The officers were ultimately acquitted of all charges.[58]

CHICAGO, ILLINOIS. On October 20, 2014, Laquan McDonald, a seventeen-year-old male, was shot sixteen times by Chicago police officer Jason Van Dyke. McDonald was being pursued by the Chicago Police after calls and complaints reported him to be carrying a knife and breaking into cars parked in a trucking yard. When confronted by police, McDonald took out his knife and slashed the tires of a police patrol car and damaged the windshield. He was told by the police to drop the knife but he continued to walk away. A police cruiser's dash-cam captured the last few minutes of McDonald's life. He is seen walking away and avoiding all officers on the scene when he is shot by Van Dyke, who fired all sixteen rounds in the magazine of his weapon. The video shows McDonald's limp body was shot while lying on the ground. According to the toxicology report, McDonald had PCP in his system, which contributed to his erratic behavior. Officer Van Dyke was charged with first-degree murder a few hours after the video was released. Van Dyke was charged with first-degree murder and turned himself in to authorities. He was indicted for six counts of first-degree murder and one count of official misconduct. Van Dyke is awaiting trial.[59]

STATEN ISLAND, NEW YORK. On July 17, 2014, Eric Garner, a forty-three-year-old Black male, was being questioned and pursued by police for selling untaxed cigarettes, something for which he had been reprimanded numerous times in the past. After confronting a verbally combative Garner, several police officers went to arrest him. When Officer Daniel Pantaleo took Garner's wrist behind his back, Garner resisted. Pantaleo then put his arm around Garner's neck and pulled him backward and down onto the ground. After Pantaleo removed his arm from Garner's neck, he then pushed Garner's face into the ground while four officers moved to restrain Garner. Throughout the video, which was recorded by a bystander, who was also a friend of Garner, Garner is repeating "I can't breathe" during the altercation and while lying face down on the sidewalk. After he lost consciousness, officers turned Garner onto his side to help ease his breathing. Garner remained lying on the sidewalk for seven minutes while the officers waited for an ambulance to arrive. Neither police officers nor the EMTs performed CPR because they believed him to still be breathing.

According to the medical examiner, Garner was killed by the compression to his neck but there was no damage to his windpipe or his spine. While Officer Pantaleo would not be indicted, a separate investigation of the entire department in regards to police brutality resulted in the Garner family settling their lawsuit with the city for $5.9 million. This ruling ignited protests that led to the shooting of two Brooklyn police officers.[60]

CHARLESTON, SOUTH CAROLINA. On April 4, 2015, Walter Scott, a fifty-year-old male, was fatally shot by North Charleston police officer, Michael Slager. Scott was stopped by Slager for a minor traffic violation. After Slager approached the car and was heading back to his patrol car, Scott exited his car and fled from the scene. Slager pursued Scott on foot. After hitting Scott with his Taser, Slager then pulled out his handgun and fired eight rounds at Scott, hitting him five times. Controversy arose after the video was released showing Slager planting his Taser on Scott. Slager's reasoning for shooting Scott was that Scott had taken his Taser and Slager feared for his safety.

After reviewing the video, Officer Slager was arrested and charged with murder. Slager was later indicted for the charge. In January 2016, Slager was released on a $500,000 bond and was under house arrest until his trial in October 2016.[61] In December 2016, a mistrial was declared in the case after jurors could not unanimously agree on a verdict. The jurors deliberated for four days and had three options: murder, voluntary manslaughter, or acquittal. One juror declared that he refused to convict Slager of anything and several other jurors were conflicted about a decision during deliberations as well. While state prosecutors have expressed an intention to retry the case, Slager is also facing three federal charges and the government may bring those charges if the state fails to prove its case against him.[62]

BATON ROUGE, LOUISIANA. In July 2016, two White officers were arresting Alton B. Sterling, a Black man, after responding to a call about an armed man. The caller allegedly told police that a Black man in a red shirt selling music CDs outside a convenience store had threatened him with a gun. Mr. Sterling had a long criminal record, including convictions for battery and illegal possession of a gun, but it is not clear whether the officers knew any of that when they tried to arrest him. As the officers wrestled with Mr. Sterling and brought him to the ground, someone in the video can be heard saying "He's got a gun! Gun! And one officer can be seen pulling his weapon. While there is more than one video and the facts of the case have not been conclusively determined, the officers shot Sterling, killing him. The incident prompted protests and demonstrations in cities across the country. A federal investigation has also been launched.[63] Several days later, in response to the shooting, three police officers were killed and three others were wounded by a former U.S. Marine. The suspect, who was African American (the officers killed were White), and whose motive for the murders is still unknown, was killed by police.[64]

DALLAS, TEXAS. In July 2016, in response to deadly shooting incidents in Baton Rouge, Louisiana, and suburban St. Paul Minnesota, police officers were ambushed by a sniper with a rifle in Dallas, Texas. Five police officers were killed and seven officers and two civilians were wounded. These officers were killed while providing protection to demonstrators who were protesting police violence against Black people. The suspect, Micah X. Johnson, a former soldier, and alleged supporter of the Black Lives Matter movement, died after a standoff with police. The suspect said he was upset about the recent police shootings of African Americans in Baton Rouge, Louisiana, and Minnesota.[65] While the details of each episode is still under investigation, the situations raise questions about the appropriateness of police actions as well as perceptions of African Americans by police officers.[66]

ST. PAUL, MINNESOTA. On July 6, 2016, in a suburb of St. Paul, Minnesota, Jeronimo Yanez, a Hispanic police officer, pulled over Philando Castile, an African American male. Castile fit the description of an armed robbery suspect that the police were searching for. Castile told officer Yanez that he had a gun permit and was armed. As he was allegedly reaching for his ID, officer Yanez shot Castile. Castile's girlfriend videotaped the incident and streamed it on Facebook. In response, protestors marched causing traffic jams on

Tensions between the police and the Black community stem from the perception of excessive violence by officers against African American males.

Interstate 35 in Minneapolis and Interstate 94 in St. Paul, causing an estimated $1.5 million in damages. In all, more than 150 arrests were made as a result of the demonstrations.[67]

On almost any given day, we hear of instances like the ones just described. These dramatic episodes raise questions about the role of the police in our society, particularly in their interactions with minority groups. Some minority leaders, as well as nonminorities, this isn't strictly true . . . there are other minorities who are not in leadership roles who have made this assertion. So to say they are nonminorities isn't factually correct. have asserted that the police, and to some extent the entire criminal justice system, are prejudiced and racist. These individuals argue that situations like the ones described above are indicators that the police target minorities and treat them differently. Is there any truth to these assertions? Are the police racist? Do they treat minorities differently? How does the public perceive the police?

Public Opinion and the Police

According to a 2013 Justice Department report, an estimated 63 million people in the United States—about 26 percent of the population—have some form of contact with the police every year. This contact was about equally likely to be initiated by residents as by the police. The latter include traffic stops or stopping persons in public places. The majority of persons with in contact with the police thought the police behaved properly during the contact. Approximately 93 percent of those who requested police assistance, 88 percent of drivers pulled over in traffic stops, and 71 percent of persons involved in street stops, felt the actions of officers were appropriate.

As it related to traffic stops, Black drivers (13 percent) were more likely than White and Hispanic (10 percent each) to be pulled over by police in a traffic stop; however

Blacks, Whites, and Hispanics were equally likely to be stopped in a street stop. This is quite different from data in the early 1990s that reflected a tendency to "stop and frisk" minorities more often than Whites. Further, about 80 percent of drivers in traffic stops and 60 percent of those involved in street stops believed they were stopped for a legitimate reason.[68]

While this latest study from the Department of Justice shows some promising trends, it is important to note that these findings have been consistent since 2005.[69] These figures indicate that, in general, a significant proportion of the population thinks the police are doing a good job; however, minorities generally feel less confident in the police and are generally less satisfied with police services. Another important factor is the characteristic of the neighborhood. One study found that people living in high crime neighborhoods and low income communities tend to have more contact with the police and report less overall satisfaction. Furthermore, because minorities tend to live in these types of neighborhoods, it is not surprising that the confidence in the police is lower than that of Whites.[70]

A 2003 study found that neighborhood characteristics and interactions with police officers were the most influential factors in assessing the public's opinion of the police. The study, conducted in four diverse neighborhoods in Los Angeles, found that residents from neighborhoods perceived to be crime-ridden, dangerous, and disorderly were less likely to approve of the police. In contrast, residents who had informal personal contact with police were more likely to express approval.

While race and ethnicity had been cited as influential factors in other studies, neither was as important as the level of social and physical disorder in the community in determining the public's satisfaction with police. Where race and ethnicity did matter concerns the perception of how the police treated minorities. For example, African Americans were more likely to say that officers acted unprofessionally toward them than toward Whites. This study also found that the media had little influence on public opinion of the police. While limited in its ability to make an overall assessment of the public's opinion of the police, this study nevertheless raised a number of questions about how to change the public's perception of police officers.[71]

Why do police officers have more contact with low-income and minority neighborhoods? Part of the answer is that this group makes greater use of police services than other groups. Police departments assign more patrol officers to these neighborhoods because of greater calls for service and because minority groups in these areas have higher crime rates. Another reason is that minorities and low-income people are more likely to call the police to solve a variety of non-criminal matters. Compared to middle-class Americans, for instance, people in the low-income category are more likely to call the police for assistance with medical emergencies and family problems. This means that the police are more actively and intrusively involved in the daily lives of people from these areas. Greater contact also means that the decisions made by officers may not be what the members of these neighborhoods prefer, resulting in lower levels of satisfaction. In sum, evidence suggests differential treatment of minorities by police on a variety of indicators, including violent crime, deadly force, arrests, and other minor forms of abuse.[72]

Violent Crime

Perhaps due to the distortion of crime and criminals in the media, as well as their own experiences with crime, many people, including the police, believe that African Americans and other minorities are more involved in violent crime than Whites. Moreover, this perception affects how officers respond to violent crimes. For instance, using data from the *National Crime Victimization Survey*, one study examined the relationship between the victim and the offender's race on three police responses to robbery and aggravated assault. The variables considered were the response time to the scene, the amount of effort made by officers to investigate these crimes at the scene, and the likelihood of arrest.[73]

Officers were quicker to respond and invested more effort in the investigation (e.g., searches) when the incident consisted of African American offenders and White victims. This relationship held even when variables such as poverty, the victim's gender, and whether or not the victim was injured were taken into account. With regard to aggravated assault, particularly those involving strangers, officers were more likely to be more thorough at the scene if it involved a White victim and an African American offender. Officers were also more likely, all other things being equal, to respond more quickly and to put forth a more determined effort if there was an injury to the White victim, particularly by an African American offender. None of these findings applied when the victim was an African American and the offender was White. Thus, evidence suggests that the race of the victim and the offender plays a role in how the police respond to violent crime. If the crime involves a White victim and African American offender, officers seem to respond more quickly to the scene of the crime and investigate it more thoroughly, and arrests are more likely to occur.[74]

Arrests

Is race a factor in the arrest of a suspect? The answer appears clear as minorities are arrested out of proportion to their representation in the population. According to the *Uniform Crime Reports*, in 2014, African Americans represented about 14 percent of the population but approximately 28 percent of all arrests and 39 percent of arrests for violent crime. In 2014, approximately 70 percent of all individuals arrested were White, with the remaining 2 percent from other races. White individuals were arrested more often for violent crimes than individuals of any other race and accounted for approximately 60 percent of those arrests. Of adults arrested for murder, about 51 percent were Black and 47 percent were White, with other races making up the remaining percentage. As it relates to juveniles, Blacks comprised nearly 53 percent of all juveniles arrested for violent crime while White juveniles accounted for nearly 60 percent of all juveniles arrested for property crimes.[75] However, there is a great deal of controversy surrounding this issue. What are the reasons for this apparent differential treatment? Do police officers arrest African Americans more frequently due to racial bias or because Blacks commit more crimes? What variables are considered in the decision to arrest?

Donald Black (1971) in his famous article "The Social Organization of Arrest," found that, in general, the decision to arrest was predicated on a number of factors, including the strength of the evidence, the seriousness of the crime, whether or not the complainant or victim wanted the suspect arrested, and whether the suspect was disrespectful toward the officer. The decision to arrest was also based on the relationship between the victim and the offender. If the suspect was a stranger to the victim, the officers were more likely to arrest him or her.[76]

Interestingly, Black found that race was not a factor in the decision to arrest. He did find that African Americans were arrested more often than Whites, but this was mainly due to the fact that Whites were more likely to show deference to the officer. As he describes, this creates a vicious cycle, where the African American men who are arrested more often have negative feelings toward the police. When these feelings are demonstrated, they are more likely to be arrested, which increases the hostility felt by African Americans.[77]

Much research following Black's earlier work found that race does matter. In the 1980s, for instance, race was considered in terms of the decision to arrest. One study found that in those instances where the suspect was African American and the victim was White, officers were more likely to make an arrest.[78] Similar to Black's findings, in these situations, officers were also more likely to arrest the suspect upon the victim's request to do so.[79]

Another study found that African Americans and Hispanics were more likely to be arrested on less evidence than Whites. The study also found that Blacks and Hispanics were more likely to be released without the case going to the prosecutor. While at first glance this may appear to be advantageous, arrest still represents a form of punishment even though formal charges may not be filed.[80]

Another study examined 718 police officers in Ohio and examined the extent to which a suspect's race influenced an officer's behavior. The results of the study showed that officers did not feel race was a significant factor in determining the officer's behavior. What was significant was the suspect's demeanor—how they acted toward the officer. However, care should be taken in interpreting this finding since it may be related to race in that African Americans may be more likely to have a negative attitude toward the police, which can lead to a similar outcome. The evidence seems to suggest then, that the race of the victim and of the offender play an important role in the decision to arrest.[81]

Use of Force

The Rodney King example is perhaps the most visible and memorable reminder of excessive use of force by police officers. King, who was driving while intoxicated, led the police on a high- speed car chase in 1991. After he eventually stopped, four officers were videotaped beating King, while several other officers observed the beating. The video, one of the first of its kind, was sent to the media and resulted in the arrest of four officers who were charged with assault with a deadly weapon and excessive use of force. Three officers were eventually acquitted of all charges and the fourth officer was acquitted of the assault charge but the jury deadlocked 8–4 in favor of acquittal on the excessive use of force. These decisions were said to be the reason for the subsequent riots that occurred in Los Angeles that led to millions of dollars in property damage and other crimes. After the state trial, federal charges were brought against the officers for violating King's civil rights. The result was that two of the officers were acquitted again and two officers were found guilty.[82]

However, prior to 1991, there was considerable academic interest in the use of force topic prior to the King incident.[83] In his classic study of the police, Albert J. Reiss (1971) found that race per se was not a determining factor in the use of excessive force. Instead "Class rather than race determines police misconduct."[84] The typical victim of excessive force is a lower-class male, regardless of race. Others however, disagree and see excessive use of force as particularly prevalent against African American men. According to a 1999 Bureau of Justice Statistics report on police-citizen contacts, there were substantial racial and ethnic disparities in police use of force. African Americans are three times as likely to experience force or threatened force than Whites. Hispanics were more likely than Whites but less likely than African Americans to experience police use of force.[85]

The implications of this trend are particularly significant for African Americans. Even if the overall rate of the use of force comprises one percent of all police-citizen encounters, if those incidents are concentrated in low-income neighborhoods and consist of lower-class men, who are likely to be African American, the effects of these incidents accumulate over time to create a perception that the police routinely harass African Americans.[86] The symbolic significance of the excessive use of force should not be overlooked. As representatives of the larger system, police officers who engage in excessive use of force serve as a reminder of the larger problems of discrimination and exploitation felt by African Americans.[87] More recently, according to a U.S. Department of Justice report, large state and local law enforcement agencies received approximately 26,000 complaints from citizens about the excessive use of force by officers. This number translates into a rate of about 6.6 complaints per 100 full-time sworn officers. About 8 percent of these complaints were officially sustained, meaning there was sufficient evidence to justify disciplinary action against the officer or officers; about 34 percent were not sustained; 25 percent were declared unfounded or the complaint was not supported by the facts (or the incident did not occur); and 23 percent ended in exonerations because the officers acted properly.[88]

Deadly Force

Despite the notoriety when such events occur, there has been a general decline in the incidence of deadly force by the police.[89] However, a great deal of attention has been given to the frequency with which police officers use deadly force against minorities.[90] When compared with their numbers in the population, African Americans are disproportionately killed by the police. However, these findings also suggest that when compared with rates of police-citizen contacts, arrest rates and resistance to or attacks upon the police, there is no apparent racial disparity in the use of deadly force by the police.[91]

By the mid-1980s, when many departments adopted a "defense of life rule," which allows officers to use deadly force only when attempting to protect themselves or the lives of others, the number of persons shot and killed by the police decreased significantly. Part of the reason for the general decline in the use of deadly force has come from more restrictive policies at the departmental level as well as from the Supreme Court decision in *Tennessee v. Garner*.[92] One study found that from 1970 to 1984, the police use of deadly force declined substantially, particularly against African Americans.[93] More recently, the data indicate that the racial disparity in the number of people shot and killed by the police has decreased from about seven African Americans for every White to about three to one.[94]

Another situation in which deadly force is justified occurs when the officer prevents the escape of a person who is extremely dangerous.[95] In *Tennessee vs. Garner* (471 U.S. 1. 1985), two officers used deadly force against an African American juvenile who was fleeing the scene of a burglary. At that time, the officers were justified in using deadly physical force against a fleeing felon. However, the Court ruled that this was no longer acceptable. As a result, many departments were required to modify their policies concerning use of force against fleeing felons. Thus, while there was a time when officers were given wide latitude in using deadly force, since 1980 departments all over the country have changed their policies regarding the use of force and the number of incidents have declined considerably.

In 2011, the U.S. Department of Justice released a report on arrest-related deaths, which noted that between 2003 to 2009, 4,813 persons died during or shortly after law enforcement personnel attempted to arrest or restrain them. About 60 percent were classified as homicides by law enforcement personnel and 40 percent to other manners of death, such as suicide, death by intoxication, accidental injury, or natural causes.

Of those person who died during the process of arrest, 95 percent were male, about 42 percent were White, 32 percent were Black, and 20 percent were Hispanic or Latino. More than 55 percent were between the ages of twenty-five and forty-four. And among male arrest-related deaths (62 percent) were attributed to homicide. Of those who committed suicide during the process of arrest, 60 percent were White, 15 percent were Black and 20 percent Hispanic or Latino. Among those deaths by intoxication, 41 percent were Black while 34 percent were White, with Hispanics comprising 21 percent.[96]

Profiling and Other Forms of Abuse

The issue surrounding discriminatory treatment of African Americans extends beyond serious offenses. In fact, one might argue that it is the minor forms of abuse that create a climate of fear and hostility between the police and minorities. These indignities, or what sociologist Elliot Liebow has referred to as the "little murders of everyday life,"[97] characterize the attitudes the police have toward minorities in some circumstances. The difference between this type of abuse and the others discussed, however, is that there is no tangible reminder that the incident occurred.

Minor forms of abuse such as profiling usually end with the interaction between the officer and the suspect. These forms of abuse usually occur on the street and typically involve no witnesses. This makes sustaining allegations very difficult and results in continued tension between the police and minorities.[98]

In the mid-1990s, the New Jersey State Police were investigated for allegedly ordering officers to concentrate on stopping Black drivers. Three state troopers stated they were instructed by their superiors to single out African American drivers for traffic stops. Additionally, a 1992 study of traffic stops in Florida found that while 5 percent of the drivers on the road were African American or Hispanic, nearly 70 percent of those stopped and 80 percent of those searched were African American or Hispanic. Further, nationally, from January 1993 to August 1995, almost 90 percent of the individuals subjected to search and seizure operations on buses and trains were people of color. Another study of all reported federal decisions from 1993 to 1995 involving bus and train sweeps found that nearly 90 percent of those targeted were minorities.[99]

About ten years later, another controversy was created when, in April 2005, a report on racial profiling was scheduled to be released by the Department of Justice's Bureau of Justice Statistics. Based on interviews with 80,000 people in 2002, the study found that White, Black, and Hispanic drivers nationwide were stopped by the police that year at about the same rate, roughly 9 percent. But, the Justice Department report also found that once they were stopped, Hispanic drivers were searched or had their vehicles searched by the police 11.4 percent of the time and Blacks 10.2 percent of the time, compared to only 3.5 percent for White drivers. The study found that officers were more likely to threaten or use force against Blacks and Hispanics more often than Whites, and the police were much more likely to issue tickets to Hispanics rather than simply giving them a warning.

The authors of the study said they were not able to draw any conclusions about the reason for the differing rates, but they said the gaps were notable. The research "uncovered evidence of Black drivers having worse experiences—more likely to be arrested, more likely to be searched, more likely to have force used against them—during traffic stops than White drivers." The inflammatory nature of these findings allegedly led the Justice Department to try to suppress some of the information or to change the findings. While strenuously arguing that the results should not be altered for political purposes, the director of the Bureau of Justice Statistics was demoted.[100] What should also be considered in reviewing the trends cited in the earlier studies is the more recent data highlighted at the beginning of this chapter. While it may be reasonable to assume that some form of profiling may exist at an individual officer level, the fact that the trends are far different from what was discovered during the 1990s indicates that the changes were made in police practices as it relates to police-citizen interactions.

Another study explored the extent to which there are racial differences in getting hassled as well as what the researchers identify as **vicarious hassling**—knowing someone who has experienced this type of treatment by the police. The main finding of the study was that African Americans are more likely to perceive they are being hassled by the police individually and vicariously. Nearly one-half of African Americans in the study had experienced a negative police interaction and two-thirds knew someone who had a similar experience, compared to the 10 percent of Whites who experienced this type of treatment in the same way. While such a discrepancy could be a result of different patrol practices, which focus on minority neighborhoods, it could also be that some of these perceptions may be a result of frequent police contact. A third explanation may be that there exists a perception by officers that African Americans and other minorities are more likely to commit crimes and thus are potential offenders that warrant police attention.[101]

Finally, there is verbal abuse. Many complaints are filed each year against officers who verbally abuse citizens. The **Christopher Commission**, created to investigate allegations of abuse in Los Angeles following the beating of Rodney King by White officers, found that officers frequently use abusive language. This may occur during the interaction with citizens or it may happen between officers. For example, the Commission's investigation discovered computer messages were sent between officers that contained racially offensive comments.

Research on police behavior suggests that derogatory comments and the stigmatizing labeling of people is a way for officers to control suspects. Profanity serves several functions: to gain the individual's attention when interacting with officers, to keep them at a social distance while the interaction occurs, and to psychologically dominate the individual.[102]

What does all this tell us? It should remind us that the relationship between the police and African Americans is complex. As some conservative researchers, such as Heather MacDonald point out, African Americans may be arrested disproportionately, in part, because of their more pronounced involvement in criminal activities;[103] it may also have to do with the way African Americans respond to police contact. Structural issues such as poverty and overcrowding in urban areas may contribute to greater police contact in that the problems experienced in those areas require a more frequent police presence. Minority involvement with the police may also have something to do with the attitudes of police officers—some officers believe minorities are more likely to become involved in criminal activities so they merit greater police attention. Finally, African American overrepresentation may also have something to do with the perceptions of the police which tend to inflame the nature of the interaction between the two groups.

In response to problems stemming from police interactions in low-income African American communities, and after being accused of racially-motivated excessive use of force, some officers in several cities around the country have employed **de-policing** as a strategy. De-policing is a tactic employed by some officers who answer only 911 calls instead of engaging in routine patrol. This is done to avoid contact with minorities and to prevent routine situations from escalating into charges of racial profiling or discriminatory treatment of minorities. By only answering emergency calls, such contact is limited, but crime rates also increase dramatically.[104]

Some experts have noted that some officers are responding to the anti-police riots and media coverage in a similar fashion, which is showing up in crime data. Other anecdotal evidence reflects the concerns about the potential backlash. In August 2015, a Birmingham, Alabama, detective pulled over a car because of erratic behavior by the driver. The officer told the driver to stay in the car while he called for backup. Instead, the driver got out and confronted the officer, repeatedly asking him why he'd been stopped. The driver, a convicted felon, then allegedly grabbed the detective's gun and pistol-whipped him, knocking him unconscious. The driver, who fled the scene but was later arrested, has a long record of felony convictions including robbery, assault, and attempted-murder. The officer later stated that he hesitated in how he handled the situation because he was concerned about how the police are being portrayed in the media and did not want to be responsible for additional negative publicity. He added: "A lot of officers are being too cautious because of what's going on in the media. I hesitated because I didn't want to be in the media like I am right now."[105]

As mentioned, the concern by law enforcement about its relationship with community residents is seen in crime data. In Baltimore, for example, according to some observers, following the riots and the indictment of six officers for the death of drug dealer Freddie Gray, arrests have seen a 60 percent decrease compared with arrests the previous year. In New York City, criminal summonses, which are an important tool for the police to maintain order, decreased by 24 percent through July 2015, compared with the same period the previous year; and the total number of arrests decreased by 16.5 percent.[106]

These problems are particularly troubling given that the media does not appear to cover attacks on the police with the same enthusiasm or dedication as they do when an officer is perceived to attack a citizen. There have been several incidents where officers have been attacked and killed by citizens, such as the assassination of two NYPD officers in New York City, Wenjian Liu and Rafael Ramos, who were shot and killed while sitting in their patrol car in Brooklyn. This extraordinary event occurred as a result of retaliation for the deaths of Michael Brown in Ferguson, Missouri, and Eric Garner in Staten Island, New York. The suspect, Ismaaiyl Abdullah Brinsley, has written that "putting wings on pigs today" to avenge Brown and Garner's death. "They take one of ours . . . let's take two of theirs." Curiously, the media coverage was not nearly as extensive but the impact this could have on police-community relations is significant. A similar sentiment was felt after police officers were ambushed in Dallas and other officers were killed in Baton Rouge, Louisiana, in apparent retaliation for incidents involving the deaths of African Americans.[107]

What seems to be missing from the discussion of the perception that White officers are racist and on a mission to kill Blacks, a sentiment that created the Black Lives Matter movement, is the data about the extent of this trend. As one article points out, in New York City, which has had a Civilian Review Board, created in the 1990s to address police abuse of authority and excessive force, the data for 2014 indicates the number of complaints filed against the police have decreased 10 percent and the number of excessive force claims decreased by 11 percent. Additionally, profanity accusations dropped by 20 percent. Further, according to the NYPD's 2013 Annual Firearms Discharge Report, NYPD officers killed eight people in 2013, and five of these cases involved a suspect with a handgun, one of whom fired six times at two officers on a subway, one with a knife. In comparison, in New York City in 2013, 335 citizens were murdered and in 63 percent of those cases the suspect was Black. According to the Uniform Crime Reports for 2013, 90 percent of Black murder victims nationally are killed by Black assailants.[108]

So while questions about police misconduct are worthy of an in-depth discussion and require specific action by departments and other agencies, it is not completely clear about the extent to which the police are responsible for the number of Blacks killed each year. Some data show, for instances, that while Blacks were more than six times likelier than Whites to have been murder victims in 2011, Blacks were also almost eight times likelier than Whites to have committed murder.[109] Thus, care must be taken to ensure that all of the data has been presented and interpreted in a fair and unbiased way. To do otherwise is to create a climate of mistrust, fear, and an unwillingness to work collaboratively to solve the larger problems in the Black community.

THE COURTS AND AFRICAN AMERICANS: SENTENCING ISSUES

Not only is there some evidence to suggest that Blacks are more likely than Whites to be stopped, searched, arrested, and killed by police officers, they are also more likely to receive harsher treatment once they arrive in court. In fact, there are many who contend that the War on Drugs is really a war on African Americans.[110] For instance, there is evidence to suggest that African Americans are more likely to receive harsher penalties and sentencing for similar crimes than Whites. This is most apparent in the different penalties for selling crack cocaine compared to powder cocaine, designer drugs, or even steroids. The federal sentencing guidelines are substantially harsher than the penalties provided by many state statutes, suggesting that state prosecutors are more likely to refer crack cases involving racial minorities to the federal system for prosecution.[111] In fact, an analysis of sentences by the U.S. Sentencing Commission found that prison sentences of Black men were almost 20 percent longer than those of White men for similar crimes.[112] The Sentencing Commission report recommended that federal judges give the guidelines more significance. This analysis has come under some scrutiny, where one law professor claims racial disparity has not increased since 2005, when the U.S. Supreme Court struck down the 1984 federal law that required judges to use the federal sentencing guidelines. In the case of *U.S. v. Booker*, the Court ruled that the law, while originally designed to address disparity in sentencing, limited judges in rendering decisions that were based on laws that were inherently biased in the first place. The most common example used involved federal law that created longer sentences for crack cocaine offenses compared to sentences for powder cocaine offenses, which were more frequently committed by Whites. While Congress reduced the disparity in 2010, in 2007 sentences of Blacks were about 15 percent longer than similarly convicted Whites. The latest study by the U.S. Sentencing Commission, which focused on the period between 2007 and 2011, found that Black males were serving about 20 percent longer sentences than Whites for similar crimes and that Black males were 25 percent less likely than Whites to receive a sentence below the guidelines' range. While this study does not, by itself, prove that judicial discretion caused greater Black-White federal sentencing disparity, it nevertheless is an improvement in the understanding of what happens to similar types of offenders in terms of the outcome of their cases.[113]

Part of the explanation for the dramatically different punishment for cocaine and crack is likely a result of the fear of drugs and those who sell drugs rather than pure discrimination and prejudice. Because of the perception by members of mainstream culture that crack cocaine represents a more serious and immediate threat to way of life, particularly when crack cocaine left the inner-city and appeared in the suburbs, more punitive measures were easily justified. Given that African Americans were already perceived to be responsible for the "drug problem" nationwide, the perceptions that the problem was being brought into middle-class suburbia resulted in panic and more punitive actions.[114]

A related conclusion appears in murder cases. Researchers found that when the level of seriousness is controlled for, such as the degree of severity and the number of persons killed, prosecutors and juries are more likely to demand the death penalty if the victim is White and the offender is Black than in any of the other possible racial combinations (e.g., White offender/Black victim; Black offender/Black victim; White offender/White victim).[115]

Further, a number of studies indicate that Whites receive a higher proportion of plea bargain deals than Blacks. One study found that Whites were more successful in getting charges reduced or dropped, diversion, probation, or fines instead of incarceration.[116] However, other studies indicate inconsistent results with regard to the effects of race on plea bargaining and prosecution strategies.[117]

A number of studies demonstrate racial bias in sentencing. A study in 39 states found that Blacks typically serve longer sentences than Whites for robbery, rape, and murder.[118] A growing body of research indicates that in many cases the key factor is the race of the victim. Preliminary evidence suggests that when the victim of rape or robbery is White, the sentence is likely to be more severe.[119] More recently, a meta-analysis of 85 research studies revealed that, after taking into account the defendant's criminal history and the seriousness of the offense, Blacks and Latinos were generally sentenced more harshly than Whites. However, the research available on sentencing patterns of Whites compared to those of Asians or Native Americans does not reveal significant differences between these groups. In general, there appears to be some evidence to suggest that disparities in sentencing still occur, even involving sentencing guidelines.[120]

In 1991, the seventeen-member New York State Judicial Commission on Minorities composed of judges, lawyers, law professors, and an official from the New York State Department of Education concluded that the state court system showed signs of racism. The commission found that minority group members were less likely than Whites to receive favorable actions from the courts; that judges and prosecuting attorneys, more than other court employees, were more hostile and racially biased toward minorities; and that minority lawyers were often subjected to opposing attorney's racial stereotyping and racist jokes.[121] Further, a recent report from the Sentencing Project, a nonprofit organization that conducts research on criminal justice issues, noted that part of the challenge of understanding the sentencing disparity issue relates to how people in general perceive Blacks and their involvement in crime. For instance, one of the findings form the report indicate that,

A large proportion of Black men are under the supervision of the criminal justice system.

based on their 2010 survey, Whites overestimate the proportion of crimes committed by people of color and associate people of color with criminality. In fact, the survey showed that this overestimation ranges between 20 and 30 percent for burglaries, drug sales, and juvenile crime. Similarly, the report showed that Whites, who associate crime with Blacks and Latinos, are also more likely to support punitive policies, including capital punishment and mandatory minimum sentencing, than Whites. The report also showed disparities in police stops, prosecutorial decision-making, and issues relating to bail and sentencing, which suggests an implicit racial bias within the criminal justice system.[122]

The conclusions from such findings, naturally, explain varying racial perceptions of crime and criminals, and foster the basis of understanding why Blacks and Latinos, while accounting for 30 percent of the general population, account for nearly 60 percent of the prison population. These perceptions also drive the belief by some groups that the criminal justice system is biased against Blacks. Such a belief is underscored by the results of the survey, which showed that over two-thirds of African Americans saw the system as biased compared to only 25 percent of Whites.[123]

THE DEATH PENALTY AND AFRICAN AMERICANS

African Americans' overrepresentation in sentencing and incarceration is also found among those sentenced to death. According to the Bureau of Justice Statistics, in 2013 about 42 percent of inmates on death row were Black. This percentage has been consistent since 1968, and 53 percent of all people executed since 1930 have been African American.[124]

Perhaps the most graphic illustration of the relationship between race and criminal justice involves the use of capital punishment. When the *Furman v. Georgia* (408 U.S.238; 1972) decision was first handed down by the Supreme Court, many scholars interpreted the finding as the abolition of capital punishment in the United States. However, in 1976 the Court heard three cases, the most important of which is the *Gregg v. Georgia* (428 U. S. 153; 1976). In this case, the state of Georgia provided the Court with a set of procedural safeguards designed to guide the discretion of the judge or jury when faced with a capital case. For instance, the Georgia statute provided an automatic appeal of all death penalty cases. It was argued that separate trials, one trial to determine guilt and another for punishment, guarded against irrelevant evidence that might influence sentencing decisions. The Georgia statute made it mandatory that the death penalty could not be imposed unless a jury unanimously (and beyond a reasonable doubt) found that the offender used excessive force or engaged in behavior that escalated the severity of the crime. The Court argued in *Gregg* that capital punishment does not necessarily amount to cruel and unusual punishment as long as certain procedural safeguards are carried out that are designed to curb arbitrary and capricious application of the death. In short, where discretion is reasonable and controlled, capital punishment is constitutionally permissible for the crime of murder.

Studies have revealed that, despite the significance of this case, the guidelines established in *Gregg* have not eliminated racial disparities in capital cases. One study examined patterns of death sentencing in Florida, Texas, Ohio, and Georgia. In each of these states, killers of Whites were sentenced to death more consistently than killers of Blacks. Also, Black defendants with White victims were more likely to receive the death penalty than White defendants with Black victims. The implication, of course, is that the decision to execute in these states reflects the same arbitrariness that has characterized the imposition of the death penalty in the past.[125] Federal statistics show that 84 percent of White victims and 93 percent of Black victims between 1980 and 2008 were murdered by someone of the same race. However, although roughly half of all U.S. homicide victims are Black, more than three-quarters of victims of death-row defendants executed since 1976 were White.[126]

Another study found a clear pattern of racial disparity in South Carolina death penalty cases when the race of the offender and the race of the victim were considered together. This study found that Blacks who kill Whites had over 4.5 times greater risk of having the death penalty sought than did Black killers of Blacks. Whites who killed Blacks were 1.1 times more likely to have the death penalty sought by the prosecutor than Whites who killed other Whites. This study concluded that the race of the victim may be a more important consideration of public prosecutors than the race of the offender.[127]

In *McCleskey v. Kemp* (481 U.S.279; 1981), Warren McClesky, a Black man, was convicted in Fulton County, Georgia, of murdering a White police officer during an armed robbery of a furniture store. The conviction was consistent with the Georgia statute concerning aggravating circumstances. At trial, McClesky failed to present any mitigating evidence to the jury and was subsequently sentenced to death.

On appeal to the U.S. Supreme Court, McCleskey claimed that the Georgia capital sentencing process is administered in a racially discriminatory manner which violated the protections provided by the 8th Amendment to the U.S. Constitution. He also argued that the discriminatory system violated the 14th Amendment's equal protection clause. To support his claim, McCleskey offered the results of an empirical study documenting evidence of a racial bias against African Americans. The study showed that from 1973 to 1979 there were 2,484 murder and nonnegligent manslaughter cases in Georgia. Defendants who killed Whites were sentenced to death in 11 percent of the cases, while defendants who killed Blacks were sentenced to death in only about 1 percent of the cases.[128]

This study also discovered that the death penalty was imposed in 22 percent of the cases where an African American defendant was convicted of murdering a White victim; 8 percent of the cases with White defendants and White victims; 3 percent of the cases with White defendant and Black victims, and only 1 percent of the case involving Black defendant and Black victims. In this detailed analysis, the researchers controlled for some 230 nonracial variables and found that none could account for the racial disparities in capital sentences among the different racial combinations of defendant and victim. People who killed Whites were 4.3 times more likely to be sentenced to death than those who killed Blacks.[129]

McCleskey claimed that race had infected the administration of capital punishment in Georgia in two ways. First, offenders who murder Whites were more likely to be sentenced to death than offenders who murder Blacks. Secondly, Black murderers were more likely to be sentenced to death than White murderers.

In 1987 the Supreme Court handed down its 5–4 decision. The essential question before the Court was whether a complex statistical study that indicates a risk that racial consideration enters into capital sentencing determinations is unconstitutional under the 8th and 14th Amendments. The Court held that the study does not prove that the administration of the Georgia system violates these amendments.

The essence of the Court's ruling is that there are acceptable standards of risk of racial discrimination in imposing the death penalty. The Court held that the study simply shows that discrepancies appear to correlate with race in imposing death sentences, but that, according to the Court, the statistics did not prove that race is a factor in any capital sentencing decisions nor that race was a factor in this particular one.[130] The Court was also concerned that a finding for the defendant would open other claims that "could be extended to other types of penalties and to claims based on unexplained discrepancies correlating to membership in other minority groups and even to gender." The dissenters in the ruling argued that whether McCleskey could prove racial discrimination in his particular case is totally irrelevant in evaluating his claim of a constitutional violation because the Court has long recognized a pattern of substantial risk of arbitrary and capricious capital sentencing suffices for a claim of unconstitutionality.

CORRECTIONS AND AFRICAN AMERICANS

There is a long history of disproportionality in the criminal justice system with regard to race and this is clearly reflected in statistics regarding incarceration. In 2014, according to the U.S. Department of Justice, there were an estimated 1,561,500 prisoners in state and federal correctional facilities, a decrease of one percent from 2013. It seems fairly evident, by any measure, that African Americans are disproportionately incarcerated. While they represented approximately 14 percent of the overall population in this country in 2014, African Americans represented 36 percent of those incarcerated in state and federal prisons. Whites represented about 75 percent of the population yet they only constituted 34 percent of the inmate population. Hispanics represented about 17 percent of the population, but about 22 percent of those incarcerated in 2014.[131]

According to the Bureau of Justice Statistics, at the beginning of 2014, American federal among those inmates with a sentence of more than one year, Black males comprised 516,900 inmates, White males made up 453,500 and Hispanic males consisted of 308,700. More than 36 percent of all sentenced males were Black, about 32 percent were White, and about 22 percent were Hispanic. Female prisoners reflected a slightly different distribution, with Whites comprising the largest percentage of female inmates at 53,100, followed by African Americans, with 22,600 inmates and Hispanics, with 17,800 prisoners. This means that of all sentenced females, 50 percent were White, 22 percent were Black, and 17 percent were Hispanic.[132]

According to the Bureau of Justice Statistics in 2014, Black males had higher imprisonment rates than prisoners of other races or Hispanic origin in every age category. The rates for Black males were between 3.8 and 10.5 times greater than White males and 1.4 to 3.1 times greater than rates for Hispanic males. Among female prisoners, Black females were between 1.6 and 4.1 times more likely to be imprisoned than White females of any group.[133]

Types of offenses also varied by race and ethnicity, although compared to violent and property offenders in state prisons, those serving time for drug offenses had very little racial disparity. Overall About 48 percent of White male prisoners, 57 percent of Black and 59 percent of Hispanic male inmates were convicted of violent offenses. However, White offenders were more likely serving time for a property offense (25 percent) compared to Blacks (16 percent) and Hispanics (14 percent). As was mentioned, drug offenders were about evenly distributed with Blacks representing the largest percentage of offenders (16 percent) followed by Whites and Hispanics equally (14.5 percent each).

African Americans' interaction and involvement in the three primary components of the criminal justice system (police, courts, and corrections) are further discussed in the latter part of this book. To be sure, controversy exists with respect to African American and other minority group involvement in the criminal justice system. Below we comment on factors that generate and perpetuate the controversy and discrepancy.

RACE, FEAR, AND CRIME

Given evidence that clearly suggests that African Americans are stopped, frisked, arrested, prosecuted, convicted, sentenced to longer prison terms, and more likely to be given the death penalty, how can such a distinctive set of trends be explained?

One theory is that African Americans are more likely to engage in criminal activity, more likely to get caught, and given their repeated patterns of behavior, receive harsher treatment at every level of the criminal justice system. This is perhaps the most popular theory since it focuses the blame squarely on the people who are adversely affected. Arguably, African Americans are punished more because they commit more acts against society and this is reflected in the arrest, conviction, and incarceration statistics.

Another theory places the blame for the misrepresentation of African Americans in the criminal justice system on the structure of society and on the system itself. Arguments on this side contend that the system is racist, and African Americans are treated unfairly largely because of public fears. As a result, a self-fulfilling prophecy develops. Motivated by the perception that African Americans represent a greater threat than White offenders, police, judges, and other court officials treat African Americans more harshly. Blacks, in turn, perceive this treatment as biased and are likely to become a more substantial threat than they would have been without exposure to racism in the criminal justice system. This reinforces the public's fears that African Americans pose a greater threat to safety than White offenders.

IS THE CRIMINAL JUSTICE SYSTEM RACIST?

In contrast to the prevailing view about the system being biased against African Americans in particular and minorities in general, William Wilbanks, in his book, *The Myth of a Racist Criminal Justice System* (1987), presents a somewhat different argument about the relationship of race to the criminal justice system. He contends that the explanation is not found in a racist system that systematically singles out Blacks for special treatment. Rather, there are other factors at play, that contribute to the involvement of Blacks in the justice system, namely poverty, negligence, and previous involvement in crime. It seems fairly clear that Whites and Blacks differ sharply over whether the criminal justice system is racist. The vast majority of Blacks appear to believe that the police and the courts unfairly discriminate against Blacks, whereas a majority of Whites rejects this charge. This disparity also appears to exist among those who work in the system.

Some Blacks have suggested that the criminal justice system is so characterized by racism that Blacks are outside the protection of the law. A sizable minority of Whites, in contrast, think that the system actually discriminates *for* Blacks out of fear of being charged with racism from the Black community. White police officers have reported often ignoring criminal activity by Blacks out of a fear of criticism from the department, the Black community, and/or the media.[134]

Wilbanks contends that these contrasting perceptions regarding the fairness of the system have at least four important consequences. First, research shows that Blacks may turn to criminality or engage in more crime because of a perception that the criminal law and its enforcement is unfair and even racist. Thus, in a way, Blacks believe they are justified in breaking the law. The second consequence relates to civil disturbances. Many riots occur because of a perception that the system is unfair and unjust. The Kerner Commission, which investigated the civil disturbances in American cities in the 1960s, found a widespread belief among Blacks that the criminal justice system was racist and concluded that negative perceptions of Blacks by the agents of the criminal justice system, particularly the police, were a major cause of the violence.

A third consequence of these opposing perceptions is a heightened sense of hostility toward the police. As mentioned, many Blacks view the criminal justice system as racist and the police as prejudiced. The greater intrusiveness by police officers into the lives of people in low-income areas often leads to heightened tensions and resentment of the police. It also creates an impression that the police are intentionally harassing people in these neighborhoods, looking for a reason to arrest them.[135]

The fourth consequence is that the White backlash to civil rights programs such as affirmative action and racial quotas may be due in part to a White perception that Blacks complain about racism, when, in fact, Whites provide excessive preferential treatment to African Americans. Wilbanks takes the position that the perception of the criminal justice system as racist is a myth. He argues that the question of whether the criminal justice system is racist must not be confused with Blacks committing crimes at a higher rate than Whites because of discrimination in employment, housing, education, etc. It may be that racial discrimination produces a gap in offending between Blacks and Whites but this gap is not increased as Black and White offenders move through the system. If the gap does not increase after the point at which offenses occur, the system cannot be held responsible for the gap that results at the end of the system (e.g., prison).

Wilbanks says that Blacks believe the system is racist for several reasons. The most important of which he calls **negative attribution**. This suggests that, in response to the history of how Blacks have been treated, African Americans have developed a negative view of Whites that attributes evil motives and traits. Whites are an "out group" intent on denying

Blacks equal rights and opportunities. This attribution leads to the tendency to look for "facts" to confirm this view of Whites.

Second, Wilbanks explains that the suspicions of African Americans of the entire criminal justice system are not an abstract or intellectual argument. The mistrust of the system in general, and of the police in particular, come from their direct personal experiences with police officers. Such personal experiences tend to confirm what people commonly hear in the Black community; thus, Blacks often express the view that they do not need statistical proof of racial discrimination since they have experienced it.

In short, Wilbanks offers the idea that the disparity in the legal system has more to do with poverty levels than race. The argument suggests that crimes like assault, drugs, burglary, and robbery are a function of the adversity families and individuals are facing as a result of being poor. Empirical support for this position was offered in the 1990s when researchers noted that a decrease in poverty levels were related to reductions in crime rates, particularly in the early part of the twentieth century. To be fair, some studies suggested a link between poverty and crime, but other evidence began to emerge that suggested race was playing a role in the justice process. Thus, while Wilbanks's approach garnered some credibility for a time, and perhaps today with conservative thinkers, the weight of the evidence suggests that something is amiss with regard to the relationship between race and the justice process.

A third position is offered by Walker, Spohn, and DeLone (1996). After an extensive review of the literature, they suggested a more moderate theory that contends the system is neither completely free of racial bias nor does it contain the type of systematic bias that other experts assert. Walker, Spohn, and DeLone agree that racial and ethnic groups are in fact treated more harshly at some (or many) stages of the system but at other points they are not singled out compared to Whites who are going through the justice process.[136]

SUMMARY

This chapter explored the historical experience of African Americans in the United States and how this group has found itself in a disadvantaged position for some time. From the early days of slavery to discrimination as they fought in world conflict to the civil rights movement, the African American has played an important role in the history of the United States. Reconstruction also played a role in the current position of African Americans as many formal and informal norms and laws were created to distance African Americans from Whites even when they were forced to live in close proximity to one another. The legacy of slavery, Jim Crow, segregation, and the denial of equal protection under the law, as found in U.S. Supreme Court cases, have fundamentally shaped the position of African Americans in the United States. A byproduct of this treatment and legacy of slavery is seen in the disproportionate representation of African Americans in the criminal justice system.

While the topic remains controversial, there can be little doubt that African Americans are overrepresented in crime statistics. This is true despite the fact that there is a growing Black middle class of educated, professional, and politically savvy African Americans. Whether it involves arrest, use of force, searches, convictions, sentences, or executions, Blacks are disproportionately represented in the criminal justice system. Not only do

Blacks have different experiences with the criminal justice system than Whites, there is a general sense of mistrust of the system in general and of the police in particular.

In many low-income neighborhoods there is a significant amount of tension between African Americans and the police. Part of the reason for this mutual mistrust is due to the fact that police officers intervene into the lives of many African Americans perhaps more so than Whites living in suburban neighborhoods. As a result, not only do African Americans perceive the police as intrusive, this frequent contact can also make it more likely that they become involved in the criminal justice system.

The reasons for the overrepresentation of African Americans in the criminal justice system range from individualistic theories, which contend that African Americans commit more crimes, get caught, and are punished, to structural explanations, which suggest there are factors outside the control of the individual which result in their involvement in the system. Finally, as Wilbanks points out, there also exists a debate concerning the racism embedded in the criminal justice system itself.

YOU MAKE THE CALL

Consider the following scenario. Debate the pros and cons of all options and decide what you would do.

You are a White, middle class, male police officer with less than one year's experience in law enforcement. You have been assigned to a high crime, low-income neighborhood. There are many calls for service and a significant amount of violent crime in this area. In fact, several times this year the SWAT team has been called to rescue officers who have been attacked by armed residents. Your partner is an eight-year veteran officer who has been involved in many disturbances in this neighborhood and dislikes many of the citizens who live in this neighborhood. In fact, during the course of several conversations, your partner uses racial epithets against African Americans and talks about "nuking the entire area" and starting all over with a group of "civilized" people. In the eleven months since you've been a police officer, you have heard rumors that this officer has engaged in acts of excessive violence toward citizens and has even planted evidence on suspects in order to arrest them.

While working late one night, the two of you answer a call from a resident that a domestic disturbance is taking place. Your partner says, "I know these people, we get called here all the time. I'll handle this." You enter the home of an African American family and your partner rushes into another room. Three shots are fired and when you come into the room, you find a Black man lying on the floor with gunshot wounds to his chest. Your partner is standing over him with his weapon drawn, smoke coming from the barrel of his pistol. He tells you that the dead man reached for a gun, but none is found. The man's family begins to scream that your partner shot an unarmed man.

Later, when detectives take your statement, they ask if your partner used excessive force against the victim. The investigators also tell you that the deceased family members claim they did not own a gun and one was not found at the scene. Does your partner's attitudes toward African Americans factor into his behavior? Do you think your partner might be prejudiced against minorities in general? What about in this particular case? How do you know? What do you say to the detectives?

KEY TERMS

abolitionists	de-policing
Black middle class	Emancipation Proclamation
Black nationalism	Freedom Schools
Black Power	fugitive slave acts
Christopher Commission	Jim Crow
Civil Rights Act	Nation of Islam
Civil Rights Movement	negative attribution

racial profiling
Reconstruction
Reconstruction Act of 1867
restrictive covenants

slave codes
vicarious hassling
Voting Rights Act

DISCUSSION QUESTIONS

1. Why do you think African Americans are overrepresented in the crime statistics? Is it because they commit more crimes or is it due to greater police presence in their communities?
2. What role, if any, does the legacy of slavery play in the involvement of African Americans in crime?
3. Do you think the criminal justice system is racist toward African Americans or does it show that individual people within the system discriminate against African Americans?
4. What role does the media play in assessing the importance of race and the criminal justice system?
5. What role do you think the Black middle class should play in resolving some of the problems in low-income neighborhoods?
6. Assume you are a U.S. Supreme Court Justice and are hearing a case on the death penalty. Do you think studies examining the race factor in executions should be used to determine if discrimination exists? Why or why not?

FOR FURTHER READING

Hay, J., ed. *The Montgomery Bus Boycott*. New York: Greenhaven Press, 2011.
Alexander, M. *The New Jim Crow: Mass Incarceration in the Age of Color Blindness*. New York: The New Press, 2012.
Isenberg, N. *White Trash: The 400-Year Untold History of Class in America*. New York: Viking, 2016.
Stuart, F. *Down, Out, and Under Arrest: Policing and Everyday Life in Skid Row*. Chicago, IL: University of Chicago Press, 2016.

NOTES

1. J. Scott and G. Marshall, *A Dictionary of Sociology*, 3rd edition (New York: Oxford University Press, 2005),183. Available online at http://www.oxfordreference.com/view/10.1093/acref/9780199533008.001.0001/acref-9780199533008-e-1859?rskey=BVTpmt&result=1859.
2. M. Tarver, S. Walker, and H. Wallace, *Multicultural Issues in the Criminal Justice System* (Boston, MA: Allyn and Bacon, 2002), 33–40.
3. J. H. Franklin and A. A. Moss, *From Slavery to Freedom: A History of African Americans*, 8th ed. (New York: McGraw-Hill, 2000), 220–43.
4. W. E. B. Dubois, *The Negro American Family* (Cambridge, MA: MIT Press, 1970), 18.
5. Ibid.
6. F. Frazier, *The Negro Church in America* (New York: Schocken, 1974), 20–29; K. Stampp, *The Peculiar Institution: Slavery in the Ante-Bellum South*. New York: Vintage, 1956/1989), 322.
7. G. P. Rawick, *From Sundown to Sunup: The Making of the Black Community* (Westport, CT: Greenwood Press, 1972), 123.
8. Franklin and Moss, *From Slavery to Freedom*.
9. J. Oakes, "Slavery," in *Encyclopedia of American Social History*, ed. M. K. Clayton, E. J. Gorn and P. W. Williams (New York: Scribners, 1993), 1407–19.
10. L. M. Killian, *The Impossible Revolution? Phase 2: Black Power and the American Dream* (New York: Random House, 1975), 57.

11. Ibid.

12. R. D. Abrahams, *Singing the Master: The Emergence of African American Culture in the Plantation South* (New York: Pantheon, 1992), 22; M. D. Free, *African Americans and the Criminal Justice System* (New York: Garland, 1996), 88.

13. L. Bennett, "The White Problem in America" *Ebony* (August, 1965): 29–45.

14. D. Lacy, *The White Use of Blacks in America*. New York: McGraw-Hill, 1972, 83–98.

15. P. Lewinson, *Race, Class, and Party: A History of Negro Suffrage and White Politics in the South* (New York: Universal Library, 1965), 94, 157; Lacy, *The White Use of Blacks in America*.

16. Free, *African Americans and the Criminal Justice System*.

17. Tarver et al., *Multicultural Issues in the Criminal Justice System*.

18. Scott and Marshall, *Dictionary of Sociology*.

19. A. Oberschall, "The Los Angeles Riot of August 1965," *Social Problems* 15 (1968): 322–41.

20. Ibid.

21. R. Kluger, *Simple Justice* (New York: Random House, 1998).

22. Oberschall, "The Los Angeles Riot."

23. Killian, *The Impossible Revolution*.

24. A. Oberschall, "The Los Angeles Riot of August 1965," *Social Problems* 15 (1968): 322-341. doi: 10.2307/799788

25. J. S. Butler, "The Return of Open Debate," *Society* 33 (March/April 1996): 11–18.

26. "What if I Don't Move to the Back of the Bus?" Available at https://www.thehenryford.org/explore/stories-of-innovation/what-if/rosa-parks/

27. Franklin and Moss, *From Slavery to Freedom*.

28. Ibid.

29. Scott and Marshall, *A Dictionary of Sociology*.

30. Oberschall, "The Los Angeles Riot."

31. Ibid.

32. Ibid.

33. Scott and Marshall, *Dictionary of Sociology*.

34. K. Cleaver, "How TV Wrecked the Black Panthers," *Channels of Communication* (November-December 1982): 98–99.

35. T. Watnabe, "Righting Islam's Image in America" *Los Angeles Times*, May 18, 1999, B2.

36. Ibid.

37. Ibid.; E. Allen, "Religious Heterodoxy and Nationalist Tradition: The Continuing Evolution of the Nation of Islam," *Black Scholar* 26, no. 3/4 (1996): 2–34.

38. J. P. Crank, *Understanding Police Culture* (Cincinnati, OH: Anderson, 1998).

39. Scott and Marshall, *Dictionary of Sociology*.

40. D. J. Besharov, "The Economic Stagnation of the Black Middle Class." Testimony before the U.S. Commission on Civil Rights, July 2005.

41. W. J. Wilson, *The Truly Disadvantaged* (Chicago: University of Chicago Press, 1987); E. Anderson, *Streetwise* (Chicago: University of Chicago Press, 1990).

42. J. P. Crank, "Understanding Police Culture" *American Journal of Criminal Justice* 24, no. 1 (September 1999): 151–54.

43. W. J. Wilson, *The Declining Significance of Race* (Chicago: University of Chicago Press, 1978).

44. See the Black Lives Matter website at: http://blacklivesmatter.com/about/

45. Ibid.

46. F. C. Harris, "The Next Civil Rights Movement?" *Dissent Magazine*, Summer 2015, accessed from https://www.dissentmagazine.org/article/black-lives-matter-new-civil-rights-movement-fredrick-harris

47. D. Cole, *No Equal Justice: Race and Class in the American Criminal Justice System* (New York: The Free Press, 1999), 88–109.

48. Ibid.

49. Ibid.

50. Ibid.

51. J. Harris, "Fathers Behind Bars and on the Street," Prison Fellowship, available at https://www.prisonfellowship.org/2014/10/fathers-behind-bars-the-problem-solution-for-americas-children/.

52. Ibid.

53. Ibid.

54. Ibid.

55. Ibid.

56. Cole, *No Equal Justice*; Harris, "Fathers Behind Bars."

57. Emily Brown, "Timeline: Michael Brown Shooting in Ferguson, Mo.," *USA Today*, August 14, 2014, available at http://www.usatoday.com/story/news/nation/2014/08/14/michael-brown-ferguson-missouri-timeline/14051827/

58. L. Bui, "Baltimore Officer Acquitted of Murder, Other Charges in Freddy Gray Case." *The Washington Post*, June 23, 2016, available at https://www.washingtonpost.com/local/public-safety/judge-to-deliver-verdict-for-police-officer-charged-with-murder-in-freddie-gray-case/2016/06/22/7a0e015b-3b12-4294-8b72-84a36e1715cd_story.html?utm_term=.64a0a51371f5; P. Hermann and J. W. Cox, "A Freddie Gray Primer: Who Was He, How Did He Die, Why Is There So Much Anger?" *Washington Post*, April 28, 2015, available at https://www.washingtonpost.com/news/local/wp/2015/04/28/a-freddie-gray-primer-who-was-he-how-did-he-why-is-there-so-much-anger/; Kevin Rector, "The 45-Minute Mystery of Freddie Gray's Death," *Baltimore Sun*, April 25, 2015, available at http://www.baltimoresun.com/news/maryland/freddie-gray/bs-md-gray-ticker-20150425-story.html

59. Annie Sweeney and Jason Meisner, "A Moment-by-Moment Account of What the Laquan McDonald Video Shows," *Chicago Tribune*, November 25, 2015, available at http://www.chicagotribune.com/news/ct-chicago-cop-shooting-video-release-laquan-mcdonald-20151124-story.html; Anne Swaney, "Chicago Police Officer Jason VanDyke Charged with 1st-Degree Murder in Laquan McDonald Shooting," *ABC7 Eyewitness News*, November 24, 2015, available at http://abc7chicago.com/news/cop-charged-with-1st-degree-murder-in-laquan-mcdonald-shooting/1097312/

60. "Medical Examiner Rules Eric Garner's Death a Homicide, Says He Was Killed by Chokehold," *NBC4 New York*, August 21, 2014, available at http://www.nbcnewyork.com/news/local/Eric-Garner-Chokehold-Police-Custody-Cause-of-Death-Staten-Island-Medical-Examiner-269396151.html; Al Baker, J. David Goodman, and Benjamin Mueller, "Beyond the Chokehold: The Path to Eric Garner's Death," *New York Times*, June 13, 2015, available at http://www.nytimes.com/2015/06/14/nyregion/eric-garner-police-chokehold-staten-island.html.

61. Catherine Shoichet, "Walter Scott Shooting Case: Court Documents Reveal New Details," *CNN*, September 10, 2015, available at http://www.cnn.com/2015/09/08/us/south-carolina-walter-scott-shooting michael-slager/; Alex Johnson, "Michael Slager, S.C. Cop Who Killed Unarmed Motorist Walter Scott, Released on $500,000 Bond," *NBC News*, January 4, 2016, available at http://www.nbcnews.com/storyline/walter-scott-shooting/michael-slager-s-c-cop-who-killed-unarmed-motorist-walter-n490066; Andrew Knapp, "Feds Seek to Charge

North Charleston Police Officer in Walter Scott Shooting," *Post and Courier*, December 3, 2015 http://www.postandcourier.com/article/20151204/PC16/151209762

62. A. Knapp, "Federal Civil Rights Trial for Michael Slager Anticipated This Spring," *Post and Courier*, December 14, 2016. Available at http://www.postandcourier.com/news/federal-civil-rights-trial-for-michael-slager-anticipated-this-spring/article_c7f64bd2-c183-11e6-b628-373f8053c64c.html

63. R. Fausset, R. Perez-Pena, and C. Robertson, "Alton Sterling Shooting in Baton Rouge Prompts Justice Department Investigation," *New York Times*, July 6, 2016, available at: http://movile.nytimes.com/2016/07/06/alton-sterling-baton-rouge-shooting.html?

64. B. Jansen, "Three Police Officers Fatally Shot in Baton Rouge; Dead Suspect Identified," *USA Today*, July 7, 2016, available at http://www.usatoday.com/story/news/2016/07/17/reports-baton-rouge-police-officers-shot/87218884/

65. G. Lopez, J. Williams, and L. Nelson, L. "Dallas Shooting Kills Multiple Police Officers: What We Know," *Vox*, July 9, 2016. Available at: http://www.vox.com/2016/7/7/12125740/dallas-shooting-police-protests.html

66. See Lopez et al., "Dallas Shooting"; Jansen, "Three Police Officers Fatally Shot"; Fausset et al., "Alton Sterling Shooting."

67. K. Potter, and A. Forliti, "AP News Guide: More Unrest as Police Shooting Probe Goes On," *Los Angeles Times*, July 28, 2016. Available at http://www.latimes.com/nation/sns-bc-us-police-shooting-minnesota-news-guide-20160727-story,amp.html

68. L. Langton, and M. Durose, M. 2013. *Police Behavior During Traffic and Street Stops* (Washington, DC: Bureau of Justice Statistics, 2013), available at http://www.bjs.gov/content/pub/pdf/pbtss11.pdf

69. M. R. Durose, E. L. Smith, and P. A. Langan, *Contacts Between the Police and the Public 2005*, April 2007, available at https://www.bjs.gov/content/pub/pdf/cpp05.pdf

70. D. A. Smith and C. Visher, "Street-Level Justice: Situational Determinants of Police Arrest Decisions," *Social Problems* 29, no. 2 (1981): 167–77.

71. C. Maxon, K. Hennigan, and D. Sloane, *Factors That Influence Public Opinion of the Police* (Washington, DC: National Institute of Justice, 2003), available at https://www.ncjrs.gov/pdffiles1/nij/197925.pdf

72. S. Walker, C. Spohn, and M. Delone, *The Color of Justice: Race, Ethnicity and Crime in America* (Belmont, CA: Wadsworth, 1996, 2000, and 2004), 108–32.

73. R. Bachman, "Victims' Perceptions of Initial Police Responses to Robbery and Aggravated Assault: Does Race Matter?" *Journal of Quantitative Criminology* 12, no. 4 (1996): 363–90.

74. Ibid.

75. U.S. Department of Justice, Federal Bureau of Investigation. *Crime in the United States*, Table 43, Fall 2015, available at https://www.fbi.gov/about-us/cjis/ucr/crime-in-the-u.s/2014/crime-in-the-u.s.-2014/tables/table-43

76. D. Black, "The Social Organization of Arrest," *Stanford Law Review* 23 (1971): 1087–111.

77. Ibid.

78. Smith and Visher, "Street-Level Justice."

79. Ibid.

80. J. Petersilia, *Racial Disparities in the Criminal Justice System* (Santa Monica, CA: RAND, 1983), available at http://www.rand.org/pubs/reports/R2947.html

81. I. S. Son, M. Davis, and D. M. Rome, "Race and its Effect on Police Officers' Perceptions Of Misconduct." *Journal of Criminal Justice* 26, no. 1 (1998): 21–28.

82. Public Broadcasting System. 2015. "The Legacy of Rodney King," *Frontline*, May 2001, available at http://pbs.org/wgbh/pages/frontline/shows/lapd/race/king.html

83. R. J. Friedrich, "Police Use of Force: Individuals, Situations, and Organizations," *Annals of the American Academy of Political and Social Science* 452 (1980): 82–97; K. Adams, K. 1995. "Measuring the Prevalence of Police Abuse of Force" In *And Justice for All*, ed. William Geller and Hans Toch (Washington, DC: The Police Executive Research Forum, 1995); H. Cohen. and L. Sherman, "Exploiting Police Authority," *Criminal Justice Ethics* (Summer/Fall 1986): 23–31.

84. A. Reiss 1971. *The Police and the Public*. New Haven, CT: Yale University Press, p.122.

85. Adams, "Measuring the Prevalence."

86. Walker et al., *The Color of Justice*.

87. Ibid.

88. M. Hickman, *Citizen Complaints About Police Use of Force*, Department of Justice, Bureau of Justice Statistics, June 2006, available at https://www.bjs.gov/content/pub/pdf/ccpuf.pdf.

89. Ibid.

90. J. G. Shoop, "National Survey Suggests Racial Disparity in Police Use of Force," *Trial* 34, no. 1 (1998): 97; J. J. Fyfe, "Police Use of Deadly Force: Research and Reform," *Justice Quarterly* 5, no. 2 (1988): 165–205; R. Dunham and G. Alpert, *Critical Issues in Policing: Contemporary Readings* (Cincinnati, OH: Waveland, 1992); W. Westley, *Violence and the Police: A Sociological Study of Law, Custom, and Morality* (Cambridge, MA: MIT Press, 1970).

91. Fyfe, "Police Use of Deadly Force"; W. A. Geller and M. S. Scott, "Deadly Force: What We Know" in *Thinking About Police*, ed. C. B. Klockars and S. D. Mastrofski (New York: McGraw-Hill, 1993), 446–76.

92. Walker et al., *The Color of Justice*.

93. Cohen and Sherman, "Exploiting Police Authority."

94. Walker et al., *The Color of Justice*.

95. R. R. Roberg and J. Kuykendall. *Police and Society* (Belmont, CA: Wadsworth, 1993).

96. A. Burch, *Arrest-Related Deaths 2003–2009*. U.S. Department of Justice, Bureau of Justice Statistics, November 2011, available at https://www.bjs.gov/content/pub/pdf/ard0309st.pdf

97. E. Liebow, *Tell Them Who I Am*. Chicago, IL: University of Chicago Press, 1999.

98. Walker et al., *The Color of Justice*.

99. Cole, *No Equal Justice*.

100. E. Lichtblau, "Profiling Report Leads to Demotion." *New York Times* (August 24, 2005), B1.

101. S. L. Browning, F. T. Cullen, L. Cao, R. Kopache, T. J. Stevenson. "Race and Getting Hassled By the Police: A Research Note," *Police Studies* 17, no. 1 (1994): 1–11.

102. M. F. White, T. C. Cox, and J. Basehart, "Theoretical Considerations of Officer Profanity and Obscenity in Formal Contacts with Citizens," in T. Barker and D. L. Carter, eds., *Police Deviance*, 2nd edition (Cincinnati, OH: Anderson, 1991), 275–97.

103. H. MacDonald, *The War on Cops* (New York: Encounter Books, 2015). See also T. Lynch:"The War on Cops Flawed Logic and Fantasy" *Newsweek*, July 31, 2016, available at http://www.newsweek.com/war-cops-flawed-logic-fantasy-485546.

104. R. Sutton, "The Dangers of Depolicing: Will Cops Just Stand Down?" *New York Post*, May 5, 2015. Available at http://nypost.com/2015/05/05/the-dangers-of-de-policing-will-cops-just-stand-down/

105. H. McDonald, "Officer Beaten by a Convicted Felon Hesitated for Fear of Being Called Racist: Welcome to Post-Ferguson Policing," *The National Review*, August 16, 2015, available at http://www.nationalreview.com/article/422605/Birmingham-cop-beaten-unconscious-feared-racism-charge

106. Ibid.

107. See Lopez et al., "Dallas Shooting"; Jansen, "Three Police Officers Fatally Shot"; Fausset et al., "Alton Sterling Shooting."

108. D. Murdock, "An Assassination of Truth," *National Review*, January 8, 2015. Available at http://www.nationalreview.com/article/395919/assassination-truth-deroy-murdock.html

109. Ibid.

110. Tarver et al., *Multicultural Issues in the Criminal Justice System.*

111. Walker et al., *The Color of Justice.*

112. J. Palazzolo, "Racial Gap in Men's Sentencing," *Wall Street Journal*, February 14, 2013. Available at http://www.wsj.com/articles/SB10001424127887324432004578304463789858002

113. Ibid.

114. C. Crawford, T. Chiricos, and G. Kleck, "Race, Racial Threat and Sentencing of Habitual Offenders," *Criminology* 36, no. 3 (1998): 481–511.

115. S. Ekland-Olson, "Structured Discretion, Racial Bias, and the Death Penalty: The First Debate after Furman in Texas," *Social Science Quarterly* 69 (December 1988): 853–73.

116. R. Weitzer, and S. A. Tuch, "Race, Class and Perceptions of Discrimination by the Police," *Crime and Delinquency* 45, no. 4 (1999): 494–507.

117. Tarver et al., *Multicultural Issues in the Criminal Justice System.*

118. A. Hacker, "Affirmative Action: The New Look." *New York Review of Books* 36 (October 12, 1989): 63–68.

119. G. LaFree, "The Effect of Sexual Stratification by Race on Official Reactions to Rape," *American Sociological Review* 45 (October 1980): 842–54.

120. O. Mitchell and D. L. MacKenzie, *The Relationship Between Race, Ethnicity, and Sentencing Outcomes: A Meta-Analysis of Sentencing Research* (Washington, DC: National Institute of Justice, 2014). Available at https://www.ncjrs.gov/pdffiles1/nij/grants/208129.pdf

121. J. Gray, "Panel Says Courts are Infested with Racism." *New York Times* (June 5, 1991): B1.

122. N. Ghandnoosh, *Race and Punishment: Racial Perceptions of Crime and Support for Punitive Policies* (The Sentencing Project, 2014). Available at: http://sentencingproject.org/doc/publications/rd_Race_and_Punishment.pdf

123. Ibid.

124. Walker et al., *The Color of Justice.*

125. W. J. Bowers and G. Pierce, "Deterrence or Brutalization: What is the Effect of Executions?" *Crime and Delinquency* 26 (1980): 453–84.

126. M. Ford, "Racism and the Execution Chamber," *Atlantic*, June 23, 2014. Available at http://www.theatlantic.com/politics/archive/2014/06/race-and-the-death-penalty/373081/

127. R. Paternoster, "Prosecutorial Discretion in Requesting the Death Penalty: A Case of Victim-Based Racial Discrimination," *Law and Society Review* 18 (1984): 437–78.

128. D. Baldus, G. Woodworth, and C. A. Pulaski, *Equal Justice and the Death Penalty: A Legal and Empirical Analysis* (Boston: Northeastern University Press, 1990).

129. Ibid.

130. *McCleskey v. Kemp* (481 U.S.279; 1981)

131. E. A. Carson, *Prisoners in 2014.* U.S. Department of Justice, Bureau of Justice Statistics, September 2015, available at: http://www.bjs.gov/content/pub/pdf/p14.pdf

132. Ibid.

133. Ibid.

134. See for instance MacDonald, *War on Cops*, 105.

135. Walker et al., *The Color of Justice.*

136. Ibid.

CHAPTER 4

HISPANIC AMERICANS AND THE CRIMINAL JUSTICE SYSTEM

CHAPTER OBJECTIVES

After reading this chapter, you should be able to:

- Understand the significance of the Hispanic/Latino influence in America
- Understand the historical importance of immigration for Chicanos, Cubans, Puerto Ricans, and those from Central and South America
- Describe the current position in American society for Chicanos, Cubans, and Puerto Ricans
- Describe the overrepresentation of Hispanic Americans in the criminal justice system, including arrests and sentencing

The group label *Hispanic Americans* includes a population of people who share a common language heritage but have many significant differences. More than one in eight people in the U.S. population are of Spanish or Latin American origin.[1] Collectively this group is called *Hispanics* or *Latinos*, terms we will use interchangeably in this chapter. The U.S. Census Bureau estimates that by 2060, Hispanics will constitute 119 million people, about 29 percent of the U.S. population. According to the Census Bureau, in 2014 there were 55 million people of Hispanic origin in the United States, making it one of the nation's largest ethnic or racial minorities. Hispanics constituted 17 percent of the nation's population. About 64 percent of those identifying with Hispanic heritage were Mexican, followed by about 10 percent who were of Puerto Rican background, about 4 percent were Cuban, about 3 percent Salvadoran, about 3 percent were Dominican and about 2.5 percent were Guatemalan. The remainder was of some other Central or South American origin.[2]

Financially, the median household income for Hispanics in the United States in 2014 was $40,963 with a poverty rate of about 24 percent. Another 24 percent of Hispanics lacked health insurance in 2014. Nearly two-thirds of Hispanics age twenty-five and older had at least a high school education. About 14 percent, or about 4.2 million people, had a bachelor's degree or higher, with another 1.3 million with advanced degrees. About 67 percent of Hispanics or Latinos sixteen years and older were in the labor force in 2014 and another 20 percent worked in management, business, science or artistic occupations.[3]

The problems of identity are evident from the outset of the discussion. How does one define this group of diverse people—are they Hispanic, Latino, or something else? People of Spanish or Latin origin share the group labels Hispanic or Latino and a common ancestral home, Central and South America. The Hispanic label combines the offspring of colonized natives, the *Hispanos*, with the descendants of foreigners, and with political and economic refugees.[4] The term *Hispanic* is not universally used and some people, particularly from Latin America, prefer the term **Latino**. Also, even among the cultures of Latin America, significant differences exist.[5]

In addition to the countries of origin, some sense of the Hispanic population can be made by examining where different groups tend to live. Chicanos, those who are Americans of Mexican origin, for example, are found primarily in the Southwest, whereas Puerto Ricans tend to live in the New England area, and Cubans tend to congregate in Florida. Given their diversity both in background and regionalism, groups in the West tend to use the term *Latino* whereas the term *Hispanic* is more often used in the East.[6]

There is even diversity found in the one area thought to be common for all Hispanics: language. Because of different dialects and nuances in pronunciation, while Spanish might be the way to generally identify the group, perhaps it is more accurate to say that Hispanics or Latinos are a non–English speaking group.

CHICANOS AND MEXICANS

Chicanos, who are Americans of Mexican origin, are the largest ethnic group in the United States. Numbering more than 39 million, with more than 55 percent living in California, Florida, and Texas in 2014. About 15 million live in California. Chicanos have a long history in the United States dating back to the early days of European exploration. The Chicano people trace their ancestry to the merging of Spanish settlers with Native Americans of Central America. In fact, evidence of Chicano history can be traced to the Mayan and Aztec civilizations.[7] Thus, the Spaniards conquered the land and merged with Native Americans over several centuries to form the Mexican people.

In 1821, Mexico obtained its independence but domination from the north began less than a generation later. After the conclusion of the Mexican American War, treaties were signed which gave the United States Texas, California, and most of Arizona and New Mexico for $15 million. In exchange, the United States granted citizenship to about 75,000 Mexicans.[8]

The beginning of the Chicano experience was varied but the one thing they had in common was that they were regarded as a vanquished people. Although maltreatment and discrimination existed, more serious issues arose when Whites began to encroach on Chicano land. Prior to 1869, Chicanos in California owned all parcels of land valued at more than $10,000. By the 1870s they owned only 25 percent of the land.

A widely accepted, and ironic, explanation for this trend was that many Whites felt justified in taking Chicano land because of the land grabbing that some Mexican governors perpetrated against American Indians. That Whites perpetuated this same type of behavior against American Indians somehow is lost in the justification in the treatment of Chicanos.[9]

IMMIGRATION

Immigration from Mexico is unique in several respects. From about 1901 to 1913, large numbers of Mexicans came into the country to work in the growing agricultural industry. The Mexican population grew significantly after the Mexican Revolution of 1909–1922, which brought even more refugees into the United States. When World War I began, fewer people from Europe came to this country, which opened the proverbial door in the labor market for Mexican workers. More Mexicans emigrated to the United States after the Mexican Revolution due to the political conflicts in their native country.[10]

The influx of Mexicans into the United States slowed after 1929 as the Great Depression was felt all over the country. Consequently, Mexicans were not needed for labor and the ones already in the United States were considered competition for existing jobs. In an attempt to reduce the labor force, the government embarked upon a deportation program, referred to as **Repatriation**, to effectively send Chicanos back to Mexico.[11]

The legal justification for Repatriation was that deportation only applied to illegal immigrants. However, one of the problems this program created stemmed from the poorly kept records concerning immigrants prior to 1930. Because the United States had little interest in whether Mexicans entered with the proper credentials, preferring their labor to their papers, many Mexicans who could be classified as illegal aliens had resided in the United States for decades. And, because many Mexicans had children who were citizens at birth, technically, they could not be legally deported. Regardless, many Chicanos were deported because they could not produce sufficient documentation that they were U.S. citizens.[12]

As a result, about half a million people were deported to Mexico. For the Chicanos and Mexicans who were allowed to remain, they could not find work and many lost the property they owned because they were unable to pay taxes. As a result, a large number of Chicanos flocked to growing concentrations of segregated areas, called **barrios**, of the Southwest.[13]

When the Depression ended, Mexican laborers again became attractive to industry. In 1942 the United States and Mexico agreed to a program allowing migration across the border by contracted workers called **Los Braceros**. Minimum standards were maintained for the transportation, housing, wages, and healthcare of the Braceros. Ironically, these safeguards placed the Braceros in a better economic situation than Chicanos, who often worked alongside the protected Mexican nationals.[14]

CHICANOS TODAY

Perhaps the two most significant areas that demonstrate the current status of Mexican Americans in this country relate to education and healthcare. Both Mexican Americans

Many of the problems experienced by African Americans are also felt by the Hispanic/Latino community.

and Puerto Ricans have seen some progress in terms of educational achievement; however both groups lag behind Whites.

Particularly in the 1960s and 1970s, strong campaigns were launched to ensure that Whites and Blacks were provided equal educational opportunities. The momentum for equality had lessened at a time when more Hispanics were entering congested, minority-dominated schools.[15]

Not surprisingly, Mexican Americans and Puerto Ricans are underrepresented in higher education. As an illustration, according to the U.S. Census, in 2014, 51 percent of Mexican Americans and 64 percent of Puerto Ricans aged twenty-five and over had completed high school. This compares with 88 percent of non-Hispanic Whites.[16]

Hispanics are also adversely affected by issues surrounding healthcare. According to the U.S. Census Bureau, despite the efforts to improve the number of Americans who have health insurance, and despite the fact that Hispanics and Latinos have seen an increase in the number of people who have obtained it, there still remains a size-able portion of the population that remain uninsured. According to a 2016 report, *Health Insurance Coverage in the United States*, In 2015, Hispanics had the highest uninsured rate in 2015, at 16.2 percent.[17] Not only is the quality of healthcare limited for many Hispanics, particularly those who are poor, there is no continuity of care since they must often rely on clinics for their medical needs. It also means preventive healthcare is limited. An added problem is the language barrier. Even with translators, communication with Hispanic patients is difficult since many medical terms are not easily translatable, particularly for interpreters who are not familiar with medical terminology.[18]

ILLEGAL IMMIGRATION, FENCING, AND THE MINUTEMAN DEFENSE CORPS

Illegal immigration is one of the most pervasive and controversial social issues among U.S. citizens. People are primarily concerned about the rise in illegal immigration, particularly from Mexico into the United States. Strategies to contain illegal immigrants consist of stricter enforcement of immigration laws or, the construction of a fence across the border between Mexico and the United States. This fence stretches over a 70-mile area and cost nearly $55 million. This fence was built using the fiber optic mesh produced by FOMGuard, USA, also currently in use on U.S. military installations, the Demilitarized Zone in Korea, and the West Bank in Israel. Perhaps most important, this fence was built on private ranch land through private donations.

Another strategy is referred to as the Minuteman Project (TMP). Beginning in April 2005, TMP was created as a way for citizens to actively take part in addressing the immigration problem from Mexico and Canada. The name of the group comes from the Minutemen who fought in the American Revolution. Essentially, the Minuteman Project is a citizen patrol group, which is a form of a community crime prevention program. The law enforcement community typically does not support citizen patrol groups, such as the Guardian Angels, because of concerns about the lack of adequate training and the threat of vigilante or "mob" justice. The U.S. Border Patrol, the primary agency responsible for the control of illegal immigration into the United States, supports the Minuteman Project. Supporters of TMP also include union leaders, who see illegal immigrants as a threat to job security, and former California governor Arnold Schwarzenegger, who, in 2005, said he thought that the group has been doing a good job and were an asset to the community.

Critics of TMP, including former Mexican president Vicente Fox, former president George W. Bush, and the Anti-Defamation League. The concern about TMP is that the program has been infiltrated with white supremacist groups, such as the Neo-Nazi party and the Ku Klux Klan. An added problem is that some TMP members have carried weapons while on patrol, lending to the perception that they are confrontational and do not supplement the border patrol. In response, TMP members argue that some members bring weapons while on patrol to kill snakes and other animals that present a threat to their personal safety. TMP members also point out that they have provided medical treatment to people they encounter while waiting for the border patrol to arrive. Most important, TMP members often engage in activities with border patrol agents. A spokesperson for the Tuscon, Arizona, sector of the border patrol says there have been no incidents where Minutemen volunteers have used their firearms to harm illegal immigrants.

The Minuteman Project is controversial for many reasons, but it does demonstrate the willingness of some citizens to recognize the limitations of the border patrol as well as their willingness to address the issue of illegal immigration. There is a fine line between citizen responsibility and vigilante justice and the debate about the Minuteman Project is at the heart of the issue.

CUBANS

Third in population only to Chicanos and Puerto Ricans, Cuban Americans represent a significant ethnic minority in the United States. The Cuban influence in this country was seen as early as 1831, with small close-knit communities organized around a single enterprise such as a cigar manufacturing factory.[19]

Until recently, however, the number of Cuban Americans was relatively small. In 1960 79,000 people who were born in Cuba lived in the United States. By 1990, this number grew to over one million. This increase followed Castro's rise to power after the 1959 Cuban Revolution. Since then, immigration to the United States has come in four distinct waves. First, there was an initial exodus of approximately 200,000 following Castro's claim to power. The first wave lasted for a period of about three years and ended as a result of the Cuban missile crisis in 1962.[20]

The second stage of immigration was informal, but important. Between 1962 and 1965, there was no direct sanctioned transportation, but nearly 30,000 Cubans came via private planes, boats, and other forms of transportation. The third stage occurred between 1965 and 1973, when the Cuban government permitted approximately 300,000 immigrants to arrive in the United States.[21]

The fourth wave has been the most controversial. In 1980, more than 124,000 refugees fled Cuba to Key West, Florida seeking asylum in the United States. President Carter, reflecting the nation's hostility toward Cuba's communist government, welcomed the refugees "with open arms and an open heart." Castro saw President Carter's claim as an opportunity to deport a host of inmates, criminals, and drug addicts. However, while refugees from this last wave of immigration have been somewhat historically stigmatized, it should be noted that the majority of refugees were not social deviants.[22]

Unfortunately, this group of refugees was given the name **Marielitos**. The word, meant to suggest that they were undesirable, refers to Mariel, the fishing port west of Havana where Cuban authorities herded people on to boats. The negative reception by the Cubans who were already here, coupled with the group's lack of formal education, resulted in a great deal of difficulty for many Marielitos in adjusting to life in America.[23]

CUBANS TODAY

Compared to other recent immigrant groups, and Hispanics as a whole, Cuban Americans have made a successful transition to American culture. Unemployment rates are low for Cuban American women, who are less likely than other groups to seek employment. The close-knit structure of Cuban American families encourages women to follow traditional roles of homemaker and mother.

Probably no ethnic group has had more influence on the fortunes of a city in a short period of time than the Cubans have had on Miami. It is the only city in the country where

While relations have improved between the United States and Cuba, many Cuban Americans are still concerned about human rights violations in their home country.

more than 57 percent of the inhabitants, an estimated two million Cuban Americans, are foreign-born. This is an increase from the 1.2 million in 2000.[24] The early immigrants were generally well-educated and many had professional or managerial backgrounds. Consequently, many Cubans used their talents and skills in the United States to achieve economic success.

However, the recent wave of immigration from Cuba, more than 500,000 since 1990, according to the U.S. Department of Homeland Security, has changed the fabric of the Cuban experience and Cuban American views of Cuba. While Cuban immigrants who came to the United States before 1990 generally think there is little in common between Cuban Americans and people living in Cuba, in 2013 almost half of current immigrants think that Cuban Americans and people living in Cuba have a lot in common.[25]

According to a 2014 study by the Cuban Research Institute at Florida International University, almost 75 percent of Cubans living in Miami-Dade County do not believe the economic embargo has worked. In fact, only a slight majority of Cubans oppose continuing the embargo, and a large majority favor diplomatic relations with Cuba, with nearly 70 percent of respondents favor lifting the travel restrictions from the United States to Cuba. Additionally, nearly 90 percent of the respondents support the Cuban Adjustment Act. This law, which began in 1966, states that Cuban citizens and their spouses and children may get a green card and become residents of the United States one year after arriving in the country. This automatic application is unusual for other immigrant groups. Additionally, a large majority of respondents (63 percent) favor the "wet foot/dry foot" immigration policy. That is, Cubans who leave by raft or boat are sent back to Cuba if they are caught before they reach U.S. soil.[26]

These demographic shifts are seen in political views. About 57 percent of recent Cuban immigrants say they identify with or "lean toward" the Democratic party, while 19 percent feel that same way about the Republican party. In contrast, about half of older immigrants, those who arrived before 1990, say they are Republican while 35 percent identify with Democrats.[27] This is a significant shift since among Latinos, those of Cuban origin have some of the highest voter turnout rates. In 2012, more than two-thirds of Cuban Americans voted nationally. This is far lower than the 48 percent of Latinos overall.[28]

According to data by the Pew Research Center, in 2013 only 47 percent of registered Cuban voters say they identify with the Republican Party, down from 64 percent in 2003. While only about 22 percent identified themselves as Democrats in 2003, that number has more than doubled in a decade. In 2004, for example, George W. Bush won 78 percent of the Cuban vote in Florida, but in 2012 the Cuban vote was split, with 49 percent supporting Barack Obama and 47 percent supporting Republican Mitt Romney.[29]

As was mentioned, this political shift is related to shifts in immigration patterns. While the wave of Cubans who arrived in the 1960s benefitted from the changes taking place in Miami and the state as a whole, the slowly recovering economy in South Florida, coupled with an influx of uneducated and less fluent Cubans, has led to greater poverty among the current wave of Cuban immigrants. A 2014 poll conducted by the Robert Wood Johnson Foundation, the Harvard School of Public Health, and NPR, showed that 45 percent of Cuban Americans say their finances are not so good or poor. Many Cuban Americans now see themselves as financially troubled at higher rates than other Latinos, and nearly two-thirds were worried about possible unemployment. Of those who find work, it is often in the lowest-paying sectors of the labor market.[30]

In 2015, President Obama announced that he planned to visit Cuba and did so in 2016. This was the first time in ninety years that a sitting U.S. president visited the island. This comes on the heels of breaking the diplomatic freeze between the two countries. In addition, both the United States and Cuba have reopened embassies in both Washington, DC, and Havana, and the Obama administration has developed a series of rule changes to allow U.S. businesses to export products to Cuba. Additionally, a deal was also reached regarding the reestablishment of commercial airline flights and cellular service by U.S. companies.[31]

However, not everyone embraces the Obama plan. Opponents of this change in relations between the two countries cite the continued human rights violations and political persecutions that remain a feature of life in Cuba. According to the Cuban Commission of Human Rights and National Reconciliation, there were 8,616 arrests of Cuban citizens who were deemed political prisoners in 2015, slightly less than the 8,899 arrests in 2014.[32]

PUERTO RICANS

Puerto Rico represents an interesting case because they are a group left in limbo with regard to their status in the United States. The island was taken by the United States during the Spanish-American War in 1898. During the time Spain controlled the island, which lasted for about four centuries, slavery was prominent as many Puerto Ricans were enslaved by the Spanish and there was an influx of Africans to the island. This legacy of slavery and intermarriage can be seen in the skin tone of many Puerto Ricans, who appear darker than other Hispanic or Latino groups.

The subsequent economic, social and political colonization, which was enhanced in 1948 when Puerto Rico became a commonwealth, left the people in a state of ambiguity in terms of status. While they are United States citizens and elect their own governor, Puerto Ricans cannot vote in presidential elections and have no representation in Congress. However, they are subject to military service and all federal laws.[33]

Historically, many Puerto Ricans came to the mainland during World War II to work on railroads and in manufacturing. New York City represented a haven for many Puerto Ricans since there was a large group who had already settled there. More recently, while many Puerto Ricans remain in New York City, others have migrated to New Jersey, Florida, Connecticut, and Pennsylvania. This latter group of Puerto Ricans is much more familiar and comfortable with American culture, making the migration easier. Perhaps most significant has been the loss of manufacturing jobs in many cities, necessitating a move to other areas of the country.[34] Puerto Ricans who return to the island after spending time away, typically in New York, have come to be called **Neoricans**. This group represents a better-educated, more affluent segment of the population who returned to Puerto Rico.[35]

However, recent changes have impacted all of Puerto Rico. A slow economic recovery has led many Puerto Ricans to leave the island for the United States in the largest numbers since World War II. The Census Bureau calls attention to the impact this massive migration has had on the island, showing its first sustained population decline since the island became a United States territory. While the number of Puerto Ricans living on the mainland reached a record of 4.9 million in 2012, since 2006 it has exceeded the number of those living on the island (3.5 million in 2012). In fact, the overall population in Puerto Rico was 3.6 million in 2013—a significant decline from the 4.5 million in 2000.[36]

Puerto Ricans who arrived from the island since 2000 are less likely than earlier migrants to settle in the Northeast and more likely to live in the South, particularly Florida. This new wave of immigrants are different from its counterpart of the past, according to a recent study by the Pew Research Center. This group is also more likely to live in poverty than older groups and were more likely to have been born on the island.[37]

The challenges facing the island, both in terms of negative migration and economic challenges, stems from a nearly decade-old recession, during which the public debt reached over $72 billion and unemployment reached 14 percent, higher than any United States state. In January 2016, Puerto Rico defaulted on its $37 million payment due on bonds issued by two government agencies. Still, the Commonwealth was able to pay off the $328 million in general obligation debt, but it had to use more than $100 million in reserve funds to make the payments.[38]

However, unlike a United States state in a severe economic decline, Puerto Rico cannot declare bankruptcy. This mountain of debt impacts its ability to jumpstart the economy and put people back to work. Tax laws were once generous to United States companies seeking to do business in Puerto Rico, which generated the growth of factories and jobs on the island, particularly in textiles and pharmaceuticals. But after a phase-out of these

Historically and currently many Puerto Ricans came to New York in search of jobs and a better life, but they maintain their Puerto Rican heritage.

incentives, coupled with the worldwide recession, the number of jobs dwindled. In response to these challenges, little was done to ensure Puerto Rico's future. Deficits increased and pensions absorbed much of the government's revenue. In 2006, the government ordered a two-week shut down because it could not meet its financial obligations. The governor reduced taxes and instituted massive layoffs and the government began to borrow in order to pay its expenses.[39]

The impact of these decisions were seen in employment and poverty rates of Puerto Rican citizens. According to one estimate, the per capita income is $15,200, half that of Mississippi, the poorest state in the United States. Moreover, 37 percent of all households in Puerto Rico receive food stamps. This is in contrast to Mississippi, where that figure is 22 percent. While jobs are scarce, pension benefits continue to shrink, all leading to a sense of malaise about the future of the island. This is what triggered the massive migration to the mainland.[40] In short, in virtually all social areas, such as housing, healthcare and education, Puerto Rico falls far short of acceptable minimal standards.[41]

THE INFLUENCE OF CENTRAL AND SOUTH AMERICA

When most people think of Hispanics and Latinos, they usually think only of the groups mentioned thus far in this chapter. However, an essential part of the Hispanic and Latino presence in this country is occupied by immigrants and citizens with a background from Central and South America. In fact, as was mentioned, the influence of this group on the culture of Little Havana in Miami or even the changing face of New York City is considerable.

For instance, people from Chile and Costa Rica have very little in common with other Hispanic and Latino groups other than the Spanish language and geographic location. In the case of Brazil, natives do not speak Spanish; the official language is Portuguese. For some reason, Americans tend to lump groups from Central and South America into a single category despite a wide range of cultural differences. In addition, instead of making distinctions between group membership based on light or dark skin tones, as is done in this country, Latin Americans make distinctions in terms of group membership based on a light to dark skin continuum sometimes called a **color gradient**. These differences are significant in terms of identifying social class and religious differences between South American and Central American groups. Thus, not only do people from these regions of the world not fit into a simple category of "Hispanic" or "Latino," there are enough differences to render any type of generalization difficult.[42]

HISPANIC INVOLVEMENT IN THE CRIMINAL JUSTICE SYSTEM

The impact of the criminal justice system on the Hispanic population has been studied since the 1970s. Several significant studies have been conducted including the following: a report by the U.S. Commission on Civil Rights entitled *Mexican Americans and the Administration of Justice in the Southwest* (1970); a report from the National Minority Advisory Council on Criminal Justice entitled *The Inequality of Justice: A Report on Crime and the Administration of Justice in the Minority Community* (1982); a report by the Population Research

Institute at Penn State University entitled *Hispanics Penalized More by Criminal Justice System Than Whites and Blacks* (2001). In these reports, the involvement and treatment of Hispanics in the criminal justice process has been highlighted and has shown a consistent trend of discrimination.

In 2002, Charles Kamasaki, senior vice president of the National Council of La Raza, testified before the United States Sentencing Commission on the impact of drug sentencing and the Latino community. He argued that there was increasing evidence that Hispanics were being held to a standard of accountability far exceeding any other segment of the population in the criminal justice system. For instance, the 2010 census showed that Latinos represented 17 percent of the U.S. population, but according to the U.S. Sentencing Commission, they constituted 52 percent of the total number of offenders in 2014.[43]

Additionally, Kamasaki argued that Hispanics were discriminated against at every stage of the criminal justice process. For example, Hispanic and Black federal defendants were more likely than White defendants to be charged with drug offenses. Compared to 29 percent of Whites charged with drug offenses in U.S. District Courts, 46 percent of Hispanic offenders and 48 percent of Black offenders were charged with drug offenses. Perhaps most important, three times as many Hispanic men ages 25–29 were sentenced to prison than Whites. Additionally, Hispanic men were a third less likely to be released before trial than Whites—approximately 23 percent of Whites were released before trial compared to 63 percent for non-Hispanic defendants. As further evidence of this disparity, half of Hispanic federal prison inmates had no previous criminal history, compared to 29 percent of Blacks and 38 percent for Whites. Finally, of all federal inmates to receive some type of substance abuse treatment, Hispanics were least likely to receive treatment. Compared to 54 percent of Whites and 48 percent of African Americans, only 36 percent of Hispanics received any type of substance abuse treatment.[44]

In sum, Kamasaki argued that despite the fact that Latinos were no more likely than other groups to use illegal drugs, they were more likely to be arrested and charged with drug offenses and less likely to be given pre-trial release. Once convicted, Latinos received harsher sentences even though the majority of offenders have no criminal history.[45]

In October 2004, a report issued by the **National Council of La Raza**, the nation's largest Hispanic civil rights organization, also found more systematic discrimination against Hispanics in the criminal justice system. The report, entitled *Lost Opportunities: The Reality of Latinos in the U.S. Criminal Justice System*, was heralded as the first comprehensive examination of Hispanics in every facet of the criminal justice system. The study was based on data from government sources, including the Bureau of Justice Statistics and the U.S. Census Bureau, and is coauthored by the Center for Youth Policy Research and Michigan State University's Office of University Outreach and Engagement. According to Nancy Walker, president and senior research fellow of the Center for Youth Policy Research, "This study conclusively documented the criminal justice system's discriminatory practices against the nation's largest and fastest growing minority population. . . . [T]his indictment of the system comes from the government's own statistics. Our nation cannot afford to ignore the compelling case that these numbers make for reforming our system."[46]

Among the many key findings from the report was that Hispanics experience discrimination during arrest, prosecution, and sentencing and were more likely to be incarcerated than Whites when charged with the same offense. Some of the findings related to the circumstances surrounding police contact with Hispanics, which can often lead to arrest, but Hispanics were also disproportionately represented by public defenders, who are often overwhelmed with cases. Compared to defendants with private attorneys, 71 percent who were represented by public counsel, compared to 54 percent with private attorneys, were sentenced to incarceration. The report also highlighted problems stemming from harsh mandatory minimum sentences, which give prosecutors the upper hand in plea negotiations and are inconsistent with the severity of the offense. The report was also critical of courts that do not provide documents written in Spanish or fail to provide translators to defendants.[47]

Another important finding of this study was that Hispanics were disproportionately charged with nonviolent, low-level drug offenses. Similar to a report in 2002, where health statistics showed similar rates of drug use, Hispanics were three times more likely to be arrested for drug offenses than Whites and accounted for nearly half of all offenders convicted of drug offenses in 2000.[48]

Since the publication of the La Raza study in 2004, these trends have continued to reveal a pattern of a problem. According to a 2014 report by the Tomas Rivera Policy Institute at the University of Southern California, research showed that Latinos receive harsher treatment in arrests, pretrial proceedings, and sentencing than Whites, even when they were charged with the same offense.[49] Other key findings include that Latinos were murdered in California at twice the rate of Whites (5.1 per 100,000 compared to 2.4). Latinos of any age were more likely to have been killed by strangers in California than Whites (40.5 percent vs. 26.1 percent of homicide victims). Latinos were also more likely to experience multiple crimes—a 2013 survey found that 43 percent of Latinos had experienced three or more crimes within the past five years, compared to 36 percent of crime victims overall.[50]

A report from the Bureau of Justice Statistics shows that from 1994 to 2011, Latinos were more likely to be shot than Whites[51] and had generally higher burglary rates than Whites.[52] Being victimized is exacerbated by a fear of reporting the crime. However, some data indicates that Latinos are reluctant to report a crime even when they have experienced one. In a 2012 survey, 44 percent of Latinos said they would be hesitant to report being victimized for fear that the police would ask them or others about their immigration status.[53]

As offenders, there appears to be some evidence to suggest unequal treatment of Latinos/Hispanics in the criminal justice system. For instance, a 2011 meta-analysis of forty different reports found that suspects of color were more likely to be arrested than White suspects.[54] Another study found that police officers search Latino/Hispanic drivers more often than White male drivers and White officers conducted more searches than African American and Latino police officers.[55] A 2014 study found that 80 percent of Latinos in California felt that racial disparities in drug enforcement is a serious problem.[56]

As it relates to Latino/Hispanic experiences with the courts, one study of felony defendants found that Latinos/Hispanics were less likely to be released on their own recognizance and when they were offered bail, it was approximately $25,000 higher than

African Americans or Whites in similar cases.[57] At the sentencing stage, a 2011 study by the United States. Sentencing Commission found that Hispanics and Latinos were more likely to be convicted of a crime with a mandatory sentence, more than any other group.[58]

According to the Bureau of Justice Statistics, in 2013 there were 1,158 Latino men in prison for every 100,000 in the United States, 2.5 times the rate for White men. This does not include those who are in county jails or cannot make bail. In California, nearly 70 percent of prison inmates are Latino or Black, with the former comprising 41 percent of those in prison. Whites make up 23 percent, according to the California Department of Corrections and Rehabilitation.[59] Additionally, California Latinos pointed to the amount of money spent on prisons and the use of incarceration for minor crimes as their main concern with the criminal justice system.[60]

Like their African American counterparts, not only are Hispanics likely to commit more crimes and engage in other forms of unacceptable behavior, they are significantly overrepresented in many of the crime statistics in this country. The same arguments that are used to explain why African Americans are overrepresented in the crime figures can be applied to Hispanics/Latinos. That is, on one hand, the treatment of Hispanics and Latinos demonstrates the fact that the system discriminates against minority groups. A counterargument is that Hispanics and Latinos have fewer opportunities to obtain well-paying jobs, have poorer educational experiences, and fewer overall chances to succeed than Whites. All of these factors, in turn, result in some segments of the population turning to crime.

IMMIGRATION AND CRIME

While Hispanics and Latinos engage in a wide assortment of crimes, three of the most noted crimes involve illegal immigration. The extent and characteristics of illegal immigration were discussed in a 2005 report by the Pew Hispanic Center, in Washington, DC. In 2004, naturalized citizens represented just under one-third of the estimated 35.7 million foreign-born population in the United States. About 10 percent of all immigrants living in this country are called Legal Permanent Resident aliens (LPRs or "legal immigrants") and have yet to become permanent citizens. Almost a third of the foreign-born population (29 percent) in the United States is identified as "unauthorized," meaning they have either entered the country without going through conventional or legal channels (such as applying for a visa and beginning the process of becoming a citizen), or have done so with forged documents. More commonly, unauthorized immigrants have remained in this country after their visas have expired.[61]

The unauthorized population has been steadily increasing in size since the last half of the 1990s. Similarly, the naturalized citizen population has grown rapidly in recent years as increasing numbers of legal immigrants have taken advantage of the opportunity to naturalize. The LPR alien population, on the other hand, actually decreased for several years as the number who naturalized (or left the United States or died) exceeded the number being admitted. In 2004, there were an estimated 10.3 million unauthorized migrants living in the United States, of which about 57 percent were from Mexico. The rest were from mainly Central America, which accounted for another 25 percent of the total. The remaining

20 percent was made up of immigrants from countries from all over the world.[62] There were an estimated 11.7 million unauthorized immigrants living in the United States in 2012, according to Pew Research Center estimates.[63] Most, about three-quarters, are from Latin America.[64] Virtually all of the unauthorized are either visa **overstayers**, persons admitted on temporary visas who either stay beyond the expiration of their visas or otherwise violate their terms of admission, or *EWIs* ("entries without inspection" or clandestine entrants).[65]

More recently, in 2014 the Pew Research Center conducted an analysis on the issue of immigration crime. Using data from the U.S. Sentencing Commission, researchers discovered that the trends identified more than a decade earlier are even more pronounced today.

For instance, dramatic growth over the past two decades in the number of offenders sentenced in federal courts has been driven primarily by enforcement of a particular immigration offense—unlawful reentry into the United States. In the ten years between 1994 and 2012, the number of offenders sentenced in federal courts more than doubled, (from 36,564 to 75,867). At the same time, the number of unlawful reentry convictions increased from 690 cases in 1992 to 19,463 in 2012. This increase accounts for 48 percent of the growth in the total number of offenders sentenced in federal courts over the period and is twice as much as the growth for the second fastest growing type of conviction: drug offenses, which accounted for 22 percent of the growth.[66]

As the number of convictions for unlawful entry increased, so did the configuration of sentenced offenders. For example, in 1992, 23 percent of sentenced offenders were Latino, but by 2012, that percentage increased to nearly half (48 percent). Similarly, in 1992, 12 percent of sentenced offenders in were unauthorized immigrants, but by 2012 it

Despite recent promises by President Trump about building a wall to thwart illegal immigration, a border fence that covers a portion of the border has already been built.

had increased to 40 percent. This impact was seen throughout the entire federal system. Between 1998 and 2010, immigration offenders accounted for 56 percent of the increase in the number of federal prison inmates.[67]

The federal government has deported nearly 400,000 unauthorized immigrants a year since the start of the Obama administration. A growing share of those deported were convicted of a criminal offense, including some related to immigration crimes. What is perhaps most significant about the explosive growth of illegal immigration is the increase in criminal activity committed by this segment of the population. Perhaps even more fascinating has been the way the United States has tried to address illegal immigrant crime in major cities. According to Heather MacDonald of the Center for Immigration Studies,[68] little has changed in recent decades regarding this policy. She states: "not only do illegal criminals represent a significant threat to public safety, but in places like Los Angeles, California, police policy to arrest illegal immigrants has run into a political windstorm."[69]

In response to the increase of illegal aliens, Special Order 40 was enacted in Los Angeles in 1979. The order prohibits officers from "initiating police action where the objective is to discover the alien status of a person." In practice, this means that the police may not even ask someone they have arrested about his or her immigration status until after criminal charges have been entered.[70] Additionally, the police may not arrest someone for immigration violations. Officers may not check a suspect's immigration status prior to arrest nor may they notify the Bureau of Immigration and Customs Enforcement (ICE) about an illegal alien picked up for minor violations. Officers can inquire about a suspect's immigration status or report the offender to immigration only after he or she has been booked for a felony or multiple misdemeanors.

Laws like this one, often referred to as **sanctuary laws**, contradict much of what has been learned about crime reduction strategies, One of the most significant discoveries in law enforcement in the last decade has been the potential effectiveness of community policing. The broken windows theory, on which much of community policing is based, suggests that arrests for minor offenses often lead to reductions in serious crimes.

In a similar way, some experts believe that enforcing immigration violations against known felons is arguably effective in reducing crime committed by illegal immigrants, but sanctuary laws inhibit this type of preventative enforcement. Only if the felon has given the officer some other reason to stop him or her, such as the officer observes a crime being committed, can the offender be detained, and only for that non-immigration-related reason. The officer cannot arrest for the immigration felony.[71]

Critics argue that such a policy is extraordinarily inefficient and puts the community at risk.[72] The rationale behind enacting sanctuary policies is to encourage illegal alien crime victims and witnesses to cooperate with the police without fear of deportation and to encourage all illegal aliens to take advantage of city services like health care and education.[73]

Critics argue that there has never been any empirical verification that sanctuary laws actually increase cooperation with the police or other city agencies. Critics of sanctuary laws also say the real reason cities prohibit police officers from immigration reporting and enforcement is a fear of alienating the population of illegal aliens, on whom the country relies so heavily.[74]

However, in 2015, an analysis of data from Immigration and Customs Enforcement in 2014, found that more than 8,100 immigrant offenders who were sought by the U.S. Bureau of Immigration and Customs Enforcement in sanctuary jurisdictions were released instead of deported. Approximately 1,900 of these deportable convicts committed an additional 4,300 crimes during that same time period, including violent crimes such as homicide, sexual assault, and rape.[75]

In trying to come to grips with the illegal immigrant–crime connection, cities such as L.A. have found that not only are the laws designed to limit the scope of investigative abilities, but even when local police officers require the assistance of the ICE agents, immigration officials are so overwhelmed that officers often do not get the assistance they need. This lack of assistance, coupled with the sanctuary laws, sends a message to the offender population that they are not likely to be punished or deported.

This issue is far from over, as the newly elected president Donald Trump has vowed to deport nearly 3 million immigrants who have criminal records. In an interview President-elect Trump stated:

> What we are going to do is get the people that are criminal and have criminal records—gang members, drug dealers, we have a lot of these people, probably two million, it could be even three million. We are getting them out of our country or we are going to incarcerate," Mr. Trump said. "But we're getting them out of our country; they're here illegally."[76]

There are a host of issues relating to this challenge, including the practical realities of how to deport 3 million immigrants. Almost certainly theses cases will have to be tried in Immigration Courts, which already have lengthy backlogs of cases. A deportation order is required from a judge for an immigrant to be deported. Such delays could take months or even years to process. Second, some immigrants identified for deportation are already incarcerated and those sentences must be completed before deportation could occur. Third, the Obama administration has already undertaken a considerable effort to deport what are being referred to as removable criminal aliens. However, this list of potential deportees also includes people with green cards for permanent legal residence, those with temporary visas, and those who have committed minor, but nonviolent crimes. By 2016, the Obama administration had already deported nearly 2.5 million immigrants since 2009, but only about 250,000 in 2015, about 40 percent of whom were charged with immigration violations, not criminal acts.[77]

Thus, the logistics and processes needed to follow through on Trump's promise contains many unknowns and impracticalities, particularly since the Obama administration has been engaging in this process for the past eight years. Finally, there is the backlash from cities and states regarding the enforcement of deportation laws. Not only will the police be required to engage in intrusive and previously unheard of search activities to locate unauthorized immigrants, many state and local officials are refusing to cooperate with federal authorities.[78] Despite the threat to withhold federal funding from cities and states that refuse to cooperate, mayors of cities such as Chicago, Minneapolis, and the state legislature in California have refused to work in conjunction with federal authorities on deportation issues. In fact, Los Angeles Police Chief Charlie Beck has gone on record that he does not feel this function should be assigned to his officers. He has stated: "That is not our job nor will I make it our job."[79]

Clearly this issue will continue to unfold in the months to come, but as the debate continues, there will undoubtedly be a great deal of controversy and discussion about immigration status for many Latinos and Hispanics.

SUMMARY

This chapter explored the changing face of American society as an increasing number of Hispanics, both legal and illegal, become a fixture of the social landscape. Estimates by the Census Bureau suggest that Hispanics will constitute the largest minority group by 2050. The Latin and Hispanic influence on American culture can be seen in a host of ways. Perhaps the best example exists in Miami, which has been transformed by the influx of Cuban immigrants over the years. Moreover, the way that Hispanics and Latinos have been historically treated in this country has resulted in many subgroups remaining mired in a life of poverty and crime. As we have seen, part of the problem for Chicanos stems from the isolation they experience with regard to education as well as the limited access to quality healthcare in this country. For Puerto Ricans, the main issue is also related to economics and the poor economy on the island. These challenges, along with a lack of optimism for the future, have led many foreign-born residents to flee the island for the mainland.

As it relates to criminal justice, Hispanics, as a general category, are overrepresented in virtually every area of criminal justice. Whether it is treatment by the police, sentences relating to drugs, or the increase in the number of Hispanic inmates in prison, clearly the trend with this group's experience in the criminal justice system looks remarkably like that of their African American counterparts.

YOU MAKE THE CALL

PRESIDENT TRUMP'S IMMIGRATION POLICY

Imagine that you are a police chief in a city that contains a large number of Hispanics and Latinos. Under president Trump's new immigration policy, there is no sanctuary for illegal immigrants, even for children born in the United States to undocumented immigrants. President Trump has threatened to withhold federal funding to any state or municipality that does not support his position and he demands that your department collaborate with federal ICE agents to "round up" undocumented and other immigrants. The mayor is a member of Trump's party and has pledged his support for the effort, but you feel that this is not only an unreasonable use of your officers (since the department is responsible for dealing with crime in your city, not addressing the immigration problem), and you feel that the policy violates the constitutional protections of citizens born in this country even though their parents might have entered illegally.

However, you work at the pleasure of the mayor, who orders you to comply. What do you do?

Questions

1. Can you refuse a direct order from a superior? Will it lead you to be terminated from your position?
2. What happens if you comply with the order but it negatively impacts morale within the department?
3. If you decide to cooperate, what steps could you consider that fulfills your responsibilities but does not embrace the policy? In other words, can you put forth a half-hearted effort to demonstrate cooperation but does not yield much success? Is such a tactic ethical?
4. What do you think the role of the media can play in this situation that might assist you in leveraging your opposition to the policy?

KEY TERMS

barrios

Chicano

color gradient

Latino

Los Braceros

Marielitos

National Council of La Raza

Neorican

overstayers

Repatriation

sanctuary laws

DISCUSSION QUESTIONS

1. Why have Cubans been so successful in assimilating into American society yet retaining elements of their native culture?
2. How can the high rates of illegal immigration be curtailed? Is simply granting citizenship to those who have entered illegally the solution? Why or why not?
3. Why is drug use so high among Hispanic adolescents?
4. Why do you think some Hispanic groups continue to struggle economically, politically and socially in the United States? Is it the language barrier or some other set of factors?
5. What do you think is needed for Hispanic/Latino groups to assimilate and be accepted by mainstream society? Why does it appear that Americans are reluctant to treat them fairly?
6. Are the experiences of African Americans similar or different from that of Hispanics in this country? Give several examples from your point of view.

FOR FURTHER READING

Song-Ha Lee, S. *Building a Latino Civil Rights Movement: Puerto Ricans, African Americans and the Pursuit of Racial Justice in New York City*. Chapel Hill, NC: University of North Carolina Press, 2014.

Foley, N. *Mexicans in the Making of America*. Cambridge, MA: Belknap Press, 2014.

Logan, J. *The New Latinos: Who They Are, Where They Are*. Albany, NY: Lewis Mumford Center for Comparative Urban and Regional Research, 2001.

Rodriquez, C. E. *Puerto Ricans: Born in the USA*. Boston, MA: Unwin Hyman, 1989.

Abrahamson, M. *Urban Enclaves: Identity and Place in America*. New York: St. Martin's Press, 1996.

NOTES

1. J. Logan, *The New Latinos: Who They Are, Where They Are* (Albany, NY: Lewis Mumford Center for Comparative Urban and Regional Research, 2001), 1. Available at http://mumford.albany.edu/census/HispanicPop/HspReport/MumfordReport.pdf
2. B. Guzman, *The Hispanic Population* (Washington, DC: U. S. Census Bureau, 2001).
3. U.S. Department of Commerce, United States Census Bureau. *Hispanic Americans By the Numbers*. Available at http://www.infoplease.com/spot/hhmcensus1.html
4. J. Scott and G. Marshall, *A Dictionary of Sociology*, 3rd edition (New York: Oxford University Press, 2005). Available online at http://www.oxfordreference.com/search?btog=chap&pageSize=

10&q0=hispanic&sort=relevance&source=%2F10.1093%2Facref%2F9780199533008.001.000 1%2Facref-9780199533008

5. D. Gonzalez, "What's the Problem with 'Hispanic'? Just Ask a 'Latino.'" *New York Times,* November 15, 1992, E6.

6. Scott and Marshall, *Dictionary of Sociology.*

7. Logan, *The New Latinos.*

8. Z. Vargas, *Crucible of Struggle: A History of Mexican Americans* (New York: Oxford University Press, 2011), 152.

9. Ibid, 102.

10. Ibid., 144–65.

11. Ibid., 213–36.

12. Ibid.

13. Ibid.

14. Scott and Marhsall, *Dictionary of Sociology.*

15. H. A. Moore and P. Iadicola, "Resegregation Processes in Desegregated Schools and Status Relationships for Hispanic Students," *Aztlan* 12 (September 1981): 39–58.

16. Scott and Marshall, *Dictionary of Sociology.*

17. U.S. Census Bureau, U.S. Department of Commerce. *Health Insurance Coverage in the United States: 2015,* by Jessica C. Barnett and Marina S. Vornovitsky, Open-file report 2016, U.S. Census Bureau (Washington, DC, 2016), https://www.census.gov/content/dam/Census/library/publications/2016/demo/p60-257.pdf

18. R. P. McNamara and K. M. McNamara, *Hispanic Healthcare Needs in Greenville, South Carolina* (Center for Social Research, Furman University, 2001), Executive Summary.

19. R. J. Chaskin, "Urban Enclaves: Identity and Place in America," *Social Science Review,* 70(4), December 1996): 662–64.

20. L. Perez, "Growing Up in Cuban Miami: Immigrants, the Enclave, and New Generations," in R. G. Rumbaut and A. Portes, eds., *Ethnicities* (Berkeley, CA: University of California Press, 2001), 91–125.

21. Ibid.

22. Ibid.

23. M. Clary, "Black, Cuban Racial Chasm Splits Miami," *Los Angeles Times,* March 23, 1997, A1, A20.

24. M. H. Lopez, "As Cuban American Demographics Change, So Do Views of Cuba," Pew Research Center, December 23, 2014, available at http://www.pewresearch.org/fact-tank/2014/12/23/as-cuban-American-demographics-change-so-do-views-of-cuba/See also G. Allen, "Poll Findings: On Cuban Americans and the Elusive 'American Dream'" *Morning Edition— NPR* January 22, 2014.

25. Ibid.

26. G. J. Grenier and H. Gladwin, *Cuba Poll: How Cuban Americans in Miami View U.S. Policies Toward Cuba* (Miami, Florida International Cuban Research Institute, 2014), available at https://cri.fiu.edu/research/cuba-poll/2014-fiu-cuba-poll.pdf.

27. M. H. Lopez, "As Cuban American Demographics Change, So Do Views of Cuba," Pew Research Center, December 23, 2014, available at http://www.pewresearch.org/fact-tank/2014/12/23/as-cuban-American-demographics-change-so-do-views-of-cuba/See also G. Allen, "Poll Findings: On Cuban Americans and the Elusive 'American Dream'" *Morning Edition— NPR,* January 22, 2014.

28. Ibid.

29. Ibid.

30. Allen, "Poll Findings."

31. A. Gomez and G. Korte, "Obama Reportedly Plans to Visit Cuba Soon," *USA Today*, February 18, 2016, 2.

32. Ibid.

33. D. Christopulos, "Puerto Rico in the Twentieth Century: A Historical Survey," in A. Lopez and J. Petras, eds., *Puerto Rico and Puerto Ricans: Studies in History and Society* (New York: Wiley, 1974), 123–66.

34. M. Navarro, "Puerto Rican Presence Wanes in New York," *New York Times* February 28, 2000, A1, A20.

35. C. G. Muschkin, "Consequences of Return Migrant Status for Employment in Puerto Rico," *International Migration Review* 27, no. 4 (1993): 13; C. G. Muschkin, "With a Vote for 'None of the Above' Puerto Ricans Endorse Island's Status Quo," *New York Times*, December 14, 1998, A12.

36. D. Cohn, E. Patten, and M. H. Lopez, "Puerto Rican Population Declines on Island, Grows on U.S. Mainland," Pew Research Center, August 6, 2014, available at http://www.pewhispanic.org/2014/08/11/puerto-rican-population-declines-on-island-grows-on-u-s-mainland/ph-2014-08-11-puerto-rico-0-01/

37. Ibid.

38. J. Zarroli, "Puerto Rico Says It Will Miss $37 Million in Bond Payments this Week," *NPR*, December 30, 2015.

39. L. Alvarez, "Economy and Crime Spur New Puerto Rican Exodus," *New York Times*, February 8, 2014, available at http://nyti.ms/1aHmGNS

40. Ibid.

41. D. A. Hemlock, "Puerto Rico Loses Its Edge." *New York Times*, September 21, 1996, pp. 17, 30.

42. A. Orlov and R. Ueda, "Central and South Americans," in S. Thernstrom, ed., *Encyclopedia of American Ethnic Groups* (Cambridge, MA: Belknap Press, 1980), 210–17.

43. U.S. Department of Justice, U.S. Sentencing Commission. Annual Report, 2014, available at http://www.ussc.gov/sites/default/files/pdf/research-and-publications/annual-reports-and-sourcebooks/2014/2014-Annual-Report.pdf

44. C. Kamasaki, *Testimony on Drug Sentencing and its Effects on the Latino Community. U.S. Sentencing Commission*, February 25, 2002, available at http://www.ussc.gov/sites/default/files/pdf/amendment-process/public-hearings-and-meetings/20020225-26/kamasaki.pdf

45. Ibid.

46. National Council of La Raza, *Lost Opportunities: The Reality of Latinos in the Criminal Justice System*. Executive Summary, 2004, ix.

47. Ibid.

48. Ibid.

49. Californians for Safety and Justice, *Latino Voices: The Impacts of Crime and Criminal Justice Policies on Latinos* (California: Tomas Rivera Policy Institute, University of Southern California, 2014). Executive Summary, ix.

50. David Binder Research, California Crime Victims Quantitative Research Summary, 2013. Available online at http://www.njjn.org/uploads/digital-library/CA_CSJ_CA-Crime-victims-voices_March-2014.pdf

51. *Firearm Violence, 1993–2011*, U.S. Department of Justice, Bureau of Justice Statistics, 2013.

52. *Household Burglary, 1994–2011*, U.S. Department of Justice, Bureau of Justice Statistics 2013.

53. N. Theodore, *Insecure Communities: Latino Perception of Police Involvement in Immigration Enforcement* (Chicago, IL: University of Illinois at Chicago, 2013). Executive Summary, i. Available online at http://www.policylink.org/sites/default/files/INSECURE_COMMUNITIES_REPORT_FINAL.PDF

54. T. R. Kochel, D. B. Wilson, and S. D. Mastrofski, "Effect of Suspect Race on Officers' Arrest Decisions," *Criminology* 49, no. 2 (2011): 473–512.

55. B. L. Withrow, "Race-Based Policing. A Descriptive Analysis of the Wichita Stop Study," *Police Practice and Research* 5, no. 3 (2004): 223–40.

56. A. Pantoja, "Poll Shows Major Support Among Latinos for Sentencing Reform," *Latino Decisions*, 2014.

57. T. Schlesinger, "Racial and Ethnic Disparity in Pretrial Criminal Processing," *Justice Quarterly* 22, no. 2 (2005): 170–92.

58. United States Sentencing Commission. *Report to the Congress: Mandatory Minimum Penalties in the Federal Criminal Justice System*, 2011, Executive Summary, i–ix.

59. United States Department of Justice, Bureau of Justice Statistics, 2013. See also California Department of Corrections and Rehabilitation, 2013.

60. David Binder Research, *California Latino Voters and Criminal Justice Reforms*, 2014, Research Brief. Available online at http://safeandjust.uscmediacurator.com/key-finding-1-california-realignment/

61. Pew Hispanic Center, *Unauthorized Migrants: Numbers and Characteristics*. Washington, DC, 2005. Available online at http://www.pewhispanic.org/2005/06/14/unauthorized-migrants/

62. Ibid.

63. J. Passel, D. Cohn, and A. Gonzalez-Barrera, *Population Decline of Unauthorized Immigrants Stalls, May Have Reversed*. Pew Research Center, September 23, 2013, available at http://www.pewhispanic.org/2013/09/23/population-decline-of-unauthorized-immigrants-stalls-may-have-reversed/

64. Ibid.

65. Ibid.

66. M. L. Light, M. H. Lopez, and A. Gonzalez-Barrera, *The Rise of Federal Immigration Crimes*. Pew Research Center, March 18, 2014, available at http://www.pewhispanic.org/2014/03/18/the-rise-of-federal-immigration-crimes/

67. Ibid.

68. H. MacDonald, *Crime & the Illegal Alien The Fallout from Crippled Immigration Enforcement* (Center for Immigration Studies, Washington, DC, 2004) available online at http://cis.org/IllegalAliensCrime

69. Ibid.

70. Los Angeles Police Department, Understanding Special Order 40, January 27, 2011. Available at http://www.lapdonline.org/newsroom/news_view/47036

71. "What are Sanctuary Cities?" *The Economist*, November 22, 2016. Available at http://www.economist.com/blogs/economist-explains/2016/11/economist-explains-13

72. J. Vaughn, "Sanctuary Laws Risk Americans' Safety," *New York Times*, July 9, 2015, available at http://www.nytimes.com/roomfordebate/2015/07/09/should-immigrant-sanctuary-laws-be-repealed/sanctuary-laws-risk-amercians-safety

73. Ibid.

74. Ibid.

75. Ibid.

76. J. H. Davis, and J. Preston, "What Donald Trump's Vow to Deport Up to 3 Million Immigrants Would Mean," *New York Times*, November 14, 2016, available at http://www.nytimes.com/2016/11/15/us/politics/donald-trump-deport-immigrants.html?_r=0

77. Ibid.

78. Ibid.

79. Ibid.

CHAPTER 5

ASIAN AMERICANS AND THE CRIMINAL JUSTICE SYSTEM

CHAPTER OBJECTIVES

After reading this chapter, you should be able to:

- Understand the differences between Far East Asians, Southeast Asians, and Pacific Islanders, and why this distinction is important
- Understand the historical importance of immigration for Chinese, Japanese, Korean, Filipino, and other Asian groups
- Understand the current position in American society for Japanese, Chinese, Korean, Southeast Asians, and Pacific Islanders
- Understand the representation of Asian Americans in the criminal justice system, including involvement in different forms of criminal activity such as drugs, gangs, human smuggling, and transnational crime

The U.S. Census uses the label Asian American to refer to people from the Far East (including China, Japan, and Korea) Southeast Asia (including Thailand, Cambodia, Vietnam, Laos, Malaysia, and Indonesia), and the Indian subcontinent (including India, Pakistan, Burma, Sri Lanka, Bangladesh, and Nepal). The term Pacific Islander refers to people who have origins in Hawaii, Guam, Samoa, or other Pacific Islander groups.[1]

Asian Americans, like Hispanics/Latinos and Native Americans, represent a vast array of people who are quite diverse in their customs, language, and culture. However, as with most minority groups in this country, those differences tend to be simplified, and groups are often put into a generic and overly broad category.

In fact, the term Asian American covers a wide breadth of people, who, in some cases, are nothing like each other. This collection of individuals from different backgrounds is one of the fastest growing segments of the U.S. population. One of the topics this chapter will explore are the differences between these groups and their impact on American culture. Like other groups, Asian Americans have made a concerted and successful effort at assimilating into mainstream America. Unfortunately, there are many

Americans who have stereotypical perceptions of Asian Americans and this has over-shadowed the hard work, determination, and sacrifice many members of these populations have achieved.

In some ways, then, Asian Americans are different from other minority groups in the sense that they have made the transition, retained much of their native culture, and while some are involved in criminal activity, Asian Americans are one of the minorities that is generally underrepresented in crime statistics. This underrepresentation not only means they do not appear to represent a large portion of the data collected on crime, it also means that Asian Americans have not been studied in as much depth as other minority groups in terms of their involvement in crime. In terms of their participation in the criminal justice system, there is less of a presence than, say, African Americans, Whites, or Hispanics. Specifically, this chapter will discuss Chinese Americans, Japanese Americans, Southeast Asians, specifically Vietnamese Americans, and Asian Indians. Because they represent the largest group of Pacific Islanders in this country, Hawaiians and Filipinos will also be discussed.

In a recent report by the Pew Research Center, Asian Americans have surpassed Hispanics/Latinos as the fastest growing immigrant group in the United States. In 2010, 36 percent of immigrants to the United States were Asian Americans, compared to 31 percent for Hispanic/Latinos. According to the report, there are an estimated 18,205,898 people listed under the category of Asian/Pacific Islander, which constitutes about 5.8 percent of the U.S. population.

Of this group, there were about 4 million Chinese Americans; 3.4 million Filipinos; 3.1 million from India; 1.7 million Vietnamese and another 1.7 Korean; 1.3 million Japanese Americans. This represents the five largest groups under this classification. The Census Bureau expects that the Asian American population will be about 38 million people by 2050, which will constitute about 9 percent of the total U.S. population.[2] Some of this growth will be attributed to immigration by certain groups, while another source of this increase will be due to higher birth rates.

The influx of Asians in the United States can be divided into two distinct periods. The first occurred roughly from the middle of the 1800s to the early years of the twentieth century.

Table 5.1 Asian American Population in the United States, 2010

Group	Population
Chinese	4.0 million
Filipino	3.4 million
Indian	3.1 million
Vietnamese	1.7 million
Korean	1.7 million
Japanese	1.3 million
Other	2.8 million

The Chinese were the first Asian group to arrive, followed by the Japanese, with Koreans and Filipinos arriving in much smaller numbers afterward. The first wave of immigrants were mostly recruited for construction and work in the agricultural industry.

The second wave of immigration was different from the first in that most of the new immigrants came from a higher socioeconomic status. Changes in immigration laws prevented many Asians from entering into this country until after 1965.[3] This latter group of immigrants has also been more diverse in national origin, coming from all areas of Asian society.[4]

A BRIEF PROFILE OF ASIAN AMERICANS

Generally speaking, according to a 2011 survey by the Pew Research Center, people who identify as Asian Americans value hard work, are highly educated, have higher median incomes than the general population, and believe their outlook for the future is bright. They generally believe in the value of hard work as a pathway to success, and while some have experienced discrimination, the group has a tendency not to see these experiences as inhibiting their drive toward success.[5]

Moreover, most Asian Americans do not identify with the Asian American label; most prefer to self-identify as a member of their racial subgroup. Asian Americans tend to believe that they are different from the typical American, with 53 percent believing they are very different from Americans in general. Moreover, being Asian does not appear to have an impact on their perceived potential for success. Almost two-thirds of Asians felt that their race made no difference in getting accepted to schools, acquiring a job, or in obtaining a promotion. While about 20 percent said they experienced discrimination within the last year, only about 13 percent felt that it was a problem for them as a group—83 percent felt it was only a minor hindrance or not one at all.[6]

Asian Americans collectively also have median family incomes higher than the general population: $66,000 compared to $49,800 for the rest of the United States. Moreover, Asian Americans are more likely to hold a bachelor's degree or higher than the rest of the general population (61 percent vs. 28 percent). Asian Americans have a poverty rate as a group that is slightly lower than the national average (11.9 percent vs. 12.8 percent) and are also more likely to intermarry with some other racial group. About 30 percent of Asian Americans have married a non-Asian and about half of all Asian Americans say there were comfortable with the idea of a family member marrying a non-Asian.[7]

There is also a strong emphasis on family relations and Asian children are more likely than any other group to live in a household with two married parents. Asian Americans also place a higher priority on having a successful marriage than the general population. Asian Americans are also more likely to vote Democrat than Republican (50 percent vs. 28 percent).[8]

While there are a number of promising trends for some Asian Americans, for others the transition to the United States has resulted in more difficult circumstances. A number of issues have arisen for all Asian Americans, particularly those who have achieved some level of societal success. These issues include the model minority myth, the glass ceiling in the labor market, hate crimes, and racial profiling.

MODEL MINORITY MYTH

The **model minority myth** states that Asian Americans constitute an ideal minority because they have endured political, economic, and social obstacles. Some experts even argue that Asian Americans are no longer considered a marginal minority.[9] However, to effectively determine whether the apparent success can be extended across all Asian American groups, we must examine the data.

Although the term model minority might seem to be complimentary, at one time many Asian Americans saw it as a condescending and damaging stereotype. Some Asian Americans have pointed out that this positive image tends to minimize or ignore some of the social and economic problems that continue to prevent many Asian Americans from succeeding. This is particularly true of Southeast Asian refugees, who remain poor, uneducated, and relatively unsuccessful.[10] Additionally, approximately 12 percent of Asian American families live below the poverty line, compared to 13 percent of White families. Thus, in many ways, when President Ronald Reagan called Asian Americans the model minority, he set in motion a series of expectations that ignored the wide diversity of educational talent among this segment of the population.

However, given the recent data from the Pew Research Center, where most Asian Americans self-identify as their respective group than as an Asian American, and given recent opinion data that suggests their belief in the value of hard work as a key component to success, many Asian Americans do not appear to embrace this categorization.

The model minority myth suggested that many Asian Americans had adequately assimilated into American society.

DOES EDUCATION PAY OFF FOR ALL ASIAN AMERICANS?

While most Americans agree that education is the path out of poverty and is the best way for minorities to achieve success, some evidence exists that problems occur even when minority groups embrace education. Asian Americans have been identified as an ethnic minority group that has successfully overcome racism and achieved the American dream, primarily through education. It's true that 61 percent of all Asian American adults have at least a college degree, the highest of all the major racial and ethnic groups. It's also common for Asian American students to have the highest test scores and/or GPAs within any given high school or college cohort.[11] However, Southeast Asians are still struggling to adapt to their lives in the United States. For example, Vietnamese Americans only have a college degree attainment rate of 26 percent, only about a third the rate for other Asian American ethnic groups and about on par with Whites. Further, Laotians, Cambodians, and Khmer only have rates around 13 percent. Those Asian Americans who are struggling tend to be immigrants who have limited English proficiency. Most are relatively fluent in English but a large portion are not.[12]

Therefore, similar to other immigrant minority groups, Asian Americans still have a need for bilingual education that is also culturally sensitive to their immigration experiences and family situations.

Even for those who make it to college, challenges have been presented. Beginning in the 1980s, many more Asian Americans were applying to college than before. Soon, it became common for 10 percent, 15 percent, or more of a given university's student population to be of Asian ancestry at a time when Asians were only about 3 percent of the general population. Many universities responded by rejecting Asian students once their Asian student population reached 10 to 15 percent of the student body. Soon, Asian Americans were accusing universities such as U.C.–Berkeley, UCLA, Stanford, Harvard, Princeton, and Brown of imposing a quota or upper limit on their admission numbers. After several protests and investigations, these universities admitted that there were problems with these admission procedures but never admitted any deliberate wrongdoing.[13] Thus, Asian Americans may appear to be succeeding in assimilating into American society, but the reality is that many still face a host of problems.

INCOME DATA

Another sign of the apparent success of Asian Americans are the figures concerning median family incomes. While the median family income of Asian Americans might seem significant to many outsiders, the total number of family members working should also be factored into the analysis. The reason for this is that the median family income figure only counts total family income, not the number of people working within that family. It is one thing if a family consists of a single parent earning most of the money, such as a corporate executive, which should suggest a certain socioeconomic position for that family. However, in many Asian American families, the total family income requires several people, all working full-time, to earn that same amount. This suggests a different economic picture for that family.

There is also the issue of the **glass ceiling**. in business. While it appears promising that Asian Americans work in the same professions as Whites, Asian immigrants are found disproportionately in the lower paying service occupations. Even in managerial positions, few Asian Americans ever reach the very top of the corporate ladder.[14]

In an effort to explain this unusual trend, Jane Hyun, whose book *Breaking the Bamboo Ceiling: Career Strategies for Asians*, offers her insight into why so few Asian Americans obtain top management positions. She says that part of the reason is cultural. Many Asian American employees are taught to respect authority. Consequently, they remain quiet in meetings and this is interpreted by their White colleagues as aloofness, arrogance, or inattention, when it is simply a general Asian habit of respecting authority.[15]

Many Asian American executives experience a glass ceiling, or limited opportunities.

Thus, while Asian Americans have done well in small businesses, because of the long hours, the income from these businesses may be below prevailing wages. Examples include Chinese restaurants, Korean American convenience stores, and Asian Indian–owned motels and gasoline stations.[16] In sum, while it might appear that Asian Americans are doing well, this is an oversimplification of the diversity of the group and its experiences. Further, this simplification also changes the public's perceptions of the need to help many Asian Americans in terms of social programs.[17] A recent study of the United States Equal Employment Opportunity Commission examining 2013 employment data from Google, Yahoo, and Facebook revealed more evidence of a glass ceiling for executive positions in those companies. In this study, while Asian Americans made up one-third of the workforce of these three companies, far surpassing the representation of African Americans or Hispanic/Latinos, Asian Americans were significantly underrepresented in leadership roles. The analysis of the data showed that there were both race and gender implications regarding Asian Americans. Overall, White males had a 42 percent advantage over White women when it came to being promoted to the executive level, and a 260 percent advantage over Asian women. Whites generally had a 150 percent advantage over Asians regardless of gender, suggesting the presence of a glass ceiling at the higher levels of business.[18]

HATE CRIMES AND RACIAL PROFILING

The perception that Asian Americans are accepted in the United States is not completely congruent with their experiences in America. For instance, reports by the National Asian Pacific American Legal Consortium demonstrate an anti-Asian sentiment in this country. Moreover, the hostility against Asian Americans is not limited to violent episodes or individual hate crimes. Part of the problem stems from the apparent success of many Asian Americans in education, business and professions, which creates a backlash of resentment from Whites.

Another reason for the resentment of Asians by Whites was due to the economic growth of some Asian countries, such as Japan, in the early 1990s. So strong was the resentment that ad campaigns were launched that encouraged people to buy "American," meaning American-made products, in order to save American jobs.

The trend of hate crimes against Asian Americans can be seen in official statistics. According to the Uniform Crime Reports in 2014, approximately 47 percent of the hate crimes in this country are motivated by racial bias. In 2014, law enforcement agencies reported 6,385 hate crime offenses. Of these offenses, about 6 percent were due to an anti-Asian/Pacific Islander bias. In terms of offenders, of the total hate crime offenses committed in 2014, 52 percent of the offenders were White, while 23.2 percent were African American. Asian offenders comprised less than one percent of hate crime offenders, the lowest of any group.[19]

Many Asian Americans also report evidence of a new form of **racial profiling**. A 2014 poll by the *Los Angeles Times* indicated that many Asian Americans support the position of Blacks and Hispanic/Latinos on perceptions of police effectiveness and racial profiling. While 18 percent of Whites felt that the police were ineffective, 47 percent of Blacks, 40 percent of Latinos, and 24 percent of Asians felt that way about the police. The findings of this study are similar to results about the attitudes towards the policy by Asian Americans nearly thirty years ago. However, these perceptions are not necessarily based on negative interactions between Asian Americans and the police.

While 28 percent of African Americans and 20 percent of Latinos said they had been treated unfairly by the police, only about 11 percent of Asians had similar experiences. Additionally, about 12 percent of Whites had experiences or interactions with the police where they felt they had been treated unfairly.[20]

Thus, while it may appear that Asian Americans have succeeded in their attempts to assimilate into mainstream American society, there are noticeable differences between the groups as well as a tendency to overgeneralize the level of success they have achieved. Perhaps the place to begin is to examine a selection of these groups that make up Asian Americans and explore their history as well as their current situations.

FAR EAST ASIAN AMERICANS

CHINESE AMERICANS

Early immigration from China into the United States was initiated largely because of economic and political unrest in China coupled with discovery of gold in California in the 1840s. Added to this was the construction of the transcontinental railroads, which drew many Chinese immigrants to the United States.[21] At the time, Chinese immigrants were welcome because they provided a sizeable group of hard-working employees. In a very short time, however, the influx of Chinese workers created a backlash of anti-Chinese sentiment. Based partly on the perceived threat by White workers, the hostility towards Chinese immigrants led to the passage of the **Chinese Exclusion Act**, which lasted in various forms for over sixty years. In 1882, Congress enacted the Chinese Exclusion Act, which outlawed Chinese immigration for ten years. The act also denied naturalization rights to immigrants already in the United States. There was little debate in Congress, in part because of the general belief in the threat the Chinese posed to American workers.[22]

In 1892, Congress extended the Exclusion Act for another ten years and added that Chinese laborers had to obtain certificates of residence within a year or face deportation. The ban against the Chinese was made permanent in 1907, and marked a significant moment in United States history when for the first time a specific group was formally prohibited from entering the country.[23]

When the act was initially passed in 1882, there were approximately 125,000 Chinese immigrants in the United States. By 1910 the number of immigrants had dropped to about 70,000, and did not really change until after 1965. Part of the reason for this had to do with the fact that most of the people coming into this country at that time were males. By one estimate, before 1882, more than 100,000 men but fewer than 9,000 women had emigrated to the United States from China.[24] Because of this imbalance between the sexes, it was quite difficult for Chinese immigrants to create ethnic communities. As a result of this sense of isolation, both from the discrimination felt by larger society as well as feeling disconnected ethnically, many were forced to live in urban ghettos or Chinatowns. In fact, many immigrants did not leave Chinatowns in great numbers until after the end of World War II.[25]

After the Exclusion Act was repealed in 1943, Chinese nationals were gradually permitted to enter the United States, first as spouses of servicemen and later as college students who were allowed to complete their education. Immigration continued slowly until the 1965 Immigration Act was passed, allowing more Chinese citizens to immigrate into the United States. The influx has recently become fairly robust, with numbers approaching 100,000 annually. In fact, in the 1990s the number of immigrants entering the United States actually exceeded the total number of Chinese immigrants already within United States that were present in 1980.[26] Today, as was mentioned, Chinese Americans represent the largest subgroup of Asian Americans, totaling nearly 4 million immigrants.

At least on the surface, Chinese Americans appear to have lower unemployment rates and are represented in many professional occupations. However, most of the jobs are found in Chinatowns around the country. The reason for this had to do with the fact that Chinese Americans were prohibited for generations from working anywhere else. While Whites did not object to Chinese immigrants in domestic occupations, largely because White men were unwilling to participate in such menial jobs, for the most part, Chinese Americans had few opportunities to work outside of the Chinatowns in most large urban areas.

Chinatowns have played an important part in the assimilation of many Asian immigrants since they have provided places where many Asians already lived and worked.

JAPANESE AMERICANS

The Japanese American experience in the United States is a fascinating case of how minority groups appear to be a threat to the mainstream way of life even when they have made efforts to assimilate and belong. While it appears that the "threat" of minority groups often drives much of our fears about whether we should allow certain immigrant groups into this country, what is more fascinating is the source of those fears and how they dictate our perception of certain groups. As we will see, the **yellow peril** was largely based on fear of Asians. This "threat" actually resulted in strict immigration laws and the imprisonment of American citizens.

The First Wave of Anti-Japanese Resentment

The Japanese who immigrated to the United States in the 1890s took jobs as laborers at low wages with poor working conditions. Their industriousness in these situations made them popular with employers but unpopular with unions and other employees. The Japanese had the misfortune of arriving just as bigotry toward the Chinese had been formalized in the Chinese Exclusion Act of 1882. While this legislation limited opportunities for Chinese workers, Japanese workers, at least initially, replaced the dwindling number of Chinese laborers in some industries, especially agriculture. Over time, however, once the threat and presence of Chinese workers disappeared, it was replaced with an anti-Japanese sentiment.

In 1913 California enacted the **Alien Land Act**. The act prohibited anyone who was ineligible for citizenship to own land and limited leases to three years. The land laws drove many first-generation Japanese into cities. However, government and union restrictions prevented Asian immigrants from taking jobs. As a result, many Japanese immigrants embarked upon self-employment to earn a living. More than any other group, Japanese immigrants opened grocery stores and other types of small businesses. The Japanese differed in many respects from the Chinese in terms of how they were treated. For instance, Japanese Americans had the benefit of witnessing what happened to the Chinese and were able to understand what changes had to occur for their treatment to be different from the experiences of the Chinese.

Second, Japanese Americans were much more vocal about the unfair treatment they received. First and second generation Japanese Americans often organized demonstrations, held boycotts, and enlisted the support of sympathetic Whites. Finally, in their native land, Japan took a more active interest in what was happening to its citizens in the United States than did China. The knowledge of how Japan felt about the treatment of their immigrants in this country, coupled with the fear of retaliation for the way Japanese Americans had been treated, led many Americans to be concerned about Japanese Americans' loyalty once Japan attacked Pearl Harbor on December 7, 1941.

The Second Wave: Internment

Almost immediately after the attack on Pearl Harbor, fear and concern about the war led people to feel threatened by Japanese Americans living on the West Coast. Many feared that Japanese Americans would fight on behalf of Japan, resulting in a successful invasion of the United States. Rumors mixed with racist bigotry, rather than facts, explain the events that followed. Japanese Americans in Hawaii were alleged to have cooperated in the attack by using signaling devices to assist pilots in locating their targets. Newspapers covered in detail FBI arrests of Japanese Americans allegedly assisting the attackers. They were accused of poisoning drinking water, cutting sugar cane fields to form arrows directing enemy pilots to targets and blocking traffic along highways to the harbor. None of these charges was substantiated despite thorough investigations.[27]

The executive order signed by Roosevelt authorized the removal of anyone considered a threat to national security in defined strategic military areas. All people on the West Coast of at least one-eighth Japanese ancestry were taken to assembly centers for transfer to concentration camps. This order covered 90 percent of the 126,000 Japanese Americans on the mainland. Of those evacuated, two-thirds were American citizens and three-quarters were under the age of twenty-five. Ultimately 120,000 people were interned in the camps: 113,000 from the mainland, 1,100 evacuated from Hawaii, about 200 voluntary residents (Caucasian spouses) and 5,900 who were born in the camps.[28]

What is interesting is that the evacuation order did not arise from any court action. No trials took place, no indictments were issued. Merely having a Japanese great-grandparent was enough to mark an individual for involuntary confinement. Perhaps even more fascinating was the fact that many Japanese Americans did not fight the order. The governing body for Japanese Americans and immigrant groups, the Japanese American Citizens League, believed that, given the emotional climate surrounding the attack as well as the suspicions of Japanese Americans, if any of those interned tried to flee or defied the order, it would likely confirm that Japanese could not be trusted.

As a result of fears that Japanese Americans would side with Japan during World War II, the government required that many Japanese Americans live in internment camps for the duration of the war.

Those that were to be interned were instructed to carry only personal items. No provision was made for shipping their household goods. The federal government took a few steps to safeguard the belongings internees left behind but the evacuees assumed all risks and agreed to turn over their property to the government for an indeterminate length of time. Internment caused merchants, farmers, and business owners to sell their property at any price they could get. Precise figures of the loss in dollars are difficult to obtain, but the Federal Reserve Bank estimated it to be approximately $400 million by 1941 standards. Today that amount would easily be billions of dollars.[29]

A few Japanese Americans resisted the evacuation and took legal action. Several cases arising out of the evacuation and detention reached the United States Supreme Court during the war. The Court upheld lower court decisions on Japanese Americans without even raising the issue of the constitutionality of the internment. Finally, in *Mitsuye Endo v. the United States*, the Supreme Court ruled that the defendant, and, presumably all evacuees, must be granted their freedom. Two weeks later, Japanese Americans were allowed to return to their homes for the first time in three years.[30]

As the *Endo* case demonstrates, our attitudes about the appropriateness of internment remained steadfastly strong. No legal action granting compensation to the evacuees for property lost was taken until 1948, with the Japanese Americans Evacuation Claims Act. Even when Americans recognized the injustice, little was done to remedy the problem. Two years after the Evacuation Claims Act's passage, only seventy-three people had received any money. Eventually there were approximately 23,000 claims and the government paid $38 million, less than 10 percent of the Federal Reserve Bank's estimate of the cost to Japanese Americans. All claims were settled with no interest or consideration of the increase in land values. Moreover the settlements were delayed so that by 1967, when the final payments were made, many of the claimants had died.[31]

In the late 1970s, President Carter created the Commission on Wartime Relocation and Internment of Civilians. The final Commission recommendation in 1983 was for a formal apology from the government and a tax-free payment of $20,000 to each of the approximately 66,000 surviving internees. Congress began hearings in 1986 on the bill and President Reagan signed the Civil Liberties Act in 1988, which authorized the payments.[32] Still the payments were slow in coming, and the internees were dying at a rate of two hundred per month. In 1990, the first checks were finally issued, accompanied by President George Bush's letter of apology.[33]

Today, only about a third of Japanese Americans are foreign-born, and they have a median family income of $65,000 per year. This group is highly educated, with 16 percent having earned advanced degrees and 31 percent having earned a bachelor's degree. More than half, 55 percent intermarry, often to non-Asians.[34]

KOREAN AMERICANS

In the early part of the twentieth century, a few thousand Koreans were recruited to work the sugar plantations in Hawaii. They were needed, in fact, to replace the Chinese workers who had been prohibited from remaining in the United States by the 1882 Chinese Exclusion Act. Still, the number of Korean immigrants remained small until after the Korean War in the 1950s, when many came as either refugees or as spouses of American servicemen returning home. However, the growth of the population exploded in the 1970s. Between 1970 and 1980, the Korean American population increased fivefold, from 70,000 to 355,000. According to the 2010 Census, Korean Americans numbered over 1.7 million.[35] However, in the late 1990s many Korean Americans chose to return to Korea. Part of the reason had to do with the political and economic growth in Korea, while for others who had difficulty adapting to American culture, the chance to feel "at home" was very appealing. For still others, operating a small business was considered too risky as tensions between Koreans and African Americans rose during the Los Angeles riots in 1992.[36]

In L.A.'s poor areas, the only shops in which to buy groceries or liquor or gasoline were owned by Korean immigrants. They had largely replaced the White-owned businesses. Scores of White business owners left the ghetto area after the 1965 Watts riots. African Americans were well aware of the dominant role Korean Americans played in their local retail market. Many African Americans expressed resentment that had been previously fueled by the 1991 shooting of a fifteen-year-old Black girl by a Korean grocer. The resentment grew when the grocer, convicted of manslaughter, had her prison sentence waived by a judge in favor of five years probation.[37]

During the riots one thousand Korean businesses valued at $300 million were destroyed. In a post-riot survey of African Americans who were arrested, 80 percent felt that Korean Americans were disrespectful, compared to 56 percent who felt similarly about Whites. Korean Americans' desire to succeed led them to the inner-city, where they did not face competition from Whites, but it also meant that they had to deal on a daily basis with the frustration of African Americans.[38]

During the L.A. riots, many Korean businesses were damaged due to a backlash against Korean Americans by African American residents.

Recent Census data indicates that nearly 80 percent of Korean Americans in the United States are foreign-born, with about 40 percent who speak English well. Korean Americans are also more likely to marry other Koreans (61 percent) than other Asian American groups. Korean Americans have a median family income of approximately $50,000 per year.[39]

SOUTHEAST ASIAN AMERICANS

The people of Southeast Asia, the Vietnamese, Cambodians, and Laotians, were once part of the former French Indochinese Union. Southeast Asian is only a term of convenience, especially since the people of these areas are ethnically and linguistically different. Numbering more than 2.8 million in 2010, Vietnamese Americans are the largest group with 1.7 million, which is approximately 9 percent of the total Asian American population.[40]

The catalyst to understanding this group of people for many Americans has been the Vietnam War. Historically, Southeast Asia consisted of many different tribes and countries such as Vietnamese, **Hmong tribes**, Cambodians, and ethnic Khmer. These and many other tribal groups came together in the early 1860s under the label "Indochina" as the French colonized the region. Because of the dissatisfaction with the political, cultural, economic, and social dominance by the French, civil wars broke out and communist influence began to take hold in the mid 1950s. In 1954, the United States sent 16,000 military advisors and support personnel in an effort to prevent communism from taking over South Vietnam. By 1962, military involvement escalated in the forms of air strikes and the use of Special Forces units to infiltrate the area. By 1964, most Americans believed that the United States had an obligation to free the people of Vietnam.[41]

By 1965 over 550,000 troops had been sent to Southeast Asia. At about the same time, the communist government in Laos attempted to eliminate any support for United States efforts in that country. The civil unrest that followed led to over 3 million Cambodians being killed by the Khmer Rouge government between 1975 and 1979. The United States withdrew from Southeast Asia in 1975 leaving 58,000 American soldiers dead and thousands more wounded. While the U.S. withdrawal left the region under communist control, thousands of refugees were brought into this country.[42] In 2010, Hmong and Cambodians represent about 530,000 in the United States.[43]

The problems for Vietnamese Americans, like that of all immigrant groups, were essentially based on the perceived threat they represented to Americans. This is true even though the initial U.S. involvement in the Vietnam War was intended to protect the South Vietnamese from the spread of communism. When the war ended and the idea of many refugees coming to America became a reality, public opinion about Vietnamese presence was negative and hostile.

Some people thought that allowing more immigrants from different cultures would cause the United States to lose its identity as a country. This same attitude was found in the mid-1970s with regard to Southeast Asians. Some experts believed that the news media created an unflattering image of the South Vietnamese, which led Americans to believe the Vietnamese were not worth saving.[44]

Approximately one million refugees fled Vietnam after the war in an attempt to escape religious persecution. In a scene similar to what was experienced in the 1980s and 1990s in Cuba, many of the people attempting to leave their native country took to the ocean in overcrowded vessels, hoping that some ship would pick them up and offer sanctuary. Hundreds of thousands were placed in other nations or remained in overcrowded refugee camps administered by the United Nations.[45] In fact, like Cuban immigrants, there were four distinct waves of immigration to the United States from Vietnam.

The first wave, which occurred between 1975 and 1977, resulted in over 130,000 refugees, the vast majority of which were Vietnamese. For the most part, these were people from upper- and middle-class backgrounds. Educated and professional, this group had perhaps the easiest time making the adjustment to life in a new country.

The second wave occurred between 1978 and 1979, bringing nearly 60,000 Vietnamese, Chinese from Vietnam, Cambodians, and Hmongs to the United States. Because this group of immigrants was more diversified in terms of their social class and educational backgrounds, the difficulty in transitioning to America was considerable. The third wave, which occurred between 1980 and 1981, had perhaps the greatest impact on American society. This group of immigrants consisted of peasants, farmers, and others who had no formal education or experience with Western culture.[46] Included in this wave of immigrants were nearly 200,000 Hmong tribal members. This is a group that lived in the highlands of Laos, Vietnam, and Cambodia and was intimately involved in the U.S. efforts in Laos. In fact, some estimates indicate that the Hmong experienced nearly a 50 percent casualty rate during the war. Because the Hmong tend to migrate and had no written language until the 1950s, this group experienced significant problems in adjusting to American culture.[47]

The fourth wave of immigration is associated with people who lived in refugee camps in Thailand and other relocation centers. Between 1987 and 1993, the number of refugees admitted from Vietnam was 173,116, from Laos (including the Hmong), 75,554 and approximately 9,000 from Cambodia.[48] Fortunately, Hmong children in these camps were exposed to English and American culture at an early age, which made the transition to America easier.

Despite the fact that it has been over thirty years since the end of the Vietnam War, Americans still seem to have mixed feelings about Southeast Asians. Surveys in the late 1980s and early 1990s show that although few Americans regarded this group as undesirable, about 50 percent still worried that they would be an economic drain. Even though most Southeast Asian children spoke no English upon arrival here, they have done extremely well in school. Many families place a heavy emphasis on education for their children.[49] However, many adult immigrants have experienced what is called **downward social mobility**. This means that the jobs Southeast Asian immigrants take are often occupationally below what they were doing in their native country.

However, Census Bureau data suggests that refugees from Vietnam have increased their family incomes when compared to what they made back home. Part of the reason for this, however, may be due to working longer hours or having more members of the family working full-time.[50] According to recent Census data, this group has one of the highest percentages of foreign-born residents, approximately 84 percent, and one of the lowest percentages of members who feel they speak English well, at 31 percent. Further, the median family income is one of the lowest of all Asian American groups ($53,800 compared to $66,000 for all Asian Americans).[51]

PACIFIC ISLANDER AMERICANS

HAWAIIANS

Historically, Hawaiians have been very tolerant of missionaries and plantation operators. Hawaiians were united under a monarchy, were respected by European immigrants, and this developed into a spirit of goodwill. In the late 1800s, a revolution occurred and the monarchy was overthrown. The United States got involved and five years later, Hawaii was annexed as a territory to the United States. During that time, citizenship had a mixed impact. Laws were passed that granted civil rights to all those born on the islands, but the anti-Asian laws still applied, which excluded the Chinese and Japanese from voting or running for office.

Hawaii has become a strategic military outpost and while most demographers contend that people marry others with similar backgrounds, sometimes known as **endogamy**, a high incidence of marrying outside one's group, called **exogamy**, can be taken as an indicator of acceptance of other groups. In Hawaii, there is a general acceptance of intermarriage or exogamy. The rate of intermarriage varies by group but consists of about 45 percent of all marriages in Hawaii, 62 percent of which include at least one Chinese American spouse.[52]

But Hawaii has its share of social problems. The pineapple and sugar cane plantation legacy persists, and native Hawaiians tend to struggle financially, often working land they do not own. The economy is dominated by Japanese Americans. Chinese Americans have had some success in business in Hawaii, but the top positions are almost all filled by Whites. The conclusion from these trends suggests that, in an absolute sense, Hawaii is not a racial paradise. The future of race relations in Hawaii is uncertain, but relative to the mainland and much of the world, its race relations more closely resemble harmony than bigotry.[53]

FILIPINOS

Few people think of Filipinos when they consider Asian Americans. Yet this group is the second largest of the Asian American population. During the past thirty years, only Mexicans have outnumbered Filipinos as immigrants to the United States.[54] After the Spanish-American War the United States took possession of the Philippines. Following the country's independence in 1946, political ties with the United States remained close. As evidence, English is one of the country's major languages and is spoken by most educated people. Moreover, like the early Koreans, Filipinos were brought to Hawaii as agricultural workers to replace the excluded Chinese, and many immigrated to the mainland in the 1920s.

Interestingly, because the Philippines was a U.S. territory at the time, immigrants were considered American nationals and as such, they were not subject to the same kind of restrictions and resentment as other Asian groups.[55] Added to the gentler attitude towards Filipinos was the fact that the Philippines became an important ally in the Pacific war against Japan. Consequently, Americans were much more tolerant of immigrants from this country than perhaps any other.

The long history and cultural compatibility, not to mention the U.S. military presence in the Philippines over the last forty years, resulted in a great deal of overlap between the two cultures.[56] This is reflected in the percentage of Filipinos who feel they speak English well—at 69 percent it is significantly higher than most other Asian groups and higher than the overall Asian American average of 53 percent. This group has one of the highest median family incomes, approximately $75,000 per year, and is generally open to intermarriage, particularly with non-Asians.[57]

INDIAN SUBCONTINENT

ASIAN INDIANS

Like the Asian American category as a whole, it is important to understand that people classified as **Asian Indian** represent a wide range of populations. India itself is a diverse nation with dozens of languages and ethnic enclaves. While most observers of India might note the religious divisions of Hindus, Muslims, and Sikhs, there are many other distinctions as well. The majority of Asian Indian immigrants have come from India, but sizable numbers come from Pakistan, Bangladesh, and Sri Lanka as well as other countries, such as Trinidad and Tobago and Guyana.[58]

As with other Asian groups, changes in immigration policies in the 1960s allowed many Asian Indians to enter the United States legally. Those who have come in recent times have been highly educated and from professional classes in their native countries. In fact, many Asian Indian immigrants have been students at American universities who find employment in the United States after graduation. This is particularly true in the computer industry.[59]

Like some other immigrant groups, Asian Indians have witnessed two types of experiences once arriving in the United States. On one hand, Asian Indians have played a significant role as entrepreneurs in the small business sector. For instance, by one estimate, more than half of all motels in the United States are owned by Asian Indians.[60] This group has the highest median family income of all Asian Americans, $88,000 per year, and is the best educated: 38 percent have advanced degrees, compared to 20 percent for all Asian Americans and 10 percent for Americans in general. Additionally, 32 percent of Asian Indians have bachelor's degrees. This compares to 29 percent for all Asian Americans and 18 percent of Americans in general.[61] On the other hand, there is a segment of this population that has not fared as well, being relegated to the lower paying industries such as restaurant workers, taxi drivers, and truck drivers. As one study concluded, Asian Indians are as likely to be cab drivers or managers of convenience stores as they are to be physicians or college professors. Many of the jobs in the service sector place them at higher risk to victimization by crime.[62]

ASIAN AMERICANS AND THE CRIMINAL JUSTICE SYSTEM

CRIME STATISTICS

According to the Uniform Crime Reports for 2014, Asian Americans represented 100,067 of the 8,730,665 arrests made by the police. This represents 1.1 percent of all arrests, even less than Native Americans, who represent 1.6 percent of all arrests for that year. This low representation in crime statistics has been a consistent trend for many years. Essentially, Asian Americans are a small proportion of those arrested by the police. Further, the percentage of arrests committed by Asian American or Pacific Islander juveniles was similar to that for all offenses, approximately 1.3 percent of all arrests for those eighteen years old and younger. Further, while Asian Americans represent about 4 percent of the total population in this country, they represent only about 1 percent of those arrested.[63] Unlike African Americans, Hispanics/Latinos, or even Native Americans, Asian Americans are underrepresented in the crime statistics.

Since 1990 the literature on crime and offenders has changed its focus from the larger minority groups, such as African Americans and Hispanics, to smaller groups of minorities, such as Native Americans and Asian Americans. While there is still a great deal less information, scholars and experts have begun examining the criminal behavior patterns among Asian Americans,[64] and some of the evidence from these studies show that certain Asian groups are more likely to be involved in criminal activity than others.

One study examined the odds of arrest for various offenses of seven different Asian groups. The findings revealed that Southeast Asian immigrants were more likely to be arrested for criminal activity than Whites. Vietnamese immigrants were overrepresented in every arrest category, while Cambodians, Laotians, and Vietnamese were more likely to be arrested for property crimes such as larceny and auto theft.[65]

A few trends also appear when examining the data on Asian Americans as victims of crime. However, one of the problems in assessing the victimization rates among Asian Americans is that the indicator used, primarily the National Crime Victimization Survey (NCVS),

Table 5.2 Five Year Arrest Trend for Asian Americans

Year	Total Arrests	Arrests	Percentage
2014	8,730,665	100,067	1.1%
2013	9,014,836	106,108	1.2%
2012	9,390,473	112,322	1.2%
2011	9,499,725	81,631	0.09%
2010	10,177,907	119,279	1.2%

collapses all the categories of Asian Americans into one group. As we have seen, there is a great deal of difference in the types of groups under this heading, and aggregating the cases obscures their differences and minimizes the overall impact of any single group. In fact, the NCVS collapses all racial groups into three categories: White, Black, and Other. They also include a separate category comparing Hispanics to non-Hispanics. Because of the aggregation of the data, any real analysis of Asians is virtually impossible, but the data does suggest that Asians are not victimized to the same extent as other groups.

As was mentioned, data from the Uniform Crime Reports in 2014 shows a low level involvement in reported crime. Only about 100,000 arrests of Asian offenders occurred, representing less than 1 percent of all arrests. What is important to note is that a comparison with Uniform Crime Report data since 2009 shows that this trend has been consistent for more than five years.[66]

Thus, while Asian Americans as a group are underrepresented in crime statistics, both as offenders and as victims, some attention has been given to the types and extent of criminal activity by some Asian American groups.

ASIAN GANGS

Growing concern about Asian crime stems from several factors, such as the legal and illegal immigration of Asians into the United States over the past twenty years. This has provided new opportunities for immigrants to engage in criminal activities such as youth gangs.[67] Some research suggests that younger Chinese Americans, unlike their elders, are not content to be grateful for what they have been given in exchange for their labor but expect the full rights and privileges of citizenship. More than their parents, they refuse to tolerate continued discrimination and unemployment.[68] Upward mobility is not in the future of many of these alienated and angry youth who, with the prospect of low wage work in restaurants and laundries, turn to gangs to achieve some level of success.

Chinese Gangs

In perhaps one of the most thorough examinations on the subject, Ko-Lin Chin, a professor at Rutgers University in New Jersey and an expert on Chinese culture, describes what is known about Chinese gangs. While there is some research to contradict Chin's findings, Chin argues that Chinese gangs are closely associated with, and are controlled by, powerful community organizations. In other words, they are an integral part of community

Asian gangs are closely connected to the Triads subculture.

life. These gangs are also influenced, to a great extent, by Chinese secret societies and the norms and values of the **triad subculture**.[69]

The primary activity of Chinese gangs is making money. Members invest a considerable amount of money in legitimate businesses and spend a lot of time negotiating business deals. Chinese gangs develop in communities in which adult criminals serve as role models and mentors for gang members. In keeping with their entrepreneurial efforts, drug use among Chinese gang members is rare. Although involved in drug trafficking, gang members rarely use drugs. In fact, if a member begins using drugs, he is expelled from the gang. Thus, unlike Black and Hispanic gangs, the establishment of Chinese gangs is not based on illicit drug use or fads.

Additionally, Chin found that Chinese gangs do not experience the deterioration and poverty prevalent with other types of gangs. Rather, Chinese gangs grow and become economically prosperous by maintaining ties with the economic and political structure of their communities. In other words, there is a cultural component to the success of Chinese gangs: they have a certain legitimacy within the community based on the historical experience of the **triad societies**.[70]

More recently, a study in New York City found that, like Chin's findings, Chinese gangs are characterized by a highly structured and disciplined manner. However, unlike the conclusions drawn by Chin, while Chinese gangs maintain close ties to adult organizations they are not controlled by them. Adult criminals also provide opportunities for gang members to advance within the larger criminal organization and to become apprentices of crime.[71]

Chinese gangs also typically engage in nonviolent forms of extortion of merchants in the area. The pervasiveness of extortion comes from a cultural understanding that extortion is a part of regular business activity. When gang violence is evident, it usually involves intergang rivalries. Popular wisdom about gang wars stemming from drug trafficking or gangs being used to leverage political control is not supported by empirical research. Also popular but unsupported by the research is the organized nature of human trafficking. While the activity is fairly common, it is not controlled by gangs. Rather, human smuggling is often a loosely organized, entrepreneurial activity.[72]

Vietnamese Gangs

While still part of an overall "Asian" category, Vietnamese youth gangs, especially in Southern California, are quite different in their characteristics from Chinese gangs. This group of immigrants, having experienced racism and discrimination both in the job market as well as in the classroom, has had a number of significant problems assimilating into mainstream American culture. Essentially, the following three themes that best characterize Vietnamese gangs: mistrust, hiding, and self-control.

A pervasive cultural theme of mistrust runs through Vietnamese communities, one that gang members exploit. For example, many members of the Vietnamese community distrust American banks and, as a result, keep their valuables and money at home. This creates a host of opportunities for gangs to rob Vietnamese citizens. As a result, robbery is a primary activity for gangs. Drug dealing in Vietnamese gangs is perceived as too risky and is avoided; thus, very few Vietnamese gang members are involved in drug dealing. Drug use, however, is heavy. The drug of choice is cocaine, while heroin is avoided since it is perceived to make one unreliable and crazy.

Vietnamese gang members continue their low-profile approach to social life by avoiding conspicuous gang tattoos or hand signs. Those that are used as indicators of gang affiliation (such as tattoos) are designed so that they can be easily concealed. Moreover, in regard to dress, Vietnamese gangs tend to opt for clothing similar to other youth in Southern California. In this way, they are able to blend in to the social landscape and more easily avoid the attention of the police. Finally, the structure of Vietnamese gangs tends to be unorganized and fluid. Membership changes constantly, and the rituals and practices of traditional gangs are noticeably absent.[73]

A recent study of Laotian/Hmong gangs in California reveals that these groups have become one of the latest threats to social life in Southern California. Laotian and Hmong gangs are an understudied area in the gang literature yet they appear to have a greater willingness to engage in violence. Members of these gangs have been involved in homicide, armed robbery, and aggravated assaults, making them a cause for considerable concern.[74]

In sum, Vietnamese gangs are loosely defined in terms of an organizational structure, disdain drug trafficking, and essentially attempt to conceal their gang affiliation to others. Vietnamese gangs do not claim turf, do not adopt similar modes of dress, and in some cases, avoid the use of gang names and "signs."[75]

HUMAN SMUGGLING

As was mentioned, one of the main areas of criminal activity for Asian Americans involves illegal immigration. For Chinese immigrants in particular, the problems are similar to illegal entry into the United States by Mexicans. However, given the distance that must be traveled, as well as the unique nature of the activity, some attempts have been made to learn more about human smuggling organizations, particularly in China.[76] While human smuggling into the United States has been going on for more than twenty years, its prevalence is based on the overwhelming numbers of Chinese nationals who wish to enter this country. As a result, when legitimate avenues were blocked, illegitimate opportunities were created.

People who leave China illegally are often called "**human snakes.**" Chinese human smugglers who lead illegal immigrants across the borders are called **snakeheads**. This has actually become an industry term to describe human smugglers either in China or overseas. As was mentioned, few have studied this subject empirically, largely because of the difficulties of finding and interviewing research subjects.

There are three main smuggling methods with estimated costs ranging from $35,000 to $65,000 to transport each illegal immigrant. Often, these methods are used in combination to transport Chinese nationals into the United States. One method is to travel to Mexico or Canada and then illegally cross the border into the United States. This method would be similar in many respects to what illegal immigrants in Mexico do to enter the country. There, the term *coyote* is used to describe the guides or facilitators who bring Mexican immigrants into the country. A second method is to have immigrants obtain false documents certifying they are citizens of another country, and then fly into the United States through transit points outside China. A third method, the one best popularized in the media and Hollywood movies, is to use fishing trawlers or freighters to smuggle immigrants into the United States.[77]

While conventional wisdom suggests that this type of activity would be sponsored and carried out by organized crime syndicates, largely because of the logistical details involved, the research seems to suggest that human smuggling is run by individual entrepreneurs, most of whom operate independent of one another. That is, snakeheads come from a host of different backgrounds and occupations, do not affiliate with any particular organized crime group, and individual teams of smugglers may work together, usually in groups no larger than five, largely based on their particular skill or networks at different points in the smuggling process.[78] In addition to the loose affiliation many snakeheads have in terms of cooperation, they also generally do not remain involved in smuggling for longer than six years, making discovery, study, or even prosecution of snakeheads exceptionally difficult.[79] Finally, the absence of a figurehead or leader of this activity, what some researchers have called a "godfather," prohibits the police from any meaningful intervention to minimize this type of criminal activity.

TRANSNATIONAL ORGANIZED CRIME

In 2012, in an attempt to assess the impact of Asian transnational organized crime in the United States, as well as to lay the foundation for a research agenda that will help the United States better understand the potential threats of international crime, two researchers, Ko-Lin Chin and James Finckenauer, conducted a study to explore the extent of Asian transnational organized crime.[80] While agreement on the particular problems as well as the scope of activities relating to organized crime is difficult, leading experts on organized crime in eight Asian countries (Cambodia, China, Hong Kong, Japan, Macau, the Philippines, Taiwan, and Thailand), have agreed that there are a few common issues.

In China, for example, law enforcement officials and other authorities consider drug distribution to be the most serious problem in that country. The increase in the number of heroin addicts in China have led officials to believe that local drug syndicates are importing heroin from the Golden Triangle area (Burma, Thailand, and Cambodia) and distributing it locally. Gambling is also considered a serious problem in China. According to officials, even though the problems of gambling and prostitution were thought to be eradicated when China began a communist reign in 1949, today these two industries appear to be thriving. Finally, Chinese authorities are concerned about the escalating levels of violence in their country. Perhaps more importantly, the violence extends beyond criminal gangs or organized crime syndicates and are affecting ordinary citizens and business owners.[81] Chinese officials are also concerned about the problems stemming from the human smuggling industry.[82]

In Japan, the most serious organized crime problem relates to this country's version of organized crime, the **yakuza**. Their involvement in gambling, prostitution, drug trafficking, particularly in amphetamines, and extortion are cause for considerable concern by authorities. Additionally, because of the large number of wealthy businessmen, Japan has become a major destination for women in the sex industry.[83]

In the Philippines, the main concern relates to human trafficking and kidnapping for ransom, the drug trade, and illegal gambling and firearms smuggling. While the country recently passed an anti-trafficking law, little priority is given to enforcing such laws despite the sexual exploitation that occurs there. Thus, while the official position is that something needs to be done about these crimes, the reality is that little emphasis is being given to solving the problem.

With regard to the drug trade, in response to improved law enforcement interdiction efforts to control the influx of amphetamines from China, Filipino authorities have discovered local laboratories have been established to manufacture the drugs. Thus, the problems in the Philippines relating to drugs have shifted from an international focus to a local concern. Authorities contend that much of this trade, like a great deal of criminal activity in general, is controlled by organized crime syndicates who are protected by local politicians.[84]

In 2014, the United Nations Office on Drugs and Crime (UNODC) issued a report on human trafficking. Similar to the trends discovered ten years earlier, the challenges involved in identifying and prosecuting traffickers remains, along with a wide variety of organizations and structures. One of the more recent trends has been the involvement of women as offenders as well as their traditional role as victims of human trafficking. The UNODC reports that about a third of all offenders are now women.[85]

Additionally, about 50 percent of victims are adult women, although this number may be skewed since girls are not counted in the tabulation. According to the UNODC, in 2012, children now represent about a third of all trafficking victims, two-thirds of which are girls. Further, while sex remains one of the primary activities of human trafficking victims, forced labor is also becoming a common feature. While women are typically victimized for sexual purposes, with male victims usually involved in forced labor, in China many women are also used for the purposes of forced labor as well.[86]

The UNODC also found that only four in ten countries have reported ten or more convictions for human trafficking, with about 15 percent of countries reporting no convictions at all. Part of the challenge relates to the discovery and prosecution of human trafficking crimes, but given the enormous profits generated from this industry, one could also assume that some countries have ignored human trafficking for economic reasons.[87]

SUMMARY

This chapter explored several of the most common Asian American groups in the United States. Many of these groups listed under the general heading of "Asian American" cover a broad spectrum of groups, with different attitudes, values, beliefs, and languages, making the category more of convenience than actual understanding. Additionally, diversity is evident in the experiences of Asian Americans and success in assimilating into mainstream American culture. Historically, most of these groups, particularly the Chinese and Japanese, have been initially perceived as beneficial since they provided cheap labor in expanding industries. However, as immigrants demonstrated their willingness to work hard and work for very little money, the group became perceived as threatening to American workers. As a result, legislation was passed to limit their immigration into the United States.

The willingness to work hard, sacrifice, and persevere has resulted in some success for groups of Asian Americans, particularly in the area of education. In fact, in more recent times, Asian Americans were given the label "model minority" to describe how well they assimilated into American culture. This label is a myth largely because it does not address the wide range of experiences for Asian Americans. While some have achieved a level of societal success, there are other groups who remain mired in poverty and discrimination. Thus, for some groups of Asian Americans, many have been able to successfully integrate themselves into American society, for others however, the problems of poverty and crime are readily self-evident. Thus, while it appears from an examination of the crime statistics as well as victimization surveys that Asian Americans are underrepresented in terms of their involvement in crime, there remains a portion of the population that is actively involved in criminal activity.

YOU MAKE THE CALL

Consider the following scenario. Debate the pros and cons of all options and decide what you would do.

You are a young prosecutor with only two years of experience trying criminal cases. A gang fight erupts in an Asian neighborhood which results in the deaths of two rival gang members. Upon interviewing residents of the area who might have seen what happened, police officers cannot find anyone willing to make a statement. They, do, however, recover substantial physical evidence that links two particular suspects to the crime. While you are trying to decide what to do, local Asian Americans protest the treatment citizens receive from police officers, causing a major uproar at City Hall. As a result, your supervisor tells you to drop the case since it will likely result in a political disaster. Given that the gang problem has become a topic of interest for

(continued)

(continued)

the police and is of some concern to the courts as well, what do you do? Assume also that you have what you think to be enough evidence to obtain a warrant for the arrest of the suspects.

Questions

1. What do you do? Do you proceed despite your supervisor's orders? What is the dilemma for you?
2. What kind of repercussions might you experience if you decide to continue with the case? What would they be if you decided to drop it?
3. Why would the police chief, the district attorney, and the mayor want you to drop the case?
4. Can a group such as Asian Americans, which typically represent a small percentage of the crime statistics and are usually less vocal than other minority groups, really have an impact on local politics? How?

KEY TERMS

Alien Land Act
Asian gangs
Asian Indians
Chinese Exclusion Act
downward social mobility
endogamy
exogamy
glass ceiling
Hmong tribes

human snakes
internment
model minority myth
racial profiling
snakeheads
triad societies
triad subculture
yakuza
yellow peril

DISCUSSION QUESTIONS

1. What do Chinese, Japanese, and Koreans all have in common in terms of their immigration into the United States?
2. How does the media contribute to the model minority myth for many Asian American groups?
3. Why do you think Asian Americans are underrepresented in the crime statistics? Is it because they commit fewer crimes or are they simply better at avoiding the police?
4. Do you think that hate crimes against Asian Americans are common? Why is it that when people think of hate crimes, they usually think of African Americans?

FOR FURTHER READING

Hyun, J. *Breaking the Bamboo Ceiling: Career Strategies for Asians*. New York: HarperCollins, 2005.

Long, P. D., and L. Ricard. *The Dream Shattered: Vietnamese Gangs in America*. Boston, MA: Northeastern University Press, 1996.

Takaki, R. *A Different Mirror: A History of Multicultural America*. New York: Back Bay Books, 2008.

Weglyn, M. *Years of Infamy: The Untold Story of America's Concentration Camps*. New York: Quill, 1976.

NOTES

1. K. Humes, and J. McKinnon, *The Asian and Pacific Islander Population in the United States: Population Characteristics*, U.S. Census Bureau, Current Population Reports (Washington, DC: U.S. Government Printing Office, 2000).

2. United States Census Brief, *From the Mideast to the Pacific: A Profile of the Nation's Asian Foreign-born Population* (U.S. Department of Commerce: Census Brief 100-4, 2000).

3. American Immigration Center, *Asian American History Timeline.* Available at https://www.us-immigration.com/asian-american-history-timeline/

4. Ibid.

5. Pew Research Center, *Asian Americans*, June 18, 2012. Available at http://www.pewsocialtrends.org/asianamericans-graphics/st_12-06-17_aa_pop-2/

6. Ibid.

7. Ibid.

8. Ibid.

9. J. Guo, "The Real Reasons the U.S. Became Less Racist Toward Asian Americans," *Washington Post*, November 29, 2016. Available at https://www.washingtonpost.com/news/wonk/wp/2016/11/29/the-real-reason-americans-stopped-spitting-on-asian-americans-and-started-praising-them/?utm_term=.30b90a7a5d7e.

10. J. Calma, "Forty years After Resettlement, Thousands of Southeast Asian Refugees Face Deportation," *NBC News*, November 23, 2015. Available at http://www.nbcnews.com/news/asian-america/forty-years-after-resettlement-thousands-southeast-asian-refugees-face-deportation-n466376.

11. Pew Research Center, *Asian Americans.*

12. Ibid.

13. Ibid.

14. T. Lien, "Asian Americans Face Glass Ceiling at Tech Firms, Report Shows," *Los Angeles Times*, May 6, 2015, available at http://www.latimes.com/business/la-fi-tech-diversity-asians-20150507-story.html.

15. J. Hyun, *Breaking the Bamboo Ceiling: Career Strategies for Asians* (New York: HarperCollins, 2005), 73–92.

16. T. Varadarajan, "A Patel Motel Cartel?" *New York Times Magazine*, July 4, 1999. Available at http://www.nytimes.com/1999/07/04/magazine/a-patel-motel-cartel.html

17. Ibid.

18. See for example, T. Lien, "Asian Americans Face Glass Ceiling at Tech Firms, Report Shows," *Los Angeles Times*, May 6, 2015, available at http://www.latimes.com/business/la-fi-tech-diversity-asians-20150507-story.html

19. Department of Justice, Federal Bureau of Investigation, *Crime in the United States, Incidents and Offenses Hate Crime Statistics*, (Washington, DC: U.S. Government Printing Office, 2014). Available at http://www.fbi.gov/about-us/ciis/ucr/hate-crime/2014/topic-pages/offenders_final

20. "Asian Americans Side with Blacks and Latinos in Opinions about Police Effectiveness and Racial Profiling." Available at http://reappropriate.co/2014/09/asian-americans-side-with-blacks-latinos-not-whites-in-opinions-on-police-effectiveness-racial-profiling/

21. National Archives. 2017. *Chinese Exclusion Act*, Available at https://www.archives.gov/research/chinese-americans.

22. Ibid.

23. Ibid.

24. I. Light, "Chinese Americans." *American Journal of Sociology* 81, no. 2 (September, 1975): 432–35.

25. Chinese Historical Society of South Carolina., "Chinatowns in the United States of America." Available at http://www.chssc.org/History/ChinatownsInAmerica.aspx.

26. J. Batalova and A. Terrareas, "Frequently Requested Statistics on Immigrants and Immigration in the U.S." *Migration Policy Institute*, December 9, 2010. Available at http://www.migrationpolicy.org/article/frequently-requested-statistics-immigrants-and-immigration-united-states-1

27. Ibid.

28. M. Weglyn, *Years of Infamy: The Untold Story of America's Concentration Camps* (New York: Quill, 1976), 316.

29. S. Caudill and F. Mixon, "Human Capital Investment and Internment of Japanese Americans During WWII: A Public Choice Approach," *International Journal of Applied Economics* 9, no. 1 (2012): 1–14.

30. Ibid.

31. Ibid.

32. "Redress to WWII Internees Complete," *Chicago Tribune* September 11, 1998. Available at http://articles.chicagotribune.com/1998-09-11/news/9809110328_1_civil-liberties-act-internees-japanese-americans.

33. Commission on Wartime Relocation and Internment of Civilians, *Recommendations*, June 1983. Available at https://archive.org/details/Personal-Justice-Denied

34. Pew Research Center, *Asian Americans.*

35. Ibid.

36. Ibid.

37. S. Mydans, "Shooting Puts Focus on Korean-Black Tensions in Los Angeles," *New York Times*, October 6, 1991, available at http://www.nytimes.com/1991/10/06/us/shooting-puts-focus-on-korean-black-frictions-in-los-angeles.html

38. Pew Research Center, *Asian Americans.*

39. Ibid.

40. Ibid.

41. Ibid.

42. J. Zong and J. Batalova, "Vietnamese Immigration in the U.S." *Migration Policy Institute*, June 8, 2016. Available online at http://www.migrationpolicy.org/article/vietnamese-immigrants-united-states

43. Pew Research Center, *Asian Americans.*

44. C. B. Luce, "Refugees and Guilt," *New York Times*, May 11, 1975, E19.

45. Zong and Batalova, *Vietnamese Immigration in the U.S.*

46. Ibid.

47. F. Ng, "Towards a Second Generation Hmong History," in F. Ng, ed., *Adaptation, Acculturation, and Transnational Ties among Asian Americans* (New York: Garland, 1998), 99–117.

48. A. Portes and R. G. Rumbaut, *Immigrant America: A Portrait,* 2nd ed. (Berkeley: University of California Press, 1996).

49. F. Ng, "Towards a Second Generation Hmong History"

50. J. Zong and J. Batalova, *Vietnamese Immigration in the U.S.*

51. Pew Research Center, *Asian Americans.*

52. Ibid.

53. Zong and Batalova, *Vietnamese Immigration in the U.S.*

54. Ibid.
55. Ibid.
56. Ibid.
57. Pew Research Center, *Asian Americans.*
58. Zong and Batalova, *Vietnamese Immigration in the U.S.*
59. B. Boxall, "Asian Indians Remake Silicon Valley," *Los Angeles Times,* July 6, 2001.
60. Varadarajan, "A Patel Motel Cartel?," 36–39.
61. Pew Research Center, 2015, *Asian Americans.*
62. Varadarajan, "A Patel Motel Cartel?"
63. Department of Justice, *Crime in the United States 2015,* Federal Bureau of Investigation, Uniform Crime Reports, available at https://ucr.fbi.gov/crime-in-the-u.s/2015/crime-in-the-u.s.-2015.
64. E. B. Penn and S. L. Gabbidon, "Race and Justice," *Criminal Justice Studies* 18, no. 1 (2005): 1–121.
65. A. J. Kposowa and G. T. Tsunokai, "Offending Patterns Among Southeast Asians in the State of California." *Journal of Ethnicity in Criminal Justice* 1, no. 1 (2003): 93–113.
66. U.S. Department of Justice, *Crime in the United States,* 2015.
67. J. Z. Wang, "Asian Gangs: New Challenges in the 21st Century," *Journal of Gang Research* 8, no. 1 (2000): 51–62.
68. Ibid; See also K. Chin, "Chinese Gangs and Extortion" in *Gangs in America,* ed. C. Ron Huff (Newbury Park, CA: Sage, 1990), 129–45.
69. D. Joe and N. Robinson, "Chinatown's Immigrant Gangs," *Criminology* 18 (1980): 337–45; K. Joe, "Myths and Realities of Asian Gangs on the West Coast," *Humanity and Society* 18, no. 2 (1994): 3–18; P. Takagi and T. Platt, "Behind the Gilded Ghetto," *Crime and Social Justice* 9, no. 2 (1978): 2–25.
70. Chin, "Chinese Gangs and Extortion." See also V. Webb, L. Ren, J. Z. Zhao, "A Comparative Study of Youth Gangs in China and the United States," *International Criminal Justice Review* 21, no. 3 (2011): 225–52.
71. See Federal Bureau of Investigation, *2011 National Gang Threat Assessment,* 2012. Available at https://www.fbi.gov/stats-services/publications/2011-national-gang-threat-assessment/2011-national-gang-threat-assessment; Wang, "Asian Gangs."
72. Ibid.
73. F. P. Lopez, *Gang 102: A Way Out,* 2014, available at http://www.sanjoseca.gov/Document Center/View/28048; P. Wyrick, *Vietnamese Youth Gang Involvement* (Washington, DC: Office of Juvenile Justice Delinquency Prevention, 2000). Available at https://www.ncjrs.gov/pdffiles1/ojjdp/fs200001.pdf; J. D. Vigil, "Cholos and Gangs: Culture Change and Street Youth in Los Angeles," in Huff, *Gangs in America,* 106–28; J. D. Vigil and Steve Chong Yun, "Vietnamese Youth Gangs in Southern California," in Huff, *Gangs in America,* 146–62.
74. J. Z. Wang, "A Preliminary Profile of Laotian/Hmong Gangs: A California Perspective." *Journal of Gang Research* 9, no. 4 (2002): 1–4.
75. Long and Ricard, *The Dream Shattered.*
76. See U.S. Department of State, *Trafficking in Persons Report,* June 2014. Available at https://www.state.gov/j/tip/rls/tiprpt/2014/index.htm.
77. Ibid.
78. Ibid.
79. Ibid.

80. K. Chin and J. O. Finckenauer, *Selling Sex Overseas: Chinese Women and the Realities of Prostitution and Global Sex Trafficking* (New York: NYU Press, 2012).

81. Ibid.

82. Zhang and Chin, *Characteristics of Chinese Human Smugglers.*

83. Chin and Finckenauer, *Selling Sex Overseas.*

84. Ibid.

85. United Nations, Office on Drugs and Crime. *Trafficking in Persons,* 2014. Available at http://www.unodc.org/documents/human-trafficking/2014/GLOTIP_2014_full_report.pdf

86. Ibid.

87. Ibid.

CHAPTER 6

NATIVE AMERICANS AND THE CRIMINAL JUSTICE SYSTEM

CHAPTER OBJECTIVES:

After reading this chapter, you should be able to:

- Identify the significance of the historical treatment of American Indians in this country;
- Understand the importance of federal intervention in the form of laws and agencies in regulating life both on and off the reservation;
- Describe the current condition of many Native Americans in this country;
- Understand the involvement of Native Americans in the criminal justice system, particularly in light of the tension between self-governance of tribes and the influence of federal laws.

As with the other groups discussed thus far, it is impossible to describe the many American-Indian cultures of North America, let alone those in Central and South America and the islands of the Caribbean. The term "Indian culture" is a generic term that includes a vast array of cultures and ways of life of the group we call "American Indians." For simplicity's sake the term Native Americans or American Indian will be used interchangeably, but, as we saw with the discussion of Hispanics and Latinos, know that there are a host of differences that make any sweeping generalizations impractical.

HISTORICAL PRESENCE OF NATIVE AMERICANS

The U.S. has had a stormy history with Native Americans. In 1500, the number of American Indians north of the Rio Grande was estimated at about 7 million. This number gradually decreased as food sources disappeared or they died due to diseases such as measles and small pox. Between 1800 and 1900, the Native American population was reduced from about 600,000 to approximately 250,000.[1]

The government's policy towards Native Americans has historically been one of expediency. If the needs of the tribes interfered with Whites' needs or desires, the sentiment was that Native Americans should capitulate to Whites. The tribes were viewed as separate nations to be dealt with by government treaties. While one may think this is a civilized approach, history clearly shows that American Indians were either exploited by cooperating with the federal government or eliminated if they refused to give up their land.[2]

For instance, as settlers moved west, the need for land increased. The government believed that Indians had no right to interfere with societal progress. To that end, the **Indian Removal Act of 1830** called for the relocation of all Eastern tribes to west of the Mississippi River. The act not only disrupted Native American culture, but it did not move the tribes far enough to stay ahead of the growing population of settlers. In an effort to elicit cooperation, peace commissioners were sent out in 1867 in an attempt to create reservations for Native American tribes.[3]

The 19th Century proved to be a difficult time for Native Americans as the U.S. continued to claim land that belonged to tribes. The treatment of the Sioux Nation serves as an example of this insensitivity. In 1868, the U.S. signed the **Fort Laramie Treaty** with the Sioux. The government agreed to keep Whites from hunting or settling on the newly established Great Sioux Reservation, which included all of the land that is now South Dakota. In exchange, the Sioux relinquished most of the remaining land they occupied at that time.[4]

Urged on perhaps by George Custer's claims of gold in the Black Hills, a flood of White people eventually infiltrated the Sioux reservation. As one might expect, conflict between the Sioux and Whites occurred. In response, the U.S. violated the parameters of the Fort Laramie Treaty and demanded that the Sioux move out of the Black Hills. When the Sioux failed to move, General George Custer was sent into the area to remove them physically. Custer underestimated the strength of the Sioux warriors, which led to the now famous **Battle at Little Big Horn** in 1876, where Custer and his men were defeated.

The Battle of Little Big Horn was an historic moment in the history of the treatment of Native Americans.

Afterward, the army redoubled its efforts to eliminate the Sioux. The tribe eventually sold the Black Hills to the federal government and agreed to the reduction of the Great Sioux Reservation to five smaller reservations.[5] The Sioux had a difficult time adjusting to life on the reservation. They sought escape through the **Ghost Dance religion**, a religion that included dances and songs proclaiming the return of the buffalo and the resurrection of dead ancestors in a land free of the White people. Although the Ghost Dance was essentially harmless, Whites feared that the social solidarity encouraged by the movement would lead to renewed warfare. As a result, more troops were summoned to areas where the Ghost Dance had become popular.[6]

In late December 1890, anticipating that a massive Ghost Dance would occur, a cavalry division arrived at a reservation of Sioux at Wounded Knee Creek on the Pine Ridge, South Dakota. While an exact account of what happened is not known, a battle ensued that left about 300 Sioux and 25 U.S. soldiers dead. This conflict is known as the **Battle of Wounded Knee**. The event was not the deadliest for Native Americans, but the battle is heralded by historians as significant because it extinguished the hope of the Sioux Nation of ever returning to a life of freedom.[7]

LEGISLATING FOR THE PEOPLE

As the death toll mounted and the conflict between Native Americans and White settlers continued, the federal government attempted a different strategy: assimilation. The idea was that if cultural differences were the source of the problem, meaning that the attitudes, values and beliefs of the tribes were in conflict with the progressive ideas of the government and settlers, then the solution was to weaken the influence of tribal culture. If tribal institutions were weakened, then Native Americans would be more likely to assimilate and subscribe to the ideas the federal government proposed. Evidence of assimilation strategy was seen in the General Allotment Act of 1887, also known as the **Dawes Act** of 1887.[8]

The General Allotment Act proposed to make landowners of individual tribe members without consulting tribal leaders. Advocated largely by community activists who sought to empower tribal members by helping them to become more like Whites, each family was given 160 acres of land. However, like programs for the poor that attempt to empower families as homeowners but do not properly equip them with the skills necessary to maintain a home, no effort was made to acquaint Native Americans with the skills necessary to make the land productive. As a result, eventually much of the land initially deeded under the act came into the possession of Whites when Native Americans became victims of fraudulent land transfers. By 1934 Native Americans had lost approximately 90 million of the 138 million acres in their possession prior to the General Allotment Act.[9]

John Collier was appointed to head the Bureau of Indian Affairs during President Franklin D. Roosevelt's first term. Collier proposed major changes in Indian policy that included the preservation of Native American culture. Perhaps most significant was his proposal to end the allotment system. In 1934 Congress passed the Indian Reorganization Act, which, among other things, prohibited further allotments of tribal lands and encouraged Native Americans to create self-governing systems within their tribes.[10]

TERMINATION

In the mid 1940s, Whites realized the significance of mistreating Native Americans, especially those who lived on reservations. However, instead of improving the quality of life on reservation land, many Americans mistakenly thought that part of the solution was to force Native Americans to assimilate into mainstream society.[11] This was accomplished by simply eliminating official recognition of tribes. The **Termination Act** was passed by Congress in 1953 which led to the termination of 13 tribes between 1945 and 1962. The Termination Act also meant that certain tribes would lose tax exempt status for their lands. Consequently, many tribal members who lost their status had to sell their land to pay the taxes on it and to pay for health and educational services for their communities.[12] Consequently, Termination laws forced nearly 35,000 displaced former land owners to urban areas. The Bureau of Indian Affairs Employment Assistance Program offered reimbursement for transportation, low-cost housing, and incidental expenses to Native Americans who agreed to resettle in cities. Soon, Indian populations in cities exceeded those of some reservations. According to the Census Bureau, in the 1960s more than half of all Native Americans live in cities. Most Native Americans strongly resisted the Termination Act, realizing that tribes would lose their lands as well as their native culture.

During the 1970s the **Red Power Movement**, which was similar to the Black Power movement for African Americans in that they tried to gain economic, social, and political equality for Native Americans, pressured the federal government to address Native Americans' concerns and to reaffirm tribal rights as set out in the Indian Reorganization Act. The effect was a renewed effort by the U.S. government to give more control back to the tribes.

The more radical American Indian Movement (AIM), which became the most visible reminder of the Red Power movement, was originally to monitor the police and to document evidence of police brutality. Eventually, AIM turned their attention to solving problems within the Native American community like programs that focused on reducing the high incidence of alcoholism among Native Americans as well as educational programs for Native American children to improve academic performance.

The 1970s, a time of great protest in the United States, was also a time when Native Americans made dramatic efforts to have their rights preserved. Perhaps the most dramatic confrontation between Native Americans and the federal government occurred in 1973. Known as the Battle of Wounded Knee II, the leader of AIM and nearly 300 supporters began a 70-day standoff with authorities in Wounded Knee, South Dakota, the site of the first famous battle with General Custer in 1890. While the event drew a great deal of media attention, it had little effect on the federal government's policy on Native Americans.[13]

GOVERNMENT INVOLVEMENT IN INDIAN AFFAIRS

In recent years, many of the policies instituted by the **Bureau of Indian Affairs**, the primary regulatory arm of the federal government as it relates to Native Americans, have been designed with the idea that the government should be less involved in Indian life. In an attempt to relinquish control over Indian affairs the federal government formed the **Indian Claims Commission** (ICC) to handle disputes. Until 1946, Native Americans could not bring any land claim against the federal government without a special act of Congress.

Like other minority groups, many Native Americans have protested the government's discrimination against them.

Although not an official U.S. court, the ICC operates somewhat like one in that lawyers present evidence for both sides. If the commission agrees with the tribe, it then determines the value of the land at the time it was illegally seized. This is of critical importance since the value of the land at the time of loss could be pennies an acre. Payments are then decreased by what are called **setoffs**. These are deductions from the money due equal to the cost of federal services provided to the tribe. It is not unusual to have a case decided in favor of the tribe only to have its settlements exceeded by the set offs.[14] In other words, while the tribe may have won the moral and legal victory by having the case decided in their favor and being entitled to compensation, the costs of using government services often left tribes in a deficit because the value of the land was not calculated at current market value.

More recently, but particularly in the 1980s, which is recognized as a decade of progress in Indian Law, Native Americans have increasingly succeeded in winning their lawsuits. The U.S. Supreme Court has ruled on nearly eighty cases between the 1960s and 1980s, most of which have gone in favor of the tribes and have reasserted such basic principles as tribes as separate governments. The 1990s were heralded as a time of new tribal sophistication, where **Tribal Courts** were increasing in quantity and in political standing, spawned perhaps by the economic wealth of some tribes due to[15] Tribal courts are courts of jurisdiction designed to allow the tribes the authority to hear and decide cases relating to life on the reservation without interference of traditional U.S. Courts.

NATIVE AMERICANS TODAY

We must again emphasize the diversity of Native Americans. Besides the variety of tribal heritages, it is important to recognize there is a distinction between Native Americans that live on and off reservations, as well as tribal members who live in small towns and in central cities, and those living on one coast or the other. Native American life has generally shifted from several hundred reservations to small towns and big cities. Life in these places is quite different, but there are enough similarities to draw a few broad conclusions about the status of Native Americans in the U.S. today. Let's look at a couple of dimensions.

EMPLOYMENT AND INCOME

According to the 2012 American Community Survey conducted by the U.S. Census, there were 5.2 million people, or about 1.7 percent of the total U.S. population. Problems emerge, however, when the categories are examined. The Census Bureau implemented a new method for collecting data on race and ethnicity. Respondents were given the option of selecting one race to indicate their identity or they could select a number of categories. Thus, in looking at the American Indian and Alaska Native category, 2.9 million listed only one race and 2.3 million listed American Indian in combination with one or more other races.[16]

According to Census officials, the number of people who self-identify in this category is growing. There were 170,110 people who identified as Sioux in the 2010 census. The largest group, Cherokee, had 819,105 people. Of those who identified as Native American or Alaska Native as their only race, about a third live on reservations or tribal lands. Among all American Indians and Alaska Natives, about 22 percent live on reservations or tribal lands.[17]

In terms of identifying with a particular tribe, with 43 percent living on reservations, the Cherokee, followed by the Navajo and Sioux are the largest tribes today. The increase in population size over the past twenty years is primarily due to a greater willingness for Native Americans to claim their heritage, either by moving back to reservations or simply claiming their heritage within an official survey. Some experts contend that the increases are due to the growth of the casino gambling industry.[18]

By the U.S. standard of living, Native Americans are quite poor. In an absolute sense of dollars earned or quality of housing, Native Americans are no worse off now than in the past. However, when making comparisons between minority groups and the larger society, most experts always use a relative standard, not an absolute one. In other words, poverty is not defined by the percentage of people who have no food, clothing, or housing. Poverty is determined by a standard that is relative to some larger group. In a relative sense, Native Americans are far behind on all standards of income and occupational status when compared to Whites. In the 1980s, for example, according to the U.S. Census, Native American families were three times more likely to live below the poverty level and much less likely to have anyone in that family working full-time. When Congress passed the Personal Responsibility Work Reconciliation Act in 1997, more commonly known as welfare reform, a major part of the act focused on chronic poverty, of which many Native Americans experience. Today, the problems seem to be getting worse for Native Americans, who generally have higher poverty and unemployment rates when compared to the national average. According to the U.S. Census Bureau, the median income of American Indian and Alaska Native alone in 2011 was $35,192—in contrast, the median income for the entire population is $50,502.[19]

For example, in South Dakota, the poverty rate at Standing Rock Reservation is 43.2 percent according to the Pew Research Center, nearly triple the national average. About 25 percent of

Poverty rates on Native American reservations are alarmingly high, largely due to the lack of employment opportunities.

American Indians and Alaska Natives were living in poverty in the United States in 2012.[20] According to the 2013 American Indian Population and Labor Force Report by the Bureau of Indian Affairs, the highest rate of poverty is in South Dakota, with about 45 percent of Native American families with incomes falling below the poverty line. Other states with high rates of poverty include Arizona, Minnesota, Montana, and Nebraska.[21]

Another marker of economic success is home ownership. According to the U.S. Census, only 54 percent of American Indian and Alaska Natives alone householders owned their own home in 2011—compared to 65 percent of the overall population. Additionally, while about 15 percent of the country lacked health insurance in 2011, the percentage of American Indians and Alaska Natives who lacked health insurance was nearly 28 percent.[22]

People living on reservations also have the highest rates of unemployment in the United States. Some of the most commonly cited reasons for high unemployment among Native Americans are lack of education, discrimination, and the scarcity of jobs and industry on and near reservations. In fact, many American Indians move to cities in search of better schooling, improved housing, and higher-paying jobs. Despite the fact that many American Indians want to obtain an education, few are prepared to do so. According to one estimate, in 2013 only about half of the 14, 217 American Indian students who took the ACT met none of its four college readiness benchmarks. This compared to just 31 percent of students overall. Only about 10 percent of American Indian students met all four, compared to 26 percent of the general population.[23]

Further, high school graduation rates continue to improve, the national average in 2009-2010 was 78.2 percent, according to the National Center for Educational Statistics. However, American Indian and Alaska Native students have the second lowest high school graduation rate of any racial or ethnic group; they are only slightly higher than African Americans at 69 percent compared to 66 percent for African Americans. For Native

INSULTS, MASCOTS, AND NATIVE AMERICANS IN SPORTS

There is little question that racism affects all aspects of American society. On one hand, Americans seem willing to avoid the use of derogatory terms because they evoke such a strong and offensive reaction on the part of the targeted group. Americans have also become more sensitive to racial slights in sports and advertising, where depictions of African Americans and Hispanics that, in the past, would seem funny or entertaining, are now no longer considered. However, the same sensitivity seems lacking for Native Americans.

For example, would anyone ever consider naming a sports team the Frito Banditos or the Little Black Sambos? Would any team consider using these characters as mascots? It does not seem likely. Many colleges and universities as well as professional sports teams frequently use Native American terms to do just that. This is particularly true in professional baseball and football. Examples include the Cleveland Indians and the Atlanta Braves, who are famous for their tomahawk chop to rally the team. Professional football uses Native American logos for the Kansas City Chiefs and the Washington Redskins.

It would be unconceivable to purposely insult the racial and religious values of African Americans, Hispanics, or even women. However, according to the National Coalition on Racism in Sports and Media, very little progress has been made to educate teams, fans, coaches, and the general public about the offensive nature Native American logos and mascots present. The public has historically been conditioned by the sports industry, educational institutions and the media to trivialize indigenous culture as common and harmless entertainment. These groups somehow fail to recognize that using Native American names and depictions to identify teams, particularly caricatures, shows a lack of respect for the history of Native Americans and diminishes the importance of certain social positions, such as the tribal leader or "chief."

Apparently this inconsistency is being noticed as at least six universities have changed their logos and/or mascots of the university athletic program, including the University of Illinois. Perhaps Americans are realizing that the historical insensitivity towards Native Americans has to stop and that they should be treated like other minority groups in this country.

American students, there are other factors at play. According to Theresa Pouley, the chief judge of the Tulalip Tribal Court in Washington, "Their substance abuse rates are higher. They're twice as likely as any other race to die before the age of 24. They have two times the reate of abuse and neglect."[24] According to the National Center for Education Statistics, Native American students comprise less than 1 percent of students in the U.S. public school system, and less than one-third of Native American students earned a diploma in 2012.[25]

While urban areas provide better opportunities for some evidenced by the lower unemployment rates for Native Americans who live in cities compared to those on the reservation, moving to these locations often entails other costs. Native Americans in cities do not always improve their standard of living because housing, food, clothing, and health care are more expensive in urban areas.[26]

CASINO GAMBLING

One area that has served as a respite for some tribal members has been the increase of gambling casinos on reservations. For many tribes, commercial gambling is the only viable source of employment and revenue. Under the 1988 Gaming Regulatory Act, states must negotiate gambling agreements with reservations and cannot prohibit any gambling already allowed under state law. In 2000, 201 tribes in over 21 states were operating a variety of gambling operations, such as Blackjack, roulette tables, sports betting, slot machines, and high stakes bingo. In 2013, according to the National Indian Gaming Commission, about 250 tribes and villages operated casinos. The booming gambling industry netted almost $11 billion in 2000, $22 billion in 2006, and $28 billion in 2013.[27]

While some tribes have done well, some recent research has found that casino revenue can actually increase the poverty of some tribal members. While many of the factors discussed earlier play a role in steady employment, such as poor health—Native Americans have the highest rates of any group of obesity and diabetes and more than 14 percent of Native Americans are in poor health according to the Department of Health and Human Services, compared with 10 percent of the general population. Added to the problem is the lack of access to adequate medical care—27 percent of Native Americans under the age of 65 lack health insurance compared to 17 percent for non-Native Americans, and the realities of steady employment become apparent. However, even those tribes that have been successful with casino gambling may be inadvertently contributing to the problem. As the casinos have become more successful, whereby tribal members receive their share of the profits, the incentive to find steady employment decreases. This problem becomes readily apparent if the profits received are not sufficient to live on.

A few successful casinos have had staggering success like the 493 members of the Connecticut Mashantucket Pequot Indians, whose Foxwoods Resort Casino provides generous benefits to anyone who can establish that he or she is at least 1/16 Pequot. In fact, the impact of the Pequot casino extends far beyond individual tribal members. The casino is now one of the largest taxpayers in the state and also one of its largest employers.[28] The tribe has also donated money to a variety of charities and paid for many improvements in the state's infrastructure, such as roads leading to the casino and being indirectly responsible for a host of ancillary industries surrounding the area.

In other states, Native American casinos have contributed money to create childcare programs, housing, roads, scholarships, health clinics, and water systems for their people. Revenues also fund tribal law enforcement, fire fighting, and other services.

While the success of casinos owned by Native Americans seems readily apparent, the National Indian Gaming Association states that the tribes that make substantial profits from gambling amounts to less than one percent of total Native Americans. The more typical picture is of moderately successful gambling operations associated with tribes whose social and economic needs are overwhelming.[29]

The main criticism against Indian casinos is the concern that organized crime will infiltrate the industry, and that casinos will become a magnet for other criminal activities. While only limited research exists on a direct relationship between Indian gaming and criminal justice on reservations, limited evidence exists that shows the relationship between Indian gaming and organized crime.[30]

Allegations of corruption, money laundering and loan sharking have been made against various tribes. For example, Asian-based organized crime has been linked to loan sharking and other forms of exploitation of Asian customers at the Mohegan Sun and Foxwoods Casinos in Connecticut.[31] An added problem, critics point out, is that Indian casinos are self-regulated and the supervision offered by the National Indian Gaming Commission, the Internal Revenue Service, and other regulatory agencies is limited due to funding and jurisdictional issues.[32] Despite these claims, no definitive evidence exists of a connection between Indian gaming and organized crime.[33]

Despite the public's perception that Native American casinos earn huge profits, only a few tribes see substantial rewards for their efforts.

What is significant about the research linking Native American gaming and crime on reservations relates to the delay between the startup of a tribally owned casino and a large increase in crime and gambling in counties near an Indian casino.[34]

EDUCATIONAL ACHIEVEMENT

As it has been with the rest of their lives, education for Native Americans has been in the control of the federal and state governments. Unfortunately, the lack of understanding of the social, cultural, political, and economic differences between Native Americans and other groups has resulted in poor management of Native American children's educational experiences. Part of the problem has been funding; Indian education programs are typically ignored or underfunded. Additionally, there are few Native American teachers, and curriculum decisions do not take into account the unique position of Native American students. As with the way Whites have always treated this group, U.S. educational policies appear to reflect the insistence that Native Americans should assimilate and ignore the celebration of their heritage. It is not surprising that Native American students have the highest dropout rate of any racial or ethnic group. This comes at a time when the national graduation rate for public schools is at an all-time high of 74.7 percent. In a 2013 report titled *Second Chances: Turning Dropouts into Graduates*, there has been considerable success in addressing dropout rates since 2000. In fact, from 2000 to 2010, the graduation rates for African Americans increased more than 16 percent, while for Hispanic/Latino students, it increased 13 percent. The only group that did not narrow the gap with White students were Native Americans. Even today, Native Americans have the lowest high school graduation rates of any group, 46 percent. The next lowest group are Hispanics/Latinos at 63 percent.[35]

The problems associated with the educational achievement of Native Americans extend beyond elementary and high school. College graduation rates for Native Americans are also low. According to a recent report by the Lumina Foundation, while about 40 percent of working Americans hold a college degree, African Americans, Hispanic/Latinos, and Native Americans lag far behind that figure. In their report, *A Stronger Nation Through Higher Education*, Lumina Foundation officials note that only about 28 percent of African Americans, 23 percent of Native Americans and 20 percent of Hispanics/Latinos have a college degree. Of further note is the fact that enrollments for African Americans and Native Americans have decreased and enrollments for Hispanics/Latinos have remained stagnant. Only Asian Americans have exceeded Whites in the percentage of people with a college degree.[36] In response to this problem, federal legislation was enacted to create institutions that recognize the importance of Native American culture. In 1968 the Navajo Nation created the first tribally controlled college, now called Diné College. Other tribal colleges quickly developed. Most of these tribal colleges began as two-year institutions and have open admissions policies.

HEALTHCARE

From the beginning of their interactions with Whites, Native Americans have been susceptible to disease and illness. In the early part of the 20th century, there were a number of epidemics, particularly tuberculosis that killed thousands of American Indians. By the end of the 20th century, the health of Native Americans improved due to increased standard of living and an increase in immunizations. While physical diseases such as measles and diphtheria were brought under control, social problems have gripped this population. Alcoholism, domestic violence, and mental disorders have plagued Native Americans, particularly in the 1980s and 1990s.[37]

For instance, in the late 1980s, the **Indian Health Service**, a division of the Public Health Service, reported that the number of deaths of Native Americans due to alcoholism was four times greater than what was reported for the general population. Additionally, suicide rates among Native Americans were 77 percent higher than the national average. More recently, diabetes and HIV have become prominent issues for Native Americans.

In the mid-1990s, the Indian Health Service reported that Native Americans were about three times more likely to be diagnosed with diabetes than Whites. Healthcare is provided by the Indian Health Service, which itself is a division of the Department of Health and Human Services.

Today, according to the Indian Health Service, about 20 percent of American Indians and Alaska Natives have two or more chronic health problems, including obesity, diabetes, smoking, and alcoholism. American Indians and Alaska Natives have an infant death rate that is 60 percent higher than the rate for Whites and in 2012, the tuberculosis rate for American Indians was more than six times the rate for Whites.[38] While these health problems are primarily related to lifestyle, meaning they can be effectively remedied, the challenge is that most American Indians and Alaska Natives have limited or no access to health care. According to the Indian Health Service, more than 40 percent of American Indians have no access to medical care.[39]

It is important to note that not all Indian Health Services facilities meet the health-care needs of Native Americans. Moreover, not all reservations or communities have medical clinics or hospitals and the ones that exist are often small with outdated equipment.[40]

Part of the problem stems from a lack of funding. Because of the poor salaries and inadequate equipment, there is a shortage of doctors, nurses, and pharmacists in clinic reservations which affects the quality and continuity of healthcare for Native Americans. For example, according to a report by the United States Commission on Civil Rights, the mental health challenges facing Native Americans, including suicide, depression and other needs, are considerable. This calls for the need for mental health professionals to treat such conditions. However, Native Americans have approximately 101 mental health professionals per 100,000 people, compared to 173 per 100,000 people for Whites.[41]

One promising note is President Obama's new proposed budget for fiscal year 2017. This $6.6 billion budget attempts to address many of the long-standing problems facing Native Americans. Included in this budget are initiatives to address the suicide rates of Native Americans, along with the Domestic Violence Prevention Initiative. This $4 million effort attempts to target one of the most looming challenges among Native Americans. Additionally, $360 million of this budget targets substance abuse, behavioral and mental health issues, along with the creation of a Tribal Crisis Response Fund, which will provide communities with staff and technical assistance in the aftermath of a crisis event, such as a mass school shooting, high rates of alcohol-related deaths or increased rates of suicides.[42]

As it relates to healthcare, substantial increases are proposed to address the lack of adequate facilities and equipment, along with improved sanitation facilities to address chronic health problems in communities without adequate sanitation, along with the augmentation of the Purchase/Referred Care program, which is designed to provide essential healthcare services to tribal members. In all, this ambitious effort attempts to address many of the challenges Native Americans currently face.[43]

NATIVE AMERICANS AND THE CRIMINAL JUSTICE SYSTEM

One of the more intriguing aspects about Native Americans relates to the study of crime. While there is data collected on victims, arrests, crimes known to the police, and information on inmates, one must remember that these individuals are typically not those who live on reservations. Rather, they are Native Americans and Alaska Natives who live off the reservation. This may seem like a subtle difference, but crime reporting and the administration of justice on tribal lands is a different proposition than what occurs in U.S. cities and towns. While data is collected on crime that occurs on tribal land, and while the FBI does get involved in criminal cases on reservations, historically, accurate data has been difficult to come by.

Fortunately, in 2010, the Tribal Law and Order Act requires the Bureau of Justice Statistics to create a tribal data collection system and to support tribal participation in national records. The law requires the director to consult with Indian tribes to determine the best ways of collecting the data, who then must report to Congress about what is known about tribal crime. In one of the first technical reports, published in July 2015, the Bureau of Justice Statistics found that at midyear 2014, a total of 566 tribes in the 48 contiguous states and in Alaska participated in the project. The tribes, in turn, were eligible for funding and services from the Bureau of Indian Affairs.

The tribal justice system in Indian country varies across tribal nations and regions. The authority to prosecute, to make arrests, and other jurisdictional matters, along with whether or not the reservation is a federally recognized one, if there exist tribal communities and identified trust lands, all contribute to how a crime is investigated and prosecuted. What also matters is the type of crime committed, whether the offender or the victims is a tribal member, and the state in which the offense occurred. Because federally recognized tribes are sovereign, crimes committed in Indian country are often subject to concurrent jurisdictions among multiple agencies.[44]

In response to the new legislation and in collaboration with the Urban Institute, the Bureau of Justice Statistics also produced a report in 2014 using some of the data collected in an effort to examine crimes in the federal system. This report showed that the FBI investigated about half of the 6,137 Indian country suspects on various incidents referred to the U.S. Attorney's office from 2009 to 2011. The number of suspects in such cases increase from 1,940 to 2,220 between 2009 and 2011. Additionally, the number of defendants in 48 federal district courts increased from 1,235 in 2009 to 1,395 in 2011. These figures suggest that the cooperation between Tribes and the federal authorities has improved since the tribes were willing to have an increased number of cases resolved in federal court and not in tribal ones.[45]

Also promising were the number of tribal law enforcement agencies that were willing to submit crime information to the FBI for the purposes of crime data analysis. According to the Department of Justice, since 2009 the number of tribal law enforcmeent agencies with idenfitiable crime data increased from 12 agencies in 2008 to 158 in 2012. These agencies reported that about 28,230 violent and property crimes occurred on tribal lands in 2013. To understand the significance of this development, prior to 2008 most of the reports from tribal law enforcment agencise could not be distinguished by type of crime, whichi also limited agencies' ability to apply for federal funding. In 2013, 88 percent of violent crimes and 83 percent of property crimes reported by tribal law enforcement agencies could be traced back to the originatl reservation, up from 13 percent in 2008.[46]

An important element of tribal self-government is jurisdiction over incidents that take place on reservations. For instance, there are currently separate laws governing the prosecution of Native American and non-Native American offenders for crimes that take place on reservations. Another area of concern involves the lack of attention paid to the victimization of Native Americans. As the data show, the rates of violent crime against Native Americans is substantially higher than for other minority groups. A third area of concern relates to the type and frequency of crimes committed by Native Americans. Clearly, crime appears to have become a consistent feature of social life for Native Americans.

CRIME RATES

There is substantially less information regarding Native Americans and crime compared to African Americans and Hispanics. In a report issued by the U.S. Department of Justice in 1997, the homicide rate for Native American males was almost three times higher than those for White males. Between 1992 and 1996, while the rest of the country was experiencing a decline in violent crime, the Native American population witnessed a dramatic increase in violent crime. According to the Bureau of Justice Statistics, the annual average violent crime rate among Native Americans was twice as high as that of Blacks (50 per 1,000 persons) and 2.5 times higher than that for Whites (41 per 1,000 persons) and 4.5 times than that for Asians (22 per 1,000 persons).[47]

In 2014, according to the Uniform Crime Reports, American Indians and Alaskan natives committed 135,599 of the estimated 8,730,665 arrests, about 1 percent of the total non-reservation arrests. The types of arrests included those for assault (17,990) liquor law violations (9,539), larcenies (15,869) and public drunkenness 6,952 were the most common.[48] These crimes relate to alcohol, which will be discussed in a section later in the chapter.

VICTIMIZATION

According to information collected by the Bureau of Justice Statistics (BJS), during the 1990s, American Indians were likely to experience violent crimes at more than twice the rate of all other U.S. residents. The BJS reported that between 1992 and 1996 the average annual rate of violent victimizations among Indians (including Alaska Natives and Aleuts) was 124 per 1,000 residents aged 12 years old and older, compared to 61 violent victimizations per 1,000 Blacks, 49 per 1,000 Whites, and 29 per 1,000 Asians.[49]

More recently, a BJS report on Native American crime between 1992 and 2002 found that the violent crime rate in every age group below 35 was significantly higher for Native Americans than for all persons. The report also found that among Native Americans age 25 to 34, the rate of violent crime victimization was more than 2.5 times the rate for all persons the same age. Rates of violent victimization for both males and females were higher for Native Americans than for all races. Further, the rate of violent victimization among Native American women was more than double that among all women.[50] According to a study by the Bureau of Justice Statistics, the most recent data available on victimization rates for Native Americans, with regard to age, in all age groups Native Americans had higher rates of violent crime victimization than other groups. The rate was highest at 155 per 1,000 people for Native Americans 18 to 24, compared to the highest rate in the 12 to 17 age group for all races (94 per 1,000). Among the elderly, Native Americans age 55 or older had a violent crime rate that was three times that for all races (22 per 1,000 compared to 8 per 1,000).[51]

As previously mentioned, in terms of the race of the offender and the relationship with the victim, Native Americans who were victims of violent crime were more likely to be victimized by a stranger than an intimate partner. Strangers committed 42 percent of the violent crimes against Native Americans from 1992-2001, while an acquaintance committed about 1/3 of all violence against Native Americans. Only about 20 percent of the victimizations of Native Americans came as a result of a relationship between the victim and the offender.[52]

With regard to race, crime against Native Americans also tends to be interracial, whereas other forms of victimization with other races tends to be intraracial. Nearly 88 percent of the victimizations against Native Americans were committed by White or African American offenders. Victims stated that Asians and other Native Americans were responsible for only13 percent of violent acts.

The problems relating to criminal behavior by Native Americans is not episodic; rather, it reflects the chronic condition many members of this population experience. For example, the recidivism rate of Native Americans was similar to those for all offenders, whether for a new arrest, conviction, or sentence to prison. An estimated 60 percent of Native Americans are arrested for a new crime, a felony or a serious misdemeanor within three years of their release from state prison. Related to this is the fact that over a third of Native Americans released from prison were returned to prison due to a parole or probation violation.[53]

THE ROLE OF ALCOHOL AND NATIVE AMERICAN CRIME

Alcohol use among Native Americans is not a recent development. Historically its use was limited to ceremonies and religious rituals.[54] Some tribes, for example, believed that drunkenness brought a purification of one's mind and heart which would also produce rain for crops.[55] However, the impact of alcohol abuse among Native Americans can be seen in physical diseases. One study found that alcoholism kills Native Americans at a rate five times higher than other Americans. It also kills people between the ages of 25 to 35 at ten times the rate of other young adults.[56] The relationship between alcohol consumption and violence is particularly noteworthy among Native Americans. Crimes such as rape, homicide, and suicide occur with a much higher frequency among this segment of the population than other segments. Alcohol is also involved in 75 percent of all fatal accidents, a number three times higher than non-Native Americans.[57]

Unfortunately, there is no single explanation for alcohol abuse among Native Americans. One of the most prevalent theories is due to the loss of their culture. That is, in an attempt to deal with the psychological problems relating to being isolated by society and unable to achieve their goals, many Native Americans use alcohol to relieve feelings of anxiety and depression. The living conditions for many Native Americans also contribute to the need for self-medication through alcohol.

On the other hand, there are experts who contend that Native Americans do not live in a cultural vacuum. That is, every culture undergoes changes and even though Native Americans might have lost their culture over generations of time, it could also be the case that as they assimilate and move to cities, their identification with American culture can ease the stress they are experiencing because they have some type of cultural mooring.[58] This school of thought argues that alcohol abuse is more of a function of poor choices than as a coping mechanism to the loss of one's culture.

According to some researchers, the government's response to alcohol abuse among Native Americans has been minimal despite the physical and social risks related to it. The government often criminalizes the byproduct behavior that comes as a result of alcohol abuse, such as homelessness, public intoxication, and liquor law violations.[59] Unfortunately, the solution then becomes arresting and incarcerating people for these symptomatic behaviors instead of addressing the larger issue of alcoholism and its causes.

QUESTIONING THE RELATIONSHIP BETWEEN NATIVE AMERICANS AND CRIME STATISTICS

A number of researchers question the official statistics regarding Native American crime. In fact, some go so far as to question whether Native Americans are actually overrepresented in the crime data. One group of scholars is critical of a widely cited report published by the Bureau of Justice Statistics (BJS) entitled *American Indians and Crime*. This report contends that American Indians over the age of twelve are twice as likely to be victims of violent crime than are members of all other racial and ethnic categories combined. Critics of this report contend that the actual rates of arrests for violence among American Indian youth are the same as those for White youth, and the murder rates of Indian people has remained constant for the last twenty years. Further, one must consider that American Indian victims of violent crime are most likely attacked by non-Indian offenders—which makes the prosecution of crimes against American Indians difficult, especially if it occurs on Indian land. Finally, critics of the BJS report argue that the highest rates of violence occur in urban settings, not on reservations. Nevertheless, the perception that Native Americans perpetuate a higher proportion of crime is a common assertion in the media.[60]

Some experts even believe that federal surveys may not be the most effective tool to measure crime among Native Americans on reservations due to a host of logistical and methodological problems. For instance, the number of crimes known among Native Americans and the size of the population on the reservation used to calculate arrest rates can produce exaggerated crime estimates.[61] This can easily create the impression that crime is more common, and a more serious problem, on reservations than in other places.

In an attempt to remedy the methodological problems stemming from using aggregated data, particularly with small populations, an in-depth analysis of a decade of arrest data for one tribe on one reservation was conducted by a team of researchers. The findings showed that violent and non-violent juvenile crime was far below the estimates in the BJS report. They also showed that juvenile crime in this community, like many communities across the country, was the result of a small group of repeat offenders.[62]

NATIVE AMERICANS AND THE POLICE

Perhaps the most fascinating, and complicated issue surrounding Native Americans relates to the jurisdiction and composition of tribal courts. When Congress passed Public Law 280 (PL 280) in 1953, criminal and civil jurisdiction over tribal lands was transferred to local governments. This gave local law enforcement the authority over Indian communities. In places where PL 280 did not apply, either the Bureau of Indian Affairs or the tribal councils were to provide law enforcement officers.[63]

As was mentioned, these varying jurisdictional boundaries present problems related to the prosecution of offenders depending on whether the person is a Native American, whether the crime took place on Indian land, and whether or not local law enforcement, tribal councils, or the Bureau of Indian Affairs, has authority over that particular area. Problems emerge, for example, when a non–Native American commits a crime on Indian land. In those situations, a criminal act normally prosecuted by state and local governments is considered an Indian issue, rendering no criminal charges against the offender. When a Native American commits a crime on Indian land and is convicted by tribal courts, the Indian Civil Rights Act of 1968 usually applies, which means tribal criminal sentences can last no more than one year in custody and a $5,000 fine, regardless of the crime.[64] Clearly both sets of circumstances are not in the interest of justice nor do they send the appropriate message about accountability of offenders' behavior.

According to the National Congress of American Indians, law enforcement on tribal lands is difficult to say the least. Police in Indian Country not only have jurisdictional challenges, meaning they must answer to multiple authorities, they patrol some of the most desolate parts of the country, often without resources or backup. For instance, there are only 2,380 Bureau of Indian Affairs and tribal uniformed officers available to serve millions of Native Americans covering over 56 million square miles. It is estimated that in order to provide a minimum of coverage to this area, at least 4,290 officers are needed. Compared to officers in non-Indian communities, tribal lands have half the number of officers per 1,000 residents.

Law enforcement authority varies by the location of where the crime was committed, whether or not the victim and/or the offender are tribal members, and the nature of the crime, whether it a felony or a misdemeanor was committed. Officers who have jurisdiction on reservations include the following:

> *Tribal Security Officers.* These are employed by the tribe and have security-related duties. At times they are given the ability to enforce tribal law and order codes by the tribal government, but they do not have arrest powers.
>
> *Tribal Police Officers* are also employed by tribal governments but these officers have arrest powers over tribal members committing violations of tribal law and other codes committed on reservations. Such officers are trained at a formal police academy.
>
> *Federally Deputized Police Officers.* These officers present a type of hybrid police presence in that they are hired by the tribal governments but are also deputized by and work for federal agencies, such as the Bureau of Indian Affairs and Special Law Enforcement Commissions. They are able to enforce federal laws both on and off the reservation and can arrest non-Indians and Indians for violation of federal laws.[65]

THE ADMINISTRATION OF JUSTICE: TRIBAL COURTS

There are also differences in philosophy between tribal courts and American criminal courts. Over the past two hundred years, the federal government has established a pattern of taking over the jurisdiction of an increasing number of crimes, removing them from tribal authority, and giving itself the power to punish offenders. This contradicts the parameters of treatises signed by the federal government giving Native tribes the right to have their own separate system of justice.[66] In 1953, Congress passed Public Law 280, without tribal consent, which offered states the opportunity to assume jurisdiction over reservations within their borders. This law stipulates that law enforcement for Native reservations is typically handled by state police and county or state courts rather than through the tribe. This law has created concern that courts are treating Native people and whites unequally.[67]

As sovereign entities, Native tribes have the right to organize and maintain their own laws and law enforcement agencies; however, not every tribe in the United States has the funding for their own tribal court or police system. Essentially, a Tribal Court is established for American Indian and Alaska Native tribes for resolving civil, criminal, and other legal matters. There is significant variation in the types of tribal courts and how they apply tribal laws. Some are like Non-Indian courts, where court procedures are used, while others use traditional Native means of solving disputes.

Finally, there are also a number of Courts of Indian Offenses. These are established by the Bureau of Indian Affairs for those tribes who do not have their own tribal courts. In 2012, 39 tribes of the 109 federally recognized tribes in California either have a tribal court or access to one through a tribal coalition. The number of tribal courts in California has more than doubled since 2002, from 9 to 22.[68]

NATIVE AMERICANS AND THE CORRECTIONAL SYSTEM

According to the Bureau of Justice Statistics, in 2014 there were an estimated 2,380 inmates confined in 79 Indian country jails at midyear 2014, a 4 percent increase from 2013. The average number of inmates per facility increased from 26 to 30 in 2014. Further, the average length of stay in an Indian country facility was about six days. About 30 percent of the inmates in Indian country jails were confined for violent offenses, a substantial decrease from 2007. Of the 30 percent confined for violence, about 12 percent were inmates for domestic violence and another 10 percent for simple assault. About 20 percent were held for public intoxication in 2014. Inmates held for DUI declined by half between 2000 and 2014. Like crime across the country, there has been a decrease in offending by Native Americans on reservations as well.[69]

SUMMARY

This chapter examined the history of Native Americans in this country as well as the ways in which they become involved in the criminal justice system. The position of Native Americans is rather unique in that while they are supposed to have a separate system of justice to address problems relating to crime, increasingly, the federal government is encroaching upon tribal authority to handle a variety of tasks. We have also seen that in many ways Native Americans are a forgotten people. Historically, the U.S. seemed to have a sense of entitlement when it came to taking land that belonged to Native Americans. Social progress was seen as more important than preserving the heritage and authority of Native Americans. Even when treaties were signed that stipulated the rights and privileges of Native Americans, Whites historically ignored the agreements and used force when Native Americans refused to capitulate.

Control over Native Americans has historically fallen to the federal government who has created the Bureau of Indian Affairs to regulate most of the aspects of life on and off the reservation. Other agencies, such as the Department of Health and Human Services, the Public Health Service, and the Indian Health Service, all attempt to address the many issues surrounding Native Americans.

While Native Americans have made an effort to assimilate, their experiences have resulted in a number of social problems. Many Native Americans still lag behind Whites economically and educationally. There are higher dropout rates for Native Americans than other minority groups, fewer who graduate from college, and even fewer in professional careers. Moreover, a large percentage of Native Americans live at or below the poverty level. Native Americans also suffer from a variety of health problems, including tuberculosis, alcoholism, mental illness and other disorders.

Many of these limitation and problems result in a significant involvement with the criminal justice system, either as victims or as offenders. As was mentioned, jurisdictional problems confuse the issues of justice. Thus, while not a large segment of the population in terms of victimization or as offenders, like their African American and Hispanic counterparts, they are overrepresented in the crime statistics.

YOU MAKE THE CALL

NATIVE AMERICAN INMATE RITUALS

Consider the following scenario. Debate the pros and cons of all options and decide what you would do.

Imagine you are the Cultural Diversity Officer with the federal Bureau of Prisons. Part of your responsibilities center around ensuring that correctional institutions remain sensitive to the cultural and religious needs of inmates. You receive a complaint from a Native American inmate in a federal correctional institution who states that his religious beliefs are being denied. This particular inmate, along with several other Native Americans in the institution, practice what is known as the Pipe Religion. Pipe Religion revolves around the use of the Sacred Pipe in seven specific rituals, in particular, the sweat lodge ceremony, which is the traditional way of cleansing body, mind, and spirit. By sweat and prayer, Native Americans cleanse their bodies of toxins, their minds of negativities, heighten their spirits, and come into a balanced relationship with themselves, the earth, and everything that surrounds them.

Although other correctional facilities provide a sweat lodge for Indian inmates, the prisoners are restricted as to when and how long the sweat lodges can be used. As a result, Sacred Pipe ceremonies—that normally span several days—cannot be performed.

Many correctional officials and other experts hold the position that freedom of religion is inferior to the state's interest in maintaining security and order within the prison.

Questions

1. How do you respond to the inmate's complaint? Do you allow the religious practice or do you argue that inmates lose some of their constitutional protections once they are convicted?
2. What liability does the institution bear if someone becomes ill or injured during the course of one of these rituals?
3. Should taxpayer money be used to allow inmates to practice their religion?
4. Are correctional officials as well as the public at greater physical risk by denying inmates the opportunity to practice their religion?

KEY TERMS

Battle at Little Big Horn
Battle at Wounded Knee
Bureau of Indian Affairs
Dawes Act
Fort Laramie Treaty
Ghost Dance religion

Indian Claims Commission
Indian Health Service
Indian Removal Act 1830
Red Power Movement
Termination Act
Tribal courts

DISCUSSION QUESTIONS

1. What role, if any, does casino gambling have on improving the lives of Native Americans? Is it really a solution to the problems relating to poverty and unemployment that is characteristic of Native Americans?
2. In the recent era of celebrating individual differences and cultures, why do you think the federal government has forced Native Americans to assimilate into mainstream American culture? What implications do you think this has on the preservation of Native American culture?
3. Should there be a separate system of justice for Native American tribes or should the federal government retain authority to hear all cases? Should there be a distinction between crimes committed on reservations compared to those outside those areas?
4. Do you think Native Americans should have their own educational system, such as tribal colleges? Why or why not?
5. Should Native Americans who commit crimes on reservations be judged differently than those off the reservation? Why or why not?
6. What obligation, if any, should the federal government have to improve the lives of Native Americans on reservations? Defend your position one way or the other.

FOR FURTHER READING

Brown, D. *Bury My Heart at Wounded Knee*. New York: Holt, Rinehart and Winston, 1971.

Nagel, J. *American Indian Ethnic Renewal: Red Power and the Resurgence of Identity and Culture*. New York: Oxford University Press, 1996.

Nielsen, M. O., and R. A. Silverman, eds. *Native Americans, Crime and Justice*. Boulder, CO: Westview Press, 1996. 58–74.

Ross, Luana. *Inventing the Savage: The Social Construction of Native American Criminality*. Austin: University of Texas Press, 1998.

NOTES

1. R. Strickland, "The Eagle's Empire: Sovereignty, Survival, and Self-Governance in Native American Law and Constitutionality," in R. Thorton, ed., *Studying Native Americans: Problems and Prospects* (Madison, WI: University of Wisconsin Press, 1998), 247–70.

2. Ibid.

3. Ibid.

4. R. Thorton, "Demographic Antecedents of the 1890 Ghost Dance," *American Sociological Review* 46 (Feb. 1981): 88–96.

5. B. Duran, E. Duran, and M. Yellow Horse Braveheart. "Native Americans and the Trauma of History," in Thorton, *Studying Native Americans*, 60–78.

6. Ibid.

7. Ibid.

8. Henry C. Dennis, *The American Indian 1492–1970: A Chronology and Fact Book* (Dobbs Ferry, NY: Oceana, 1971).

9. Indian Land Allotment Foundation, *General Allotment Act*. Available online at https://www.iltf.org/resources/land-tenure-history/allotment.

10. Native Voices, "President Roosevelt Signs the Indian Reorganization Act." Available online at https://www.nlm.nih.gov/nativevoices/timeline/452.html.

11. Ibid.

12. Judith Nies, *Native American History: A Chronology of the Vast Achievements of a Culture and Their Links to World Events* (New York: Ballantine Books, 1996), 357.

13. W. Washburn, "A Fifty-Year Perspective on the Indian Reorganization Act," *American Anthropologist* 86 (1984): 279–89.

14. J. Nagel, *American Indian Ethnic Renewal*; D. Drabelle, "The Trade of the Tribes," *Washington Post National Weekly Edition* 24 (September 8, 1997): 34.

15. S. W. Perry, *Tribal Crime Data Collection Activities*, U.S. Department of Justice, Office of Justice Programs (Washington, DC: Bureau of Justice Statistics, 2015). Available at https://www.bjs.gov/index.cfm?ty=pbdetail&iid=5323.

16. United States Bureau of the Census, "Resident Population Estimates of the United States," (Washington, DC: U.S. Government Printing Office, 2000).

17. Jens Manuel Krogstad, "One in Four Native Americans and Alaska Natives are Living in Poverty," Pew Research Center, June 13, 2014, available at http://www.pewresearch.org/fact-tank/2014/06/13/1-in-4-native-Americans-and-alaska-natives-are-living-in-poverty/

18. Luana Ross, *Inventing the Savage: The Social Construction of Native American Criminality* (Austin: University of Texas Press, 1998), 16–19.

19. U.S. Department of Commerce, 2012.

20. Krogstad, *One in Four Native Americans*.
21. U.S. Department of the Interior, 2013 American Indian Population and Labor Force Report (Washington, DC, 2012), 11, https://www.bia.gov/cs/groups/public/documents/text/idc1-024782.pdf
22. Krogstad, *One in Four Native Americans*.
23. A. Bidwell, "Are American Indian Students the Least Prepared for College?" *U.S. News and World Report*, March 13, 2014, available at https://www.usnews.com/news/blogs/data-mine/2014/03/13/are-American-indian-students-the-least-prepared-for-college
24. Ibid.
25. K. Sheehy, "Graduation Rates Dropping Among Native American Students," *U.S. News and World Report*, June 6, 2013, available at https://www.usnews.com/education/high-schools/articles/2013/06/06/graduation-rates-dropping-among-native-American-students
26. Ibid.
27. "Of Slots and Sloth: How Cash Casinos Make Native Americans Poorer," *The Economist*, January 17, 2015, available at http://www.economist.com/news/united-states/21639547-how-cash-casinos-makes-native-Americans-poorer-slots-and-sloth
28. F. Carstensen, *Economic Impact of the Mashantucket Pequot Tribal Nation Operations in Connecticut* (Storrs, CT: Connecticut Center for Economic Analysis, 2000).
29. Ibid.
30. M. Rezendes, "Gambling and Crime," *CitizenLink*, December 27, 2000. Available at http://www.family.org; J. Unseem, "The Big Gamble: Have American Indians Found their New Buffalo?" *Fortune*, October 2, 2000.
31. M. Burgard, and R. Green, "More Arrests in Loan Scheme: Casino Patrons Are Victimized," *Hartford Courant*, March 13, 2002.
32. Rezendes, "Gambling and Crime."
33. H. M. Buffalo, "Indian Gaming Success in the North," in *Oklahoma Supreme Court Sovereignty Symposium 2002: Language and the Law* (Oklahoma City, OK: Supreme Court of Oklahoma, 2002), III 22-III, 40.; G. A. Fine, *Review of Indian Gaming Crimes*, Office of Inspector General, Report Number 1-2-1-06, July 3, 2001.
34. W. N. Evans, and J. H. Topeleski, "The Social and Economic Impact of Native American Casinos," National Bureau of Economic Research Working Paper 9198, 2002. Available at http://wnetc.mcc.ac.uk/WoPEc/data/Papers/nbrnberwo9198.html
35. Diplomas Count, *Second Chances: Turning Dropouts into Graduates*, 2013. Available at http://www.edweek.org/media/diplomascount2013_release.pdf
36. Lumina Foundation, *A Stronger Nation Through Higher Education*, 2015. Available at http://www.luminafoundation.org/report/main-narrative.html
37. L. Gould, "Alcoholism, Colonialism, and Crime," in *Native Americans and the Criminal Justice System*, ed. J. I. Ross and L. Gould (Boulder, CO: Paradigm Publishing, 2006), 87–102.
38. Bureau of Indian Affairs, Indian Health Services. *Minority Health*. Available at http://minorityhealth.hhs.gov/omh/browse.aspx?lvl=3&lvlid=62
39. U.S. Department of Health and Human Services, Office on Women's Health. *American Indians/Alaska Natives*, July 16, 2012, available at http://www.womenshealth.gov/minority-health/American-indians/
40. R. Garcia Cano, "Watchdog: Staff Issues Affect Care at Reservation Hospitals," Associate Press, October 7, 2016. Available at http://bigstory.ap.org/article/68b5a09034c24c9a8a29fc4c46773889/watchdog-staff-issues-affect-care-reservation-hospitals

41. United States Commission on Civil Rights, *Broken Promises: Evaluating the Native American Healthcare System*, 2012. Available online at https://www.law.umaryland.edu/marshall/usccr/documents/cr122004024431draft.pdf

42. Indian Health Service, "Proposed Budget for 2017 for Indian Health Service Expands Quality Care, Behavioral Health." Available online at https://www.ihs.gov/newsroom/ihs-blog/march2016/proposed-budget-for-2017-for-indian-health-service-expands-quality-care-behavioral-health//

43. Ibid.

44. Ibid.

45. Ibid.

46. Ibid.

47. L. Greenfield and S. K. Smith, *American Indians and Crime*, 1999, U.S. Department of Justice, Office of Justice Programs, Bureau of Justice Statistics., Available at *https://www.bjs.gov/content/pub/pdf/aic.pdf* /

48. U.S. Department of Justice, Federal Bureau of Investigation. 2014. Crime in the United States, Table 43. Available at https://ucr.fbi.gov/crime-in-the-u.s/2014/crime-in-the-u.s.-2014/tables/table-43.

49. Greenfield and Smith, *American Indians and Crime.*

50. Perry, *A BJS Statistical Profile, 1992–2002: American Indians and Crime.*

51. Ibid.

52. Ibid.

53. *Sourcebook of Criminal Justice Statistics*, 2004.

54. R. Snake, G. Hawkins, and S. LaBoueff, *Report on Alcohol and Drug Abuse: Final Report to the American Indian Policy Review Commission* (Washington, DC: U.S. Government Printing Office, 1976).

55. J. H. Parry, "Spanish Indian Policy in Colonial America: The Ordering of Society," in *Three American Empires*, ed. J. J. TePaske (Durham, NC: Duke University Press, 1967), 109–26.

56. C. Grim, *Responding Through Collaborations*, a report delivered at the Tribal Leader Summit on Alcohol and Substance Abuse, Albuquerque, New Mexico, 2002.

57. Gould, "Alcoholism, Colonialism, and Crime."

58. S. Saggers and D. Gray, *Dealing with Alcohol: Indigenous Usage in Australia, New Zealand and Canada* (Cambridge, UK: Cambridge University Press, 1998).

59. Gould, "Alcoholism, Colonialism, and Crime."

60. Eileen Luna-Firebaugh, *Tribal Policing: Asserting Sovereignty, Seeking Justice* (Pheonix, AZ: University of Arizona Press, 2007).

61. R. A. Silverman, "Patterns of Native American Crime," in M. O. Nielsen and R. A. Silverman, eds., *Native Americans, Crime and Justice* (Boulder, CO: Westview Press, 1996), 58–74.

62. Luna-Firebaugh, *Tribal Policing.*

63. Ibid.

64. Ibid.

65. Hon. Marcy L. Khan, *New York Federal-State-Tribal Courts and Indian Nations Justice Forum*, 2014–2015, available at http://www.courts.ca.gov/documents/forum-20140821-materials.pdf.

66. Ross, *Inventing the Savage.*

67. Ibid.

68. Khan, *New York Federal-State-Tribal Courts.*

69. Minton, 2014.

CHAPTER 7

WOMEN AND THE CRIMINAL JUSTICE SYSTEM

CHAPTER OBJECTIVES

After reading this chapter, you should be able to:

- Understand the differential treatment of males and females in the criminal justice system
- Recognize the differences between male and female criminality and victimization
- Understand how females have overcome and also continue to face barriers with regard to being accepted as law enforcement officers
- Contrast the role of males and females with regard to courtroom practices
- Understand the particular challenges facing women under correctional supervision

Women have faced much adversity in their fight for equal rights. Toward this end, much progress has been made, yet much work remains. Regarding criminal justice, females have historically been an afterthought, with a few "evil women" entering the system. The situation is much different today. An increasing number of females are entering the criminal justice system, in turn providing distinct challenges for the system and multiple hurdles for female offenders.

THE FIGHT FOR RIGHTS

Females were largely taken for granted in the early part of U.S. history. The limited consideration of females is evidenced in the prohibition of females from voting, serving on juries, holding property, or making legal contracts. Further, the 1776 Declaration of Independence noted that all men are created equal and the only reference to sex in the Constitution is in the **Nineteenth Amendment**, signed in 1920, which gave women the right to vote. Women were not considered persons protected by the Fourteenth Amendment to the Constitution which provides equal protection of the law.[1]

The advancement of females in relation to these and related restrictions is largely attributable to **feminist movements**, which generally promote the idea that males and females

Table 7.1 Influential Females in The History of U.S. Criminal Justice

Mary Weed – The first women administrator in U.S. corrections, she was the principal keeper of the Walnut Street Jail in 1793.

Charlotte E. Ray – In 1872 she became the first African-American woman admitted to the bar in the United States.

Lola G. Baldwin – In 1908 she became one of the United States' first female policewomen.

Alice Stubbins Wells – In 1910 she became one of the United States' first female policewomen.

Jane Addams – Her work improving social and living conditions for the poor was among the contributions that earned her a Nobel Peace Prize in 1931.

Dorothea Dix – During the nineteenth century she was extremely influential in advocating humanitarian reform in American mental institutions.

Sandra Day O'Connor – In 1981 she began serving as the first female Associate Justice of the Supreme Court of the United States.

Penny Harrington – In 1985 she became the first woman in the United States to become chief of police in a large city when she was appointed to head the Portland Police Bureau.

should be politically, socially, and economically equal. The beginning of the first feminist movement of the nineteenth century is traced to a convention in Seneca Falls, New York, attended by roughly three hundred women intent on achieving equal rights for women. The group's focus was on property and suffrage. Attendees adopted a women-specific Declaration of Independence highlighting women's concerns. In the end, their efforts went formally unrecognized.[2] However, their voices were heard, in turn, opening the doors for additional women's rights movements and the ultimate advancement of female interests.

Other forms of activism in support of woman's rights emerged following the gathering in Seneca Falls. For instance, in 1916, a group of feminists, then known as suffragists, organized into the National Women's Party and picketed the White House. This group of feminists consisted of two factions with differing goals. One faction sought reform of all institutions of society, while the other faction focused on winning the right to vote for females. The latter faction dominated the movement, and with passage of the 1920 amendment that gave women the right to vote, the group disintegrated. The United States lagged behind many other countries in granting women the right to vote, including New Zealand (women were first permitted to vote in 1893), Norway (1913), Canada (1917), Germany (1918), the United Kingdom (1918), and Sweden (1919).

Support for women's rights re-emerged in the 1960s and continues today. This wave has broad goals ranging from increasing employment opportunities for females to reducing the amount of violence against women. This movement is focused on meeting the needs of today's women and continues to shape public policy as it relates to gender equality. These movements have paid off in terms of the advancement of females. Figure 7-1 highlights the accomplishments of several females who significantly impacted the criminal justice system.

To be sure, many other females have impacted the development of the criminal justice system. The above-noted individuals are among those who have made the most significant contributions.

Despite the progress, females continue to face discrimination and challenges involving the criminal justice system. Among the problems currently faced by females are increased levels of drug addiction, poverty, racism, and incarceration. These troubles are pronounced with regard to the marginalized females in society.[3]

WOMEN AS A DISTINCT CULTURE

Family therapist and author John Gray earlier published the best-selling book *Men are From Mars, Women are From Venus.* In the book, Gray discusses the differences between males and females, suggesting that men and women are as distant as planets of the solar system, and offers advice on how the differences between males and females can be overcome. Whether one agrees with Gray's assertions that there are substantial differences between men and women is their own prerogative. However, it cannot be denied that men and women are different in several forms and fashions.

There is some debate regarding whether or not women's culture is distinct from men's culture. At the most basic level, **culture** involves the sharing of norms, language, beliefs, values, behaviors, and material objects. Thus, the question is asked, do females differ from males with regard to culture? Researchers have identified differences between males and females with regard to each of these criteria, yet are the differences significant enough to warrant a women's culture distinct from men's culture? We believe there indeed exists a distinct women's culture, thus a chapter on females is included in this book. Nevertheless, we recognize the great number of similarities between males and females and appreciate the arguments of those who suggest females are not culturally distinct from males. The deciding factor in our decision to include a chapter on females in this work was the distinct nature, treatment, and plight of females entering the criminal justice system. In many ways, the females who enter the justice system are different from the males who do so. Accordingly, females are worthy of directed scholarly attention.

Gender is a master status as it cuts across all walks of life. It is a social characteristic that varies from one group to another and refers to femininity or masculinity. We are all labeled either male or female, and with that label comes expectations of our behavior and images of what we are like. The labels often guide our behavior. Related to gender is **sex**, which relates to the biological characteristics that distinguish between males and females. You inherit your sex; you are socialized into your gender by the expectations and standards of the culture in which you live.

Females are considered a minority group in the United States despite there being more females than males in the population. How can this be? As mentioned earlier in this book, a minority group consists of a group of individuals who face discrimination based on members' cultural or physical characteristics. While progress has been made with regard to societal acceptance of women as equal to men, there remains a great deal of discrimination against females solely on the basis of gender.

The distinction between sex and gender generates debate regarding whether human behavior is mostly a product of biological or sociological influences. For instance, are females distinct from males in many ways due to biological factors, or are the differences attributable to the manner in which society treats both males and females? The issue of nature versus nurture is alive and well.

Aside from the obvious biological differences, females differ from males in a variety of ways. The psychological, biological, and sociological research literatures are filled with studies highlighting differences between males and females. Differences between males and females with regard to social factors are evident and relevant to the study of crime and justice. For instance, along with education levels, a major predictor of poverty is the sex of the individual who heads the family. Females, compared to males, are more likely to be poor and poverty rates are highest for families headed by single women. Figure 7.1 depicts the income disparities for males and females.[4] Divorce, births to single women, and the lower wages paid to females largely contribute to the increased level of poverty among females.[5] These factors ultimately contribute to increased incarceration rates.

The criminal justice system has been mixed in its approach to recognizing distinctions between male and female criminals and crime. For example, there exists a wealth of research suggesting that females, more so than males, are given preferential treatment by police, prosecutors, and judges. On the other hand, the lack of consideration of female needs in prison and the belief that what explains male crime also explains female crime suggests that criminal justice professionals and criminologists believe females are no different from males.

The continuously emerging field of feminist criminology has aptly changed society's interpretation of differences between males and females regarding criminality. Too often,

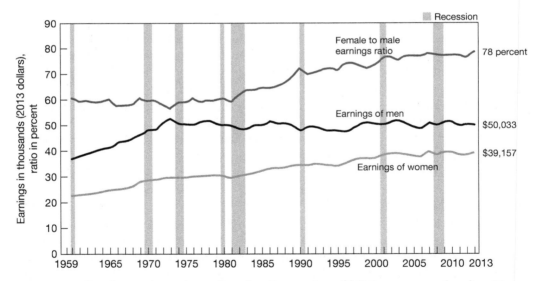

FIGURE 7.1 Female-to-male earnings ratio and median earnings of full-time, year-round workers 15 years and older by sex: 1960 to 2013

Note: Data on earnings of full-time, year-round workers are not readily available before 1960. For information on confidentiality protection, sampling error, nonsampling error, and definitions, see <ftp://ftp2-census.gov/programs-surveys/cps/techdocs/cpsmar14.pdf>

Source: U.S. Census Bureau. Current Population Survey. 1961 to 2014 Annual Social and Economic Supplements.

females are considered as only a control variable in criminological research.[6] While the consideration of male/female differences is appropriate, merely including females as a control variable says little of the distinct nature of female involvement in crime and criminal justice practices. The fields of criminology and criminal justice lag behind many other disciplines with regard to the acceptance of female scholarship as vital to the field of study. While feminist scholarship has grown in the past three decades, much of the work has been marginalized and relegated to specialty journals.[7] Females have been underrepresented in sociological and criminological journals dating back to 1895, with both male and female researchers more likely to focus on males rather than females.[8]

Recent evidence suggests increased female involvement in crime.

FEMALE ARRESTEES AND VICTIMS

Females have historically been underrepresented in criminal behavior. Recent evidence suggests increased female involvement in crime, however, males continue to be responsible for the bulk of criminal behavior. Data from the 2014 Uniform Crime Report (UCR) suggests females constituted 26.7 percent of all arrests. There was a notable difference in arrest patterns with regard to violent and property crimes. Specifically, females constituted 38.2 percent of arrests for property crimes, yet only 20.2 percent of arrests for violent crimes. Females accounted for 21.9 percent of arrests for drug abuse violations.[9]

Arrest trend data highlight the increased level of female involvement in crime and the criminal justice system. Nationwide, there was a substantial decrease in the number of people arrested between 2005 and 2014. There were, however, substantial differences between males and females. The number of males arrested decreased 22.7 percent between 2005 and 2014, compared to a decrease of 9.6 percent in the number of females arrested. During the same time frame, the number of males arrested for violent crime fell 18.6 percent, yet the number of females arrested for violent crime decreased by only 4.7 percent. The number of males arrested for property crimes decreased 12 percent from 2005 through 2014, however the number of females arrested increased 12.6 percent.[10] Again, despite the substantial increases in arrests of females, it remains that men constitute the bulk of offenders and arrestees. Nevertheless, these findings must be considered in light of the fact that arrests do not necessarily explain criminal behavior. For instance, it is believed by some researchers that despite increased arrests for females committing violent crimes, the typical female offender has not become increasingly violent in recent history.[11] Arrests are largely influenced by police officer discretion, which certainly influences arrest statistics.

Increased female involvement in the criminal justice system has not happened by chance. To be sure, there are several explanations why females are increasingly represented in arrest statistics. Prominent among the explanations for recent trends in female arrests include:

- Less biased responses by criminal justice practitioners to criminal behavior,
- Changes in law enforcement practices targeting less serious offenses,
- Gender equality and more desire and opportunity to commit crime,
- Increased economic marginalization of women,
- Increased inner-city community disorganization,
- Expanded opportunities for female-type crimes, for instance as they relate to increased consumerism,
- Changes in the criminal underworld, for instance, the reduced supply of male crime partners due to increased incarceration, and
- Trends in drug dependency, with drug addiction encouraging income-generating crime.[12]

Each of these items helps explain the rise in female involvement in the criminal justice system and each is worthy of greater empirical evaluation to determine the extent to which they have impacted females and the criminal justice system.

The distinction between males and females in the criminal justice system is obvious with regard to victimization rates, for instance, as females are notably more likely than males to be victimized by someone known to them rather than a stranger. The increased likelihood of women being violently victimized during domestic abuse cases largely contributes to these findings. Females are also far more susceptible to sex offenses than are males. **Acquaintance rape**, which involves an individual raping an acquaintance; **marital rape**, in which a man or woman rapes their spouse; and sexual abuse (including that against children) are of particular

Females are more likely to be victimized by someone they know rather than by a stranger.

concern to females, who are also particularly vulnerable to specific types of violent crime, such as domestic violence and stalking. Females in some countries are not protected from domestic violence to the extent they are in the United States, for example, as some Latin American countries excuse a man who murders his wife if she is caught engaging in adultery, and many countries around the globe offer limited protection for females in domestic violence cases. Such cases are often viewed and treated as family, private matters.[13]

WOMEN AND POLICING

There is debate regarding who deserves the title of the first female police officer. Alice Stebbens Wells arguably became the world's first policewoman when she began her career with the LAPD in 1910. Others claim Portland's Lola Baldwin became the nation's first policewoman following her 1908 appointment as an officer in Portland, and more recently it was suggested the Marie Owens was the first policewoman in the United States when she was employed as a police officer in Chicago in the 1890s.[14] Regardless of who deserves the distinction, female involvement in policing prior to the time of Wells was restricted to roles as jailers and police matrons. By 1915 female police officers worked in twenty-five different U.S. cities, and in 1918 Ellen O'Grady became police commissioner of New York City.[15] The pioneering work of these and other female officers has paved the way for enhanced female involvement in policing, yet for several reasons, females remain very underrepresented in policing. A primary reason for the underrepresentation of females in policing is the nature of police work. It is likely that many females may not wish to work in policing. Females and minorities have historically been underrepresented on police forces, although proactive efforts by police departments have sought to increase the representation of both groups.

Females have made great progress in policing since the **Civil Rights Act of 1964**, which prohibited discrimination in hiring on the basis of color, race, sex, religion, or national origin, and the **Equal Employment Opportunity Act of 1972**, when protections of women and minorities were extended to local governments. Women have moved beyond primarily assuming the administrative assignments and matron-like duties to increasingly engaging in traditional police officer practices. Nevertheless, much work remains.

Females remain underrepresented in all ranks of policing, constituting only about 12 percent of local law enforcement officers as of 2013. This percentage has remained about the same in recent years, although it is much higher than it was years ago (it was 8 percent in 1987). Figure 7.2 notes female representation among full-time sworn personnel from 1987 to 2013.[16]

Higher percentages of female officers are generally found in larger departments rather than small, rural departments. Research in the area noted that females have higher levels of representation in departments that emphasize community policing, have higher education requirements, have more incentives and benefits, do not have physical fitness screening criteria, and have no collective bargaining rights. They are also more likely to be employed by departments that serve larger and more racially and ethnically diverse communities.[17] Females are more represented in non-sworn law enforcement positions (e.g., as dispatchers).[18] Unfortunately, some male officers and members of the general public maintain the misperception that females are unsuited for the difficulties associated with police work.

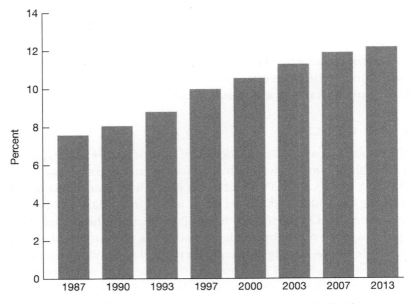

Females are underrepresented in federal law enforcement, constituting roughly 15.5 percent of all sworn federal law enforcement officers (Reaves, 2012). They did not enter federal law enforcement until 1971[19], although it was not until 2002 that a women headed a federal law enforcement agency, when Teresa Chambers became the chief of the U.S. Park Police.[20] In a study of female federal law enforcement officers, it was noted that all respondents (n=168) reported at least one occupational barrier in the workplace, with 24.1 percent of respondents citing negative attitudes from male colleagues, and over half (59.1 percent) noting the lack of female role models. Other concerns included the perceived glass ceiling to promotions (19.4 percent), sexual discrimination (21.3 percent), and non-family-friendly care policies (34 percent).[21]

POLICEWOMEN

Despite the perception of some individuals in society and some male police officers, females have much to offer police work. For instance, the research literature in policing suggests females tend to use less force, and thus face fewer excessive force complaints, have better communications skills than males, are better able to address situations of violence against women, and could change the climate of policing to reduce the number of claims regarding sexual harassment and sex discrimination.[22]

Policewomen have often faced difficulty overcoming the barriers associated with being accepted as "legitimate" police officers. For instance, some male officers (and their wives) perceive that females may not provide adequate backup during dangerous encounters.

Females have become increasingly involved in policing, although they remain largely underrepresented compared to males.

Some officers believe policewomen often are unwilling or unable to provide the appropriate level of enforcement when needed.[23] The police culture, which emphasizes masculinity and toughness, provides a notable obstacle for females wishing to be accepted among the ranks. Women officers are perceived by some in policing and general society to lack the physical and emotional strength to tackle the rigors of police work.[24] Females are sometimes required to "prove" themselves and mitigate traditional stereotypes early in their careers by using force in the presence of male officers.[25] Research examining officer use of force in St. Petersburg, Florida, and Indianapolis, Indiana, suggest that compared to male officers, female officers were not reluctant to use physical force and few differences were found with regard to the extent to which officers used verbal and physical violence and the reasons for doing so.[26] Another study examining female officer use of force found no statistically significant differences between male and female officers with regard to the overall rate of force or in the rate of unarmed physical force.[27] Table 7.2 highlights several barriers females have had to overcome in being accepted as a police officer.

Female officers from other minority groups sometimes face a sense of **double marginality**, for instance, when their race and gender pose particular challenges not faced by many other officers.[28] Hostility, separation, intimidation, and implicit and explicit discriminatory behaviors of fellow male officers contribute to the underrepresentation of African American female officers on many forces.[29] Double marginality is not restricted to African American females in policing, as female officers from other minority groups face similar challenges. For instance, researchers found that lesbian police officers in a large municipal police department faced a notable sense of social exclusion and overt sexist and anti-gay behavior from coworkers. Lesbian officers in a small department sensed that their greatest barriers were attributable to their gender rather than their sexual orientation.[30]

Table 7.2 Barriers to Females in Policing

- Stereotypes, for instance, that females are not strong enough for police work;
- Discrimination in the hiring process;
- Sexual harassment;
- Social isolation;
- A double-standard in performance evaluations, as females feel they must outperform their male counterparts;
- Receiving less desirable assignments;
- Limited opportunities for promotion, and;
- Lack of family-friendly policies such as those pertaining to child care.*

* Harrington, P.S. & Lonsway, K.A. (2004). "Current Barriers and Future Prospects for Women in Policing." Pp. 495–510 in B. R. Price & Natalie J. Sokoloff (Eds.), *The Criminal Justice System and Women: Offenders, Prisoners, Victims, & Workers* (3rd ed.). New York: McGraw-Hill.

The misperception that females are less effective police officers than males hampers efforts of females to become more ingrained in policing. Very few individuals in society would seek to work in an area where one's colleagues and "customers" are skeptical of one's abilities to perform the job. The term "misperception" is used as it is well documented that females perform as well as, or better than males in particular aspects of policing. To be sure, there are aspects of policing that are better suited to males. For instance, males are generally better suited to wrestle offenders given the likelihood of male officers having more muscle mass than females. Yet, wrestling offenders is a small, albeit important, aspect of the job. The inability of females to physically interact with offenders on par with males is tempered by the fact that some male offenders won't engage in physical contact with females, and female officers are better able than male officers to verbally, as opposed to physically, quell a confrontational situation.

THE INTERNATIONAL ASSOCIATION OF WOMEN POLICE

In 1915 the International Policewomen's Association was established to support the advancement of females in policing. The group would later reorganize and change its name to the International Association of Women Police (IAWP). Among other contributions to supporting women's involvement in policing, the IAWP annually hosts a five-day forum for researchers and practitioners from around the world to share their views and disseminate information on females in policing. Currently, the IAWP has members from more than sixty different countries.

The IAWP, like other professional associations that promote the advancement of females in policing, offers its members educational, networking, and mentoring opportunities. Further, the IAWP seeks to enhance the prestige and professionalism of policewomen, encourage officers to learn new things about themselves and their career, and provide a sense of belonging for the officers. Primary among the goals of the IAWP are to promote fairness and equity in workplaces and encourage a work environment that's free of harassment and discrimination.[31]

The adoption of an international component of a professional policewomen's association demonstrates the awareness of the need to promote cross-national interaction in policing, particularly with regard to females. Understanding the challenges faced by female officers in other countries, and the responses to those challenges, provide numerous benefits to policing in general. Along these lines, the existence of the IAWP and other professional associations designated for policewomen (such as the National Association of Women Law Enforcement Executives, the National Center for Women and Policing, and various state- and regional-level groups) provides invaluable support for female officers and demonstrates the significant advancement of females in policing.

INTERACTION WITH THE POLICE

It is well established in the criminology literature that males commit the bulk of crime in society. Accordingly, it is expected that males would more often be in contact with the police. In 2011, over 62.9 million U.S. residents (or 26 percent) over the age of fifteen had one or more contacts with the police. Females were far less likely than males to be the targets of both street and traffic stops.

Most police-citizen encounters occur while officers are on patrol. Patrol is considered the backbone of policing. Among other functions, patrol enables officers to quickly respond to calls, promotes positive police-community relations, deters would-be offenders, and helps control crime through traffic stops. The U.S. Bureau of Justice Statistics noted that male drivers were more likely than females to be stopped by police, and more punitive actions were taken against males than females. Males were more likely to be ticketed and searched.[32] During all types of contacts (including street and traffic stops), males were far more likely than females to have force used against them.[33] These numbers do not prove differential treatment of males and females, as one must consider the actions and behaviors of the motorists stopped by, and individuals in contact with, the police. Nevertheless, the numbers do suggest that interactions between police and motorists differ based on gender.

FEMALES AND THE COURTS

Discretion is inherent in the criminal justice system, and is perhaps most obvious in the legal arena where critical decisions are often made. The decision to file charges, grant pretrial release (including the nature of the release), engage in plea bargaining, convict or acquit, and impose a punitive or soft sentence are among the most critical decisions made by courtroom personnel. To be sure, consideration of cultural factors influences some decisions. For instance, the double marginality faced by minority females in the criminal justice system, based on their status as female and minority, dictates that courts ought to make concerted efforts to release female minority defendants on their own recognizance since they are often low-income and unable to post bail.[34] If bail is required, it should be reasonable given that many minority females who enter the criminal justice system are single parents and detention would have secondary effects on the defendant's children.[35] Similarly, poor minorities entering our courts also face challenges, as a lack of resources increases the difficulties associated with, among other things, obtaining competent representation and/or securing release from detention.

Gender-based decisions are notably obvious in the legal arena, as evidenced in the criminal justice research literature and our discussion of females and the courts. We focus on several critical areas of gender differences as they exist in the courts. Specifically, we examine decision-making and gender as it relates to sentencing and the imposition of capital punishment. The section concludes with a look at the nature and challenges of females working in the courtroom.

SENTENCING

Historically, female offenders generally received more lenient sentences than their male counterparts. The difference was more pronounced with regard to less serious crimes, as more serious, violent crimes decreased the likelihood of differential treatment. Some research suggests there is no gender neutrality in the sentencing process, as females face much lower odds than males of being incarcerated. Female offenders are sometimes viewed as less culpable, less likely to re-offend, and more amenable to rehabilitation than male offenders, and sentenced accordingly.[36] There is debate, however, regarding whether or not females continue to receive preferential treatment in the courts, and whether or not paternalism or chivalry on behalf of criminal justice officials persists. In light of increasing numbers of females entering the criminal justice system, some researchers suggest females are no longer treated differently from males.

It appears that with regard to judicial decision-making and sentencing decisions, judges consider both legally relevant and irrelevant factors when sentencing females, yet only legally relevant factors when sentencing males.[37] Judges typically consider dangerousness, blameworthiness, and social costs in their sentencing decisions, with the latter consideration most often benefiting female defendants. Judges are more likely to take child care into consideration in processing females convicted of less serious crimes.[38] **Sentencing guidelines**, designed to provide consistency and parity in sentencing decisions, are seemingly undermined by judges who deviate from the sentencing schedule while treating females more leniently than males.[39] Nevertheless, sentencing guidelines have largely contributed to the increased rate of female incarceration.

CAPITAL PUNISHMENT AND FEMALES

In 1998 Karla Faye Tucker generated worldwide attention. Tucker, a born-again Christian, was scheduled for execution in Texas. Prior to the execution, Waly Bacre Ndiaye (the United Nations Commission on Summary and Arbitrary Executions), Pope John Paul II, Italian Prime Minister Romano Prodi, and others offered support of Tucker who was convicted of committing murder with a pickaxe. Why the controversy, given that Texas executes many offenders? For starters, Tucker was to be the first female executed in Texas since the Civil War. To be sure, other females in Texas committed offenses worthy of capital punishment between the Civil War and 1998. Yet, why didn't they face execution? Karla Faye Tucker was executed on February 3, 1998.

It is suggested that receiving the death penalty (i.e., "capital punishment") is akin to a crapshoot which is dependent upon a variety of variables. Judicial discretion, jury makeup, and the state in which the capital offense was committed largely contribute to one's likelihood of being executed. Needless to say, capital punishment remains one of the more controversial issues in society. The small number of females executed or facing execution in relation to the number of males adds to the controversy.

Males undoubtedly commit more violent crime and more capital offenses than females. Thus, it is not surprising that only 2 percent of the roughly 3,000 of the inmates on death row were female at the beginning of 2014. African American females were notably overrepresented among the female inmates sentenced to death.[40]

FEMALE COURTROOM PERSONNEL

Courtroom personnel have traditionally consisted of White males, although recent trends suggest an increase in the numbers of women assuming law-related careers as public defenders, prosecutors, and judges.[41] For instance, the percentage of female lawyers increased from 23 percent in 1994 to 36 percent in 2016, and female attorney salaries as a percentage of their male counterparts' have increased.[42] Further, the enrollment of females in law school has increased and constituted roughly half of all law school enrollments in 2016. Until the 1950s and 1960s, women had been denied entry to some law schools, which contributed to them constituting less than 5 percent of the legal profession as late as 1970.[43]

Females have increasingly become represented as judges, as they comprise over one-third of the U.S. Supreme Court Justices, federal Circuit Courts of Appeals judges, and federal District Court judges. They comprise 31.1 percent of all state court judges in the United States.[44] An increasing number of females have assumed positions as federal judges beginning with Jimmy Carter's presidency, with females constituting 18 percent of former president Bill Clinton nominations to the federal judiciary.[45] President Barak Obama nominated two females to the U.S. Supreme Court: Justice Sonia Sotomayor and Justice Elena Kagan. Nevertheless, females remain underrepresented as practitioners in the legal system.

The lack of representation in the legal arena is pronounced for minority females who face the double marginality of being female and a minority group member. For instance, as of 2014, only 7.4 percent of attorneys were women of color.[46] Research on this population noted that compared to White men, women attorneys of color felt excluded from informal and formal networking opportunities, were more likely to believe they met with clients only when their gender or race would be advantageous to the firm, and more often felt their accomplishments didn't receive due consideration.[47]

Unfortunately, women of all races who have "broken the barrier" and entered the inside world of working within the courts continue to face particular challenges such as limited advancement opportunities due to stereotyping females and lack of access to the male socialization process.[48] Gender bias is primary among the concerns addressed by the women's rights movement, and certainly evident in our courts as the U.S. legal system is by no means exempt from claims of gender bias. Task forces were created in thirty-six states to investigate gender bias in the legal system. Such bias can come in the form of decision-making based on stereotypes regarding gender, for instance, in believing that domestic violence is a private matter that should be addressed at home. Gender bias also comes in the form of comments and actions toward individuals based on gender. Referring to female attorneys by their first names or making sexist remarks or jokes fall in this category and were common among the claims addressed by the task forces. Bias based on gender is also evident in claims that females face more difficulty than males in being hired and promoted, and that they are paid less than their male counterparts.[49]

The increased number of females working in the legal arena may or may not lead to changes in our courtrooms. The possibility and/or extent of these changes is open to debate. Particularly, some feel that gender differences will result in differential treatment of those entering our courts. There is also the possibility that any possible differences due to gender would be tempered by the background of the females entering the courts and the socialization process found in our courts. Put simply, there is uncertainty regarding if and how biological (i.e., differences due to gender) or sociological factors (e.g., the influences of law school and working directly within the court system) will influence future courtroom practices in light of the increasing number of females working in our courts.

Of particular interest with regard to the increased number of females working within our courts is the changing practices associated with judicial discretion. Speculation and assumptions regarding the behaviors of female judges tend to suggest that female judges are less punitive than male judges, although more likely than male judges to act more harshly toward sex offenses. There is also the belief that male judges are more paternalistic than female judges toward female defendants. However, limited empirical research has examined the on-the-job differences between male and female judges. To address the lack of research in the area, professors Darrell Steffensmeier and Chris Hebert examined the sentencing practices of male and female judges and found both similarities and differences in the sentencing practices of males and females on the bench. Particularly, they found that female judges were somewhat more punitive and more considerate of defendant characteristics (specifically, race, sex, and age) and prior record than male judges. They also found that female judges were more punitive than male judges when sentencing repeat Black offenders.[50]

FEMALES AND CORRECTIONS

As more females are arrested and convicted it follows that a greater percentage of women will be under correctional supervision. The increased presence of females in correctional facilities and under correctional supervision provides particular challenges to correctional staff and administration. Females under correctional supervision have special needs distinct from male offenders. Female prisons and jail administrators must continue to consider the special needs of female inmates and ensure that the goals of the correctional agency or institution are met. Too often in corrections, it is believed that simply applying male-based correctional practices to females will suffice. This approach is limited at best.

The increased number of incarcerated females has encouraged corrections officials to adjust to a series of issues and concerns as they relate to females. For instance, many female inmates have children they must care for while incarcerated. Traditional correctional practices and procedures are not well-suited to address the special needs of females. Addressing, at least in part, the challenges posed by an increasingly female correctional population has changed the face of corrections, and helped address what has been termed **collateral damage**, or the harms suffered by children of incarcerated parents.[51] At the very least it has forced correctional agencies to consider ways to best adapt to the changing demographics of their population.

FEMALE INCARCERATION

The United States has experienced a dramatic increase in its incarceration rate beginning in the early 1980s. Increased incarceration of both males and females has impacted females in several ways. For example, the high cost of building prisons takes resources away from the social services from which females often benefit. Further, enhanced focus on incarceration takes resources from social services which are typically offered by female professionals. In turn, there are fewer professional employment opportunities for women.[52]

One of the more notable developments in society pertains to the increased number of females incarcerated in U.S. prisons and jails. Although the number of males incarcerated far outnumbers the number of females, the percentage of incarcerated females is increasing at a higher rate than males. Three competing hypotheses are offered to explain the increased rate of female incarceration: the demise of chivalry or the paternalistic treatment of women; women as becoming increasingly involved in crime; and the equal treatment of females.[53]

Primary among the reasons for the increased presence of females in the criminal justice system are the substantial impact the war on drugs has had on females, and the merging of society's move to become tough on crime with a backlash against women's equality.[54] Other factors influencing the increased number of females being incarcerated include:

- Increased poverty of women
- Income inequality
- Selective enforcement of drug crimes disproportionately targeting minority and the poor
- An overall more punitive societal and criminal justice system approach to crime
- Increased use of sentencing guidelines and less use of judicial discretion
- Increased drug use and addiction among women
- A political switch to the right in which criminal behavior is believed to be caused by evil self-will, and
- racism, sexism, homophobia, and class bias.[55]

With regard to prison statistics, men, at year end 2014, were roughly fourteen times more likely than females to be incarcerated. However, the female prison population grew at a higher rate than males between 2004 and 2014. Females comprised approximately 7.2 percent of the prison population at mid-year 2006, compared to 6.1 percent at year end 2000.[56]

The increases noted in the prison population are also found with regard to jails. One doesn't get to prison without having first passed through jail. Accordingly, the female jail population has also recently increased. The female local jail population increased by 48 percent from 1999 to year end 2013, when females accounted for 14 percent of the local jail population.[57]

With regard to race and gender, minority females are more likely than White females to be incarcerated. There were more White women than Black or Hispanic women in state and federal prisons at year end 2014, however, the rate of incarceration for Hispanic (64 per 100,000 Hispanic women) and Black women (109 per 100,000) was higher than it was for White women (53 per 100,000).[58] This discrepancy is largely attributable to the war on drugs, which has been very influential on women's involvement in the criminal justice system. The war has had a particular influence on Black and Latina women. Along these lines, women of color are more often the mothers of dependent children, and economically marginalized and disadvantaged. The increased level of female incarceration has heavily impacted Black and Latina women.[59]

WOMEN IN JAIL

With a relatively transient population, jails offer more limited treatment opportunities and services than prisons. This problem has been compounded by the increasing number of females incarcerated. Jails have been forced to adapt to a changing inmate population. While several areas of policy and procedure in jails remain constant regardless of inmate gender (e.g., searches, housing, and transportation), special accommodations are needed for females. Inmate mental and physical well-being is of concern, as is the need to consider that many female inmates are single parents who must consider the well-being of their children. These considerations are by no means restricted to jails, as female prison inmates face these and other struggles.

Jails need to consider several issues as related to the increasing involvement of females in the criminal justice system. Particularly, females generally have a more difficult time than males raising money for pretrial release, and female inmates may not receive proper medical and mental health attention, as jails have traditionally been structured toward serving male inmates. Visiting hours with their children is also of concern, as are appropriate jail-issued clothing, hygiene supplies, recreational activities, work training programs, and inmate worker positions.[60]

These concerns have not always been addressed. For example, in 1999 the U.S. General Accounting Office published a report, *Women in Prison: Issues and Challenges Confronting U.S. Correctional Systems*, which highlighted the failure of the state to meet the special needs of women and provide adequate medical care.[61] Again, many of these issues also apply to females in prison, however, these concerns are more likely to be addressed in prison than in jails given that those in prison stay for longer periods of time and the problems may be more noticeable and more likely addressed in prison. Unfortunately, females in jail have been referred to as an "afterthought" that pose burdens on the staff.[62] Experienced jail staff who convey to new recruits the stereotype that women in jail are difficult perpetuate a culture of bias.[63]

FEMALES IN PRISON

Female prisoners were housed in institutions designed for males until the early nineteenth century. In some institutions females were housed in separated sections. The initial step toward creating prisons specially designed for women didn't occur until 1835, when the Mount Pleasant, New York, Female Prison was attached to Sing Sing, a male prison. The twentieth century brought about females being incarcerated exclusively in female prisons, which were less threatening and smaller than male prisons. Unfortunately, their small size resulted in a decreased number of facilities for the inmates.[64]

Prisons contain inmates facing long-term stays (more than one year). Accordingly, the opportunity for inmates to receive specialized treatment and recognition of cultural differences is generally of greater consideration in prison than in jails. However, the burden is on prison officials to provide the specialized treatment and recognize and respond to the various cultural differences.

One of the more notable differences between male and female prisons concerns the social world of prison life. The social structure of male prisons is largely built around the

The female inmate population has increased in recent history. Female prisons differ to some extent from male prisons, for instance in terms of the social atmosphere, health needs, and programming.

ideas of masculinity, manhood, and homophobia, while female prisons are more structured around kinship, open expression of affection, and family-type structures.[65] **Prison play-families**, in which inmates assume the roles of different family members, are more often found in female prisons than in male institutions, where such structural arrangements are frowned upon. Latina prisoners are particularly active in play-families given their likelihood of being from families with strong kinship ties outside of prison.[66]

Concern for familial ties extends beyond the prison walls. Of particular concern regarding female prison inmates is care for their children. Roughly two-thirds of the women in prison in the United States have a child under age eighteen.[67] While female jail inmates must also contend with caring for their children while incarcerated, prison stays are longer than the time spent in jail and, accordingly, family concerns are amplified among female prisoners. The social, psychological, and economic effects of an increasing number of children with incarcerated parents will have significant societal impacts for years and generations to come.[68] More children are likely to encounter the incarceration of a father rather than a mother, however, children of female inmates are more likely than their counterparts to suffer from problems associated with being separated from their parent and more trauma as the mother is often the primary caregiver.[69] Pertinent among the factors influencing the ability of a child with an incarcerated mother to avoid involvement with the criminal justice system include the age of the child at the time of the mother's incarceration, the child's relationship with their custodian, the strength of the mother-child bond, the type of crime committed by the mother, and the length of the mother's sentence.[70]

The increasing number of parents, particularly mothers, incarcerated leads to two concerns: What becomes of the children upon incarceration of their parent(s) and how can prisons facilitate continued parental contact with their children? The children of inmates most often live with the child's other parent. However, there is a notable difference between male and female inmates with regard to who assumes custody of their children while the parent is incarcerated. Particularly, the children of male inmates are most often cared for by the child's mother, however females most often leave their children in the care of the child's grandparent.[71] The large number of males being incarcerated leaves behind a greater percentage of troubled children living in single-parent families with marginal economic resources.

Female inmates are more often in contact with their children than are males. The bond between mothers and their children is particularly important for newborns, however it is often difficult for women who give birth while incarcerated to establish and maintain that bond. Some prisons take efforts to address this concern, for instance as ten states permit mothers with infant children to care for them in prison nurseries.[72] Criminal justice officials concerned with promoting close contact between incarcerated parents and their children need to consider placement issues, with the goal of keeping parents as close as possible to their children while maintaining the goals of incarceration. Close family ties during incarceration are related to lower recidivism, improved mental health of inmates, more enhanced unification of the family following release, and enhanced success on parole.[73]

Avenues to address the negative impacts upon children of incarcerated parents include:

- Crisis nurseries to address acute trauma such as a parent's incarceration
- Crisis intervention counseling following the arrest of a parent
- Therapeutic interventions to help children address the effects of disturbing situations and promote coping skills
- Therapeutic visitation to reduce the likelihood of domestic violence upon reentry
- Community-based mother-infant correctional programs to foster maternal bonding
- Parent-child visitation programs to encourage positive interactions between child and incarcerated parent, and
- Children's support groups, which help children confront the concerns they may face while having an incarcerated parent.[74]

The varied cultural background of incarcerated females generates several issues of concern. Consideration of cultural concerns regarding Latina, African-American, and Asian American female inmates is documented in the criminology and criminal justice literatures. For instance, Native American females were identified as having several unmet needs while in prison, despite the fact that females and Native Americans are among the groups with the fastest growing incarceration rate. Unfortunately, little is known about Native American female inmates. In response, Native American scholar Luana Ross studied the troubles faced by Native American women in a Montana prison, and noted how these inmates resist prison due to the institutional lack of recognition or honoring of Native American culture. Ross found that Native American female inmates lacked access to native spiritual leaders and culturally relevant betterment programs in prison. The desistance of these women led to them receiving more punitive treatment in the facility.[75] To be sure, these and related cultural challenges exist not only within the institution Ross studied, but in many other correctional institutions as well. Further, cultural concerns are not restricted to Native American females, as other groups face a variety of challenges.

Treatment, counseling, and other therapeutic approaches in correctional facilities have historically been designed and targeted toward male offenders. Further, prison staff should be well-versed in multicultural counseling awareness, training, and sensitivity as they pertain to females. Failure to recognize and address the special needs of females, in conjunction with a lack of concern for aftercare, contributes to the re-incarceration of female (and other) offenders.[76] Females entering the criminal justice system are more likely than other women to have substance abuse problems, yet correctional institutions often lack adequate substance abuse treatment. In some cases, substance abuse counseling is offered absent additional treatment approaches such as group therapy, family counseling, reunification programs, mental health assistance, and other ailments faced by female inmates.[77] Greater focus on issues such violence against females, childhood sexual abuse, and caring for children while incarcerated is needed in today's prisons.

Our discussion of females under correctional supervision has centered primarily on institutional corrections. However, we should not neglect the substantial and increasing number of females under correctional supervision in the community. As expected in light of the increasing number of females being arrested and convicted, women are increasingly being supervised in the community. The increased presence of females in the criminal justice system is evident in the percentage of females on probation and parole. For instance, at year-end 2014, females constituted 25 percent of all probationers, which was an increase from 22 percent in 2000.[78] The percentage of females on probation increased from 21 percent in 1995 to 23 percent in 2005.[79] Further, the percentage of females on parole increased from 10 percent to 12 percent of all parolees between 1995 and 2005, and remained at 12 percent in 2014.[80]

To be sure, females face particular challenges and issues as both offenders under community corrections and as professionals supervising offenders in the community. Consider the particular challenges faced in supervising Hispanic males in the community. The emphasis on machismo in the Hispanic community may pose particular challenges for female probation officers. For example, it is suggested that female probation officers initially establish their official role due to Hispanic males often basing their relationship with women according to roles.[81] Further, understanding cultural differences with regard to language can facilitate interactions with clients. Hispanics are typically more immediate in their vocal communications, which may, inaccurately, sound intimidating to some. Interactions are enhanced if parole officers are concise and to the point when communicating with Hispanic clients.[82] Women face particular issues when working in all areas of corrections, particularly prisons.

FEMALES WORKING IN CORRECTIONS

While not completely absent from correctional facilities, females working in prisons were historically restricted to clerical duties. Things changed with Title VII of the Civil Rights Act of 1964, which prohibited sex discrimination by governments in hiring and promotion practices. Among many other accomplishments, this act enabled females to increasingly assume positions in correctional facilities. By 1998, females constituted over 20 percent of the correctional officers in U.S. prisons.[83] By 2005, the percentage of females working in federal and state correctional institutions increased to 33 percent.[84]

Females have had to overcome a series of obstacles to gain acceptance as correctional officials. Females were notably under-represented in the ranks of jail employees until the 1980s and 1990s.[85] Despite the increase in numbers, females have not been particularly well-received as employees working in jails. Discrimination, harassment, and the belief that females are unable to fulfill the need for authoritativeness and occasional aggressiveness are but a few of the factors working against females employed in jails.

The introduction of female staff members into male prisons initially generated controversy among inmates and (male) prison staff. Much of the controversy stemmed around the belief that female prison officers were not strong enough to guard male inmates, and that they were more sympathetic to inmate causes.[86] Further, some male officers believe the long shifts and need to put in overtime as a correctional officer render females unsuitable as prison officers, primarily because women are viewed as having to be accountable to family needs.[87] Among other effects, the resentment faced by early female corrections officers limited women officers' opportunities to learn from the social networks established by experienced male officers.[88] These and related concerns subsided over time, yet some believe corrections remains the most male-dominated, sex-segregated component of the criminal justice system.[89]

Inmates had their own set of concerns with regard to the presence of females on the prison staff. Some male prisoners were sensitive to having to use toilets and showers in plain view of female correctional officers. Sexual harassment of female officers also generated concern, as inmates (and male correctional officers) would have to learn, and abide by the rules surrounding sexual harassment.[90] Today, female and male prison officers are viewed by prisoners as similar with regard to arbitrariness, fairness, and empathy.[91]

Consider the struggles of a female warden of a male prison. Females have historically been absent from the top level of administration in prisons, although more females today are assuming positions as wardens of men's (and women's) prisons.[92] Tekla Miller, who was appointed warden of the maximum-security Huron Valley Men's Facility in Michigan, documented the challenges she faced upon assuming the role.[93] Male prison staff, some of whom were opposed to female employees in a male prison, viewed the appointment of Miller as Warden with disdain. Miller was able to successfully overcome the opposition of the officers through remaining diplomatic and encouraging a team-oriented approach from her subordinates. In general, females have had success as wardens of male (and female) prisons.[94] However, the number of female wardens will remain low until females are more openly accepted among the ranks of correctional officers, an important stepping stone for one who wishes to become a warden. Females have had a much easier time being accepted among the ranks of probation and parole officers.

Probation emerged from the treatment model of corrections in the early part of the twentieth century, and was led by White female probation officers who had a background in social services. Probation took a slight turn in focus during the late 1960s and early 1970s when the emphasis on rehabilitative services turned toward **reintegration**, or helping offenders adjust to society. In the 1980s and 1990s the focus of probation would change again, this time adopting an emphasis on risk assessment and increased surveillance. The latter change has negatively impacted probation officer morale and involvement.[95]

Through all of these changes female probation officers have remained active in probation services. For several reasons, female probation officers have not faced the same level of rejection and harassment they face in law enforcement and to a lesser degree, the legal arena. First, male probation and parole officers have not established a culture that excludes females. Second, the historical need for treatment and professionally-trained social workers in probation and parole fares well for the acceptance of females. Third, probation has never truly been recognized as a male-dominated profession; thus male officers often have little concern when working with female colleagues.[96]

Increased diversification in correctional staff provides greater encouragement for multicultural training. For instance, correctional agencies were forced to offer specialized training for prison officers upon the increased presence of females in male prisons. Issues such as sexual harassment, supervising men in prison, and management strategies increasingly became part of correctional officer and administrator training programs.[97] Similar training concerns appeared as more racial and ethnic minorities joined the staffs of our prisons. There has been a notable increase in the overall number of African American females working in criminal justice, particularly in corrections. Among the reasons for the increase are civil rights legislation, welfare reform, national and local changes in public assistance programs, and national movements promoting awareness and support for diversity and inclusion.[98]

SUMMARY

Women may or may not be culturally distinct from males. Regardless of one's view, females are distinct from males when it comes to crime and justice. As both practitioners and "participants" in the system, females face specific hurdles not faced by their male counterparts.

Criminal justice in the United States is undergoing significant changes that will impact generations to come. Prominent among the changes is the increased involvement of women in all aspects of our justice systems. Females are increasingly assuming roles as police officers, police chiefs, attorneys, judges, probation officers, parole officers, and correctional officers, wardens, defendants, inmates, and clients. Responding to these changes has been and continues to be a work-in-progress that will hopefully result in fruitful benefits for all. As practitioners, females have much to offer the criminal justice system. The goal is to recognize and utilize the many benefits females have to offer. Equally important is the need to recognize and respond to the fact that male and female offenders differ and accommodations for these differences should not be ignored.

YOU MAKE THE CALL

FEMALE CORRECTIONAL OFFICER

Consider the following scenario. Debate the pros and cons of all options and decide what you would do.

As a female, you are a bit apprehensive about becoming a prison officer. Particularly, you wonder how the inmates will treat you. You know that tension exists between prison officers and prisoners, but you don't expect tension from your colleagues. As you begin your career in corrections, several male officers make off-the-cuff comments about you being a female prison officer. One officer asks you why you want to do a "man's job." Not one to put up with such shortsightedness, you report their behavior to your supervisor. The supervisor notes that the officers are "testing" you, to see if you can handle the ridicule . . . to see if

(continued)

(continued)

you are "one of them." He says the comments will cease after you've been on the job for awhile—"once you prove yourself."

Word gets out that you complained about the comments to the supervisor, and you begin to feel increasingly isolated among the prison officer ranks. The officers stop making comments to your face, but they also stop speaking to you unless communication is absolutely necessary. You can sense that the officers are making derogatory comments behind your back. Although you're not a quitter, it becomes increasingly difficult for you to continue working in such an atmosphere.

Questions

1. Do you believe the situation would have improved if you stood up for yourself and ridiculed the male officers in response?
2. Should the supervisor have reacted differently?
3. What steps, if any, can you take in this instance to improve your working conditions?
4. Was it appropriate for you to complain about the comments or should you have simply brushed them off?

KEY TERMS

acquaintance rape
Civil Rights Act of 1964
collateral damage
culture
double marginality
Equal Employment Opportunity Act of 1972
feminist movements

gender
marital rape
Nineteenth Amendment
prison play-families
reintegration
sentencing guidelines
sex

DISCUSSION QUESTIONS

1. Why have females become increasingly involved in the criminal justice system?
2. What barriers do females face with regard to being accepted as police officers? What can be done to address these barriers?
3. Discuss the differences between males and females as they relate to: (1) courtroom personnel, and (2) defendants being sentenced.
4. What are the special needs of females undergoing correctional supervision?
5. What can prison officials do to reduce the harms on children with incarcerated parents?

FOR FURTHER READING

Adler, F. *Sisters in Crime.* New York: McGraw-Hill, 1975.

Barberet, R. *Women, Crime and Criminal Justice: A Global Enquiry.* London: Routledge, 2014.

Chesney-Lind, M., and L. Pasko. *The Female Offender: Girls, Women, and Crime,* 3rd ed. Thousand Oaks, CA: Sage, 2013.

George, E. *A Woman Doing Life: Notes from a Prison for Women,* 2nd ed. New York: Oxford University Press, 2014.

Muraskin, R. *Women and Justice: It's a Crime,* 5th ed. Upper Saddle River, NJ: Pearson, 2012.

NOTES

1. Roslyn Muraskin, "Ain't I a Woman?" in *It's a Crime: Women and Justice,* ed. R. Muraskin (Upper Saddle River, NJ: Prentice Hall, 2007), 2–12.
2. Ibid.
3. B. R. Price and Natalie J. Sokoloff, "Preface," in *The Criminal Justice System and Women: Offenders, Prisoners, Victims & Workers,* 3rd ed., ed. B. R. Price and Natalie J. Sokoloff (Eds.), (New York: McGraw-Hill, 2004), xiii–xxii.

4. Carmen DeNavas-Walt, Bernadette D. Proctor, and Cheryl Hill Lee, "Income, Poverty, and Health Insurance Coverage in the United States: 2005," U.S. Department of Commerce, U.S. Census Bureau, August 2006, 60–231.

5. Ibid.

6. Susan F. Sharp and Kristen Hefley, "This is a Man's World . . . Or Least That's How It Looks in the Journals [sic]," *Critical Criminology* 15 (2007): 3–18.

7. Ibid.

8. L. A. Hughes, "The Representation of Females in Criminological Research: A Content Analysis of American and British Journal Articles," *Women & Criminal Justice* 16 (2005): 1–28.

9. "Arrests, by Sex, 2014—Table 42." *Crime in the United States, 2014.* U.S. Department of Justice, Federal Bureau of Investigation. Accessed online May 24, 2016 at https://www.fbi.gov/about-us/cjis/ucr/crime-in-the-u.s/2014/crime-in-the-u.s.-2014/tables/table-42.

10. "Ten-Year Arrest Trends, by Sex, 2005–2014—Table 33." *Crime in the United States, 2014.* U.S. Department of Justice, Federal Bureau of Investigation. Accessed online May 24, 2016 at https://www.fbi.gov/about-us/cjis/ucr/crime-in-the-u.s/2014/crime-in-the-u.s.-2014/tables/table-33

11. E.g., Darrell Steffensmeier and Jennifer Schwartz, (2004). "Contemporary Explanations of Women's Crime," in Price and Sokoloff, *The Criminal Justice System and Women*, 113–26.

12. Ibid.

13. Fred E. Jandt, *An Introduction to Intercultural Communication: Identities in a Global Community*, 6th edition (Thousand Oaks, CA: Sage, 2010), 240.

14. C. Mastony, "Was Chicago Home to the Country's 1st Female Cop?" *Chicago Tribune*, September 1, 2010. Accessed online at: http://articles.chicagotribune.com/2010-09-01/news/ct-met-first-police-woman-20100901_1_female-officer-police-officer-female-cop

15. Michael D. Lyman, *The Police: An Introduction*, 4th edition (Upper Saddle River, NJ: Pearson Prentice Hall, 2010).

16. B. A. Reaves, *Local Police Departments, 2013: Personnel, Policies, and Practices*, U.S. Department of Justice, Bureau of Justice Statistics, 2015, NCJ 248677, 4.

17. A. M. Schuck, "Female Representation in Law Enforcement: The Influence of Screening, Unions, Incentives, Community Policing, CALEA, and Size," *Police Quarterly* 17, no. 1 (2014): 54–78.

18. "Full-Time Law Enforcement Employees—Table 74," *Crime in the United States, 2011*, U.S. Department of Justice, Federal Bureau of Investigation. Accessed online May 24, 2016 at https://www.fbi.gov/about-us/cjis/ucr/crime-in-the-u.s/2011/crime-in-the-u.s.-2011/tables/table_74_full-time_law_enforcement_employees_by_population_group_percent_male_and_female_2011.xls

19. D. M. Schulz, "Women Special Agents in Charge: The First Generation," *Policing: An International Journal of Police Strategies & Management* 32 (2009): 675–93.

20. D. M. Schulz, *Breaking the Brass Ceiling: Women Police Chiefs and Their Paths to the Top* (Westport, CT: Praeger, 2004).

21. H. H. Yu, "An Examination of Federal Law Enforcement: An Exploratory Analysis of the Challenges They Face in the Work Environment," *Feminist Criminology* 10, no. 3 (2015): 259–78.

22. See Eugene A. Paoline III and William Terrill, "Women Police Officers and the Use of Coercion," *Women & Criminal Justice* 15, no. 3/4 (2004): 97–119 for elaboration on the ability of women to perform as police officers.

23. Paoline and Terrill, "Women Police Officers."

24. Ibid.

25. J. Hunt, "Police Accounts of Normal Force," in *The Police and Society*, 3rd edition, ed. V. Kappeler (Prospect Height, IL: Waveland, 1999), 306–24.

26. Paoline and Terrill, "Women Police Officers."

27. P. B. Hoffman and E. R. Hickey "Use of Force by Female Police Officers," *Journal of Criminal Justice* 33 (2005): 145–51.

28. S. E. Martin, "'Outsiders Within' the Station House: The Impact of Race and Gender On Black Women Police," *Social Problems* 41 (August 1994): 383–84, 389.

29. Ibid; also G. T. Felkenes and J. R. Schroeder, "A Case Study of Minority Women in Policing," *Women and Criminal Justice* 4 (1993): 65–89.

30. S. L. Miller, K. B. Forest, and N. C. Jurik, (2004). "Lesbians in Policing: Perceptions and Work Experiences Within the Macho Cop Culture," in Price and Sokoloff, *The Criminal Justice System and Women*, 511–25.

31. International Association of Women Police. "Past & Present, 1915–Today." Accessed July 4, 2016, online at http://www.iawp.org/history/pastpresent.htm.

32. L. Langton and M. Durose, *Police Behavior During Traffic and Street Stops, 2011*. U.S. Department of Justice, Bureau of Justice Statistics, 2013. NCJ 242937, 9.

33. C. Eith and M. R. Durose, *Contacts Between the Police and the Public, 2008*. U.S. Department of Justice, Bureau of Justice Statistics, 2011, NCJ 234599.

34. Coramae M. Mann, "Minority and Female: A Criminal Justice Double Bind," *Social Justice* 16 (1989): 95–114.

35. Ibid.

36. Cassia Spohn and Dawn Beichner, "Is Preferential Treatment of Female Offenders a Thing of the Past? A Multisite Study of Gender, Race, and Imprisonment," *Criminal Justice Policy Review* 11, no. 2 (2000): 149–84. See also C. C. Spohn and J. W. Spears, "Gender and Case-Processing Decisions: A Comparison of Case Outcomes for Male and Female Defendants Charged with Violent Felonies," *Women & Criminal Justice* 8 (1997): 29–59.

37. Marian R. Williams, "Gender and Sentencing: An Analysis of Indicators," *Criminal Justice Policy Review* 10, no. 4 (1999): 471–90.

38. Spohn and Beichner, "Preferential Treatment."

39. Ibid.

40. Tracy L. Snell, *Capital Punishment, 2013—Statistical Tables*. U.S. Department of Justice, Bureau of Justice Statistics, 2014. NCJ 248448, 10–11.

41. Darrell Steffensmeier and Chris Hebert, "Women and Men Policy Makers: Does the Judge's Gender Affect the Sentencing of Criminal Defendants?" *Social Forces* 77, no. 3 (1999): 1163–96.

42. American Bar Association, "Charting Our Progress: The Status of Women in the Profession Today," *A Current Glance at Women in the Law* (Chicago, IL. American Bar Association, 2016). Accessed online at: http://www.americanbar.org/content/dam/aba/marketing/women/current_glance_statistics_may2016.authcheckdam.pdf

43. R. L. Abel, "The Transformation of the American Legal Profession," *Law & Society Review* 20, no. 1 (1986): 7–18.

44. American Bar Association, *A Current Glance at Women in the Law*.

45. R. Spill, and K. Bratton, "Clinton and Diversification of the Federal Judiciary," *Judicature* 84 (2001): 256–61.

46. Vault Career Intelligence, *Vault/MCCA Law Firm Diversity Survey Report*, Minority Corporate Counsel Association and Vault, 2016. Accessed online at: http://www.mcca.com/_data/global/downloads/research/reports/VaultMCCA_Survey-2015-v03.pdf

47. American Bar Association, "Visible Invisibility: Women of Color in Law Firms—Executive Summary" (Chicago, IL, 2006).

48. Steffensmeier and Hebert, "Women and Men Policy Makers."

49. D. W. Neubauer and H. F. Fradella, *America's Courts and the Criminal Justice System*, 12th ed. (Boston, MA: Cengage, 2017), 140.

50. Steffensmeier and Hebert, "Women and Men Policy Makers."

51. J. Crawford, "Alternative Sentencing Necessary for Female Inmates with Children." *Corrections Today* (June 2003), 8–10.

52. M. J. E. Danner, "Three Strikes and It's *Women* who are Out," in Muraskin, *It's a Crime*, 723–33.

53. J. Belknap, *The Invisible Women: Gender, Crime, and Justice*, 2nd edition (Belmont, CA: Wadsworth, 2001).

54. Meda Chesney-Lind, *The Female Offender: Girls, Women, and Crime* (Thousand Oaks, CA: Sage, 1997).

55. Price and Sokoloff, *The Criminal Justice System and Women*.

56. William J. Sabol, Todd D. Minton, and Paige M. Harrison, *Prison and Jail Inmates at Midyear 2006*. U.S. Department of Justice, Bureau of Justice Statistics, June 2007. NCJ 217675; E. A. Carson, *Prisoners in 2014*. U.S. Department of Justice, Bureau of Justice Statistics, 2015. NCJ 248955.

57. T. D. Minton, S. Ginder, S. M. Brumbaugh, H. Smiley-McDonald, and H. Rohloff, *Census of Jails: Population Changes, 1999–2013*. U.S. Department of Justice, Bureau of Justice Statistics, 2015. NCJ 248627, 1–2.

58. Carson, *Prisoners in 2014*, 15.

59. Z. T. McGee, E. Joseph, I. Allicott, T. A. Gayle, A. Barber, and A. Smith, "From the Inside: Patterns of Coping and Adustment [sic] among Women in Prison," in Muraskin, *It's a Crime*, 507–27.

60. Susan W. McCampbell, "Gender-Responsive Strategies for Women Offenders," *American Jails* (September/October 2005): 39–41, 43–46; 43.

61. General Accounting Office, *Women in Prison: Issues and Challenges Confronting U.S. Correctional Systems* (Washington, DC: U.S. Department of Justice, 1999).

62. Ibid.

63. Ibid.

64. F. Adler, G. O. W. Mueller, and W. S. Laufer, *Criminal Justice: An Introduction*, 6th edition (New York: McGraw-Hill, 2012), 335–336.

65. K. S. Van Wormer and C. Bartollas, *Women and the Criminal Justice System*, 2nd edition (Boston, MA: Allyn & Bacon, 2007).

66. J. Diaz-Cotto, *Gender, Ethnicity, and the State: Latina and Latino Prison Politics* (Albany, NY: New York State University Press, 1996).

67. NPR, "For Some Mothers in Prison, a Sentence Doesn't Mean Separation," February 22, 2015. Accessed online at: http://www.npr.org/2015/02/22/388262646/for-some-mothers-in-prison-a-sentence-doesnt-mean-separation

68. Diane F. Reed and Edward L. Reed, "Mothers in Prison and Their Children," in Price and Sokoloff, *The Criminal Justice System and Women*, 261–73.

69. E.g., B. Bloom and D. Steinhart, "Why Punish the Children?: A Reappraisal of the Children of Incarcerated Mothers in America" (San Francisco: National Council on Crime and Delinquency, 1993); S. H. Fishman, "Impact of Incarceration on Children of Offenders," *Journal of Children in Contemporary Society* 15 (1983): 89–99.

70. McGee et al., "From the Inside."

71. L. E. Glaze and L. M. Maruschak, *Parents in Prison and their Minor Children*. U.S. Department of Justice, Bureau of Justice Statistics, 2008. NCJ 222984.

72. Jessica Pishko, interview by Arun Rath, All Things Considered, *NPR*, February 22, 2015. Accessed online at: http://www.npr.org/2015/02/22/388262646/for-some-mothers-in-prison-a-sentence-doesnt-mean-separation.

73. E.g., C. F. Hariston, "Family Ties During Imprisonment: Important to Whom and for What?" *Journal of Sociology and Social Welfare* 18, no. 1 (1991): 87–104; N E. Schaefer, "Prison Visiting Policies and Practices," *International Journal of Offender Therapy and Comparative Criminology* 35, no. 3 (1991): 263–75.

74. D. Johnston, "Intervention," in *Children of Incarcerated Parents*, ed. K. Gabel and D. Johnston (New York: Lexington Books, 1995), 199–236.

75. Luana Ross, "Resistance and Survivance: Cultural Genocide and Imprisoned Native Women," in Price and Sokoloff, *The Criminal Justice System and Women*, 235–47.

76. J. B. Morton, *Working with Women Offenders in Correctional Institutions* (Lanham, MD: American Correctional Association, 2004).

77. McGee et al., "From the Inside."

78. D. Kaeble, L. M. Maruschak, and T. P. Bonczar, *Probation and Parole in the U.S., 2014.* U.S. Department of Justice, Bureau of Justice Statistics, 2015. NCJ 249057, 5.

79. Lauren E. Glaze, and Thomas P. Bonczar, *Probation and Parole in the United States, 2005*, U.S. Department of Justice, Bureau of Justice Statistics, November 2006. NCJ 215091.

80. Glaze and Bonczar, *Probation and Parole*. Kaeble, et al., *Probation and Parole*, 7.

81. Marsha Bailey, "Georgia Parole Officers Confront Language and Cultural Barriers," *Corrections Today* (December 1991): 118, 120–21.

82. Ibid.

83. Criminal Justice Institute, *The Corrections Yearbook* (Middletown, CT: Author, 1998).

84. J. J. Stephan, *Census of State and Federal Correctional Facilities, 2005.* U.S. Department of Justice, Bureau of Justice Statistics, 2008. NCJ 222182.

85. M. R. Pogrebin and E. D. Poole, "The Sexualized Work Environment: A Look at Women Jail Officers," *The Prison Journal* (March 1997) 77: 41–57.

86. John Irwin, *The Warehouse Prison: Disposal of the New Dangerous Class* (Los Angeles, CA: Roxbury, 2005).

87. J. Pollock, *Women, Prison & Crime*, 2nd ed. (Belmont, CA: Wadsworth, 2002).

88. N. Jurik, "An Officer and a Lady: Organizational Barrier to Women Working as Correctional Officers in Men's Prisons," *Social Problems* 32 (1985): 375–88.

89. Mary V. Leftridge Byrd, "African-American Women in Corrections," in *The Full Spectrum: Essays on Staff Diversity in Corrections*, ed. C. Smalls (Lanham, MD: American Correctional Association, 2004), 105–16.

90. Irwin, *The Warehouse Prison*.

91. Ibid.

92. Van Wormer and Bartollas, *Women and the Criminal Justice System*.

93. Tekla S. Miller, "Woman Warden's Assignment Offered Rewarding Challenges," *Corrections Today* (December 1991): 110–11.

94. Van Wormer and Bartollas, *Women and the Criminal Justice System*

95. Ibid.

96. Van Wormer and Bartollas, *Women and the Criminal Justice System*.

97. Ilene R. Bergsmann, (1991, December). "ACA Women in Corrections Committee Examines Female Staff Training Needs." *Corrections Today* (December 1991): 106, 108–109.

98. Byrd, "African-American Women in Corrections."

CHAPTER 8

THE LGBT COMMUNITY AND THE CRIMINAL JUSTICE SYSTEM

CHAPTER OBJECTIVES

After reading this chapter, you should be able to:

- Describe the characteristics of the lesbian, gay, bisexual, and transgender (LGBT) populations in the United States
- Describe the history of the LGBT movement in the United States
- Understand hate crimes and the nature of victimization for LGBT people
- Discuss the issues and challenges in the criminal justice system in dealing with LGBT people. This includes gay police officers, juror bias against gays, and issues relating to prison experiences.

- "I was standing on the street talking with some friends and a police officer approached me. She asked me for my ID and I gave it to her. She took a picture of my ID and sent it to the sixth precinct. The dispatcher told her my record was clear but instead of letting me go, she said wanted to look inside my purse. I didn't know my rights then or I would not have consented to the search. When she looked inside she saw two condoms. She called the precinct back and asked for a police car to come to her location. I asked her 'Why are you locking me up? I can't carry condoms?' She replied, 'You are getting locked up for prostitution.' I was taken to the precinct and put in with the men. I was seventeen years old. For my community, it is not only being put at risk for HIV, STDs, or unwanted pregnancies, but having to be harassed and assaulted by police officers for being transgender or queer."[1]
- "I spent three and a half years in federal prison on a drug charge. As a Black-trans woman, I experienced sexual violence while in prison. When I went to tell the prison staff, I was told that if I reported the assault the only place he could house me was in the SHU, which is isolation. I knew that being housed there would prevent me from participating in the drug program that was allowing me to qualify for early release and I would not be able to attend school programs that I was involved in. I chose to keep

quiet about what was happening to me so that I could be part of the program and be released from prison eighteen months early."[2]

- "In 2006 I was jailed and eventually sentenced to a ten-year state prison term for aggravated assault on a police officer with a deadly weapon or dangerous instrument—the deadly weapon was my 'HIV-infected saliva.' After a six-year appeal, the charge was vacated by the New York State Court of Appeals and I was released. I remained on parole until 2014, where I was not allowed to leave my small county without my parole officer's permission. I cannot drive and was under a 9:00 pm curfew. I lost my health insurance and now rely on Medicare and Medicaid. I find myself having to explain my criminal history over and over again, from applying for housing to registering for classes at my local college. All of these things are a consequence of being charged with an HIV-related crime. I never realized the stigma attached to those with HIV and especially those who also have a criminal record."[3]

PUBLIC ATTITUDES ABOUT LESBIAN, GAY, BISEXUAL, AND TRANSGENDER PEOPLE

According to recent research by the National Opinion Research Center (NORC), an independent research organization affiliated with the University of Chicago, public attitudes towards gays and lesbians are changing. Based on the available evidence, the position of gays and lesbians in the United States has improved in recent decades.

For example, in the United States, approval of gay marriage, while still a hotly debated topic, a majority of Americans (55 percent) support same-sex marriage compared with 39 percent who oppose it. Younger generations have higher levels of support for same-sex marriage while older Americans have only recently become more supportive of same-sex marriage. Among other demographic variables, such as religious affiliation, race, gender, and political affiliation, a few trends should become clear.

Among Catholics and White mainline Protestants, about 60 percent support same-sex marriage, but it is much lower among Black Protestants and White evangelical Protestants. Politically, approximately two-thirds of both Democrats and Independents favor same-sex marriage and even though only about a third of Republicans support it, like other groups these numbers have increased in the past decade as well. Approximately 58 percent of Whites and 39 percent of Blacks support same-sex marriage, along with 58 percent of women and 53 percent of men.[4]

These trends are quite different from what was seen in 2005. During that time, public opinion polls revealed that Americans were divided on same-sex marriage and the acceptance of homosexuals. A 2005 *USA Today*/CNN/Gallup poll found that, when asked whether same-sex relations between consenting adults should be legal, 48 percent agreed while 46 percent disagreed. Experts note that some of the factors relating to the general tolerance towards gay couples in general and same-sex marriages in particular involve a U.S. Supreme Court case that struck down anti-sodomy laws. Additionally, corporations have also become more accepting of the homosexual lifestyle.

For instance, Walmart expanded anti-discrimination protection to gay workers, while the Walt Disney Company changed its policy regarding the Fairy Tale Wedding program to include gay couples. Disney's prior policy was that only couples with a valid marriage license could purchase the service, which ranges in cost from $8,000 to more than $45,000. Disney Parks and Resorts Spokesman Donn Walker said, "We believe this change is consistent with Disney's long-standing policy of welcoming every guest in an inclusive environment. We want everyone who comes to celebrate a special occasion at Disney to feel welcome and respected."[5] Others see the change in acceptability of same-sex marriages as a function of the growing visibility of gays in the media, politics, and as cultural leaders.[6]

Still another issue relates to how LGBT people and people living with HIV (referred here as PLWHIV) are involved in the criminal justice system. According to a recent national study, about 73 percent of all LGBT people and PLWHIV surveyed have had face-to-face contact with police officers during the past five years. About 5 percent report having spent time in jail or prison, a much higher rate than the 3 percent of the general U.S. adult population.[7] In fact, according to some advocacy groups, there is a consistent pattern of discrimination against LGBT and PLWHIV that is similar to many of the other minority groups discussed in this textbook. Like their African American, Hispanic, Native American, Asian, and elderly counterparts, part of the challenge of the disproportionate involvement in the criminal justice system can be understood in the context of issues relating to employment, education, social services, healthcare, and responses to violence. The difference, perhaps, between these other groups and LGBTs and PLWHIV, is that there may be less attention paid to their plight and less advocacy in terms of policy changes.[8]

In this chapter we will focus on how homosexuality affects the criminal justice system. While homosexuals are sometimes victimized because of their lifestyle, in what are known as hate crimes, there are other dimensions of this phenomenon, such as how the system perceives and responds to LGBTs and PLWHIV, and what are the internal challenges facing gay police officers within the system.

Disney has always maintained a level of sensitivity towards LGBT people.

OPERATIONALIZATION OF TERMS: GAY VERSUS HOMOSEXUAL

On one hand, defining homosexuality seems simple. Part of the difficulty in defining a topic like homosexuality, however, relates to the distinction between a person's behavior and their identity. Teenagers, for example, might vandalize an abandoned piece of property but are normally obedient and considerate to others. Or they might experiment with drugs but are not really drug abusers. This distinction between behavior and identity is found in the discussion of homosexuality. While people may engage in homosexual behavior, this does not mean they have taken on a homosexual identity.

The word **homosexual** first appeared in German in a 1869 political pamphlet by Karl Kertbeny intended to protest the inclusion of Prussian sodomy statutes in the German constitution. The term coincided with the discovery of an extensive network of gay males in European and North American cities. While it is not clear which came first, the discovery of a group of men with same-sex attractions or the label to identify them, by the mid-twentieth century, homosexual was frequently used to identify this segment of the population. The term also became compared to heterosexuality, which initially was understood to be connected to a desire for sexual contact with both sexes. Over time, however, heterosexual came to mean a desire for sexual contact exclusively with members of the opposite sex.[9]

The phrase **sexual orientation** is used to describe a sexual attraction toward people either of the same gender, the opposite sex, or both. The question of when someone is considered a heterosexual, homosexual, or bisexual is difficult to answer. Determining one's sexual orientation is not simply a matter of observing one's behavior since there is evidence that many heterosexuals have had homosexual encounters and vice versa. This runs counter to conventional wisdom since many people believe that if a person engages in homosexual activity, it is taken as evidence that he or she must be a homosexual. However, there is substantial evidence to suggest this is not the case.[10]

For example, Alfred Kinsey's controversial study in the late 1940s of American males and his study of American females in the 1950s found that 37 percent of the males and 13 percent of females in his sample had at least one homosexual encounter. However, when does a man who has had a sexual encounter with another man become classified as a homosexual? The problem is further complicated by the fact that research shows many people engage in sexual experimentation before confining themselves to one type of sex partner. An added complication relates to a person's thoughts as well as their behaviors. What if a person is a heterosexual but has sexual fantasies about a homosexual encounter? How does one label that person? Sigmund Freud, for example, argued that one's sexuality is determined by their thoughts and images when becoming sexually aroused. Thus, a man who has same-sex fantasies while having sex with his wife would be classified as a homosexual even though there is nothing in his behavior that would indicate homosexual tendencies.

There is also the problem of what one might call **situational homosexuality**. These are instances in which homosexual behavior occurs between two otherwise heterosexuals. In this type of situation homosexual behavior is contingent upon the environment in which a person finds themselves. Examples would include prisons, ships at sea, monasteries and convents, or even boarding schools. Moreover, situational homosexuality consists of behavior that ranges from sexual experimentation, such as what might be found on a college campus, to prison rape. Even more complicated is the notion of **bisexuality**, where the person is attracted to both sexes. Like homosexuality, this sexual orientation has been stigmatized by both heterosexuals and homosexuals, making bisexuals feel pressured to "choose" one sexual preference or another.

The psychiatric literature on sexuality have several theories about why people become homosexuals. For some, homosexuality is a regression to Freud's oral stage of development, meaning that most families of homosexuals are characterized by an overprotective mother and an absent father or that homosexuals fear a dominant mother in the pre-Oedipal stage.[11] Other experts have suggested that homosexuality may be an expression of nonsexual problems, such as a fear of adult responsibility, or it may be triggered by various sexual experiences, such as an enjoyable homosexual encounter at an early age. Theories to explain lesbianism include memories of abusive relationships with men or disappointing heterosexual relationships.[12]

There may also be cultural factors at work to explain homosexuality. The need to fit in may drive some people into a particular orientation when their preferences are for members of the same sex. Thus, it is not clear how one goes about choosing a sexual orientation. It may be that people choose heterosexuality because are attracted to the opposite sex or it may be that they feel pressured to be "normal" even though their thoughts, fantasies, and attraction are toward people from the same sex. Others may choose a homosexual orientation because they feel the need to be honest with who they are and in what they believe. Still others may not be able to decide and choose bisexuality.

An added problem is that the research is not clear about whether sexual orientation is an actual choice. Some researchers have explored whether or not there is a biological connection to homosexuality. This is a very controversial topic, with biologists on one side and religious groups on the other. Biological proponents argue that homosexuality might be related to hormonal imbalances in the mother during pregnancy.[13] Others argue that homosexuality might be related to brain functioning.[14] Some research suggests that the hypothalamus in homosexual men is between 25 and 50 percent smaller than in heterosexual men.[15] Other studies have shown that homosexual men react differently to human pheromones than heterosexual men. Whatever the explanation, most theorists agree that homosexual orientation tends to arise at an early age.[16]

DIFFERENCES BETWEEN MALE AND FEMALE HOMOSEXUALITY

The incidence of female homosexuality appears less than males. Female homosexuality is also much less visible. This is largely due to American social customs such as the greater tolerance for two females to hold hands in public, to dance, to kiss, or to share an apartment. Consequently, Americans are less likely to ascribe homosexuality to females than to males, making it much easier for females to conceal it if they choose to do so.

Lesbians tend to have fewer sexual partners than do male homosexuals. For example, while most males have "cruised" looking for sex with strangers, fewer than 20 percent of lesbians have done so. Lesbians tend to avoid the bar scene and tend to look for continuing durable relationships. This may in part explain why male homosexuals, who tend to have numerous partners, have a larger representation in the numbers of AIDS cases. This is not to say that homosexual men do not form lasting gay relationships, it simply means that male homosexuals are more likely to "hook up" for casual sex than women.[17]

The term "LGBT" refers to the collective group of homosexuals who identify themselves as either lesbian, gay, bisexual, or transgender. It is a designation that reflects the larger community rather than a specific group. In this chapter the terms LGBT and gay/homosexual will be used interchangeably to reflect the larger discussion, the history of the development of this movement, and some consideration to those who may be less informed about the recent stigma connected to the term homosexual. Included, although not necessarily directly, are those individuals who are living with HIV/AIDS. While not all LGBT individuals suffer from this illness, some that do fall into one of these classifications. Thus, people living with HIV, or PLWHIV, are incorporated into the larger discussion since they too often experience some levels of discrimination and mistreatment.

THE HISTORY OF HOMOSEXUALITY AND GAY IDENTITIES IN THE UNITED STATES

The general pattern of how American culture has perceived homosexuality over the sweep of history is best summarized by a transition from a sinful conduct view, to a disease model, to the development of gay identities.[18] Churches have been largely responsible for the overall condemnation of homosexuality. In early America, colonial ministers spoke of an angry God who would rain fire and brimstone and destroy this segment of the population much in the same way He destroyed Sodom and Gomorrah. Citing scripture that deplores homosexuality, the distaste for homosexuality was a very powerful element in holding people accountable for their actions. Bible scripture also justified the harsh punishment inflicted on homosexuals. In every colony, sodomy was a capital offense while other homosexual acts, such as lewdness between women, were punished with whippings and fines.[19]

After the American Revolution, although Enlightenment philosophy largely dictated how laws were created, there was resistance to removing sodomy statutes as "crimes against nature." As time went on, legislatures and courts included a wider range of activities, such as oral sex between men and sexual activity between women. In the late nineteenth century, the medical profession diagnosed homosexuality as a form of mental illness. The development of Freudian psychoanalysis led many physicians and psychiatrists to conclude that homosexuality was an acquired affliction that required medical treatments, some of which were barbaric and torturous. Examples included electroshock therapy, lobotomy, hysterectomy, and even castration.[20]

The development of psychiatry during this period also reinforced the medical model used to understand and treat homosexuality. Reflecting the attitudes, values, and beliefs about homosexuality at the time, many states enacted sexual psychopath laws to regulate consensual sex among same-sex partners. This medical model translated into criminal behavior for some adults. Not only were homosexuals determined to be in need of treatment, and more likely to spend time in mental institutions, district attorneys often used the sexual psychopath laws to criminally prosecute them.[21]

Despite these risks, in the late nineteenth century, some people began to organize their lives around a homosexual orientation. At first certain parks, streets, and bath houses became meeting places for men. Bars and clubs also appeared in or near **red-light districts** or centers for prostitution, of major cities. As a result, a hidden urban gay subculture began to be seen in the 1920s and 1930s.[22]

After World War II ended, many men returned to the cities rather than going home to small towns. This, in turn, allowed many cities began to see the increase in the number of gay bars in the 1940s.[23] In the 1950s, during the time of the Cold War, not only were communists a threat to the American way of life, Senate investigations portrayed homosexuals in the same way. In fact, this perception was so pervasive that President Dwight D. Eisenhower issued an executive order barring gay men and lesbians from all federal jobs. In response, state and local governments followed suit as did many companies in the private sector. The FBI created a surveillance program against homosexuals and local police departments conducted undercover operations in gay bars, making mass arrests on a regular basis. Wichita, Dallas, Memphis, and Seattle were among the cities that most intensely attacked the gay community, averaging one hundred misdemeanor charges against gay men and lesbians per month.[24]

In the 1960s, influenced perhaps by the successful protests against other causes, such as the Civil Rights Movement and the Vietnam War, the gay community began to

The Stonewall Rebellion is a landmark moment in the history of the gay community's attempt to secure equal protection under the law.

organize politically. By 1969, nearly fifty gay rights organizations existed in the United States, with membership running in the thousands. However, on June 27, 1969, at the Stonewall Inn, a gay bar in New York City's Greenwich Village, the police conducted a raid. This time, members of the gay community resisted and violence broke out between citizens and the police. The angry response from patrons resulted in three nights of rioting and violence in the city. The Stonewall incident also spawned the "Gay Power" movement. A massive grassroots gay liberation movement began, similar to that of Blacks, women, and college students of that era.

Like their militant counterparts, gay people challenged the public's perception of them, the way they were treated by the larger society, with the proclamation that gays lived "alternative" rather than "deviant" lifestyles. The phrase "coming out of the closet" was born during this time to solidify their identity and value to the larger society. By 1973, there were almost eight hundred gay and lesbian organizations in the United States. By 1990, the number was several thousand.[25]

This politicalization of the gay community resulted in changes in legislation, public policy, and the way gay people were perceived by American society. Not only did half the states decriminalize homosexual behavior over the next twenty years, public and political pressure reduced the number of police raids, harassment, and arrests as well. Many cities included sexual orientation in their civil rights statues and in 1974, the American Psychiatric Association removed homosexuality from its list of mental illnesses. In 1975, the Civil Service Commission eliminated the ban on the employment of gays for federal jobs. In short, the gay and lesbian world was no longer hidden from public view. Gay individuals were very visible: there were gay businesses, political clubs, community centers, even gay candidates ran for public office.[26]

However, the "coming out" experience and identity was not universally welcomed. Mainstream society still had difficulty adjusting to the visible and militant presence of gays. The late 1970s and 1980s were a turbulent time for this community. Singer Anita Bryant, most known for her commercials regarding orange juice, began an anti-gay campaign in Dade County, Florida. The basis of her efforts centered on her opposition of equal rights for gays. Building off of her efforts, by the 1980s, a conservative, Christian based anti-gay movement had begun. Fundamentalist ministers such as Jerry Falwell, who formed the Moral Majority, Inc., worked with other groups to oppose gays.

The threat of the AIDS epidemic in the early 1980s intensified anti-gay groups' efforts against homosexuals, this time from a public health perspective. However, the threat of AIDS also galvanized the homosexual community. As a result, many gay organizations were created to address the practical consequences of infection with the disease as well as its treatment. While initially perceived as a catastrophic event in the pursuit of equality for gays, AIDS was actually instrumental in shaping and changing the gay rights movement.[27]

The current issue in the gay rights movement focuses primarily on same-sex marriage. While the issue of legalizing gay marriage was decided by the U.S. Supreme Court in the case of *Obergfell v. Hodges*,[28] the backlash against gays can be seen in the ways that they are victimized and discriminated against in the criminal justice system.

LGBT PEOPLE AND THE CRIMINAL JUSTICE SYSTEM

HATE CRIMES AND VICTIMIZATION

On April 23, 1990, Congress passed the Hate Crime Statistics Act, which mandated that data be collected "about crimes that manifest evidence of prejudice based on race, religion, sexual orientation, or ethnicity." Management of this data was given to the FBI and the Uniform Crime Reporting program. The first report on hate crimes was issued in that same year, entitled *Hate Crime Statistics 1990: A Resource Book*, which drew from data in eleven states.

In 1994, Congress augmented the Hate Crime Statistics Act by passing the Violent Crime and Law Enforcement Act of 1994. This act expanded the scope of the Hate Crime Statistics Act by including bias against persons with disabilities. In 1996, Congress further expanded its efforts to understand and prevent hate crimes by passing the Church Arson Prevention Act. It also mandated that hate crime data become a permanent part of the Uniform Crime Reporting program.[29]

Methods of Collecting Hate Crime Data

In an effort to provide comprehensive coverage of hate crime information, the program merged the normal Uniform Crime Report information submitted by law enforcement agencies with hate crime data. The types of hate crimes reported include offense type, location, bias motivation, victim type, number of offenders, and the race of the offender.[30]

There are a number of challenges presented to collecting information on hate crimes. For instance, because motivation is subjective, it is difficult to know whether a crime resulted from an offender's bias or some other factor. Additionally, even if the offender was

Hate crime legislation is an important component of protection for the gay community.

biased towards a particular group or individual, their actions do not necessarily qualify as a hate crime. The only way an act is considered a hate crime is if the investigation into the incident reveals sufficient evidence to conclude that the offender's actions were motivated in some way by his or her bias.

As was mentioned, part of the data collection of hate crime information consists of the crimes known to the police as a normal part of the UCR program. This would include **crimes against persons**, or violent crimes. Examples include murder and non-negligent manslaughter, forcible rape, assaults, and intimidation. **Crimes against property**, or economic crimes, include burglary, larceny-theft, motor vehicle theft, vandalism, and arson. For those agencies that participate in the National Incident-Based Reporting System (NIBRS) an additional category is added, **crimes against society**, which include offenses such as gambling, prostitution, drugs, or weapons violations.[31]

Incidents and Offenses

The UCR program collects data about single-bias and multiple-bias hate crimes. For each offense reported, the police must indicate the motivation or bias on which it is based. A single-bias incident occurs when one or more offenses within the same incident are motivated by the same bias. A multiple-bias incident occurs when more than one offense occurs in the incident and at least two offenses are motivated by different bias. This means that there can be more incidents than offenses because for each incident, multiple crimes may occur.[32]

For instance, if a gay man is in a bar and a homophobic male attacks him, steals his wallet, and, as he leaves the bar, vandalizes the gay man's car, three separate crimes occurred: an assault, a robbery, and vandalism. However, because all three offenses were based on the fact that the victim was gay, the UCR would consider that a single-bias (sexual orientation) incident. In the same scenario, if the gay man is on a date with a Black man, and during the course of the same events, the offender shouts a racial slur at the Black man and threatens to kill both of them, now there is an assault, a robbery, threatening, and vandalism. For the purposes of data collection, that would be a multiple bias incident since two different types of bias are present: racial bias and sexual orientation bias.

Of the 15,494 agencies that participate in the hate crime program, 1,666 reported the occurrence of 5,479 hate crime incidents in 2014. These incidents involved 6,385 offenses, 6,681 victims and 5,176 offenders.[33]

What the Data Shows

The UCR program's analysis of the 6,385 incidents in 2014 showed a number of easily identifiable trends. That is, when hate crimes occur, they seem to consistently occur against particular groups. For instance, overall, nearly 47 percent of hate offenses were racially motivated; 19 percent were motivated by religious bias, and 19 percent occurred due to sexual-orientation bias. The data also revealed that the majority of hate crimes, 63 percent, consisted of crimes against persons while 37 percent were crimes against property (the designation of crimes against society accounted for only 1 percent of hate crime offenses).[34]

Of the racially-based hate crime offenses in 2014, nearly 64 percent were the result of anti-Black bias and another 23 percent were motivated by anti-White bias. The remainder was divided up between multiple race groups, anti-Asian/Pacific Islander bias (about 5 percent each) and bias against Native Americans (2 percent). Religious bias, which represents about 17 percent of all hate crimes, consists of nearly 58 percent anti-Jewish motivations. About 16 percent were anti-Islamic and another 11 percent were biased against some unknown religion.

With regard to sexual orientation, in 2014, there were 109 gender identity bias incidents, 69 of which were against transgendered victims. Almost 58 percent were biased against gay males. Another 24 percent were generically anti-gay motivated and about 14 percent targeted female homosexuals. In terms of ethnicity, there appears to be an increase in anti-Hispanic sentiment in the United States. Of the 790 offenses based on the perceived ethnicity of the victim, almost 52 percent were anti-Hispanic. Finally there is disability bias. Recall that Congress included bias against disabled people in the hate crime statistics in 1994. Only 95 offenses in 2014 were based on disability, with 69 of them against mentally disabled victims.

In terms of the type of victimization, about 43 percent of the offenses in 2014 consisted of intimidation while another 38 percent consisted of vandalism to property, and approximately 19 percent consisted of some type of assault, either a simple assault or one of a serious and aggravated nature. Further analysis of crimes against persons revealed that of the 4,048 hate crimes against persons, about 43 percent consisted of some form of intimidation, while another 37 percent were simple assaults. The remaining 20 percent were serious assaults. Hate crimes against property consisted primarily of vandalism or destruction of property, which comprised 82 percent of the 3,109 bias crimes in that category.

Of the 5,192 known hate crime offenders in 2014, 52 percent were White, while 23 percent were African American. The remaining percentages were primarily unknown race or multiple race categories. Finally, of the reported hate crime incidents in 2014, about 32 percent occurred in or near residences or homes. About 18 percent occurred on highways, roads, alleys, or streets and about 9 percent happened at schools or colleges. Another 20 percent occurred in other locations, such as public buildings or restaurants. Of the 1,017 hate crimes incidents from a sexual orientation bias, about a third occurred in or near residences or homes and a quarter happened on highways, roads, alleys or streets. Another 8 percent took place at schools or colleges and another 12 percent occurred in various locations.[35]

In sum, the picture of hate crimes consists primarily of anti-Black, anti-Jewish, anti-Hispanic, and anti-gay male bias. The majority of events consisted of intimidation or assault and frequently occurred in or near the victim's home.

GAY BASHING

On October 7, 1998, Matthew Shepard, age twenty-one, a student at the University of Wyoming, met Russell Henderson and Aaron McKinney in a bar in Laramie, Wyoming. Around midnight, Shepard asked the two men for a ride home. Subsequently, Shepard was robbed, severely beaten, and tied to a fence is a remote area, where he was left to die. About eighteen hours later, a bicyclist discovered Shepard,

(continued)

(continued)

barely alive. Shepard suffered a fractured skull and had severe brain damage. Shepard never regained consciousness and died four days later. Police then arrested Henderson and McKinney.

There was an outcry of sympathy for Matthew Shepard. While he was in the hospital, candlelight vigils were held across the country. Moreover, people in the entertainment industry responded by making films about the case and writing songs in support of Shepard as a way of expressing their outrage over what happened.

Both defendants attempted to use the "gay panic defense" arguing that they were driven temporarily insane by Shepard's

sexual advances towards them. Henderson subsequently pleaded guilty and agreed to testify against McKinney to avoid the death penalty. In exchange, he received two consecutive life sentences. The jury found McKinney guilty of two counts of felony murder. As deliberations on whether to execute McKinney began, Shepard's parents intervened, which resulted in McKinney receiving two consecutive life terms without the possibility of parole.

The two defendants were not charged with a hate crime since Wyoming had no such statute. A year after the trial, the Wyoming legislature introduced such a bill but it was defeated on a 30-30 tie in the Wyoming House of Representatives.

Is Hate Crime Legislation Really Necessary?

Some researchers contend that hate crime legislation is not only unnecessary, it sets in motion a double standard of accountability that can create a host of problems. These problems stem largely from the way hate crime legislation is interpreted. Critics also contend that many state legislatures have passed laws to expand the general categories of hate crimes. As one author noted, "ethnic intimidation" legislation, which was originally targeted for people who are gay, and transgender, have now expanded to include groups such as the elderly and the disabled. These "special status" crimes can include categories such as blindness, sensory handicap, involvement in human or civil rights activities or even marital status and political affiliation."[36]

The main argument against hate crimes is that they are unnecessary. The logic behind the legislation in the first place, opponents argue, was that hate crimes are worse than other forms of violence against a particular group of people. However, critics contend that some advocacy groups exaggerate the extent of hate crimes, creating a climate of fear about persecution, exploitation, and victimization that requires greater protection by the law. As evidence of this claim, one commentator noted that

> a careful look at hate crimes data shows that such crimes are a tiny fraction of major violent crimes and that many "hate crimes" are nonviolent personal conflicts. The federal Hate Crimes Reporting Act of 1990 requires that "intimidation" be included as a reported crime. This category, which consists of threats that are never carried out, accounts for 56 percent of the FBI's annually reported hate crimes against persons. In 2001, the FBI reported that there were 9,730 hate crime incidents. The fact that there were over 11,849,006 crimes reported to the police in 2001 suggests that less than one percent (0.09 percent) of personal or property crimes is a hate crime in the United States.[37]

In 2014, a similar trend showed that there were 6,385 hate crimes out of a total of 10,443,213 offenses known to the police. This, too, consists of less than 1 percent of all personal and property crimes (0.06 percent). In general, then, some experts contend a special category of hate crimes is not needed since existing criminal law adequately protects victims. As evidence, one opponent to hate crimes argues that:

> Wyoming has no hate crime laws but the killers of Matthew Shepard were sentenced to life in prison without parole and would have been sentenced to death, but for the request of Shepard's parents. Likewise, when James Byrd was dragged to his death by three men in Texas, the Texas criminal justice system reacted with its characteristic severity; two of the killers are on death row and the third was sentenced to life imprisonment. A hate crimes law in Texas could not have increased their punishment by one iota, nor could it have deterred their acts any more than the existence of the death penalty did.[38]

As evidence of the problems in highlighting hate crimes, consider the case in which a man and his wife were camping at an Ohio campground. The couple played their radio too loudly, disturbing the family in the next campground. When the park ranger told the couple to turn the radio down, they did but fifteen minutes later they turned it up again. The husband who was asked to lower his radio then yelled that he ought to shoot the campers at the next campsite. During his diatribe towards his fellow campers, the man used the word "nigger" and another racial epithet. He did not take any steps to carry out his threat nor did he act in a violent way. While the man should have been prosecuted for disturbing the peace and of making a threat, he was convicted of a hate crime felony and sentenced to a year and a half in prison. If he had not said those words, his offense would have been a misdemeanor, subject to a sentence of perhaps no jail time or up to six months.[39]

Another potential problem with hate crimes, say critics, is that while ordinarily laws regarding harassment, disturbing the peace, and other forms of minor misbehavior require a fact finding about the offender's behavior, the legislation often requires judges to determine a person's motives, their opinions, and whether they acted upon statements made, either in the present or past.

Critics of hate crimes point out that once the government begins to identify some groups for special treatment, it is difficult to determine which groups should and should not be given the same consideration. For instance, the number of women with a divorced spouse who stalks them is greater than the number of gays who are attacked because of their sexual orientation; however, no such special crime is identified for domestic violence. Why does one group merit special consideration? If it is based on extensive harm or violence, should women and other groups have similar protections?

Finally, critics of hate crime legislation argue that these statutes infringe upon freedom of thought. To punish someone because of his or her bad political thoughts or because of his inappropriate political words expressed during a crime, is to punish him more because of the beliefs he holds.

CHALLENGES FOR LGBT PEOPLE AND PLWHIV IN THE CRIMINAL JUSTICE SYSTEM

While the issues discussed in previous sections provide a broad context of understanding relating to how this group is affected by policies and practices within the criminal justice system, it would be a mistake to think of gays as a homogenous group. What is consistent, however, is that gender and sexuality impacts law enforcement practices, interactions with court personnel and its operation, and the correctional system has a host of challenges related to gender and sexuality. Each agent of the criminal justice system will be considered, along with how sexuality impacts practitioners within the system as well.

LGBTS/PLWHIV AND THE POLICE

Much of the literature regarding the relationship between LGBTs or PLWHIV and the police suggests that there may be a different set of standards used to stop and search suspects. For example, as one study pointed out, it is often common for LGBT people, but particularly women and youth, to be perceived as involved in sex work. As such, police in some jurisdictions use possession of condoms as evidence supporting arrests for prostitution-related offenses.[40] Another study pointed out that LGBT people and PLWHIV are often targets of harassment by the police. Transgender people of color in particular are three times more likely to be victims of harassment and assault than non-transgender people. However, according to the National Coalition of Anti-Violence Programs, about half of the survivors who reported the violence to the police also reported incidents of police misconduct.[41]

In this recent national survey of LGBT people, a quarter of respondents who had recently had contact with the police reported at least one type of misconduct or harassment, including false arrests, verbal or physical assault by officers. Moreover, LGBT people of color were five times more likely to be asked about their immigration status by police officers than White survey respondents.

In light of these studies, it should not be surprising that many LGBT respondents in the study were uncomfortable seeking the help of the police should they need it.[42] Yet given the nature of their existence, where homelessness, poverty, and other social challenges serves to marginalize this group, the likelihood of victimization is much higher than the rest of the population. In fact, one study found that, over the past decade, the police have been among the top three categories of offenders against LGBT people.[43] As was mentioned, many LGBT youth are homeless or housing-challenged—by one estimate LGBT youth make up 40 percent of all homeless youth in the United States.[44] As a result, LGBT people are impacted by police sweeps as well as by laws that address the use of public spaces. According to one report, about half to two-thirds of homeless LGBT in New York reported that they had been stopped, searched, threatened with arrest, or falsely arrested by police, compared to only 25 percent of LGBT youth who live in their own apartments.[45]

Further, challenges exist when LGBT people are arrested. According to the National Prison Rape Elimination Commission, as well as reports by human rights organizations, women and LGBT people in police custody often experience unlawful searches and sexual assaults while in detention. Some of these searches and assaults, either on the street or in lockup, are ostensibly for the purpose of assigning a gender to detainees, but it is a short step from that to abuse.[46]

GAY POLICE OFFICERS

The idea of the police being a subculture is not new and has been well documented.[47] For our purposes, a **subculture** may be defined as the meanings, values, and behavior patterns unique to a particular group in a given society. Entry into the police subculture begins with a process of socialization whereby recruits learn the values and behavior patterns characteristic of experienced officers. The development and maintenance of attitudes and values by police officers have both positive and negative implications.

In addition to a certain **homogeneity**, or similarity in attitudes, values, and beliefs in policing, many experts have argued that law enforcement embraces ideas of masculinity, strength, bravery, with femininity being equated with weakness. It should not be surprising, then, to realize that there is also a tendency for police officers to be homophobic, particularly towards gay males. Essentially there are two issues relating to the relationship between gays and police officers. The first relates to how heterosexual police officers treat gay suspects, victims, and citizens, while the second focuses on the way gay police officers are treated by their law enforcement colleagues.

Homophobia and Policing

While **gay bashing**, or unprovoked attacks on people with gay identities, remains a fundamental problem for this group, one area of concern relates to the way police officers treat gays and lesbian victims. Recall the recent surveys, where many LGBT people have claimed harassment, threats, and misconduct by police officers. In fact, many police officers have observed the differential treatment at times.

One study showed that officers believe that a correlation exists between general attitudes toward gays and lesbians and actual discriminatory behavior. Between 30 to 40 percent of officers indicate that gays and lesbians will not be treated the same or will not be taken as seriously as heterosexuals by the larger society. Although the study points out that this might be an improvement over how gay people have been treated in the past, the implication is that problems will still be evident for gays and lesbians and they will remain relatively easy targets for harassment.[48]

Another study examined police officers' responses to incidents of domestic violence involving same-sex couples compared to opposite-sex couples. Although members of the gay and lesbian community believe that police officers respond differently to same-sex couples, this study offered four versions of a scenario depicting an incident of domestic violence to which two imaginary police officers responded. The study found that the sexual orientation of the couple played a role in how the officers handled the situation. While this study could not predict how officers would respond to an actual incident, the findings do raise a number of questions about traditional law enforcement interactions with same-sex couples.[49]

Homophobia Within Policing

Historically, gay police officers felt that they could not reveal their sexual orientation among colleagues since law enforcement is known to be male-dominated and portrays a macho image. Gay officers feared embarrassment, harassment, or isolation if their sexual identities became known. In the past, one of the attractions to law enforcement as a career was the sense of brotherhood and camaraderie. To be excluded from that community, particularly since police officers often feel isolated from the larger society, would make it difficult for officers to function effectively. It also meant that officers might not receive assistance in emergency situations from their fellow officers. Thus, many homosexual officers felt they could not reveal their identities and had to hide behind a more macho image.

Some of the early research on homosexuality in policing suggested there was a lot of truth to these perceptions. For instance, in perhaps one of the most thoughtful books on the subject of gay police officers, Steven Leinen interviewed forty-one gay officers from the New York City Police Department (NYPD). In the vast majority of cases, homosexual officers described the fear of being discovered by other officers as well as the struggles of passing themselves off as heterosexuals.[50]

More recently, in response to court cases, many police departments that had previously refused to hire known homosexuals and did not offer any type of support mechanisms for gay cops began to develop programs to address their needs. There appear to be mixed findings about how gay police officers are treated. On one hand, there appears to be evidence that officers remain hostile toward gay officers. Being an openly gay officer once meant being subject to overt ridicule, including anti-gay graffiti painted on an officer's locker or having their uniform soaked in urine. Like much of the overt racism against Blacks, outright anti-gay behavior in law enforcement has become more subdued. However, there is some evidence that discriminatory treatment remains. One study of the San Diego Police Department found that while having openly gay and lesbian officers does not undermine the effectiveness of the department, some forms of discrimination and harassment do exist. This means that openly gay officers face a number of challenges.[51]

Two groundbreaking court decisions made it easier for gay officers to publicly proclaim their sexual orientation. In *Romer v. Evans* in 1996, the U.S. Supreme Court struck down a Colorado constitutional amendment that denied gay men and lesbians anti-discrimination protections. Some legal experts argued that this case cleared the way for other states to protect gay employees. In 2003, the U.S. Supreme Court struck down anti-sodomy laws, which essentially took away termination for cause options for police departments. Prior to 2003, departments could refuse to hire gays and could fire officers who came out because they were presumed to be engaging in illegal behavior.[52]

Some gay officers have successfully sued police departments for discriminating against them. For instance, a California Highway Patrol officer won $1.5 million in damages after other officers used derogatory names to describe him and urinated on his uniform and stuffed it in his locker. In 1993 a Los Angeles Police Department (LAPD) officer sued the department and settled once the department agreed to create anti-gay harassment policies. He sued the department again in 1996 for failure to implement those policies. In 2005, a New Jersey police officer sued his department for failing to protect him from taunts and harassment by his coworkers.

Additionally, if the number of gay police officers is any indication of a willingness to reject traditional views of homosexuality in law enforcement, there may be reason for optimism. Gays and lesbians have become an increasingly larger part of policing over the past two decades. In fact, some departments have actively recruited gay officers, particularly in areas heavily populated by gay and lesbians.

While the law has granted gays some protections, there remains a considerable level of fear among gay officers. While some officers argue that being gay is less stigmatizing than ever before, pointing to the creation of liaison officers between departments and the gay community[53] as well as the creation of gay officers' associations in many agencies across the country, other officers contend that problems occur even when departments seem to be attempting to minimize the effects of homophobia in their organizations. Gay officers argue they are still the target of harassment, jokes, and, perhaps most importantly, other officers will not provide them "backup" on calls for service.[54]

There is also the issue of the type of homosexuality to consider. Some male officers feel that lesbians in policing are more likely to be accepted, partly, they say, because of their common interest in women. As one gay female officer put it, "It's plain to me that it's much easier for women to be accepted. We work mainly with men and are treated like one of the guys. They'll joke around with you, like saying 'check out that hot chick over there.'"[55]

Some gay officers believe that their sexual orientation is actually an asset in the performance of their duties. One study in a Midwestern police department found that gay officers viewed themselves as particularly qualified to work with marginal groups, largely because they understand the implications and consequences of being stigmatized by the larger society. Officers in this study described the double marginality they experience: as police officers they are prevented from being fully integrated into the larger community and they are also gay, which creates a host of problems in terms of their place in the larger culture.[56]

Other gay officers believe that sexual orientation matters less than people think in policing. Rather, these officers argue that acceptance by non-gay officers has more to do with professional competency. There may be some empirical support for this perception. One study found that gay officers balance the stigma of "homosexual" with the value of being a "good cop." This study found that officers did not view themselves in terms of men, women, or even as homosexuals or heterosexuals. Rather, they believed that officers who worked hard and proved themselves to be competent were more likely to be accepted by other officers. This study also found that gay officers viewed their sexual orientation as a professional asset rather than as a liability in dealing with the public.[57]

To be designated a "good cop," police officers must have professional skills that are needed to survive the work environment. Among police officers, a good cop was characterized by the following general terms:

- An officer who backs up a partner and coworkers in emergency situations
- An officer who covers up coworkers' indiscretions or misconduct at work, or at the very least, does not betray a fellow officer who is accused of having engaged in misconduct
- An officer who is a risk-taker and not afraid to deviate from departmental rules to get the job done
- An officer who shares in the workload, especially in the handling of routine or tedious jobs; and who does not look for others to do his or her work.[58]

Increasingly, more gay police officers feel free to publicly celebrate their sexual orientation.

A fascinating dimension to the study of gay police officers is the fact that the issue of stigmatization, discriminatory practices, and the lack of legal protections are rather unique to American policing. Other countries, particularly the United Kingdom, have dealt with the issue of homosexuality in law enforcement for some time. One example of this acceptance is the popularity of the Gay Police Association (GPA) in England. Formed in 1990, it has grown into a formidable agency with members in all of the police forces in England. Focusing on policy development, hate crimes, victim care, and training in cultural diversity, the GPA has been a leader not only on issues relating to homosexuality, but also for those with physical disabilities, minority groups, and women. Other studies in England point to the ways in which police officers are treated as compared to those in the United States.[59]

THE COURTS AND LGBTS/PLWHIV

The courts also appear to have some difficulty in dealing with the gay community. Some scholars argue that the status of homosexuals in society is reflected in the kind of treatment they get by the courts. This is particularly true with regard to jury bias. The jury is one of the most important parts of the legal system in this country and they are required to be composed of a fair cross-section of the population. If a jury is biased against gays, a defendant might be convicted for being a homosexual rather than for the crime they have committed. Further, jury bias against gays can raise questions about the credibility of a gay witness despite the fact that this should have no bearing on whether they are telling the truth. Bias against gays can also result in reduced sentences against an offender who victimizes a gay person since the jury might perceive the victim as deserving of what happened to him or her.[60] Thus, the composition of juries, their perceptions of homosexuals, and how sexuality factors into jury decisions, play a pivotal role in understanding the relationship between gays and the justice system.

Perhaps one of the most obvious instances of jury bias relates to the ways defendants are treated who victimize gay people. One controversial legal aspect of homophobia occurred in the 1990s, called the **homosexual advance theory**, in which courts allow a nonviolent homosexual advance to constitute sufficient provocation to incite a reasonable man to "lose his self-control and kill in the heat of passion, thus mitigating murder to manslaughter." The homosexual advance theory is different from self-defense in that it does not attempt to justify the behavior of the offender. Rather, the theory states that it is a mitigating factor that should reduce the severity of the crime. While not all courts allow this theory to be introduced in homicide cases, the fact that some do raise concerns that perhaps some juries and judges allow their individual preferences on sexuality to interfere with equality of justice.[61]

For example, in *Schick v. State* (570 N. E. 2d 918 (Ind. Ct. App. 1991), the defendant, Schick, claimed that after being propositioned by a man for sex, Schick attacked him, knocking him to the ground. When Schick stopped hitting and kicking the man, he heard "gurgling noises" coming from the main's chest. Schick took the man's wallet and left the scene. The man later died. At trial, Schick argued that he was so repulsed by being propositioned by another man that he lost control. The jury found Schick not guilty of murder while attempting to commit robbery, but he was convicted of voluntary manslaughter.

In other cases, however, the homosexual advance played no part in the decision at trial. For example, in *State v. Volk* (421 N.W. 2d 360 Minn. Ct. App. 1988) the defendant was convicted of second-degree murder after the trial court refused to give a manslaughter instruction to the jury. Volk allegedly was hitchhiking with his friend, who testified that they planned to pose as prostitutes, pick up a gay man, and rob him. They found the victim at a store and he invited Volk and his friend to his apartment. Volk allegedly hit the victim over the head with a liquor bottle and tied him up. When Volk's friend left to search the victim's car for money, the victim freed himself, attacked Volk and during the fight, Volk shot him twice. At trial Volk argued that, in part, he was revolted by the victim's homosexual advance and this should serve, like intoxication and exhaustion, as a mitigating factor in the crime. The court found that there "was no provocation sufficient to elicit a heat of passion response." The court further found that a reasonable person finding themselves in such circumstances would have simply walked away from the scene.

These cases show how divided the courts are in deciding which set of circumstances warrant the homosexual advance criteria as a mitigating factor. The most important point with regard to the homosexual advance theory is that if juries are allowed to use a homosexual advance as a mitigating factor in the commission of a crime, courts reinforce the idea that gay men do not have the same protections afforded to nonhomosexuals in the criminal justice system.[62]

While the homosexual advance theory remains controversial, where there is greater agreement about the likelihood of jury bias against homosexuals is found in the selection process. This is not to say that all juries are biased against gays, however, there is greater concern over how and in what ways jury bias can creep into the process, causing a host of problems in the administration of justice. The main question surrounding **voir dire**, or the jury selection process, concerns jurors' sexuality and how such information should be used.

In some cases, sexual orientation is one of the main issues presented to the jury, such as hate crimes or in cases of sexual discrimination. Thus, in those cases where sexual orientation is a central issue, potential jurors' attitudes toward homosexuality may affect whether attorneys can select an impartial jury. What is less clear are those cases in which jurors should be questioned about homosexuality when sexual orientation is not an issue in the case, but where the defendant or the victim is gay. Considering that jury bias against gays plays a crucial role in the outcome of such cases, is it fair for a court to ask individual jurors about their sexual orientation or is it an invasion of privacy?

The courts have indicated that jurors have some privacy rights when asked to serve on juries. It appears that two conditions must be met if a juror can legitimately be asked about his or her sexual orientation. First, it must be clear that sexual orientation–related bias might bear on deliberations. As was mentioned, in those cases involving hate crimes or sexual discrimination suits, clearly the jurors' sexual orientation is a significant factor in the case. However, in those cases where the victim or the defendant is gay, and there is no legal question about sexual orientation, it is unlawful for attorneys to ask jurors about their own sexuality.

The second condition relates to the first in that it is an invasion of privacy to ask jurors about their own sexuality when any bias against gays could be discovered simply by asking jurors about their attitudes towards homosexuality. In other words, the attorney cannot circumvent a juror's right to privacy under the guise of trying to determine juror bias by starting with a round of questions about how they feel about homosexuality and then asking them about their own sexual orientation. The best way to avoid jury bias against gays appears to be to allow the questioning of jurors about their attitudes towards homosexuality in general.

Some experts believe that an unbiased jury will not allow evidence of sexuality of the victim or the defendant to affect the outcome of the case. They will not care if the defendant in a rape case is gay or if the murder victim made a homosexual advance.[63] Jury bias and homophobia by court personnel sometimes affects decision-making. While the courts have never provided a constitutional protection of a jury of one's peers (meaning that a gay person cannot ask for a jury made up of only other gay people), they have provided that a jury will come from a cross-section of the population and there are steps that can be taken to minimize the bias many people feel towards gay defendants and victims.

LGBTS/PLWHIV AND PRISON LIFE

Certain places, such as prisons, induce situational homosexual behavior, which includes acts of homosexuality by people who do not otherwise practice it. The first ethnographic study of sex by male inmates was conducted in 1934. Joseph Fishman, a former inspector for federal prisons, found that inmates engaging in homosexual activity were divided into different categories based on whether or not the behavior was coerced or consensual.[64]

In the late 1950s, Gresham Sykes wrote a book on prison life entitled, *The Society of Captives*. Sykes describes the process by which a person becomes socialized into prison life. He refers to it as **prisonization**. It is a social and physical transformation of the individual in an effort to compensate for the pains of imprisonment, one of which relates to sexual behavior. Sykes argues that being deprived of heterosexual outlets leads him to find ways to alleviate the stress associated with it.[65]

Building off of Sykes's and Fishman's work, research in the 1970s on prison life included homosexual behavior. The findings of several studies resulted in a number of typologies to describe participants who engage in homosexual activities. The first is the **queen**. Inmates and staff use the term to refer to a male inmate who prefers male sexual partners. The Queen is not really engaged in situational homosexual behavior, for "she" would prefer male partners in prison or on the outside. To attract partners, the queen exaggerates aspects of female sexuality. She may take on a feminine nickname and let her hair grow long, wear jewelry, makeup etc. The queen is accorded some social status in the prison, but not much.

The second type of participant is called the **punk**. This group of homosexual inmates are accorded one of the lowest statuses in the institution. Punks are despised by inmates who see his homosexual behavior as the result of either weakness in the face of pressure or a willingness to sacrifice his manhood to obtain goods and services. There are essentially two types of punks: **canteen punks**: who perform oral or anal sex for candy, cigarettes, or other items purchased at the prison store or canteen; and **pressure punks**, who are inmates that submit to homosexual behavior because they have been threatened or raped by other prisoners. There are generally two ways to become a pressure punk. An inmate may offer help of some sort to a new inmate or "fish." If the fish accepts the offer, he then becomes indebted to his benefactor. The second way is to rig a gambling game so that fish loses. In either case, when debt is called, the fish cannot usually pay so the inmate demands sex as payment. This leaves fish with two choices: fight the inmate or submit to the sexual advances. Anyone who does this must continue to submit for the rest of his prison term.

The third type of participant in prison is called the **wolf** or **jocker**. This type of inmate is viewed by his colleagues as a "man." To remain a "man" and still engage in homosexual acts, the jocker has to present an image of exaggerated toughness. So the jocker uses force: he rapes. The more violence that surrounds his sexual acts, the more he is seen as masculine. To maintain his status, he must also keep his sexual acts emotionless and impersonal. It is not uncommon for a wolf to own a punk and to prostitute him much in the same way a pimp uses a female prostitute on the street.[66]

As was mentioned, the research on situational homosexual behavior indicates that men in single-sex environments such as the military, correctional institutions, boarding schools, or remote work sites have been known to engage in sexual activities with one another yet maintain a heterosexual identity. The behavior was simply defined as a response to the deprivation or lack of mixed sex interactions. The general belief was that most men who engage in this type of activity would return to heterosexual sexual activities once they return to a mixed-sex environment.

The early explanations for homosexual behavior in prison focused on environmental influences. That is, the social structure of the prison produces and promotes homosexual behavior. First, the lack of female companionship may drive some men towards homosexual behavior, particularly if this type of behavior is tolerated by prison officials and understood as necessary by other inmates.

Another factor relating to prison homosexuality is idleness. Without opportunities to work or engage in distracting activities, some research suggests homosexual behavior is more likely. Another reason for homosexual behavior in prisons relates to overcrowding. Currently many prisons exceed their maximum capacity for inmates. Overcrowding means more inmates per cell, less privacy, and the greater likelihood of inmates acting upon their sexual urges. Finally, experts note that when prisons prohibit pornography or conjugal visits, which can act as release methods for prisoners to achieve some of their sexual desires, the incidence of homosexual behavior and prison rape increases. Currently, only a few states allow conjugal visits in their correctional facilities.[67]

Another significant issue with regard to homosexual behavior in prisons relates to HIV/AIDS. Clearly the spread of sexually transmitted diseases is an important area of concern for all institutions, particularly those that house violent inmates, where prison rape is more common. While abstinence is clearly the most effective method to preventing the transmission of HIV/AIDS or other sexually transmitted diseases, this is less likely to occur in prison. The other primary method to prevent the spread of diseases is through safe sex practices. However, many prison officials are reluctant to promote safe sex since it suggests that they are supplying condoms to inmates for the purpose of engaging in prohibited behavior inside the institution.[68]

While the subject of coerced sexual behavior in prison has been studied extensively, consensual homosexual behavior has been largely ignored in the literature. Most of the research on this subject focuses on the formation of surrogate families in female prisons. What appears to be missing from the literature is research on masturbation and consensual sex among males in prison. While these two practices appear to be vastly more common than prison rape or some type of coerced sex, only a few studies exist on consensual homosexual activity in U.S. male prisons, four of which were conducted in the 1980s or early 1990s. The general findings of these studies showed that the vast majority of inmates masturbated on a regular basis and if consensual homosexual behavior occurred, inmates who considered themselves heterosexuals almost always took on the masculine role in the interaction, while the feminine role was associated with being a gay or bisexual person.[69]

A more recent study explored the dynamics of these activities in an attempt to understand how and in what ways the prison environment induced changes in one's sexual identity both inside the institution as well as once the inmate was released. The findings of this study showed that race significantly affected an inmate's decision to engage in homosexual behavior. Whites were more likely to engage in homosexual activity than non-Whites. Additionally, White inmates were more likely to be targeted for sexual approaches than non-White inmates. The explanation for this may be that non-White inmates perceive homosexual activity as a threat to their identity as both males and heterosexuals. In fact, there are some studies that show Black inmates are more likely to rape White inmates while incarcerated.[70]

It is important to note that whether or not inmates remain involved in homosexual activity after their release is unclear. While the prison environment can explain why some inmates engage in homosexual activity, whether as consensual partners or due to the threat of violence, what is unclear is what happens after they are released.[71]

WOMEN, HOMOSEXUALITY, AND PRISON LIFE

The early research on same-sex behavior among female inmates suggested that, in an effort to replace lost family roles, "pseudo families" or kinship networks dominated life in women's prison. The relationships formed in prison dominated social life for inmates and the social structure it created simulated life outside prison walls. "Marriages," "divorces," "infidelity," and other evidence of family drama were found in prisons among women.[72] Although the relationships women form in prison continue to reflect early research trends discovered in the 1960s, 1970s, and even 1980s, there is some evidence that these types of prison relationships have diminished in recent years. One researcher noted that while female offenders still participate in "pseudo families" and form homosexual relationships with other inmates, it is not considered acceptable nor is it practiced by all inmates.[73]

The dynamics of social interaction among female inmates suggests that the move away from rehabilitation as a philosophy of punishment, which has been replaced with a more punitive orientation, has had an impact on the types of social relationships inmates form with each other. Rather than forming caring relationships, or extended networks of quasi-families, female inmates are more reluctant than before to become involved with others. Preferring instead to "doing time" alone, many female inmates are beginning to resemble their male counterparts in that they prefer to avoid common areas in the prison and rely only on a few trusted friends. This is done in an attempt to survive an increasingly violent and unstable environment in women's prisons.

Some of the changes in female inmates' relationships are structural: in the past, women's institutions were designed to be more conducive to social interaction. The cottage system of the 1960s was designed to facilitate a more rehabilitative approach to women largely because it was felt that if the prison environment was more like a home than a cell, inmates would be more successful in being rehabilitated. With the change in orientation, from rehabilitation to an emphasis on punishment, many women's prisons now resemble male prisons. Additionally, prisons are less isolating than in the past. Inmates can continue to be influenced by the larger culture through television, movies, radio, visits with family members and, in some cases, conjugal visits.

This makes the aforementioned "pains of imprisonment" different than what it was in the past. It also means the need for a single unifying inmate subculture that provides surrogate roles for inmates to emulate the outside, unnecessary. Thus, inmates simply do not need the same types of relationships they did in the past and given the wider diversity of female offenders entering prisons, there is less cohesiveness and greater levels of violence. Consequently, while homosexual relationships still occur in women's prisons, their need and pervasiveness has declined.[74]

For LGBT people and PLWHIV, prison life presents additional challenges. For instance, a 2009 study found that transgender prisoners experience sexual victimization at a rate thirteen times higher than non-transgender prisoners.[75] This is what led to the National Prison Rape Elimination Commission to mandate that correctional facilities take more pronounced steps to protect this segment of the inmate population from harm. While the violence and victimization that occurs in prison has been well documented, the issues related to protecting and providing adequate care for LGBTs and PLWHIV are significant and many correctional institutions are limited in their ability to provide adequate care.

The solution by many correctional facilities has been to place LGBT people and PLWHIV in solitary confinement for their protection. However, such a practice results in a lack of access to mail, job opportunities, and programs while incarcerated. Some reports indicate that LGBT people remain in protective custody for years, meaning that they are likely to serve much of their sentence in isolation and are more likely to serve the maximum time since they are not eligible for good time credit and early release.[76]

Another dimension relating to the incarceration of LGBT people and PLWHIV relates to immigration. According to one estimate, there are at least 267,000 undocumented LGBT immigrants in the United States. While an exact figure cannot be determined, it is estimated that a significant percentage of those detained in immigration detention and holding facilities are LGBT people.[77]

Further, because of changes in immigration policy in the United States, the number of persons detained by immigration officials has dramatically increased in recent years. Advocates estimate that almost 70 percent of the 420,000 persons detained by Immigration and Customs Enforcement (ICE) were held in state and local facilities. While the same issues for LGBT immigrants occurs for natives, meaning the discrimination, use of solitary confinement, and so on, there is the added challenge of filing a claim for asylum during the one year window, which impacts nearly 20 percent of those people fleeing persecution.[78]

SUMMARY

There can be little doubt that the debate over gay identity and same-sex marriage in this country remains controversial. Public opinion polls in past years showed a general tolerance for gay lifestyles, and, more recently Americans have been found to be more willing to grant gays equal rights. Evidence of the intolerance of gays is seen throughout American history and it was only in the 1960s with the famous Stonewall incident, that the gay community began to assert themselves and organize politically in an effort to change people's understanding of their lifestyle. Despite the apparent progress, gays remain a stigmatized and victimized group. Hate crime legislation, which was enacted in 1990 to provide additional protection against offenders motivated by a racial, religious, or sexual orientation bias, made it a federal crime to victimize gays. Despite the small number of crimes, the symbolic importance of hate crime legislation is an important illustration of the position of gay people in America.

The gay community has also experienced discrimination and other problems when they have entered certain professions such as law enforcement. Like the society as a whole, while it appears progress is being made in terms of equal treatment, gay police officers still encounter problems in their profession. Similarly, when homosexuals find themselves in court, either as defendants, victims, or witnesses, a number of unique challenges are presented. Juror bias in particular is perhaps the greatest problem in the courts in the administration of justice for gays.

Finally, homosexual behavior in prison has been a long-standing problem. Prison rape as well as consensual sex have created numerous problems for prison officials, particularly as it relates to sexually transmitted diseases such as HIV/AIDS. Additionally, the changing nature of prison life for women, with a greater emphasis on punishment rather than rehabilitation, has also affected the nature of social interaction. The nature of gay relationships in women prisons historically took on the characteristics of pseudo-families, with less violence and more cooperative roles. As the philosophy of punishment shifted to a model in prison with an emphasis on punishment, the prevalence of pseudo-families appears to have decreased. Female inmates now resemble their male counterparts in terms of their relationships to other inmates.

YOU MAKE THE CALL

HATE CRIMES

Consider the following scenario. Debate the pros and cons of all options and decide what you would do.

You are a criminal defense attorney who has been asked to represent two youths who engaged in "gay bashing" against a homosexual male. The two defendants, both males, were propositioned by the victims in a bar near a college campus. In response to the solicitation by the victim, your clients brought the victim to a motel under the guise of a romantic encounter but once the three arrived, the two youths attacked the victim, beating him with fists, feet, and clubs. The victim sustained serious injuries and was in a coma for ten days. The two suspects were arrested a few days after the assault and contacted you to represent them. You have taken a strong and very public stance against gay people and same-sex marriage. You have also tried to influence Congress to repeal hate crime legislation, stating

that it unfairly discriminates against some types of victims. This public stance was the main reason the two suspects contacted you to represent them.

Questions

1. Do you agree to represent the two suspects or turn them down? Why?
2. If you agree to represent the two suspects, could you separate your personal biases against gays and adequately represent them?
3. Do you think your public (and personal) stance on homosexuality will adversely affect the jury? If so, in what ways?
4. Should there be a different standard of justice on the basis of race, religious beliefs, or sexual orientation? Why or why not?
5. Would you use the homosexual advance theory in this case? Why or why not?

KEY TERMS

bisexuality
canteen punk
crimes against persons
crimes against property
crimes against society
gay bashing
homogeneity
homosexual advance theory
homosexuality
jocker

queen
pressure punk
prisonization
punk
red-light districts
sexual orientation
situational homosexuality
subculture
voir dire
wolf

DISCUSSION QUESTIONS

1. Do you think the change in the structure of women's prisons, where they now resemble male institutions, has affected the nature of social interaction and sexual behavior? Is this a good thing or does it present more serious problems for prison officials?
2. As homosexual behavior continues to gain some level of acceptability in society, do you think the police subculture will become more tolerant of gay police officers? Why or why not?
3. Do you think that jurors are biased against gay people? What do you think about the homosexual advance theory—should offenders' responsibility be reduced for the crime they committed if the victim made a sexual advance toward them?
4. Why do you think many Americans are opposed to same-sex marriage? Is it simply based on religion or are gays perceived as a threat in some ways?
5. Some people argue that if a person engages in homosexual behavior, then they must be a homosexual. Do you think there is really a difference? Why or why not?

FOR FURTHER READING

D'Emilio, J. *Sexual Politics, Sexual Communities: The Making of a Homosexual Minority in the United States 1940–1970*. New York: Basic Books, 1983.

Katz, J. *Gay American History*. New York: Avon Books, 1978.

Leinen, S. *Gay Cops*. Brunswick, NJ: Rutgers University Press, 1993.

Sykes, G. *The Society of Captives: A Study of a Maximum Security Prison*. Princeton, NJ: Princeton University Press, 1958.

Owens, B. *In the Mix: Struggle and Survival in a Women's Prison*. Albany, NY: State University of Albany Press, 1989.

NOTES

1. Z. Ford, Z. "Five Stories of LGBT People Being Unfairly Treated by the Criminal Justice System," Think Progress, 2014, available at http://thinkprogress.org/lgbt/2014/05/07/3435157/5-stories-of-lgbt-people-being-unfairly-treated-by-the-criminal-justice-system/
2. Ibid.
3. Ibid.
4. Pew Research Center, *Changing Attitudes on Gay Marriage*, May 12, 2016, available at http://www.pewforum.org/2015/07/29/graphics-slideshow-changing-attitudes-on-gay-marriage/
5. G. Gentile, "Disney Opens Weddings to Gay Couples." Associated Press. April 6, 2007.
6. Susan Page, "Poll Shows Backlash on Gay Issues," *USA Today*, May 20, 2005.
7. Lambda Legal, "Protected and Served? Survey of LGBT/HIV Contact with Police, Prisons, Courts and Schools," Fact Sheet, 2014.
8. C. Hanssens, A. C. Moodie-Mills, A. J. Ritchie, D. Spade, and U. Vaid, *A Roadmap for Change: Federal Policy Recommendations for Addressing the Criminalization of LGBT People and People Living with HIV* (New York: Center for Gender and Sexuality Law, Columbia Law School, 2014).
9. C. J. Summers, ed., An Encyclopedia of Gay, Lesbian, Bisexual, Transgender, and Queer Culture (Chicago, Illinois: Glbtq, Inc., 2004).
10. Ibid.
11. Cheshire Calhoun, "Separating Lesbian Theory from Feminist Theory," Ethics 104, no. 3 (April 1994): 558–81.

12. Ibid.
13. Mark J. Stern, "Born this Way?" *Slate*, June 28, 2013, available at http://www.slate.com/articles/health_and_science/science/2013/06/biological_basis_for_homosexuality_the_fraternal_birth_order_explanation.html
14. Dick. F. Swaab, "Sexual Orientation and its Basis in Brain Structure and Function," *Proceedings of the National Academy of Sciences*, 105, no. 30 (July 2008), available at http://www.pnas.org/content/105/30/10273.full
15. Simon LeVay, "A Difference in Hypothalamic Structure Between Heterosexual and Homosexual Men," *Science*, 253, no. 5023 (August 1991): 1034, available at https://www.ncbi.nlm.nih.gov/pubmed/1887219
16. Ibid.
17. C. Grov, T. J. Parsons, and D. S. Bimbi, "Cruising for Sex Among Gay and Bisexual Men: Different Venues, Different Risks," *Journal of Sex Research* (February 2006).
18. J. D'Emilio, *Sexual Politics, Sexual Communities: The Making of a Homosexual Minority in the United States 1940–1970* (New York: Basic Books, 1983).
19. Ibid.
20. Ibid.
21. J. Katz, *Gay American History* (New York: Avon Books, 1978).
22. D'Emilio, *Sexual Politics*.
23. Katz, *Gay American History*.
24. D'Emilio, *Sexual Politics*.
25. Ibid.
26. Katz, *Gay American History*.
27. D'Emilio, *Sexual Politics*.
28. Obergfell v. Hodges 576 U.S. ___2015.
29. Department of Justice, Uniform Crime Reports, *Hate Crimes in the United States* (Washington, DC: U.S. Government Printing Office, 2014).
30. Ibid.
31. Ibid.
32. Ibid.
33. Ibid.
34. Ibid.
35. Ibid.
36. D. Kopel, "Hate Crime Laws: Dangerous and Divisive," Independence Institute, Jan. 13, 2003.
37. Ibid.
38. Ibid.
39. Ibid.
40. Hanssens, et al., *A Roadmap for Change*.
41. National Coalition of Anti-Violence Programs, *Report on Lesbian, Gay, Bisexual and Transgender, Queer, and HIV-Affected Hate Violence in 2012*, June 3, 2013. Available at http://www.avp.org/storage/documents/ncavp_2012_hvreport_final.pdf
42. Lambda Legal, "Protected and Served?"
43. National Coalition of Anti-Violence Programs, *Report*.
44. Human Rights Campaign. 2012. *HRC Issue Brief: Housing and Homelessness*, available at http://www.hrc.org/files/assets/resources/HousingAndHomeless_Document.pdf; see also, A. Greenblatt, "In Some Cities, Gays Face Greater Risk of Becoming Homeless," National

Public Radio, August 7, 2013, available at http://www.npr.org/2013/08/06/209510271/in-some-cities-gays-face-greater-risk-of-becoming-homeless.

45. New York Commission for Lesbian, Gay, Bisexual, Transgender, and Questioning Youth, *All Our Children: Strategies to Prevent Homelessness, Strengthen Services and Build Support for LGBTQ Youth*, (June, 2010), available at http://www.nyc.gov/html/om/pdf/2010/pr267_10_report.pdf

46. National Prison Rape Elimination Commission, *National Prison Rape Elimination Commission Report*, 2011. Available at http://static.nicic.gov/usershared/2013-03-29_nprec_finalreport.pdf; see also W. Harrell, "Prisons: The Next Frontier for LGBTI Rights," *The Life of the Law*, 2013, available at http://www.lifeofthelaw.org/prisons-the-next-frontier-for-lgbti-rights/

47. See for instance E. Bittner, *The Functions of Police in Modern Society* (Chevy Chase, MD: National Clearinghouse for Mental Health, 1970); G. Kirkham, *Signal Zero* (New York: Ballentine, 1970); Milton Rokeach, Martin Miller, and Hohn Snyder. 1971. "The Value Gap Between Police and Policed," *Journal of Social Issues* 27 (1971): 155–71; William Westley, *Violence and the Police: A Sociological Study of Law, Custom, and Morality* (Cambridge, MA: MIT Press, 1970).

48. M. Bernstein and C. Kostelac, "Lavender and Blue: Attitudes about Homosexuality and Behavior Toward Lesbians and Gay Men Among Police Officers," *Journal of Contemporary Criminal Justice* 18, no. 3 (2002): 302–28.

49. J. Younglove, M. G. Kerr, and C. J. Vitello, "Law Enforcement Officers' Perceptions of Same Sex Domestic Violence: Reason for Cautious Optimism," *Journal of Interpersonal Violence* 17, no. 7 (2001): 760–72.

50. S. Leinen, *Gay Cops* (Brunswick, NJ: Rutgers University Press, 1993)

51. A. Belkin, and J. McNichol, "Pink and Blue: Outcomes Associated with the Integration of Openly Gay and Lesbian Personnel in the San Diego Police Department," *Police Quarterly* 5, no. 1 (2002): 63–95.

52. T. Henneman, "A Gun and Badge for Gays: Becoming an Openly Gay Police Officer Used to Mean Facing Harassment and Rejection. Now Departments Across the Country are Actively Seeking Gay Recruits," *The Advocate: The National Gay and Lesbian News Magazine*, May 9, 2006.

53. See for instance the Washington DC Metropolitan Police Department's Gay Liaison Unit, January 11, 2016, available at https://mpdc.dc.gov/page/lesbian-gay-bisexual-and-transgender-liaison-unit-lgbtlu

54. Henneman, "A Gun and Badge for Gays."

55. Keegan, "Gay Police Officers."

56. S. Miller, K. B. Forest, and N. C. Jurik, "Diversity in Blue: Lesbian and Gay Police Officers in a Masculine Operation," *Men and Masculinities* 5, no. 4 (2003): 355–85.

57. K. A. Myers, K. B. Forest, and S. L. Miller, "Officer Friendly and the Tough Cop: Gays and Lesbians Navigate Homophobia and Policing," *Journal of Homosexuality* 47, no. 1 (2004): 17–37.

58. Leinen, *Gay Cops*, 79.

59. M. E. Burke, *Coming Out of the Blue: British Police Officers Talk About Their Lives in 'The Job' as Lesbians, Gays and Bisexuals* (London: Cassell, 1993).

60. H. C. Brunelli, "The Double Bind: Unequal Treatment for Homosexuals Within the American Legal Framework," *Boston College Third World Law Journal*, 2004.

61. R. Minson, "Homophobia in Manslaughter: The Homosexual Advance As Insufficient Provocation," *California Law Review* 80 (1992): 133. See also, J. Dressler, "When Heterosexual Men Kill Homosexual Men: Reflections on Provocation Law, Sexual Advance, and the Reasonable Man Standard," *Journal of Criminal Law and Criminology* 85 (1995): 726.

62. Brunelli, "The Double Bind."

63. Ibid.

64. C. Hensley, J. Wright, R. Tewksbury, and T. Castle, "The Evolving Nature of Prison Argot and Sexual Hierarchies," in *Behind Bars: Readings in Prison Culture*, ed. R. Tewksbury (Upper Saddle River, NJ: Prentice-Hall, 2006), 421–29.

65. G. Sykes, *The Society of Captives: A Study of a Maximum Security Prison* (Princeton, NJ: Princeton University Press, 1958).

66. A. I. Ibrahaim, "Deviant Sexual Behavior in Men's Prisons," *Crime and Delinquency* 20, no. 1 (1974): 38–44. See also L. Bowker, *Prison Victimization* (New York: Elsevier North Holland, 1980).

67. C. Hopper, "The Evolution of Conjugal Visiting in Mississippi," *The Prison Journal* 69, no. 1 (1989):103–109.

68. C. Saum, H. Surratt, J. Inciardi, and R. Bennett, "Sex in Prison: Exploring the Myths and Realities," *The Prison Journal* 75, no. 4 (1995): 413–30.

69. See, for instance, P. Naccis and T. Kane, "Sex and Sexual Aggression in Federal Prisons." *Federal Probation* 47, no. 4 (1983) : 31–36; Saum, et al. "Sex in Prison"; R. Tewksbury, "Measures of Sexual Behavior in an Ohio Prison," *Sociology and Social Research* 74, no. 1 (1989): 34–39; W. Wooden and J. Parker, *Men Behind Bars: Sexual Exploitation in Prison* (New York: Plenum, 1982).

70. L. Carroll, *Hacks, Blacks and Cons* (Lexington, MA: D.C. Heath, 1974).

71. C. Hensley, R. Tewksbury, and J. Wright, "Exploring the Dynamics of Masturbation and Consensual Same-Sex Activity Within a Male Maximum Security Prison," in Tewksbury, *Behind Bars*, 97–109.

72. J. Pollock, *Counseling Women in Prison* (Thousand Oaks, CA: Sage, 1998).

73. B. Owens, *In the Mix: Struggle and Survival in a Women's Prison* (Albany, NY: State University of Albany Press, 1989).

74. K. Greer, "The Changing Nature of Interpersonal Relationships in a Women's Prison," in Tewksbury, *Behind Bars*,110–28.

75. National Coalition of Anti-Violence Programs, *Report*.

76. Ibid.

77. See "Each Year, Immigration Equality Fields Inquiries from Over 1,000 LGBT or HIV-Positive Foreign Nationals and Their Loved Ones About Their Options Under U.S. Immigration Law." Available at Immigration Equality at **http://immigrationequality.org/about/**

78. National Coalition of Anti-Violence Programs, *Report*.

CHAPTER 9

THE ELDERLY AND THE CRIMINAL JUSTICE SYSTEM

CHAPTER OBJECTIVES:

After reading this chapter, you should be able to:

- Describe the characteristics of the elderly population in the United States
- Understand victimization patterns for the elderly
- Describe the types of activities elderly criminals commonly engage in
- Discuss the challenges elderly criminals and inmates pose for the criminal justice system

There can be little doubt that the population in the United States is getting older. According to *the Statistical Abstract of the U.S.*, in 2005 there were approximately 36 million people aged 65 and over, which represented about 13 percent of the population.[1] In 2012, the most current data available, that number is over 43 million, which is still about 13 percent of the U.S. population.[2] While there are problems in determining what constitutes "elderly," the generally accepted age category is 65 and older.

As a result of improvements in health and medicine, people are living longer in this country. According to the Center for Disease Control, the life expectancy of an American in 1960 was 69.7 years, in 1990 it was 75.4 years, and in 2012, it was 78.8 years.[3] Additionally, all of the age categories one might use to describe the elderly: 55 and over, 65 and over, and 75 and over, witnessed dramatic increases in size since 1980. The 55 and over category increased by 42 percent, the 65 and over category increased by 44 percent while the 75 and over category witnessed an 82 percent increase.

This explosive growth is expected to continue. According to the U.S. Census Bureau, by 2050, people age 65 years and over will almost double its size in 2012, to 83.7 million. The Census Bureau has included a new category, 85 years and over, in making its projections for the next fifty years. In fact, by 2050, the Census Bureau expects that the surviving baby boomers will be over the age of 85.[4] The implications of the population getting older means that the elderly population will become more racially and ethnically diverse and programs like Social Security and Medicare, as well as healthcare providers, families, and businesses will be affected by this trend.

The Census Bureau notes of the 43 million people in the 65 and over age group, 18.8 million were men and 24.3 million were women. The majority of this group were married, 58 percent, while 26 percent were widowed and 26 percent were divorced. About 81 percent in this age category were high school graduates and 24 percent had a college degree. Only about 9 percent of the 65 and over age group were living below the **poverty line**, the income level at which people are entitled to public assistance such as welfare.[5] The low poverty rate among the elderly is primarily due to Social Security benefits. Without programs like Social Security, most experts believe that about half the elderly would be poor.[6]

The racial composition of the elderly in 2012 consisted of Whites, who comprised about 37 million of the total 43 million people age 65 and older (85 percent). Similarly, African Americans comprised about 8 percent of the elderly population in the U.S. in 2012 (about 3.7 million people) and those who were identified as having Hispanic or Latino origin represented about 7 percent of the elderly population in 2012 (about 3.1 million people).[7]

In general then, the population as a whole is getting older, the numbers of people considered elderly is growing, and they are living longer. There can be little doubt that as the elderly population continues to grow, the social and economic issues that they represent are considerable. One of those costs relates to healthcare, another relates to crime.[8]

BABY BOOMERS, GENERATION X, AND GENERATION Y

After World War II ended, the United States experienced an explosion of births, nearly 76 million from 1946 to 1964. Sociologists define those born during those years as **baby boomers**. This group represents about 28 percent of the U.S. population and is responsible for some of the most dramatic changes in American history. From the Vietnam War protests to the Civil Rights Movement to the rise of feminism and the hippie movement, baby boomers have been at the center of the debate, discussion, and social change. This group, many of whom turned sixty years old in 2006, comprises some of the country's leading politicians, entertainers, and social activists. Baby boomers have also been referred to as the "Me" generation for their emphasis on narcissism and individual pleasure. In fact, this group has fundamentally altered the way in which the elderly are understood in American society. Not content to simply age gracefully like their parents, this group has remained healthy and active into their retirement years. As a result, baby boomers have changed the way most Americans conceive of normal aging.[9]

Baby boomers focused on their careers, leisure activities, and many delayed having children or remained childless. As a result, an anticipated second baby boom generation did not occur. The subsequent generation, clearly smaller in size, consisting of about 41 million, were born roughly between 1968 and 1979. These are often referred to as **Generation X** (Gen Xers). Many experts argue that this group has often been ignored and misunderstood, a disheartened generation.[10] Gen Xers are generally marked by their lack of optimism for the future and an absence of trust in traditional values. During the early 1990s, the media portrayed Gen Xers as a group of overeducated, underachieving "slackers," who are more concerned with tattoos, body piercings, and who spawned the grunge music movement.

Gen Xers grew up during the end of the Cold War, the Reagan administration, and witnessed the economic depression of the 1990s. Many members of this generation watched as their parents coped with the loss of their careers and jobs due to outsourcing, deindustrialization, and corporate mergers. This had a profound impact on many Gen Xers, who realized that company loyalty and sacrifices to get ahead did not always pay off. As a result, many Gen Xers did not take advantage of their education or talents and ended up in *McJobs*, or jobs in the lowest paying sectors of the market, including many minimum wage jobs. This lack of stability in the job market left many Gen Xers with a strong sense of cynicism about their lives, future, and the country as a whole. This group is also generally critical of the baby boomer generation, whom many Gen Xers look upon as self-centered and impractical.[11]

Generation Y (Gen Yers), those born approximately between 1977 and 1994, make up over 20 percent of the U.S. population or 70 million people. This generation is a large one and they are likely to have a significant impact on this country's social and economic landscape in the future. Generation Y is characterized by three main elements. First, members are comfortable and tolerant of the racial and ethnic diversity around them and feel comfortable interacting with people outside their own ethnic group.

Second, one of the most noted trends in the Generation Y segment of the population is that for parents of Generation Y children, much of the family focus is on them. That is, unlike parents of Generation X, parents of Generation Y kids are very involved in the daily lives and decisions of their children. Parents often help Gen Yers plan their achievements, take part in their daily activities, and strongly encourage their children to succeed. This encouragement by parents make members of the Y Generation believe they can accomplish anything. Their relationship with their parents also make it more likely for Gen Yers to feel they can always return home to their parents for support and assistance.

Third, an important characteristic of this generation is that its members are technologically savvy—Gen Yers tend to be more sophisticated in their computer skills than previous groups. This is largely due to being exposed to and using technology at an early age. For instance, three out of four teenagers are online and 93 percent of those ages 15 to 17 are computer users. The time spent online consists of gaming, emailing, and instant messaging according to the National Center for Health Statistics.[12] This generation is ambitious and have high expectations of themselves and those around them. It also means this group is accustomed to instant gratification and tend to be overly confident. This group is also often characterized as those who are willing to cheat, if necessary, to achieve their goals. On the positive side, this group is very adaptable in a variety of settings, efficient at multitasking, and they possess the technological skills and educational talents to achieve significant goals.[13]

ELDERLY CRIME

Since the early 1970s some attention has been paid to the relationship between crime and the elderly.[14] The majority of this focus has been on fear of crime as well as elderly victimization. While conventional wisdom has been that the elderly are at the greatest risk of becoming the victims of crime, research has consistently shown that they have the lowest rates of actual victimization.[15] However, fear itself can be seen as a form of victimization, and the elderly, along with females, express the highest levels of fear. Moreover, the consequences of actual victimization can be more severe for the elderly than other age groups because of their physical limitations as well as their limited economic ability to recover from the financial losses sustained by crime.

ELDERLY VICTIMS

As a general rule, as a person ages, rates of victimization tend to decline. According to the National Crime Victimization Survey (NCVS), elderly persons, those over the age of 65, experienced less violence and fewer property crimes than younger persons between 1993 and 2013. Property crime provided the greatest threat to those age 65 or older. Elderly persons age 65 or older had substantially lower victimization rates of violent crime (3.6 victimizations per 1,000 persons) compared to younger people age 12 to 24 (49.9 victimizations per 1,000 persons or people ages 25 to 49 (27.6 per 1,000). While the elderly made up about 21 percent of the population age 12 or older during 1993 to 2013, they accounted for less than 4 percent of all serious crime during that same period.[16]

The NCVS for 2014 showed that between 1993 and 2013, the victimization of the elderly for violent crime such as homicide is quite low. The data also reveals that older teens and young adults (18 to 24 years old) experienced the highest homicide rate, however this trend has shown a decline since its peak in the early 1990s. In general nonfatal violent crime rate for the elderly declined 41 percent from 1994 to 2013 and the homicide rate declined 44 percent. Moreover, the elderly homicide rates were lower than the rates for all other age groups between 1994 and 2011.[17]

Similarly, property crime committed against the elderly decreased by 48 percent from 1994 to 2013. Like violent crime, the rate of property crime for all age groups saw a decrease during this ten-year period, but the percentage decrease for the elderly was lower than for other age groups. For instance, property crime decreased by 48 percent for the elderly compared to declines of 55 percent for those ages 12 to 24, 60 percent for those ages 25 to 49, and 52 percent for those ages 50 to 64.[18] With regard to identity theft, persons age 65 or older had higher incidents than persons ages 16 to 24 (5.0 percent vs. 3.8 percent), but this could be due to the fact that the elderly generally have more assets and resources than this younger group. The rates for the elderly were still lower than identity theft for other age groups such as persons ages 25 to 49 (7.9 percent) or ages 50 to 64 (7.8 percent).[19]

While the elderly are much less likely to experience victimization for either violent or property crimes, they are much more likely to report crimes to the police than their younger counterparts. About 56 percent of the elderly reported incidents of violent crime and 38 percent of property to the police compared to 38 percent of those who were ages 12 to 24. Interestingly, no differences were shown between the elderly and other age groups.

ELDERLY ABUSE

Another type of victimization concerns elderly abuse. No one knows exactly how many older Americans are abused, neglected, or exploited each year; part of the reason for this has to do with the problems of defining elder abuse. Additionally, there is no uniform reporting system, rendering any type of comprehensive national database difficult to obtain. A study funded by the National Institute of Justice of more than seven thousand elders living in a community, found that approximately one in ten reported experiencing at least one form of elder mistreatment in the past year. The study found that financial exploitation by a family member occurred in the past year by about 5 percent of participants.[20] Another NIJ funded study of abuse in assisted living facilities found that verbal and psychological abuse were the most common forms of abuse reported by care workers.[21] Finally, in another study, based on both staff accounts of incidents as well as responses by residents themselves, there appears to be an increasing trend toward elder mistreatment by patients themselves in residential care facilities.[22]

Elder abuse is one of the most underreported crimes.

Like many crimes, elder abuse often goes unreported. According to the National Center on Elder Abuse, for every case of elder abuse, neglect, or exploitation, or self-neglect reported to authorities, about five more go unreported.[23] Additionally, the types of abuse vary. One type involves financial exploitation. This is usually the result of some sort of confidence game or fraud committed against the elderly. According to one study, the overall reporting of financial exploitation is about 1 in 25 cases, which translates into about 5 million financial abuse victims each year.[24]

Another type of elderly victimization is physical abuse. A study of nursing homes found that among seven types of abuse, physical abuse was the most common type reported.[25] The National Center on Elder Abuse found that older women were far more likely than men to suffer from physical abuse or neglect—almost two-thirds (65.7 percent) of elder abuse victims were women. This study also found that 43 percent of abuse victims were age 80 or older. The abusers in this study were primarily females (52.7 percent) and three-fourths of offenders were under age 60. About half of the perpetrators of elderly abuse were members of the victim's family—a third of the perpetrators were adult children and another 21 percent were other family members. Spouses or intimate partners accounted for only 11 percent of the total number of offenders. According to the study, caregiver neglect accounted for about 20 percent of all neglect cases.[26]

ELDERLY OFFENDERS

While a great deal of attention has been given to elderly victims, relatively little has been offered on elderly offenders. The image of the elderly offender is filled with stereotypes and misinformation. Because people think of the elderly as infirm or limited in mobility, it is relatively easy to conclude that these individuals commit relatively "harmless" crimes, such as shoplifting or other nonviolent acts. However as was mentioned, there is no consensus in determining when someone is considered "elderly." Most people use sixty-five years old as the cutoff point. This is the usual retirement age, the point at which one is eligible for Social Security benefits, pensions, retirement income, Medicare, and so on. But the number is rather arbitrarily designated. Additionally, the agencies that collect data on crime vary considerably in their **operationalization** of age, or how they define it for the purpose of analysis.

For example, the FBI, in their analysis of crime statistics, uses "65 and over" as the upper most category in arrest data, but include 55 to 59 and 60 to 64 age groups as well. Other agencies in the criminal justice system, such as the Federal Bureau of Prisons, use forty-five as their cutoff point, while some state systems use sixty. More recently, some states have taken to using the degree of disability in their definition rather than chronological age. An added problem is that the elderly population tends to overlap with two other special needs categories: the chronically and terminally ill.[27] In general, the criminal justice system often classifies those "55 and over" as elderly. Opinions vary as to why this is the case, but many researchers contend that the reason for the differences has to do with collapsing intervals in order to have enough people in the respective categories.[28] However, this variability makes it difficult to compare information about elderly criminals from one study to the next.

To complicate the problem further, some researchers relate age categories to the type of crime committed. For instance, "joyriding" tends to be committed by teenagers. If a person 35 years of age is arrested for joyriding, for the purpose of statistical analysis, he or she could be defined as an elderly offender, largely because people in this age group typically do not engage in this type of activity. As a result of these problems, most researchers rely on the chronological categorization of age, but even here, problems emerge.[29]

The classification based on age is but one part of the problem. There is also the problem of defining a crime. When people typically talk about the "crime problem" they are referring to street crime. Using this definition, crime statistics reflect the image that crime tends to be a young, minority, male phenomenon. However, this is an overly simplistic definition of crime since it does not take into account white collar or organized crime, nor does it include professional criminals, most of whom tend to be older. While crime is generally considered a "young man's game," it is important to account for when, and under what circumstances, the elderly become involved in criminal activity. As was mentioned, according to the Uniform Crime Reports, which classifies arrests by age, there are three general categories to use in assessing elderly criminals: 55 to 59, 60 to 64, and 65 and older. Given the problems of operationalizing the term "elderly," for the purpose of this chapter, all three categories will be used.

AGING MOBSTER, 96, SENTENCED

Ninety-six-year-old Albert "The Old Man" Facchiano, a "made member" of the Genovese crime family, the nation's largest and most powerful Mafia family for decades, pleaded guilty to charges of racketeering, conspiracy, and jury tampering. According to prosecutors, Facchiano supervised robberies, money laundering, bank fraud and stolen merchandise from 1994 to 2006. He also pled guilty to trying to locate and intimidate a government witness in New York in 2005. Facchiano becomes one of the oldest criminals to plead guilty to federal crimes and one of the oldest to have committed crimes at such an advanced age. During the court hearing, Facchiano used a special headset to hear questions from the U.S. District Court judge. When asked by the judge "Is your mind okay?" Facchiano eventually responded "Oh yes, I can't hear, but I can understand, your honor." Facchiano's attorney stated that his client sees a doctor four times a week, suffers from back pain and a host of other ailments. While the charges against Facchiano carried a prison sentence of up to thirty years and $500,000 in fines, by pleading guilty, prosecutors recommended Facchiano serve house arrest, citing that any form of incarceration would be a form of capital punishment.

Elderly Criminals and the Criminal Justice System

While the research on elderly criminals is relatively small, it is worth noting that each phase of the criminal justice system is confronted with the challenges presented by elderly criminals. For the police, there is ample research that the age of the suspect, along with other factors, plays a role in how the officer evaluates a situation. However, this applies mostly to young offenders—few, if any, police departments provide training on how to deal with elderly suspects. However, it could be that some officers might take a more lenient view of elderly offenders, particularly if the crime is not a serious one. However, what about the elderly criminal who continues to commit crimes without any remorse or concern for the victims? Or when a respectable citizen who is elderly commits a crime such as a sex crime against a minor, a crime involving the sale of drugs, or even a DUI charge? While it may be that conventional wisdom assumes that the elderly are given a more gentle touch when they engage in minor offenses, not all officers or suspects are, or should be treated the same.[30]

Similarly, as it relates to how the courts deal with elderly criminals, while the decision to pass sentence should include factors such as the seriousness of the crime, the suspect's criminal record, and other factors relating to the activity, should the age of the offender and his or her declining health also be factors to consider at the sentencing stage? Like the challenges facing the police, the issue is anything but clear—some argue that older offenders should know better while opponents think that this should be a mitigating factor in an offender's sentence. The research on the role of age of the offender at sentencing is mixed— the general conclusion is that age of the offender, if they are elderly, should be considered a mitigating factor for minor charges, such as shoplifting.[31]

Where the issue of elderly offenders becomes most significant is at the incarceration stage. While the number of studies on elderly criminals remains small, particularly after the 1980s, the most recent research continues to focus on the challenges of older inmates and the economic costs to states that are responsible for their healthcare. As a result of the harsh sentences in the 1980s and 1990s, many offenders have remained in prison for an extended period of time. The deleterious effect of prison life in general, coupled with whatever other problems inmates brought with them to prison, are the subject of considerable debate and present challenges to correctional institutions that were not designed to be ADA compliant or to contain the medical facilities necessary to treat chronically ill and aging inmates.[32] Yet, that is exactly what is occurring and many states wrestle with how to provide an adequate standard of care and to provide some level of protection to medically and emotionally disabled inmates.

What is interesting about the research on this population during the 1980s was that many experts were looking at elderly criminals as the onset of a social problem.[33] In their seminal text, *Constructing Social Problems*, John Kitsuse and Malcom Spector state that **claimsmaking** is a fundamental aspect of how social problems are defined in a given society.[34] When people, particularly experts, assert that an event or phenomenon is problematic for a society, the process of making a claim occurs, and a social problem is created. This same process occurred in the literature on elderly criminals. Because it seemed logical at the time, and because many researchers were pointing to the inevitability of an increase in elderly offenders, many criminal justice researchers and sociologists were convinced of the validity of these claims. As an illustration, the authors of one of the most comprehensive texts on the subject of elderly criminals offered this prediction:

> It is a rare opportunity to see a social problem coming with enough lead time to do something about it. We are very sure that the demographic balance of our population will shift so that more people will be in the upper age ranges. As this occurs, the elderly crime problem can only assume a more important position on our list of domestic problems. It seems particularly appropriate to begin developing policies of control and prevention right now.[35]

However, just as the research in the 1980s intensified in anticipation of a significant social problem, the research nearly stopped in the 1990s. As was mentioned, while some assessment of this subject continues, it is usually much more focused on the effects of incarceration rather than the incidence of elderly crime.[36] Few studies make reference to the expectations of a decade earlier. However, this is not to say what was discovered during this time period was flawed—a great deal was learned about the range of activities of many elderly offenders.

At first glance, the dramatic decrease in the number of studies suggests a wavering interest in the topic, which could be taken as evidence that the elderly crime wave failed to occur. However, a better indicator of the accuracy of this prediction would be an analysis of arrest statistics much in the same way that they were conducted in the 1980s. One study, for example, analyzed arrest statistics from the Uniform Crime Reports between 1964 and 1979, and found a dramatic increase of arrests for serious crimes among those 55 years old and over. The findings of this study showed a significant increase in the percentage of elderly arrests for property crime, motor vehicle theft, and sex offenses, especially when compared to the rest of the offender population. The conclusion drawn from this study was that while the elderly constitute only a small part of the total arrests, there was every reason to expect the number of elderly arrests would increase dramatically as the entire population grew older.[37] An analysis of the Uniform Crime Reports arrest statistics was done from 1990 to 1994 in an effort to assess these predictions over time. The findings from this study showed that the percentage of arrests for the population increased from 1990 to 1994, but the overall arrest rate for elderly offenders decreased by 5 percent.[38]

Table 9.1 Violent and Property Crime by Age Group, 2004 and 2014

	2004			2014		
	55–59	60–64	65 and over	55–59	60–64	65 and over
Violent Crime	5,899	2,930	2,710	11,276	5,056	4,246
Property Crime	13,259	5,897	5,576	30,176	13,441	9,518
Total Arrests	1,186,390			1,226,608		

There was also a difference from the previous research with regard to violent crime, which increased almost as much for elderly offenders as it did for the rest of the population, while property crimes witnessed a dramatic decrease. In comparing arrest statistics between 2004 and 2014, the property crime and violent crime rates showed an increase, even though the total numbers of arrests for all categories declined for violent crime. On average, elderly criminals represented a small percentage of the total number of arrests in both 2004 and 2014. In virtually every age category, whether it was property crime or violent crime, the number of arrests nearly doubled. In 2004, there were 5,899 arrests in the 55 to 59 age group, 2,930 in the 60 to 64 category, and 2,710 in the group 65 and over. In 2014, for each respective category, those numbers were 11,276 for the 55 to 59 age group, 5,056 for those 60 to 64, and 4,246 for those over age 65. The same trend can be seen in property crime arrests.

Thus, the current trends in crime committed by the elderly, as well as the types of crimes, are somewhat supported from what was known in the 1980s. Recall that the research predicted the number of offenders would increase as the population got older, and the data seems to suggest that arrests on the upswing.[39]

Because of the complexity of the issues involving elderly criminals, some advocates promote the idea of a separate court system for this population.

TYPES OF ELDERLY OFFENSES

SHOPLIFTING

As was mentioned, the image of the elderly criminal strikes most people as incongruous with their understanding of crime in society. When Americans think of elderly criminals, it is not uncommon to envision a rather passive and benign type of offender: one who does not injure his or her victims and commits economic crimes rather than violent ones. Shoplifting is one type of crime that fits this image. It is passive, it does not usually lead to injuries to bystanders, and one does not need a great deal of dexterity or mobility to commit it.

Many people also attempt to deflect the culpability of the elderly offender by offering exculpatory reasons for committing this act, such as economic hardship or lack of intent. In other words, elderly shoplifters are simply those people who forget to pay for their purchases and then are apprehended when they attempt to leave the premises. Loneliness is also used as an explanation by some scholars, in that the elderly criminal is in need of contact with others and, like a young child, steals for the attention they receive.[40]

But what do we really know about elderly shoplifters? One of the few studies of this population examined 191 first time offenders in Florida who agreed to participate in a court-ordered diversion program. In trying to answer the question that elderly shoplifters steal because they are poor, researchers in this study collected data on the offenders' income, occupation, and whether or not they owned a home. With regard to income, the median monthly income level was approximately $7,500 and about half of those cases (45 percent) derived their incomes from three or more sources: interest from savings, stocks and bonds, and Social Security benefits. Most were white-collar workers, professionals, and administrators in their former careers. Moreover, 83 percent of offenders owned their place of residence. Thus, the vast majority of elderly shoplifters in this study were homeowners and had sufficient resources, which runs counter to the indigent argument.

Additionally, of the objects stolen, the most common were clothing items and cosmetics rather than subsistence or need-based items such as food or drugs. Researchers in this study also attempted to document the "lack of intent" explanation, where shoplifting cases by the elderly were due to forgetfulness rather than intentionally stealing them. While there are instances where people innocuously take items and forget to pay for them, this explanation loses much of its validity when multiple items are taken. That is, most people can understand forgetting one item, but the intent to shoplift becomes more credible as the number increases. In this study, about half (48 percent) of the cases involved two or three stolen items.

Finally, as was mentioned, a popular explanation for elderly shoplifting involves loneliness. In these cases, the elderly offender is isolated from social interaction and craves attention. However, the findings of this particular study showed that approximately 70 percent of the offenders did not live alone, and 65 percent were married. In addition, approximately 80 percent indicated that they have family members or close friends living in the area. Other tests of social isolation given to offenders supported the conclusion that the offenders were not stealing due to loneliness or feeling isolated from the larger community.[41]

Table 9.2 Larceny-Theft by Age, 2004 and 2014

| | 2004 | | | 2014 | | |
	55–59	60–64	65+	55–59	60–64	65+
Larceny-Theft	11,555	5,256	55,138	26,879	11,940	8,735
Total Arrests		858,821			978,033	

In sum, the research on the elderly shoplifter, while still quite scant, runs counter to popular understanding of why these individuals engage in this type of criminal activity. They are not indigent, are not without other resources, and appear to have adequate social and emotional support networks. Moreover, elderly shoplifters do not appear to be retaliating against businesses they patronized. In fact, many rate the establishments from which they steal rather high in terms of the services they provided.

While no formal category of shoplifting exists in official statistics, according to the Uniform Crime Reports, there has been a dramatic increase in the number of arrests for crimes like shoplifting. In 2004 there were a total of 858,821 larceny-theft arrests. This included 11,555 larceny-theft arrests for those in the 55 to 59 age group, 5,256 in the 60 to 64 category, and 55,138 in the over 65 age group. In 2014, there were a total of 978,033 arrests, a 12 percent increase. This included 26,879 arrests for the 55 to 59 age group, a 57 percent increase since 2004. There were also 11,940 arrests in the 60 to 64 age group, a 6 percent increase since 2004, and in the over 65 age category, there were 8,735 arrests in 2014, a substantial decrease from the 55,138 in 2004.[42]

HOMICIDE

While relatively few homicides occur in the United States each year, the number and proportions of violent crime committed by the elderly remains less than 2 percent on any given year, according to arrest statistics from the Uniform Crime Reports.[43]

While a great deal of attention is given to older victims of homicide, information is generally lacking on older homicide offenders. In the quest to demystify some of the notions about this topic, one study examined elderly homicide using *Supplemental Homicide Reports* by the Federal Bureau of Investigation to profile elderly homicide offenders. The study showed that, like the fluctuation in the overall homicide rate, the rate for the elderly is not stable across jurisdictions. As a result, the elderly offender is affected by the same sociological factors that create different murder rates among younger adults from state to state.

Some experts argue that elderly offenders would be more likely to kill those of their own age than offenders in other categories. Some of the research on this topic shows that many young homicide offenders kill people older than they are as a result of robberies or the commission of other felonies.[44] Since the data shows that the elderly are not as likely to be involved in these kinds of activities, one might conclude that older people *would* be more likely to kill within their own age group. However, the data suggests that the opposite is true. According to the Uniform Crime Reports for 2014, people in the 60 to 64 and

65 to 74 group were actually less likely to kill someone their own age and about 21 percent of those age 50 and over kill victims of the same age.

Finally, it was argued that elderly offenders would be more likely to use firearms than offenders in other age groups. The logic, of course, is that since the elderly are not as strong as younger people, they would be more likely to use a gun to commit the crime. Twenty years ago a study found that this was supported by the data: elderly offenders were more likely to use firearms than the nonelderly. In the mid 1990s, another study of elderly homicide offenders was conducted in Detroit.[45] Many of the trends identified in initial study of elderly homicide remained constant almost ten years later. This study found that older homicide offenders were more likely to use firearms in the commission of a crime than their younger counterparts. The author of this study also found that "Proportionally fewer homicides perpetrated by older persons appear to be committed between 8:00 pm and 1:59 am. For some reason, the elderly are less inclined to kill late at night than are the nonelderly."[46]

An analysis of homicide statistics from 1976 to 2004 revealed that only about 8 percent of offenders age 50 and older used a firearm to commit a homicide.[47] This data suggests that elderly homicide offenders are not significantly different in many ways from other types of murderers, although some of the practical aspects of committing the crime account for some differences in their rates. For instance, unlike younger offenders, older killers commit many of their crimes within their own residences. This may be due to a variety of reasons, but perhaps the most significant is that elderly people tend to spend more time at home than in public or commercial establishments. Finally, the low incidence of murders by the elderly may have something to do with the shorter life span of violent individuals. Some research suggests that people with predispositions toward violence are less likely to reach the age of fifty-five and thus are at lower risk to become an elderly offender. Thus, while it is true the elderly commit fewer homicides, in general the patterns are similar to younger offenders.

The most recent data available on elderly homicide shows some changes in the 55 to 59 age group category. According to the Uniform Crime Reports, in 2004, there were approximately 328 elderly arrests for homicide. This includes 137 for offenders in the 55 to 59 age category, 88 in the group aged 60 to 64, and 103 for those 65 and older. However, the overall number increased 21 percent in 2014 to a total of 416. The distribution of arrests for each category was 213, 103, and 100 respectively.[48]

SEX OFFENSES

As with other crimes, stereotypical images exist about elderly sex offenders that interfere with an accurate understanding of this phenomenon. Some people believe, for instance, that sexual offenses involving children are the most often committed by old men.[49] The

Table 9.3 Homicide by Age, 2004 and 2014

	2004			2014		
	55–59	60–64	65+	55–59	60–64	65+
Homicide	137	88	103	213	103	100
Total Arrests		9,554			8,267	

media has also created a climate in which the image of a sexual predator is an elderly man, likely a Catholic priest, who preys upon innocent children. In fact, there is a great deal of distortion of sex offenses among the elderly and the pedophilia of priests in particular. Much of what has been called pedophilia is actually non-forcible sex among older boys, not child abuse or sexual assault as has been portrayed in the media. This trend does not suggest that pedophilia is acceptable or what some priests have done is appropriate. However, the media's distorted image does suggest that perhaps the elderly are not as involved in sex offenses as is commonly believed.[50]

One study attempted to synthesize the information on the subject by examining eighty-six old and young sex offenders (young was defined as 30 years old or younger, while elderly was defined as those 60 years or older). The results were that elderly offenders had more stability in terms of their marital status, occupational income, and ties to the community. Younger sexual offenders were more likely to have higher education levels, a history of drug and alcohol abuse, and were likely to have a sexual encounter with a child in a public place, such as a local park. Elderly offenders were more likely to be a passive recipient in the exchange with a child and to engage in this activity in the privacy of their own home.[51]

In virtually all of the cases, there was some sort of relationship between the victim and the offender and the nature of the activity was usually nonviolent. This study and others have found that mental disorders, organic brain dysfunctions such as dementia and delirium, as well as neurosis, personality disorders, and alcoholism are much more common among the elderly than younger offenders.[52]

For the purposes of analysis, according to the Uniform Crime Reports, sex crimes include all activities except prostitution and forcible rape. While this covers a wide range of activities, the data suggests that this trend decreased considerably in 2014, but remained relatively stable for elderly offenders. The total number of those arrested for sex offenses in 2004 was 64,671. This included 1,915 for those 55 to 59 and 1,109 arrests in the 60 to 64 category. For those age 65 and over, the number of arrests was 1,343. In 2014, the total number of arrests for sex offenses was 43,422, an increase of approximately 33 percent. This included 2,105 in the 55 to 59 category, an increase of about 9 percent from 2004. In the 60 to 64 group, the numbers increased from 1,109 to 1,299, about 15 percent. In the over 65 category, the numbers were slightly different (1,343 compared to 1,593 in 2014, a 16 percent increase).[53]

DRUNK DRIVING

Unlike other forms of elderly crime, the evidence on the relationship between alcohol use and criminal activity among the elderly has a larger empirical foundation. The questions and controversy surrounding this type of criminal behavior stems largely from

Table 9.4 Sex Crimes by Age, 2004 and 2014

	2004			2014		
	55–59	60–64	65+	55–59	60–64	65+
Sex Crimes	1,915	1,109	1,343	2,105	1,299	1,593
Total Arrests		64,671			43,422	

Table 9.5 DUI and Drunkenness by Age, 2004 and 2014

	2004			2014		
	55–59	**60–64**	**65+**	**55–59**	**60–64**	**65+**
DUI	28,655	14,264	12,050	41,325	21,550	16,285
Drunkenness	11,928	5,634	3,802	19,947	8,970	4,599
Total Arrests:		1,012,651			872,184	

whether or not elderly people drink more than young people—while some experts argue that older people drink to alleviate feelings of isolation, emotional loss, or to derive some sense of satisfaction in life, others contend that the incidence of these types of crimes decreases with age.[54]

Alcohol-related arrests, such as driving while intoxicated and public drunkenness, account for the majority of criminal behavior of people 55 or older. Other research on alcohol-related crime by the elderly has shown that the majority of offenders are males with long-term, chronic drinking problems and equally long histories of crime while under the influence of alcohol.[55] However, there is also data that suggests older people generally drink less than their younger counterparts. In fact, in contrast to these prevailing theories, some studies suggest that the very old, those 75 or older, are more likely to abstain from alcohol altogether.[56] While there remains a great deal of debate about this issue, the research suffers from methodological problems and often lacks comparability with other studies. However, the weight of the evidence suggests that the problems of alcohol-related crime by the elderly is not of epidemic proportions. While the data shows that if older people are arrested for crimes, they are very likely to be alcohol-related ones. However, alcohol-related offenses, such as drunk driving and public drunkenness, account for only a small percentage of all reported arrests of older adults.[57]

According to the Uniform Crime Reports in 2004, there were over a million arrests for driving under the influence (DUI). This breaks down into 28,655 for those in the 55 to 59 age category, 14,264 for those 60 to 64, and 12,050 for those 65 and over. In 2014, there were 872,184 DUI arrests of the elderly. This includes 41,325 fo013 in the 60 to 64 age group, and 11,663 in the over 65 category. Public drunkenness also witnessed a slight decrease between 2004 and 2014. There were 21,364 elderly arrests for public drunkenness in 2004 compared to only 33,516 arrests for that crime in 2014, about a 36 percent increase. So even though the total number of arrests decreased, the percentage related to the elderly actually increased between 2004 and 2014.[58]

FORMAL REACTIONS TO THE ELDERLY CRIMINAL

It should be clear at this point that the "problem" of elderly crime is really not a problem in terms of the actual numbers of offenders or offenses. It is unlikely, either now or perhaps even in the future, that an "elderly crime wave" will occur. Despite its limitations and flaws, the Uniform Crime Reports has consistently shown that elderly criminals do not represent a significant crime problem. However, perhaps the problem should not be understood in terms of its volume or magnitude, but rather in terms of its uniqueness. The fact that elderly individuals commit various types of crime, including violent offenses, raises a number of questions about the pursuit of justice, the goals of punishment, and the purpose of the criminal justice system.

The problem is somewhat similar to the juvenile justice system in that society recognizes young people as being different from adults when they commit criminal acts. Consequently, this system has a different philosophy than the adult system: one that tempers the culpability of the offender while still holding youth accountable. Add to the fact that since most of the recent research focuses on the particular problems elderly criminals encounter when they are processed through the system,[59] many criminal justice experts have argued that perhaps one way to alleviate these problems is to establish a separate system for the elderly, or what is sometimes referred to as a **geriatric court**.[60]

Proponents of this type of change argue that elderly criminals are inherently different and merit special consideration in the justice process. Moreover, the pains of punishment are more taxing on elderly offenders. Advocates of the geriatric court also contend that there should be a more lenient attitude by the courts in sentencing, a more lax approach by law enforcement, and a sympathetic approach to punishment by the correctional institutions. The logic of course, is that neither society nor the individual benefits from the unilateral treatment of offenders. What good does it serve society for example, if a sixty-five-year-old man is given a thirty-year prison sentence? The same punishment to a fifteen-year-old does not end his life, however, in the former case this sentence for an elderly criminal may in fact be a form of capital punishment. Moreover, since the legal precedent for a separate system has already been established for juveniles, and the particular needs and problems of older offenders are similar to juveniles (in terms of vulnerability and risks, as well as the issue of rehabilitation), why not create a separate system?

It may very well be that a geriatric court can lead to improvements in meeting the needs of the elderly population. While the answers to these questions cannot be found without additional and extensive research, the idea of a geriatric court requires an examination of many current policies and practices involving the administration of justice.

On the other hand, opponents of this approach argue that distinctions of crime cannot be based on chronological age. In other words, a person is ultimately responsible whether they are eighteen years old or eighty. In this model, one that clearly fits within the **just deserts** philosophy, which argues that every person is equally responsible for their actions and should be punished according to what they have done, the symbolic and practical consequences of taking a lenient attitude toward the elderly may encourage other potential offenders to commit crime.

Finally, as was mentioned, while there is much left to be done in terms of understanding elderly crime, the vast majority of the research has focused on how and in what ways offenders are forced to cope with the pains of imprisonment. This includes the organizational and logistical problems faced by correctional institutions with an increasingly older inmate population. The problems are many, quite diversified, and they will likely increase with time. Thus, the handling of elderly inmates, both in terms of physical safety as well as healthcare, will likely remain a central feature in the study of elderly offenders.

ELDERLY INMATES

The research on elderly criminals shows that the number of offenders over the age of 55 going to prison is increasing and the ones already in prison are getting older. Added to the aging of the inmate population is the fact that tougher sentencing laws mean that younger offenders who commit serious crimes will also likely spend longer periods of time in prison. According to the National Institute of Corrections, the number of state and federal inmates age 50 or older increased 173 percent from 1992 and comprised about 8 percent of the overall prison population. In 2005, elderly inmates 55 and over comprised 10 percent of the total inmate population in state and federal prisons. In 2012 a study by the American Civil Liberties Union found that of the nation's 1.5 million state and federal prisoners, around 246,600 were age 50 and over, about 16 percent of the overall prison population. [61]

The National Institute of Corrections uses age 50 due to the stress of incarceration and the lack of appropriate healthcare prior to and during incarceration.[62] The real problem with the aging of the inmate population relates to escalating healthcare costs. In 2013, according to a study by the Pew Charitable Trusts, the costs of incarcerating an aging inmate population is an estimated $16 billion per year, including $3 billion in medical care. While it costs taxpayers approximately $34,000 per year on average to incarcerate a prisoner, it costs over $68,000 to care for elderly prisoner. Moreover, the problem appears to be getting worse. By one estimate, by 2030, nearly a third of the entire prison population in the U.S., nearly 400,000 inmates, will be elderly.[63]

The most common health-related problems elderly inmates experience include incontinence, respiratory illnesses, cardiovascular disease, and chronic problems such as arthritis, high blood pressure, prostate problems, and ulcers. Elderly inmates also suffer from typical age-related illnesses such as cognitive impairment, reduced vision and hearing, loss of physical strength, and emotional disorders.[64]

The special circumstances surrounding the incarceration of elderly inmates also create a number of challenges for correctional institutions. For example, older inmates have

One of the most pressing issues in corrections is providing healthcare to an aging inmate population.

greater healthcare needs, may require a number of structural changes in the facility to accommodate them, such as single beds instead of bunk beds, fewer inmates per cell, and even the creation of geriatric units within the prison. Healthcare needs also require correctional institutions to either establish or contract comprehensive healthcare services.[65] Even the day-to-day stressors and risks associated with institutional life are exceptionally hard on elderly offenders. Elderly inmates also require more protection from correctional officers from younger predators.

Across the country, some states are attempting to address the escalating healthcare costs for elderly inmates. For example, at least sixteen states have established separate facilities to house older inmates and many are offering hospice care for dying prisoners. In Texas, for example, about two hundred inmates over the age of sixty-five receive round-the-clock care. The state of Nebraska offers nursing home living for some inmates while Oklahoma is also creating a separate unit for older inmates.[66]

In California, where there are 172,000 prisoners in the state system, the problem has become acute, with jails releasing convicted felons because of overcrowding. In the state prisons, inmates are stacked three high in cells and housed in hallways and converted gyms. Some California prisons are even 200 to 300 percent over capacity. In order to provide space for inmates, some facilities have had to rent cell space from other, less crowded prisons. As prison officials struggle to find solutions to the problems of overcrowding, they are faced with a 70 percent **recidivism rate**, which is also known as the re-offending rate. California's recidivism rate is currently the highest in the nation. This means that 70 percent of the inmates convicted of a crime will commit another one within three years of release.

In California, the number of prisoners 55 and older has doubled since 1997, with almost 20,000 prisoners over age 50 and almost 750 over 70 years old. In fact, California, Texas, and Florida combined accounted for 43 percent of the nation's entire elderly prison population in 2013.[67] As one expert on prisons noted, there is evidence that prisoners are physiologically ten years older than their chronological age. This means that inmate needs are increasing as are the costs of their incarceration.[68] Because of this, some have suggested that the best way to alleviate overcrowding in prison would be to release the inmates who pose the least risk to the community. Given that recidivism rates generally drop around the age of 30 and continue to fall after that, an argument can be made that releasing elderly criminals makes sense in that they are least likely to commit another crime against the community.[69]

As the current research tries to show, there are a number of practical issues surrounding elderly inmates. These range from the pragmatic difficulties of maneuvering a wheelchair in a prison cell to the importance of improved healthcare facilities. For example, it seems obvious that planners did not, and perhaps could not, have foreseen these issues when prisons were being constructed ten, twenty, or even forty years ago. Prison cells were simply not designed for offenders who were limited in mobility. However, the realities of incarcerating older inmates, as well as caring for those who become ill, needs to be incorporated into the design and construction of new facilities. While this will increase the costs, it may be one of the consequences of punishing older offenders or keeping people incarcerated for longer periods of time.

Related to the issues surrounding elderly inmates are several philosophical and pragmatic questions raised by many criminal justice scholars. David Newman, a noted expert on elderly crime, makes an interesting point about the practical problems for police officers who encounter elderly criminals. He questions whether handcuffing or shackling a 75-year-old is really in line with the goals of the criminal justice system. Newman also questions whether or not booking procedures, including fingerprinting, photographing, and lineups are really necessary and appropriate for seventy-year-old suspects. In addition, Newman argues against monetary bail as the only way elderly offenders can be released while awaiting trial. He asks, "Are they likely to flee? Do many or most elderly offenders really need to be jailed or imprisoned?"[70] In short, Newman calls into question the issue of whether or not the criminal justice system effectively addresses the problems of elderly offenders.

While Newman raises some interesting points, does this mean chronological age should play a factor in these issues? There are many instances in which exceptions are made for all types of offenders. If the person is violent, whether they be elderly or not, one would think that the safety of the arresting officers, the citizens of that community, and the well-being of the individual offender, would override any embarrassment or humiliation the particular suspect might feel. In short, it is not clear whether older offenders should be given special considerations with regard to the early stages of the justice process. Where there is stronger support in Newman's argument concerns the pragmatic problems of being imprisoned. Given that cells are not designed for the elderly, this presents a number of problems for the correctional institution as well as the inmate.

The subject of elderly criminals presents one of the most interesting juxtapositions of the disciplines of criminology, criminal justice, and gerontology. Despite the fact that it has not grown in the way the research had predicted, the issues and problems surrounding this phenomenon will continue to have an impact on the understanding and perceptions of aging in American society as well as how and in what ways crime influences social life.

SUMMARY

This chapter explored the phenomenon of elderly crime. There can be little doubt that as the population gets older, the number of people involved in crime, whether as victims or as offenders, will likely increase. Baby boomers, those born between 1946 and 1960, represent the newest group of elderly in this country. As a generation, they have redefined the face of America with the Civil Rights Movement and protests against the Vietnam War, and they represent some of the leading figures in politics, economics, and social activism. As this generation becomes older, it is likely that they will also redefine the criteria used to evaluate the concept of aging. Generation X or Gen Xers are those individuals born between 1968 and 1979. This group is generally considered an underachieving generation, critical of the self-indulgence of baby boomers, and who grew up amid a host of social problems in the 1980s and 1990s. Generation Y is the latest group of young people in this country, born approximately between 1977 and 1994, and are characterized by their willingness to embrace cultural diversity, are educationally and technologically sophisticated, and have a strong sense of self including feelings of entitlement, self-confidence, and impatience in climbing the ladder of success.

Conventional wisdom concerning elderly crime typically focuses on elderly victimization. As this chapter has shown, the elderly are the least likely to be victimized of any other age group but this should not be interpreted to mean the elderly are not victimized. There is a great deal of empirical evidence on elderly abuse as well as research on elderly offenders.

Early predictions of an elderly crime wave, based largely on population and demographic shifts, have failed to emerge. However, the research on elderly criminals, found primarily in the official crime statistics, shows that elderly crime is not as frequent as crime committed by younger offenders, however, it is sufficient to warrant more attention. Generally speaking, most of the elderly crime noted in the data relates to minor forms of crime, usually alcohol-related or some type of larceny. Despite noted cases where elderly criminals commit violent acts, these instances are relatively rare.

Where most of the research interest on elderly criminals has focused has been in the area of incarceration and prison life in general. As inmates are sentenced to longer prison terms, issues relating to healthcare and the overall quality of life for inmates become a topic of keen interest to researchers.

YOU MAKE THE CALL

ELDERLY CRIMINALS

Consider the following scenario. Debate the pros and cons of all options and decide what you would do.

You are a federal judge who has received an appeal from a 65-year-old inmate, who was convicted of murdering his terminally ill wife. Knowing that she was going to endure extraordinarily painful treatments, the man, overcome with emotion, decided to throw his wife off of the balcony of his ten-story apartment. Upon conviction, he received a thirty-year sentence for his crime, but appealed on the basis that this constituted cruel and unusual punishment. The reason for this, obviously, is that such punishment is, effectively, a death sentence given

his age. The public is supportive of a merciful approach, particularly given the fact that the offender's crimes, while heinous, merit some consideration.

Questions

1. What do you do?
2. Should there be a different standard of justice on the basis of the man's age?
3. Should the way the man killed his wife factor into the sentencing decision?
4. Does the public's sentiment towards the man merit consideration? Why or why not?

KEY TERMS

baby boomers
claimsmaking
elderly abuse
Generation X
Generation Y

geriatric court
just deserts
operationalization
poverty line
recidivism rate

DISCUSSION QUESTIONS

1. Do you think a geriatrics court would be helpful in the processing of elderly offenders? Can it be used in a similar fashion as the juvenile justice system? Why or why not?
2. What responsibility does the government have to provide comprehensive healthcare to elderly inmates? Should correctional agencies be forced to meet serious and chronic healthcare needs of elderly inmates or should they only be responsible for routine care or emergencies?
3. In what ways do you think the baby boomer generation will change the way the elderly are perceived? Is this characterization of baby boomers seen in a positive or negative light?

4. How is elderly abuse different from child abuse? Should offenders be given the same punishments as child abusers? How do you think elderly abusers would be perceived in prison compared to child abusers?
5. Given the role that alcohol plays in elderly crime, do you think society should be able to restrict its use among the elderly in the same way it limits access for minors? Why or why not?
6. Given the public's perception of elderly criminals, what steps can you think of to help merchants prevent elderly shoplifting?

FOR FURTHER READING

Zemke, R., C. Raines, C. and B. Filipczak. *Generations at Work: Managing the Clash of Veterans, Boomers, and Xers and Nexters in your Workplace.* New York: American Management Association, 2000.

Castle, N. *Examination of Resident Abuse in Assisted Living Facilities. Final Report to the National Institute of Justice.* 2013. Grant number 2010-IJ-CX-00223.

Shimkus, J. *The Graying of America's Prisons: Corrections Copes with Care for the Aged.* Washington, DC: National Commission on Correctional Healthcare, 2007.

Newman, E. S., D. J. Newman and M. L. Gerwitz *Elderly Criminals.* Cambridge, MA: Oelgeschlager, Gunn, and Hain, 1984.

Wolfgang, M. *Patterns of Criminal Homicide.* Philadelphia: University of Pennsylvania Press, 1958.

NOTES

1. Department of Commerce, U.S. Census Bureau, *Statistical Abstract of the United States: 2004–2005.* August 2004. Available at https://www.census.gov/prod/2004pubs/04statab/pop.pdf
2. Department of Commerce, U.S. Census Bureau, *Statistical Abstract of the United States: 2012.* August 2011. Available at http://www2.census.gov/library/publications/2011/compendia/statab/131ed/2012-statab.pdf
3. U.S. Department of Health and Human Services, Center for Disease Control and Prevention, *Trends in Health and Aging: Life Expectancy,* Atlanta, GA, 2004.
4. Department of Commerce, Census Bureau, *Statistical Abstract of the United States, 2012,* (Washington, DC: U.S. Government Printing Office, 2011).
5. Department of Commerce, U.S. Census, *Older Americans Month: May 2013,* 2013. Available at https://www.census.gov/data/tables/time-series/demo/income-poverty/historical-poverty-thresholds.html
6. C. Renzetti and D. Curran, *Social Problems* (Boston: Allyn and Bacon, 2004).
7. J. M. Ortman, V. A. Velkoff, and H. Hogan, *An Aging Nation,* Department of Commerce, U.S. Census Bureau. 2014. Available at https://www.census.gov/prod/2014pubs/p25-1140.pdf
8. Ibid.
9. Department of Commerce, U.S. Census Bureau, *Oldest Baby Boomers Turn 60,* Facts for Features (Washington, DC: U.S. Government Printing Office, 2014).
10. Deborah Rothberg, "Generation Y for Dummies," *eWeek,* August 24, 2006, available at http://www.eweek.com/c/a/IT-Management/Generation-Y-for-Dummies
11. R. Zemke, C. Raines, and B. Filipczak, *Generations at Work: Managing the Clash of Veterans, Boomers, and Xers and Nexters in your Workplace* (New York: American Management Association, 2000).

12. NAS Recruitment Communication, "Generation Y: The Millennials, Ready or Not, Here They Come," *NAS Insights*, 2006.

13. Ibid.

14. See for instance L. J. Seigel, *Criminology* (New York: West Publishing, 2005); G. M. Sykes and F. T. Cullen, *Criminology* (New York: Harcourt Brace and Jovanovich, 2005).

15. J. Livingston, *Crime and Criminology* (Clifton Hill, NJ: Prentice-Hall, 1992); F. Adler, G. O. W. Mueller, and W. S. Laufer. *Criminology* (New York: McGraw-Hill, 1995).

16. J. L. Truman and Lynn Langton, *Criminal Victimization, 2014*, Department of Justice, Bureau of Justice Statistics (Washington, DC: U.S. Government Printing Office, 2015).

17. R. Morgan, *Crimes Against the Elderly, 2003–2013*, U.S. Department of Justice, Bureau of Justice Statistics, 2014. Available at http://www.bjs.gov/content/pub/pdf/cae0313.pdf

18. Ibid.

19. Ibid.

20. R. Acierno, M. Hernandez-Tejada, W. Muzzy, and K. Steve, National Elder Mistreatment Study, *Final Report to the National Institute of Justice*, grant number 2007-WG-BX-009, March 2008, NCJ 226456.

21. N. Castle, *Examination of Resident Abuse in Assisted Living Facilities. Final report to the National Institute of Justice*, 2013, grant number 2010-IJ-CX-00223.

22. M. Lachs, J. A. Teresi, and M. Ramirez, *Documentation of Resident to Resident Elder Mistreatment in Residential Care Facilities. Final Report to the National Institute of Justice*, 2014, grant number 2009_IJ-XC-0001.

23. National Center on Elder Abuse, *National Elder Abuse Incidence Study* (Washington DC: U.S. Government Printing Office, 2005).

24. J. Wasik, "The Fleecing of America's Elderly," *Consumer's Digest* (March/April 2000).

25. *National Ombudsman Reporting System Data Tables* (Washington, DC: U.S. Administration on Aging, 2003).

26. National Center on Elder Abuse, *Abuse of Adults Age 60+: 2004 Survey of State Adult Protective Services* (Washington, DC, 2004).

27. J. Shimkus, *The Graying of America's Prisons: Corrections Copes with Care for the Aged*, National Commission on Correctional Healthcare (Washington, DC, 2007).

28. See for instance D. J. Newman, "Elderly Offenders and American Crime Patterns," in *Elderly Criminals*, E. S. Newman, D. J. Newman, and M. L. Gerwitz (Cambridge, MA: Oelgeschlager, Gunn and Hain, 1984), 3–16.

29. Ibid.

30. R. H. Aday and J. J. Krabill, "Aging Offenders in the Criminal Justice System," *Marqueet Elder's Advisor* 7, no. 2 (2006). Available at http://scholarship.law.marquette.edu/elders/vol7/iss2/4

31. See for instance, Aday and Krabill, "Aging Offenders"; C. Cushall and K. Adams, "Responding to Older Offenders: Age Selectivity in the Processing of Shoplifters," *Criminal Justice Review* 1, 1 and 4 (Fall 1983); G. Feinberg and D. Khosla, "Sanctioning Elderly Delinquents," *Trial* (1985): 46, 47–49.

32. See for instance, Aday and Krabill, "Aging Offenders"; J. Rudolf, "Elderly Inmate Population Soared 1,300 Percent Since 1980s: Report." *Huffington Post*, June 13, 2012. Shimkus, *The Graying of America's Prisons*; H. Deluca, "Managing Elderly Inmates: It's More Than Just Time," in *Social Gerontology*, ed. R. P. McNamara and D. E. Redburn (Westport, CT: Auburn House, 1997), 209–20.

33. Newman et al., *Elderly Criminals*.

34. Malcolm Spector and John I. Kitsuse, *Constructing Social Problems,* (New Jersey: Transaction Publishers, 2000).

35. Newman et al., *Elderly Criminals,* 209.

36. See for instance G. Jones, M. Connelly, and K. Wagner, *Aging Offenders and the Criminal Justice System,* Maryland State Commission on Criminal Sentencing, 2001; M. T. Harrison, "True Grit: An Innovative Program for Elderly Inmates," *Corrections Today Magazine* 68, no. 7 (2006): 46–49; S. Wallace, "Health Status of Federal Inmates: A Comparison of Admission and Release Medical Records," *Journal of Prison and Jail Health* 10, no. 2 (1992): 133–51; L. Long, "A Study of Arrests of Older Offenders: Trends and Patterns," *Journal of Crime and Justice* 15, no. 2 (1992): 157–75.

37. D. Shichor, "The Extent and Nature of Lawbreaking by the Elderly: A Review of Arrest Statistics," in Newman, et al., *Elderly Criminals,* 17–32.

38. M. A. Ames and D. A. Houston, "Legal, Social, and Biological Definitions of Pedophilia," *Archives of Sexual Behavior* 19, no. 4 (1990): 333–42.

39. U.S. Department of Justice, Federal Bureau of Investigation. *Crime in the United States, 2004.* Available at https://ucr.fbi.gov/crime-in-the-u.s/2004/crime-in-the-u.s.-2004; and *Crime in the United States 2014.* Available at https://ucr.fbi.gov/crime-in-the-u.s/2014/crime-in-the-u.s.-2014

40. D. Curran, "Characteristics of the Elderly Shoplifter and the Effect of Sanctions on Recidivism," in *Elderly Criminals,* ed. W. Wilbanks and P. K. Kim (New York: University Press of America, 1984), 123–42.

41. G. Feinberg, "Profile of the Elderly Shoplifter," in Newman et al., *Elderly Criminals,* 35–50.

42. *Crime in the United States,* 2004 and 2014.

43. Ibid.

44. See for instance A. Blum and G. Fisher, "Women Who Kill," in *Violence: Perspectives on Murder and Aggression,* ed. I. L. Kutash, S. B. Kutash, and L. B. Schlesinger and Associates (San Francisco: Jossey-Bass, 1979); A. Goetting, "Patterns of Homicide Among the Elderly," *Violence and Victims* 7, no. 3 (1992): 203–15; S. J. Hucker and M. H. Ben-Aron, "Violent Elderly Offenders: A Comparative Study," in Wilbanks and Kim, *Elderly Criminals,* 69–82; R. A. Silverman and L. W. Kennedy, "Relational Distance and Homicide: The Role of the Stranger," *Journal of Criminal Law and Criminology* 78 (1987): 272–308; W. Wilbanks and D. D. Murphy, "The Elderly Homicide Offender," in Newman, et al., *Elderly Criminals,* 79–92; M. Wolfgang, *Patterns of Criminal Homicide* (Philadelphia: University of Pennsylvania Press, 1958); M. A. Zahn and P. C. Sagi, "Stranger Homicides in Nine American Cities," *Journal of Criminal Law and Criminology* 78 (1987): 377–97.

45. Goetting, "Patterns of Homicide," 203–15.

46. Ibid., 212.

47. Department of Justice, Federal Bureau of Investigation, *FBI Supplementary Homicide Reports 1976–2004* (Washington, DC: U.S. Government Printing Office, 2005).

48. *Crime in the United States,* 2004 and 2014.

49. S. J. Hucker, "Psychiatric Aspects of Crime in Old Age," in Newman et al., *Elderly Criminals,* 67–78.

50. See for instance Ames and Houston, "Legal, Social, and Biological Definitions," 333–42; J. Briere and M. Runtz, "University Males' Sexual Interest in Children: Predicting Potential Indices of 'Pedophilia' in a Nonforensic Sample," *Child Abuse and Neglect* 13, no. 1 (1989): 65–75.

51. Hucker and Ben-Aron, "Violent Elderly Offenders," 69–82.

52. See for instance E. Revitch and R. Weiss, 1962. "The Pedophiliac Offender," *Diseases of the Nervous System* 23, no. 2 (1962): 1–6; J. Mohr, R. E. Turner, and M. B. Jerry, *Pedophilia and Exhibitionism* (Toronto: University of Toronto Press, 1964).

53. *Crime in the United States*, 2004 and 2014.

54. See for instance C. Burnett, and S. T. Ortega, "Elderly Offenders: A Descriptive Analysis," in W. Wilbanks and P. K. Kim (eds.) *Elderly Criminals*, 17–40.

55. See for instance United States Department of Justice, *Jailing Drunk Drivers: Impact on the Criminal Justice System* (Washington, D.C: U.S. Government Printing Office, 1984); D. Calahan, *Problem Drinkers* (San Francisco: Jossey-Bass, 1970).

56. See for instance U.S. Department of Justice, *Jailing Drunk Drivers*; J. H. Atkinson, "Alcoholism and Geriatric Problems, I and II," *Advances in Alcoholism* 11, no. 8–9 (1981): 1–3; E. Gomberg, *Drinking and Problem Drinking Among the Elderly* (Ann Arbor, MI: Institute for Gerontology, University of Michigan, 1980).

57. Ibid.

58. *Crime in the United States*, 2004 and 2014.

59. See for instance P. C. Kratcoski and S. Babb, "Adjustment of Older Inmates: An Analysis by Institutional Structure and Gender," *Journal of Contemporary Criminal Justice* 6, no. 4 (1990): 264–81; R. H. Aday, "Golden Years Behind Bars: Special Programs and Facilities for Elderly Inmates," *Federal Probation* 58 (21): 47–54; Long, "A Study of Arrests," 157–75; Wallace, "Health Status of Federal Inmates," 133–51.

60. See for instance A. J. Abrams, "Foreword," in Newman et al., *Elderly Criminals*.

61. American Civil Liberties Union, *America's Expense: The Mass Incarceration of the Elderly*, 2012.

62. "Reports on Elderly Prisoners Spur Call for Reforms," *Prison Legal News*, 2014. Available at https://www.prisonlegalnews.org/news/2014/may/19/reports-elderly-prisoners-spur-call-reforms/

63. Ibid.

64. Shimkus, *The Graying of America's Prisons*.

65. C. M. Lemieux, T. B. Dyeson, and B. Castiglione, "Revisiting The Literature on Prisoners Who are Older: Are We Wiser?" *Prison Journal* 82, no. 4 (2002): 440–58.

66. K. Leonard, "Is Medicaid the Answer to Crushing Health Care Costs for Inmates?" *U.S. News and World Reports*, May 19, 2015. Available at https://www.usnews.com/news/articles/2015/05/19/is-medicaid-the-answer-to-crushing-health-care-costs-for-inmates; Pew Charitable Trusts, *Managing Prison Health Care Spending*, October 2013. Available at http://www.pewtrusts.org/~/media/legacy/uploadedfiles/pcs_assets/2014/pctcorrectionshealthcarebrief050814pdf.pdf; C. W. Johnston and N. O. Alozie, "Effect of Age on Criminal Processing: Is There an Advantage to Being Older?" *Journal of Gerontological Social Work* 34, no. 4 (2001): 65–82.

67. "Reports on Elderly Prisons."

68. Jonathan Turley, "Release Elderly Inmates," *Los Angeles Times*, October 7, 2006. See also U.S. Department of Justice, Office of Inspector General, *The Impact of an Aging Inmate Population on the Federal Bureau of Prisons*, February 2006. Available at https://oig.justice.gov/reports/2015/e1505.pdf; Florida Institute of Government, Project on Accountable Justice, *Florida's Aging Inmate Population* (March 2015). Available at http://www.iog.fsu.edu/paj/documents/Florida%20Aging%20Prisoners%20March%2027%202015.pdf

69. Ibid.

70. Newman et al., *Elderly Criminals*.

CHAPTER 10

JUVENILES AND THE CRIMINAL JUSTICE SYSTEM

CHAPTER OBJECTIVES

After reading this chapter, you should be able to:

- Define juvenile delinquency and *parens patriae*
- Trace society's historical development of the juvenile justice system
- Discuss crime data as it relates to juveniles, particularly African Americans, Hispanic/ Latino Americans, Asian Americans, and Native Americans
- Describe current social policies relating to addressing disproportionality of minority involvement in the juvenile justice system

A review of any major news outlet regularly offers stories about young offenders who commit violent acts. Also included are stories about children who are victimized by adults, other youth, and a host of other forms of maltreatment. Still other websites and blogs offer opinions about the failure of the juvenile justice system to protect society from hard-core violent offenders. Often, positions are presented about why the United States should disband the entire juvenile justice system and treat young offenders who commit crimes like adults. Other accounts point to the disproportionality of minority youth who are arrested, convicted, and incarcerated for their involvement in crime. Like their counterparts in the adult criminal justice system, minorities in the juvenile justice system face many distinct challenges.

In many ways, some of the same trends we see with adult minorities in the criminal justice system can be applied to juveniles, but there are a number of significant differences. Societal attitudes about juveniles are different, and there is ample evidence that the current juvenile justice system adequately deals with the problem of juvenile misbehavior. However, a "get tough" approach to crime in the United States during the 1980s and 1990s impacted all types of offenders. What we have seen for the past twenty years has been a steady decline in delinquency offending, similar to what we have seen in the adult population.

Victimization patterns are different for juveniles simply based on the types of crimes that are committed against them, where they occur, and how they are prevented. In addition to different types of offenses and forms of victimization, American attitudes about children and youth in general require us to think differently about juvenile crime. As mentioned, while there is an element within society that views serious juvenile offenders as miniature adults, for the most part, juvenile crime is qualitatively different from adult crime and is handled in a different manner. Perhaps most importantly, some of the trends remind us that there are a host of factors beyond race and ethnicity that impact juvenile delinquency.

In this chapter we will examine the juvenile population in the United States as well as how delinquency is defined and addressed by the justice system. Since there are crimes that only youths can commit, such as status offenses, we explore these activities as well.

DEFINITIONS OF JUVENILE DELINQUENCY

Juvenile delinquency is a complex issue that requires a thorough understanding of the physical, social, economic, legal, and political context in which it occurs. Delinquency also encompasses a wide range of activities, making it difficult to define. How one defines delinquency has much to do with how it is measured, understood, and addressed. Sometimes we apply the legal definition. Although this definition works to standardize the behaviors associated with delinquency to some degree, it is not always inclusive of what the general public believes delinquency to be.

In most states, the legal definition of delinquency consists of behavior that violates the criminal code and is committed by youth who have not reached majority age of eighteen.[1] Because each state has its own definition of delinquency, there is a wide variation in the age at which youths remain under the jurisdiction of the juvenile court. Historically, many states have failed to distinguish between youths who commit criminal acts and youths who are victims of abuse, neglect, or other mistreatment.[2] With the passage of federal legislation separating minor offenders from serious ones—most notably, the Juvenile Justice and Delinquency Prevention Act—many states began to distinguish between delinquents and **status offenders**, those who engage in activities that could only be committed by youths, such as truancy, running away, or underage drinking.[3]

Legally, delinquent acts are those for which youths can be arrested and sentenced—a process referred to in juvenile court as **adjudication**. While legal definitions provide narrower designations for delinquent acts, others define *delinquency* much more broadly. Parents and siblings, for example, may use the term *delinquent* to define a wide array of behaviors, such as refusing to complete household chores, hanging out with people they think are troublemakers, or listening to rap music. The way that youths dress and talk, and the people with whom they associate do not necessarily mean they are breaking any laws. While parents may complain to social workers, counselors, or even probation officers, these types of behaviors are not likely to be considered delinquent acts by the juvenile justice system.

HISTORY OF JUVENILE DELINQUENCY IN THE UNITED STATES

The law has historically differentiated juveniles from adult offenders, but the degree of that distinction has varied during different eras and for many reasons. In early U.S. history, the law was heavily influenced by the common law of England, which governed the American colonies.

One of the most important English lawyers of the time was William Blackstone, whose *Commentaries on the Laws of England*, first published in the late 1760s, was read widely by the nation's founders.[4] Blackstone identified two criteria by which to hold someone accountable for a crime. First, the person had to have a "vicious will," the intent to commit a crime. Second, the person had to commit an unlawful act. If either the will or the act was lacking, no crime had occurred.[5]

Blackstone felt that there were groups of people who were incapable of committing a crime based on these two criteria. One group consists of infants, or children who were too young to fully understand their actions. Those under the age of seven were classified as infants and could not be guilty of a felony or serious crime such as burglary, kidnapping, or murder. Children over the age of fourteen were said to be able to understand the significance of their actions and so were treated like adults if found guilty of a crime.[6]

For Blackstone and his contemporaries, the ages between seven and fourteen were more difficult to categorize, because children in this age range were generally presumed incapable of committing crimes. If, however, children appeared to understand the difference between right and wrong, then they could be convicted and suffer the full consequence, such as a prison sentence, or even the death penalty in a capital crime.[7]

NINETEENTH-CENTURY UNITED STATES

In the early nineteenth century, the United States experienced significant social and economic changes as a result of the Industrial Revolution. Economic growth, coupled with immigration, urbanization, and industrialization had an adverse effect on many families. Many poor families had to migrate from farms to cities and take jobs in factories in order to survive. Many children were forced to work long hours in those same factories to help their families. Child labor laws were developed to prevent the exploitation of children, but because parents were working long hours, many children did not receive adequate supervision, which led to a rise in neglect and abuse of children, as well as increases in crime and delinquency.

During this time, several reform movements emerged in an effort to protect children. One of the earliest came in New York City, which had many orphans, runaways, and throwaway children. To remedy the problem, Reverend Charles Loring Brace, who established the **Children's Aid Society** to help homeless children, came up with an innovative idea. Believing that one of the main reasons for juvenile crime stemmed from the negative influence of the urban environment, Brace created **orphan trains**, which transported city youths to rural farms, where families assumed custody of and responsibility for them as apprentices.

At regularly scheduled dates, farming families would go to their local train stations and select orphaned children to live with them. The children and their families had one year to decide whether they would stay together. At the end of the year, if either party decided to part ways, the child would be returned to the Children's Aid Society and board the next train, to be selected by a family in another location.[8]

The orphan trains strategy was a popular one since many families were moving west and could use help operating their farms. It also provided orphans with a family environment and got them away from dangers found in cities. Unfortunately, some host families considered orphans to be little more than cheap labor, and so treated them harshly. While the practice of shipping children to unknown families was questionable, with some evidence that this was yet another form of exploitation by adults, some experts cite success stories associated with the experience.[9]

Another attempt to address juvenile crime and child exploitation was the **Child Savers Movement**, which consisted primarily of philanthropists and social reformers who felt that the exploitation of children ultimately resulted in juvenile crime and a host of other problems. Child Savers attempted to enact laws that would allow children to be placed in reformatories or other institutions. As with the orphan trains, the thought was that if children were placed in country settings where they could be taught the value of hard work, away from the negative influences of the city, their lives could be improved.

Unfortunately, the noble goal of creating a better life for children often resulted in youths being warehoused in institutions where they were treated poorly and their needs were not met. Some experts note that the Child Savers were unrealistic in their efforts to reform troubled youths. The false expectation that urban, immigrant children would easily and willingly adopt rural Protestant values often resulted in misbehavior.[10]

For those youths who did not participate in orphan trains or reside in institutions in rural areas, **houses of refuge** were created. The first house of refuge opened in New York

Orphan trains, houses of refuge, and other organizations attempted to remove delinquents from the deleterious conditions of the city.

in 1825 as a facility exclusively for children. By the 1840s, an additional fifty-three houses had been built around the country. Houses of refuge did not limit their services to children who had committed crimes. They were also homes for poor children, orphans, and any children thought to be incorrigible or wayward. The average number of children in a house was two hundred, but some, like the New York House of Refuge, housed over one thousand youths at any given time.[11]

As the needs of children surpassed the ability of the houses of refuge to safely care for them, with problems such as overcrowding, deplorable living conditions, and reports of abuse by staff, training schools were developed in the mid-nineteenth century. **Training schools** were larger facilities that placed a greater emphasis on education and vocational training. Consistent with contemporary thinking at the time, the city was the source of temptation, and a rural setting would offer youths a simpler and more virtuous way of life. Such thinking led to many of the new facilities being built outside of cities.[12]

While the twentieth century brought the development of individualized diagnosis and treatment, new kinds of rehabilitative therapy, and improved educational programming, the training school model of concentrating large numbers of juvenile offenders in one institution has persisted.[13]

DELINQUENCY IN THE EARLY TWENTIETH CENTURY

In the late nineteenth century, in response to continuing problems associated with juvenile delinquency, child neglect, and the exploitation of children, the Child Savers and other reformists attempted to establish a separate court for juveniles. In 1899, after years of development and months of compromise, the Illinois legislature passed a law permitting counties in the state to designate one or more of their circuit court judges to hear all cases involving dependent, neglected, and delinquent children younger than age sixteen. The law stipulated that these cases were to be heard in a special courtroom that would be designated as the juvenile courtroom, generally referred to as the juvenile court. Thus, the first juvenile court in Cook County, Illinois, was not a new court, but a division of the existing circuit court with original jurisdiction over juvenile cases.

By 1910, thirty-two states had established juvenile courts and/or probation services. By 1925, all but two states had followed Illinois's lead in creating a separate court for juveniles. Borrowing from British thinking, the doctrine *parens patriae* (the state as parent) served as the foundation for the state to intervene and to provide protection for children whose parents did not provide adequate care or supervision.[14]

In line with their "parental" role, juvenile courts tried to focus on the best interests of children. They emphasized an informal, nonadversarial, and flexible approach to cases—there were few procedural rules that the courts were required to follow. Cases were treated as civil (noncriminal) actions, and the ultimate goal was to guide juvenile offenders through adolescence to become responsible, law-abiding adults. The juvenile court could, however, order that young offenders be removed from their homes and placed in juvenile reform institutions as part of their rehabilitation program.[15]

In subsequent years, most juvenile courts had exclusive jurisdiction over all youths under age eighteen who were charged with violating criminal laws. Only if the juvenile court decided to waive its jurisdiction in a case could children be transferred to criminal court and tried as adults. **Transfer** decisions were made on a case-by-case basis, using a "best interests of the child and public" standard.[16]

By this stage in the development of the juvenile court, there were significant differences in the juvenile and adult criminal court systems. The focus of the juvenile court was on the offender, not on the offense, and the juvenile court could be much more flexible and informal than the adult criminal court. Additionally, the focus was on rehabilitation rather than punishment. There was a wide range of options available to judges at the sentencing phase: judges were not limited to punitive sanctions stemming from the particular offense.[17]

DELINQUENCY IN THE 1960S–1970S

In the 1950s and 1960s, treatment strategies available to juvenile justice professionals were called into question. Although the goal of rehabilitation through **individualized justice**— the basic philosophy of the juvenile justice system—was not in question, professionals were concerned about the growing number of juveniles who were being institutionalized indefinitely in the name of treatment. In a series of decisions beginning in the 1960s, the U.S. Supreme Court required that juvenile courts become more formal, like the criminal courts.[18]

Formal hearings were required in waiver situations, and delinquents facing possible confinement were given protection against self-incrimination and rights to receive notice of the charges against them, to present and question witnesses, and to have an attorney present during the proceedings. The burden-of-proof standard for adjudication changed from merely a preponderance of evidence to the much more rigorous proof beyond a reasonable doubt. The Supreme Court, however, still held that there were enough "differences of substance between the criminal and juvenile courts…to hold that a jury is not required in the latter."[19]

Take, for example, the case of Morris Kent, whose circumstances set precedent in the landmark Supreme Court decision known as *Kent v. the United States*, 383 U.S. 541 (1966). Kent first entered the juvenile court system at the age of fourteen, following several housebreakings and attempted thefts. Two years later, his fingerprints were found in the apartment of a woman who had been robbed and raped. Detained and interrogated by police, he admitted to the crimes. Kent's mother hired a lawyer, who arranged for a psychiatric examination of the boy. The examination concluded that Kent suffered from "severe psychopathology" and recommended that he be placed in a psychiatric hospital for observation.[20]

The juvenile court judge had authority to **waive jurisdiction** in Kent's case to a criminal court, where Kent would be tried as an adult. Kent's lawyer opposed the waiver and offered to prove that if Kent was given proper hospital treatment, he would be a candidate for rehabilitation. The juvenile court did not respond to the motions made by Kent's lawyer and, without a hearing, waived jurisdiction to adult court.[21]

The U.S. Supreme Court ruled that Kent was entitled to a hearing and to a statement of the reasons for the juvenile court's decision to waive jurisdiction. The majority of the justices also expressed concerns that the juvenile courts were not living up to their potential and speculated "that there may be grounds for concern that the child receives the worst of both worlds [in juvenile courts]: that he gets neither the protections accorded to adults nor the solicitous care and regenerative treatment postulated for children."[22]

A year after the Kent decision, the case of *in re Gault* 387 U.S. 1 (1967) was heard by the U.S. Supreme Court and fundamentally changed the way juvenile courts processed cases. Gault, a fifteen-year-old Arizona boy, was accused of making an indecent phone call to a neighbor. The victim, who recognized Gault's voice, called the police. Officers arrived at Gault's home and took him into custody, without leaving notice to Gault's parents that their son had been arrested. Before Gault's adjudication hearing, neither Gault nor his parents received notification of the specific charges against him. At the hearings, there were no sworn witnesses, and no record was made of the proceedings. Not even the neighbor who had made the complaint about the phone call was present.[23]

At the end of the hearings, the judge committed Gault to Arizona's State Industrial School until he turned twenty-one, a six-year sentence. An adult convicted of using vulgar or obscene language would have received a maximum penalty of a $50 fine and imprisonment for no more than two months. Gault's parents argued that he had been denied due process of the law and that his constitutional rights to a fair trial had been violated. The case eventually made its way to the Supreme Court, which ruled in Gault's favor.[24]

While the U.S. Supreme Court was protecting the constitutional rights of juveniles accused of committing crimes, Congress was attempting to determine the types of crimes and offenders that warranted special attention. In 1968, Congress passed the **Juvenile Delinquency Prevention and Control Act**, recommending that children charged with noncriminal (status) offenses be handled outside the court system. A few years later, Congress passed the **Juvenile Justice and Delinquency Prevention Act of 1974**, which prohibited states from incarcerating status offenders and required them to detain juvenile offenders in separate facilities from adult offenders.[25]

Most youths who enter the juvenile justice system tend not to return as repeat offenders.

DELINQUENCY FROM THE 1980S AND INTO THE NEW MILLENNIUM

During the 1980s and 1990s, many politicians and policy makers asserted that not only were instances of serious juvenile crime increasing, but the juvenile justice system was too lenient with offenders. In response, many states attempted to limit the authority of the juvenile courts over some types of delinquents. Changes included mandatory waivers and/or sentences for certain offenses, and a reduction in protections normally afforded to juveniles, such as having confidentiality laws, fingerprinting and photographing suspects during booking procedures, using a juvenile's prior record at the sentencing stage of the process, and allowing juvenile hearings to be open to the public.

Over the past thirty-five years, the media have painted a picture of juveniles as violent and chronic offenders, and many policymakers and politicians claim that delinquency is out of control. But the vast majority of juvenile offenders are not violent, nor are they chronic in their misbehavior, and the juvenile justice system appears to be able to adequately deal with the challenges they present to their respective communities.[26] Ample research also suggests that incarceration does not rehabilitate juvenile offenders.[27] Instead, it may contribute to the delinquency problem, as youths are more likely to commit additional crimes after being incarcerated.[28]

THE JUVENILE POPULATION

According to recent data, in 2014 there were approximately 73.6 million children and youth under the age of 18 in the United States. Older youth, those aged 12 to 17, represent about 25 percent of that population, or about 18.4 million. Other age groups, such as those aged 0-5 or 6-11 years old, represent 23.9 percent and 24.7 percent respectively, making the distribution along these classifications somewhat evenly distributed.[29] As mentioned, from the outset it is important to note that most youths do not engage in delinquent acts and if they do, the situation is handled long before the juvenile justice system becomes involved. However, even when youths are referred to the system for formal processing, there are a host of places along the way where a diversion or resolution can occur. Given all this, most who progress through the system do not return as repeat offenders. This finding alone should raise questions about the arguments made that the juvenile justice system is ineffective—perhaps what is needed is a more in-depth understanding of the types of offenders the juvenile justice system is designed to handle—it is not focused on the hard-core offenders. Let's look at the role of juveniles in the justice process, both as victims as well as offenders. What we will find is that the trends noted in previous chapters regarding a race and ethnicity disproportionality exists among juveniles as it does with adults.

JUVENILE VICTIMS

Of all the discussions of background factors that contribute to crime, such as poverty, poor educational achievement, abuse, neglect, and others, most use these variables to explain adult criminality. Moreover, race and ethnicity play important roles in understanding the disproportionality found in the crime data. However, a closer look at this data shows that experiences such as exposure to violence at an early age, being neglected or abused, or poor academic achievement are all early onset factors for adult offenders. They also contribute to a juvenile's engagement in crime as well. Thus, while one could make the argument, as has been done in virtually every chapter in this book, that discriminatory practices against certain groups results in an increase frequency of involvement in the criminal justice system, we could also say that many of the same background factors are crucial to understanding delinquency patterns.

According to the National Center for Juvenile Justice and the Office of Juvenile Justice and Delinquency Prevention, in their 2014 report, *Juvenile Offenders and Victims: 2014 National Report*, child maltreatment occurs "when a caretaker (a parent or substitute) is responsible for, or permits, the abuse or neglect of a child. The maltreatment can result in actual physical or emotional harm, or it can place the child in danger of physical or emotional harm. The acts include physical abuse (caused or could cause physical injury to a child), sexual abuse (involvement of a child in sexual activity, either forcefully or without force), emotional abuse (verbal threats or emotional assaults, willful cruelty or exploitation), physical neglect (disregard of a child's physical needs, including failure to seek healthcare, inadequate supervision, food, hygiene, or clothing), emotional neglect (inadequate affection, exposing a child to domestic violence or other inattention to emotional or developmental needs), or educational neglect (permitting chronic truancy or inattention to educational needs)."[30]

While the rates of child maltreatment have not substantially changed in the last decade, the rates of neglect, specifically emotional neglect, have increased. This increase is related to a significant rise in the number of children exposed to domestic violence, which tripled between 1993 and 2006. An examination of the data also shows that Black children have higher rates of maltreatment. See Table 10-1.

Generally speaking, maltreatment rates vary by parents' employment status and economic situation. That is, children with an unemployed parent or those with parents not working have a higher risk of experiencing maltreatment compared to children who has one or both parents in the labor force. Similarly, children who lived in families with low household incomes, below $15,000 per year, or those who received food stamps,

Table 10.1 Child Maltreatment Victims per 1,000 Children, 2005–2006

Maltreatment Type	White	Black	Hispanics
All	28.6	49.6	30.2
All Abuse	8.7	14.9	9.4
Physical	4.6	9.7	5.9
Emotional	3.5	4.5	2.4
All Neglect	22.4	36.8	23.0
Physical	12.2	17.9	9.9
Emotional	12.1	17.9	12.2[i]

public housing, or any type of public assistance, were five times more likely to be maltreated in some way, three times more likely to be abused, and seven times more likely to be neglected as children who did not live in these types of families.[31]

Similarly, children who lived with two married biological parents fared much better than children who live in single-parent families or in adoptive or step-parent families. In fact, children living with two married biological parents have the lowest rates of maltreatment of any group whereas children who lived with a single parent, or those who had a cohabiting partner, have the highest maltreatment rates.[32]

According to the National Center for Juvenile Justice, neglect was the most common form of maltreatment for victims, a trend that has remained consistent for the past several decades. While children are often the victims of more than one type of maltreatment, if they are separated into independent categories, 78 percent of all victims experienced neglect, where about 18 percent experienced physical abuse, 9 percent were sexually abused, 8 percent were emotional maltreated and 10 percent experienced some other form of maltreatment.[33]

The breakdown of this trend is that just over 51 percent of maltreatment victims are girls and most victims were White (44.8 percent) followed by Black (21.9 percent) and Hispanic (21.4 percent). Asian/Pacific Islanders, along with American Indian/Alaska Natives, accounted for about 1 percent each. Black children had the highest maltreatment rates (14.6 per 1,000), which is about twice the rate of White children (7.8 per 1,000). Although they only accounted for a small percentage of reported maltreatment victims, American Indian/Alaska Natives had victimization rates higher than 10 per 1,000.[34]

The overwhelming majority of maltreatment offenders are parents of the victims. In 2010, the National Child Abuse and Neglect Data System recognized over 500,000 unique offenders of child maltreatment. Women are disproportionately represented in these

Most offenders of child neglect are parents.

statistics—they accounted for more than half (54 percent) of maltreatment offenders. Further, nearly half of offenders were White, 20 percent were Black and 20 percent were Hispanic. Not too surprisingly, this distribution is similar to the race profile of victims of maltreatment.[35]

Other types of victimization relate to a child's exposure to violence. According to the National Survey of Children's Exposure to Violence, 61 percent of youth surveyed had been either victims of or witnesses to violence in the prior year, with nearly half (46 percent) reporting being victims of assault in the past year. About 25 percent report being victims of robbery, vandalism, or theft. About 13 percent report being physically bullied within the last year. Overall, about 6 percent of youth stated they have been sexually victimized in the past year, with the age group 14 to 17 being the most common one to experience this.[36]

According to the National Crime Victimization Survey, which monitors levels of violent crime in the U.S., between 1994 and 2010, youth ages 12 to 17 were about twice as likely to be victims of serious violent crime than adults. However, the rate of serious violent crime was greater for Hispanic youth than for Whites (87 percent vs. 79 percent). Black youth experienced a 66 percent decline in this crime, but it seems clear that violence among Hispanic youth declined at a steeper rate. So while crime decreased overall, other groups had greater reductions in offending than African Americans. Still, the rate of serious violence against Black youth was twice that of either Whites or Hispanics. The simple assault rates for Black youth were also significantly higher than for Whites or Hispanic youth.[37]

Homicide is one of the leading causes of juvenile deaths in the United States. According to the National Center for Injury Prevention and Control, homicide is the fourth leading cause of death for children ages 1 to 11, and it is the third leading cause of death for juveniles ages 12 to 17. An estimated 1,450 persons under age 18 were murdered in the United States in 2010, about 10 percent of all persons murdered that year. Nearly half of these victims were Black, while 47 percent were White and 3 percent were either American Indian, or Asian. Given that White youth comprise 76 percent of the U.S. resident juvenile population in 2010, while Blacks represented 17 percent, the murder rate for Black youth was nearly five times the rate for White youth.

Finally, youths age 7 to 17 are about as likely to be victims of suicide as they are to be a victim of homicide. Between 1990 and 2010, the juvenile suicide rate for White non-Hispanic youth was 28.3 per 100,000 youths. The suicide rates for Hispanics (17.3) and Blacks (16.4) and Asian (15.4) youth is much lower. However, the juvenile suicide rate for Native Americans (66.6) was more than double the White rate and more than triple the rate for other groups. The good news is that the juvenile suicide rate in general has steadily declined since 1990. Nevertheless, the disproportionality among different racial and ethnic groups has remained.

JUVENILE OFFENDERS

While the image of the hard-core, violent juvenile offender is popular in the media and perhaps colors the public's images about delinquents in general, the reality is that the vast majority of offenders in the juvenile justice system do not return to it, and most offenders in general never enter the system in the first place. This suggests a very different portrait of juvenile delinquents, as well as the overall effectiveness of the juvenile justice system. Additionally, the range of activities in which youths become involved might be classified as criminal vary substantially—it can be a fight at school, vandalizing someone's property, underage drinking and/or smoking tobacco, illicit drug use, or it can be more serious crimes such as gang activity and violent crime. For the purposes of this discussion, we will focus on the more serious crimes since they are most likely to demonstrate a more pronounced racial and ethnic distribution. At every stage of the juvenile justice process, we see evidence of a similar type of disproportionality that we saw in chapters for adult minorities.

JUVENILES AND THE POLICE

When examining the crime data presented by the Uniform Crime Reports, it is important to note that arrest information is divided by race and by ethnicity. That is, there is one table that captures arrest information for Whites, Blacks, Asians, Native Americans, and those from Hawaii and Pacific Islanders. There is another table that contrasts arrests for Hispanics and Latinos, comparing it to nonHispanics/Latinos.[38]

In 2014, according to the Uniform Crime Reports, there were a total of 797,229 arrests for individuals under the age of 18. This is a significant decline from 2010, when there were 1,642,500 juvenile arrests. However, in examining some of the demographic trends, little difference is found among those groups who were arrested during either period. For instance, in 2010, 66 percent of juveniles arrested were White, with Blacks representing 31 percent of all arrests. In 2014, 63 percent of all juveniles arrested were White and 35 percent were Black. In presenting these data, the Uniform Crime Report divides arrests by race (White, Black, Asian) and also by ethnicity (Hispanic/Latino compared to non-Hispanic/Latino). In the latter case, the percentages are slightly different because the total number of arrests made varies. In 2014, for example, there were a total of 569,908 arrests by ethnicity, of which 136,000 were classified as Hispanic/Latino. This represented about 24 percent of all arrests by ethnicity. Non-Hispanic/Latino comprised about 76 percent of all arrests. This division applies for specific crimes as well as for all arrests, and the trends noted in 2014 are similar to those in 2010.[39]

Of course, these proportions vary according to the type of crime committed, but on balance, what we see is a fairly consistent portrait of juvenile arrests in the United States. For instance, for those arrested under the age of 18, White juveniles accounted for about two-thirds of rape arrests, whereas Black juveniles made up nearly three-quarters of robbery arrests. Similarly, nearly 75 percent of White juveniles were arrested for arson, while only about 24 percent of Black juveniles were arrested for this crime. Arrests for homicide were higher among Black juveniles than Whites (57 percent vs. 41 percent), and more Whites were arrested for aggravated assault than Black juveniles (55.3 percent vs. 42.4 percent).[40]

The ratio of White-Black arrests for rape was 2 to 1, with Whites comprising 1,667 arrests for this crime compared to 844 for Black juveniles. Hispanic/Latinos represented 383 rapes, far lower than for either Whites or Blacks. The robbery ratio for Blacks to Whites was 2.5 to 1, while the ratio of Blacks to Hispanics is closer to 4 to 1. The juvenile arrest rate for robbery has seen a consistent decline since 2000. In 2010, the rate for Black youth was ten times the rate for White youth, fifteen times the rate for Native American youth, and nineteen times the rate for Asian youth. This trend still applies in 2014, despite dramatic declines in the number of overall arrests.[41]

Interestingly, arrests for aggravated assault have continued to decrease since their peak in 1994, by as much as 53 percent in 2010. However, what is noted in the data, including in 2014, has been the increase in the number of females arrested for this crime. There may be several explanations for this, but as one author noted, the reason may have to do with a modification of policy that encouraged arrests of females, particularly for domestic violence situations. Similar trends are noted for simple assaults. This trend can also be attributed to policy changes, where many schools have enacted zero tolerance policies, which result in arrests for incidents that would normally be handled informally.[42]

Schools provide unique settings for juveniles as they spend much time there and they are the setting for much delinquency and related activities. Researchers assessed the impact of various protective measures, such as law enforcement, security policies, and school/neighborhood characteristics on school violence with consideration of the racial composition of schools and grade levels. The researchers noted that minority schools often faced higher levels of reported violence and had a heavier law enforcement presence. The enhanced law enforcement efforts at predominantly minority schools had mixed or counterproductive results for reducing school violence, leading the researchers to suggest that the environments in which the schools are located and the characteristics or culture of the schools should be considered in efforts to reduce violence on campus.[43] The increased presence of law enforcement at schools results in many behaviors that were once handled informally becoming part of a youth's official record, and contributes

For some youths, gang life is a means of survival.

to the **"school-to-prison pipeline,"** which refers to the increasing patterns of students having contact with the justice system as a result of more punitive approaches to addressing school-related problems.

Ultimately, with regard to arrests, there appears to be a consistent trend of disproportionality with regard to African Americans and Whites. While Whites still represent the majority of arrests for most crimes, minorities, particularly African Americans and Hispanics, are overrepresented in the arrest data.

JUVENILES AND THE COURTS

A 2014 report, *Juvenile Court Statistics*, provides information on delinquency and status offense cases handled by juvenile courts, including demographic profiles of the trends in the volume and characteristics of court activity. U.S. courts with the authority to hear juvenile cases handled approximately 1.4 million cases in which a youth was charged with a delinquency offense. This is a significant decrease from the previous years, which is in line with the decrease in the number of juvenile arrests during that period. In fact, trends in juvenile court cases parallel the arrest trends in the FBI data.[44]

In terms of a demographic distribution, females represented about 25 percent of all delinquency cases handled by juvenile courts in 2010, although they did have higher rates based on specific offenses, such as larceny-theft (45 percent) or simple assault (36 percent) or disorderly conduct (35 percent). In 2010, Black juveniles represented about 16 percent of the juvenile population and about a third of all delinquency cases. In 2010, White youth made up 76 percent of the juvenile population and about 64 percent of all delinquency cases. Similarly, American Indian represented about 2 percent of the population and about the same percentage of cases, whereas Asian youth represented about 5 percent of the juvenile population and 1 percent of delinquency cases. These percentages were about the same ten years earlier, indicating that the disproportionality problem is a chronic one in the juvenile court system.[45]

While White youth accounted for the largest number of delinquency cases involving detention as an outcome, they were also the group least likely to actually experience it. In contrast, the likelihood of detention was highest for Black juveniles for all crimes except public order ones. In those cases, American Indian and Asian youths had slightly greater proportions of detention (30 percent and 29 percent) than Black youth (26 percent). Of those cases that involved progressing through the system to the adjudication stage, an interesting trend is revealed. While the likelihood of adjudication in 2010 was higher for males than for females, Black juveniles were less likely to be adjudicated compared to other groups, but once they are adjudicated, they are much more likely to be detained than other adjudicated youth. Table 10-2 shows that there has been a consistent trend where Black juveniles have not had their cases adjudicated even though there has been some indicators of a disproportionality regarding arrest and other aspects of the justice process.[46]

Interestingly, until 2016, information on Hispanic involvement in delinquency cases was not well known, despite the growth of the overall Hispanic population in the United States. In a recent publication titled, *Delinquency Cases Involving Hispanic Youth 2013*, researchers from the National Center on Juvenile Justice explored the participation of

Table 10.2 Percent of Petitioned Delinquency Cases Adjudicated by Race, 2010

Race	2001	2010
White	63%	60%
Black	58%	55%
American Indian	67%	69%
Asian	60%	58%

Hispanic youth in juvenile court. The findings of the study, based on a sample of cases, showed that Hispanic youth accounted for 26 percent of all cases processed in 2013. Property and public order offense cases each accounted for about one-third of the Hispanic delinquency caseload during that time period, and younger teens, those under the age of 16, accounted for about half of the caseload. The study concluded that, compared with White youth, Hispanic youth were 20 percent more likely to be referred to juvenile court and equally as likely to have their case handled formally. Once adjudicated, Hispanic youth were as likely as White youth to be placed on probation, but 30 percent more likely to be ordered to out-of-home placement.[47]

However, given that most adjudicated delinquency cases result in either residential placement or formal probation as a disposition, one question this data may raise is whether or not there is a racial distribution regarding this outcome. The data indicates that White youth were less likely than Black youth or American Indian youth to be ordered to residential placement as a result of a finding of adjudication of delinquency. However, there are many factors to consider when making a decision to place a youth in a residential facility, including criminal history, severity of the offense, and other factors.[48]

What should policymakers do about these apparent disparities? In 1988 Congress passed an amendment to the Juvenile Justice and Delinquency Prevention Act that required states to address the problem of disproportionality, particularly as it relates to confinement. Known as DMC, for disproportionate minority confinement, this amendment was expanded in 2002 which required states to create systems to reduce the problem of minorities who come into contact with the juvenile justice system. That is, measuring disparity can occur at multiple points in the system and can build upon itself in terms of the severity of outcomes. The research suggested that disparity is most pronounced at arrest, and as youth continue through the system, the differential treatment they receive is cumulative—disparity at arrest impacts disparity treatment in the court system, and so on.[49]

RELATIVE RATE INDEX

To address these problems, in 2010 the Office of Juvenile Justice and Delinquency Prevention created the Relative Rate Index (RRI) to measure disparities across the stages of the system by comparing rates of juvenile justice contact experienced by different groups of youth. The RRI includes the size of each subgroup (White, Black, Asian, etc.) at each stage and compares it to the preceding stage that occurs before it.

The idea is to quantify the nature of the decisions at each point and then compare the decisions in an effort to identify any influence disparity at one point impacts the next phase. While imperfect and given that not all states contribute to the database, the idea of having some sort of index or indicator of disparity is an important step in uncovering the reasons why disparity exists in the system as well as identifying specific "sticking points" for certain groups. In 2010, RRI data show that Black youth were arrested for delinquency offenses at more than twice the rate for White youth; and the diversion rate (meaning a case is diverted from further processing) for Black and other minority groups was less than the rate for White offenders. In general, there is more disparity for Black juveniles at arrest, detention, and waiver to criminal court than at other stages of the juvenile justice process.[50]

JUVENILES AND CORRECTIONS

The emphasis on individualized justice as a guiding philosophy of the juvenile justice system lends itself to a variety of resolutions to delinquent behavior. While most cases are handled informally and do not even come to the attention of the juvenile justice system, when they do, solutions such as probation and other less punitive measures are often provided. These are sometimes referred to as community-based programs and can include forestry camps, wilderness programs, mentoring programs, and other alternative measures. While they have their place and some have been shown to be notably effective in reducing repeat delinquent behavior, in other cases the offense committed by the juvenile is too serious to warrant such an approach.

In these instances, more formal detention is required. Institutional facilities are generally designed to serve youths awaiting a detention or adjudication hearing or those who were committed to detention by a juvenile court or some other administrative body, such as a social service agency. Youths referred to detention facilities under these circumstances are sometimes called **voluntary placements** because either their parents turned them over to a social service agency or the agency placed them because they committed delinquent acts but were not formally adjudicated. However, voluntary placements are rare, consisting of less than one percent of all detained youth.[51] Far more common are situations in which a judge orders a youth to a residential facility for committing a delinquent act. There are a wide range of options for institutional detention, including reception centers, ranches and forestry camps, boot camps, and traditional training schools, and adult prisons.

According to a report by the Office of Juvenile Justice and Delinquency Prevention, there were 79,166 juveniles in residential placements in the United States in 2010. About 24 percent of these youth were detained for violent crimes, 24 percent for property crimes, and only 7 percent for drug offenses.[52] In most cases, delinquents are held in publicly operated facilities while most status offenders are held in private ones. While about 80 percent of public juvenile detention facilities are considered secure, only about 20 percent of private institutions are high-security facilities.[53] However, while the number of juveniles serving time in detention centers has decreased since 2003, when the total number was nearly 97,000 youths, this number should be viewed with caution as it may not accurately reflect all youths who are detained. For example, the data do not include many minors

Table 10.3 Juvenile Offenders in Placement, 2010

Race/Ethnicity	Number	Percent	Percent Change 1997–2010
Total	70,792	100%	−33%
White	22,947	32	−42
Black	47,845	68	−27
Hispanic	15,590	22	−19
Am. Indian	1,236	2	−23
Asian	728	1	−67
Two or More	1,315	2	134

who are incarcerated after they are waived to adult courts or who have been tried as adults. In addition, some youths may be placed in private mental hospitals and substance-abuse clinics, but these are not typically included in official statistics on juveniles in detention.[54]

As with other phases of the juvenile justice process, race plays a role when it comes to detention. In 2010, nearly 48,000 minority offenders were in residential placement in juvenile facilities in the United States. Black youth accounted for 41 percent of all offenders in placement. While the population of offenders in residential placement dropped by a third between 1997 and 2010, fewer minorities were impacted by this decrease. White youth declined by 42 percent compared to 27 percent for minority youth.[55] (See Table 10-3.)

The research suggests that the reason for the difference stems from early stages of case processing—Black youths are less likely to be diverted from the court system and more likely to receive sentences involving detention. About 60 percent of all juveniles in custody are minorities and almost three-fourths of youths held in custody for a violent crime are minorities.[56]

In some cases, especially for serious offenders, juveniles can be sent to training schools or state institutions for longer periods of detention. They can also be sent to adult prisons, depending on a number

One unintended consequence of detention for some youths is that incarceration actually improves their standard of living.

of factors. The main difference between an adult prison and a training school is that there is a greater emphasis placed on rehabilitation and counseling in the juvenile facility. However, the emphasis on maintaining order and control of individual behavior is relatively the same in both places.[57]

In juvenile facilities, there is an emphasis placed on altering the individual's behavior so that he or she does not commit additional crimes in the future. It is often difficult to assess the success of programs with this goal in mind since participants have committed serious offenses or are repeat offenders. Thus, this group represents perhaps the worst of the delinquency population, making success a relatively difficult concept to evaluate. The fact that many serious offenders go on to adult careers in crime is not necessarily an indication that such programs are ineffective—it may be that the population they serve is the most difficult to change.[58]

Whether they look like prisons or college campuses, or even when attempts are made to create a home environment, training schools, which are being used increasingly in the United States to house juveniles, are an expensive way to handle delinquent youths. This is particularly true given the fact that only a small percentage of youths sentenced to secure detention have committed a violent crime. The vast majority of offenders have committed property crimes, such as burglary or larceny-theft.[59] In addition to the expense, like their adult counterparts, overcrowding has become problematic for juvenile training schools and gangs are becoming a feature of the training school landscape.[60]

Short-Term Facilities

In addition to long-term secure facilities, a youth can be placed in a short-term one as well. Essentially, there are two types of short-term facilities: those that house youths awaiting adjudication or dispositional hearings, which are similar in many ways to jails, and short-term facilities for adjudicated offenders. Examples of the latter are boot camps, forestry camps, or ranches. Part of the problem with this type of approach is that they offer little in the way of therapy nor do they contribute to correcting the behavior that caused youths to be arrested in the first place.

Additionally, there is no follow-up care from this type of program; youths are simply sent back to the environments and neighborhoods from which they originally came with few tools to cope with the problems that got them into trouble. While the popularity of boot camps peaked around the mid 1990s, with several hundred programs operating across the country, the evaluations of these programs demonstrated that they have little in the way of long-term positive effects. In sum, given their short duration, the absence of consistency of the message after they leave the program, and few opportunities to understand the significance of what happened to them during the process, this type of intervention falls quite short of the mark in terms of changing youths' behavior.[61]

INSTITUTIONAL LIFE FOR DELINQUENTS

Everyone responds to stress in different ways: some confront it head-on, others withdraw, while still others develop a variety of coping mechanisms. The sad truth is that while detention is supposed to be a place where constructive work can occur despite the coercive setting, for many youths, time spent in a detention facility actually improves their social standing, a term sociologists refer to as **upward social mobility**. The reason for this is that many youths come from dysfunctional families, where living arrangements are chaotic, and going to jail or prison is actually an improvement in their quality of life since they are provided with shelter, food, and clothing, something often lacking at home.[62]

Still, despite its potential social benefits, institutional life can be quite unsettling for youths. Not only must they adapt to an inflexible structure, where their freedom, meals, and time are regulated by others, perhaps for the first time in their lives, youths must confront a wide range of issues often brought out during therapy sessions.[63]

Institutionalized youths are also likely to suffer from underdeveloped social and communication skills, which often translate into anti-social behavior. Because the structure of the institution forces youths to interact with others, juveniles need a great deal of encouragement and support as they begin to learn how to effectively deal with others.[64] There are also a number of other issues, such as coping with various forms of mental illness and suicide.

MENTAL ILLNESS AND DETENTION

Many youths enter the prison system suffering from a host of emotional and psychological disorders. One meta-analysis of the literature on psychological and mental disorders in juvenile detention facilities found that adolescents, particularly boys, were ten times more likely to suffer from psychosis than the general population. Girls in detention were most often diagnosed with major depression, and males were more likely to be diagnosed with ADHD, conduct disorders, bipolar disorder, and other illnesses.[65] According to some studies, between 50 and 90 percent of youths in confinement suffer from conduct disorders, about half from attention deficit disorder, 40 percent suffer from anxiety disorders, nearly 50 percent are substance abuse dependent, 80 percent suffer from affective disorders and between one and five percent have a psychotic disorder.[66] All of these figures are higher for detained youth than for those in the general population.[67] These problems can result in disciplinary issues while incarcerated as well as limit youths' participation in programs designed to address their disorders. One of the challenges facing most public institutions is the provision of such services. While this may not seem to be that important at first glance, in that youths are increasingly being detained for the purpose accountability and punishment rather than treatment, the end result is likely a higher rate of recidivism once they are released.

SUICIDE AND INSTITUTIONALIZED YOUTH

The risk of suicide is an important factor in how youths are treated while detained. According to the surgeon general of the United States, youth suicide in the general population is a national tragedy and a major public health problem.[68] A recent national survey found that more than 3 million youths are at risk for suicide each year, with 37 percent of surveyed youths reporting that they attempted suicide during the previous twelve months.[69]

Despite the fact that youth suicide in the general population is considered a major public health problem, comparable research has not been conducted regarding juvenile suicide in confinement.[70] A review of the literature on suicide among detained juveniles shows only a few studies on this topic, but the information available suggests that self-harm and suicide attempts happen rather frequently in juvenile correctional facilities. For example, according to one study, more than 11,000 juveniles are estimated to engage in more than 17,000 incidents of suicidal behavior in juvenile detention facilities each year.[71]

The research also shows that White youths appear to attempt suicide in confinement or think about it more often than African American, Hispanic, or Asian youths.[72] It should be noted that while isolation often occurs in detention centers as a disciplinary measure, as well as a safety precaution to prevent victimization, it can also be an important factor in suicide. Further, a report by the Office of Juvenile Justice and Delinquency Prevention notes that youths sent to secure detention facilities are unlike the vast majority of offenders who come to the attention of the juvenile justice system. As such, they bring with them unique problems, behaviors, and perspectives that may make them a higher risk for extreme behavior such as suicide. This underscores the need for staff working in confined environments to receive additional training on handling these types of offenders.[73]

DELINQUENCY, DETENTION, AND PUBLIC POLICY

Not only do the fears and concerns about serious juvenile offenders translate into practices and programs that focus more on punishment than treatment, what is available to youths who have been detained is also limited by the public's perception of who they are and what they need. The research suggests that detention does little to effectively rehabilitate youths, and perhaps the need for accountability supersedes any therapeutic benefit. What is missing from the discussion, however, are the long-term effects of the "get-tough" approach to delinquents. Similar to adult offenders, eventually inmates must be released and in the absence of effective methods to reintegrate them back into society (e.g., life skills, job training, housing, healthcare), it is likely that those who have experienced incarceration will return to the justice system. The same can be said for juveniles who have been detained; the difference is that their criminal careers are likely to be much longer than their older counterparts. At the same time, there may not be effective alternatives to detention for serious and violent juvenile offenders, leaving incarceration, perhaps in adult facilities, the only viable option for some states.

SUMMARY

This chapter explored the history of the treatment of juveniles who committed delinquency as well as the development of the juvenile justice system in the United States. Included in the discussion was an assessment of the disproportionality of minorities for juveniles, either as victims or offenders. Like their adult counterparts, African American and Hispanic juveniles are more likely than White youth to be involved in each stage of the juvenile justice process, from arrest, to adjudication, to sentencing, to detention. Also included in the discussion about juveniles was the influence of emotional disorders and suicidal tendencies for detained youth. From a public policy standpoint, the issue of the overall "get tough" approach to crime, popular since the 1980s, has impacted how the general public views juveniles, despite the fact that most youths who enter the juvenile justice system do not return. The remaining small number of hard-core, violent juvenile offenders has shaped public policy in all aspects of the juvenile system, with a greater emphasis on treating youth like adults for many offenses.

YOU MAKE THE CALL

ZERO TOLERANCE POLICIES AND DELINQUENCY

You were recently hired as an elementary school teacher in an inner-city urban area. As part of the school's zero tolerance policy, you were instructed by your principal to call the police in the event students engage in fighting or combative behavior. As you are supervising the cafeteria at lunch, a group of students gather around in a circle to observe a fight between two males. You make your way over to the location where the fight is taking place and separate the two young men, one of whom is White and the other is Black. The White student begins to protest that he was only defending himself and that he wants to press charges against his African American colleague. The other youth is silent and says nothing to anyone. A more experienced teacher is present who tells you to have the office call the police. When they arrive, the officers place the Black youth in custody and take a statement from the White youth, but do not place him in handcuffs. You notice this and ask the officers about it—they inform you that they plan to bring the African

American youth to the station for processing. When you ask why, the officers are a bit evasive, stating only that they believe the African American initiated the fight. Given that you were the only one who really saw what happened, you wonder how the officers could know that.

Questions

1. Do you think the officers are being fair in the assessment of the confrontation and if so why?
2. Do you think you should try to persuade the officers to take both youths into custody until the matter is resolved?
3. Why do you think the African American youth remained silent throughout the experience while the White youth made the case that he was the victim?
4. Do you think the African American youth will be formally processed through the juvenile justice system? Why or why not?
5. What can you do as a teacher to address this issue?

KEY TERMS

adjudication
Child Savers Movement
Children's Aid Society
houses of refuge
individualized justice
juvenile delinquency
Juvenile Delinquency Prevention and
Control Act
Juvenile Justice and Delinquency Prevention
Act of 1974

orphan trains
parens patriae
school-to-prison pipeline
status offenders
training schools
transfer
upward social mobility
voluntary placements
waive jurisdiction

DISCUSSION QUESTIONS

1. What are some of the primary differences between the juvenile justice system and the adult system?
2. Do you think that the juvenile justice system should be abolished and all offenders handled by the adult system? Why or why not?
3. Why is *parens patriae* such an important feature of the juvenile justice system? How does it operate in practice?

4. What is it about the life of many delinquents that suggests that detention is actually an improvement in their standard of living?

5. How do the statistics about the disproportionality in the adult system compare to what is seen among juveniles who enter the juvenile justice system?

6. What do you think about the connection between juvenile detention and suicide and mental illness?

FOR FURTHER READING

McNamara, R. H. *The Lost Population: Status Offenders in America*. Durham, NC: Carolina Academic Press, 2008.

O'Connor, S. *Orphan Trains*. Boston: Houghton Mifflin, 2001.

Tanenhaus, D. S. *Juvenile Justice in the Making*. New York: Oxford University Press, 2005.

Marrus, E. *Children and Juvenile Justice*. Durham, NC: Carolina Academic Press, 2007.

NOTES

1. Robert H. McNamara, *Juvenile Delinquency: Bridging Theory to Practice* (New York: McGraw-Hill, 2013).

2. Juvenile Justice and Delinquency Prevention Act of 1974. P.L. 93-415, 88 Stat. 1109.

3. See Robert H. McNamara, *The Lost Population: Status Offenders in America* (Durham, NC: Carolina Academic Press, 2008).

4. See A. W. Simpson, *Blackstone's Commentaries on the Laws of England* (New York: Nabu Press, 2010).

5. Ibid.

6. Ibid.

7. Ibid.

8. See for instance, S. O'Connor, *Orphan Trains* (Boston: Houghton Mifflin, 2001).

9. Ibid.

10. Ibid.

11. D. S. Tanenhaus, *Juvenile Justice in the Making* (New York: Oxford University Press, 2005).

12. Ibid.

13. E. Marrus, *Children and Juvenile Justice* (Durham, NC: Carolina Academic Press, 2007).

14. See for instance, the Center on Juvenile and Criminal Justice at http://www.cjcj.org/juvenile/justice/juvenile/justice/overview

15. Tanenhaus, *Juvenile Justice*.

16. Ibid.

17. Marrus, *Children and Juvenile Justice*.

18. H. N. Snyder and M. Sickmund, *Juvenile Offenders and Victims 2006: A National Report*. U.S. Department of Justice, Office of Justice Programs, Office of Juvenile Justice and Delinquency Prevention, 2006. Available at https://www.ojjdp.gov/ojstatbb/nr2006/

19. Ibid.

20. *Kent v. United States*, 383 U.S. 541 (1966).

21. Ibid.

22. Ibid.

23. Ibid.

24. Ibid.

25. Ibid.
26. Marrus, *Children and Juvenile Justice.*
27. See R. A. Mendel, 2002. *Less Hype , More Help: Reducing Juvenile Crime: What Works and What Doesn't* (Washington, DC: America Youth Forum, 2002); also B. Krisberg, *Juvenile Justice: Redeeming Our Children* (Los Angeles: Sage, 2005); D. L. Mackenzie, *What Works in Corrections* (Boston: Cambridge University Press, 2006), 271–303.
28. Ibid.
29. ChildTrends.org. "Appendix 1—Number of Children Under 18 in United States as a Percentage of the Population," *Child Trends Databank*, November 2015. Available at http://www .childtrends.org/wp-content/uploads/2012/07/53_appendix1.pdf
30. M. Sickmund and C. Puzzanchera, eds, *Juvenile Offenders and Victims: 2014 National Report* (Pittsburgh, PA: National Center for Juvenile Justice, 2014).
31. Ibid.
32. Ibid.
33. Ibid.
34. Ibid.
35. Ibid.
36. Ibid.
37. J. Truman and L. Langton, *Criminal Victimization 2014*, U.S. Department of Justice, Bureau of Justice Statistics, 2014. Available at http://www.bjs.gov/content/pub/pdf/cv14.pdf.
38. U.S. Department of Justice, Federal Bureau of Investigation. 2014. *Crime in the United States 2014*. Table 43B. Available at https://www.fbi.gov/about-us/cjis/ucr/crime-in-the-u.s/2014/ crime-in-the-u.s.-2014
39. Ibid.
40. Ibid.
41. *Crime in the United States, 2014.*
42. McNamara, *Juvenile Delinquency.*
43. C. Crawford and R. Burns, "Reducing School Violence: Considering School Characteristics and the Impacts of Law Enforcement, School Security, and Environmental Factors," *Policing: An International Journal of Police Strategies & Management*39, no. 3 (2016): 456–77.
44. Sickmund and Puzzanchera, *Juvenile Offenders and Victims.*
45. Ibid.
46. Ibid.
47. U.S. Department of Justice, Office of Justice Programs, *Delinquency Cases Involving Hispanic Youth 2013*, by Sarah Hockenberry and Charles Puzzanchera, Office of Juvenile Justice and Delinquency Prevention, (Washington DC, 2016), http://www.ncjj.org/pdf/249915.pdf
48. Sickmund and Puzzanchera, *Juvenile Offenders and Victims.*
49. Ibid.
50. Ibid.
51. Ibid.
52. Ibid.
53. Office of Juvenile Justice and Delinquency Prevention. *Juveniles in Residential Placement*. 2014. Available at *https://www.ojjdp.gov/ojstatbb/corrections/qa08201.asp?qaDate=2014*
54. See R. H. McNamara, *The Lost Population: Status Offenders in America* (Durham, NC: Carolina Academic Press, 2008).
55. Sickmund and Puzzanchera, *Juvenile Offenders and Victims.*
56. Office of Juvenile Justice, *Census of Juveniles.*

57. See S. M. Taroola, E. F. Wagner, J. Rabinowitz, and J. L. Tubman, "Understanding and Treating Juvenile Offenders: A Review of Current Knowledge and Future Directions," *Aggression and Violent Behavior* 7, no. 2 (2002): 125–43.

58. See R. Haapanen, L. Britton, and T. Croisdale, "Persistent Criminality and Career Length," *Crime and Delinquency* 53, no. 1 (2007): 133–55.

59. Sickmund and Puzzanchera, *Juvenile Offenders and Victims*.

60. Ibid.

61. See D. L. Mackenzie, *What Works in Corrections: Reducing the Criminal Activities of Offenders and Delinquents* (Cambridge, MA: Cambridge University Press, 2006).

62. For some inmates, life improves substantially when they are incarcerated in that their immediate needs are met. For an interesting discussion of the economics of incarceration, see Vera Institute of Justice, *The Unintended Consequences of Incarceration*, 1996, Available at http://archive.vera.org/sites/default/files/resources/downloads/uci.pdf

63. See for instance, M. Petersen-Badali and C. J. Koegl, "Juveniles Experiences with Incarceration: The Role of Correctional Staff in Peer Violence," *Journal of Criminal Justice* 30, no. 1 (2002): 41–49.

64. Ibid.

65. S. Faze, H. Dole, and N. Angstrom, "Mental Disorders Among Adolescents in Juvenile Detention and Correctional Facilities: A Systematic Review and Meta Regression Analysis of 25 Surveys," Journal of American Academy of Child and Adolescent Psychiatry 48, *no. 9 (2008)*: 1010–19.

66. R. Otto, J. Greenstein, M. Johnson, and R. Friedman, "Prevalence of Mental Disorders Among Youth in the Juvenile Justice System," in *Responding to the Mental Health Needs of Youth in the Juvenile Justice System* (Seattle, WA: National Coalition for the Mentally Ill in the Criminal Justice System, 1992), 7–48; J. Eden and R. Otto, "Prevalence of Mental Disorders Among Youth in the Juvenile Justice System," *Focal Point* (Spring 1997): 1–8.

67. See for instance J. Coosa and K. Skiwear, "Youth with Mental Health Disorders: Issues and Emerging Responses," *Juvenile Justice* 7, no. 1 (2000): 3–13.

68. R. H. Carmona, MD, MPh, FACS, *Suicide Prevention Among Native American Youth*. Testimony of Surgeon General Before the Indian Affairs Committee, U.S. Senate, June 15, 2005. Department of Health and Human Services, *The Surgeon General's Call To Action To Prevent Suicide, 1999* (Washington, DC: U.S. Department of Health and Human Services, 1999).

69. Substance Abuse and Mental Health Services Administration, *Summary of Findings From the 2000 National Household Survey on Drug Abuse*, NHSDA Series: H-13, DHHS Publication No. SMA 01-3549. (Rockville, MD: U.S. Department of Health and Human Services, 2001).

70. L. Hayes, "Prison Suicide: An Overview and a Guide to Prevention," *The Prison Journal* 75, no. 4 (1995): 431–55; L. M. Hayes, *Suicide Prevention in Juvenile Correction and Detention Facilities: A Resource Guide* (South Easton, MA: Council of Juvenile Correctional Administrators, 1997).

71. D. Parent, V. Leiter, S. Kennedy, L. Livens, D. Wentworth, and S. Wilcox, *Conditions of Confinement: Juvenile Detention and Corrections Facilities* (Washington, DC: Office of Juvenile Justice and Delinquency Prevention, 1994).

72. T. Kempton and R. Forehand, "Suicide Attempts Among Juvenile Delinquents: The Contribution of Mental Health Factors," *Behaviour Research and Therapy* 30, no. 5 (1992): 537–41. N. Alessi, M. McManus, A. Brickman, and L. Grapentine, L. 1984. "Suicidal Behavior Among Serious Juvenile Offenders" *American Journal of Psychiatry* 141, no. 2 (1984): 286–87.

73. U.S. Department of Justice, Office of Justice Programs, *Juvenile Suicide in Confinement: A National Survey*, by Lindsay M. Hayes, Open-file report NJC 213691, Office of Juvenile Justice and Delinquency Prevention (Washington, DC, 2009), https://www.ncjrs.gov/pdffiles1/ojjdp/213691.pdf

PART III

INTERNAL ISSUES IN THE CRIMINAL JUSTICE SYSTEM AND MULTICULTURALISM

CHAPTER 11

POLICING AND MULTICULTURALISM

CHAPTER OBJECTIVES:

After reading this chapter, you should be able to:

- Understand how the historical development of policing relates to current concerns regarding multiculturalism
- Understand the extent, nature, and need for multiculturalism among police personnel
- Recognize how police practices exist with regard to multiculturalism, and how those actions affect police-community relations and perceptions of the police
- Understand the significance of police-community relations

In April 2014, the U.S. Department of Justice (DOJ) concluded a two-year investigation of the Albuquerque (NM) Police Department, and found that the officers engaged in a pattern or practice of use of excessive force, including deadly force, which violated the Fourth Amendment. A DOJ investigation of the Cleveland Division of Police in December of the same year found similar results, and in 2015, the DOJ identified a pattern of clear racial disparities and discriminatory intent in the Ferguson (MO) Police Department.

These DOJ findings emerged during a time when various other acts of seemingly biased and unprofessional policing have caused many in society to reconsider the role of the police, police practices, police training, police-community relations, and a host of other issues related to policing. Police practices have undergone increasing scrutiny, as tensions between the police and certain groups in society (primarily minority groups) have suffered from the exposure of questionable police practices, including but not restricted to racial profiling and seemingly wrongful deaths.

The nature of police work, including the regular social interaction with varied groups, sometimes results in claims of officer misbehavior. Put simply, police practices are sometimes controversial and failure to recognize cultural diversity is sometimes a primary contributing factor. Scholars have noted that: "Some of the most problematic encounters involving the police occur between White police officers and minority citizens. Encounters between the police and Blacks, Hispanics, Native Americans, and, increasingly, Asians indicate that a good deal of hostility remains as a result of racist attitudes, historical distrust, and past discrimination."[1] The diverse culture in which policing is practiced requires officers to maintain, at minimum, a base-level recognition and understanding of cultural differences in order to ensure justice, personal safety, and the safety of others.

The police are the primary agents of formal social control in our society. Charged with the dubious and vague tasks of "serving and protecting," officers must find a balance between controlling and preventing crime, and preserving individual rights. It could be argued that too often the police sacrifice individual rights for the sake of crime control, and vice versa. Finding an approach that suits everyone is much easier said than done.

Modern police practices largely reflect the roots of historical policing. In their insightful and thorough work, *Police in a Multicultural Society*, authors David and Melissa Barlow discuss the historical evolution of policing and tie it to modern police practices.[2] They comment on police practices such as **underpolicing**, which involve the police denying "equal protection to racial and ethnic minorities in the United States by failing to protect them from violent racist actions by Whites, by declining to ensure their basic human rights, and by inadequately responding to problems of crime and neglect in minority neighborhoods."[3] Barlow and Barlow also discuss **overpolicing**, which involves "the oppressive and often brutal treatment of marginalized groups by police."[4] These styles of policing highlight the historical and recent conflict between police and underrepresented groups in society.

Throughout this book there are numerous accounts of how multiculturalism affects policing. This chapter focuses specifically on how policing came to be, why it exists, and how diversity and multiculturalism have shaped modern policing. Included is discussion of policing, and multiculturalism as it pertains to critical issues in policing. Of particular interest is the history of policing, police personnel issues, police practices and behavior, and police-community relations. As demonstrated throughout this book, police officers, as the primary gatekeepers to the criminal justice system, should be well-versed in recognizing and understanding cultural diversity.

HISTORICAL POLICING

Much of what police do today is similar to what was done when formal policing began. In other words, policing has not changed much in the roughly 180 years of its existence. There have been alterations and developments in the manner in which policing exists and occurs. However, there have been few, if any, major changes to policing in general. With regard to policing in the United States, the activities and practices of the earliest periods of policing largely reflect those found in England. The following discussion of the history of policing maintains a primary focus on diversity and multiculturalism.

THE ROOTS OF U.S. POLICING

The history of formal policing dates back to the development of the Metropolitan Police, the name for the police department established in London in 1829 and organized by Sir Robert Peel.[5] Prior to formal policing, social control was primarily the responsibility of the citizens. Citizens lived communally for several reasons, including the need for en-hanced farming practices and for safety and security. With regard to the latter, it became evident to citizens that there was strength in numbers. Under what was known as the **Frankpledge system**, or the practice of informal social control in which community members protected one another, citizens raised the **hue and cry** upon being victimized.[6] Raising the hue and cry, or call to arms, generated a response from every able-bodied male in attempts to bring the offenders(s) to justice. Failure to respond to the hue and cry could result in punitive sanctions. Citizens also protected one another through night watch and day ward systems in which constables and/or citizens were expected to watch out for danger—whether it be in the form of weather, fires, or individuals. Such informal social control was initially effective given the small population sizes and the homogene-ity of groups living communally.

The need for formal social control became evident as small towns became large cities and England began transitioning from an agrarian society to one focused on industrial-ism. Numerous individuals migrated to cities in hopes of great success, only to find a great deal of social disorganization, poverty, and difficulty in attaining their goals. Many individuals abandoned their lifestyles and belongings in their attempt to find success in the big city, only to find limited opportunities and great difficulties upon their arrival. The increased cultural diversity during this transitional period also contributed to the difficul-ties. No longer could informal social control (e.g., fellow citizens) serve the purposes of law enforcement. The need for formal social control (e.g., policing) became increasingly evident as rioting occurred, and populations and culture conflict significantly increased in the cities as industrialization took hold.

London magistrate Sir Henry Fielding is credited with creating the **Bow Street Runners**, a precursor to the first formal police department.[7] Fielding noticed the frequency with which particular individuals were brought into his court and decided something needed to be done. Mind you, bringing someone to justice during this time (circa 1750) was not as easy as it is today. Citizens had to hire private security to bring the accused before the court, or do it themselves. Fielding decided to hire individuals to seek law violators in the Bow Street region of London, and paid a sum of money to those who brought suspects before the court. The limitations of this approach are clearly evident (e.g., unethically bringing forth suspects in efforts to make money); however, the Bow Street Runners helped cleanse the area of much crime, and inspired the **Metropolitan Police Act**, which was passed in 1829. This act led to the first formal police department, the Metropolitan Police, led by Sir Robert Peel. Peel's approach was very reactive and centered on serving the public. Much of what Peel proposed is evident in the commu-nity policing approaches found in many of today's police departments. His principles generally emphasized crime prevention, police cooperation with the public, and police professionalism.

The London police initially were not well-accepted by Londoners, who believed that their rights were being violated. To proactively seek law violators and monitor societal be-havior was a new practice at the time, and not all citizens appreciated the perceived intru-sion. Such public disapproval of policing would eventually subside as citizens recognized that the police provided citizens with protection. Such frustration in public approval of the police was a sign of things to come, as throughout the history of policing we've seen peaks and valleys regarding public approval of police and police actions. The development of policing in England would mirror the development of policing in the United States, and the Metropolitan Police would provide a blueprint for all police practices.

HISTORICAL U.S. POLICING

Policing in the United States developed in much the same manner as policing in England. Informal social control in which citizens protected one another, and relied on the hue and cry and the watch and ward system, was used prior to the development of large cities. Formal policing emerged in areas where small towns grew into larger ones. Cities along the eastern seaboard were among the first to have formal police departments, as settlers eventually recognized the need for formal law enforcement. Formal policing would soon extend across the entire country, as settlers moved west and small towns grew into large ones.

SLAVE PATROLS AND BLACK CODES

Policing in Southern states, however, took a notably distinct approach compared to elsewhere in the United States. The roots of policing in the South are found in the **slave patrols** used in the Southern states and colonies prior to and following the Revolutionary War. Slave patrols are considered by some as the first American police departments,[8] and were established as early as the 1740s. By 1750 every Southern colony maintained a slave patrol.[9] The patrols were tasked with preventing slave revolts and apprehending runaway slaves. The large population of slaves in the South prompted plantation owners to create special codes of laws and, subsequently, special forces to ensure that slaves abided by the laws. These laws, for instance, prevented slaves from having weapons, leaving plantations without permission, gathering in groups, and resisting punishment.[10] Southern states also made it legal for any White freeman to stop, search, and apprehend any Black person, regardless of whether or not they were a slave.[11] Most states and colonies permitted slave patrols to enter any slaves' dwellings, punish slaves who were away from their plantation, and search, punish, and perhaps even kill slaves found to be in violation of the slave code.[12]

The emancipation of the slaves did not provide an end to the enhanced levels of social control faced by African Americans in the South. Southern states circumvented the emancipation by creating **Black codes**, laws designed to nullify the rights granted to the newly freed slaves. Among the restrictions found in Black codes were the prohibition of interracial marriage, renting land in urban areas, preaching the gospel without a license, and assuming any occupation other than servant or farmer unless the newly freed slave paid a tax. The mission of Southern police departments was to protect the White population from the violent threats of slaves, and later, freed slaves.[13] The **Civil Rights Act of 1866**, passed by Congress despite President Johnson's veto, was targeted to address the Black codes by defining all persons born in the United States, with the exception of

Table 11.1 Three Eras of U.S. Policing

The Political Era (1840–1930)

The Reform Era (1930–1980)

The Community Era (1980–present)

Native Americans, as national citizens who were to enjoy specific rights. These rights included permission to make contracts, bring lawsuits, and enjoy the full and equal benefit of the law.[14]

THREE ERAS OF POLICING

The history of policing in the United States has been categorized into three eras: The political era, the reform era, and the community era.[15] While the history of a complex institution such as policing can be difficult to categorize into three periods, there are several identifiable characteristics of these eras, particularly as they relate to multiculturalism. While such a categorization provides for interesting discussion of the historical intervals of policing, it is argued that the categorization fails to consider the development of policing with regard to segregation, slavery, discrimination, and racism,[16] factors which have undoubtedly influenced modern U.S. policing. To understand our police requires understanding of the barriers they've overcome, the obstacles they've provided, and their relationship to the communities they serve.

The Political Era

The **political era of policing** (1840–1930) is characterized by police officers establishing intimate relationships with the community and politics heavily influencing police departments and police practices. The police had limited technology during this time, thus they walked beats which encouraged police-community interaction. In addition to crime control, officers provided a significant amount of general services to the public, and relied on their problem-solving skills, as there was no radio to call for backup and no police car to provide rapid assistance.

Police practices during this period were also influenced by politics, with those holding political power rewarding those who supported them during their candidacy and when in office. The "spoils system" was evident during this period and certainly influenced who worked for the police department and in what capacity they served. **Patronage**, or the practice of politicians rewarding friends, created police departments that often reflected the communities they served.[17] For instance, the Irish Americans began appointing their friends as police officers once the Irish Americans began to win political power.[18]

Police officers during the political era were not exempt from the lack of cultural sensitivity existent at the time, and minority police officers were treated differently from White officers. For instance, Black officers were prohibited from patrolling in predominantly White areas, were required to call a White officer to arrest a White suspect, and were given assignments in high-crime, predominantly minority neighborhoods. The virtual absence of Black police officers resulted in less police attention and protection in areas heavily populated by minorities.[19] Other racial and ethnic groups, as well as women, were also underrepresented, if not absent, from early police departments. Society in general at this time was largely unaware of the impending social unrest that would result from cultural insensitivity.

Police corruption was problematic during the political era, especially during the years of **Prohibition** (1919–1933), which criminalized the sale, transport, or manufacturing of alcohol. It was during Prohibition when police officers sometimes took advantage of "favors" offered in exchange for them looking the other way while alcohol was served. Prohibition had a significant impact on the history of policing, particularly with regard to police corruption and public perceptions of the police because officers were charged with enforcing an unpopular law.

Race riots and racial disorder, especially those in New York City, Boston, and Philadelphia also significantly shaped policing during the political era, as departments developed and assumed the responsibility of quelling the disturbances. Unfortunately, little professional training existed for addressing civil disorders. The level of violence accompanying the unrest was sometimes agitated by officers too quickly resorting to violence. Civil disorder would not end with the political era.

The Reform Era

The **reform era of policing** (1930–1980), also known as the progressive era, was a time when police-community relations suffered and police became increasingly reliant upon technology and overly concerned with efficiency. It was during the reform era that police departments began heavily using police cars to enhance overall police practices. Although the automobile and other technological advances (e.g., the two-way radio) enhanced policing, police-community relations suffered as officers became distant from the public. Officers were no longer primarily walking beats and interacting with the public. Instead, they largely focused on crime fighting. The "just the facts ma'am" approach to policing may initially enhance the efficiency of crime control, but it does very little for police-community relations, which became problematic during this period.

Several turbulent incidents occurred during the reform era, which in turn impacted policing. Many of these events have direct relationships with policing a multicultural society. Among the happenings was the civil rights movement, which began in the late 1950s and set in motion a series of actions that would change policing, and more generally, society.

The civil rights movement initially began as a grassroots effort to highlight economic, political, and social inequality in the United States. Blacks who chose to protest were confronted by police officers who were typically White males with limited training in how to confront such collective action. The officers' actions in handling protest marches and general civil disobedience often aggravated the situation.[20] The assassinations of several prominent figures such as Martin Luther King Jr., Malcolm X, President Kennedy, and Medgar Evers contributed to the unrest during this period, as did the protest of those opposed to the war in Vietnam. Police were charged with handling, among other responsibilities, a series of race and antiwar demonstrations. The underrepresentation of African Americans and other minorities in policing contributed to clashes between the groups and certainly played a role in the hundreds of riots that occurred between 1966 and 1971. The unrest further separated the police from the public and created danger for officers, as police practices such as providing public protection sometimes generated collective violence in the form of rioting. We've seen several similar incidents in more recent times.

A wave of riots occurred between 1964 and 1968 due in part to tensions between the police and the Black community. Many of the riots followed a situation involving police.[21] For instance, the New York City riot began following the shooting death of a Black teenager by an off-duty police officer. The Watts, California, riot was initiated by a traffic stop.[22] Rioting during this time was largely perpetuated by negative public attitudes toward the police, the lack of preparedness of police to address civil unrest, and racial tensions between Blacks and Whites.[23] Racially selective policing exacerbated protest demonstration most significantly in areas with strained police-minority community relations.[24] The potential harm and costs of such unrest was alarming. For instance, the week-long rioting in Detroit in 1967 resulted in forty-three deaths and roughly $40 million in property damage. In 1966, forty-three riots were identified in major urban areas across the United States.[25] These numbers say little about the damage done to police-community relations.

The lack of police training, particularly with regard to addressing cultural diversity, contributed to the police being seen by many as the enemy. A confusing array of social movements, including the emerging drug culture, contributed to the problems faced by police.[26] Officers were commonly referred to as "pigs," and the isolation that was emerging between police and society was enhanced by the overall social unrest of the times. The White male police officers tasked with maintaining the peace in the predominantly minority urban ghetto faced numerous challenges, especially in light of the officer's symbolic representation of power and control. Many angry and frustrated Blacks viewed the police as symbolic of a criminal justice system that had been largely unresponsive to their needs.[27] To compound the situation, an increasing number of viewers across the United States could watch the events in the comfort of their own homes as televisions were becoming increasingly common in households.

The tension and conflict between police and minority groups led to intense focus on the problems underlying the social unrest. Prominent among the national commissions formed to examine the situation and to offer recommendation for change was the 1965 **President's Commission on Law Enforcement and Administration of Justice** (also known as the President's Crime Commission).[28] The Commission focused on enhancing professionalization of policing and police officers by hiring greater diversity in policing and encouraging departments to become more community-oriented. Another commission, the **National Advisory Commission on Civil Disorders** (also known as the Kerner Commission), was created to study the causes behind the rioting. The commission identified a series of issues that contributed to the collective violence, including unequal justice, institutional racism, unemployment, and discrimination. With regard to policing, the Kerner Commission noted the lack of Black police officers, inadequate training and supervision, brutal and abrasive police conduct, and poor police-community relations.[29] The police during this period faced criticism from every direction.

Police practices were also the target of several landmark Supreme Court decisions made during this period. The decisions restricted police powers and provided greater rights to defendants. Beginning in the 1950s, several Court decisions under the direction of Supreme Court Justice Earl Warren influenced police-community relations and the lives of many individuals from underrepresented groups. The Supreme Court ruled in cases such as *Mapp v. Ohio*,[30] which extended the **exclusionary rule**, or the prohibition of introducing in court illegally seized materials, to apply in all courts and jurisdictions in the United States. The Court also ruled in *Gideon v. Wainwright*,[31] which mandated that all defendants charged with a felony are entitled to legal representation, and *Miranda v. Arizona*,[32] in which the Court ruled that any evidence obtained by police during a custodial interrogation cannot be used in court unless the suspect is informed of his or her basic rights. In *Terry v. Ohio*[33] the Court clarified the law surrounding when a police officer can stop and question a person. These cases restricted police discretion and provided numerous protections to individuals.

The reform era was influential in the history of U.S. policing. Police officers initially shifted their focus away from interacting with the public, yet, at the end of the era they were forced to confront violent reactions. Many of these reactions resulted from what were perceived as intrusive and/or biased police practices. It was also a time when police departments were forced to reassess their relationship with the community. In turn, many departments recognized the need to get back in touch with the roots of policing, and begin to once again more positively interact with citizens.

The Community Era

The **community era of policing**, which began around 1980 and continues today, involves efforts by the police to reconnect with the public primarily through the adoption of the **community policing** philosophy. Clearly defining community policing, however, is not easily done. The problems associated with defining community policing largely stem from the different approaches to community policing taken by various departments, and the difficulties departments face when implementing the community policing philosophy. Generally, the term has been defined as "a philosophy that promotes a decentralized

Community policing encourages positive police-community relations and encourages citizens to take a more active role in crime fighting. Neighborhood Watch programs are an example.

organizational design; a proactive approach to policing that encourages partnerships and problem-solving to address public concerns."[34]

Community policing is by no means solely focused on public relations at the expense of crime fighting. One can easily recognize how the community era of policing combines the positive elements of the political era with the strengths of the reform era. Getting back in touch with citizens and doing so in an effective manner, for instance, through problem-oriented policing, highlights one of the strengths of community policing. **Problem-oriented policing**, a component of community policing, involves a four-step approach to addressing specific crimes in the community. These steps include scanning communities to identify problems, analyzing the nature and extent of the problems, responding to the problems, and assessing whether or not the problems are properly addressed. It can be stated with confidence that police getting back in touch with the public while maintaining a concern for crime control was needed in light of events occurring during the latter part of the reform era.

Regardless of its strength and good intentions, community policing has not solved society's problems and not all departments have adopted a community-oriented approach. Because some departments have adopted the philosophy on a piecemeal basis, and it is difficult to measure a philosophical approach to policing, it remains unclear whether or not community policing meets all of its goals. We do know that the approach improves police-community relations, which certainly provides optimism for police as they continuously engage in an increasingly multicultural society. The Bureau of Justice Statistics reported that in 2013, roughly 68 percent of local police departments had a mission statement that included a community policing component.[35] The percentage has increased from 2003, when only 47 percent of departments mentioned community policing in their mission statements.[36]

Despite the progress made with regard to police-community relations following the reform era, many of the issues that contributed to the rioting in the 1960s remain.[37] The 1992 riots in Los Angeles following the acquittal by a mostly White jury of the Los Angeles Police Department (LAPD) officers seen beating Black motorist Rodney King sent a message that racial tensions had not disappeared. The riot, which led to forty-three deaths, was perpetuated by economic tensions of residents in South Los Angeles and historical strains in police-community relations, especially with regard to claims of officers engaging in racial profiling and excessive force against minorities. The **Christopher Commission**, assembled in the wake of the Rodney King incident in response to claims of LAPD officer misbehavior, stated in its report that "there is a significant number of officers in the LAPD who repetitively use excessive force against the public and persistently ignore the written guidelines of the Department regarding force."[38] They added that "the problem of excessive force is aggravated by racism and bias," and noted that "failure to control (problem) officers is a management issue that is at the heart of the problem."[39]

Later, rioting in Cincinnati began in April 2001 following the fatal shooting of nineteen-year-old Timothy Thomas by a White Cincinnati police officer. Similar to other riots, the riot stemmed from tension among the minority community and police. Fifteen Black males under the age of forty were killed by Cincinnati police officers between 1995 and 2001, compared to no other males from other races during the same period. Claims of officers engaging in racial profiling with regard to traffic stops also contributed to the violence. The police argued that they were doing their job and reacted in an appropriate manner, yet protestors claimed the police were biased and unjust. The rioting, which lasted three days, resulted in hundreds of thousands of dollars in property damage and over eight hundred arrests.

These and related incidents have occurred throughout the history of the police. More recently, in July 2014, Eric Garner was killed on Staten Island (NY) due to a chokehold used by an officer. The death was ruled a homicide. A month later, the fatal shooting of Michael Brown by a Ferguson (MO) police officer set off a series of protests around the country, with the primary focus on police misusing their powers against minorities. During the same month of Mr. Brown's death, Freddie Gray died while in police custody in Baltimore (MD), which further ignited the social unrest. Similar incidents were brought to the public's attention during this tumultuous period, including a shooting death caught on video in South Carolina, and the police shooting of twelve-year-old Tamir Rice, who was playing with a toy pistol when police shot him.

These incidents were followed by several other shootings of Black males by White officers, including those in Minnesota, Florida, and Louisiana. The tension and frustration generated by the shootings led to several acts of retaliation against the police, including a 2016 incident in Dallas (TX) in which five police officers were killed by a gunman. The shootings occurred at the conclusion of a peaceful Black Lives Matter march in the city, as citizens bound together to protest the shootings. The officers were accompanying the

Police practices can be very controversial. Several high-profile shootings generated a series of protests and acts of retaliation against police officers following the events, which drew national attention.

protestors. Ten days later, a gunman killed three law enforcement officers in Louisiana in what was believed to be an act of retaliation against the police for the shootings.

The short history of policing in the United States is rife with conflict between police and society. Much of the conflict involves members of underrepresented groups who feel the police overstep the boundaries of procedural law, which dictates how the police are to use their powers. To be sure, negative police-citizen interactions are often brought to the public's attention. It is rare that society hears how an officer successfully overcame cultural barriers and quelled a situation. Perhaps public opinion of police-minority contacts would improve if we heard more about the successes. Arguably, many of the previously-discussed problems with regard to police-community relations were intensified and/or perpetuated by the historical lack of minority representation in policing. In response, efforts have been made to better diversify police departments.

POLICE PERSONNEL ISSUES

Police departments are regularly hiring new officers. The expansion of local-level policing duties to address terrorism and homeland security has also led to the increased need for officers. The challenges of recruiting and selecting officers who maintain awareness of cultural diversity pose several difficulties for local law enforcement agencies.

Historically, White males have been overrepresented on police forces across the United States, meaning that non-Whites and females have been largely underrepresented. Part of the problematic relationship departments and officers has with the public stem from the limited representation of underrepresented groups. Further, the relationship is hampered by the influences of the **police subculture**, which promotes a distinct working personality that encourages solidarity, authoritarianism, and sometimes the exclusion of females and minority officers. The causes of the historical underrepresentation of minority people in policing include:

- Minority individuals were not aggressively sought by police departments until the 1980s;
- Police work has not been attractive to many minorities;
- Minority individuals have reason to doubt they will be accepted in policing;
- For social rather than racial reasons, numerous young African Americans have a criminal record, limiting their options for a career in policing; and
- Many educationally better-qualified Blacks have sought and taken more attractive employment opportunities.[40]

Much has been done to increase the diversity of police departments. Addressing issues pertaining to the demographic makeup of officers is necessary for effective policing in a multicultural society. Among other contributions, increased diversity in policing promotes tolerance of different groups and helps defuse historical concerns regarding the under-representation of particular cultures in policing. Legislation and affirmative action programs influenced police departments to increase diversity and proactively seek and hire candidates from underrepresented groups.

LEGISLATING DIVERSITY IN POLICING

Title VII of the **Civil Rights Act of 1964** prevents governments, unions, employment agencies, and private employers with fifteen or more employees from discrimination based on color, race, sex, religion, or national origin. The 1972 **Equal Employment Opportunity Act** extended the 1964 Act to state and local governments and placed further restrictions on hiring practices. Table 11-2 depicts other influential acts that promoted equal employment opportunities for women and minorities. A series of **affirmative action** programs designed to promote the hiring of minority applicants accompanied these and related pieces of legislation.

Historically, police departments have needed greater female and minority representation. Recall that the National Advisory Commission on Civil Disorders reported that poor police-minority relations were prominent among the causes underlying the rioting. As noted below, there's been notable success in this area as the number of females and racial minorities working in police departments steadily increased following passage of the Equal Employment Opportunity Act of 1972.[41]

Government agencies that receive public funds and all private employers must have affirmative action plans. Affirmative action plans require employers to: (1) conduct a census of current employees, (2) identify underutilization or concentration of minorities and women, and (3) develop a recruiting plan to correct any underutilization.[42] Affirmative action plans have undoubtedly shaped the look of today's police departments.

Failure to comply with affirmative action policies could result in an agency facing civil suits from the parties excluded and a loss of funding from major grant bodies. Affirmative action policies are controversial in that they generate charges of **reverse discrimination**, or claims that minorities are being hired at the expense of those in the majority. Further, some individuals from underrepresented groups are being hired as "**tokens**" or officers who received their position solely because of affirmative action policies.[43] In policing, tokens were often treated differently by those in the majority race and gender, which often led to discrimination in assignments and evaluations, exclusion from the police culture, and harassment.[44]

Table 11.2 Promoting Equal Employment Opportunities

Equal Pay Act, 1963—Prohibited unequal pay for men and women who performed the same work.

Age Discrimination in Employment Act of 1967—Prohibited employment discrimination against those over age forty.

Executive Order, 1969—Prevented the federal government from using gender as a qualification for hiring.

Crime Control Act, 1973—Ensured that police departments didn't discriminate against women in hiring practices by threatening to withhold funding should departments do so.

Americans with Disabilities Act, 1990—Prevented agencies from discriminating against any person otherwise qualified for a job because of a disability.

Family and Medical Leave Act of 1993—Required employers with fifty or more employees to grant eligible employees with up to twelve weeks of unpaid, job-secured leave for medical and family reasons.

INTEGRATING POLICING

Many police agencies seek to establish a department that reflects, from a race and ethnicity standpoint, the community in which they operate. Doing so helps gain the public's trust and confidence in the police, and better enables individuals from minority groups to provide insight from different backgrounds and cultures into policing. Bilingual officers provide important contributions to policing in situations in which language barriers pose problems. Departments have become increasingly diverse, however there have been, and remain to some extent, particular obstacles associated with hiring members of minority groups. Prominent among the obstacles are: (1) police departments failing to make their job searches extensive enough to attract the most qualified individuals to the job, (2) some African Americans failing to possess the minimum qualifications for the position, and (3) many African Americans possessing a negative impression of police officers and police work.[45] One could claim outright discrimination against underrepresented groups in hiring practices contributed to some part of the failure. These difficulties are not restricted to African Americans, as individuals from many minority groups historically experienced difficulty obtaining and retaining positions in policing.

Both females and minorities have become increasingly represented in policing. For instance, roughly 27 percent of local police officers were members of a racial or ethnic minority in 2013, compared to 15 percent in 1987. The biggest increase has been with regard to the hiring of Latino or Hispanic officers. From 2007 to 2013 the number of Hispanic or Latino local police officers increased by 16 percent. As of 2013, this group constituted an estimated 11.6 percent of local police officers, which is an increase from 1987, when only 4.5 percent of officers were in this category. Black or African American officers comprise roughly 12 percent of local officers, which is an increase from 1987 when only 9 percent of officers were Black or African American.

Females remain largely underrepresented in policing, although their representation has increased. In 2013, females comprised roughly 12 percent of local police officers compared to 1987, when only 8 percent were female.[46] "Though women have made progress in law enforcement and many agencies have taken action to eliminate and reduce occupational barriers, much work remains.[47] Figure 11-1 highlights recent changes in the makeup of police departments.

Compared to the U.S. population in general, African Americans are not notably underrepresented in policing anymore. Particularly, in 2015 African Americans comprised 13.2 percent of the U.S. population, and 12 percent of all local police officers. Hispanics and Latinos are somewhat underrepresented, as they comprised 17.4 percent of the U.S. population, yet only 11.6 percent of local police officers. Females remain largely underrepresented relative to their presence in society, due in large part to issues such as workplace harassment, family issues, recruitment and selection biases, females generally not being interested in a career in policing, and the general non-acceptance of females in policing.

Comparing the demographics of the United States to the demographics of policing provides some insight regarding the inclusiveness of policing, however it also masks some problems. Of particular concern are cities in which African Americans and members of other minority groups remain underrepresented in policing. For instance, the Ferguson

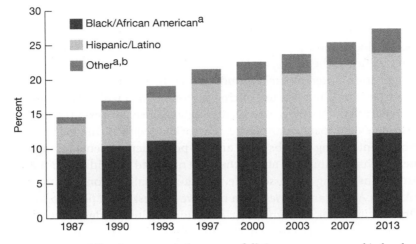

FIGURE 11.1   Minority representation among full-time sworn personnel in local police departments, 1987–2013
Note: Figure includes all years for which data were collected.
[a]Excludes persons of Hispanic or Latino origin.
[b]Includes Asian, Native Hawaiian, or other Pacific Islanders; American Indian or Alaska Natives; and Persons identifying two or more eaces.
Source: Reaves, Brian A. (2015). *Local Police Departments, 2013: Personnel, Policies, and Practices.* Bureau of Justice Statistics, U.S. Department of Justice. NCJ 248677.

Police Department, which was at the center of controversy in 2015 following the shooting death of Michael Brown, had fifty-three officers on its force, four of whom were Black. Ferguson's population was 66 percent Black.[48]

There is limited information regarding Hispanic police officers and officers from other cultural backgrounds simply because it is only recently that policing has become more diversified. We do know that the Hispanic population in the United States is increasing and their presence in police departments is beginning to keep pace. Hispanics in the United States come from various areas and bring with them diverse cultural backgrounds. Of particular importance to police is the ability of Hispanic officers to speak Spanish and to better understand different cultures.

Hispanics have faced many of the same limitations as other underrepresented groups in policing, including difficulties in gaining employment with police departments. The historical underrepresentation of Hispanics in policing can be attributed to the language barrier, the physical size requirements of police departments, the belief that many Hispanics may not wish to become police officers, and Hispanics not being sought after by police departments.[49]

Other racial and ethnic groups have much to offer policing, although their presence in police departments has been relatively limited. For instance, Asian Americans and gay and lesbian officers offer specific contributions that assist police work. Asian American officers, akin to Hispanic officers, offer insight into different cultures, and help address language barriers, although they are poorly represented in police departments across the

Policing has become increasingly diverse, as departments have made notable efforts to hire officers from historically underrepresented groups.

United States. This is due, in part, to the lack of Asian Americans applying for police positions, given the influences of parents who may not wish for their children to seek this line of work given the limited professionalism of policing in their homelands.[50]

The number of gay and lesbian officers is difficult to determine as many departments do not ask about sexual orientation, and officers may mask the fact that they are members of these groups out of concern for differential treatment. The historical mistreatment and underrepresentation of LGBT officers may be dissipating, as some departments have made proactive efforts to hire gay and lesbian officers. These efforts are particularly evident in cities where there are large gay and lesbian populations, including Key West (FL), where the police chief openly admitted that he is gay. The strengths and contributions of other underrepresented groups in policing are discussed throughout this book.

STEPS TO DIVERSIFY POLICING

Departments actively recruit in minority communities to increase their diversity. For instance, in 2008, 21 percent of local police agencies used special officer recruitment efforts to attract racial and ethnic minorities, as did 85 percent of state agencies. Similar percentages used special efforts to target females (21 percent, and 83 percent, respectively). Sixteen percent used special recruitment efforts to attract multilingual persons.[51]

Departments may offer incentive pay to bilingual officers with the intent to address existing and potential cultural and communication problems. Qualified individuals are often available, but departments sometimes face difficulty finding, attracting, and hiring them. If faced with difficulties, it is argued that departments should not lower their standards to find suitable minority candidates. Instead, they should suspend hiring practices to do more effective targeted recruiting.[52] Departments may enhance their search practices when faced with obstacles in hiring. Advertising in minority-specific media outlets, utilizing religious and community groups, and employing the services of bilingual recruiters can help departments become more diverse. **Market segmentation**, or marketing practices "focused on a subset of prospects to identify individuals who will provide the greatest return for the efforts"[53] is common in many occupations, including policing.

Retaining and promoting underrepresented groups in policing is critical for diversifying a department. Too often women and minorities in policing, and many other occupations, experience the **glass ceiling**, or an abstract barrier preventing certain groups and/or individuals from moving beyond entry-level positions. The lack of minority promotion in policing is well-documented in the research literature, for instance as one in eight local police officers were female in 2013, however only one in ten females were first line supervisors.[54] It is assumed that there will be more diversity among the higher ranks of law enforcement as it is only somewhat recently that departments have become increasingly diverse, and years of service are required for promotions and assuming command positions.

Recent developments suggest hope for a more positive future regarding the promotion of underrepresented groups in policing. For instance, females serve as police chiefs in several major cities, and have directed several prominent federal law enforcement agencies (e.g., the DEA, Secret Service, and U.S. Marshals Service), and Beverly Harvard became the first African American female to head a large municipal police department in 1994.

One cannot overlook the problems within police departments stemming from historical failures to diversify. Affirmative action policies, the civil rights movement, and the demand for increased diversity in policing following the 1960s riots contributed to greater multiculturalism in our police departments. Evidence of the progress is noted in minority officers approaching representation in policing commensurate with their representation in society. Police departments are to be commended for their actions with regard to more culturally sensitive hiring practices.

As noted in Table 11-3, there are many organizations and associations that promote the interests of women and cultural/racial/ethnic groups in policing. These organizations and

Table 11.3 Examples of Organizations and Associations Promoting Interests of Women and Cultural/Racial/Ethnic Groups in Policing

Gay Officers Action League

Hispanic National Law Enforcement Association

International Association of Women Police

Irish American Police Officers Association

National Asian Peace Officers' Association

National Association of Black Law Enforcement Executives

National Center for Women and Policing

National Coalition of Italian American Law Enforcement Organizations

National Latino Peace Officers Association

National Native American Law Enforcement Association

Polish American Police Association

associations provide officers opportunities to share concerns, issues, and related aspects of the job with officers of similar backgrounds from around the country and sometimes internationally.

POLICE PRACTICES

Recent incidents involving controversial police practices in Ferguson, New York, Baltimore, and other cities once again directed societal attention toward policing. Accounts of poor relations between the police and various minority groups, and reports of controversial police practices are continuously brought to public attention. It could be argued that such practices have long occurred, although we hear about them more frequently due in part to the increased accessibility and use of technology such as cell phones with video cameras that have increasingly documented questionable and unprofessional police practices. The use of cameras provides a new layer of accountability for police officers who may wrongfully enforce the law, and officers who may subscribe to the **blue wall of silence**, which is the unwritten rule among officers to not report other officers' wrongful behavior. Cameras also provide protection for officers and the public, as video footage can provide powerful evidence of both good and bad police practices.

Having special powers to actively enforce social control puts police in a notably difficult position. The profession has progressed with regard to the methods, strategies, and overall practices employed by departments and officers, yet controversy remains. Police field practices pose the greatest sources of tension between minorities and police.[55] Among the most important types of police practices that contribute to the tension are:

- Delays in responding to calls for service
- Verbal abuse, such as the use of racially offensive epithets or other forms of disrespect
- Excessive stopping, questioning, and frisking of African-American citizens
- Discriminatory patterns of arrest and traffic citations
- Excessive use of physical force
- Excessive use of deadly force, and
- Systematic underenforcement of the law and the failure to protect law-abiding citizens.[56]

This list is significant and identifiable in modern policing. To what extent each practice exists is unknown. Research on policing has largely increased following the research revolution of the 1960s when substantial government funding was allocated toward police sciences, yet it remains unclear to what extent police behave differently toward various groups in society.

Among the more recent controversial police practices involved the New York Police Department's stop-and-frisk program which largely targeted high-crime areas and hot spots of crime. Some argue that the policy contributed to reductions in crime, while others argued that it violated individual rights. The policy, which began in the 1990s, involved stopping suspicious people and questioning them about their activities. It also involved searching them for weapons or contraband. An analysis of the practice found that the police increasingly stopped citizens, most of whom were African American or Hispanic. The police found nothing illegal and took no further action in the large majority (89 percent) of the stops.[57]

There is ongoing debate regarding whether police treat groups differently. For instance, consider the following scenario. *A young man steals a clock radio from a department store. The police catch the suspect as he enters the parking lot of the store and arrest him.*

Seems pretty straightforward. The police did their job. Now, let's alter the variables a bit. Suppose the young man is ten years old and admitted stealing the radio so he could buy food for his younger sister. His mother is always away from home and his father is in prison. His sister was painfully hungry. What should the police do in this case? What would you do? Arrest him? Give him a stern lecture? Hold his mother accountable? There are no easy answers to these questions. The young man obviously had good intentions, but went about his business in an inappropriate manner. Should his motive, age, or race influence police practices? Police officers are often required to use their discretion and are criticized when they use it poorly or not in accord with community standards.

Consider the following findings extracted from two Bureau of Justice Statistics reports with regard to traffic and street stops, and police use of nonfatal force:

Traffic and street stops:

- Of the individuals involved in traffic and street stops, Blacks were less likely than Whites to believe the police behaved properly during the stop
- Drivers pulled over by an officer of the same race or ethnicity were more likely than drivers pulled over by an officer of a different race or ethnicity to believe that the reason for the traffic stop was legitimate
- White drivers were both ticketed and searched at a lower rate than Black and Hispanic drivers.[58]

Police use of nonfatal force:

- Blacks were more likely to experience nonfatal force during their most recent contact with police than Whites and Hispanics
- Blacks were far more likely than Hispanics and Whites to experience nonfatal force during street stops
- Traffic stops involving an officer and driver of different races were more likely to involve force than traffic stops involving an officer and driver of the same race, and
- Blacks were twice as likely as Whites to experience force during contacts involving a personal search.[59]

These findings suggest that certain groups, particularly African Americans, are more likely to be treated punitively by the police (as emphasized in Chapter 3 of this book). Of course, we must consider the context of police-citizen encounters, for instance, as it may be the case that the police acted appropriately during a particular encounter, and it was the actions of the individuals they stopped and used force against that warranted the more punitive behavior. Or, it may be the case that the police misuse their powers by treating groups differently. Arguably, it is a combination of both, although it is difficult to discern the extent to which one factor plays a more significant role than the other.

American policing has become increasingly militarized in nature, largely due to federal funding. Special Weapons and Tactics (SWAT) teams have become increasingly common among police departments, and their use has been subject to little scrutiny. A 2014 report by the American Civil Liberties Union (ACLU) noted that SWAT teams, which were created primarily to deal with emergency situations such as hostage, barricade, and shooter situations, have commonly been used to search suspect's homes for drugs. Analyzing over 800 SWAT deployments among twenty law enforcement agencies, the ACLU noted that most (79 percent) of the incidents involved the use of a SWAT team to search someone's home, with more than 60 percent of the cases involving a search for drugs.

The report further noted that the use of paramilitary tactics and weapons largely impacted people of color. For instance, 42 percent of the people affected by a SWAT deployment to execute a search warrant were Black, and 12 percent were Latino. The report noted that SWAT deployments involving drug searches primarily involved people of color, while deployments in hostage or barricade scenarios (which constituted 7 percent of all deployments) primarily involved Whites.[60] These numbers add support to the argument that different styles of policing may exist for different groups. To address the continued militarization of the police, in May 2015 President Obama banned the federal government from providing some military-style equipment to local police departments, and put stricter controls on other weapons and gear provided to law enforcement. These restrictions were designed to prevent law enforcement agencies from misusing or overusing the items, which are often viewed as militaristic in nature, and prevent further damage to the tenuous police-community relations in some areas.

POLICE DISCRETION

Police discretion, which involves officer decision-making, is evident in all aspects of police practices and at times is recognized as a necessary evil. Discretion is necessary in policing as officers are consistently faced with difficult situations involving multiple

Police officers maintain a great deal of discretion throughout the course of each shift. We expect them to always make the correct choices, and they do so appropriately the large majority of the time. There are times, however, when discretion is abused.

variables. It can be harmful when police misuse their discretion, regardless of whether it was intentional or accidental. While police training provides the nuts and bolts for doing the job, no amount of formal training can ever fully prepare officers to properly handle all situations they encounter. Much of what is learned in policing comes from on-the-job experience.

It is hoped that an officer's formal training and street experience encourage him or her to properly exercise discretion. Researchers categorized the factors that influence an officer's use of discretion with the goal of better understanding police practices. These factors include: (1) organizational influences (e.g., guidance from the department), (2) situational characteristics (e.g., time of day, presence of witnesses, race of suspect), (3) officer characteristics (e.g., male or female, minority or nonminority), and (4) neighborhood or community influences (e.g., poor or wealthy community). The research literature contains many accounts of how these factors influence police practices. Ultimately, many variables influence policing.

Organizational Variables

Several organizational factors influence police discretion, including the professionalism or bureaucratic nature of the department, the size of the department, supervision levels, and the rotation of officers.[61] There is evidence that how closely a department adopts a militaristic style influences how officers police. Researchers found that officers in more bureaucratic departments tend to focus more on law and order rather than providing general services.[62] Another study found that an officer's continued presence in a neighborhood promoted community relations and an understanding of community problems.[63]

Situational Factors

Situational factors are closely related to police practices. Factors such as suspect characteristics and behaviors, and the characteristics of the settings in which police and citizens interact provide the most powerful explanations of police violence.[64] Of particular interest with regard to policing in a multicultural society are findings that African Americans are overrepresented in arrests, use of force, and police shootings. Currently there exist two explanations for the disproportionality: (1) African Americans commit a disproportionate amount of crime, and (2) police treat African Americans more punitively than they treat other groups. Both explanations address the disproportionate level of interactions between African Americans and police, and both have been used as excuses, explanations, and justifications for racial profiling. To what extent each contributes to the disproportionality is open for debate.

Officer Characteristics

Officer characteristics, in general, are not strong predictors of officer discretion and behavior. With regard to police violence, a National Institute of Justice report stated with modest confidence that "use of force appears to be unrelated to an officer's personal characteristics, such as age, gender, and ethnicity."[65] However, some research suggests that officer race is related to arrest practices,[66] but others found no relation.[67] Other findings suggest African American officers are overrepresented in police shootings, but the notable level of deployment of African American officers in predominantly minority neighborhoods likely accounts for the differences.[68] A study of police use of force in predominantly minority communities suggested that patrol officer education was related to their use of force, as officers with higher levels of education less frequently used force, and used lower levels of force compared to patrol officers with lower levels of education.[69]

Earlier research suggested that Black officers were less lenient to Black suspects than were White officers.[70] More recent work in this area, however, found no strong evidence that African American or Hispanic officers police differently than White officers. Minority officers may find interacting with minority suspects more difficult in that the officers may be viewed as representing a biased criminal justice system that imposes its will upon minority groups. It was argued that Black officers sometimes suffer from **double marginality**, meaning that they are viewed as traitors by some in the Black community, while White officers may distrust them as colleagues.[71] Nevertheless, Black officers report that their on-duty relationships with White officers are satisfactory and are confident that their White partners would back them up if needed.[72]

Neighborhood and Community Influences

There is a significant need to consider neighborhood-related variables when discussing policing and multiculturalism. For example, the research literature covering police use of deadly force highlights the impact of neighborhood or community variables on police discretion. Further, the literature highlighting inequities in wealth distribution suggests that income inequalities among groups promote instability in the social order. Responses to the instability in social order sometimes involve the use of force or coercion by the dominant class.[73] It is argued that the economic power maintained by some individuals and groups provides the basis for formal social control, for instance, as income inequality appears to be the strongest explanation for police killings.[74]

Population variation also appears to influence police use of deadly force. It is well-established in the criminology literature that population stability typically results in greater intimacy among members of society. Conversely, social disorganization prompts instability. Aside from stability, the presence of particular minority groups appears to influence police practices. Research suggests that cities with more African-Americans have higher police killing rates of African-Americans.[75]

Police practices range from simple police-citizen verbal exchanges to police use of deadly force. Police use of deadly force is obviously the most scrutinized aspect of policing and generates much concern with regard to policing in a multicultural society. Two explanations are offered for police killings: (1) political threat explanations, which suggest that such acts are more likely to occur where racial or economic differences are greater, because of the threat resultant from the divisions between the groups, and (2) reactive explanations, which suggest that police killings are more likely to occur in areas experiencing high violent crime rates, or where officers must respond to urban conditions such as enhanced levels of poverty, thus making their job more difficult.[76] These explanations facilitate understanding the influences of neighborhood and community variables with regard to police practices in a multicultural society.

The rate of African Americans shot or killed by police far exceeds the rate for Whites. However, as noted, there remains debate as to why this is the case. Several researchers subscribe to the belief that police discretion or "differential policing" largely explains the disproportionality. Others hold that racial imbalance is a reflection of the struggles associated with being a member of a disadvantaged class, including social inequality and economic deprivation. Such a situation is evidenced in the extensive research literature which suggests that lower-class suspects receive harsher treatment from the police. Looking to the future of policing, author David Bayley argued in his article "Policing in America: Social Science and Public Policy in America" that the possibility of group violence in the U.S. is real, largely as a result of inequities in race, class, and ethnicity.[77] The civil unrest we've more recently witnessed in response to questionable police practices, such as racial profiling and seemingly wrongful deaths, provides evidence for his claim. (For further discussion of these events, see Chapter 3, "African Americans and the Criminal Justice System.")

Many examples throughout this book highlight the complexities and controversial practices involved with policing a multicultural society. This chapter highlights but a few of the many facets of police practices. As noted in Chapter 14 ("Preparing for Multiculturalism in the Criminal Justice System: Training and Policies"), it is perhaps with more efficient and effective training and policies that police can overcome the many obstacles and challenges they face on a daily basis. Further, police practices can be enhanced through stronger relations with the communities they serve.

POLICE-COMMUNITY RELATIONS

Police-community relations have become increasingly important, as departments seek to gain the trust of the communities they serve. Doing so has become notably difficult in light of the aforementioned events around the United States in which many citizens perceived the police misused their powers, particularly against less powerful groups. Strong police-community relations, which provide the foundation for many community-policing efforts, generally enable the police to more effectively perform their job, assist with crime reporting practices, facilitate crime prevention efforts, facilitate effective communication between groups, and encourage more individuals to consider careers in policing.

Most people in society are supportive of the police. There are, of course, segments of society that are less supportive of the police, and have less confidence in them. Police-community relations have been controversial throughout history, particularly in light of the suggestion that "The police have had a long history of discriminating against members of minority groups because of their own prejudices, ignorance, or official responsibility for enforcing laws that restricted some people's civil rights (such as segregation laws).

Numerous civil disturbances in the United States have been precipitated by police be-havior considered inappropriate or offensive by minority groups."[78] Various factors have hampered police-community relations. For instance, the war on drugs has had notable impacts on many minority communities, as has the increased militarization of the police, and decreased civil liberties in a time of concerns for homeland security and immigration.

There are discernable trends with regard to public approval of and confidence in the police. Generally, Americans are supportive of the police, although there are notable dif-ferences in levels of support for and confidence in the police among groups, and the levels of support fluctuate on a regular basis. Several Gallup polls offer insight into the nature of police-community relations. Results from these polls suggest that Black Americans are not particularly supportive of the police compared to other groups, and do not maintain confidence in them. For instance, a 2015 poll found that 52 percent of Blacks noted that the police treat racial minorities very fairly or fairly, compared to the national average of 73 percent who felt the same way. Hispanics (71 percent) and Whites (78 percent) were far more likely than Blacks to believe the police were fair or very fair. Further, Blacks (38 percent) were more likely than Hispanics (30 percent) and far more likely than Whites (18 percent) to prefer a larger police presence in their area than existed at the time of the poll.[79]

Muslim Americans have received increased attention from the police following the 2001 terrorist attacks against the United States. Members of these groups have increasingly been the targets of hate crimes, and police have more closely monitored these groups out of concerns for homeland security. As such, there have been concerns regarding their civil rights and the suspicion they generate within their communities. They have requested additional law enforcement attention, and departments have responded by providing pro-tection and training officers with regard to Muslim beliefs and traditions in efforts to minimize misunderstandings.[80]

A different Gallup poll assessed confidence in the police during 2014–15, and found that over half (52 percent) of all Americans had a great deal or quite a lot of confidence in the police, however this percentage was the lowest it has been since 1993 when it was also 52 percent. The poll conducted in 1993 was arguably impacted by the ongoing trial of the four police officers who were being tried for beating Rodney King. With regard to differences among groups in the more recent poll, males (51 percent), females (53 percent), and Hispanics (52 percent) all had roughly the same levels of confidence in the police. However, only 30 percent of Black respondents reported having a great deal or quite a lot of confidence in the police.[81] A comprehensive literature review of empirical studies that have examined perceptions and attitudes of police across ethnic and racial groups noted that individuals who identified themselves as Black, non-White, or Hispanic were more likely to maintain negative perceptions of the police than self-identified Whites. Hispan-ics tended to have more negative views of the police than Whites, yet more positive views than Blacks.[82]

Immigration, both legal and illegal, has also provided challenges for police officers. New immigrants bring with them various cultural beliefs that may conflict with the norms of the dominant groups in the United States, and they may have pre-established perceptions of policing based on practices in their homeland. Illegal immigrants warrant specific attention given their status as being in the United States illegally, and local police are often placed in the difficult position of enforcing laws that seem controversial. The lack of clear and consistent federal, state, and local laws regarding how to respond to illegal immigration places police officers, who are at the front line of addressing issues pertaining to illegal immigration, in particularly difficult situations.

Evidence of the rift in the relationship between some minority groups and the police is noted with the 2013 "Black Lives Matter" activist movement in the United States that originated following the 2013 acquittal of George Zimmerman after he shot African American teenager Trayvon Martin. The movement gained greater attention after the 2014 deaths of two unarmed African Americans (Michael Brown in Ferguson, and Eric Garner in New York City) and the failure of grand juries to indict the officers involved in the shootings. The group campaigns against police brutality against African Americans.

In light of several events which highlighted the rifts between local police and some communities they serve, President Barack Obama signed an executive order establishing the *Task Force on 21st Century Policing* in December 2014. The task force was charged with finding best practices and providing recommendations on how police practices can promote effective crime fighting while building public trust. Among other contributions, the task force identified six areas of recommendations for policing. The areas include:

- Building trust and legitimacy (e.g., treating people with respect, and being neutral in decision-making)
- Policy and oversight (e.g., working with community members to create strategies in high-crime areas to reduce crime by improving relationships, and promoting community engagement and cooperation)
- Technology and social media (e.g., striving to identify new technology to assist with policing, and finding best practices to use social media)
- Community policing and crime reduction (e.g., developing and adopting policies and strategies that promote the importance of community engagement with regard to public safety)
- Training and education (e.g., encouraging the federal government to support the development of partnerships with training facilities to promote consistent standards for high quality training), and
- Officer wellness and safety (e.g., being wary of the harmful effects of policing on officers, and proactively addressing potential problems).[83]

These areas are certainly important to the future of policing, and several have direct implications for policing in a diverse society. Particularly, the need to build trust and legitimacy, for effective policy and oversight, for community policing and crime reduction, and for enhanced training and education can all serve to better improve police-community relations, and ultimately enhance policing.

The aforementioned Department of Justice (DOJ) report that found that the Cleveland Division of Police (CDP) regularly violated Fourth Amendment protections resulted in an agreement between the two groups, which focused on "building community trust, creating a culture of community and problem-oriented policing, officer safety and training, officer accountability, and technological upgrades." Among the provisions of the agreement were the creation of the Community Police Commission, which consists of representatives from the community and various police personnel, the integration of bias-free policing principles to all levels of the organization, including training of officers and supervisors, and the development of a recruiting policy and strategic recruitment plan in efforts to attract well-qualified applicants from a broad cross-section of the community.[84] Each of these provisions highlight the importance of multiculturalism in policing.

Police departments must consider future developments with regard to multiculturalism and demographic changes. For instance, the percentage of Hispanics is expected to continue increasing in the United States, and departments must be prepared for the change. Another demographic change involves an increasingly older U.S. population. People are living longer, healthier lives, and the police must be prepared to respond to the special needs of an increasingly aging population. Such needs include dementia, deterioration of driving skills, elder abuse, and self-neglect. Training and preparing officers to best respond to these and related issues will facilitate police-community relations, and result in more effective police practices.

Steps have been taken to address the concerns of older populations. The National Association of Triads, a partnership created by the American Association of Retired Persons (AARP), the International Association of Chiefs of Police (IACP), and the National Sheriffs' Association (NSA), seeks to promote adult safety and reduce the fear of crime among the elderly. Triads involving partnerships between the police and senior citizens exist in many communities, and assist older residents through education, offering support, uniting agencies, and offering opportunities for volunteers to become involved in policing.

SUMMARY

The news media is filled with stories involving police practices. Unfortunately, we often hear of the negative aspects of policing and failure to prevent crime. For instance, we rarely hear of the police officer who arrested the drunk driver and possibly saved several lives, or the officer who successfully defused a sticky situation verbally instead of violently. Instead, we hear of the officer who was arrested or the officer accused of racial profiling. To be sure, these events occur and should not be tolerated. However, those reading this chapter should bear in mind that most police officers abide by the law and are professional in their practice. Most are not racist, biased, or hateful. They perform a difficult and controversial job that grants them special powers and often places them in the spotlight. Unfortunately, the negative actions of a few officers are often reflected on all. As a society, one of our primary goals with regard to social control remains to identify and remove from policing those who fail to appropriately do their job.

YOU MAKE THE CALL

ETHICAL POLICING?

Consider the following scenario. Debate the pros and cons of all options and decide what you would do.

You're an African American rookie police officer patrolling a community heavily populated by Hispanic Americans. There is ongoing tension between the police and Hispanic American residents in the area following claims of police abuse of young Hispanic males. You stop a car that made an illegal U-turn in the street. The car pulls over. You notice three young Hispanic males in the car as you approach the vehicle. The driver rolls down the window and you smell marijuana. The driver seems agitated that you pulled him over and begins making claims of racial profiling. You're somewhat sympathetic to his claims as you've personally seen officers profile minority drivers. The others in the car chime in. You ask the driver to step out of the car and he refuses, claiming he wants a lawyer. You call for backup. As you're making the call, the three individuals step out of the car in what you perceive to be an aggressive manner. They're angry and not listening to your commands. Your backup is three minutes away. You reach for your baton

and command the individuals to get on the ground. They refuse and move toward you. Their aggressive demeanor prompts you to use your baton on them. Your backup arrives as you wrestle with the suspects. You and the other officers successfully place the suspects in custody. The suspects claim you targeted them based on their ethnicity, used excessive force by using a baton, and said derogatory terms during the tussle. You don't recall saying anything of that nature, and believe you were fully justified in your actions.

Questions

1. How should your supervisor respond to the claims that you used derogatory terms?
2. How could you have prevented this incident from escalating into violence?
3. To what extent do you believe the tensions in the community contributed to the unfortunate outcome of this incident?
4. What steps, if any, should the police chief take to ensure that an incident such as this does not occur again? What should you do, if anything?

KEY TERMS

affirmative action
Black codes
blue wall of silence
Bow Street Runners
Christopher Commission
Civil Rights Act of 1866
Civil Rights Act of 1964
community era of policing
community policing
double marginality
Equal Employment Opportunity Act
exclusionary rule
Frankpledge system
glass ceiling
hue and cry
Market segmentation

Metropolitan Police Act
National Advisory Commission on Civil Disorders
overpolicing
patronage
police discretion
police subculture
political era of policing
President's Commission on Law Enforcement
   and Administration of Justice
problem-oriented policing
Prohibition
reform era of policing
reverse discrimination
slave patrols
tokens
underpolicing

DISCUSSION QUESTIONS

1. Discuss significant events in the history of policing that contributed to current problematic relations between underrepresented groups and the police.
2. Identify the three eras of policing and discuss the impact of each on public perceptions of the police.

3. What significant events have helped diversify police forces?
4. Identify and discuss the four categories of variables that influence police discretion. How do these factors affect policing in a multicultural society?
5. What steps do you believe are most important in building and maintaining strong police-community relations?

FOR FURTHER READING

Barlow, David, and Melissa Hickman Barlow. *Police in a Multicultural Society: An American Story.* Prospect Heights, IL: Waveland Press, 2000.

Palmer, Darren, Michael M. Berlin, and Dilip K. Das, eds. *Global Environment of Policing.* Boca Raton, FL: CRC Press, 2012.

Perez, D. W. *Paradoxes of Police Work*, 2nd ed. Clifton Park, NY: Cengage, 2011.

Skolnick, J. *Justice Without Trial: Law Enforcement in a Democratic Society.* New York: John Wiley & Sons, 1966.

Wells, S. K., and B. L Alt. *Police Women: Life with the Badge.* Westport, CT: Prager, 2005.

NOTES

1. S. M. Cox, W. P. McCamey, W.P., and G. L. Scaramella, *Introduction to Policing*, 2nd ed. (Thousand Oaks, CA: Sage, 2014), 324.
2. David Barlow and Melissa Hickman Barlow, *Police in a Multicultural Society: An American Story* (Prospect Heights, IL: Waveland Press, 2000).
3. Ibid., 53.
4. Ibid, xii.
5. Philip Smith, *Policing Victorian London* (London: Greenwood Press, 1985).
6. Craig Uchida, "The Development of the American Police: An Historical Overview," in *Critical Issues in Policing: Contemporary Readings*, 2nd ed., ed. R. Dunham and G. Alpert (Prospect Heights, IL: Waveland Press, 1993), 16–32.
7. Philip Stead, *The Police of Britain* (Macmillan, 1985).
8. W. Marvin Dulaney, *Black Police in America* (Bloomington, IN: Indiana University Press, 1996).
9. Ibid.
10. Linda S. Miller and Karen M. Hess, *Community Policing: Partnerships for Problem Solving*, 4th ed. (Belmont, CA: Wadsworth, 2005).
11. James A. Fagin, *Criminal Justice*, 2nd ed. (Boston, MA: Allyn and Bacon, 2007).
12. Miller and Hess, *Community Policing*, 9.
13. Fagin, *Criminal Justice*.
14. Hubert Williams and Patrick V. Murphy "The Evolving Strategy of Police: A Minority View." U.S. Department of Justice, National Institute of Justice. No. 13 (January 1990).
15. George L. Kelling and Mark H. Moore, "From Political to Reform to Community: The Evolving Strategy of Police," in *Community Policing: Rhetoric or Reality*, ed. Jack R. Greene and Stephen D. Mastrofski (New York: Praeger Publishers, 1991), 3–25.
16. Williams and Murphy, "The Evolving Strategy."
17. Samuel Walker and Charles M. Katz, *The Police in America*, 7th ed. (New York: McGraw-Hill, 2011), 31.
18. Ibid.
19. Williams and Murphy, "The Evolving Strategy.".

20. Miller and Hess, *Community Policing.*
21. Walker and Katz, *The Police in America,* 42.
22. Ibid.
23. Anthony D. Perez, Kimberly M. Berg, and Daniel J. Myers, "Police and Riots, 1967–1969," *Journal of Black Studies* 34, no. 2 (2003): 153–82.
24. Ibid, 177.
25. Michael D. White, *Current Issues and Controversies in Policing* (Boston, MA: Allyn and Bacon, 2007).
26. Miller and Hess, *Community Policing,* 12.
27. Williams and Murphy, "The Evolving Strategy," 11.
28. Miller and Hess, *Community Policing,* 13.
29. National Advisory Commission on Civil Disorders. *Report of the National Advisory Commission on Civil Disorders.* (New York: Bantam Books, 1967).
30. *Mapp v. Ohio,* 367 U.S. 643 (1961).
31. *Gideon v. Wainwright,* 372 U.S. 335 (1963).
32. *Miranda v. Arizona,* 384 U.S. 436 (1966).
33. *Terry v. Ohio,* 392 U.S. 1 (1968).
34. R. G. Burns, *Policing: A Modular Approach* (Upper Saddle River, NJ: Pearson, 2013), 8.
35. Brian A. Reaves, *Local Police Departments, 2013: Personnel, Policies, and Practices,* Bureau of Justice Statistics, U.S. Department of Justice, 2015. NCJ 248677, 8.
36. Matthew J. Hickman and Brian A. Reaves, *Local Police Departments, 2003.* Bureau of Justice Statistics, U.S. Department of Justice, 2006. NCJ 210118, 19.
37. Perez, et al., "Police and Riots," 179.
38. *Report of the Independent Commission on the Los Angeles Police Department,* July 9, 1991, p. iii.
39. Ibid., iv.
40. David L.Carter and Louis A. Radelet , *The Police and the Community,* 6th ed. (Upper Saddle River, NJ: Prentice Hall, 1999), 298–99.
41. Robert H. Langworthy and Lawrence P. Travis III, *Policing in America: A Balance of Forces,* 2nd ed. (Upper Saddle River, NJ: Prentice Hall, 1999), 244.
42. Walker and Katz, *The Police in America.*
43. H. B. Grant and K. J. Terry, *Law Enforcement in the 21st Century,* 4th ed. (Upper Saddle River, NJ: Pearson, 2017).
44. Ibid.
45. Michael D. Lyman, *The Police: An Introduction,* 4th ed. (Upper Saddle River, NJ: Pearson, 2010), 96.
46. Reaves, *Local Police Departments, 2013,* 4.
47. H. H. Yu, "Overcoming Tokenism and Gender Barriers: the Critical Role of Nongovernmental Organizations for Women in Federal Law Enforcement," *The Police Chief* (January 2015): 50.
48. Y. Alcindor and N. Penzenstadler, "Police Redouble Efforts to Recruit Diverse Officers," *USA Today,* January 21, 2015. Accessed online at: http://www.usatoday.com/story/news/2015/01/21/police-redoubling-efforts-to-recruit-diverse-officers/21574081/
49. Ibid., "Police Redouble Efforts."
50. J. S. Dempsey and L. S. Forst, *An Introduction to Policing,* 7th ed. (Clifton Park, NY: Cengage, 2014), 209.
51. B. A. Reaves, *Hiring and Retention of State and Local Law Enforcement Officers, 2008—Statistical Tables.* U.S. Department of Justice, Bureau of Justice Statistics, 2012. NCJ 238251, 13.
52. White, *Current Issues.*

53. Burns, *Policing*, 104.

54. Reaves, *Local Police Departments, 2013*, 1.

55. Kenneth J. Peak and Ronald W. Glensor, *Community Policing & Problem Solving: Strategies and Practices*, 2nd ed. (Upper Saddle River, NJ: Prentice Hall, 1999), 218–20.

56. Ibid.

57. Jennifer Fratello, Andres F Rengifo, and Jennifer Trone, *Coming of Age with Stop and Frisk: Experiences, Perceptions, and Public Safety Implications* (NY: Vera Institute of Justice, 2013).

58. L. Langton and M. Durose, *Police Behavior During Traffic and Street Stops*, U.S. Department of Justice, Bureau of Justice Statistics, 2013. NCJ 242937, 1.

59. S. Hyland, L. Langton, and E. Davis, *Police Use of Nonfatal Force, 2002–2011.* U.S. Department of Justice, Bureau of Justice Statistics, 2015. NCJ 249216, 1.

60. American Civil Liberties Union, *War Comes Home: The Excessive Militarization of American Policing*, June 2014. Accessed online at: https://www.aclu.org/sites/default/files/assets/jus14-warcomeshome-report-web-rel1.pdf

61. Laure Weber Brooks, "Police Discretionary Behavior: A Study of Style." in *Critical Issues in Policing: Contemporary Readings*, ed. R. G. Dunham and G. P. Alpert (Long Grove, IL: Waveland, 2005), 89–105.

62. J. Skolnick, *Justice Without Trial: Law Enforcement in a Democratic Society* (New York: John Wiley & Sons, 1966).

63. S. Mastrofski, "Policing the Beat: The Impact of Organizational Scale on Patrol Officer Behavior in Urban Residential Neighborhoods," *Journal of Criminal Justice* 9 (1981): 343–58, 1981).

64. Ronald Burns and Charles Crawford , "Situational Determinants of Police Violence," in *Policing and Violence*, ed. R. Burns and C. Crawford (Upper Saddle River, NJ: Prentice Hall, 2002), 76.

65. National Institute of Justice , Executive Summary. *Use of Force by Police: Overview of National and Local Data.* (NCJ 176330). (Washington, DC: U.S. Department of Justice, 1999), viii.

66. L. Sherman, "Causes of Police Behavior: The Current State of Quantitative Research," *Journal of Research in Crime and Delinquency* 17 (1980): 69–100.

67. R. E. Worden, "Situational and Attitudinal Explanations of Police Behavior: A Theoretical Reappraisal and Empirical Assessment," *Law and Society Review* 23 (1989): 667–711.

68. R. Geller and K. Karales, *Split Second Decisions: Shootings of and by the Chicago Police*, Chicago Law Enforcement Study Group, 1981.

69. C. Chapman, "Use of Force in Minority Communities Is Related to Police Education, Age, Experience, and Ethnicity," *Police Practice and Research* 13, no. 5 (2012): 421–36.

70. N. Alex, *Black in Blue: A Study of the Negro Policeman* (New York: Appleton-Century-Crofts, 1976).

71. Alex, *Black in Blue.*

72. Cox et al., *Introduction to Policing.*

73. D. Jacobs and R. O'Brien, "The Determinants of Deadly Force: A Structural Analysis of Police Violence," *American Journal of Sociology* 103 (1998): 837–62.

74. D. Jacobs and D. Britt, "Inequality and the Police Use of Deadly Force," *Social Problems* 26 (1979): 403–12.

75. Jacobs and O'Brien, "The Determinants of Deadly Force."

76. Ibid.

77. David Bayley, "Policing in America: Social Science and Public Policy in America," *Society* (Nov./Dec. 1998): 16–19.

78. R. Roberg, K. Novak, G. Cordner, and B. Smith, *Police and Society*, 6th ed. (New York: Oxford University Press, 2015), 98.

79. A. Swift, *Blacks Divided on Whether Police Treat Minorities Fairly*. Gallup, August 6, 2015. Accessed online at: http://www.gallup.com/poll/184511/blacks-divided-whether-police-treat-minorities-fairly.aspx

80. Dempsey and Forst, *Introduction to Policing*, 325–326.

81. J. M. Jones, "In U.S., Confidence in Police Lowest in 22 Years," Gallup, June 19, 2015. Accessed online at: http://www.gallup.com/poll/183704/confidence-police-lowest-years.aspx

82. J. H. Peck, "Minority Perceptions of the Police: A State-of-the-Art Review," *Policing: An International Journal of Police Strategies and Management* 38, no. 1 (2015): 173–203.

83. President's Task Force on 21st Century Policing, *Final Report of the President's Task Force on 21st Century Policing* (Washington, DC: Office of Community Oriented Policing Services, 2015).

84. U.S. Department of Justice, "Justice Department Reaches Agreement with City of Cleveland to Reform Cleveland Division of Police Following Finding of a Pattern or Practice of Excessive Force," May 26, 2015. Accessed online at: http://www.justice.gov/opa/pr/justice-department-reaches-agreement-city-cleveland-reform-cleveland-division-police

CHAPTER 12

COURTS AND MULTICULTURALISM

CHAPTER OBJECTIVES:

After reading this chapter, you should be able to:

- Discuss how pretrial processes maintain potential biases against underrepresented groups
- Identify potential biases working against minorities with regard to the manner in which prospective jurors are identified and the manner in which jurors are ultimately selected
- Discuss the steps of a trial, including areas where the prosecution may have an unfair advantage
- Identify how sentencing practices and sentencing structures have contributed to the overrepresentation of minorities in prison
- Explain why we need diversity among the courtroom personnel and identify whether race influences judicial practices

The U.S. criminal court system consists of state and federal courts. State courts process those charged with state violations. Federal courts process those accused of committing federal offenses. The U.S. Supreme Court, the highest court in the land, hears cases from both state and federal courts. Most criminal case processing occurs in state courts. Multiculturalism plays a significant role in our court systems given the large number of defendants processed each year.

In their book *American Cultural Pluralism and Law*, Jill Norgren and Serena Nanda note that as the United States increasingly diversifies, "it faces a fundamental tension: on one hand there is the need to create national institutions, including law, which unify culturally different groups, and on the other, the need to protect human rights by allowing some degree of religious, personal, cultural, and local political autonomy."[1] They add that "law...is one of the most important mechanisms for addressing this inevitable tension between the needs of the nation-state for some growing consensus around a dominant set of cultural values and institutions, and the needs of groups to enact and increase their

The U.S. Supreme Court is the highest court in the United States. It is an appellate court that it hears cases that originate in both state and federal courtrooms.

autonomy."[2] U.S. courts interpret, create, and apply criminal and civil law, and are particularly vulnerable to the previously described tensions.

Increased diversity in the courtroom perpetuates interpersonal misunderstandings. For example, the verbal and body language of non-English speaking defendants and witnesses are sometimes misinterpreted by English speaking courtroom personnel. In response, courts have become increasingly sensitive to the needs of those unable to speak English.[3] Some suggest holding trials in Spanish should a defendant choose to do so.[4]

In a recent newspaper article titled "Courts Asked to Consider Culture," author Richard Willing commented on the role of culture in U.S. courts, suggesting that "Immigrants with roots in Africa, Asia, and other non-Western cultures are winding up in America's courts after being charged with crimes for acts that would not be offenses in their home countries."[5] Incidents involving animal sacrifices, ritual mutilations, and other customs of foreign cultures are increasingly showing up in our courts, leading to the suggestion that the courts permit defendants from non-Western backgrounds to offer a 'cultural defense' in response to being charged with a crime.[6] Cultural defenses have been reluctantly allowed in court, although, as Willing notes, "Exceptions have come when groups have been able to argue that their religious as well as cultural rights have been violated."[7]

Research addressing felony defendants in large urban counties found an overrepresentation of Blacks and an underrepresentation of Whites entering criminal court. Black defendants accounted for 45 percent of those entering courts on felony charges, while Whites constituted 30 percent of those charged with felony offenses and 24 percent were Hispanic. Of particular interest is the finding that over half (55 percent) of those under age eighteen and entering felony court were Black males. Black males were also largely overrepresented (37 percent) among the felony defendants who were age forty or older when entering criminal court. Males were far more likely than females to end up in felony court (83 percent compared to 17 percent).[8]

The following discussion of multiculturalism in the courts is organized according to the stages of criminal case processing in criminal courts. The discussion begins with a look at multiculturalism in the events occurring at the initial appearance, followed by discussion of preliminary/grand jury hearings, arraignments, trials, sentencing, and appeals. This chapter concludes with discussion of the diversity of those working in our courts. Due to their overrepresentation in the courts, African Americans are the focus of much discussion regarding multiculturalism and the courts.

INITIAL APPEARANCE

At the **initial appearance**, also referred to as the first appearance, defendants are:

- brought before the court
- informed of the formal charges against them
- advised of their rights, including the right to retain a lawyer or have one appointed to them
- possibly granted pretrial release, and
- made aware of the upcoming steps in their case.

In general, felony criminal case processing is more complicated than misdemeanor processing. The difference stems from the more severe or harmful circumstances typically involved in felonies than in misdemeanors. The more severe penalties associated with felonies also contribute to the differences in the resources devoted to each type of case. Misdemeanor processing often begins and ends with the initial appearance. Felony processing is more drawn out and more likely to involve the steps occurring after the initial appearance.

NOTICE OF CHARGES

Decisions to charge a defendant and the nature of the charges are sometimes controversial. Prosecutors typically examine the evidence provided to them following an arrest and preliminary investigation and use their discretion to determine whether or not to file charges. If they choose to file charges, they must then determine what charge(s) to file. Prosecutors depend heavily on police reports and input from those involved with the incident to make their assessment. The power to make several key decisions, especially as they relate to filing charges, offers avenues for prosecutorial abuse of discretion.

Prosecutors primarily rely on the strength of the evidence in their decisions to file charges against a defendant. However, there is evidence that variables such as race and ethnicity may play a factor in this stage of the criminal justice system. Several studies found that African American and Hispanic suspects were more likely than White suspects to face criminal charges. An evaluation of thirty-four research studies that considered the decision to charge found inconsistent results, as some suggested that minorities were the recipients of more punitive practices, while other studies suggested they weren't.[9] In their assessment of race and the decision to charge, authors Walker and colleagues noted: "that there is compelling evidence of racial *disparity* (italics in original) in charging and plea bargaining," and further added that the "disparity frequently reflects racial discrimination."[10]

COUNSEL AND THE INITIAL APPEARANCE

Defendants entering court are commonly represented by counsel. Very few defendants choose to represent themselves. Counsel comes in two forms: private counsel secured by the defendant and state-provided counsel. In *Gideon v. Wainwright* the U.S. Supreme Court ruled that all who enter our courts have the right to counsel at all critical stages of the criminal justice process.[11] Prior to *Gideon*, only defendants in federal courts had the right to counsel, as decided in *Johnson v. Zerbst*.[12]

State-issued counsel is provided in the forms of assigned counsel and public defenders. Both groups are tasked with providing legal representation to **indigent defendants**, those who cannot afford representation. The **assigned counsel** involves the court appointing indigent cases to practicing attorneys. Attorneys are assigned indigent cases in return for a statutorily-determined fee. In many cases, these attorneys have a caseload in their private practice that generates more income than the indigent cases. The statutorily-prescribed fee for indigent representation is far below what attorneys earn in their private practice. Such a situation may result in attorneys devoting greater attention to their private practice than to the assigned cases, given the need for private entities to generate profit for their financial survival.[13]

Although most U.S. counties use the assigned counsel system, most defendants are represented by **public defenders** who work in offices that exist solely to provide indigent representation. Public defenders face many challenges, including responsibility for large caseloads and limited resources. Their offices are primarily located in large urban cities where large volumes of criminal cases require their services.

Racial and ethnic minorities are more likely than Whites to receive state-issued counsel upon entering court.[14] The economic differences between minorities and nonminorities significantly contribute to this finding. It is important to take the limitations of indigent representation very seriously as public defenders and appointed counsel face several challenges in providing quality defense. Those representing the poor are threatened by a lack of financial support, large caseloads, and questionable training and supervision.[15] Indigent defendants are often represented by overworked, underpaid, and unqualified attorneys.[16] Prosecutors typically have more resources than indigent defense attorneys, thus putting defendants with fewer means at a clear disadvantage.

The Supreme Court requires that indigent defendants receive "effective assistance," but the standard for "effectiveness" is subjective. The subjectivity of the term is evident in cases where lawyers representing the indigent showed up in court drunk or fell asleep during the proceeding yet were deemed effective.[17] Those purchasing the services of private attorneys can shop around and determine for themselves who they wish to represent them, but indigent defendants are provided attorneys by the state. Such a situation has resulted in inexperienced lawyers with limited knowledge of the complex law pertaining to capital punishment trials representing some indigent defendants facing the death penalty.[18] Nevertheless, the research literature has not consistently demonstrated that those represented by public defenders receive harsher sentences than those who use private counsel.[19]

PRETRIAL RELEASE

Arrestees are sometimes detained following arrest and prior to trial. The severity of the offense for which they've been arrested largely determines whether or not they are detained. Those arrested for the more serious offenses and posing the greatest threats to society are most likely to be detained. While detained, most arrestees will be granted **pretrial release** at their initial appearance. Pretrial release can be secured monetarily, as in the case of bail, or nonfinancially, such as release on recognizance, which involves the accused being relaeased with no financial obligations, however they promise, in writing, to appear at all later court hearings. Judges typically determine whether or not the accused will be released prior to trial and the nature of the release. Among the considerations related to the nature of one's pretrial release are ensuring that the defendant will stay out of trouble while released and he or she will return to court for further processing.

Judicial discretion in setting or denying bail and the circumstances surrounding release generates controversy. Judges typically consider a variety of factors in the release decision, such as the seriousness of the offense, the defendant's criminal record, their likelihood of returning to court, and the anticipated behavior should they be released. Part of the controversy involves the uncertainty of how variables such as race, gender, and ethnicity influence judicial discretion. Studies observing the effect of race on bail-setting decisions provide contradictory results. Much has improved with regard to the unfair treatment of racial minorities who are arrested and detained; however, evidence suggests that some judges still consider race and other extralegal variables with regard to decisions concerning bail;[20] for instance as one study found that Blacks and Latinos, at both arrest and prior to trial, were more likely than Whites to be denied bail and detained in urban courts and county jails across the United States.[21]

Research suggests that Black and Hispanic detainees are more likely than Whites to be detained in jail while awaiting trial.[22] Other research found that Hispanics received significantly higher bail amounts than their African American and White counterparts.[23] Financial bail poses more of a challenge to the poor than it does to those with means. The inability to secure release provides many challenges for defendants, including the increased likelihood of being found guilty, and a longer sentence.[24]

PRELIMINARY HEARING/GRAND JURY

A preliminary hearing or grand jury hearing is required in felony cases due to the more severe circumstances associated with felonies than with misdemeanors. Preliminary hearings differ from grand jury hearings in several ways, although their primary goal remains the same: to determine if the accused should remain in the system. **Preliminary hearings** involve a prosecutor demonstrating to a judge why charges have been filed and justification for continued processing. The prosecutor bears the burden of demonstrating guilt.

Grand jury hearings are also used to determine if continued case processing may be necessary. Grand jurors are laypersons selected to serve on the jury. In grand jury hearings jurors basically replace the judge used in a preliminary hearing. The grand jury's task is to determine if the prosecutor's case is strong enough to warrant an **indictment**.

An indictment is the charging document used by grand juries to suggest enough evidence exists to proceed with case processing. Grand juries are also permitted to engage in evidence collection of their own, should they choose to do so. Some states rely on preliminary hearings; others use grand juries or both types of hearings.

It is argued that preliminary hearings and grand jury hearings are somewhat insignificant in criminal case processing due to the unfair advantage maintained by prosecutors. While there are no implications of racism or cultural bias with regard to grand jury and preliminary hearings, defendants are arguably at a disadvantage in both types of hearings.

Let's consider grand jury hearings as a potential setting for bias or discrimination. Prosecutors maintain great discretion in jurisdictions that use grand jury hearings. They are the only legal officers permitted in the room when grand jury members consider evidence.[25] Prosecutors assess what types of evidence will be presented to grand juries, which undoubtedly influences grand jury decisions to indict. The absence of defendants during grand jury hearings typically works to their disadvantage, as does the low level of proof required (probable cause) for an indictment. Other factors influencing the outcomes of grand jury hearings include the need for only one-half to two-thirds of grand juror votes to find probable cause in most states, the permissible use of hearsay evidence in grand jury deliberations, and the effective screening practices on behalf of prosecutors who drop cases they perceive as unworthy of grand jury consideration. In light of these variables, it is understandable why a grand jury indictment is referred to as little more than a rubber stamp.[26] While the advantages provided to the prosecution by no means exemplify overt racism, the disproportionate number of minority defendants, particularly African Americans, entering our courts is most directly affected.

ARRAIGNMENT

An **arraignment** is the step in criminal case processing when the accused is formally notified of the charges against them, and he or she enters a plea. At an arraignment, defendants enter a plea, pretrial motions are offered, and **discovery** may occur. Discovery is the sharing of information among the attorneys with the goal of helping attorneys adequately prepare their cases. None of these steps has proven challenging with regard to multiculturalism. Nevertheless one must remember that the use of discretion inherent during the arraignment and throughout all stages of adjudication could pose problems for underrepresented groups entering our courts.

It is not until the arraignment that felony defendants enter a plea. As noted earlier, misdemeanor processing is more informal than felony processing. Thus, defendants charged with a misdemeanor often have their cases disposed of more quickly. Many individuals charged with a misdemeanor enter a plea upon first entering the court. Felony cases are typically more formal; a defendant's case may come up in court several times prior to the individual entering a plea.

Defendants typically enter one of three pleas during the arraignment: guilty, not guilty, or *contendere*. Most who enter our courts enter a guilty plea after having engaged in **plea bargaining**, or an exchange between the prosecution and defense which would encourage a guilty plea in exchange for a benefit for the defendant. Defendants sometimes enter a plea of ***nolo contendere***, or "no contest," which has the legal effect of a guilty plea. Defendants may choose to enter a plea of *nolo contendere* instead of admitting guilt in attempt to cooperate with the court (through essentially pleading guilty), but they do not wish to directly admit guilt. Pleading "no contest" is sometimes done in cases in which a forthcoming civil trial may occur between the defendant and the victim and/or their family. The civil trial would be brief and perhaps unnecessary if a defendant earlier admitted guilt in criminal court, as evidence used in the criminal court case (e.g., the admission of guilt) could be introduced in the civil case. Defendants sometimes enter a *nolo contendere* plea out of principle; they do not believe they are guilty, yet they are attracted to the benefits of the plea bargaining negotiations. Defendants may stand mute or refuse to recognize the court, which is typically done when one is protesting the actions of the criminal justice system. The court recognizes standing mute as a "not guilty" plea.

Plea bargaining is continuously replacing the criminal trial. Pleading guilty facilitates case processing and rewards defendants. By eliminating the need for a trial through pleading guilty, defendants generally receive reduced sentences or other beneficial treatment by the court (e.g., a less-stigmatized type of crime). Roughly 90 to 95 percent of felony defendants plead guilty, many of whom are minorities. Similar to other steps of the adjudication process, there is evidence that African Americans are treated differently, for instance as they appear to be less likely than Whites to receive a reduced charge, and shorter or reduced sentences.[27]

The level of justice inherent in plea bargaining is a topic of scholarly debate. To be sure, our court system would collapse if all defendants who entered a courtroom requested a jury trial or even a **bench trial** in which the judge serves as both judge and jury. Our court system simply does not have the resources to provide everyone a trial. Plea bargaining encourages certain individuals to admit guilt when they are innocent. Further, there's evidence of discriminatory practices with regard to the deals offered and the opportunities to engage in plea bargaining.[28] Defendants have no right to plea bargaining; it occurs only when both attorneys agree to an arrangement and a judge approves the deal.

Research regarding the impact of race on plea bargaining suggests that bias does exist. For instance, using data on plea bargaining in relation to misdemeanor marijuana cases, researchers found that compared to Whites, Black defendants were less likely to be offered reduced charge offers, and Latino and Black defendants were more likely to receive custodial sentence offers. These disparities, however, were primarily explained through evidence, legal factors, court actor characteristics, and arrest circumstances. After removing these controls, Black defendants were still more likely than Whites to receive custodial sentence offers. Given the large role of plea bargaining, biases in this aspect of the court process have significant impacts on minority representation in prison and other correctional sanctions.[29]

Pleading not guilty means one is willing to go to trial. In preparation for the trial, attorneys may begin, at the arraignment, offering **pretrial motions**. These motions help ensure that each side's interests are recognized by the court. Among the more common motions are:

- Motion to dismiss—typically filed by the defense in hopes that the case will be dismissed, for example, based on due process violations or insufficient evidence.
- Motion to determine the competency of the accused to stand trial—designed to protect mentally ill persons from improperly being held responsible for their acts.
- Motion to suppress evidence obtained through an unlawful search or seizure—designed to protect a defendant's Fourth Amendment rights.
- Motion to suppress confession, admissions, or other statements made to the police—protects against violation of the suspect's legal rights.
- Motion to require the prosecution to disclose the identity of a confidential informant—enables the defense to better understand the sources of information and evidence to be used against them.
- Motion for a change of venue—offered in attempt to relocate the setting for a trial with the goal of ensuring that a fair verdict can be rendered. This motion is sometimes offered in response to pretrial publicity.
- Motion for a continuance—provides attorneys more time to prepare their case.

These motions are presented to a judge and can be a determining factor in the outcome of a case. For example, should a judge deny a defendant's motion to suppress illegally obtained evidence, a defense attorney may wish to initiate plea negotiations since their likelihood of winning a case may be severely diminished. The discretion inherent in judicial decisions to grant or deny particular motions provides further evidence of the need for cultural awareness in the criminal justice system.

TRIALS

The events involved with criminal trials largely reflect our society's quest for justice. The formality associated with the criminal trial, including much of the symbolism found in the courtroom (e.g., the judge's robe and gavel), suggests that justice will be served. History suggests, however, that our courts suffer from several limitations, not the least of which is the desire of attorneys to "win" cases as opposed to finding justice. Further, there's evidence of the differential treatment of certain groups that enter our courts. While the modern day criminal trial is certainly more civil than earlier forms of seeking justice, there is great room for improvement. For example, the substantial levels of prosecutorial and judicial discretion inherent in trials have, on occasion, generated ethical concerns and questions of misbehavior.

Judges and prosecutors play significant roles in the adjudicatory process. Judicial discretion is evident in many areas, especially in bench trials where judges serve as both judge and jury. Judges are also influential with regard to certain sentencing decisions, their directions to jurors, the decision to allow or disallow evidence to be introduced or objections to be acknowledged, and many other areas. Prosecutorial discretion at trial includes decisions such as whether or not to introduce particular pieces of evidence and whether continued case processing is warranted. Among the key decisions made by the defense at trial are whether or not to put the suspect on the stand and what type of defense, if any, they should offer. Defense attorneys represent the accused and typically don't have to prove much of anything; their client enters court innocent until proven guilty.

Trials involve a series of events that have generated controversy with regard to multi-culturalism. Trials begin with the selection of jurors, followed by opening statements, the presentation of evidence, closing arguments, the judge's charge to the jury, jury deliberations, the jury offering a verdict, and sentencing. Although some level of controversy exists at each of these steps, several steps are more controversial than others.

Steps in a Criminal Trial

Jury Selection → Opening Statements → Presentation of Evidence → Judge's Charges → Jury Deliberations → Verdict

---

JURY SELECTION

Jury selection has an influence on the outcome of many criminal trials. The selection of jurors and unethical jury behavior have unfortunately hampered the effectiveness of jury trials. For instance, we sometimes hear statements such as "he was convicted by an all-White jury," suggesting that race may have impacted the jury's decision. Further, as noted in Chapter 8, victim characteristics appear to influence jury decision-making. It is argued that Whites are more punitive in cases involving defendants of color,[30] especially when Whites constitute the majority of the jury.[31]

There are many arguments for having diverse juries. To begin, jury members from di-verse backgrounds provide broader views and experiences, and are more reflective of the communities in which trials are conducted. Diverse juries also have the potential to sen-sitize other jury members of the potential for prejudice,[32] and discourage attorneys from using stereotypical arguments and other biased arguments.[33] Further, excluding racial and ethnic minorities from serving on juries denies members of these groups the opportunity to participate in the judicial process and reduces their confidence in the legal system,[34] and diverse juries tend to deliberate longer and have higher-quality discussions of cases than do all-White juries.[35] This occurs despite the fact that members of some groups (e.g., Asian Americans)[36] exhibit lower levels of participation during jury deliberations than members from other groups.

Controversy with regard to jury selection and multiculturalism exists primarily in the manner in which potential jurors are identified and the process of questioning jurors known as *voir dire*. A series of changes in jury selection practices attempted to overcome the historical underrepresentation of minorities and other groups; however, racial dis-crimination in the selection of jurors remains problematic.[37]

CONSTRUCTING THE VENIRE

States use various means to assemble a jury pool, or **venire**, from which prospective jurors will be selected and questioned. Voter registration lists are most commonly used, and are

Jury selection is an integral part of the adjudication process. In light of claims that juries lack diversity, efforts have been made to ensure greater representation of members from all groups on juries.

often supplemented with driver's license lists, automobile registration lists, and property tax rolls. The **Federal Jury Selection and Services Act of 1968** prohibited the exclusion of individuals based on religion, race, gender, national origin, or economic status. Nevertheless, the ability of currently-used lists to adequately provide a cross-section of society has been questioned by scholars. Minorities and low-income individuals are less likely than their counterparts to be identified for jury selection, as they are less likely to own property and cars, be registered voters, or have a driver's license. Further, minorities and the poor are more likely than their counterparts to switch residences[38]; thus, they are less likely to receive a **summons**, a document informing individuals of their call to jury duty.

An example of the limitations of current jury selection practices is found in research in a southeastern district in the United States, which noted that the selection process systematically Whitened juries, which produced frequently all-White juries or ones that contained only one minority member. It was noted that the limitations associated with minority groups receiving summons were the primary reason; a problem that was compounded by racial disparities in the use of peremptory strikes and removals for cause. The researcher suggested the use of a broader range of sources to identify potential jurors, encouraging or requiring employers to pay full days' wages to those who are called to jury duty, and addressing language barriers to assist those for whom English is a second language.[39] Consideration and the implementation of these practices widens the pool of potential jurors and increases the likelihood of adequate representation of all groups.

Those targeted for potentially serving on a jury are required to report to a particular location on a specified date for jury duty. At this point, names will be randomly selected and prospective jurors will be instructed to report to a specific courtroom for questioning regarding their suitability to serve. Accordingly, not all who are included in the venire will be selected for participation on a jury. Potential jurors may not even make it to *voir dire*, and others will be excused following *voir dire*. Some will be excluded due to legal stipulations surrounding participation on a jury. Virtually all states have provisions requiring jurors to be U.S. citizens, residents of the locality, a certain minimum age, and able to understand English.[40] Most states do not permit convicted felons or insane persons from serving. Certain states maintain statutory exemptions for select individuals (e.g., government officials, lawyers) who are excused.[41] These restrictions have implications for creating culturally diverse juries. Excluding those unable to understand English, non–U.S. citizens, and convicted felons (who are disproportionately minority) all pose problems in a multicultural society.

VOIR DIRE

Voir dire is the final step in jury selection. During this process, prospective jurors are questioned by a judge and/or attorneys to determine their suitability for serving on a jury. The questioning seeks to identify whether jurors have any familiarity with the primary actors in the case, the individual's beliefs or attitudes regarding specific issues that may arise in the trial, and any other matters that may influence the prospective juror's ability to render a fair decision in the case. Unsuitable jurors are dismissed by the defense attorney or the prosecution during *voir dire* via one of two manners: challenges for cause and peremptory challenges. These options are designed to promote the assemblage of an unbiased jury.

Attorneys who wish to eliminate a juror because of an identifiable bias, or a juror's apparent inability to judge a case fairly file a **challenge for cause** motion. The judge rules on the motion and if sustained the prospective juror is dismissed. Judges assessing the appropriateness of a challenge for cause demonstrates the presence of judicial discretion in jury selection. **Peremptory challenges**, on the other hand, generate much greater controversy with regard to multiculturalism in U.S. courts.

Peremptory challenges, similar to challenges for cause, enable attorneys to eliminate seemingly unfit or inappropriate members of the jury pool. Attorneys typically do not need to justify using a peremptory challenge. They are provided an unlimited number of challenges for cause, although they are limited in the number of peremptory challenges they can use. Controversy surrounds the use of peremptory challenges, leading author David Neubauer to state that "based on hunch, prejudice, knowledge of psychology, or pseudoscience, attorneys use peremptory strikes—without having to give a reason—to eliminate the jurors they feel might not vote for their side."[42]

In 1965 the Supreme Court ruled in *Swain v. Alabama* that a prosecutor who used peremptory challenges to remove all six African Americans in the jury pool did not violate the Equal Protection Clause of the Constitution.[43] Years later, in 1986, the Court ruled in *Batson v. Kentucky* that a prosecutor's use of peremptory challenges may not include the dismissal of members of the jury pool based solely on their race.[44] The Court ruled that doing so was in violation of the Equal Protection Clause found in the Fourteenth Amendment. Despite the positive intentions of the *Batson* decision to enhance jury selection practices, the decision hasn't eliminated the use of race-based peremptory strikes.[45] In *Batson* the Court sought to retain a great deal of the freedom inherent in peremptory challenges, while excluding challenges based strictly on race. In turn, attorneys have much freedom in their use of peremptory challenges as courts must accept any explanation for exclusion that is not race-based.[46]

Additional Supreme Court cases[47] following *Batson* have sought to control the use of peremptory challenges from violating the Equal Protection Clause, however there is evidence that the challenges continue to be used in a discriminatory manner.[48] Minorities continue to be excluded from juries, as lawyers offer spurious reasons for the dismissal of minority individuals.[49] In discussing the jury selection practices as a barrier to the participation of racial and ethnic minority in trials, Professor Jennifer Hunt noted: "Despite the prohibition on race-based peremptory challenges, there is considerable evidence that they continue to be used in a discriminatory manner."[50] In response, there is an overrepresentation of White middle- and upper-class jurors and an underrepresentation of the poor and racial minorities.[51]

Recent reform in the pretrial stages of adjudication has reduced discrimination such as reconsideration of the sources via which potential jurors are identified, and it has become less likely that minority defendants will be tried by an all-White jury.[52] Attorneys seek to assemble a jury that will view a case according to the attorney's interest. Put simply, jury selection is sometimes more about winning a case than seeking justice. To be sure, discrimination exists with regard to both prosecutors and defense attorneys as the practices of using peremptory challenges to eliminate minorities from a jury pool could just as easily be used to eliminate Whites from a jury. The bottom line is that racial, ethnic, and cultural considerations are prevalent in jury selection. Such is the nature of seeking justice in a multicultural society.

THE BODY OF THE TRIAL

Scarce scholarly attention has addressed multiculturalism as it pertains to select steps of a trial. Limited attention has focused on the impact of various cultural groups with regard to opening statements, the presentation of the evidence, closing arguments, and the judge's charge to the jury. These important stages often impact the outcome of criminal cases.

Once the trial stage is set, attorneys offer opening statements. The prosecution typically offers the initial opening statement to the jury (or the judge, depending on whether it's a bench or jury trial), followed by the defense. It could be argued that being permitted to make the "first impression" with the jury is an unfair advantage for the prosecution. However, someone has to go first, and the prosecution seems suitable given their task of having to prove guilt. Opening statements permit attorneys to outline their case for the jury.

Potential obstacles for attorneys during opening statements include understanding the background of the jury and being able to effectively speak in comprehensible terms. Attorneys are encouraged to avoid "legal speak" and to recognize that the jury may not have a large working vocabulary. These suggestions hold true throughout all stages of a trial.

Both the prosecution and defense present evidence following opening statements. The presentation of evidence can be controversial in several ways. Some public defenders don't have the resources to thoroughly investigate their cases. As mentioned earlier, public defenders are often overworked and have limited resources. The impact of their situation may be evident during the presentation of the evidence. For instance, technology is influencing our courtrooms, and those with greater resources can sway juries with impressive technology-based presentations. Limited resources also hamper a public defender's ability to locate witnesses or to obtain other helpful information.

Notable judicial and attorney discretion exists with regard to the presentation of evidence. For example, judges may allow or disallow particular pieces of evidence to be introduced. Legal guidelines certainly assist with judicial discretion, as judges must abide by a code of conduct. The failure of judges to properly use their discretion, for example regarding the introduction of key evidence, can be grounds for a case to undergo appeal. Cases are sometimes won or lost depending on a judge's decision regarding the introduction of key pieces of evidence.

Among the many decisions they face at trial, defense attorneys must decide whether or not to put the defendant on the stand. Juries would seemingly like to hear from the defendant,[53] but it may not be strategically advantageous for the defense if the defendant is not an effective communicator. Defense attorneys should assess both at trial and during *voir dire* whether or not a jury will be receptive to their client. Cultural differences could certainly influence whether or not a defendant takes the stand.

At trial, defendants offer one of two defenses. They may offer an **alibi** that suggests that they did not commit they crime (e.g., they were in another location at the time of the crime), or defendants may also offer an **affirmative defense**, in which they admit committing the action in question, although they have legal justification for doing so. Entering an affirmative defense requires defendants to demonstrate that their action was justified. Self-defense, insanity, coercion, and entrapment are affirmative defenses. Although not widely used, the defense "**Black rage**" attempts to provide legal justification for criminal behavior by some African Americans frustrated by oppression resulting from living in a White-dominated society.

Closing arguments are offered once the defense and prosecution present their evidence and cross-examination of that evidence is completed. Closing arguments allow attorneys to make a final impression on the jury by recapping their arguments.

Following closing arguments, the judge prepares the **charge to the jury**, a written document that explains how the law applies to the case. Charges to the jury are typically assembled in an informal conference involving the judge and trial attorneys. The charge generally:

- reminds the jury of the prosecution's responsibility to prove guilt beyond a reasonable doubt,
- provides procedural directions for deliberations,
- identifies evidence that may or may not be considered during deliberations, and
- lists the options of verdicts for jury consideration.

Cultural differences and general familiarity with trial procedure and the law are of importance at this point. It is important for judges to provide clearly defined and readable instructions for jury members. Scholars have questioned the ability of jurors to clearly understand the directions provided by judges.[54] In turn, there have been calls for improving jury instructions. Providing visual aids to jury members[55] and offering instructions in multiple languages are among the suggestions for improvement.

Juries leave the courtroom and begin deliberating upon receiving the judge's instructions. A foreperson is elected by the jury, or one is appointed by the court prior to deliberations. This individual presides over jury deliberations and ultimately reads the verdict in the courtroom. One stronghold of jury deliberations is the secrecy involved. No outsiders are permitted in deliberations. The secrecy prohibits much understanding of the dynamics involved in deliberations. What we know about jury deliberations comes mostly from mock juries, interviews of jurors following their dismissal, and the questions asked during deliberations.[56] Research on jury decision-making suggests that jurors are sometimes influenced by implicit biases with regard to minority defendants.[57] Such biases are subtle, making them difficult to identify or address.

Unanimity is not necessary in non-capital cases although most jurisdictions require it. Federal cases must be unanimous. It can be challenging to have a group of strangers from various cultural backgrounds come to agreement. Juries may be requested to further deliberate if not enough members concur with the verdict, or a judge may rule the case a mistrial causing preparation for a new trial with new jurors to begin. Juries sometimes fail to reach agreement due to **jury nullification**, which is the practice of jurors acquitting particular defendants despite strong evidence suggesting guilt.

JURY NULLIFICATION

Jury members are charged with assessing the facts of the case and rendering a verdict. Juries are permitted to acquit even when the facts of the case suggest they convict in what is known as **jury nullification**. Jury nullification enables the community to actively participate in criminal law enforcement. It is rooted in English common law,[58] and is sometimes used in cases where the jury believes a prosecutor enforced an unpopular law or a jury sympathizes with the defendant. Jury nullification has become controversial as several prominent African American scholars encouraged Blacks to acquit other Blacks due to perceived mistreatment of African Americans by the courts and more generally the criminal justice system.

Former U.S. attorney Paul Butler commented on the power involved with jury nullification. He suggested that African American jurors should consider jury nullification in cases involving victimless, nonviolent offenses (e.g., drug possession). He argues that White jurors have historically engaged in jury nullification, and that Black jurors should follow suit. He adds that jury nullification would generate controversy and call into question the existing problems in the use of juries. Such attention could lead to methods of correcting the injustices faced by African Americans and other minorities.[59] Butler's comments are controversial and have generated critical responses. It is argued that race-based jury nullification further damages race relations, has moral implications, and generates greater racial discrimination.[60]

ENHANCING JURY TRIALS

The limitations inherent in the selection for juries have led to suggestions of alternatives, or enhancements of current practices. Professional juries, which involve full-time, trained, salaried professional jurors, purportedly address many of the problems associated with the use of laypersons serving as jurors. Professional jurors would provide the benefits of dependability, knowledge, and equity. Allowing jury members to write notes during the trial and participate more in trials by posing questions to witnesses are also feasible options for enhancing jury trials. Some California courts present jurors with notebooks containing trial exhibits and legal papers to help them render a fair verdict.[61] Other courts provide legal instructions to jurors before trial, instead of at the conclusion of the trial, to enable them to better understand their roles.

The need for effective verbal and nonverbal communication is evident throughout the trial. Attorneys must be clear and concise when addressing the court, especially in communication with jurors who have limited experience in legal terminology or courtroom procedures. As noted earlier, communication is largely conveyed nonverbally. Accordingly, the ability to speak clearly and "visually appeal" to those in the courtroom is important. This point should be noted by defense attorneys who should prepare their clients for trial, but preparing defendants for trial is much easier said than done. Jury members are often unfamiliar with legal terminology and the overall legal culture of the courtroom. Enhanced use of interpreters and an overall needs assessment related to enhancing jury practices would help.

Much of the needed change with regard to trials, and more generally, our criminal justice system, stems from the misuse of individual discretion. As evidenced throughout this book, discretion is inherent in the criminal justice system. Although most criminal justice professionals use their discretion in a very professional manner, there remains controversy when one makes decisions that appear to, or are intended to, negatively impact certain groups.

SENTENCING

What purposes are to be served through criminal sentences? The primary purposes of criminal sanctions include offender rehabilitation, retribution, deterrence, and incapacitation. **Rehabilitation** involves attempts to "cure" or "fix" the ills leading to the offender's behavior. **Retribution**, or punishment, adopts the "eye for an eye" approach. **Deterrence** seeks to dissuade the offender (specific deterrence) or society in general (general deterrence) from engaging in acts for which the offender is being punished. **Incapacitation** involves physically preventing one from committing similar criminal acts in the future. Incarceration is the most widely used form of incapacitation. Each sentence has a purpose or perhaps several purposes. For instance, a judge who orders an offender to life in prison without the possibility of parole is intent on incapacitation and/or retribution. The drug offender who receives treatment is targeted for rehabilitation. Multiple goals may be evident in a criminal sentence. For example, the offender who receives house arrest has likely been targeted for punishment and rehabilitation.

Does our justice system treat various groups differently? The answer to that question largely depends on who is asked. A 2013 Gallup poll found that over two-thirds (68 percent) of Blacks noted that the American justice system is biased against Blacks, however only 25 percent of Whites concurred. Forty percent of Hispanic respondents believed that the justice system is biased against Blacks.[62] Of note, it seems those most affected by the courts are the ones most likely to be critical of justice-based practices.

DISCRIMINATORY SENTENCING?

Early research on the sentencing of minorities suggested discrimination in the types of sentences and sentence severity, but recent research produced conflicting findings. For example, the research literature provides conflicting results regarding the possibility of discrimination regarding Native Americans sentenced in court. Several studies find that Blacks receive harsher sentences than Whites, while other findings suggest the opposite is true. Still, some findings suggest no differences in sentencing practices with regard to race.

If sentencing practices are unbiased, why is there disparity in the percentages of minorities entering our prisons? An obvious response to this question concerns socioeconomic status. While race may not be evident in sentencing decisions, one's socioeconomic status certainly influences the likelihood of being punished. The disparity with which minorities are punished in our courts is explained, in large part, by unfavorable social conditions faced by many minorities. Further, the structures under which individuals are sentenced appear to unfavorably influence poor minorities. Thus, discrimination may not be evident in the actions of those imposing sentences; instead it may be located within the structural components of criminal sentencing.

SENTENCING STRUCTURES

Sentencing is perhaps the most controversial aspect of courtroom practices, primarily because of the extensive amount of discretion inherent in this part of criminal case processing. We can easily view the penalties received by various individuals in relation to their demographics, the crime(s) they committed, and their criminal history. Historically, judges maintained wide latitude in sentencing practices. Beginning in the late 1960s and early 1970s conservatives and liberals, albeit for different reasons, agreed that sentencing reform was needed. The indeterminate sentencing structure that existed provided too much discretion. Both liberals and conservatives agreed consistency was needed, as conservatives pointed to judges giving sentences that were too lenient, while liberals believed punishments were too harsh. It was agreed that determinate sentencing would reduce disparity and alleviate discrimination.[63]

A number of states have adopted **determinate sentencing** practices that involve offenders receiving a specific amount of time to be served based on the crime for which they were convicted. Determinate sentencing differs from indeterminate sentencing which relies on parole board determinations regarding an offender's readiness for reentry to society. The move to determinate sentencing is typically accompanied by the elimination of parole. Instead of relying on discretionary release from a parole board, offenders processed in jurisdictions using mandatory release are free to leave prison upon expiration of their sentence minus "good time." **Good time** is time taken off a prison sentence for good behavior. Determinate sentencing was designed to reduce discretion in the courts and help ensure equal treatment for all.

Since the 1980s legislatures have created commissions to look into sentencing practices. Among the developments are **sentencing guidelines**, which are used by some states. The guidelines provide a risk assessment of the offender based on current offense and past history. The ultimate goal is to ensure justice with limited discretion. However, sentencing guidelines prompt controversy due to the belief sentencing guidelines are harsh, haven't reduced disparities, and are too rigid and complex.[64] The federal government introduced sentencing guidelines in 1984, however it ceased using them following the U.S. Supreme Courts decision in *United States v. Booker*.[65] In *Booker*, the Court noted that the guidelines violated the Sixth Amendment, and made the guidelines advisory, meaning that federal judges must consider, but not use them. State guidelines are less controversial than the federal provisions, as states have made adjustments to accommodate particular cases and provide judges a sense of discretion as needed.

Sentencing guidelines appear to shift discretion from judges to prosecutors. Consideration of prior criminal record in sentencing guidelines leaves minorities at a disadvantage compared to nonminorities who are less likely to have a criminal history.[66]

Legislators responded to public sentiment that prison sentences are too lenient by imposing **mandatory minimum sentencing**. Mandatory minimums require offenders convicted of certain offenses to be sentenced to prison for no less than a specified term of years, and nonprison sentences (e.g., probation) are not an option. Mandatory minimum sentences are typically imposed on violent offenders. Similar to sentencing guidelines, mandatory minimum sentencing has generated criticism. African Americans are disproportionately convicted under these laws primarily due to their overrepresentation in drug offenses and the disparity in sentences given to offenses involving crack cocaine.[67] "Three strikes and you're out" penalties have been the topic of much controversy with regard to sentencing practices.

Between 1993 and 1995 many states imposed varied versions of **"three strikes and you're out"** sentences targeted toward repeat offenders. The legislation demonstrates the public's disdain for crime and an attempt to target those who seem undeterred by criminal law and punishment. Three strikes laws vary among the states that use them, with offenders in certain jurisdictions facing life sentences following a third felony. The idea behind the legislation and its application are popular, yet implementation of the legislation has posed several problems, especially for minorities.[68] One researcher commented on the "draconian results" associated with the penalties, in which some offenders have received notably stringent penalties for minor offenses.[69] Further, one cannot ignore the influence of the legislation on many offenders who are aging out of crime and don't commit a third offense until late in their criminal careers. The costs associated with the laws are also problematic as offenders serve longer sentences. Further, three strikes laws arguably increase the risks for police officers as "two-strike" defendants being pursued by officers may be willing to attempt escape at all costs.[70]

In his article "The Impact of Federal Sentencing Reforms on African Americans" author Marvin D. Free Jr. commented on the influences of sentencing practices in stating that "neither mandatory minimum sentences nor the guidelines have been effective in eliminating racial disparity in sentencing in federal court."[71] The disparity is affected by drug laws, especially with regard to crack cocaine. Selective law enforcement on the streets also impacts the disparity.[72] Recent sentencing reform involving determinate sentencing and sentencing guidelines has reduced the likelihood of overt discrimination in the courts, yet discriminatory sentencing practices have not disappeared.

There are various reasons why African American and Hispanic defendants receive harsher penalties than their White counterparts. First, differences in sentence severity could be explained by African Americans and Hispanics committing more serious crimes, and having more serious criminal histories than Whites. They could be explained through economic discrimination, with poor defendants (typically minorities) receiving differential treatment in the courts. Third, blatant racial or ethnic discrimination on behalf of those involved in sentencing could explain the disparity. Or, the disparities could be due to contextual discrimination in the sense that minorities are treated differently upon being sentenced for certain crimes (e.g., violent crimes).[73] Each explanation has merit and combined they largely explain the disparity in sentencing. The first argument, that minorities commit more serious crimes and are thus punished more severely than Whites, is the only one of the four that doesn't involve some form of discrimination.

Disparities and discrimination evident in the sentencing of minorities to the death penalty are covered in Chapter 3 of this book. As suggested earlier, evidence suggests racial minorities have disproportionately received capital punishment. Accordingly, in his book *No Equal Justice,* author David Cole stated, "Virtually every study of race and the death penalty has concluded that, all other things being equal, defendants who kill White victims are much more likely to receive the death penalty than those who kill Black victims."[74] This statement is supported by others, for instance as one researcher noted that the existing research suggests that jurors often make more punitive judgments of defendants from other ethnic and racial groups, and are more likely to impose death sentences in cases involving White victims and Black or Latino defendants.[75] Recent efforts to reform the application of the death penalty, beginning with the 1972 Supreme Court case *Furman v. Georgia,*[76] provide perhaps the best evidence of the discrepancies found in its application.

The above discussion of multiculturalism and sentencing, and more generally our court system, has focused primarily on African American and Hispanics. This is not to disregard the plight of many other underrepresented groups who enter our courts. The research in this area, especially with regard to sentencing, focuses primarily on Blacks, with less information on Hispanics and even less information on other groups.

APPELLATE COURTS

Defendants have the right to appeal following their conviction. Defendants also have the right to counsel during the appellate stage. Accordingly, U.S. courts can be categorized based on their trial and appellate jurisdiction. Among other functions, appellate courts help protect defendants' right according to state or federal constitutions, criminal court procedural law, and substantive law.

Most criminal cases do not involve an appeal given the large percentage of cases settled by plea bargaining. Defendants forfeit their right to appeal following the admission of guilt. Appeals involve the legal issues surrounding the trial, often focusing on issues such as the introduction of illegally seized evidence, improper jury instructions, and denial of counsel or a fair trial.[77]

Many of the same limitations faced by underrepresented groups in the trial court jurisdiction appear in the appellate court system. Discretion is inherent in the appellate process, and historical evidence suggests that groups have received differential treatment. For example, researchers found that a defendant's race significantly influenced an appellate court's decision to uphold a trial court's decision in which a judge departed from the sentence recommended by guidelines.[78]

High levels of judicial and attorney discretion exist in the appellate courts. For instance, discretion is involved with appellate court judges determining the significance of alleged errors at trial. The **harmless error doctrine** holds that a trial court decision will not be overturned based on small, insignificant errors that appear to have small or no impact on the trial. The term "harmless" is certainly subjective and open to interpretation by appellate judges.

MULTICULTURALISM AND COURTROOM PERSONNEL

Thus far this chapter has focused predominantly on the role of underrepresented groups who enter our courts. What about members of the various cultural groups working in our courts? Have minorities assimilated into the courtroom workgroup? Are they treated differently? Do they act in contrast to others? Progress has been made toward increasing the diversity of those working in our court system. Affirmative action programs have increased the presence of historically underrepresented groups, and it is anticipated that greater representation is forthcoming.

The lack of diversity working in the courts is well documented in the research literature. Systematic discrimination targeting females and minorities in the legal arena has been endemic in the United States.[79] Such discrimination has occurred formally, for instance via the choices and actions of courts, legislatures, law schools, and bar associations to disallow or discourage minorities from entering the legal profession, and informally through mistreating minorities in the legal field.[80]

The American Bar Association noted that minority judges are notably underrepresented in the various levels of courts. For instance, in 2015, only about 11.8 percent of judges were African American, followed by Hispanic (6.4 percent) and Asian and Pacific (6.2 percent). Women comprised 39 percent of judgeships in the United States.[81]

These percentages suggest greater diversity is needed on the bench. Further disparity exists with regard to the percentages of lawyers and others working in the courts, such as paralegals and legal assistants. Only about 5.1 percent of lawyers are Hispanic, followed by Asian (4.8 percent) and African American (4.6 percent) attorneys. Females (34.5 percent) are also underrepresented. Hispanic or Latino/as (13.4 percent) were more likely than other minority groups to work as paralegals or legal assistants in 2015, although other groups appear underrepresented, including African Americans (10.3 percent) and Asians (3.9 percent).[82] The percentages of women and minority associates and partners at law firms have grown over time, although these groups still remain underrepresented in these positions.[83]

Why are minorities underrepresented as professionals in the courts? Edward Chen, the first Asian Pacific American judge appointed to the federal bench for the Northern District of California—despite the significant number of Asian Pacific Americans in the area—noted that the lack of diversity in the judiciary is attributable to several factors. Prominent among the factors are the lack of diversity in the pool of experienced attorneys, the influences of political ties negatively affecting minorities, the limited access of networking for minorities, and overall hampered career opportunities.[84]

Progress has been made in diversifying the courts, particularly the federal courts. During his terms in office, President Barak Obama made great efforts to diversify the federal courts. Roughly 60 percent of his appointments were non-White males. As of 2014, there were ten openly gay judges on the federal bench, all of whom were appointed by President Obama.

MULTICULTURALISM IN THE WORKFORCE

Failing to promote a multicultural workforce is costly in many aspects. The courts play an integral role in ensuring that employees are treated in a fair and just manner both within and outside of the criminal justice system. Several cases highlight the important role of the courts in ensuring diversity and equal treatment in the workforce, including one involving the large brokerage firm Merrill Lynch. The company agreed to pay $160 million to settle a racial bias lawsuit originated by a longtime broker of the company who accused the company of providing better opportunities and more compensation for White employees. The case grew to include over 1,200 brokers.

In a different case, New Jersey Transit, which is the state's public transportation organization, agreed to pay $3.65 million to settle a racial discrimination lawsuit. The suit was filed by seven current and former employees who claimed that they were subjected to racial insults by supervisors. The plaintiffs claimed that they were paid less than their White coworkers, and were victims of unfair treatment while working for the organization. The agreement to settle the case came less than four years after New Jersey Transit spent $5.8 million to settle a similar discrimination lawsuit filed by minority police officers who were employed by the organization.

In 2014 case, five state corrections officers in Nebraska received $777,000 after claiming that they were subjected to taunts and discrimination because they are African American. The five plaintiffs claimed in their federal lawsuit that it was common for non-Black staff members at the prison in which they worked to make racially based taunts and jokes as the officers reported for roll call. The officers earlier reported the harassment, although they received more work or undesirable jobs in response to their complaints. Following the complaints and case in general, the state's Department of Correctional Services hired someone to work on intercultural sensitivity, updated its diversity training materials, and conducted cultural awareness training for senior corrections staff and wardens.

Unfortunately, these are but a few of the many cases in which workers must rely on the law to ensure a safe and bias-free workplace.

Why do we need greater diversity in the courts? To begin, greater diversity promotes greater cultural sensitivity and comprehension of the varied issues addressed in the courts. Courtroom personnel may be able to recognize differences within their objective context, as opposed to at face value. Further, greater diversity promotes respect for the courts from underrepresented groups. Minorities are more likely than Whites to view the courts with apprehension. Past discriminatory practices could be mended, in part, if it appeared that our court system isn't primarily staffed with nonminorities. Used in this context, the term **"symbolic representation"** refers to making our courts more representative of all groups.[85] In other words, the perceived legitimacy of the courts would be enhanced through greater diversity among courtroom personnel.

Females and racial and ethnic minorities have increasingly assumed positions as attorneys and judges, yet they remain underrepresented in these key courtroom positions. Pictured is Supreme Court Justice Sonia Sotomayor.

There is also evidence that judges may be biased in their decision-making. For instance, researchers surveyed judges in a Northeastern state in the United States regarding their beliefs as to why there exist racial disparities in the criminal justice system. In other words, they were asked why racial minorities are overrepresented in the system. Most judges attributed the disparities, in part, to differential treatment by judges and/or other criminal justice officials, while some attributed the disparities to the negative impacts of poverty and different offending rates among racial groups.[86] The differential treatment explanation incorporates implicit and overt discrimination by those tasked with enforcing the law, including police officers, judges, prosecutors, and probation officers.[87]

As noted in Table 12-1, there are many organizations and associations that promote the interests of women and cultural/racial/ethnic groups in the courts. These organizations and associations provide workers opportunities to share concerns, issues, and related aspects of the job with officers of similar backgrounds from around the country.

Recent efforts to promote diversity on the bench have resulted in greater representation of minority judges and an opportunity to better understand the behaviors of minority

Table 12.1 Examples of Organizations and Associations Promoting Interests of Women and Cultural/Racial/Ethnic Groups in the Courts

American Bar Association Commission on Women in the Profession
American Bar Association Commission on Racial and Ethnic Diversity in the Profession
American Bar Association Council on Racial and Ethnic Justice
Hispanic National Bar Association
National Asian Pacific American Bar Association
National Conference on Women's Bar Association
National LGBT Bar Association
Native American Bar Association
National Association of Women Lawyers

judges in the courtroom. There is conflicting research regarding the practices of minority and nonminority judges. One study found that African American and White judges considered case and offender information similarly when imposing punishment decisions. Black judges were more likely than White judges to impose a prison sentence on both Black and White offenders. The more punitive approach taken by Black judges may be attributable to their perceptions of themselves as "tokens" or it may be that they maintain greater sensitivity to the harms associated with crime.[88]

Researchers found conflicting results when comparing the sentencing and incarceration practices of Black and White judges. White judges were more likely than Black judges to treat White defendants more leniently. Little discrimination was found with regard to sentence severity. However, White judges treated Black and White defendants equally severely. Black judges treated Black defendants more leniently than White defendants.[89] With regard to gender, earlier research found that female judges were more likely than male judges to treat men and women defendants equally.[90]

Research on judicial practices in Detroit identified few differences with regard to race and judicial behavior. There were notable similarities in the sentencing practices of both Black and White judges, with race offering limited significant predictive powers with regard to judicial sentencing practices. It was found that both Black and White judges sentenced Black defendants more severely than their White counterparts.[91] The similarities in sentencing practices could be attributed to the judicial recruitment process which produces a somewhat homogeneous judiciary with regard to judicial practices. The socialization practices of judges and others working in the criminal justice system certainly influence the behaviors of those in the field.[92]

Defendants should and do consider cultural factors in choosing a bench or jury trial. For instance, given public sentiment, an Arab-American charged with robbery shortly after the September 11, 2001, terrorist attacks may have had a better chance of receiving a fair trial absent a jury. However, one cannot discard the elevated level of judicial discretion inherent in bench trials. It is hoped that judges are better able than jurors to put aside personal beliefs in favor of professionalism.

SUMMARY

While this discussion of the U.S. court system and multiculturalism centers on criminal courts, one cannot overlook the accomplishments of federal civil courts in shaping state and local criminal justice practices with regard to diversity. Several areas of federal civil legislation have important consequences for criminal justice officials. The more significant legislation relates to:

- Civil rights violations, which enables individuals to sue civilly city or state employees who deprive them of their constitutional rights
- Equal employment opportunities, which prohibits discrimination based on race, color, religion, sex, age, or national origin
- Sex discrimination, and
- Discrimination against the disabled, which protects Americans with disabilities from discrimination in employment in the use of public facilities and services.

Steven Vago, author of the book *Law and Society*, stated that "racism is embedded in the system and proponents recognize that its elimination is impossible but at the same time they insist that an ongoing struggle to countervail racism must be carried out."[93] To be sure, disparity and discrimination in the courtroom are not restricted to one's race, as gender, ethnicity, culture, and socioeconomic factors influence discretionary practices at all stages of the system. As an example, minority women face special concerns upon entering the criminal justice system, particularly given their high rates of poverty and unemployment, and the increased likelihood of them being a single parent. Unfortunately, the plight of minority women who enter our courts has been the subject of scant research efforts. What we do know about this group suggests differential treatment of minority women in the courts and throughout the criminal justice system.[94]

Much has changed in our courts, as numerous reforms directed at leveling the playing field for minorities and all groups have influenced courtroom practices and personnel. Nevertheless, much work remains. It is hoped that recognizing and highlighting the problems and accomplishments provides an impetus for continued progress.

YOU MAKE THE CALL

COURTROOM CONTROVERSY

Consider the following scenario. Debate the pros and cons of all options and decide what you would do.

You're a public defender assigned to represent a defendant who is charged with fifteen counts of animal cruelty involving the sacrificing of cats. The defendant claims the sacrifices were part of his religious practices, and he is not guilty of anything illegal. He cites his constitutional right to freedom of religion. Professionally, you have an obligation to provide appropriate representation for your client. Personally, you're an animal lover and have four cats. You're familiar with the judge presiding over

this case. She also loves animals. The prosecuting attorney in this case is a member of the People for the Ethical Treatment of Animals (PETA).

Questions

1. Does your client enter court at a disadvantage?
2. Will you be able to put aside your personal feelings and provide effective counsel for the accused?
3. Should you decline to defend the client (if possible) and/ or request a new judge?
4. Do you encourage your client to plea bargain, request a bench trial, or take their chances with a jury trial?

KEY TERMS

affirmative defense

alibi

arraignment

assigned counsel

bench trial

black rage

challenge for cause

charge to the jury

determinate sentencing

deterrence

discovery

Federal Jury Selection and Services Act of 1968

good time

grand jury hearing

harmless error doctrine

incapacitation

indictment

indigent defendants

initial appearance

jury nullification

mandatory minimum sentencing

nolo contendere

peremptory challenge

plea bargaining

preliminary hearing

pretrial motions

pretrial release

public defenders

rehabilitation

retribution

sentencing guidelines

summons

symbolic representation

"three strikes and you're out" sentencing

venire

voir dire

DISCUSSION QUESTIONS

1. Identify and discuss the steps of the trial. Which step do you believe involves the greatest area of controversy with regard to discrimination? Why?
2. Identify how judicial, prosecutorial, and defense attorney discretion influences the outcome of court cases.
3. How are jurors selected? Does this process seem fair to you? Discuss why or why not.
4. How have recent sentencing reform efforts failed to eliminate disparity in sentencing? What steps would you take to improve sentencing practices?
5. Are racial and ethnic minorities adequately represented among the courtroom personnel? If not, what steps could be taken to diversify our courts?

FOR FURTHER READING

Baer, J. A., and L. F. Goldstein. *The Constitutional and Legal Rights of Women: Cases in Law and Social Change*, 3rd ed. New York: Oxford University Press, 2006.

Benforado, A. *Unfair: The New Science of Criminal Injustice*. NY: Crown, 2015.

Neubauer, D. W., and H. F. Fradella. *America's Courts and the Criminal Justice System*, 12th ed. Boston, MA: Cengage, 2017.

Ramirez, L. F., ed. *Cultural Issues in Criminal Defense*. Huntington, NY: Juris, 2010.

Walsh, A., and C. Hemmens. *Law, Justice, and Society*, 4th ed. New York: Oxford University Press, 2016.

NOTES

1. Jill Norgren and Serena Nanda, *American Cultural Pluralism and Law* (New York: Praeger, 1988), 1
2. Ibid., 1.
3. Norgren and Nanda, *American Cultural Pluralism*.

4. Gaye Tuchman, Gaye, "Let's Hold Trials Here in Spanish," *New York Times*, August 28, 1979, A17.

5. Richard Willing, "Courts Asked to Consider Culture," *USA Today*, May 25, 2004, 3A.

6. Ibid.

7. Ibid.

8. B. A. Reaves, *Felony Defendants in Large Urban Counties, 2009—Statistical Tables*. U.S. Department of Justice, Bureau of Justice Statistics, 2013. NCJ 243777.

9. 9 B. Kutateladze, V. Lynn, and E. Liang. *Do Race and Ethnicity Matter in Prosecution? A Review of Empirical Studies* (New York: The Vera Institute, 2012).

10. S. Walker, C. Spohn, and M. Delone, *The Color of Justice: Race, Ethnicity, and Crime in America* 5th ed. (Belmont, CA: Wadsworth, 2012).

11. *Gideon v. Wainwright*, 372 U.S. 335 (1963).

12. *Johnson v. Zerbst*, 304 U.S. 458 (1938).

13. Frank Schmalleger, *Criminal Justice Today: An Introductory Text for the 21st Century* (Upper Saddle River, NJ: Prentice Hall, 2005), 392–93.

14. Caroline W. Harlow, *Defense Counsel in Criminal Cases*. U.S. Department of Justice, Bureau of Justice Statistics, November 2000. NCJ 179023.

15. Bennett L. Gershman, "Themes of Injustice: Wrongful Convictions, Racial Prejudice, and Lawyer Incompetence," in *Criminal Courts for the 21st Century*, ed. Lisa Stolzenberg and Stewart J. D'Alessio (Upper Saddle River, NJ: Prentice Hall, 1999), 360.

16. David Cole, *No Equal Justice: Race and Class in the American Criminal Justice System* (New York: The New Press, 1999), 89.

17. Ibid., 64.

18. Ibid., 76.

19. Walker, et al., *The Color of Justice*.

20. Ibid.

21. T. Schlesinger, "Racial and Ethnic Disparity in Pretrial Criminal Processing," *Justice Quarterly* 22 (2005):170–92.

22. Victor E. Kappeler and Gary W. Potter, *The Mythology of Crime and Criminal Justice*, 4th ed. (Long Grove, IL: Waveland, 2005), 274.

23. K. B. Turner and James B. Johnson, "A Comparison of Bail Amounts for Hispanics, Whites, and African Americans: A Single County Analysis," *American Journal of Criminal Justice* 30, no. 1 (2005): 35–53.

24. M. T. Phillips, M. T. (2008). *Pretrial Detention and Case Outcomes. Part 2: Felony Cases* (New York: New York City Criminal Justice Agency, 2008); M. Sacks and A. R. Ackerman, "Bail and Sentencing: Does Pretrial Detention Lead to Harsher Punishment?" *Criminal Justice Policy Review* 25, no. 1 (2014): 59–77.

25. Ronald G. Burns, *The Criminal Justice System* (Upper Saddle River, NJ: Prentice Hall, 2007), 41.

26. D. W. Neubauer and S. S. Meinhold, *Judicial Process: Law, Courts, and Politics in the United States*, 7th ed. (Boston, MA: Cengage, 2017), 225.

27. L. Devers, *Plea and Charge Bargaining: Research Summary*. U.S. Department of Justice, Bureau of Justice Assistance, 2011, 3.

28. Walker, et al. *The Color of Justice*. See 229–31 for discussion of race and plea bargaining decisions.

29. B. L. Kutateladze, N. R. Andiloro, and B. Johnson, "Opening Pandora's Box: How Does Defendant Race Influence Plea Bargaining?" *Justice Quarterly* 33, no. 3 (2016): 398–426.

30. S. R. Sommers, "Race and the Decision Making of Juries," *Legal and Criminological Psychology* 12, no. 2 (2007): 171–87.

31. M. Lynch and C. Haney, "Mapping the Racial Bias of the White Male Capital Juror: Jury Composition and the 'Emphatic Divide,'" *Law and Society Review* 45, no. 1 (2011): 69–102.

32. S. R. Sommers and O. O. Adekanmbi, "Race and Juries: an Experimental Psychology Perspective," in *Critical Race Realism: Intersections of Psychology, Race, and Law*, ed. G. S. Park and S. Jones (New York: New Press, 2008), 78–93.

33. H. Fukurai and R. Krooth, *Race in the Jury Box: Affirmative Action in Jury Selection* (Albany, NY: State University of New York Press, 2003).

34. Ibid.

35. J. S. Hunt, "Race, Ethnicity, and Culture in Jury Decision Making." *Annual Review of Law and Social Science* 11 (2015): 269–88.

36. E. Y. Cornwell and V. P. Hans, "Representation Through Participation: A Multilevel Analysis of Jury Deliberations," *Law & Society Review* 45, no. 3 (2011): 667–98.

37. Cole, *No Equal Justice*, 101.

38. Ibid.

39. J. M. Gau, "A Jury of Whose Peers?: The Impact of Selection Procedures on Racial Composition and the Prevalence of Majority-White Juries," *Journal of Crime and Justice* 39, no. 1 (2016): 75–87.

40. D. W. Neubauer and H. F. Fradella, *America's Courts and the Criminal Justice System* (Boston, MA: Cengage, 2017), 361.

41. Ibid., 361.

42. Ibid., 363.

43. *Swain v. Alabama*, 380 U.S. 202 (1965).

44. *Batson v. Kentucky*, 476 U.S. 79 (1986).

45. Cole, *No Equal Justice*, 120.

46. Ibid.

47. *Edmonson v. Leesville Concrete Company*, No. 89-7743, 500 U.S. 614 (Sup. Ct. 1991); *Miller-El v. Dretke*, No. 03-9659, 545 U.S. 231 (Sup. Ct. 2005); *Snyder v. Louisiana*, No. 06-10119, 552 U.S. 472 (Sup. Ct. 2007).

48. Hunt, "Race, Ethnicity, and Culture."

49. Gershman, "Themes of Injustice," 359.

50. Hunt, "Race, Ethnicity, and Culture."

51. Walker, et al., *The Color of Justice*.

52. Ibid.

53. Burns, *The Criminal Justice System*, 56.

54. E.g., R. Dattu, "Illustrated Jury Instructions," *Judicature* 82, no. 2 (Sept./Oct. 1998): 79; see also, W. D. Foglia, "They Know Not What They Do: Unguided and Misguided Discretion in Pennsylvania Capital Cases," *Justice Quarterly* 20, no. 1 (2003): 187–211.

55. Dattu, "Illustrated Jury Instructions."

56. Burns, *The Criminal Justice System*, 58.

57. J. Kang, M. Bennett, D. Carbado, P. Casey, N. Dasgupta, D. Faigman, R. Godsil, A. G. Greenwald, J. Levinson, and J. Mnookin, "Implicit Bias in the Courtroom," *UCLA Law Review* 59 (2012): 1124–86.

58. Walker, et al., *The Color of Justice*.

59. Paul Butler, "Racially Based Jury Nullification: Black Power in the Criminal Justice System," *The Yale Law Journal* 105, no. 3 (Dec. 1995): 677–25.

60. Randall Kennedy, *Race, Crime, and the Law* (New York: Vintage, 1997.

61. R. Willing, "Courts Try to Make Jury Duty Less of a Chore," *USA Today*, March 17, 2005, 17A–18A.

62. F. Newport, "Gulf Grows in Black-White Views of U.S. Justice System Bias," Gallup, July 22, 2013. Accessed online at: http://www.gallup.com/poll/163610/gulf-grows-black-white-views-justice-system-bias.aspx?g_source=justice&g_medium=search&g_campaign=tiles

63. Neubauer and Fradella, *America's Courts.*

64. M. Tonry, "The Failure of U.S. Sentencing Commission's Guidelines," *Crime & Delinquency* 39 (1993): 131–49.

65. *United States v. Booker*, 543 U.S. 220 (2005).

66. Marvin D. Free Jr.,"The Impact of Federal Sentencing Reforms on African Americans," *Journal of Black Studies* 28, no. 2 (1997): 268–86.

67. Ibid.

68. Cole, *No Equal Justice.*

69. Ibid., 147.

70. Ibid.

71. Free, "The Impact," 283–84.

72. Ibid.

73. Ibid., 286.

74. Cole, *No Equal Justice*, 132.

75. Hunt, "Race, Ethnicity, and Culture."

76. *Furman v. Georgia*, 408 U.S. 238, 245 (1972)

77. Burns, *The Criminal Justice System*, 67–68.

78. J. J. Williams, "Predicting Decisions Rendered in Criminal Appeals," *Journal of Criminal Justice* 19 (1991): 463–69.

79. Mark S. Hurwitz and Drew Noble Lanier, "Explaining Judicial Diversity: The Differential Ability of Women and Minorities to Attain Seats on State Supreme and Appellate Courts," *State Politics and Policy Quarterly* 3, no. 4 (2003): 329.

80. Ibid., 329.

81. Bureau of Labor Statistics. "Household Data Annual Averages." Available online at: http://www.bls.gov/cps/cpsaat11.pdf

82. Ibid.

83. A. Cuyler, "Diversity in the Practice of Law: How Far Have We Come?" *GP Solo* 29, no. 5 (2012). Accessed online at: http://www.americanbar.org/publications/gp_solo/2012/september_october/diversity_practice_law_how_far_have_we_come.html.

84. Edward M. Chen, "The Judiciary, Diversity, and Justice For All," *California Law Review* 91 (2003): 1109–24.

85. Susan Welch, Michael Combs, and John Gruhl, "Do Black Judges Make a Difference?" *American Journal of Political Science* 32, no. 1 (1988): 126–36.

86. M. Clair and A. S. Winter, "How Judges Think About Racial Disparities: Situational Decision-Making in the Criminal Justice System," *Criminology* 54, no. 2 (2016): 332–59.

87. K. Beckett, K. Nyrop and L. Pfingst, "Race, Drugs, and Policing: Understanding Disparities in Drug Delivery Arrests," *Criminology* 44 (2006):105–37; C. C. Spohn, C.C. (2013). "Racial Disparities in Prosecution, Sentencing, and Punishment," in *The Oxford Handbook of Ethnicity, Crime, and Immigration*, ed. S. M. Bucerius and M. Tonry (New York: Oxford University Press, 2013).

88. Darrell Steffensmeier and Chester L. Britt, "Judges' Race and Judicial Decision Making: Do Black Judges Sentence Differently?" *Social Science Quarterly* 82, no. 4 (2001): 749–64.

89. Welch, et al., "Do Black Judges Make a Difference?" 126.

90. John Gruhl, Susan Welch, and Cassia Spohn, "Women as Policy Makers: The Case of Trial Judges," *American Journal of Political Science* 25 (1981): 308–22.

91. Cassia Spohn, "The Sentencing Decisions of Black and White Judges: Expected and Unexpected Similarities," *Law & Society Review* 24, no. 5 (1990): 1197–216.

92. Ibid.

93. Steven Vago, *Law and Society*, 7th ed. (Upper Saddle River, NJ: Prentice Hall, 2003), 71.

94. Coramae Richey Mann, "Minority and Female: A Criminal Justice Double Bind," *Social Justice* 16, no. 4 (38) (1989): 95-114, http://www.jstor.org/stable/29766503

CHAPTER 13

CORRECTIONS AND MULTICULTURALISM

CHAPTER OBJECTIVES

After reading this chapter, you should be able to:

- Recognize the significance of multiculturalism with regard to institutional corrections
- Identify and discuss the significance of cultural diversity as it relates to prison life
- Understand the challenges associated with incarceration
- Recognize the importance of cultural diversity as it pertains to community corrections
- Understand the significance of ensuring that correctional staff is aware of and tolerant of cultural diversity

Enforcing formal social control over those convicted of crimes is no easy task, and current correctional practices in the United States generate controversy. The controversy largely stems from the lack of directed goals with regard to many correctional practices, the limited capacity of correctional practices to "correct" human behavior, and the problems stemming from the multicultural makeup of our correctional system. With regard to the latter, it is well documented that the demographics of those under correctional supervision are unlike the demographics of society in general. The diversity within our correctional system coupled with controversial correctional practices make for interesting study and is the focus of this chapter.

It is argued that heterogeneous countries, in which citizens differ based on race, ethnicity, religion, and other traits, are more punitive in nature than are homogenous countries. Support for this argument is found in imprisonment rates in the 1990s during which the United States, Russia, and South Africa led all other nations in the rate of incarceration. All three countries faced difficulties related to multiculturalism, compounded in the case of Russia and South Africa by changing government regimes. Law and punishment were increasingly used to formally control the disorder and conflict found in these countries.[1]

In recent years the United States has increasingly relied on incarceration and punishment as means to address crime. These approaches have disproportionately impacted many lower-income minority communities which have suffered in numerous ways. While it is argued that imprisonment and overall correctional practices help protect society, we must remember that most offenders eventually return to the same communities and environments in which they committed their offense. Some may have been "corrected," however, there are many who return to society to face the same difficulties as they did prior to correctional intervention. Their problems are often amplified in various means, not the least of which involves being labeled a "criminal," or "ex-con."

The status change from accused to offender leads to those under correctional supervision being viewed as criminals. In other words, upon being convicted they lose their status as "innocent until proven guilty." Offenders are often recognized by society as law violators who must be punished. Accordingly, our correctional system deals with individuals maintaining the lowest status of all who enter the criminal justice system. Upon release these same individuals will continue to be looked down upon by society. This is but one of the many challenges faced by those entering corrections.

The complexities of more frequently interacting with diverse groups and individuals are another difficulty faced by those under correctional supervision. Prison inmates face many struggles associated with being incarcerated, including contending with cultural biases. The situation is enhanced in jails where the classification of inmates is less of a concern than in prisons. To increase the likelihood of success in community corrections, probationers, parolees, and the officers who supervise offenders in the community must overcome cultural differences. Discussion of multiculturalism and corrections becomes more important as the number of individuals under correctional supervision increases and subsequently diversifies.

This chapter addresses multiculturalism and corrections by focusing on the main components of corrections: institutionalization in the forms of prisons and jails, and community corrections in the forms of probation and parole. This discussion is preceded by an observation of the organization and structure of corrections and characteristics of those under correctional supervision. The chapter concludes with a look at how cultural diversity impacts correctional staff.

THE ORGANIZATION OF CORRECTIONS

The organization of correctional agencies is complex in nature, due to the varied approaches comprising corrections and the different practices adopted by the fifty states and the federal government. Perhaps the best way to summarize the organization of corrections is to begin with observation of corrections at the federal level and follow with examination of how states primarily organize their correctional practices.

As of 2016, the **Federal Bureau of Prisons** within the Department of Justice operated 122 institutions and 25 community corrections offices, and contracted with 12 private companies to run private correctional institutions. The bureau oversaw roughly 190,000 federal inmates. Included in these facilities are detention centers, which, similar to jails, hold those awaiting trial. The approximately 40,000 bureau employees responsible for the day-to-day functioning of the bureau are spread throughout the United States.[2] The **U.S. Probation and Pretrial Services System** is responsible for several tasks, not the least of which is assisting the federal courts with pretrial practices and supervising federal probationers. The **U.S. Parole Commission** oversees federal parolees.

The organization of state correctional facilities is more complex, as each state designs its organizational structure. **Prisons** are state-run correctional facilities administered by the executive branch of each state government. They hold inmates serving sentences of one year or more. **Jails** hold detainees awaiting trial and those sentenced to incarceration for less than a year. In most states jails are operated by county-level officials, mostly sheriff's departments. The organization of **probation** and **parole**, both forms of **community corrections** in which offenders are supervised in the community, is more elaborate. Among the issues of concern with regard to probation is whether it should be organized in a centralized or decentralized manner meaning administered by state government or the judiciary; and combined with parole services.[3] States vary in their approach to these issues, as they consider what works best with regard to their resources and culture. Parole is administered by state parole boards, which may or may not work in conjunction with probation services. State correctional systems oversee far more offenders than the federal system as most crimes are prosecuted at the state level.

THE CORRECTIONAL POPULATION

Corrections in the United States took an interesting turn beginning in the early 1980s. Crime control became a primary focus and greater use of incarceration was a significant part of the approach. Enhanced focus on incarceration increased the number of incarcerated by

Prisons maintain very diverse populations that provide challenges for all who work or stay in them.

nearly 3.8 million between 1974 and 2001.[4] The increase has continued to a large extent, for instance as there are roughly 6.85 million adults under some form of correctional supervision, despite recent, slight decreases in the correctional population. An estimated 1 in 36 adults (roughly 2.8 percent of adults in the U.S.) was under some form of correctional supervision as of yearend 2014.[5] Much of the increased reliance on corrections to address crime was felt by minority groups.

The U.S. Bureau of Justice Statistics (BJS) provides the most accurate demographic account of prison and jail inmates. Recent reports suggest that over 2.2 million persons are incarcerated in U.S. prisons and jails, with prisons holding over two-thirds of the population.[6] Of particular interest with regard to incarceration are the overrepresentation of African Americans, the aging prison population, and the increased percentage of female offenders. Particularly, as of yearend 2014, 2.7 percent of all Black male residents in the United States were in prison, compared to 1.1 percent of Hispanic males and .5 percent of White males.[7] The median age of state prisoners in 2013 was 36, which is notably higher than the median age in previous years, for instance 1993 when the median age was 30.[8] Although females are far less likely than males to end up in prison (they account for only 7.0 percent of all prisoners), their presence in prison is growing. The number of females in prison has increased at a rate 50 percent higher than men since 1980.[9] The increased rate of incarceration for women has occurred despite recent decreases in the U.S. prison population.

Probation is the most frequently used criminal sanction. A recent BJS report noted that over 3.7 million probationers were supervised in the community in 2015, most of whom were male (75 percent). The percentage of female probationers increased from 20 percent in 2000 to 25 percent in 2015. Most probationers were White (55 percent), followed by Black (30 percent) and Hispanic probationers (13 percent).[10]

The parole population in 2015 was roughly 870,500, with males again accounting for the greatest percentage (87 percent). Of particular interest with regard to multicultural issues is the percentage of Blacks on parole (38 percent), which is largely disproportionate to their representation in the United States (about 13.3 percent). Hispanics constituted 16 percent of those on parole as of the end of 2015.[11]

These numbers provide an overview of those incarcerated and those on probation and parole. They say little of why these individuals ended up under correctional supervision and the difficulties they face. Nonetheless, the numbers provide a foundation for examination of multiculturalism as it relates to corrections. Knowing who is incarcerated or being supervised in the community facilitates discussion of the multicultural issues existent within corrections.

INCARCERATION

Incarceration, or the physical detention of an inmate, exists primarily in two forms: prison and jail. These institutions have much in common, yet they differ in several ways. Prominent among the differences is the length of sentence served by those incarcerated. Jails typically hold those serving a sentence of less than one year, while prisons hold those serving sentences of a year or more. Another significant difference is the clientele. Jails hold those unconvicted awaiting trial and those convicted of crimes.

Prisons do not hold unconvicted individuals. The demographics of jail and prison inmates are somewhat similar in the sense that one typically does not get to prison without having first entered jail. Accordingly, many of the issues associated with prisons are found in jails and vice versa.

Inmates face numerous difficulties upon being incarcerated. The challenges are so severe that several guidebooks for surviving prison life are available.[12] The loss of liberty, goods and services, autonomy, heterosexual relationships, and security are prominent among the deprivations faced by the incarcerated.[13] In his book *The Warehouse Prison*, John Irwin identifies some of the main sources of harm in the modern warehouse prison, where inmates are stockpiled much like merchandise stored in a department store warehouse. Particularly, Irwin cites the troubles associated with health and disease, psychological damages, and **prisonization**,[14] or an inmate's adaptation to the prison culture. Each of these issues makes prison life profoundly different from life outside of prison.

Female inmates face additional challenges, including concerns related to privacy, separation from their children, pregnancy, clothing and hygiene, a loss of dignity, effective programming, mental and physical health/damage, strict enforcement of prison rules, and psychological and physical safety.[15] Needless to say, institutionalization generates significant changes and demands, including forced daily interaction with individuals from diverse cultures.

Inmates from different ethnic and religious groups often have a dislike for each other, which sometimes leads to violent encounters and promotes greater separation among the groups.[16] Authors Todd Clear and colleagues noted that "Reflecting tensions in U.S. society, many prisons are marked today by racially motivated violence, organizations based on race, and voluntary segregation by inmates by race whenever possible."[17] For twenty-five years, California prisons segregated tens of thousands of inmates according to racial lines during their first sixty days in custody. The policy was designed to reduce racially motivated violence. In 2005 the state ended its practice of doing so. Ultimately, jail and prison administrators need to strategically house inmates within facilities and recognize that cultural factors influence staff and inmate safety and well-being.

Violence among inmates is of utmost concern for correctional officials. Prison rape is often mentioned with regard to prison violence, as the nature of institutionalization seems ripe for such attacks. Same-sex, regimented institutions such as prison tend to precipitate sexually deviant behavior.[18] It appears that inmate race is related to sexual violence in prison. It was found that Whites comprised 70 percent of victims of inmate-on-inmate prison and jail sexual violence; yet, they were the perpetrators in only 45 percent of such incidents. Blacks constituted 18 percent of the victims and 39 percent of the perpetrators of such attacks. Females are particularly vulnerable to sexual violence in prison, as the same research noted that between 2009 and 2011, females represented about 7 percent of all state and federal prison inmates, yet accounted for 22 percent of inmate-on-inmate victims and 33 percent of staff-on-inmate victims.[19] The **Prison Rape Elimination Act**, passed in 2003, was designed to address prison rape through developing standards to prevent incidents of sexual violence in prison, including a zero tolerance policy, emphasizing research, and information gathering.

Violence in prisons and jails extends beyond sexual attacks, and factors such as overcrowding, improper classification, and race relations certainly underlie much of the violence in prison. These and related issues, as they relate to prison and jail, are discussed below.

PRISON

You're driving along the highway after having a few too many drinks. The next thing you know you wake up in a jail cell inhaling an odor you've never smelled, nor do you care to ever again. With a heavy head, you listen to the rumblings of the other jail inmates, none of whom seem to be like you, and none seems overly friendly. Eventually, a jailer approaches your cell, only to tell you that last night you crossed the highway dividing line and killed a passing driver. Your heart drops into your stomach as you realize what you've done. Then, you realize the potential consequences of your actions, not the least of which involves taking an innocent victim's life and the fact that you're not, nor perhaps will you ever be, prepared for prison life.

You initially think and hope you'll receive a sentence of probation, as you've never been in trouble before. But, killing someone? That's pretty serious. Perhaps you can plea bargain for only a few years in prison. Still, you're not "prison material." What will you do upon entering prison, and how will you protect yourself? What about your family? What will you do upon exiting prison?

Prison life poses many difficulties for those who enter. Consider the scenario described above. Picture the offender as a middle-class, White male enrolled in college. How do you perceive this individual faring in prison? How do you envision this individual will be upon exiting prison? Would you perceive the situation differently if the offending drunk driver was an African American male with a criminal history? Do you believe that person would

Life in prison is full of many challenges, including the potential for much cultural misunderstanding and conflict.

have an easier time adjusting to prison life and life after prison? How would you fare in prison?

The detrimental effects of going to prison extend beyond the incarcerated individual. Families may struggle in response to the absence of a parent and society, in general, may experience the effects of prisonization once the individual returns to the community following incarceration. It is not unreasonable to expect that inmates will bring some effects of prison life back into society upon their release.

The impacts of incarceration are many. Of particular interest is the absence of a parent. This concern notably influences Black communities, for instance as research on incarcerated parents found that Black children in the United States were seven and a half times more likely than White children to have a parent in prison. Hispanic children were two and a half times more likely than White children to have a parent in prison.[20] The absence of a parent poses numerous challenges for all young children, particularly in relation to accountability, financial support, and overall family stress.

Have you ever visited a prison? If so, did you consider racial, ethnic, and cultural issues as they pertain to social control? If you haven't visited a prison and are interested in criminal justice you are encouraged to do so. Among the many interesting things you'll notice in prison is the diverse population under formal social control. Further, you'll notice a prisoner lifestyle that is likely much different from the one you live.

Prison Life

The prison life observed in most institutions differs from life on the outside in many facets. Prominent among the differences are the presence of a particular inmate subculture, recognition of the need to balance constitutional rights with concerns for safety and security, the enhanced influences of gang members, and the notable concerns surrounding the spread of communicable diseases. These and related issues continuously challenge prison officials, and the impact of those issues will increase as we rely on imprisonment as a primary form of social control.

Researchers have identified a subculture among prisoners that maintains characteristics different from society in general. For instance, **ultramasculinity**, or an emphasis on being strong, is a priority.[21] The **inmate code**, which involves the norms and values developed and stressed in prison, encourages toughness, insensitivity, disdain and manipulation of fellow inmates and the prison staff. The inmate code generally varies among institutions, as does inmate commitment to the code. Nevertheless, a notable trend among institutions is the social organization of inmates along racial and ethnic lines.[22] White inmates, with few exceptions, associate with White inmates, Blacks with Blacks, and Hispanics with Hispanics.[23]

Prison staff trainees often ask why prisons accommodate a large number of religions.[24] The simple answer to the question involves respect for inmates' First Amendment right to religious freedoms. Federal and state legislation may further define the religious freedoms of inmates, and prison systems have policies and procedures designed to ensure that constitutional and statutory religious rights are recognized. The American Correctional Association's standards for accreditation require that inmates be provided the right to practice religion. Such practices should be considered with concern for institutional order and safety.

Religion offers an avenue of solidarity among inmates, provides a mechanism of adjustment to incarceration for some individuals,[25] and encourages rehabilitation and overall self-improvement. Religion also provides avenues of differences among inmates and staff and sometimes generates struggles in regards to multiculturalism. The Black Muslim movement and concerns from Native Americans with regard to their religious freedoms in prisons were certainly among the factors influencing how correctional officials recognize religious practices in prison. Over the years we've seen religion play an integral role in prison organization and overall prison practices.

Many prisons permit access to religion as a form of rehabilitation. The U.S. penal system, however, has its roots in Judeo-Christian concepts of punishment and rehabilitation. Christianity is promoted and provided to Native Americans ahead of their own traditions. Judeo-Christian-based rehabilitation centers around an individual reflecting upon their own misbehavior. This contrasts the Native American belief system which involves all people, animals, and elements that constitute the universe as an interrelated force. They believe that the community contributed to some of the individual's wrongdoings, thus self-reflection and individual counseling is limited. It is argued that more effective rehabilitative approaches for Native Americans, one more in line with their cultural beliefs, would involve Native spiritual leaders to counsel inmates and the use of **sweat lodges**, which are used by many Native Americans.[26] The lodges are small huts in which ceremonies are held to cleanse spirits in a religious rite of purification and penance.

Researchers have commented on the changing nature of gangs in prisons as a new generation of inmates is incarcerated. The more-established gangs remain active in prison, although several new groups have emerged largely in response to older gang members dropping out of gang life, being segregated from the rest of prison, or going undercover.[27] These newer gangs, much like their predecessors, are heavily influenced by race and ethnicity. Table 13-1 depicts the major prison gangs and their affiliated race/ethnicity.

To be sure, street and prison gangs are largely intertwined; involvement in gang life doesn't necessarily cease upon incarceration. Pressures emanating from gang involvement on the inside or outside of prison provide numerous difficulties for any attempts to correct criminal behavior. With regard to multiculturalism, the organization and practices of prison gangs certainly highlight the significance of race and ethnicity.

Table 13.1 Major Prison Gangs

Name	Race/Ethnicity
Neta	Puerto-Rican/Hispanic
Aryan Brotherhood	White
Black Guerrilla Family	Black
Mexican Mafia	Mexican-American/Hispanic
La Nuestra Familia	Mexican-American/Hispanic
Texas Syndicate	Mexican-American/Hispanic*

*Florida Department of Corrections (n.d.), *Gang and Security Threat Group Awareness*. Accessed online at: http://www.dc.state.fl.us/pub/gangs/index.html

CULTURAL SOLIDARITY AMONG PRISON GANGS

Prison gangs increase the likelihood of violence in prison and strongly define the social structure of prison life. Gangs in prison are organized along hierarchical lines, and typically have a creed or motto, symbols signifying membership, and a constitution that guides member behavior. Further, prison gangs are divisive, adversarial factions that are largely based along racial and ethnic lines. They are more commonly found in male prisons.

The organization of prison gangs along racial and ethnic lines demonstrates the solidarity and commitment associated with various cultural groups. Examples of the divisive nature of prison gangs is found in Hispanic inmates assembling into gangs such as the Mexican Mafia and the Nuestra Familia, Black inmates belonging to the Black Guerilla Family, and White inmates being actively involved in the Aryan Brotherhood. The organization of gang-involved inmates according to race and ethnicity suggests that multiculturalism is not well-accepted among inmates.[28]

The exclusivity and seclusion associated with prison gangs prohibits in-depth understanding of prison gangs in general.

At face value, however, there is little doubt that prison gang members typically associate with those from a similar racial or ethnic background. While it is admirable that prison gang members remain committed to their ancestral heritage, aligning one's self with others simply based on race or ethnicity does little toward the advancement of multiculturalism. Almost all inmates who enter prison will return to society. Unfortunately for some former inmates, their time in prison will have been spent festering dislike and hatred for others simply based on race or ethnicity. These feelings will likely remain within the individual as they readjust to life outside prison, making it less likely that society will adopt a true appreciation of multiculturalism.

Prison life provides an excellent opportunity to test the effectiveness of pro-multicultural programs. For instance, the divisive nature of inmates among racial and ethnic lines and the captive audiences found in prisons provide ample opportunities for prison officials to "test" or "experiment" with programs that promote diversity. Promoting multiculturalism in prison has many benefits, not the least of which involves the decreased likelihood of violent behavior.

Prison life is challenging to say the least. Protecting one's self from exploitation or attack are indeed significant. Protection from disease and illness are also of concern. Consider the "cold and flu" season that occurs each winter. Both colds and the flu seem to spread quite easily, affecting large numbers of persons. Now, consider a communicable disease in prison, where individuals are confined to an institution and aren't always able to purchase over-the-counter drugs to address the ill effects of the disease.

Now, let's up the ante a bit. Let's change the communicable disease from colds and the flu to the human immunodeficiency virus (HIV) or AIDS. We most certainly need to alter our scenario in response, particularly with regard to the methods of transmitting these harmful diseases. Sharing colds and the flu is much more easily done than is transmitting HIV or AIDS. Nevertheless, inmates are at a much greater risk of obtaining and transmitting the diseases given their increased involvement in particular activities associated with transmission, including sharing dirty hypodermic needles (which have been smuggled into the facility or made from items such as pens) and engaging in unprotected sex. Absent from this discussion is the effects of other communicable diseases such as various types of hepatitis and the more easily-transmitted tuberculosis.

In 2010, the rate of AIDS-related deaths among state prisoners was lower than it was in the U.S. general population. Nevertheless, African American inmates seem to be more affected by the deadly diseases than other inmates. The rate of AIDS-related deaths for Blacks (8 per 100,000 prisoners) was notably higher than it was for Whites (5) and Hispanics (2).[29] The Centers for Disease Control and Prevention noted that the situation is more pronounced in jails, where African American men are five times as likely as White males and twice as likely as Hispanic/Latino men to be diagnosed with HIV.[30] The impacts of AIDS on African Americans is not restricted to prisons, as African Americans both within and outside of prison have a higher rate of contracting the disease than others. The fact that African Americans are overrepresented in the criminal justice system contributes to the need to recognize and treat infected individuals. The above-noted findings provide guidance for corrections officials charged with the safety and well-being of inmates.

These health and safety concerns as they relate to prison most certainly also apply to all other aspects of corrections. Those on probation and parole, and those incarcerated in jail face many of the same challenges. Jail inmates face particular challenges due to the limited amount of testing, treatment, and classification of inmates. Individuals charged with supervising offenders with communicable diseases face specific challenges, particularly as they relate to the need for face-to-face contacts, confidentiality, offenders maintaining employment, and preventing inmates from engaging in sexual contact with others.

Multiculturalism and Challenges in Prison

Prisons are full of demands, not the least of which involves the need to control a diverse group of seemingly dangerous individuals. The increasingly diverse nature of corrections poses particular difficulties, several of which are identified and discussed below. Critical issues with regard to multiculturalism and prisons involve specific needs of select groups, counseling methods that must consider cultural diversity, and overall correctional approaches designed to address cultural needs.

Many of the challenges stemming from living in a multicultural society result from society often categorizing individuals based on a particular label, trait or characteristic. Consider, for instance, the term "inmate." Many in society assume that most inmates are similar simply because they broke the law and were convicted of a crime. Yet, there are notable differences among inmates that need to be recognized before we can expect significantly positive results from incarceration or any other type of correctional intervention.

Individuals maintain several roles, belong to specific groups, and are categorized and/or stereotyped accordingly. Of particular interest in prisons and, more generally, corrections, is categorizing individuals as Hispanic. It is argued that the disaggregation of the term "Hispanic" is needed in correctional institutions in light of the diversity of the groups comprising the term. The classification of all Hispanics into one group blurs a great deal of cultural diversity.[31] Groups classified under the label "Hispanic," including Mexicans, Puerto Ricans, and Cubans show notable differences with regard to offense characteristics, criminal records, family background, and personal characteristics.[32] Prison officers and others throughout the criminal justice system should recognize the distinct characteristics of those comprising the term "Hispanic."

Perhaps one of the most effective means of observing how multiculturalism impacts corrections requires observation of how particular groups exist, coexist, and function while incarcerated. Researchers suggest that there are differences between Black and White prison inmates, perhaps due to Blacks facing discrimination from those involved in all steps of the criminal justice system.[33] Particularly, researchers have identified differences among inmates, with Black inmates more likely than White inmates to engage in conflicts with other inmates and the staff.[34] Blacks were also more likely than Whites to engage in conduct that attracted the attention of prison administrators. Racial biases on behalf of prison staff and administrators may contribute to the differential.[35]

Research on racial differences among inmates further suggests White inmates experience higher levels of fear and stress than Black inmates, and it appears that White inmates have more positive perceptions of prison officers than do their minority counterparts. It was found that Black **exmates**, those released from prison, were significantly more likely than White exmates to perceive that prison officers use too much force on inmates. Further, Whites were more likely than Blacks to believe they were treated "pretty good" in prison, and were almost twice as likely as Black or Hispanic exmates to disagree with the suggestion that prison officers treated them as if they were less than human.[36]

Race, however, is not the only variable of concern with regard to multiculturalism in corrections. Consider the prison experience of a transgendered individual. Given the emphasis on masculinity in male prisons, what obstacles does the transgendered male inmate face? Further, what challenges does this inmate pose for prison officials? At the very least, determination of what prison the inmate is sent to and the classification of the inmate are of notable significance. The inmate's right to treatment must also be considered. Should this treatment include hormones used to maintain one's transgendered appearance?

Transsexual people who haven't had genital surgery are typically classified according to their birth sex, regardless of how long they've lived as the opposite sex. Those who have had genital surgery are typically classified and housed based on their reassigned sex.[37] Some transsexual inmates are permitted to maintain their hormone treatment while in prison. Until 2010, the U.S. Bureau of Prisons provided hormones at whatever levels were maintained prior to incarceration. The policy was changed following a lawsuit, and the agency now includes transgendered women who had not started hormone therapy until after their incarceration.[38]

Homosexuality in prison poses particular difficulties for correctional officials. The extent of homosexual activity varies by prison and by the methods used to assess such behavior. Inmates report higher levels of homosexual activity than are recognized in official accounts.[39] Nevertheless, a common approach in response to homosexual activity is to do nothing or pretend it doesn't exist. This approach is limited in the sense that it may neglect nonconsensual acts of homosexuality, and it may lead to sexual discrimination claims by heterosexual inmates who may argue for conjugal visits.[40] In other words, it could be argued that heterosexual inmates are subject to sexual discrimination when they're prevented from having sexual relations while LGBT inmates are not. Other policy approaches to homosexuality in prison include providing condoms to promote safe sex, permitting conjugal visits, and the more radical approaches of establishing mixed-sex prisons (yet refraining from any physical contact), permitting homosexual activity, and promoting safe sex practices through education.[41]

Native Americans face particular problems upon entering the correctional system. As an example, Native American culture differs from the dominant culture in that maintaining eye contact may convey disrespect.[42] As noted elsewhere in this book, failure to maintain eye contact when communicating can play an integral role in miscommunication. Further, some Native Americans view being under correctional control as an extension of their ancestral experiences.[43] Many institutions limit participation in Native American healing ceremonies to individuals who are enrolled in federally recognized tribes. This policy neglects Native Americans' First Amendment right to freedom of religion and the fact that not all tribes are recognized by the federal government. The possession of items considered sacred by Native Americans is also problematic for the incarcerated and prison officials. Eagle feathers, bear claws, pipes, and other artifacts may be viewed by correctional officers as potential safety and health risks.[44] Further, Native Americans reared in traditional manners are prompted to learn through experience, which isn't always possible while incarcerated. In turn, some of the Native American culture is lost when young adults are incarcerated.[45] Gayl Edmunds, Program Director for the Indian Alcoholism Treatment Service in Wichita, Kansas, commented on the problems faced by Native Americans in the correctional system in stating that a "total lack of understanding and often, respect, for American Indian's spiritual beliefs and practices, has created fertile ground for an ethnic community that feels misunderstood, disenfranchised, and powerless."[46]

Traditional counseling methods in prison are targeted toward the White middle-class, which poses challenges for those from diverse backgrounds. Such counseling may neglect diverse beliefs, values, experiences, and behaviors maintained by the varied groups that enter prison.[47] The concentration is often focused on helping inmates adapt to the dominant culture, while neglecting multiculturalism.

The term "corrections" suggests that some form of correcting is being done. Treatment is not the primary concern of many prisons these days as punishment and deterrence have become increasingly popular. Nevertheless, counseling and therapeutic approaches are found in most, if not all prisons. Selecting a treatment approach that suits all offenders is challenging to prison officials. Particularly, inmates come from diverse backgrounds and face many obstacles. A single approach to treating the ills of all inmates will not work. Accordingly, prison officials must identify and adopt the most effective approach for each individual, something that is easier said than done.

Puerto Rican inmates, as an example, face particular challenges with regard to counseling. Puerto Rican cultural issues as they pertain to time, relationships and friends, morality, responsibility and decision making require recognition on behalf of counselors to consider how to shape their counseling efforts. For instance, cultural influences prompt Puerto Ricans inmates to believe moral issues are discussed only with family members, while in the dominant culture morality is often a public issue.[48] Recognition of these and related issues can only serve to enhance counseling inmates.

The formal and social organization of inmates highlights the significance of the classification and day-to-day functions of inmates. Multiculturalism is certainly on the minds of prison administrators who must determine, among other things, who should share a cell with whom, and what groups should eat or recreate at the same time. Failure to consider inmate hostility toward particular groups contributes to a disruptive prison. However, it could be argued that isolating inmates of different backgrounds for the sake of safety discourages tolerance and acceptance of different groups and perpetuates the associated problems.

JAIL

Jails were earlier described by some as "poorhouses of the twentieth century,"[49] "festering sores," "cesspools of crime," "teeming houses of horror," and "the ultimate ghetto."[50] These terms were offered decades ago, however it appears they remain accurate.[51] In contrast to prisons, jails are the least understood and least frequently studied component of the criminal justice system.[52] Yet, the significance of jails to the criminal justice system cannot be understated. Particularly:

- more people pass through jail than through prison
- critical decisions are often made while inmates remain in jail or are released on bond
- jail-related experiences often influence inmates' minds, and
- jail arguably imposes the cruelest means of punishment in the United States.[53]

Jails have a constantly changing population and much potential for cultural misunderstanding and conflict. Jail officials can eliminate their need to engage in physical forms of social control through greater understanding of cultural differences. Entering jail can be a traumatic experience for some who may soon realize that they face an unpleasant environment. Their reaction can be violence directed toward themselves (e.g., suicide) or others, including jail officials and/or other inmates. Effective assessment of an individual's dangerousness is facilitated through better understanding of those who enter jail.

Effectively assessing individuals requires recognition of cultural backgrounds. Behaviors or responses that seem dangerous may be attributable to cultural practices. Cultural practices seemingly influence assessment practices regarding the suicidal risks of American Indians placed in jail. Particularly, researchers found that American Indians are discomforted by the interview process involved in screening practices concerning jail inmate suicide. Many American Indians considered the screening intrusive and feared the repercussions of admitting a propensity to harm themselves. These, and related reactions were not found among non-Indian counterparts. Part of the American Indian reactions and responses to the suicide risk screening is attributed to the American Indian concept of respect, which discourages prying into the innermost thoughts and feelings of others as is done in suicide screening.[54]

Jails differ from prisons in several ways. Among the differences are the higher turnover rate of inmates, the enhanced control over inmates, and the limited influence of an inmate subculture found in jails.[55] Much of the research literature on incarceration focuses on life in prison, in contrast to the scant study of jails.[56] One area of neglect is research on violence in jails.[57] What is known, however, suggests that many of the same factors influencing prison violence affect violence in jails. Particularly, overcrowding, poorly trained correctional staffs, acts of social injustice, and offender personalities are among the factors influencing jail violence.[58] Inmate age also influences behavior, as younger inmates are generally more unruly than their older counterparts. Researchers found mixed results exist with regard to inmate misconduct and race,[59] although it appears that Black inmates are more often written up for misconduct than are other groups. The disproportionality is possibly the result of reactions to perceived mistreatment, including closer scrutinization of Black inmates by correctional officials.[60]

For some individuals, entering jail is a traumatic experience. The ones most influenced by jail placement may be most vulnerable to treatment. Accordingly, jails sometimes have chaplains, clergy, and related individuals who interact with inmates in attempts to make the most of a difficult situation. These groups are also present in prisons, however, their influence on jail inmates is of importance given the vulnerability of some inmates. Among the benefits of providing religious faith and spirituality in jails (and prisons for that matter) are positive influences on character development, recovery from various types of addiction, and overall transformation and rehabilitation.[61] Providing jail chaplains or clergy who recognize different faiths provides for a more effective jail experience[62] and demonstrates the significance of concerns for multiculturalism in the criminal justice system.

COMMUNITY CORRECTIONS

Community corrections involves correctional supervision provided outside an institution. Community corrections personnel are expected to rehabilitate, monitor, and manage offenders outside of strict institutional settings. The practice is traced back to the pre-revolutionary colonial period, although at that time the community was not viewed as either a cause of crime, nor as an avenue to correct criminal behavior.[63] Today, community corrections is used largely to reduce prison overcrowding. Correctional practices in the community include probation, parole, halfway houses, residential centers, and work furloughs.

Correctional supervision in the community is preferable to most inmates and is often used by courts and correctional personnel as an incentive toward good behavior. Offenders typically view community supervision as preferable to incarceration, yet they remain aware that misbehavior could result in (re)commitment to prison or jail. Determining who receives community corrections involves discretion and opens opportunities for differential treatment of various groups. The situation is perhaps best summed by researchers Todd Clear and Harry Dammer, who note:

> Where there is discretion, there is the possibility of abuse of decision-making authority. Judges, parole boards, and program administrators are human. When they consider an offender for a community program in place of incarceration, they are looking for attributes that give reason to believe the offender will succeed in that program. It is not difficult to imagine that some of those attributes might be correlated with social statuses we think are not permissible for them to use. The most significant problems have to do with race and ethnicity.[64]

Clear and Dammer comment on the difficulties faced by Black Americans in the criminal justice system, who are more likely than their White counterparts to be unemployed, be less educated, be younger, be less skilled, and have a more serious criminal record. These characteristics could result in a partiality that involves biases in selecting clients for community corrections.[65]

Gender discrimination is also apparent with regard to community corrections programs. Aside from having some different needs or concerns than males undergoing community corrections (e.g., a female is more likely to be a single parent), females also face difficulties stemming from community corrections programs that often structure their strategies toward males.[66] This could result in an emphasis on surveillance and control at the expense of support, the latter being of greater importance to females than males.[67]

Probation and parole are the most frequently used forms of community corrections. The terms "probation" and "parole" are often used to refer to the same thing: supervision in the community. However, they differ in several ways. Probation is a front-end strategy in which judicial bodies place conditions on offenders in lieu of incarceration. Parole is a back-end strategy that it is imposed following a period of incarceration. Many of the challenges of dealing with multiculturalism and probationers are evident with regard to parolees, as both require supervision in the community. Recognizing cultural differences in the manner in which supervision is conducted benefits both the supervising agents and the individuals under supervision.

PROBATION

Probation practices in the United States are traced back to 1841 when shoemaker John Augustus assisted minor offenders. Augustus would offer to supervise offenders in the community. Probation is defined as conditional freedom offered by a judicial officer to an alleged or adjudged offender, provided the individual abides by certain conditions of behavior. Conditions of probation may involve offenders submitting to random drug tests,

Probation and parole officers regularly work with diverse populations in ensuring that offenders are properly supervised in the community.

obeying curfews, reporting to a probation officer on a regular basis, and/or avoiding particular individuals or locations. Judges may impose a prison sentence upon an offender following a guilty verdict and subsequently suspend the sentence in lieu of probation. The offender would be accountable for their actions and subject to additional penalties should they commit another crime. Should they violate the terms of their probation, or commit what is referred to as a **technical violation**, they would serve the suspended sentence of incarceration. Technical violations involve infractions committed by those on probation or parole that are not necessarily illegal, however, they violate the terms of the probation or parole agreement. Signing a contract or changing residences without permission are two of the more recognizable types of technical violations.

Investigation and supervision are at the heart of probation. Investigation involves preparing and presenting a presentence investigation report to judges involved in sentencing hearings. Supervision involves what most people associate with probation: supervising offenders in the community. The difficulties associated with the supervisory component of probation is perhaps best summed by author Todd Clear and colleagues, who identify the informal nature of the supervisory aspect of probation "as a complex interaction between officers (who vary in style, knowledge, and philosophy) and offenders (who vary in responsiveness and need for supervision) in a bureaucratic organization that imposes significant formal and informal constraints on the work."[68]

Supervising probationers generally consists of three primary components, including the probation officer establishing a relationship with the offender and defining the roles of the probationer and probation officer; the officer and offender establishing supervision goals to assist the offender with complying with the conditions set by the court, and; the officer deciding how to the probation period will be terminated (e.g., early termination, expiration of sentence, revocation).[69] Perhaps the most significant aspect of probation involves enforcing the terms of probation. Enforcement of probationer behavior requires probation officers to properly process cases in which probationers commit new offenses or technical violations. The discretion inherent in this aspect of the job provides probation officers the power to involve or avoid judicial intervention when dealing with minor infractions. In other words, probation officers use their discretion to formally or informally confront problematic situations. They may also choose to ignore the problem. An officer's level of discretion decreases as the severity of the violation increases.

Is it possible for probation officers to use their discretion in an unfair and biased manner through bringing minor infractions of particular groups to attention of the courts, yet not doing so for other groups? Absolutely. How often this happens is unknown, although it could be argued that one time is too many. Discretion to involve or avoid contact with judges provides an avenue for the differential treatment of probationers. Probation officers working in a jurisdiction where judges closely follow the probation revocation recommendations of the probation officer maintain notable influence on the outcome of the revocation hearing. Officers possessing a solid understanding and appreciation of different cultures reduce the likelihood that probationers will be treated unfairly.

Research on probation revocation practices found that young Black male individuals received the harshest penalties, while Hispanics and Whites were generally treated the same. Further, one's employment status at the time of their probation violation seemed to offer no support for young Black males since employed young Black males received harsher treatment than their White unemployed counterparts. The lack of statutory or administrative guidelines permits wide judicial discretion with regard to probation revocation.[70]

An offender's response to the supervision they're provided influences the effectiveness of their probation sentence. Put simply, how probationers respond to a probation officer's supervisory powers greatly affects the probationer's behavior. How the roles of probationers and probation officer are initially established influences supervision practices, and differences among cultures dictate that different approaches to establish and enforce "supervisor-supervised relationships" are needed.

The diverse nature of the individuals entering our correctional agencies dictates that corrections personnel maintain a keen awareness of cultural differences, for instance, as they relate to transgendered and transsexual persons. Many probation officers will at some point encounter a transgender person. Those who lack knowledge about transgenderism feel less confident than those with more knowledge in dealing with specific issues as they pertain to transgenderism.[71] Privacy and confidentiality are primary among the issues raised when dealing with transgendered probationers. The need to understand one's transgendered status becomes important for presentence investigation reports, particularly if the punishment may involve incarceration.[72] Probation officers must appropriately confront their own perceptions of transgenderism when dealing with these individuals, and recognize that transgendered individuals have higher rates of psychological and substance abuse problems than their counterparts.[73] The difficulties associated with the social isolation of many transgendered individuals are compounded by probation officers not overly familiar with support networks for transgendered persons.[74]

The vast number of individuals entering probation comes from diverse cultures. The extensive and diverse caseloads maintained by probation officers require staff recognition of multicultural issues. Cross-cultural barriers provide a primary impediment to constructing an effective officer-client relationship.[75] Diversifying probation officer staffs is a step in the right direction, as these individuals provide many contributions to offender supervision in the community. However, there remains a significant need to ensure that field officers recognize, consider, and appreciate cultural differences. Sincerity, high service energy, knowledge of a client's culture, resourcefulness, and a nonjudgmental attitude are characteristic of a culturally competent probation officer.[76] Having a solid grasp of the innuendos of multiculturalism and actively questioning one's assumptions regarding particular groups undoubtedly contribute to the effectiveness of probation officer supervision.

RELEASE FROM PRISON AND PAROLE

Inmates are released from prison conditionally or unconditionally. Those released under conditions face community supervision for a specified time upon exiting prison. **Conditional release** can involve **discretionary release**, for instance when a parole board grants an inmate parole, or inmates can receive **mandatory release** in states that have abandoned traditional parole practices in favor of **"good time"** practices. States using mandatory release eliminate parole board discretion through a policy in which inmates earn time off of their prison sentence through various incentives, such as behaving appropriately in prison and taking advantage of self-improvement programs. Individuals released unconditionally have "maxed out" or served their entire sentence and are released from prison without conditions or supervision in the community.

Unlike probationers, parolees have spent time in prison and face particular obstacles. Prominent among the difficulties faced by those released from prison are: the influences of prisonization; being labeled a "former prisoner"; losing the right to vote, hold public office, or sign contracts in some states; and surviving without much state support. The need to find employment and re-establish ties with family and community members pose particular problems for some parolees. The financial cutbacks in many prisons have contributed to some inmates failing to address the factors leading to their incarceration. Financial concerns have led some prisons to reduce the number of counseling and treatment opportunities for inmates.

The increased number of prisoners beginning in the 1980s generated an increased focused on **reentry**, or an inmate's return to society. Providing support for inmates who are reentering society contributes to their avoiding a return to prison. Government and private groups have emerged in efforts to assist former inmates. For instance, the Ban the Box campaign emerged in the late 1990s in the United States when civil rights groups and advocates sought to encourage employers to remove the box that asks job applicants if they have a criminal record. As of 2016, over forty-five cities and counties have altered their hiring practices in public employment to limit the negative impacts of asking about arrest or conviction records.[77]

While the challenges of parole apply to all groups, cultures, and individuals, the disproportionate number of African American prisoners in the United States results in enhanced struggles for this group. One could argue that failing to address the initial causes underlying the incarceration and the difficulties of adjusting to parole perpetuate the overrepresentation of Blacks in prison and the criminal justice system in general.

Parole board members in most states are typically appointed by a governor for a fixed period of time. Members primarily assess inmate suitability for parole and assist with parole policy development. Participation on a parole board requires thorough knowledge of crime, justice, and human behavior, and recognition and appreciation of cultural diversity. A preparole investigation report, similar to a presentence investigation report, containing vital information regarding the potential parolee assists parole board members with their decision. Parole board member discretion in determining whether or not to grant an inmate parole is notable for any discussion of multiculturalism in corrections.

Those currently released on parole are being supervised by parole officers emphasizing *surveillance* over *assistance* even though both components are essential to parole. It is argued that inmates are receiving longer prison sentences coupled with limited pre-release or rehabilitation programs. This problem is compounded by the increased level of disorganization and disadvantages in the communities to which inmates are returning, inmates' families being less likely to support them upon their release, and fewer available social services for parolees.[78]

Parole officers supervise parolees and are influential in determining who is brought to the attention of the court following parole violations. Their duties are quite similar to those provided by probation officers. Parole officers provide law enforcement services and social services primarily through ensuring that parolees abide by the terms of their parole agreement and referring parolees to social services as needed.

One's parole can be revoked following the commission of a new offense or a technical violation of an individual's parole agreement. As noted, parole officers use their discretion to decide whether or not to pursue revocation of parole, an issue of particular significance with concern for multiculturalism.

Aside from parole or maxing out, inmates are released from prison via other means. Inmates may be granted **clemency**, which permits legislative action to reduce the severity of one's punishment, waive the punishment associated with a crime, or exclude certain individuals from prosecution of a specific crime. Clemency comes in the form of pardons, amnesty, commutations, and reprieves. **Pardons** involve the restoration of a former inmate's rights and privileges. **Amnesty** is similar to pardons, although it involves groups of people instead of individuals. Granting rights and privileges to illegal aliens is an example of amnesty. **Commutations** involve shortening or changing an inmate's prison sentence, for instance when one becomes terminally ill or death sentences are switched to sentences of life in prison. They may also be used for other reasons, for instance as President Barak Obama commuted the sentences of over 350 inmates who he believed were the victims of particularly harsh sentences. **Reprieves** involve the postponement of a sentence and are typically associated with delaying an execution. The decision to grant clemency is often influenced by several individuals. The extent to which cultural diversity influences such decisions remains unknown. Given historical use of discretion in the criminal justice system, it can be stated with modest confidence that multicultural issues play a role in decision-making.

CORRECTIONAL STAFF AND TRAINING

Commenting on the difficulties of working with a correctional staff, Deputy Secretary Mary Leftridge Byrd of the Pennsylvania Department of Corrections stated, "The convergence of public expectation, responsibilities of correctional professionals, and demands of the correctional environment, coupled with the cultural influence of the large world, creates incredible dynamics."[79] The hands-on approach of correctional professionals evident throughout corrections requires directed attention toward multiculturalism. Given the day-to-day interaction between those under correctional supervision and those supervising, it is important to recognize the training and preparation of correctional officials with regard to multiculturalism.

DIVERSITY AND CORRECTIONAL STAFF

Several trends have impacted the correctional workforce. Prominent among the trends are the increased number of privately-operated prisons, the continued introduction of technology, the imposition of standards on correctional facilities by outside agencies, and changes in the workforce demographics.[80] With regard to the latter, the demographic changes involve increases in the number of female and minority correctional staff.

Diversity among correctional staff was limited until about thirty to forty years ago. The infamous 1971 rioting at the Attica Correctional Facility in New York was largely encouraged by inmate perceptions of the correctional staff's inability and failure to recognize and respect varying cultures, ethnic backgrounds, and religious practices and rights.[81] The lack

The close contact between inmates and correctional staff mandates the need for all to maintain an understanding and appreciation of diversity.

of multicultural awareness contributing to the rioting is evidenced by the staff's seeming lack of concern for religious beliefs. As noted by author Howard Abadinsky:

> Attica had a large number of Black Muslims (members of the Nation of Islam) who had difficulty with a prison diet that was heavy with pork. Muslims also objected to the lack of ministers. Correctional officials would not allow the ministers, many of whom had prison records, into Attica. Black Muslims spent their recreation time in the yard engaging in worship and highly disciplined physical exercise. The correctional staff, which never understood the Black Muslims, was quite fearful of this group, who exhibited military-type discipline and remained aloof from both staff and other inmates.[82]

Accordingly, Black Muslims played a significant role in the rioting that ensued.

Since the time of the Attica prison riot there has been increased representation of various ethnic and racial minority groups among correctional staffs and the benefits have become obvious to corrections professionals. The opportunities of diverse groups to work together in correctional settings facilitate staff interaction and learning from one another. Creating a diverse correctional staff also encourages inmates to recognize that the criminal justice system does not solely consist of middle-class White men who don't understand cultural diversity.

Prisons were historically built in rural locations, often in areas with homogenous populations from which staff members were drawn. The inmates placed in these institutions, however, often hailed from urban, more heterogeneous areas.[83] Such a situation clearly encourages culture-based conflict. Differences between the traditional rural-White prison officer and the urban-minority prisoner still exist in some states, although they have largely diminished in large, more urban states.[84] Creating a diverse staff provides several challenges like encouraging minority workers to move to rural locations; minorities finding employment in more attractive public service and private industry positions; and the unwillingness of some minorities to work in a system they view as racist.[85] Equal opportunity programs have assisted in diversifying correctional staff; however, working in prisons where racial and ethnic tensions contribute to an already challenging situation discourages some minorities from seeking such work.

Non-Whites, particularly African Americans, have increasingly assumed prison staff positions. Unfortunately, they've faced many obstacles working in prison. Early resentment from White officers, many of whom hailed from rural backgrounds, was complemented by the perception that Black prison officers would be more sympathetic to inmates, particularly Black inmates.[86] Black and Latino officers would soon be accepted into the prison officer culture. Inmates currently recognize little difference among White and non-White officers.[87] It is projected that females and minorities will increasingly join correctional staffs and bring their cultural beliefs and backgrounds into an arena that has long been secluded from such input.

There is sometimes an assumption among inmates that cultural similarities will outweigh prison officer responsibilities and commitment to the job.[88] In other words, some inmates feel that prison officers will provide favoritism to inmates from similar cultures. Determining the extent to which prison officers let cultural influences dictate their actions is difficult, if not impossible. However, we would be foolish to believe that cultural influences are completely unrelated to officer discretion.

Research has produced mixed results with regard to the differences among correctional officer attitudes and practices. Some suggest minority officers assume more punitive attitudes toward inmates than do White officers.[89] Other studies suggest the opposite[90] or argue there's no difference between the groups.[91] Some suggest African American correctional officers are more likely than their White counterparts to support rehabilitative practices and are more likely to perceive the current court system as too harsh.[92] Nevertheless, there is not enough research support to comfortably state that minority correctional officers use their discretion differently than nonminority officers.

SUMMARY

None of the many facets of corrections is exempt from multicultural concerns. The diversity within our correctional system warrants significant societal attention. What type of attention is needed and what can society do? Being tolerant of diversity would break down many barriers between cultural groups. Trying to understand the many cultural lifestyles found in society may help us better understand why people commit crime and how we can correct their behavior.

Cultural intolerance has existed for some time. So has the inability of correctional practices to fully correct. These statements, taken together, do not imply that becoming tolerant of other cultures will substantially change corrections. There are far too many variables involved with correctional practices to suggest that enhanced tolerance is the solution to solving crime. However, understanding the uniqueness of individuals and groups certainly plays a significant role in correcting human behavior.

What can we expect with regard to multiculturalism and corrections in the near future? The increased presence of females and minorities on correctional staffs suggests a more diverse correctional workforce. Such diversity will seemingly coincide with an increasingly diverse correctional population. Demographic trends suggest increased minority representation in the larger society, and statistical trends suggest greater representation of minorities under correctional supervision. It is hoped that the continuous search for alternatives to crime can someday eliminate the need for correctional intervention.

YOU MAKE THE CALL

PROBATION OFFICER CHALLENGES

Consider the following scenario. Debate the pros and cons of all options and decide what you would do.

You became a probation officer because you like to help people and you appreciate the spontaneity associated with the job. As an African American male, you face particular challenges when visiting your clients, especially those who live in predominantly nonminority neighborhoods. On one occasion you were (wrongfully) stopped by police who claimed you failed to come to a complete stop at a stop sign as you approached a probationer's home. Personally, you believe the officers were engaging in racial profiling. You decide not to let it bother you. However, three weeks later, officers (again wrongfully) stopped you in the same neighborhood claiming that you failed to signal during a lane change. Again, you believe the officers were targeting you because you're a Black man in a predominantly White neighborhood. To make matters worse, you receive suspicious looks from the citizens in the community, and have had the police slowly drive by and monitor your actions as you walked toward your probationer's home. Your probationer is a blatant racist who has no respect for you and on several occasions has filed claims of impropriety on your behalf. You like the job, but begin to wonder whether the hassles are worth it.

Questions

1. Should you simply explain to the police officers why you're in the neighborhood, ignore the unjustified stops, or report the wrongful actions of the police to the police department or some other official agency?
2. Should you request to be removed from this client's case, in light of the disturbance your presence causes in the neighborhood?
3. Should you attempt to enlighten the probationer's racist attitude, adopt a more punitive approach toward him, or ignore his shortsighted racist behavior?
4. Do you believe your continuous presence as a probation officer of color in the neighborhood helps or hinders efforts toward multiculturalism? In other words, do you believe it is a positive experience for citizens to have diversity in their surroundings?

KEY TERMS

amnesty
clemency
community corrections
commutations
conditional release
discretionary release
exmates
Federal Bureau of Prisons
good time
incarceration
inmate code
jail
mandatory release

pardons
parole
prison
Prison Rape Elimination Act
prisonization
probation
reentry
reprieves
sweat lodges
technical violation
U.S. Parole Commission
U.S. Probation and Pretrial Services System
ultramasculinity

DISCUSSION QUESTIONS

1. How are correctional agencies organized? Do you believe that a centralized approach to corrections (e.g., in the form of one unified correctional system) would be more effective than our fragmented approach?
2. Discuss the difficulties of being incarcerated.
3. What particular challenges do Native Americans face upon incarceration?
4. Why is concern for multiculturalism of significance to probation and parole officers? What steps can be taken to address these concerns?
5. Discuss the evolution of diversity in corrections. Why is it important for correctional agencies to incorporate cultural diversity into their staffs?

FOR FURTHER READING

Alexander, M. *The New Jim Crow: Mass Incarceration in the Age of Colorblindness*. Jackson, TN: New Press, 2010.

Irwin, John. *The Warehouse Prison: Disposal of the New Dangerous Class*. Los Angeles, CA: Roxbury, 2005.

Petersilia, J. *When Prisoners Come Home: Parole and Prisoner Reentry*. New York: Oxford University Press, 2009.

Smalls, C., ed. *The Full Spectrum: Essays on Staff Diversity in Corrections*. Lanham, MD: American Correctional Association, 2004.

Sykes, Gresham M. *The Society of Captives*. Princeton, NJ: Princeton University Press, 1958/2007.

NOTES

1. Burk Foster, *Corrections: The Fundamentals* (Upper Saddle River, NJ: Prentice Hall, 2006).
2. "About the Bureau of Prisons." Available at: https://www.bop.gov/about/agency/.
3. T. R. Clear, M. D. Reisig, and G. F. Cole, *American Corrections*, 11th edition (Boston, MA: Cengage, 2016).
4. Thomas P. Bonczar, *Prevalence of Imprisonment in the U.S. Population, 1974-2001*. U.S. Department of Justice, Bureau of Justice Statistics, August 2003. NCJ 197976. P. 3
5. D. Kaeble, L. Glaze, A. Tsoutis, and T. Minton, *Correctional Populations in the United States, 2014*. U.S. Department of Justice, Bureau of Justice Statistics, 2015. NCJ 249513. P. 1.
6. Ibid. P. 2.
7. E. A. Carson, *Prisoners in 2014*. U.S, Department of Justice, Bureau of Justice Statistics, 2015. NCJ 248955. P. 15.
8. E. A. Carson, *Aging of the State Prison Population, 1993–2013*. U.S. Department of Justice, Bureau of Justice Statistics, 2016. NCJ 248766. P. 1.
9. The Sentencing Project, *Trends in Corrections*, 2015. Accessed online at: http://www.sentencingproject.org/publications/trends-in-u-s-corrections/
10. D. Kaeble and T. P. Bonczar, *Probation and Parole in the United States, 2015*. U.S. Department of Justice, Bureau of Justice Statistics, 2016. NCJ 250230. P. 5.
11. Ibid. P. 7.
12. E.g., Jeffrey Ian Ross and Stephen C. Richards, *Behind Bars: Surviving Prison* (Indianapolis IN: Alpha, 2002); and Jim Hogshire, *You Are Going to Prison* (Port Townsend, WA: Loompanics Unlimited, 1994).
13. Gresham M. Sykes, *The Society of Captives* (Princeton, NJ: Princeton University Press, 1958).

14. John Irwin, *The Warehouse Prison: Disposal of the New Dangerous Class* (Los Angeles, CA: Roxbury, 2005).

15. Barbara Owen, "The Case of Women: Gendered Harm in the Contemporary Prison," in *The Warehouse Prison: Disposal of the New Dangerous Class*, ed. J. Irwin (Los Angeles, CA: Roxbury, 2005), 264–89.

16. Daniel Moriarty, "Training Detention Officers to Understand Inmate Behavior," *Corrections Today* (Dec. 1991): 72, 74–75.

17. Clear, et al., *American Corrections*, 281.

18. Niyi Awofeso, "Managing Homosexuality in Prison: A Brief Review of Policy Options," *American Jails*, Jan./Feb. 2005): 79–81.

19. A. J. Beck and R. R. Rantala, *Sexual Victimization Reported by Adult Correctional Authorities, 2009–2011*. U.S. Department of Justice, Bureau of Justice Statistics, 2014. NCJ 243904. P. 1.

20. L. E. Glaze and L. M. Maruschak, *Parents in Prison and their Minor Children*. U.S. Department of Justice, Bureau of Justice Statistics, 2008. NCJ 222984. P. 2.

21. Don Sabo, Terry A. Kupers, and Willie London, "Gender and the Politics of Punishment," in *Prison Masculinities*, ed. Don Sabo, Terry A. Kupers, and Willie London (Philadelphia, PA: Temple University Press, 2001), 3.

22. E.g., Sabo et al., "Gender and the Politics of Punishment"; Ross and Richards *Behind Bars*.

23. Ross and Richards, *Behind Bars*.

24. Doris Woodruff-Filbey, "Religious Diversity: A Kaleidoscope of Faiths," in *The Full Spectrum: Essays on Staff Diversity in Corrections*, ed. C. Smalls (Lanham, MD: American Correctional Association, 2004), 53–64.

25. S. Walker, C. Spohn, and M. DeLone, *The Color of Justice*, 5th ed. (Belmont, CA: Wadsworth, 2012).

26. J. Saleem, "Native American spirituality in the United States prison system: Part 2: Legal restrictions on spirituality," MulticulturalFamilia.com, March 6, 2012. Accessed online at: http://www.multiculturalfamilia.com/2012/03/06/native-american-spirituality-in-the-united-states-prison-system-part-2-legal-restrictions-on-spirituality/

27. Geoffrey Hunt, Stephanie Riegel, Tomas Morales, and Dan Waldorf, "Changes in Prison Culture: Prison Gangs and the Case of the 'Pepsi Generation,'" *Social Problems* 40, no. 3 (1993): 398–409.

28. B. Foster, *Corrections: The Fundamentals* (Upper Saddle River, NJ: Prentice Hall, 2006).

29. Laura M. Maruschak, *HIV in Prisons, 2001–2010*. U.S. Department of Justice, Bureau of Justice Statistics, 2012. NCJ 238877.

30. Centers for Disease Control and Prevention, *HIV Among Incarcerated Populations*, 2015. Accessed online at: http://www.cdc.gov/hiv/group/correctional.html

31. D. J. Martinez, "Hispanics Incarcerated in State Correctional Facilities: Variations in Inmate Characteristics Across Hispanic Subgroups," *Journal of Ethnicity in Criminal Justice* 2, no. 1/2 (2004): 119–31.

32. Ibid.

33. Craig Hemmens and James W. Marquart, "Friend or Foe? Race, Age, and Inmate Perceptions of Inmate-Staff Relations," *Journal of Criminal Justice* 28 (2000): 297–312.

34. Ibid.

35. T. J. Flanagan, "Correlates of Institutional Misconduct Among State Prisoners," *Criminology* 21 (1983): 29–39.

36. Hemmens and Marquart, "Friend or Foe?"

37. See *Farmer v. Brennan*, 511 U.S. 825, 829 (1994); *Farmer v. Haas*, 990 F.2d 319, 320 (7th Cir. 1993).

38. J. Keenan, "Getting Hormones and Surgery for Transgender Prisoners," *The Atlantic*, Aug. 23, 2013. Accessed online at: http://www.theatlantic.com/health/archive/2013/08/getting-hormones-and-surgery-for-transgender-prisoners/278998/

39. Awofeso, "Managing Homosexuality."
40. Ibid.
41. Ibid.
42. Gary Cesarz and Joyce Madrid-Bustos, "Taking a Multicultural World View in Today's Corrections Facilities," *Corrections Today* (Dec. 1991): 68, 70–71.
43. William G. Archambeault, "The Web of Steel and the Heart of the Eagle: The Contextual Interface of American Corrections and Native Americans," *The Prison Journal* 83, no. 1 (2003): 3–25.
44. Ibid.
45. Ibid.
46. Gayl R. Edmunds, "American Indians," in C. Smalls *The Full Spectrum*, 82.
47. Edil Torres Rivera, Michael P. Wilbur, and Janice Roberts-Wilbur, "The Puerto Rican Prison Experience: A Multicultural Understanding of Values, Beliefs, and Attitudes," *Journal of Addictions & Offender Counseling* 18, no. 2 (1998): 63–78.
48. Ibid.
49. R. Goldfarb, *Jails: The Ultimate Ghetto* (Garden City, NY: Doubleday, 1975), 29.
50. J. Thompson, "The American Jail: Problems, Politics, and Prospects," *American Journal of Criminal Justice* 10 (1986): 205
51. See for example Michelle Mark and Associated Press. "Report: New York's Biggest Jail has a Huge Problem with Sexual Abuse." Businessinsider.com. Accessed online at: http://www.businessinsider.com/ap-apnewsbreak-report-assails-nyc-jails-sex-abuse-response-2016-6 (2016, June 21).
52. R. Kiekbusch, "Misinformation About the American Jail and Our Duty to Inform," *American Jails* (March/April 1999): 119.
53. J. Irwin, *The Jail: Managing the Underclass in American Society* (Berkeley, CA: University of California Press, 2013), xxii.
54. A. R. Gonzalez, T. A. Henke, and S. V. Hart, "American Indian Suicides in Jail: Can Risk Screening Be Culturally Sensitive?" U.S. Department of Justice, Office of Justice Programs, June 2005. NCJ 207326, 4.
55. J. D. Senese and D. B. Kalinich, "A Study of Jail Inmate Misconduct: An Analysis of Rule Violations and Official Processing," *Journal of Crime & Justice* 15, no. 1 (1993): 131–47.
56. R. Burns, "Assessing Jail Coverage in Introductory Criminal Justice Textbooks," *Journal of Criminal Justice Education* 13, no. 1 (2002): 87–100.
57. P. F. McManimon Jr., "Correlates of Jail Violence," *American Jails*, May/June 2004): 41–43, 45–47.
58. M. Braswell, S. Dillingham, and R. Montgomery Jr., *Prison Violence in America*, (New York: Anderson, 1985).
59. McManimon, "Correlates of Jail Violence."
60. E. D. Poole and R. M. Regoli, "Race, Institutional Rule Breaking, and Disciplinary Decision Making in Prison," *Law and Society Review* 14, no. 4 (1980): 931–46.
61. Robert Toll, "How a Multifaith Chaplaincy Program Operates in a County Detention Facility," *American Jails* (January/February 2004): 19–24.
62. Ken Kerle, "Religion and Jails," *American Jails* (May/June 2004): 5. See also Toll, "How a Multifaith Chaplaincy Program Operates."
63. Mark C. Dean-Myrda and Francis T. Cullen (1998). "The Panacea Pendulum: An Account of Community Response to Crime," in *Community Corrections: Probation, Parole, and Intermediate Sanctions*, ed. J. Petersilia (New York: Oxford University Press, 1998), 3–18.
64. Todd R. Clear and Harry R. Dammer, *The Offender in the Community* (Belmont, CA: Wadsworth, 2000), 40.
65. Ibid.

66. Ibid.

67. Ibid.

68. Clear, et al., *American Corrections*, 209.

69. Ibid.

70. Michael Tapia and Patricia M. Harris, "Race and Revocation: Is There a Penalty for Young, Minority Males?" *Journal of Ethnicity in Criminal Justice* 4, no. 3 (2006): 1–25.

71. Lindsey Poole, Stephen Whittle, and Paula Stephens, "Working with Transgendered and Transsexual People As Offenders in the Probation Service," *Probation Journal* 49, no. 3 (2002): 227–32.

72. Ibid.

73. Ibid.

74. Ibid.

75. Robert A. Shearer and Patricia Ann King, "Multicultural Competencies in Probation: Issues and Challenges," *Federal Probation* 68, no. 1 (June 2004): 3–9.

76. M. Sanders, "Building Bridges Instead of Walls: Effective Cross-Cultural Counseling," *Corrections Today* 65, no. 1 (2003): 58–59.

77. Ban the Box, About: Ban the Box Campaign, 2016. Accessed online at: http://bantheboxcampaign.org/about/#.WFfj7XeZPEY

78. R. P. Seiter and K. R. Kadela, " Prisoner Reentry: What Works, What Does Not, and What Is Promising." *Crime & Delinquency* 49, no. 3 (2003): 360–88.

79. Mary V. Leftridge Byrd, "African-American Women in Corrections," in Smalls, *The Full Spectrum*, 115.

80. Portia Hunt, "Correctional Officers Need Cultural Diversity Training," in Smalls, *The Full Spectrum*, 127–55.

81. Joe W. Booker Jr. "Staff Equality: A Welcomed Addition to the Correctional Workplace," *Corrections Today* (1999): 95.

82. H. Abadinsky, *Probation & Parole: Theory & Practice*, 12th ed. (Upper Saddle River, NJ: Pearson, 2015), 79.

83. Booker, "Staff Equality."

84. Irwin, *The Warehouse Prison*.

85. Scott Camp, William G. Saylor, and Kevin N. Wright, "Racial Diversity of Correctional Workers and Inmates: Organizational Commitment, Teamwork, and Workers' Efficacy in Prisons," *Justice Quarterly* 18, no. 2 (2001): 411–27.

86. Byrd, "African American Women."

87. Ibid.

88. Ana T. Aguire, "Latinos in Corrections: One View," in Smalls, *The Full Spectrum*, 65–74.

89. J. B. Jacobs and L. Kraft, "Integrating the Keepers: A Comparison of Black and White Prison Guards in Illinois," *Social Problems* 25 (1978): 304–18.

90. N. Jurik, "Individual and Organizational Determinants of Correctional Officer Attitudes Towards Inmates," *Criminology* 23 (1985): 523–39.

91. B. M. Crouch and G. P. Alpert, "Prison Guards' Attitudes Towards Components of the Criminal Justice System," *Criminology* 18 (1982): 227–36.

92. John A. Arthur, "Correctional Ideology of Black Correctional Officers," *Federal Probation* 58 (1994): 57–65.

CHAPTER 14

PREPARING FOR MULTICULTURALISM IN THE CRIMINAL JUSTICE SYSTEM: TRAINING AND POLICY

CHAPTER OBJECTIVES

After reading this chapter, you should be able to:

- Understand the role of education with regard to training
- Describe the types of training provided for criminal justice professionals
- Explain why training alone cannot prepare criminal justice personnel for the many diversity-related challenges they will encounter
- Demonstrate how criminal justice policies have impacted less powerful groups in society
- Explain the benefits of maintaining a global perspective with regard to policy-making

In June 2016, the Kentucky Commissioner of Corrections declared that prison policies that banned inmate mail that dealt with or promoted homosexuality were unacceptable. The policy was believed to unfairly target gay inmates. A few months earlier, the city of Allentown (PA) paid $100,000 to settle a lawsuit regarding a police officer's use of a stun gun against a fourteen-year-old girl. The lawsuit contained allegations of excessive force by a police officer, improper training, and deficient policies. These accounts are reflective of the importance of training and policy in the criminal justice system. Diversity and the need for tolerance and understanding of differences among individuals and groups pose many notable challenges for the criminal justice system. Evidence demonstrating the need for greater preparedness and understanding of differences are found everywhere—on the news, in other countries, in workplaces, and so on. This chapter addresses the training received by criminal justice officials with regard to diversity and related concepts, and highlights policy as it relates to diversity, tolerance, understanding of others, and acceptance.

To be sure, overcoming the challenges associated with diversity is not easy. The history of the United States is rife with accounts of individuals being treated differently based solely on skin color, cultural beliefs, appearance, age, sexual orientation, and related factors. To simply state that additional training and/or policies will solve all of our problems is shortsighted. Nevertheless, educating and training our criminal justice professionals, and creating policies that are inclusive as opposed to exclusive will contribute much toward improving the system and society in general.

TRAINING AND MULTICULTURALISM

In June 2016, the U.S. Department of Justice announced that over 33,000 federal agents and prosecutors will undergo training designed to prevent unconscious bias from affecting their law enforcement decisions. Similar actions have been taken by many local police departments following several shootings of unarmed African American males by White police officers.

Training, similar to formal education, seeks to impart knowledge and skills on an individual in preparation for future endeavors. It could be argued that enhanced training for all criminal justice officials could solve many problems associated with the intersection of multiculturalism and justice-based practices. It could also be argued that solid training wouldn't solve the problems. Such is the nature of trying to change human behavior. Consider a college-level criminal justice class, for example. Some students will comprehend all of the material and earn an "A" in the course. Others will get much (70–79 percent) of the information and earn a "C." Other students will get very little out of the course, and some will fail to receive credit. The students who earned a "C" or an "A" both passed the class. They've demonstrated their ability to grasp much or perhaps all of the material. However, does comprehending "much" of the material mean that you're trained in this area? And does one's ability to pass exams and/or write papers necessarily demonstrate overall comprehension of the material? Many of the challenges found in training college students are evident in training criminal justice officials.

Properly training criminal justice professionals is vital to the success of justice-based practices. Training, of course, is difficult, primarily because it seeks to alter human behavior. Training will not change everyone, but the notably large amount of resources regularly devoted to training criminal justice practitioners suggests that we rely on it heavily, and it must have many benefits. Some training programs and requirements are more effective than others, and the key to successful training is finding what works and for whom. The importance of training is noted, for instance, in the body of research which suggests that training can have positive, significant effects upon the interactions between probation officers and their clients, and can contribute to lower offender failure rates.[1]

Cultural differences and other diversity-related issues have been at the core of many problems and controversies in the criminal justice system. Evidence is noted with the 2013 **Black Lives Matter** activist movement in the United States that originated after the 2013 acquittal of George Zimmerman, who shot and killed Trayvon Martin, an African American teenager. The movement received greater attention following the 2014 deaths of two unarmed African Americans (Michael Brown in Ferguson, and Eric Garner in New York City), and the failure of grand juries to indict the officers involved in the shootings. The group campaigns against police brutality against African Americans.

In general, cultural diversity training should include four primary components: awareness of one's own cultural influences, understanding of other cultures, comprehension of the emotional challenges faced in recognizing and understanding diversity, and the basic skills needed to appropriately address cultural differences.[2] It is argued that a weakness in any of these components hampers understanding cultural diversity. Self-reflection through examination of one's own cultural influences and understanding the emotional challenges with regard to diversity facilitates individuals overcoming personal biases they may have toward other groups.

There are two basic approaches taken with respect to multicultural skills development: culture-specific and culture-general training. **Culture-specific training** addresses the practices, beliefs, and traits of particular cultural groups. **Culture-general training** emphasizes the flexibility, skills, and understanding that would apply to understanding an array of cultures.[3] Research with regard to these approaches found that the culture-general model, interactive training methods, and trainer qualifications hold viable potential for positive training impacts.[4] These finding provide guidance for future training practices.

Cultural diversity and awareness training for criminal justice practitioners should, at minimum, address:

- communication skills
- understanding and recognizing bias
- racism, bigotry, discrimination and the like
- understanding and appreciating various (or if possible, most or all) cultures
- understanding the benefits and challenges of diversity and its relationship to justice-based practices, and
- action steps to confront multicultural challenges.

Agencies faced with limited resources should tailor their training to focus primarily on the groups within their jurisdiction. For example, probation officers working in an area with a large number of Native Americans should familiarize themselves with Native American culture.

Cultural sensitivity and diversity training are generally imposed on line workers, but it is also very important for administrators and supervisors to be culturally sensitive, and to take remedial actions with those who are not. Supervisors and administrators heavily influence the agencies and departments they oversee, for instance as they are largely involved in the recruitment, selection, and training of employees. Further, their practices help establish how discretion will be used, and largely shape the overall organizational culture. Diversity is one of the more substantial issues in the workplace, yet many employers are ill-prepared to address it. The problem appears in part because many managers grew up isolated from other cultures. Accordingly, it is imperative that cultural sensitivity training be provided to all who work in criminal justice.

In discussing the importance of fairness and neutrality with regard to race and policing, police administrators Kessee and Nila noted that "The goal of effective diversity training is not simply to check the box and meet mandatory requirements, but rather to create long-lasting transformative change."[5] Ultimately, training should be designed to have long-lasting effects that shape the individual in a positive manner. The benefits of training should be emphasized to all employees, and efforts should be made to continuously engage trainees. Disinterested or bored trainees are less impressionable than those who are actively engaged in the training practices.

THE ROLE OF EDUCATION

Education is an important aspect of training. It promotes critical thinking skills, the incorporation of theory, and ethical considerations. Education is primarily concerned with learning about something, while training is much broader and encompasses learning about something, and doing it. Consider police academies for example. Officers must attend police academies to become sworn officers. At the academy (as discussed below), officers have classroom sessions in which they are educated about important aspects of policing, and they engage in field activities in which they practice what they were taught. Their training continues after the academy, for instance in the form of **field training** in which they patrol the streets under the guidance of an experienced colleague.

One of the more notable shifts in the focus of higher education involves greater consideration for diversity and multiculturalism.[6] There exists many ways to cover these topics in the classroom, and the issues covered by general university-level training regarding diversity and multiculturalism range from understanding basic concepts to interpretation of advanced statistical analyses regarding race and gender. Unfortunately, most university students will get only one course on multiculturalism.[7] Similar to those who

Classroom education is an important component of formal training. It alone, however, is not enough to ensure that those who work in criminal justice are prepared for their positions.

have taken only one semester of a foreign language, students taking only one course in multiculturalism will have a broad overview of the topic but lack substantial comprehension of the many-faceted aspects of the topic. It is not uncommon for instructors teaching a sensitive topic such as diversity or multiculturalism to sacrifice complexity for morality.[8]

Teaching about diversity, multiculturalism, and tolerance should not be restricted to university settings. Changing stereotypical images and discriminatory practices requires teaching at an early age. The onus is on both public and private educational institutions from kindergarten through college to address tolerance and diversity, as today's students are tomorrow's professionals.[9] Recognizing and incorporating the many significant accomplishments of individuals from various cultures encourages young, impressionable students to embrace multiculturalism, however, additional work is required.

The goal in teaching multiculturalism is to structure one's mind toward tolerance and acceptance of a diverse society. To do so, it is important to observe historical events that shaped current thought. Throughout this book we've commented on the historical treatment of various cultures and groups both within and outside of the criminal justice system. Teaching about diversity and multiculturalism, particularly to students of criminal justice, requires a holistic approach that encompasses, in addition to historical events, various social, political, economic, demographic, and related considerations. In other words, we can't simply consider the role of various cultures in the criminal justice system without recognizing the significance of political influences, the effects of poverty, the impact of racist attitudes, and the changing nature of our society's population.

In discussing an approach to incorporating multiculturalism into the criminal justice curriculum, researcher William Calathes argues that cultural pluralism, intergroup relations, demography, and involvement constitute the theoretical component of multiculturalism. He adds that such topics are often neglected in traditional criminal justice textbooks.[10] At the very least, concepts that highlight the contextual nature of diversity within the system should be emphasized in any discussion of multiculturalism within the criminal justice system.

Calathes argues that a multicultural approach to criminal justice would help students recognize the "present and future eventualities" and assist students in obtaining the critical thinking skills and ability to work, teach, and engage in research from that perspective.[11] Calathes offers a series of steps that would promote teaching multiculturalism in the criminal justice curriculum. Included among his suggestions are:

- informing students of the experiences of different cultures as they relate to life both within and outside of the criminal justice system
- teaching from the perspective of the subjects
- emphasizing the relationship between law and politics, including examination of the power differentials in society
- teaching students to recognize various cultures, with particular concern for racism and oppression, and
- preparing students to understand the problems of different groups and conflicts between groups.[12]

Students are often taught critical thinking skills to encourage them to consider all possibilities with regard to problem-solving. Critical thinking skills promote consideration of alternatives or solutions, and discourage individuals, including those within the criminal justice system, from acting in a manner simply because "that's the way it's always been done." Such skills could be useful in efforts to enhance our justice systems with regard to diversity and the need for understanding different groups.

Teaching tolerance for diversity should not be restricted to schools. Parents, coaches, mentors, and other role models need to stress the importance of recognizing and appreciating other groups. For instance, athletic coaches are often in ideal situations to stress teamwork among individuals from different backgrounds. The lesson that individuals need to work as a team could be generalized to society with the goal of encouraging athletes (and others) to recognize the beneficial contributions from diverse individuals. The same idea holds true for band leaders, church group facilitators, and others. There are many avenues where progress can be made with regard to accepting and appreciating diverse individuals and groups.

TRAINING AND LAW ENFORCEMENT

The police are considered the "gatekeepers to the criminal justice system," as they are involved with the initial steps of the adjudication process. The police interact with citizens more frequently than any other component of the criminal justice system, and largely shape the public's perception of justice-based practices. As such, police training is important for numerous reasons. Failing to properly train officers could result in negative police-community relations, wasted resources, dangers to the public, the failure to properly address society's problems, and lawsuits. With regard to the latter, counties and municipalities can face litigation if it is believed they are in violation of federal statute Title 42, United States Code, Section 1983, which allows individuals to hold government employees and in some cases their employers accountable for violation of rights under the U.S. Constitution. With regard to police training, individuals who believe they were treated improperly by the police can claim their rights were violated by a failure to adequately train officers.[13]

All states have mandated training for police officers. The requirements for the minimum standards of training, and general guidance for police training are provided by state organizations typically called **Police Officers Standards and Training Commissions** (POSTs). In addition to establishing minimum standards, POSTs typically provide training criteria for police officers and seek means, for instance through research, to improve police training practices. As an example, the Louisiana Peace Officer Standards and Training Council (POST) develops training standards for peace officers in Louisiana. Among other contributions, the Council develops and evaluates the curriculum of mandatory basic training courses for peace officers in the state.[14]

Cultural sensitivity training, also known as cross-cultural training, for police officers largely emerged in the 1980s. The increased focus on cultural sensitivity training was designed to improve police-community relations and address citizen complaints of police officers misusing their powers against underrepresented persons in the community.[15] Although such training largely emerged in the 1980s, there has been a historical need for sensitivity training. For example, the 1967 Kerner Report suggested that poor police-community relations were at the root of much civil unrest.

Cultural sensitivity training is imperative for today's police officers. Ideally, training should alter officer behavior, generate alternative solutions to problematic or confrontational situations, and encourage officers to adopt the values and ideals of the department.[16] With regard to the latter, one must assume and hope that the values and ideals of the department are based on tolerance and cultural sensitivity. The recent shift in policing toward greater interaction with the public in the form of community-oriented policing necessitates greater emphasis on personal communication skills, and tolerating and appreciating diversity. Accordingly, many departments and police academies have enhanced their focus on cultural sensitivity training. As noted in Chapter 11, the *Task Force on 21st Century Policing* included training and education among its six areas of recommendations to improve police practices and build public trust. In emphasizing training as it relates to interacting with diverse groups, the report noted:

> One specific method of increasing the quality of training would be to ensure that Peace Officer and Standards Training (POST) boards include mandatory Crisis Intervention Training (CIT), which equips officers to deal with individuals in crisis or living with mental disabilities, as part of both basic recruit and in-service officer training—as well as instruction in disease of addiction, implicit bias and cultural responsiveness, policing in a democratic society, procedural justice, and effective social interaction and tactical skills.[17]

Among the issues surrounding sensitivity training are gaining an understanding, recognition, and respect for the various groups and cultures in society. Training must consist of more than a briefing or cursory examination at the academy, or generic comments offered at roll call. Such training must be ongoing and reinforced by fellow officers and superiors who should also have notable appreciation of cultural diversity. Further, cultural sensitivity training is more effective when various groups outside of policing, for example civic leaders, offer input regarding their expectations and an overview of their cultural beliefs and practices.

It would be difficult for police officers, especially those in large cities where diversity is most prominent, to have a thorough understanding of all cultural beliefs and practices. Fortunately, community policing strategies emphasize police-citizen interaction, in part, by having officers consistently work in specific jurisdictions. In other words, maintaining an officer's presence in a particular neighborhood or community becomes important for officers to grasp the local culture as they become better able to understand those in the community. Learning how to grasp the local culture and how to respect cultural diversity are among the many topics addressed at the police academy.

Pre-service training for officers begins at the police academy. The academy teaches officers the technical skills required for the job, indoctrinates cadets into the social world of policing, and identifies those unfit for a career in policing. At the police academy officers spend time on law, practical skills, human relations, criminal investigations, patrol procedures, the structure and practices of policing, and more generally the criminal justice system. Officers will later be provided in-service and field training to keep them fresh and abreast of changes throughout their careers, and help them apply what they learned at the academy, respectively.

The most recent account from the U.S. Bureau of Justice Statistics regarding local and state police training noted that officers received an average of 843 hours of classroom instruction, and an average of 521 hours of field training. On average, special jurisdiction police agencies required the largest number of hours (1,075), followed by county police (1,029) and municipal police (936 hours). Municipal police departments (630) required the highest average number of field training hours.[18] These and related findings are noted in Table 14-1.

The same report included information regarding the special topics included in state and local law enforcement training academies, as well as the percentages of agencies that include such topics.[19] Many of these topics are of particular interest to the many groups discussed in this book. The findings can be viewed as both encouraging and discouraging, for instance as it is encouraging that the majority of academies address issues such as domestic violence, hate crimes/bias crimes, and elder abuse. However, the finding that only three hours on average are devoted to topics such as hate crimes/bias crimes and elder abuse, and that fact that only 78 percent and 73 percent include this as part of the training could be viewed as discouraging. These and related findings are noted in Table 14.2.

In discussing his many years of teaching cultural diversity and ethics to law enforcement groups, Daniel Carlson, author of the book "When Cultures Clash," suggested that training on topics such as ethics or cultural diversity is not popular among police officers. He states, "Very often in the heat of these classes, officers bemoan the fact that while they

Table 14.1 Duration of basic training programs in state and local law enforcement training academies, by type of academy, 2013

Type of academy	Average length in classroom	Mandatory field training component			
		Total	For all recruits	Agency specific	Average length[a]
All types	843 hrs.	81%	37%	44%	521 hrs.
State POST[b]	650	38	14	24	250
State police/highway patrol	878	94	76	18	455
Sheriff's office	706	90	37	53	506
County police	1,029	100	76	24	479
Municipal police	936	97	71	26	630
4-year college/university	903	68	15	53	321
2-year college	822	71	14	57	332
Technical school	703	65	0	65	~
Special jurisdiction	1,075	100	69	31	493
Multiagency/regional	827	95	36	60	185

Note: Detail may not sum to total due to rounding.

~Not applicable.

[a]Excludes field training segments that were not overseen by academies.

[b]Peace Officer Standards and Training.

Source: Bureau of Justice Statistics, Census of Law Enforcement Training Academies, 2013.

Table 14.2 Special topics included in basic training programs in state and local law enforcement training academies, 2013

Subject area	Percent of academies with training	Average number of hours of instruction per recruit*
Domestic violence	98%	13 hrs.
Mental illness	95	10
Sexual assault	92	6
Crimes against children	90	6
Domestic preparedness/terrorism	85	9
Gangs	82	4
Victim response	80	5
Hate crimes/bias crimes	78	3
Sexual harassment	75	3
Elder abuse	73	3
Clandestine drug labs	67	4
Human trafficking	64	3
Cyber/Internet crimes	57	3

*Excludes academies that did not provide this type of instruction.
Source: Bureau of Justice Statistics, Census of Law Enforcement Training Academies, 2013.

are 'forced' to endure training designed to improve police-citizen interactions, no such training exists for citizens." The officers argue that the public needs to better understand policing and police officers.[20] There is certainly merit to this argument, as policing arguably has a distinctive culture of its own. The dilemma exists in that it is a "give-and-take" situation that requires efforts from both sides.

So what exactly is cultural sensitivity training for police officers? Should coverage of hate or bias crime be included in such training? Departments have responded to concerns surrounding hate crimes, in part by training officers and administrators to understand how to identify hate crimes. Should cultural sensitivity training also include teaching officers to recognize the differences between those with physical ailments from the intoxicated? In discussing the best practices to improve police relations with transgender individuals, scholar Jan Redfern noted that: "Police departments should consider sensitivity training of law enforcement professionals to increase awareness and appreciation of gender diversity, to avoid personal biases and assumptions, and to avoid costly litigation from civil rights violations." Such training, Redfern argues, would assist officers by improving interactions and communications in assisting or arresting transgender individuals.[21]

Cultural sensitivity is a complex phenomenon that is created and shaped in individuals during their upbringing. What is taught in the police academy and supplemented on the streets also contributes to how officers react to multiculturalism. Police training is an ongoing process, as evidenced during an officer's probationary period following graduation from the academy. Many departments use **field training officer programs**, which pair new officers with experienced ones. Field training officers teach new officers the practical aspects of police work, building upon and reinforcing what was taught at the academy, and acclimates the officers to the department's and community's values.[22] It is at this point in the officer's new career that they gain a foundation of skills, knowledge, and expectations that shape their future. Pairing new officers with culturally sensitive officers enhances policing in many ways. Continued in-service training should reinforce earlier training and expose officers to developments in policing.

Police officer training is particularly important given the frequency with which officers engage the public and the seriousness of the encounters they sometimes face.

MULTICULTURALISM AND COURTROOM PERSONNEL TRAINING

The nature of the training for the primary actors (i.e., judges, prosecutors, and defense attorneys) in the courtroom is much different than it is in policing and corrections. Judges, prosecutors, and defense attorneys are primarily trained through law school and on-the-job experience. Training in policing and corrections is more formal in nature, for instance as corrections officers and police officers attend training academies and must complete a specified number of training courses or hours. Individuals interested in practicing law typically attend law school, and from there either join a private law firm, or become a public defender or assistant district attorney. Judges primarily have years of experience as a practicing attorney, and are elected or appointed to their positions.

Law schools provide an academic view of the law, with emphases in particular areas. The courses a law school student takes during their first year are typically prescribed, and students are often permitted to study a particular areas of law in their latter two years. These areas include criminal law, contract law, corporate law, and tax law, among others. Students typically spend three years studying various aspects of law, following which they must pass a bar exam to practice law in the state in which they took the exam.

In discussing the importance of law school students understanding civil rights issues, law professor Tamara Lawson noted that "It is optimal for students to take a specialized course in Race-in-the-Law, Critical Race Theory, or Civil Rights, but many students are unable to take such a course either due to their schedules, their university's offerings, or their lack of interest in the subject." Professor Lawson suggested that discussions of civil rights should be incorporated into the core curriculum, which would enable all law school students to have a better understanding of diversity and civil rights.[23]

New assistant district attorneys are generally granted much freedom with regard to how they handle their cases, and office policies are typically general and vague in nature. New attorneys are encouraged to observe and ask questions of the more experienced attorneys, a socialization process that helps them better understand the expectations of the position.[24] Historically, training for new assistant district attorneys was primarily conducted through on-the-job learning. It was not uncommon for recently hired attorneys to be placed in the courtroom on their first day of employment. This has changed in recent years, as prosecutors' offices have incorporated more systematic training for new employees. Such training may include introducing the new employee to the different divisions of the office, and having them attend different courtroom proceedings where they closely observe how experienced prosecutors handle cases.[25]

Similar to the training for new assistant district attorneys, training for new public defenders has largely consisted of learning through working in the courts and learning as one handles cases. This has been supplemented by some public defenders working closely with more experienced attorneys and formal training programs.[26] In noting its support for training new public defenders, the American Bar Association highlighted the importance of training and continued legal education in Principles 6 and 9 of its *Ten Principles of a Public Defense Delivery System*. Principle 6 notes:

Much of the formal training for attorneys occurs in law school. Judges are often former practicing attorneys who attended law school. The schools are increasingly incorporating experiential education to better prepare law students for a career in the courts.

- **Defense counsel's ability, training, and experience match the complexity of the case.**

  "Counsel should never be assigned a case that counsel lacks the experience or training to handle competently, and counsel is obligated to refuse appointment if unable to provide ethical, high-quality representation."

Principle 9 notes:

- **Defense counsel is provided with and required to attend continuing legal education.**

  "Counsel and staff providing defense services should have systematic and comprehensive training appropriate to their areas of practice and at least equal to that received by prosecutors."[27]

Statewide administrative offices regularly develop, update, and offer elaborate training and education programs for new judges. These programs also provide formal training for experienced judges, and may last several weeks and cover a wide range of topics.[28] For instance, New Jersey offers the "Judicial Performance Program" which provides training and guidance for new and experienced judges, for instance by keeping them abreast of developments in the law and judicial administration.[29]

Educational qualifications for appellate and general-jurisdiction judges in the state courts are largely established by state constitutional provisions. Some states give the legislature the power to set or expand on the criteria. Other states have no specific educational requirements established by statute. Although most states require a judge in courts of general jurisdiction to be a qualified attorney, over half of all states permit non-attorneys to become judges in their lower-courts. In many cases there are no educational requirements to preside over the lower courts, or the requirement may be a high school diploma or a GED. Permitting non-attorneys to become judges helps address the problems encountered in rural areas where there are typically few attorneys.[30]

Law schools have responded to the lack of hands-on experience of law school students through offering more skills-oriented classes in their curricula. The schools have increasingly added problem-based learning and community-engaged learning activities designed to better prepare students for employment in the field.[31] For instance, law professor Charlotte Alexander wrote about the hands-on experience law students receive in a course at Georgia State University College of Law in which students are paired with an attorney in solo practice or a small law firm. The fieldwork exposes students to the realities of practicing law, including the ethical decision-making practices, practice management tools, and general skills needed to be an attorney. The students are matched with attorneys who practice law in subject areas that the students anticipate entering, and the fieldwork begins with an interview of the attorney and observation of them at work. This course is one of many similarly designed courses increasingly being offered at law schools around the United States, in efforts to ensure that new attorneys are prepared for practicing law.[32]

MULTICULTURALISM AND CORRECTIONAL STAFF TRAINING

In the late 1970s, the American Correctional Association (ACA) Commission on Accreditation established the first training standards for corrections workers. Among other contributions, the commission set standards for positions within corrections, identified training topics, set specified numbers of pre-service and annual training hours, and established specific basic administrative policy support requirements for training programs.[33] States built off of the initial work of the ACA, and almost all states today require at least 120 hours of pre-service training for correctional officers working in institutions, with many states requiring more.

Aside from the ACA, other associations in corrections offer models of professionalism designed to advance the field. Among them are the American Probation and Parole Association, and the American Jail Association. These groups offer principles, guidance, and support for correctional workers and administrators. They offer training opportunities, host seminars and meetings, advertise position openings, and publish literature designed to advance correctional practices. They may also lobby legislative bodies to further a particular cause.

Training requirements for correctional officers vary among jurisdictions and institutions. State administrative agencies typically establish the standards and requirements. Standard training typically includes use of force and restraints, weapons, self-defense, first aid and CPR, report writing, testifying in court, defusing hostile situations, interpersonal communications, gang intelligence, and law.

Probation and parole officers have similar training requirements as those who work in institutions.[34] For instance, the Nevada Department of Public Safety Training Division offers training for probation and parole officers in the state, requiring them to complete 480 hours of classroom and field training during their first year of work. The training covers areas such as legal liability issues, ethics, personnel matters, department policies and procedures, and statutes.[35]

Correctional agencies typically do not have the resources to train all staff regarding the cultural differences of the incarcerated. Accordingly, training resources must be used wisely. Employees working with special populations, such as the elderly or mentally impaired receive specific sensitivity training. Those assuming leadership roles in the institution receive more advanced training in diversity.[36] In the end, exposing all staff members to as many cultural differences as feasible contributes to more effective correctional practices. Correctional leadership needs to promote tolerance and cultural diversity among the officers and encourage officers to develop the interpersonal skills necessary to operate in a multicultural institution, or work in community corrections. Effective communication skills are necessary for working in corrections since poor communication is a major source of problems.[37] The ability to speak a second language can largely contribute to a correctional or any other criminal justice officer's effectiveness. Bilingual or multilingual prison officers provide much needed safety and security in institutions with great diversity.[38] Considering cultural context in the course of communicating ultimately promotes a more effective work environment.

The use of community resources to assist correctional staff is important in many ways, particularly in cases in which there exists a notable lack of familiarity with a particular culture. Incorporating input from volunteers, guest speakers, professional associations, and specific interest groups demonstrates to correctional staff and the individuals they supervise that the agency respects cultural diversity. The onus is on correctional agencies to proactively identify means by which they can send a message of tolerance to all individuals with whom they associate.

One difficulty associated with multicultural awareness training involves a method or technique of assessing awareness or knowledge with regard to cultural diversity.[39] In other words, how do we know if someone (e.g., a probation officer) is prepared to supervise individuals from diverse cultures? Part of correctional officer training involves role-play, in which cadets act as unruly inmates demonstrating cultural idiosyncrasies that test the correctional officials' ability to properly respond. The actor's cadet colleagues learn methods of responding appropriately to the challenges. Communication skills, including interpreting and using nonverbal communication, are stressed, as is the need to recognize and appreciate culture-related symbolism. While these and related training skills will not end culture conflict throughout correctional systems, they certainly will help alleviate tensions among correctional officials and those under correctional supervision.

Correctional officers maintain a great deal of discretion in their day-to-day functions. Determining whether or not to confront troubling situations with formal or informal methods is one example of this discretion. Improper use of discretion could explain why inexperienced prison officers are more likely than their experienced counterparts to be assaulted by inmates.[40] Violent inmate reactions may be spurred by perceptions of injustice. Sensitivities to race, age, and crime-related factors of individual inmates undoubtedly factor into how corrections officers use their discretion.[41] Training officers to properly consider such extralegal factors and continuous reinforcement of that training should be of primary concern to correctional administrators.

Institutional administrators play a significant role in promoting cultural diversity. Proper recruitment, selection, and training contribute to recognizing and promoting multiculturalism in corrections. The organizational culture of the institution or agency should be one in which cultural diversity is among the primary concerns. Failure to recognize diversity results in a much greater likelihood of violence and related negative consequences. Promoting cultural tolerance among staff members is significantly important for administrators, as failure to properly resolve situational conflicts and misunderstandings is related to:

- lost productivity
- increased isolation of staff members
- enhanced suspicion and distrust among staff members
- increased staff turnover
- more disgruntled employees, and
- overall negative changes in the climate of the correctional institution.[42]

THE LIMITATIONS OF TRAINING

Despite the many benefits of training, there are some limitations. As referenced earlier, changing human behavior is sometimes difficult. The question is asked whether training is too heavily focused on critical incidents that occur relatively infrequently (e.g., shootings) at the expense of the kinds of situations that occur more frequently (e.g., interacting with diverse groups)?[43] The following common limitations appear inherent in police training, although most apply to training for many other important positions in the criminal justice system:

- Program content—programs may not cover significant areas (e.g., rape, human relations)
- Training facilities and equipment—the lack of adequate facilities in which to train
- Part-time training instructors and directors—full-time personnel with no other job duties should be provided
- Full-time attendance—officers who work and attend the academy face many difficulties
- Training prior to exercising power—this prevents untrained officers from working the streets
- Follow-up evaluation—training should occur at two-year intervals following initial pre-service training
- Field training officers—to evaluate the recruit's work in the field, and
- Quality control of instructors—instructors may not be effective teachers.[44]

The significant role played by trainers cannot be ignored, and instructors are typically expected to teach in certain areas. Race, ethnicity, gender, cultural background, and related factors could influence trainer effectiveness, for instance as it was noted that White course facilitators discussing racial profiling are often easily dismissed by trainees who generally believe the facilitator is unaware of life as an officer on the streets. Yet, a racial minority police officer who shares personal experiences of being harassed by the police generates notable attention.[45]

Despite the aforementioned and other limitations, training is an integral and vital aspect of employment in the criminal justice system. It could be argued, however, that we expect too much out of training. This dilemma presents a challenge for all employees who work in the criminal justice system, and will continue to do so until the limitations are addressed. At the most basic level, criminal justice practitioners are first and foremost human beings who were molded and shaped by various forces prior to entering the field. Various types of training may be expected to undue internal limitations or conflicts among individuals. Part of cultural sensitivity training involves "undoing" damage from the past and promoting tolerance. It is hoped that proper recruitment, selection, and training can provide criminal justice agencies individuals who won't let personal conflicts affect their ability to properly perform their job. In sum, much progress has been made to address the limitations involved in training, although much work remains.

POLICIES AND MULTICULTURALISM

Similar to the earlier suggestion that training alone cannot solve all problems related to an increasingly diverse society, no policy or group of policies will completely fix the diversity-related challenges facing the criminal justice system. This, of course, is not to say that policy cannot change some things and have positive, lasting effects. **Policy** refers to decisions or actions that address particular issues or problems. **Public policy** is supported by public resources and enforced by the legal system. **Criminal justice policy** focuses on issues or problems pertaining to policing, courts, corrections, and related areas of formal social control.

Policies should not be established simply for the sake of making policy. There must be valid reason to impose restrictions or offer guidance on human behavior. Effective policies directly address areas in which attention is needed. Policies are necessary for many reasons. They guide behavior, promote fair and just practices, and can serve as a deterrent. Their existence symbolizes concern for a particular issue. Of particular importance with regard to any policy are efforts to ensure that they are properly enforced. Failing to properly enforce or address policies is harmful in many aspects, for instance, as the policy becomes of little importance and has limited if any effect if there's no concern for it. Further, neglecting policies sends a message that the issue at the center of the policy is of limited importance.

With regard to the criminal justice system, one can simply consider findings from recent Gallup public opinion polls to identify the need for more effective policy. The following results highlight the many diversity-, justice-, and tolerance-related issues that challenge the United States today:

- For more than a decade prior to December 2014, no more than 5 percent of Americans had named racism or race relations as the top problem facing the United States, with the figure often measuring 0 percent. In December 2014 it was 13 percent.[46]
- Over one-third of Americans reported being worried a great deal about race relations in the United States in 2016. This is the highest percentage since Gallup first asked the question in 2001.[47]
- In 2016, Blacks (53 percent) were far more likely than Whites (27 percent) to report that they worry a great deal about race relations in the United States.[48]
- In 2016, Whites (62 percent) were significantly more likely than non-Whites (39 percent) to note that they had a great deal or quite a lot of confidence in the police.[49]
- Forty-three percent of Americans harbored some degree of prejudice toward Muslims in 2015.[50]

Public perception of the criminal justice system is particularly low, as noted in Figure 14-1.[51] The finding that only 23 percent of respondents had a great deal or quite a lot of confidence in the criminal justice system suggests that change is required. Such change may include altering some existing policies, eliminating others, and creating effective new ones.

Results from this poll suggest that the general public is not as confident in the criminal justice system as it is in other institutions in the United States. Interestingly, the public has a relatively high level of confidence in the police. This finding, however, should be considered in light of the notable differences in levels of confidence in the police between Whites and racial and ethnic minorities, as noted above.

The history of criminal justice in the United States is filled with policies designed to address particular problems. Some of the more recognizable policies are those that pertain to drugs, capital punishment, guns, and sentencing. Despite the fact that policies are designed to address problems, and the many benefits that policies often provide, they are

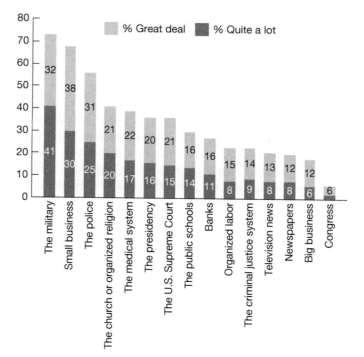

FIGURE 14.1 I am going to read you a list of institutions in American society. Please tell me how much confidence you, yourself, have in each one—a great deal, quite a lot, some or very little? *June 1–5, 2016*

often subject to criticism. Some, and perhaps much, of the criticism has been voiced by less powerful groups in society, primarily because they are often the target of criminal justice policies. For example, the punitive laws directed toward drug offenses involving crack cocaine in the 1980s and 1990s were believed to be targeted toward inner-city African American males. More generally, harsh penalties imposed on all drug offenses have been perceived to be directed toward many minority groups. Tougher sentencing policies have disproportionately impacted less powerful groups in society, leaving many to believe that they too were intentionally designed to punish groups as opposed to individuals.

Policies are subject to change, and proactive institutions, agencies, and organizations regularly create and update policies to address changes. The United States has recently experienced a change in many drug-related policies, as earlier efforts to confront drug use were viewed as overly harsh. In 2016, marijuana was permitted for medicinal purposes in twenty-five states, and four states and Washington, DC, have legalized marijuana for recreational purposes. Further, as of March 2016, President Barak Obama had granted clemency to 248 federal inmates in efforts to address overly harsh drug penalties.

Criminal justice policies are often popular because we all wish to live in a crime-free society, and we generally want those who break the law to be punished for their actions. It is often politically popular to be tough on crime, and the interconnectedness of politics and criminal justice has contributed to increasingly punitive policies and practices. Consider the fact the several key criminal justice practitioners are elected to their position in many places. For example, judges and sheriffs in many places are elected officials who often shape their political campaigns around the public's want for tough justice-based practices. What is overlooked in many instances are the repercussions or outcomes of tough policies and practices. For instance, tougher sentencing laws and practices result in higher levels of incarceration, which consumes public funding otherwise used for education, healthcare, and related services. Tougher sentencing practices have also had a disproportionate impact on particular groups, including African Americans, and contribute to more children living in single-parent households and families living in poverty. Ultimately, an important, yet often overlooked, aspect of policies is the long-term effects the policy-related actions will have.

To be sure, policies are important in society. They have been the source of criticism and many positive changes. No single policy is going to have all desired outcomes, and no policy is going to please everyone. Differences among groups, including varied interests, contribute to different perceptions of policies. Policies that may seem appropriate for one group are viewed with disdain by other groups. Policies should not consist of knee jerk reactions to pressing problems, but instead should be well thought out, with particular concern for the effects of policies.

Aside from the many high profile policies found within justice-based practices, there are many policies that go unnoticed by much of society. Consider, for instance, the placement of halfway houses and other residential correctional facilities. As used by the criminal justice system, **halfway houses** are community-based facilities that enable offenders to reside in the community while remaining under relatively close supervision. Offenders are able to maintain employment and family ties, while being supervised and undergoing programming and counseling. The residences are, however, viewed by some groups and individuals as problematic, as they contribute to the concentration of offenders in a particular area, may be perceived as harmful by residents who live in close proximity to the facilities, may decrease property values, and generally impact quality of life issues for residents who live close by. Would you be excited to hear that the house next to yours has been turned into a halfway house? Thus, the question is often asked: where should we place halfway houses?

The acronym **NIMBY** refers to "Not in my backyard," and relates to citizen concerns about the siting of something unpleasant or potentially dangerous in their vicinity. Such concerns are not restricted to the siting of criminal justice facilities, for instance as citizens have argued against the placement of hazardous waste facilities near their residences.[52] Nevertheless, there have been concerns over the location of many criminal and juvenile justice facilities, for instance, as having a prison as a neighbor is not appealing to a large number of people. The nature of community corrections becomes increasingly important, as offenders are not confined within prison walls, and are supervised in the community.

In a study of the placement of residential facilities in Connecticut, researchers noted that halfway houses were significantly more likely to be located in non-White communities with high crime rates.[53] Related research has noted that such undesirable facilities are often located in areas where there is a concentration of less powerful groups. To be sure, there is no policy which states that such facilities will be placed in particular areas.

Community resistance to the placement of halfway houses provides an example of the widespread effects of policies. Halfway houses provide helpful services for offenders residing in the community, yet many residents do not wish to have them located in their communities.

The government officials tasked with locating halfway houses and related facilities undoubtedly consider a host of factors, including resources. Simply, it's less expensive to operate a facility in a low-income area. This predicament results in concerns for **social justice**, which is defined as a "perspective of justice that evaluates how a society provides for the needs of its members and the extent to which it treats its subgroups equally."[54]

Although policy does not dictate that undesirable correctional facilities are to be located in low-income areas, it remains that they often are. Policy, however, does dictate the use of halfway houses, and the siting of them contributes to controversy. While it may be less costly to locate halfway houses in low-income areas, the repercussions of doing so are many. Citizens in these areas may believe that they are being placed at a greater risk of victimization, and may view the placement of such facilities as another example of powerful individuals lacking a concern for social justice.

The policy of using halfway houses and the associated difficulties in locating them are among the many policy-related concerns in criminal justice. This section does not provide a comprehensive account of which policies work, which policies do not, and which policies should be adopted. To do so with something as vast as criminal justice practices is notably burdensome. Instead, we seek to introduce readers to what constitute a policy, and the need for considering diversity and related issues when issuing policy. Below we offer some examples of policies that offer promise for more successful justice-based actions, and recognize that there are many others in existence.

TRANSGENDER BATHROOM DEBATE

Transgender activism became the focus of much national attention in 2016, especially in relation to the use of public restrooms. Several states introduced and one passed legislation with regard to transgender bathroom use. North Carolina's law requires all people to use the bathroom matching the sex on their birth certificate, and other states proposed legislation that would restrict which bathrooms transgendered individuals could use. Several cities passed ordinances that require people to use restrooms based on their sex, as opposed to gender identity, and some schools have rules that require transgender students to use restrooms and locker rooms that match the sex listed on their birth certificate. These and forthcoming policies will continue to be addressed in the courts.

The primary rationale behind these policies is a concern for predators who will prey on women and children in bathrooms. It is believed that some individuals may pretend to be transgender and will now have easy access to commit deviant and harmful acts. Critics argue that the policies are discriminatory in nature, and that transgender individuals pose little to no danger. Several large companies and other groups denounced the bathroom laws, including Paypal, which cancelled plans to build a global operations center in North Carolina, resulting in the loss of millions of dollars and over four hundred jobs to the state, and performing artists such as Bruce Springsteen canceled shows in the state to show their support.

One of the more promising policy approaches in policing is the increased use of **community liaison officers**, who meet with residents and business owners to discuss crime and crime prevention efforts. These officers are ideally situated to interact with citizens in a nonconfrontational manner, share information with the community, and learn about issues that may hamper police and general criminal justice practices. The officers can better understand cultural and other diversity-related differences among the citizens, and promote the benefits of the police departments. The use of such officers has increased with the incorporation of community policing, and the need for additional use of these officers is evident in the aforementioned polls regarding Black respondents' low level of confidence in the police.

Policies directed toward diversifying criminal justice agencies promote more effective justice-based practices. Many criminal justice agencies have adopted policies designed to diversify the workforce. As noted throughout this book, women and racial and ethnic minorities have been underrepresented in criminal justice agencies. Efforts have been taken to diversify the field, however much work remains. Among other benefits, a more diverse criminal justice workforce helps practitioners identify broader solutions, helps generate culturally sensitive solutions to problems, enhances trust between the agencies and the public, reduces discrimination, and encourages members of underrepresented groups to support criminal justice practices.

Similarly, policies directed toward building and maintaining positive work environments encourage more positive criminal justice practices. The term **organizational culture** refers to shared beliefs, values, and assumptions that influence how individuals behave in organizations. Much has been written about different cultures and subcultures, including the police subculture, and it appears that cultural organization has a significant impact on employee performances and behaviors. While it is easy to simply state that criminal justice agencies should create positive organizational cultures that value diversity and promote multiculturalism, it remains important that they do. Policies that encourage tolerance, acceptance, understanding of different groups, and the like would contribute much to addressing many of the issues faced in the criminal justice system. Among the means to create a more positive organizational culture are recruiting, selecting, and hiring individuals who will treat all groups and individuals with respect. Effective training, as noted above, also contributes to creating a positive organizational culture, as do specific programs designed to promote tolerance. For instance, the West Hartford (CT) Police Department adopted a policy designed to assist officers when interacting with members of the LGBT community. Among other requirements the policy notes that officers should use the person's preferred name as opposed to their legal name when interacting with them, and abide by the transgendered person's request to be searched by an officer of a specific gender.[55]

Several incidents in which the police were accused of using too much force against racial and ethnic minorities have resulted in less positive perceptions of the police. For instance, the shooting of Michael Brown by a Ferguson (MO) police officer generated protests in the city and around the country. In discussing the significance of race in contemporary urban policing, authors Jones-Brown, Moran, King-Toler, and Sudula offered three policy recommendations designed to enhance policing, including public perceptions of the police. Particularly, they suggest making multicultural competency an integral part of policing policy and practice; prioritizing constitutionality, transparency, and accountability; and analyzing the effects of police policies on racial and ethic minorities.[56] These suggestions, while offered with consideration of urban policing, could apply to all types of policing, and all components of the criminal justice system.

GLOBAL PERSPECTIVES

Consideration of the justice-based practices in other countries could enable us to adopt pieces, or aspects that could promote additional tolerance and fairness in our criminal justice system. Justice systems in the United States are based on English heritage, closely resemble criminal justice practices in some countries, and differ greatly from practices found in other countries. Our system has been refined over time, as various reforms in policing, the courts, and corrections have regularly reshaped our justice-based practices.

Consideration of other country's systems of justice may provide avenues through which we could enhance our policies and practices. Four legal traditions are recognized in countries across the globe.[57] The categories include the common tradition, the civil tradition, the Islamic tradition, and the Eastern Asia tradition. The **common legal tradition** is found in the United States and other countries and is based on feudal practices, custom, and equity. The **civil legal tradition** is based on Roman and canon laws, and codification. The **Islamic legal tradition** is based on the Qur'an and Sunna, as well as the doctrine of consensus and reasoning by analogy. The **Eastern Asia legal tradition** is grounded in the principles of Confucianism, along with collectivism, context, and informalism. The two primary legal systems today are the common law and civil law systems. Common law systems are found primarily in North American and England, while the civil law system is most often found throughout the rest of the world today.[58] Consideration of policies in other countries with similar legal traditions, and perhaps even those that differ greatly from those found in the United States, has the potential to enhance our justice-based practices.

Studying justice systems is beneficial in many ways, as it facilitates a better understanding of other people and cultures, and highlights avenues for improvement, especially with regard to policies. Further, it enables individuals to adopt a more global perspective of justice.[59] The need to better understand varying systems of justice and the ease with which transnational crimes can occur was highlighted by Thomas Friedman in his popular book *The World Is Flat: A Brief History of the Twenty-First Century*, in which he highlights how various societal changes, including those pertaining to communication and transportation, have impacted society in many important ways.[60] A primary benefit of globalization is the sharing of ideas and practices, which could benefit justice-based practices in the United States. The United States is certainly not the only country dealing with diversity-related issues both within and outside of its justice system. Identifying helpful and proven approaches to address the issues in other countries is a promising means by which to effectively address our issues.

Of particular importance when comparing international criminal justice systems is the need to consider what type of system is in place and the practices of the individuals in relation to the system. For instance, two countries may have a similar criminal justice system in design, however the laws may be applied with differing levels of severity and the use of discretion may differ. The system of justice in the United States is similar to what exists in England, however the United States is viewed as being particularly more punitive compared to England and many other countries.

SUMMARY

This chapter addressed two important issues that could help those who work in the criminal justice system in many ways: Training and policies. Training is required of all criminal justice employees, and helps prepare individuals for the situations they will encounter. Education is a very important component of training, but it alone cannot properly train an individual. Hands-on experience and guidance from supervisors and experienced colleagues are also important to one's training. Training requirements vary among the numerous positions in the criminal justice system, for instance as police officers and correctional officers attend training academies, while lawyers and judges attend law school and primarily learn from work experience and guidance. Training is limited in several ways, for instance as it cannot fully prepare individuals for what they will experience in the non-academy world.

Policies are created, implemented, and enforced with the goal to control behaviors. Criminal justice policy has been both very helpful and at times controversial. Many effective policies have been implemented, and their benefits often go unnoticed. The controversial policies draw most attention. Fortunately, policies are flexible and can be altered to address unanticipated challenges. Policies can be imposed at the agency level (e.g., with regard to decisions to prosecute) or on a much larger scale, for instance in the form of federal drug policies. Criminal justice agencies should consider policies from other countries in efforts to generate new, effective policies that could possibly be implemented in the United States.

YOU MAKE THE CALL

TEACHING DIVERSITY

Consider the following scenario. Debate the pros and cons of all options and decide what you would do.

You're a new college faculty member at a historically African American university. As part of your teaching assignment, you've been asked to teach the upper-level undergraduate "Minorities and Crime" course. As a White male, however, you're a bit apprehensive. Sure, you know all about crime and took courses and researched minority issues, but you never anticipated such a challenge this early in your teaching career. Aside from having to be current on your knowledge of crime, you also have to discuss minority issues to a large group of minorities. On the first day of class, a young man in the audience asks how you can comment on minority issues, when you have absolutely no life experience being a minority. You hoped this wouldn't be an issue, but you are prepared to answer the question.

Questions

1. How will you build credibility with the predominantly African American students?
2. How will you structure the course? In other words, would you approach the course from the views of minority groups or the views of the majority? Or, would you attempt to provide an adequate balance between both?
3. How would you answer the student's question?
4. Discuss how the following teaching tools that could assist with your situation:

- Class discussion
- Videos (what movies would you include?)
- Guest speakers
- Lecture

KEY TERMS

Black Lives Matter
civil legal tradition
common legal tradition
community liaison officers
criminal justice policy
culture-general training
culture-specific training
Eastern Asia legal tradition
field training
field training officer programs

halfway houses
Islamic legal tradition
NIMBY
organizational culture
Police Officers Standards and Training
    Commissions
policy
pre-service training
public policy
social justice

DISCUSSION QUESTIONS

1. To what extent do you believe additional training for police officers will alleviate the problems we've seen with officers allegedly misusing their powers against African American males?
2. Should prosecutors and defense attorneys be required to attend a training academy, akin to what is required of police officers? Or, do you believe law school and on-the-job experience alone appropriately prepare attorneys for working in the courts?
3. Assume you are a city manager tasked with locating a new prison in your city. What factors will you consider in placing the facility? Will you select the areas where there will be the least amount of resistance? Discuss.
4. What recent policy (since the 1980s) has most notably impacted the criminal justice system? Do you support this policy? Discuss.
5. What do you believe are the limitations in looking to other countries for guidance with regard to criminal justice policy? Should the United States consider what policies work and which ones do not in other countries? Discuss.

FOR FURTHER READING

Friedman, T. L. *The World is Flat: A Brief History of the Twenty-First Century.* New York: Farrar, Straus, and Giroux, 2005.

Haberfeld, M. *Critical Issues in Police Training,* 3rd ed. Upper Saddle River, NJ: Pearson, 2013.

Reichel, P. L. *Comparative Criminal Justice Systems: A Topical Approach.* Upper Saddle River, NJ: Pearson, 2013.

Welsh, W. N., and P. W. Harris, *Criminal Justice Policy and Planning: Planned Change,* 5th ed. New York: Routledge, 2016.

Worrall, J. L. *Crime Control in America: What Works?* 3rd ed. Boston, MA: Pearson, 2014.

NOTES

1. C. T. Lowenkamp, A. M. Holsinger, A. W. Flores, I. Koutsenok, and N. Pearl, "Changing Probation Officer Attitudes: Training Experience, Motivation, and Knowledge," *Federal Probation* 77, no. 2 (2013): 54–58.

2. R. Brislin and T. Yoshida, *Intercultural Communication Training: An Introduction* (Thousand Oaks, CA: Sage, 1994).

3. Myrna M. Cornett-DeVito and Edward L. McGlone, "Multicultural Communication Training for Law Enforcement Officers: A Case Study," *Criminal Justice Policy Review* 11, no. 3 (2000): 234–53.

4. Ibid., 234.

5. T. Keesee and M. J. Nila, "Fairness and Neutrality: Addressing the Issue of Race in Policing," *The Police Chief,* 78 (2011): 34–39.

6. D. K. Magner, "Fewer Professors Believe Western Culture Should be the Cornerstone of the College Curriculum," *Chronicle of Higher Education* (Sept. 13, 1996): 12–13.

7. T Platt, "Desegregating Multiculturalism: Problems in the Theory and Pedagogy of Diversity Education," *Social Justice* 29, no. 4 (2002): 41–46.

8. Ibid.

9. See C. M. Mann and M. S. Zatz, "A Fragile Future: Pitfalls and Possibilities," *Images of Color, Images of Crime,* 3rd edition, ed. C. R. Mann, M. S. Zatz, and N. Rodriguez (Los Angeles, CA: Roxbury, 2006), 252–64.

10. W. Calathes, "The Case for a Multicultural Approach to Teaching Criminal Justice," *Journal of Criminal Justice Education* 5, no. 1 (1994): 1–14.

11. Ibid., 4.

12. Ibid., 9–11.

13. M. J. King, "'Deliberate Indifference': Liability for Failure to Train," *FBI Law Enforcement Bulletin* 74, no. 10 (Oct. 2005): 22–31.

14. Louisiana Commission on Law Enforcement and Administration of Criminal Justice, "Peace Officer Standards and Training Council," Nov. 27, 2016. Accessed online at: http://www.cole.state.la.us/programs/post.asp

15. E. A. Thibault, L. M. Lynch, R. B. McBride, and G. Walsh, *Proactive Police Management,* 9th edition (Upper Saddle River, NJ: Pearson, 2015).

16. Kenneth W. Flynn, "Training and Police Violence," in *Policing and Violence,* ed. R. G. Burns and C. E. Crawford (Upper Saddle River, NJ: Prentice Hall, 2002), 127–46.

17. President's Task Force on 21st Century Policing, *Final Report of the President's Task Force on 21st Century Policing* (Washington, DC: Office of Community Oriented Policing Services, 2015), 4.

18. B. A. Reaves, *State and Local Law Enforcement Training Academies, 2013*. U.S. Department of Justice, Bureau of Justice Statistics, 2016. NCJ 249784. P.4.

19. Ibid., 7.

20. Daniel P. Carlson, *When Cultures Clash: The Divisive Nature of Police-Community Relations and Suggestions for Improvement* (Upper Saddle River, NJ: Prentice Hall, 2003).

21. J. S. Redfern, "Best Practices to Improve Police Relations with Transgender Individuals," *Journal of Law Enforcement* 3, no. 4 (2013). Accessed online at: http://jghcs.info/index.php/l/article/view/265/239.

22. R. M. Getty, J. L. Worrall, and R. G. Morris, "How Far from the Tree Does That Apple Fall? Field Training Officers, Their Trainees, and Allegations of Misconduct," *Crime & Delinquency* 62, no. 2 (2016): 821–39.

23. T. F. Lawson, "Mainstreaming Civil Rights in the Law School Curriculum: Criminal Law and Criminal Procedure," *St. Louis University Law Journal* 54 no. 3 (2010): 838.

24. D. W. Neubauer and H. F. Fradella, *America's Courts and the Criminal Justice System*, 7th ed. (Boston, MA: Cangage, 2017).

25. Neubauer and Fradella, *America's Courts*.

26. P. E. Mann, "Progressing from Law School to J.D. to Public Defender, Training Is the Key," National Legal Aid & Defender Association, 2010. Accessed online at http://www.nlada.net/library/articles/na_trainingisthekeyndli

27. *ABA Ten Principles of a Public Defense Deliver System*, American Bar Association, Feb. 2002, 3. Accessed online at: http://www.americanbar.org/content/dam/aba/administrative/legal_aid_indigent_defendants/ls_sclaid_def_tenprinciplesbooklet.authcheckdam.pdf

28. N. Sharp, "Judicial Formation: A Step Beyond Education or Training for New Judges," *Justice System Journal* 29, no. 1 (2008): 100–104.

29. New Jersey Courts. (2016). "Judicial Performance and Education Programs. Judicial Performance Program: A Brief Description," 2016. Accessed online at: http://www.judiciary.state.nj.us/education/

30. W. E. Raftery, "Get Thee a Law Degree! More States Are Imposing Minimum Educational Requirements for Judges," *Judicature* 100, no. 2 (2016): 7–8.

31. J. S. Bard, "Practicing Medicine and Studying Law: How Medical Schools Used to Have the Same Problems We Do and What We Can Learn from Their Efforts to Solve Them," *Seattle Journal for Social Justice* 10 (2011): 135–209.

32. C. S. Alexander, "Learning to Be Lawyers: Professional Identity and the Law School Curriculum," *Maryland Law Review* 70, no. 2 (2011): 465–83.

33. H. E. Williamson, *The Corrections Profession* (Newbury Park, CA: Sage, 1990).

34. F. Schmalleger and J. O. Smykla, *Corrections in the 21st Century*, 4th ed. (New York: McGraw-Hill, 2009).

35. Nevada Department of Public Safety, n.d., "Parole and Probation." Accessed online at: http://npp.dps.nv.gov/Employment/Officer_Training/

36. Reginald A. Wilkinson, "Diversity in Correctional Management: An Essential Tool," in *The Full Spectrum: Essays on Staff Diversity in Corrections*, ed. C. Smalls (Lanham, MD: American Correctional Association, 2004), 117–25.

37. P. Hunt, "Correctional Officers Need Cultural Diversity Training," in Smalls *The Full Spectrum*, 127–55.

38. A. T. Aguire, "Latinos in Corrections: One View," in Smalls, *The Full Spectrum*, 65–74.

39. R. A. Shearer, and P. A. King, "Multicultural Competencies in Probation: Issues and Challenges," *Federal Probation* 68, no. 1 (June 2004): 3–9.

40. P. C. Kratcoski, "The Implications of Research Explaining Prison Violence and Disruption," *Federal Probation* 52, no. 1 (1988): 27–32.

41. P. F. McManimon Jr., "Correlates of Jail Violence." *American Jails* (May/June 2004), 41–43, 45–47.

42. Linda Dillon, "Effective Communication Embraces Diversity," in Smalls, *The Full Spectrum*, 1–9.

43. S. Walker and C. M. Katz, *The Police in America*, 7th edition (New York: McGraw-Hill, 2011).

44. Thibault et al., *Proactive Police Management*.

45. Carlson, *When Cultures Clash*, 61.

46. R. Rifkin, "Racism Edges Up Again as Most Important U.S. Problem," Gallup, July 16 2015. Accessed online at: http://www.gallup.com/poll/184193/racism-edges-again-important-problem.aspx?g_source=race&g_medium=search&g_campaign=tiles

47. J. Norman, "U.S. Worries About Race Relations Reach a New High," Gallup, April 11, 2016. Accessed online at: http://www.gallup.com/poll/190574/worries-race-relations-reach-new-high.aspx?g_source=police&g_medium=search&g_campaign=tiles

48. Ibid.

49. F. Newport, "U.S. Confidence in Police Recovers from Last Year's Low," Gallup, June 14, 2016. Accessed online at: http://www.gallup.com/poll/192701/confidence-police-recovers-last-year-low.aspx

50. M. Younis, "Perceptions of Muslims in the United States: A Review," Gallup, Dec. 11, 2011. Accessed online at: http://www.gallup.com/opinion/gallup/187664/perceptions-muslims-united-states-review.aspx

51. Gallup, "Confidence in Institutions," June 1–5, 2016. Accessed online at: http://www.gallup.com/poll/1597/confidence-institutions.aspx

52. M. J. Lynch, R. G. Burns, and P. Stretesky, *Environmental Law, Crime, and Justice*, 2nd ed. (El Paso, TX: LFB Scholarly, 2014).

53. S. E. Costanza, J. C. Kilburn Jr., and S. Vendetti-Koski, "Are Minority Areas Disproportionately Targeted for Halfway House Placement?" *Journal of Ethnicity in Criminal Justice* 11 (2013): 256–76.

54. B. A. Arrigo, *Social Justice/Criminal Justice: The Maturation of Critical Theory in Law, Crime, and Deviance* (Belmont, CA: Wadsworth, 1999), 282.

55. Associated Press, "West Hartford Police Department Adopts New LGBT Policy," *Washington Times*, August 15, 2016. Accessed online at: http://www.washingtontimes.com/news/2016/aug/15/west-hartford-police-department-adopts-new-lgbt-po/

56. D. Jones-Brown, K. Moran, E. King-Toler, and S. Sudula, "The Significance of Race in Contemporary Urban Policing Policy," in *U.S. Criminal Justice Policy: A Contemporary Reader*, 2nd edition, ed. K. Ismaili (Burlington, MA: Jones & Bartlett, 2017), 21–61.

57. P. L. Reichel, *Comparative Criminal Justice Systems: A Topical Approach* (Upper Saddle River, NJ: Pearson, 2013).

58. H. Wallace and C. Roberson, *Principles of Criminal Law*, 3rd ed. (Boston, MA: Pearson Allyn & Bacon, 2006).

59. Reichel, *Comparitive Criminal Justice Systems*.

60. T. L. Friedman, *The World is Flat: A Brief History of the Twenty-First Century*. (New York: Farrar, Straus, and Giroux, 2005).

CHAPTER 15

THE FUTURE OF DIVERSITY AND MULTICULTURALISM IN CRIMINAL JUSTICE: STRATEGIES FOR SUCCESS

CHAPTER OBJECTIVES

After reading this chapter, you should be able to:

* Understand the methods by which the future is forecasted
* Recognize the drivers that influence the future of multiculturalism and criminal justice
* Identify and discuss the critical issues challenging the future of multiculturalism and criminal justice
* Discuss the extent to which progress has been made with regard to multiculturalism and criminal justice

The future of multiculturalism and diversity, particularly as it relates to criminal justice, can be viewed from many perspectives. For instance, one could observe the positive changes, such as the increased presence of minority groups working within the system, and this could be one reason to have optimism about the future of the system. Conversely, differential treatment of groups still exists in the criminal justice system, contributing to the perception that multiculturalism and diversity are simply buzzwords for something not likely to occur in criminal justice or in society in general. How, exactly, will we know what the future holds for multiculturalism?

This question can only be answered with time as the future plays out and we see what becomes of our increasingly diverse society. Yet, sitting back and waiting to see what happens (i.e., taking a reactive approach) is likely detrimental. Tomorrow's professionals are tasked with making society a better place, and doing so requires proactive efforts. Recognizing the nature and extent of the problems faced by our current justice system is the most appropriate place to begin. Accordingly, the preceding chapters have examined the hurdles and obstacles faced by different groups within the criminal justice system. The chapters have also examined how the criminal justice system has responded to an increasingly diverse society. Thus, the foundation for progress has been set. Now comes the tricky part: understanding what can be done.

FORECASTING THE FUTURE

Futurists are scientists who forecast future developments in society. Notice the term "forecast" is used in place of the term "prediction." **Forecasting** involves the use of scientific techniques regarding future developments. These developments can be topic or discipline-specific (e.g., pertain solely to criminal justice) or more general in nature. **Predictions**, on the other hand, involve instinctual feelings (aka "gut feelings") that lack scientific validity. The difference between the terms is evidenced in your local news programming when meteorologists forecast the weather through the use of various models. Meteorologists offer weather forecasts based on scientific evidence as opposed to gut feelings. As we all know, however, the forecast is not always correct. While forecasting provides a more scientific-based assessment of future developments, there is certainly an element of error involved.

Forecasting the weather and forecasting what will become of multiculturalism and the criminal justice system seem quite different and they are in many respects. Nevertheless, the incorporation of scientific methods makes both types of forecasting similar. Weather patterns are distinct from human behavior, yet science enables us to anticipate changes in the weather much like we anticipate changes in human behavior. As a social science, criminal justice is vulnerable to changes in human behavior. It differs from the hard sciences such as chemistry where it is certain that the combination of particularly substances will have a particular effect. Errors are more likely to occur in the social sciences given the varied nature of society in general.

Consider the changes that occurred following the terrorist attacks against the United States on September 11, 2001. Many forecasts made as late as September 10, 2001, were largely, and unexpectedly, impacted by the changes that ensued. The resulting reorganization of federal law enforcement agencies in the United States and an overriding concern for homeland security changed daily lives and significantly impacted the criminal justice system. For example, local law enforcement agencies now must maintain an intensified concern for homeland security and are competing for scarce personnel resources as the wars in Iraq and Afghanistan have required the services of qualified applicants.

Futurists use several techniques to forecast the future. Prominent among the methods are **quantitative analyses**, which involve the use of statistics and trends to anticipate changes in society. Demographers, for instance, observe population trends and offer input regarding the demographic nature of society in the forthcoming years. Forecasters and futurists also consider **qualitative approaches**, which largely involve examination of non-numerical trends and patterns in attempt to anticipate future developments and changes. Among the qualitative approaches to forecasting the future is the **Delphi method**, in which experts offer input regarding anticipated developments in their area of expertise. For instance, a forecaster intent on using the Delphi method to anticipate the future of criminal behavior may seek input from experts in the fields of sociology, biology, demography,

economics, and criminal justice. The collaborative efforts of professionals result in anticipated changes in the future. Futurist Gene Stephens used the Delphi method when he surveyed police experts regarding the role of the police in the future. Briefly, the group agreed
that better-educated police officers with enhanced interpersonal skills and an understanding of technology were needed for the future success of policing.[1] The use of **scenarios**, in
which a narrative is used to describe anticipated future events, is another method utilized
by forecasters. To be sure, there are other methods by which the future is forecasted. Advanced statistical analyses and the increased incorporation of technology in forecasting,
specifically computers, have improved the accuracy of future expectations.

There is debate regarding which forecasting method is most effective; however, analyses of multiple forecasts of the future may show consistencies and offer substantial confidence. In addition to selecting a forecasting method, futurist researchers must select
appropriate variables for their analyses. Of particular concern when forecasting are **drivers
of the future**, or particular issues which have significant impacts on the future. Among the
drivers of forecasting, particularly with regard to criminal justice, are economics, crime
factors (e.g., the increasing amount of international and computer crime), demographics,
technology, and politics. Timeframe is also of significance to forecasting, as researchers
must consider how far out into the future they're projecting. There are no restrictions on
how far into the future one can forecast; however, the accuracy of the forecast generally
decreases as one looks further into the future.[2]

FORECASTING MULTICULTURALISM IN THE CRIMINAL JUSTICE SYSTEM

So, what's expected with regard to multiculturalism and criminal justice? In this section
we offer our analyses, using various forecasting methods, regarding the future of criminal
justice with concern for multiculturalism. There are many limitations to our analyses, as
we provide a simplified, broad forecast of the future. For instance, we provide general
overviews of trend data and forego advanced statistical analyses of the many significant
factors that drive changes in the criminal justice system. We leave the hardcore forecasting
to futurist researchers. Our analyses, nevertheless, offer a general overview of expected
changes and demonstrate how forecasting the future is conducted.

To begin, we must first consider a time frame. Let's look at anticipated changes in
ten years. Next, we have to identify our method of forecasting the future. As mentioned,
comparing the outcomes of multiple forecasting methods generally provides a greater level
of confidence, thus, let's conduct both a qualitative and quantitative approach. We also
must consider what exactly we're trying to forecast. For instance, are we forecasting the anticipated increase or decrease in the number of minorities working in the criminal justice
system? Or, are we interested in the projected number of offenders? Let's consider diversity
and the anticipated number of prisoners.

In 1980 the incarceration rate in the United States was 139 inmates in state and federal
prisons per 100,000 population.[3] In 2007 and 2008 the rate reached 510. The incarceration rate began consistently declining in 2009, and as of 2014 was at 470.[4] Based on this
trend and the costs associated with incarcerating notably large numbers of individuals, it's
relatively safe to suggest that the incarceration rate will continue to slowly decline in the

next ten years, although it is doubtful that we will see the rates found in the early 1980s and prior. Despite the recent declines, there remain concerns with regard to multicultural-ism and diversity.

Demographics are a primary driver of change in the criminal justice system with regard to diversity and multiculturalism. Data from the U.S. Census Bureau suggests that by 2044 over half of all Americans are projected to belong to a minority group, and Hispanics will constitute nearly 29 percent of the U.S. population by the year 2060, up from 12.6 percent in 2000. The percentage of African Americans in the United States is expected to remain about the same, increasing from 13.2 percent in 2014 to 14.3 percent by 2060, however the Asian population is expected to grow (from 5.4 percent to 9.3 percent) as is the percentage of individuals who are two or more races (from 2.5 percent to 6.2 percent).[5] Given that minorities are overrepresented in U.S. prisons and the percentages of minorities in society are expected to increase, one can anticipate continued minority overrepresentation in our prisons. Thus, the importance of studying diversity within the criminal justice system is even more important and necessary.

To be sure, this is a *very* simplistic quantitative forecast. Many other factors besides historical practices influence incarceration trends. True forecasting methods take much more into account and involve more advanced analyses. This example, however, is offered to broadly demonstrate how forecasting is conducted. Below we offer an equally simplistic qualitative forecast regarding multiculturalism and incarceration. Again, hardcore qualita-tive forecasting involves much more analyses, consideration, and depth than the cursory examination we provide. Our analyses are based on recent developments in several areas that appear to have implications for the future of incarceration.

Below we discuss three significant societal trends that will likely impact the future of incarceration as it pertains to diversity and culture. Many other qualitative factors will certainly impact the nature and extent of U.S. incarceration. We've identified factors that we believe are among the most significant drivers of incarceration in the future, with par-ticular concern for diversity and multiculturalism.

First, issues pertaining to homeland security will continue to result in the expansion of law enforcement. For better or for worse, ours is a time of enhanced social control pri-marily due to terrorist threats. Accordingly, enhanced law enforcement and other social control efforts will mean continued increasing incarceration rates and the continued over-representation of minorities in the criminal justice system, as these groups are continu-ously closely monitored by law enforcement.

Second, females and other minorities will continue to be more visible in the crimi-nal justice system. For instance, Chapter 7 of this book highlighted the changing nature of the criminal justice system as females become more actively involved as arrestees/offenders and practitioners. As females become increasingly involved in everyday ac-tivities, it is expected that their presence in the criminal justice system will continue to increase.

Additionally, no signs point to decreased involvement of racial and ethnic minorities in the criminal justice system. The continued overrepresentation of minorities, particu-larly African Americans, as suspects and offenders in the criminal justice system does not seem to be waning. The social factors that contribute to the increased incarceration among minority groups persist and are perhaps becoming even more pronounced than during the past 20-30 years when incarceration rates notably impacted minority communities. Increased levels of poverty and single-parent families are prominent among the factors contributing to increased minority representation in the criminal justice system.

Another qualitative factor likely to influence the nature of U.S. incarceration in the coming years concerns the increasing frequency with which international crimes occur. Thomas L. Friedman's best-selling book *The World is Flat: A Brief History of the Twenty-first Century* documents how increased globalization has and will continue to impact the world.[6] Along these lines, it is anticipated that an increased amount of crime will have an international flavor as more opportunities for criminal behavior appear. In turn, criminal justice officials in the United States will have to continue working with other countries and promoting cooperative and collaborative efforts to ensure justice. Such efforts will result in the continued diversification of the system. For the purposes of our forecasting efforts, increased international crime will result in a greater need for multiculturalism in corrections. The need to recognize and react to various cultural backgrounds will increase as more offenders from around the globe enter our prisons.

Our forecasting efforts have targeted the future of incarceration with concern for multiculturalism. We could also observe the future of minority involvement as practitioners in the criminal justice system; and a variety of other, related issues. Regardless of our approach, the future of the criminal justice system and multiculturalism will be shaped by a variety of factors. Below we turn our attention to several critical issues that affect and are

Increased globalism will require criminal justice practitioners to overcome many challenges, including language barriers. Having them understand key phrases, or even learning different languages will contribute to more effective justice-based practices.

expected to continue impacting the criminal justice system. The mere existence of these issues provides a discouraging commentary on the current state of tolerance for diversity and multiculturalism as it exists in society in general.

CRITICAL ISSUES AFFECTING MULTICULTURALISM AND CRIMINAL JUSTICE

Several critical issues hamper, and will continue to impact, efforts toward a multicultural society in the United States. These issues are not restricted to the United States, as other countries face the same obstacles. Prominent among the issues impeding a completely multicultural society are racial profiling, hate crimes, immigration, and globalization.

RACIAL AND ETHNIC PROFILING

Racial and ethnic profiling are discussed in several chapters of this book, particularly in our focus on policing and multiculturalism. Police officers are often criticized for disproportionately targeting minority drivers in attempt to uncover drug trafficking. However, racial and ethnic profiling are not restricted to our roadways, as minorities have been unlawfully approached in their homes, while walking on public streets, at airports, in shopping areas, and in other places. An estimated 32 million Americans believe they have been subject to racial profiling in their lifetime.[7]

The practice of racial and ethnic profiling provides a gauge to determine society's concern for due process and crime control. Scholar Herbert Packer commented on these two competing models of criminal justice. The **crime control model of criminal justice** maintains an emphasis on expediency and reducing crime, yet such practices often occur at the expense of individual rights. The **due process model of criminal justice** is primarily concerned with respecting individual rights, yet doing so often comes at the expense of controlling crime.[8] In the United States, concern for homeland security and drug crimes has resulted in a criminal justice system focused on crime control that too often comes at the expense of individual rights. The notable concern about racial and ethnic profiling among minority communities provides evidence of this claim. Finding the proper balance between crime control and individual rights is often difficult in a multicultural, heterogeneous society such as the United States. A criminal justice system that recognizes and responds to multiculturalism is one that includes no racial or ethnic profiling. Future criminal justice practices will hopefully be void of race-based and culture-based crime fighting efforts.

Related to concerns for racial and ethnic profiling is implicit bias. Criminal justice agencies at all levels of government continue to try and identify, recruit, and train personnel who are bias-free. The existence of implicit bias, however, makes this difficult as it is often difficult to determine what exists inside an individual. Job candidates may appear bias-free during the selection process, however subtle (and sometimes not so subtle), biased actions after being hired may be masked by the nature of the work. For instance, a patrol officer who disproportionately runs the license plates of Hispanic motorists out of a subconscious belief that the car was stolen may go unnoticed, despite the fact that the officer is stereotyping.

HATE CRIMES

Hate crimes involve illegal actions that are motivated by hate and taken against particular groups. The term hate crime didn't exist prior to the 1980s and is sometimes used interchangeably with **bias crime**, which involves illegal acts taken against a group based on some form of bias. While the motivation, hate, is consistent in all hate crimes, the target and offender characteristics of hate crimes are not. The hatred or bias can be based on one's race, gender, religion, ethnicity, sexual orientation, disability, age, or political affiliation. Hate crimes are not, however, solely committed against minority groups, as White males have also been the target of hate-motivated incidents. That an individual would be motivated to break the law based on hatred of a particular group suggests that not everyone is tolerant of diversity. The mere existence of hate crimes in society demonstrates that much work remains with regard to creating a society that embraces multiculturalism.

Hate crime statistics, albeit controversial, speak loudly of the need for acceptance of multiculturalism. In 2014, there were over 6,100 offenses reported as being motivated by bias toward race, gender, gender identity, religion, disability, sexual orientation, and ethnicity. Most (63 percent) of these incidents involved violent crimes, including four murders and nine rapes. Race was the motivating factor for the hate crime in most cases (48.3 percent), followed by sexual orientation bias (18.7 percent) and religious bias (17.1 percent).[9]

As discussed in Chapter 8, determining what, specifically, constitutes a hate crime is difficult. Similar to the difficulties found in courtrooms when attorneys attempt to determine whether or not the accused had the intent to commit a crime, determining one's motivation for committing a crime is not always easily done. Is the White supremacist who robs an African American female guilty of a hate crime? Yes, if he admits his motivation was hatred or his actions (e.g., verbal comments) suggest hatred prompted the robbery. Otherwise, attorneys, judges, and jurors have to speculate or assume the crime wasn't hate-motivated. Perhaps the African American female provided the most opportune target for the offender.

Accordingly, one must consider hate crime statistics with caution, as there are several limitations to measuring hate crime. Particularly, the varied definitions of hate crime, the difficulty in determining one's motivation, and the sometimes unreliable data-gathering methods of researchers, the government, and advocacy groups can distort the prevalence of hate crime in society. Authors James Jacobs and Kimberly Potter argue that there is no reliable evidence pointing to an increase in hate crimes. They suggest the current hate-crime movement is motivated by increased sensitivity to prejudice and bigotry.[10]

Hate crime laws provide enhanced penalties for offenders charged with crimes involving hate-motivation. The ultimate goal is to promote tolerance and to recognize the benefits of diversity. The argument is that offenders who commit crime out of hatred or bias are morally worse, and thus more culpable, than those who engage in crime for other reasons. Hate crime laws are also justified on the grounds that hate crimes disproportionately impose injuries and harms to victims, have more substantial negative impacts on the community than do typical crimes, and facilitate the potential for retaliation and intergroup conflict. Hate crime legislation is intended to send a message that society is concerned about diversity and tolerance, and ultimately deterring criminal behavior. Whether or not the goals of hate crime legislation are being reached is the subject of debate.[11] Hate crimes would not exist in a society that embraces multiculturalism. What current and future efforts are needed to eliminate or at the very least reduce hate crime incidents? This and related questions are addressed later in this chapter.

IMMIGRATION

The multicultural makeup of the United States is one of the many strengths of the country. Accordingly, the United States takes pride in its diversity. The excerpt from Emma Lazarus's poem "The New Colossus" engraved at the bottom of the Statue of Liberty speaks loudly:

> Give me your tired, your poor,
> Your huddled masses yearning to breathe free,
> The wretched refuse of your teeming shore.
> Send these, the homeless, tempest-tossed, to me:
> I lift my lamp beside the golden door.[12]

Despite these words, there is current debate regarding immigration into the United States. When discussing immigration, a distinction must be made between legal and illegal immigration. Legal immigration can be controlled by the government, in turn providing a monitor to protect overpopulation and the economic well-being of the country, among other things. Illegal immigration is a different matter. The government attempts to protect against illegal immigrants entering the country, however, doing so has been difficult and controversial. Too often discussions of immigration intermix references to both groups and the discussion becomes clouded. Currently, there is a particular concern with illegal immigration, which is making life more difficult for legal immigrants.

Illegal immigration attracts substantial attention given the illegal status of those who enter the country without permission. In the fight against illegal immigration, those opposed to immigration are joined by those opposed to law-breakers. The fight against illegal immigration extends from the federal government to local communities. In 2006 the U.S. Congress introduced legislation to make illegal immigration a

The Statue of Liberty is a symbol of freedom and the United States' willingness to accept all groups of people. Not everyone, however, can easily enter the country.

felony and build a 700-mile fence along the Mexican border. Immigration and Customs Enforcement, under direction of the Department of Homeland Security, announced in 2006 that it would triple the number of fugitive-hunting teams, with the goal of doubling the number in 2007.[13] About 650 miles of fence currently exists with plans to build additional fences.

Critics of illegal immigration argue that the federal government hasn't done enough in response to the number of immigrants illegally entering the United States. Accordingly, state legislatures and local municipalities have taken action by considering and adopting an unprecedented number of measures to address the issue. From January through June 2007, 171 immigration bills became law in 41 states, which is twice as many as the 84 laws passed in all of 2006.[14] Tennessee made it a criminal offense, rather than a civil offense, to "recklessly employ" illegal immigrants. Fines for doing so can be up to $50,000.[15] Most states (40) require a Social Security number for obtaining a driver's license, which precludes unauthorized immigrants from driving legally; most states (30) do not permit unauthorized immigrants to attend a public college at the same in-state tuition rate that legal residents and American citizens pay, and only a few permit them to apply for financial aid, and; following the lead of Arizona, which in 2010 passed a law requiring the police to question anyone they arrest about immigration status if they suspect the person is in the United States illegally, five other states enacted similar laws. In 2014, President Barak Obama used executive orders that would give work permits and protections from deportation to roughly four million unauthorized immigrants. The action was challenged by twenty-six states as unconstitutional, and in June 2016 the U.S. Supreme Court blocked President Obama's orders.[16] These are just a few of the many steps taken by state legislatures to control illegal immigration.

City governments around the country are also responding to complaints about illegal immigrants. The city of Hazleton, Pennsylvania passed the "Illegal Immigration Relief Act" which included fines for landlords who rent to illegal immigrants and denying business permits to companies that employ them. Then-mayor of Hazleton Lou Barletta cited drug, crime, and gang problems involving illegal immigrants as the impetus behind the act. Critics of the act stated that the law usurped the federal government's power to regulate immigration, deprived residents of their constitutional rights to due process, and violated federal housing laws.[17] A federal judge voided the act. Hazleton, however, is not the only city to react to illegal immigration, as cities around the United States have responded in a similar and sometimes more punitive manner. These actions will also continue to be considered in courts around the country.

The 2016 election of Donald Trump as president of the United States further fueled discussions regarding immigration, as Trump adopted a tough stance toward immigration. Among the proposed actions Trump planned to take to curtail illegal immigration were building a wall to separate the United States from Mexico and employing additional technological devices to catch those seeking to illegally cross the border, and mass-deporting illegal immigrants currently in the United States. With regard to the latter, Trump could revoke former president Barak Obama's earlier actions which protected over 700,000 undocumented immigrants who came to the United States as children. After being elected,

Trump adopted a somewhat softer approach to some immigration issues, however immigration will likely remain at the forefront of much political discussion.

While much of the debate concerning immigration centers on illegal immigration, legal immigrants face particular challenges. For instance, from a criminal justice perspective, immigrants are victimized at rates similar to the general population, yet their rate of reporting victimization is much lower. The underreporting of criminal victimization of immigrants stems largely from the hardships associated with appearing in court, including language barriers, uncertainty regarding the U.S. criminal justice system, and general cultural differences.[18]

Among other effects, the failure to report crime fails to ensure the protection of all citizens and undermines the effectiveness of the criminal justice system. At the very least, it increases the likelihood of the offender committing further crime. Efforts have been made to address the underreporting by providing interpreters during court hearings and various victims outreach programs in communities heavily populated by immigrants.[19] It can be stated with confidence that the future of criminal justice and multiculturalism will be heavily impacted by immigration issues.

Racial and ethnic profiling, hate crimes, and immigration concerns are not the only critical issues challenging efforts toward multiculturalism. These issues were discussed based on their relevance to the criminal justice system. Several other issues are affecting multiculturalism in the larger society. For instance, there has been and continues to be debate regarding prayers in schools. Should students be permitted to express their religious beliefs in a school setting?

Bigotry, prejudice, and bias are evident in many issues and at minimum hamper efforts toward tolerance. So what can be done? Are the immigration laws and reactions to our diverse society appropriate? The criminal justice system has, in the past, responded to discrimination and diversity-related issues. Efforts to eliminate or at least reduce discrimination in the criminal justice system are evident in actions such as sentencing guidelines, the 1970s decision to nullify existing capital punishment statutes, and an increased focus on diversity training among all criminal justice practitioners. However, attempts to limit or remove the impacts of discretionary actions by criminal justice professionals do not always reduce discriminatory practices. For instance, the manner in which capital punishment is used continues to be controversial in that poor minorities are more likely than their counterparts to face execution.[20]

Is there an "American culture" to which all groups in the United States must subscribe? Given the historical development of the United States (in which waves of immigrants landed on U.S. soil and helped build the country into what it is today) and failed efforts to change cultural beliefs, one could make a strong argument that tolerance of diverse cultures is needed. To be sure, culture conflict will continue. The goal is to eliminate, or at least minimize the harms.

GLOBALISM AND INTERNATIONAL CRIME

Concerns for immigration in the United States and elsewhere largely stem from globalism. **Globalization** refers to the international integration of cultural, social, and economic issues among countries that have historically been distinct from one another. The

Concerns regarding illegal immigration in the United States have generated many enforcement actions at various levels of government. Finding an immigration policy that pleases all groups has long challenged government leaders.

increasingly international nature of crime and justice requires greater interaction among countries, particularly with regard to justice-based efforts. Simply, criminal justice agencies across the globe will need to be legally and procedurally prepared to confront such crimes.

The experienced and anticipated changes in the demographics and diversity in the United States largely stems from communication, travel, and commerce becoming increasingly global in nature. The ease with which one can travel to, or communicate with individuals in other countries has diversified the United States, but it has also created several challenges. For instance, increased globalism contributes to increased levels of international crime, and jurisdictional issues cause concerns regarding extradition, and cooperation between countries, agencies, and justice officials will continue to become increasingly important. Criminal justice agencies will likely face an increasing number of challenging situations caused by increased globalism. Anticipating these changes and challenges will help officials prepare for and respond to them in the future.

In citing the need for our justice systems to prepare for the future, one researcher noted that "there's no question that terrorism, the growth of multicultural populations, massive migration, upheaval in age-composition demographics, technological developments, and globalization over the next three or more decades will affect the world's criminal justice systems."[21] This and related comments regarding the future of the criminal justice suggest that increasing change, including an increasingly diverse society, is indeed ahead for the United States.

Differences in laws, ideology, and justice-based practices among countries hamper efforts to address international crime. Increased globalism has, to some extent, enhanced levels of cooperation among different countries, however, much work remains. Among the biggest hurdles to overcome are conflict and change. Conflict among countries hampers justice-based efforts, and changes influence justice-based practices at differing rates and in various forms, as some countries are more advanced than others.[22]

International crime has historically involved organized crime and drug offenses, including piracy and White slavery among the earliest forms. International relations between involved countries often influenced the level of cooperation and ultimate resolutions of the cases.[23] Over time, however, international crimes have expanded in scope and occur more frequently. Crimes involving harms to the environment, gang crimes, weapons trafficking, and other crimes often associated with organized crime groups that were once viewed primarily as domestic concerns have become international in nature. The increased reliance of the Internet and the associated vulnerabilities to criminal victimization, as well as human trafficking, have also expanded the scope and frequency of international crime.

Several incidents in the 1970s drew attention to the need for countries to better address global crimes. The expansion of the illegal drug trade, concerns about human trafficking and exploiting humans, and several terrorist attacks highlighted the increasingly international nature of crime.[24] International crime increased in the 1980s with trade and finance becoming increasingly international,[25] and the 2001 terrorist attacks against the United States prompted a more aggressive U.S. response to international crime concerns and homeland security in general.

International crimes are traditional forms of crime that cross borders of countries. They are difficult to detect, apprehend, and adjudicate due to the various countries involved, and while the public is more familiar with everyday street crime, it was noted "the level of transnational crime affecting the United States is not inconsequential."[26] Organized crime groups, terrorists, drug cartels, and others are expected to continued challenge criminal justice officials, as international crime becomes increasingly complex and occurs with greater frequency. For instance, various organized crime groups, including the Chinese triads, the Yakuza, La Cosa Nostra, Russian gangs, and Mexican and Colombian drug cartels, are among the many groups that have engaged in international crime and have exploited weaknesses in international crime fighting efforts.

Among the more troubling forms of international crime is **human trafficking**, which involves "the involuntary movement of people across and within borders and typically involves coercion, deception, and violence," and is not legal anywhere in the world.[27] Human trafficking has become increasingly problematic in many countries and has been deemed "a major worldwide concern" and "Likely one of the most egregious acts violating the most basic and fundamental human rights."[28] Millions of men, women, and children are trafficked around the globe, creating a $32 billion per year industry that is second only to drug trafficking as the most profitable form of international crime.[29]

Efforts to address human trafficking include specialized courts that focus directly on these cases. The Human Trafficking Intervention Courts in New York State are an example, as the statewide system of courts was created in large response to claims from criminal justice professionals and others that it is better to recognize prostitutes as victims instead of defendants or criminals. The view is largely the result of increased societal focus on human trafficking and exploitation of young girls in the United States. Upon determination by the court that a prostitute is a victim of human trafficking or sex trafficking, the defendants in the courts is provided protective services such as drug treatment, shelter, healthcare, job training, and education in efforts to prevent them from returning to the sex trade.[30]

Extradition involves a state surrendering an individual accused of a crime to the state in which the individual is accused, and is going to become increasingly used as globalism increases. The secretary of state in the United States is responsible for requesting the return of individuals from the United States who commit crimes and flee to other countries under the terms of extradition treaties the United States has with other countries. Such treaties, however, do not exist with all countries.

Efforts to better address globalism are evidenced in the 2002 creation of the **International Criminal Court** (ICC), which is a permanent international court that investigates, prosecutes, and tries individuals accused of committing the most serious crimes that are of concern to the international community. Those crimes include genocide, crimes against humanity, war crimes, and aggression. The creation of the ICC is certainly a positive step toward addressing international crime, but it has jurisdiction over only the most serious offenses. Many other international crimes occur outside the jurisdiction of the court, and it is anticipated that additional and new forms of international crime will occur in the future.

PROGRESS?

Arguably, criminal justice education has promoted assimilation, in contrast to multiculturalism, through adopting the idea that the United States is melting pot.[31] Is the United States a melting pot that welcomes individuals from different backgrounds and promotes assimilation? Or is the term "salad bowl" better suited to describe the integration and interaction of different groups in society? Earlier interpretations of ethnic relations in the United States used the term melting pot, but more recently, the term salad bowl is used. Why? The melting pot metaphor conjures images of individuals molding together or assimilating in society. The salad bowl metaphor suggests that each individual retains their flavor and integrity and contributes to the final product. References to cultural relations in terms of a salad bowl are another way of promoting multiculturalism.

Some sociologists actually use a "stew" metaphor instead of a salad since there are distinct differences between the groups, inevitably the groups affect each other in profound ways and the groups shape the overall culture. The melting pot illustration was popular among the public but never really given any credence by the academic community, largely because of the racial and ethnic conflicts that have always existed.

The power differentials in a capitalistic society are such that those without means are more often brought to the attention of the criminal justice system. Whether or not the differential power structure encourages the less powerful to commit crime, or the criminal justice system disproportionately focuses on crimes of the lower class, it remains that the less powerful constitute the vast majority of our prison population. How do we change this unfavorable situation? The answer to this question involves radical

Evidence of progress in the United States with regard to diversity is found in politics, as members of historically underrepresented groups have made notable progress. There is, however, a need for continued progress in politics and other areas.

changes in the sociocultural, socioeconomic, and sociopolitical makeup of the United States. Radical changes, however, are not beyond the capacity of any society. Consider the fact that Barack Obama, who is part African American, recently served two terms as president of the United States (2009–2017), and in 2016 Hillary Clinton (a female) became the first woman to be nominated for president by a major political party.

If indeed we haven't seen progress with regard to diversity, multiculturalism, and tolerance in the criminal justice system, then what should we do? What changes are needed to improve the system? The answer to these questions is twofold, as we must consider increasing equity, diversity, and tolerance with regard to the accused and the offenders entering and within the system, in addition to those working within the system. Several authors have commented on the changes necessary for a more equitable system of criminal justice. For instance, scholars Coramae Richey Mann and Marjorie Zatz suggest that significant changes are needed in the major social institutions in the United States to erase the stereotype of people of color. Particularly, they cite changes needed in relation to housing, health, education, family, religion, political, and economic issues. Mann and Zatz argue that changes in these institutions will eradicate the negative stereotypical images of minorities as they pertain to crime.[32]

Author David Cole offers three promising and challenging solutions to address the inequities existent in today's criminal justice system. First, Cole argues that we must acknowledge that all are not equal before the law. The privileged still maintain a distinct advantage in many aspects of the criminal justice system. Second, Cole argues that we must restore the legitimacy of criminal law to eliminate or reduce the existing double standards. He cites the differential treatment of groups in many stages of the criminal justice system (as noted throughout this text) as evidence. Further legitimizing the criminal justice system would help address the existing disparities and bring to light charges of discrimination and differential treatment. Third, Cole argues that effective community-based responses to crime are needed at both the preventative and punitive stages.[33] His call for the further integration of the community in preventing and responding to crime is supported by many others, including those supporting community policing efforts, community courts, and community corrections.[34]

With regard to increasing the diversity of the criminal justice workforce, scholar Becky Tatum offers several suggestions to achieve and maintain diversity within the criminal justice system. Particularly, she encourages criminal justice organizations to:

- understand that diversity enhances organizational effectiveness and success
- continue practicing and promoting affirmative action policies
- be committed to diversity
- establish effective recruitment, selection, training, and promotion practices
- create effective complaint policies and procedures to ensure that employees are not treated differently, and
- evaluate progress and the results of policies and procedures.[35]

To be sure, progress has been made with regard to multiculturalism in the criminal justice system. Despite existing problems, our system is fairer than it's been in the past and the criminal justice workforce is more diverse than ever. However, the continued disintegration of affirmative action policies warrants mention. Affirmative action has played an integral part in diversifying the criminal justice workforce, although recent court rulings have limited its effectiveness. Further, affirmative action programs have not corrected the underlying causes of inequality and prejudice in many arenas.[36] Accordingly, the reduced impact of affirmative action and the general climate of intolerance in the United States may contribute to increased discriminatory practices.[37]

If progress has been made with regard to multiculturalism in criminal justice, why the concern? The obvious answer is because there's more room for improvement. Progress refers to advancement and does not necessarily mean that success has been achieved. The concern regarding diversity and criminal justice relates to the work that remains, including greater sensitivity to diversity issues. Society is quite sensitive to culture-based issues.

TECHNOLOGY AND POLICY

Policies are not always large-scale in nature. Departments and agencies have policies that guide employee practices. Failure to abide by the policies can lead to the dismissal of employees. The relatively recent, widespread incorporation of technology into our everyday lives has led to departments creating and refining policies regarding its use. The increased use of cell phones and social media have created new areas that require regulation in the workplace, and have provided new means by which a lack of tolerance for diversity can be expressed. Inappropriate texting and emails, in particular, have resulted in the dismissal of criminal justice employees in several agencies. For instance, in April 2016, the chief of the San Francisco Police Department announced that all officers would be required to undergo anti-bias training after he shared nine pages of racist text messages among three officers. The discovery of the messages compounded earlier disclosure of racist emails and text messages that the department was attempting to address.

Such inappropriate behavior is not restricted to policing, the San Francisco Police Department, and texting. For instance, nine jail workers in New Jersey were terminated after the discovery of racist texts on their cell phones. The jailers exchanged over 5,700 text messages that contained inflammatory and racist comments that routinely targeted coworkers, inmates, superiors, and African Americans in general. In a different case, a Buffalo correctional officer resigned from his position after his department confronted him about derogatory comments he made on his Facebook page. Among other comments, the officer threatened to shoot gays. These are by no means the only accounts in which technology has provided a forum for hateful comments. Accordingly, departments are regularly revising their policies and guidelines with regard to texting, emails, and the use of social media.

That we are more sensitive to such issues suggests progress has been made and provides an ample opportunity for change. Nevertheless, the efforts pertaining to cultural sensitivity continue to highlight the existing challenges.

Each time we hear that an LGBT candidate was denied an employment position in criminal justice based on his or her sexual orientation we believe we're taking a step backward. In many ways, such claims and actions are a step backward. One could equally look at such claims as progress, as in years past we may not have heard of the situation. The candidate may have simply accepted the discriminatory practice and moved on. Or, perhaps even worse, the candidate wouldn't have applied for the position at all, out of a belief that they would be denied a position based on their sexual orientation. Hearing about discrimination can make the problem appear more prominent than it truly is; simultaneously, it sends a message that such practices are unacceptable.

Efforts toward multiculturalism are enhanced when individuals who have faced discrimination speak out about the mistreatment. Bringing the issue to light, in a nonconfrontational manner, draws attention. Such individuals must use caution, however, as exaggerated, or elaborated stories often hamper efforts toward progress. The media can play a vital tool in helping victims of discrimination or of mistreatment share their story.

SUMMARY

One cannot consider the future without recognizing the impact of technology, although technological changes appear to have little impact on cultural relations. Nevertheless, the future of multiculturalism and the criminal justice system will be influenced by several changes in the larger society. Demographic trends will impact the system, as will the increased international nature of crime. The increasing separation of socioeconomic classes will continue to negatively impact multiculturalism and the criminal justice system, as will the ever-prominent crime control approach we've adopted.

All is not lost, however, as positive changes may be on the horizon. The changing demographics of society will dictate greater minority involvement as criminal justice practitioners, which should promote positive changes to the system. Individuals from diverse backgrounds are increasingly assuming more powerful roles in public service, politics, and private business. While there may be current tensions between cultural groups (as evidenced in the anti-illegal immigration legislation), signs point toward greater recognition of diversity and increased acceptance of multiculturalism.

Changes in the criminal justice system begin with changes in people. The system is composed of and influenced by individuals from various backgrounds. The system, as designed on paper, is not biased, racist, or anti-multicultural. What's needed for acceptance of multiculturalism is tolerance among individuals in society. The problems and challenges faced by different cultures in the criminal justice system were created by people—including biased and unbiased people. The problems posed by the unbiased can be addressed through greater professionalism in criminal justice. Fortunately, many signs point to greater professionalism in the discipline. The problems posed by biased individuals are fixed through identifying and correcting the problems, while removing such individuals from their influential positions.

YOU MAKE THE CALL

PLANNING FOR THE FUTURE

Consider the following scenario. Debate the pros and cons of all options and decide what you would do.

You've just been promoted to the head of research and planning in the large municipal police department in which you work. While granting you the promotion, the police chief told you that she wants the department to become more proactive and better prepared for the future so the department is not in a reactionary mode. The chief mentioned that she wants you to focus on the future of several issues that currently challenge and are expected to continue challenging the department. Particularly, she wants you to create short-, medium-, and long-term plans with regard to: (1) crime, (2) diversity in the community, and (3) intercultural relations.

You eagerly accept the position, and look forward to the challenges. You tell the chief that she has nothing to worry about, that you'll start immediately and do an exceptional

job. In your mind, however, you have many uncertainties. Sure, you've worked in research and planning, but the department has historically brushed aside research efforts and forecasts of the future.

Questions

1. How will you begin the process of creating the various plans requested by the chief?
2. What methods of forecasting the future do you believe will be most effective in creating plans for the short-term? Medium-term? Long-term?
3. What scenario would you create to help with planning for the long-term?
4. What obstacles do you anticipate encountering as you create the plans?

KEY TERMS

bias crime
crime control model of criminal justice
Delphi method
drivers of the future
due process model of criminal justice
extradition
forecasting
futurists

globalization
hate crimes
human trafficking
International Criminal Court
predictions
qualitative approaches
quantitative analyses
scenarios

DISCUSSION QUESTIONS

1. Provide a scenario of the criminal justice system in the year 2075. Be sure to focus on issues pertaining to diversity, tolerance, and multiculturalism.
2. Compare and contrast the various methods of forecasting the future. Which do you believe offer the greatest accuracy? Why?
3. Discuss how racial profiling, immigration, and hate crimes will impact the future of multiculturalism and criminal justice.
4. Create an outline for an undergraduate-level course on multiculturalism and criminal justice. What topics would you include? How would you structure the course?
5. Identify and discuss three changes you believe are necessary for the criminal justice system to welcome diversity among the ranks of practitioners.

FOR FURTHER READING

Frey, W. H. *Diversity Explosion: How New Racial Demographics are Remaking America.* Washington, DC: Brookings Institution, 2015.

Parry, J. T., and L. S. Richardson, eds. *The Constitution and the Future of Criminal Justice in America.* New York: Cambridge University Press, 2013.

Simon, J. *Mass Incarceration on Trial: A Remarkable Court Decision and the Future of Prisons in America.* New York: New Press, 2014.

Stuntz, W. J. *The Collapse of American Criminal Justice.* Cambridge, MA: Harvard University Press, 2011.

Zimring, F. E., and D. S. Tanenhaus, *Choosing the Future for American Juvenile Justice.* New York: New York University Press, 2014.

NOTES

1. G. Stephens, "Policing the Future: Law Enforcement's New Challenges," *The Futurist,* (March/April 2005): 51–57.

2. R. Burns, "The Future of Delinquency Prevention and Treatment," in *Youth Violence & Delinquency,* vol. 3, ed. M. D. McShane & F.P. Williams III (Westport, CT: Praeger, 2007), 171–85.

3. T. L. Snell, *Correctional Populations in the United States, 1993.* U.S. Department of Justice. Bureau of Justice Statistics, 1995. NCJ 156241, 9.

4. D. Kaeble, L. Glaze, A. Tsoutis, and T. Minton, *Correctional Populations in the United States, 2014.* U.S. Department of Justice, Bureau of Justice Statistics, 2015. NCJ 249513, 4.

5. S. L. Colby and J. M. Ortman, *Projections of the Size and Composition of the U.S. Population: 2014 to 2060.* United States Census Bureau, 2015. Accessed online at: https://www.census.gov/content/dam/Census/library/publications/2015/demo/p25-1143.pdf.

6. T. L. Friedman, *The World is Flat: A Brief History of the Twenty-First Century* (New York: Farrar, Straus, and Giroux, 2005).

7. "Threat and Humiliation: Racial Profiling, Domestic Security, and Human Rights in the United States." (2004). Amnesty International. Accessed August 6, 2007 at www.amnestyusa.org/racial_profiling/report/rp_report.pdf

8. H. L. Packer, *The Limits of the Criminal Sanction* (Stanford, CA: Stanford University Press, 1968).

9. Federal Bureau of Investigation, *2014 Hate Crime Statistics.* Uniform Crime Reports, 2015. Accessed online at: https://www.fbi.gov/about-us/cjis/ucr/hate-crime/2014

10. J. B. Jacobs and K. Potter, *Hate Crimes: Criminal Law & Identity Politics* (New York: Oxford University Press, 1998).

11. Ibid.

12. E. Lazarus, "The New Colossus," 1883.

13. L. T. Cullen, "Mission: Search and Send Back," *Time Magazine,* March 27, 2006. Accessed August 6, 2007 at http://content.time.com/time/magazine/article/0,9171,1176999,00.html

14. S. LeBlanc, "States Enter Void Left by Immigration Bill," Associated Press, Aug. 5, 2007. Accessed August 8, 2007 at www.chron.com/disp/story.mpl/ap/nation/5029404.html.

15. J. Preston, "Surge in Immigration Laws Around the U.S.," *New York Times*, Aug. 6, 2007. Accessed August 7, 2007 at www.nytimes.com/2007/08/06/washington/06immig.html?ex=118 7064000&en=9269b383a0d29231&ei=5123&partner=BREITBART.

16. H. Park, "Which States Make Life Easier or Harder for Illegal Immigrants," *NYTimes.com*, March 29, 2015. Accessed online at: http://www.nytimes.com/interactive/2015/03/30/us/laws-affecting-unauthorized-immigrants.html?_r=0

17. "Judge Strikes Down Law Targeting Immigrants," Associated Press, July 26, 2007. Accessed August 6, 2007 at www.wfaa.com/sharedcontent/dws/wfaa/latestnews/stories/wfaa070726_wz_immigration.b2b47907.html.

18. R. C. Davis and E. Erez, *Immigrant Populations as Victims: Toward a Multicultural Criminal Justice System*. U.S. Department of Justice, Bureau of Justice Statistics. (Washington, DC, 1998), 2.

19. Ibid.

20. M. Welch, *Punishment in America: Social Control and the Ironies of Imprisonment* (Thousand Oaks, CA: Sage, 1999).

21. N. Ritter, "Preparing for the Future: Criminal Justice in 2040," *National Institute of Justice Journal* 255 (2006): 8.

22. P. Andreas and E. Nadelmann, *Policing the Globe* (New York: Oxford University Press, 2006).

23. N. Gerspacher, "The History of International Police Cooperation: a 150-Year Evolution in Trends and Approaches," *Global Crime* 9, no. 1–2 (2008): 169–84.

24. Andreas and Nadelmann, *Policing the Globe*.

25. P. Williams and E. Savona, "The United Nations and Transnational Organised Crime," *Transnational Organised Crime* 1, no. 3 (1995): 8–10.

26. J. A. Eterno, "Policing in the United States: Balancing Crime Fighting and Legal Rights," in *Police Practices in Global Perspective*, ed. J. A. Eterno & D. K. Das (Lanham, MD: Rowman & Littlefield, 2010), 12.

27. S. Aguilar-Millan, J. E. Foltz, J. Jackson, and A. Oberg, "Global Crime Case: The Modern Slave Trade," *The Futurist* (2008): 45. K. Williams, "Human Trafficking: the Return of an Ancient Malaise and What Law Enforcement Can Do About It," *The Briefing* (Aug. 2014): 1–3. National White Collar Crime Center.

28. A. L. Sciarabba and C. G. Sullivan, "Transnational Crime and the Law: An Overview of Current Practices," in Eterno and Das, *Police Practices*, 227.

29. U.S. Department of Homeland Security. (2016). *The Blue Campaign*, 2016 Accessed online at: https://www.dhs.gov/sites/default/files/publications/blue-campaign/BC%20inserts%20intro.pdf

30. W. K. Rashbaum, "With Special Courts, State Aims to Steer Women Away from Sex Trade," *New York Times*, Sept. 25, 2013. Accessed online at: http://www.nytimes.com/2013/09/26/nyregion/special-courts-for-human-trafficking-and-prostitution-cases-are-planned-in-new-york.html?_r=0

31. Welch, *Punishment in America*.

32. Coramae Richey Mann, and Marjorie S. Zatz, "A Fragile Future: Pitfalls and Possibilities," in *Images of Color*, 3rd ed., eds. C. R. Mann, M. S. Zatz, and N. Rodriguez. (Los Angeles, CA: Roxbury, 2006), 252–64.

33. David Cole, *No Equal Justice: Race and Class in the American Criminal Justice System* (New York: The New Press, 1999).

34. Among the many resources addressing community-based criminal justice are: T. Clear and E. Cadora, *Community Justice* (Belmont, CA: Wadsworth, 2003); V. E. Kappeler and

L. K. Gaines, *Community Policing: A Contemporary Perspective*, 4th edition (Cincinnati, OH: Anderson, 2005); and E. Lee, *Community Courts: An Evolving Model*, U.S. Department of Justice, Office of Justice Programs, Oct. 2000. NCJ 183452.

35. B. Tatum, "Criminal Justice Personnel in the Twenty-First Century," in *Visions for Change: Crime and Justice in the Twenty-First Century*, ed. R. Muraskin and A. R. Roberts (Upper Saddle River, NJ: Prentice Hall, 2005), 670–83.

36. R. Thomas, "From Affirmative Action to Affirming Diversity," *Harvard Business Review* (March/April 1990): 107–17.

37. E. F. Morgan, "The Administration of Justice Based on Gender and Race," in Muraskin and Roberts, *Visions for Change*, 652–69.

GLOSSARY

ABOLITIONISTS Individuals who contended that slavery was morally objectionable.

ACQUAINTANCE RAPE An act of rape involving individuals familiar with one another.

ADJUDICATION The process in which it is determined whether a youth is responsible for the illegal act(s) with which he or she is charged.

AFFIRMATIVE ACTION Programs designed to promote the hiring of minority applicants.

AFFIRMATIVE DEFENSE A defense in which the defendant admits committing the action in question, although they have legal justification for doing so. Entering an affirmative defense requires defendants to demonstrate that their action was justified. Self-defense, insanity, coercion, and entrapment are affirmative defenses.

ALIBI One of two types of defenses that may be offered at trial (affirmative defenses being the other). It states that the defendant could not have committed the crime because they were in another location at the time of the crime.

ALIEN LAND ACT Prohibited anyone who was ineligible for citizenship to own land and limited leases to three years. The land laws drove many first-generation Japanese into cities.

AMNESTY A type of clemency that restores rights and privileges of groups of people.

APPEARANCE Items that signify a performer's social status.

ARRAIGNMENT The step in criminal case processing when the accused is formally notified of the charges against them, he or she enters a plea, pretrial motions are offered, and discovery may occur.

ASIAN INDIAN A term that represents a wide range of populations. India itself is a diverse nation with dozens of languages and ethnic enclaves.

ASIAN GANGS Primarily focused on criminal activity, these gangs are made up of various Asian members, and they are connected to legitimate businesses as part of the Asian community.

ASSIGNED COUNSEL Court appointed representation for indigent cases. Attorneys are assigned indigent cases in return for a statutorily-determined fee.

ASSIMILATION The process by which the subordinate group takes on the characteristics of the dominant group and is eventually accepted as part of that group.

BABY BOOMERS A term to describe a segment of the population born between 1946 and 1964. This group represents about 28 percent of the U.S. population and is responsible for some of the most dramatic changes in American history.

BARRIOS Concentrations of segregated areas in the Southwestern portion of the U.S.

BATTLE AT LITTLE BIG HORN A battle fought in 1876 in which Custer and his men were defeated.

BATTLE OF WOUNDED KNEE The battle heralded by historians as significant because it extinguished the hope of the Sioux Nation of ever returning to a life of freedom.

BENCH TRIAL Trials in which judges serve as both judge and jury.

BIAS CRIME Illegal acts taken against a person or group based on bias.

BISEXUALITY A term used to describe an individual's attraction to both sexes.

BLACK CODES Laws designed to nullify the rights granted to the newly freed slaves. Among the restrictions found in Black Codes were the prohibition of interracial marriage, renting land in urban areas, preaching the gospel without a license, and assuming any occupation other than servant or farmer unless the newly freed slave paid a tax.

"BLACK LIVES MATTER" An activist movement in the U.S. that originated after the 2013 acquittal of George Zimmerman in the shooting of Trayvon Martin. The group campaigns against police brutality against African Americans.

BLACK MIDDLE CLASS A term used to describe relatively affluent African Americans.

BLACK NATIONALISM The philosophy that encourages Blacks to see themselves as Blacks first rather than as Americans first.

BLACK POWER A political movement that encouraged Blacks to create new institutions and emulate the political path followed by many European immigrant groups.

BLACK RAGE A defense offered in court which attempts to provide legal justification for criminal behavior by some African Americans frustrated by oppression resulting from living in a White-dominated society.

BLUE WALL OF SILENCE The unwritten rule among officers to not report other officers' wrongful behavior.

BOW STREET RUNNERS A precursor to formal policing, this group consisted of individuals who sought law violators in the Bow Street region of London. The Runners were paid a sum of money for bringing suspects before the court.

BUREAU OF INDIAN AFFAIRS The primary regulatory arm of the federal government as it relates to Native Americans.

CANTEEN PUNKS Inmates who perform oral or anal sex for candy, cigarettes, or other items purchased at the prison store or canteen.

CHALLENGE FOR CAUSE A motion through which attorneys may eliminate a potential juror because of an identifiable bias and/or an apparent inability to assess a case fairly.

CHARGE TO THE JURY A written document, prepared by a judge for a jury, that explains the parameters under which jurors may deliberate.

CHICANOS Americans of Mexican origin.

CHILDREN'S AID SOCIETY A group established by Reverend Charles Loring Brace that helped homeless children.

CHILD SAVERS MOVEMENT A movement that largely involved philanthropists and social reformers who felt that the exploitation of children ultimately resulted in juvenile crime and a host of other problems. They attempted to enact laws that would allow children to be placed in reformatories or other institutions.

CHINESE EXCLUSION ACT An act passed in 1882 that outlawed Chinese immigration for ten years. It lasted in various forms for over sixty years.

CHRISTOPHER COMMISSION A commission assembled in the wake of the Rodney King incident in response to claims of LAPD officer misbehavior. The commission identified several areas and instances of unethical behavior by LAPD officers.

CIVIL LEGAL TRADITION A justice system approach that is based on Roman and canon laws, and codification.

CIVIL RIGHTS ACT OF 1866 This act was targeted to address the Black Codes by defining all persons born in the United States, with the exception of Native Americans, as national citizens who were to enjoy specific rights. These rights included permission to make contracts, bring lawsuits, and enjoy the full and equal benefit of the law.

CIVIL RIGHTS ACT OF 1964 Prohibited discrimination in hiring on the basis of color, race, sex, religion, or national origin.

CIVIL RIGHTS MOVEMENT A movement designed to provide equal rights to minorities.

CLAIMSMAKING The process of convincing others that a social problem exists; it also addresses how social problems are defined in a given society.

CLEMENCY Legislative actions which reduce the severity of one's punishment, waive the punishment associated with a crime, or exclude certain individuals from prosecution of a specific crime.

COLLATERAL DAMAGE With regard to incarceration and children, it is the harms suffered by children of incarcerated parents.

COLLECTIVE CONSCIENCE Shared beliefs and moral attitudes which contribute to unifying society.

COLOR GRADIENT Distinctions in terms of group membership based on a light-to-dark skin continuum.

COMMON LEGAL TRADITION A justice system approach that is found in the United States and other countries and is based on feudal practices, custom, and equity.

COMMUNITY CORRECTIONS Correctional supervision in a community setting.

COMMUNITY ERA OF POLICING The era of policing that began around 1980 and continues today. It involves efforts by the police to reconnect with the public primarily through the adoption of the community policing philosophy.

COMMUNITY LIAISON OFFICERS A promising approach in policing in which designated officers meet with residents and business owners to discuss crime and crime prevention efforts.

COMMUNITY POLICING A philosophical approach to policing that stresses creating and perpetuating a sense of community. It promotes positive police-citizen interaction and focuses on quality of life issues.

COMMUTATIONS A type of clemency which involves shortening or changing an inmate's prison sentence.

CONCEALING ERRORS Nondisclosure of errors that have been made in the preparation of a performance as well as steps that have been taken to correct these errors.

CONCEALING SECRET PLEASURES Nondisclosure of activities engaged in prior to a performance or in past lives that are incompatible with a performance.

CONDITIONAL RELEASE Release from prison accompanied by community supervision.

CONTINUUM OF FORCE A concept that guides officer behavior with respect to use of force.

COURTROOM WORKGROUP Individuals who work on a regular basis in a courtroom setting.

CRIME CONTROL MODEL OF CRIMINAL JUSTICE A perspective on the administration of justice, as described by Herbert Packer, which maintains an emphasis on expediency and reducing crime.

CRIMES AGAINST PERSONS Interpersonal or violent crimes. Examples include murder and non-negligent manslaughter, forcible rape, assaults, robbery, and intimidation.

CRIMES AGAINST PROPERTY Economic crimes. Examples include burglary, larceny-theft, motor vehicle theft, vandalism, and arson.

CRIMES AGAINST SOCIETY Often referred to as victimless crimes, they are a series of crimes in which there is no easily discernable victim. They include offenses such as gambling, prostitution, drugs, or weapons violations.

CRIMINAL JUSTICE POLICY Decisions or actions that address particular issues or problems pertaining to policing, courts, corrections, and related areas of formal social control.

CULTURAL FUSION A goal of multiculturalism, where minority and majority groups come together to form an entirely new group.

CULTURE Beliefs, values, behaviors, and material goods that collectively constitute a people's manner of life. Culture shapes what we do and our personalities.

CULTURE-GENERAL TRAINING Training that emphasizes the flexibility, skills, and understanding that would apply to understanding an array of cultures.

CULTURE-SPECIFIC TRAINING Training that addresses the practices, beliefs, and traits of particular cultural groups.

DAWES ACT Legislation that made landowners of individual tribe members without consulting tribal leaders.

DELPHI METHOD A qualitative approach to forecasting the future in which experts offer input regarding anticipated developments in their area of expertise.

DE-POLICING A tactic employed by some officers who answer only high-priority calls instead of engaging in routine patrol.

DETERMINATE SENTENCING Sentencing practices in which offenders receive a specific amount of time to be served based on the crime for which they were convicted.

DETERRENCE Efforts to dissuade the offender (specific deterrence) or society in general (general deterrence) from engaging in acts for which the offender is being punished.

DISCOVERY The sharing of information among attorneys with the goal of helping them adequately prepare their cases.

DISCREDITED STIGMA A type of stigma in which the actor assumes that the differences contributing to the stigma are known by the audience members or are evident to them.

DISCRETIONARY RELEASE Involves the use of discretion in the decision to release an inmate from prison. It most commonly refers to parole board decision-making.

DISCRIMINATION The unequal treatment of people based on their membership in a particular group.

DOUBLE MARGINALITY The challenges faced by Black officers who may be viewed as traitors by some in the Black community, while White officers may distrust them as colleagues. It could also apply to females and members of other minority groups working in the criminal justice system.

DOWNWARD SOCIAL MOBILITY Individuals whose social class is diminished.

DRAMATURGICAL CIRCUMSPECTION The logistical planning involved in carrying out a performance. Examples include planning for emergencies, making only brief appearances, and preventing audiences access to private information.

DRAMATURGICAL DISCIPLINE Concise preparation of a performance. It includes such things as having the presence of mind to avoid slips, maintaining self-control, and managing facial expressions and the tone of voice of one's performance.

DRAMATURGY A view of social life as a series of dramatic performances like those performed on stage.

DRIVERS OF THE FUTURE Particular issues which have significant impacts on the future.

DUE PROCESS MODEL OF CRIMINAL JUSTICE A perspective on the administration of justice, as described by Herbert Packer, that is primarily concerned with respecting individual rights.

EASTERN ASIA LEGAL TRADITION A justice system approach that is grounded in the principles of Confucianism, along with collectivism, context, and informalism.

ELDERLY ABUSE The physical, emotional, and sometimes sexual abuse or neglect of people aged 65 and older. While no one knows the true extent of this problem, what is known is that family members, healthcare workers and others are often the perpetrators of these crimes.

EMANCIPATION PROCLAMATION A proclamation and presidential executive order that freed slaves in the Confederacy.

ENDOGAMY The practice of marrying others with similar backgrounds.

ENVIRONMENTAL JUSTICE Attempts to treat all groups, regardless of race, ethnicity, or income equally with regard to environmental protection and laws.

ENVIRONMENTAL RACISM The underregulation of environmental laws, and the disproportionate placement of hazardous materials in minority neighborhoods.

EQUAL EMPLOYMENT OPPORTUNITY ACT OF 1972 This act extended the protections of women and other minorities to local governments.

ETHNICISM Emphases on ethnic identity. Preference for a particular ethnicity.

ETHNOCENTRIC The tendency to judge other cultures by the standards of one's own, thinking the latter is superior.

ETHNOCENTRISM Believing that one's culture or group is superior to others.

EXCLUSIONARY RULE Prohibits illegally seized materials from being introduced in court.

EXMATES Former prison inmates.

EXOGAMY The practice of marrying outside one's group.

EXPLICIT BIAS The biased beliefs or attitudes an individual maintains at a conscious level. The actions associated with this type of bias are apparent to the individuals and the audience.

EXPULSION The removal of groups from an area or territory.

EXTERMINATION A process where the military attempted to wipe out entire tribes as part of the conflict between the government and Native Americans. While some of the conflicts were violent, some of the effort was accomplished by requiring Native Americans to relocate after the creation of reservations across the country.

EXTRADITION When a state or country surrenders an individual accused of a crime to the state or country in which the individual is accused.

FEDERAL BUREAU OF PRISONS A bureau within the federal government that operates 114 institutions and 28 community corrections offices across the United States. The Bureau oversees roughly 193,000 offenders convicted of federal offenses.

FEDERAL JURY SELECTION AND SERVICE ACT OF 1968 This act provided greater equity in jury selection practices in that it prohibited the exclusion of individuals based on religion, race, gender, national origin, or economic status.

FEMINIST MOVEMENTS Social movements that generally promote the idea that males and females should be politically, socially, and economically equal.

FIELD TRAINING Police officer training that follows basic training and involves officers working under the guidance of an experienced colleague.

FIELD TRAINING OFFICER PROGRAMS Programs in which new officers are paired with experienced ones who teach new officers the practical aspects of the job, build upon and reinforce what was taught at the academy, and acclimate the officers to the department's and community's values.

FORECASTING The use of scientific techniques to anticipate future developments.

FORT LARAMIE TREATY An agreement with the Sioux in which the government agreed to keep Whites from hunting or settling on the newly established Great Sioux Reservation, which included all of the land that is now South Dakota. In exchange, the Sioux relinquished most of the remaining land they occupied at that time.

FRANKPLEDGE SYSTEM The early English practice of informal social control in which community members protected one another.

FREEDOM SCHOOLS Private all-White schools that enrolled an estimated 300,000 White children by 1970. Their development occurred with the intent of evading the *Brown* decision.

FUGITIVE SLAVE ACTS Legislation that required slaves who had escaped, even to a free state, to be returned to their owners.

FUTURISTS Scientists who forecast future developments in society.

GAY BASHING Unprovoked attacks on homosexuals.

GENDER A social characteristic that varies from one social group to another and refers to femininity or masculinity. It is a master status as it cuts across all walks of life.

GENERATION X The group of individuals born between 1968 and 1979. Those born during the period are referred to as Gen Xers.

GENERATION Y The group of individuals born between approximately 1977 and 1994 Those born during this period are referred to as Gen Yers.

GENOCIDE The deliberate, systematic killing of an entire people or nation.

GERIATRIC COURT A distinct system of justice for the elderly.

GHOST DANCE RELIGION A religion that included dances and songs proclaiming the return of the buffalo and the resurrection of dead ancestors in a land free of White people.

GLASS CEILING An abstract barrier preventing certain groups and/or individuals from moving beyond entry-level occupational positions.

GLOBALIZATION The international integration of cultural, social, and economic issues among countries that have historically been distinct from one another.

GOING RATE The penalties informally associated with particular criminal offenses.

GOOD TIME Used in determinate sentencing structures, it refers to the time eliminated from an offender's sentence for good behavior.

GRAND JURY HEARING Hearings used to determine if continued case processing is necessary. In grand jury hearings jurors basically replace the judge used in a preliminary hearing. The grand jury's task is to determine if the prosecutor's case is strong enough to warrant an indictment.

GROUP GOALS Agreed-upon tasks or activities that a group seeks to complete or accomplish.

GROUP STRUCTURE The characteristics of a group. A group's structure is largely determined by group roles, and typically evolves in accord with, or from, group norms and rules. The structure is vulnerable to change as norms, goals, and other factors impacting the group change.

HALFWAY HOUSES Community-based facilities that enable offenders to reside in the community while remaining under relatively close supervision.

HARMLESS ERROR DOCTRINE A doctrine which holds that a trial court decision will not be overturned in an appellate court based on small, insignificant errors that appear to have limited or no impact on the trial outcome.

HATE CRIMES Illegal actions that are motivated by hate and taken against particular groups.

HATE SPEECH Communication that attacks individuals or groups on the basis of specific attributes, such as race, ethnicity, gender, sexual orientation, religion, or disability.

HETEROGENEOUS Something diverse in nature. Societies in which people come from a wide range of backgrounds and experiences.

HMONG TRIBES Tribal groups that came together in the early 1860s under the label "Indochina" as the French colonized the region.

HOMOGENEITY Similarity in attitudes, values, and beliefs.

HOMOGENEOUS SOCIETIES Societies in which individuals share similar attitudes, values, and beliefs.

HOMOSEXUAL An individual attracted to those of the same sex.

HOMOSEXUAL ADVANCE THEORY The justification for courts to allow a nonviolent homosexual advance to constitute sufficient provocation.

HOUSES OF REFUGE Facilities designed to house children who committed crimes, were poor, were orphans, or were thought to be incorrigible or wayward.

HUE AND CRY An early form of informal social control in which a call to arms generated a response from every able-bodied male in attempts to bring offenders(s) to justice.

HUMAN SNAKES Individuals who leave China illegally.

HUMAN TRAFFICKING The involuntary movement of people across and within borders; it typically involves coercion, deception, and violence.

IMPLICIT BIAS Covert cognitive processes that shape attitudes and stereotypes while operating at a below conscious level. The individual is not consciously aware of their biased behavior.

INCAPACITATION Physically preventing one from committing similar criminal acts in the future. Incarceration is the most widely used form of incapacitation.

INCARCERATION The physical detention of an inmate; it consists primarily of placement in prison and jail.

INDIAN CLAIMS COMMISSION Although not an official U.S. court, the commission operates somewhat like one in that lawyers present evidence for both sides. If the commission agrees with the tribe, it then determines the value of the land at the time it was illegally seized.

INDIAN HEALTH SERVICES An agency within the U.S. Department of Health and Human Services that is responsible for providing federal health services to American Indians and Alaskan Natives.

INDIAN REMOVAL ACT OF 1830 An act which called for the relocation of all Eastern tribes to west of the Mississippi River.

INDICTMENT The charging document used by grand juries to suggest enough evidence exists to proceed with case processing.

INDIGENT DEFENDANTS Defendants who cannot afford privately-secured representation.

INDIVIDUALIZED JUSTICE Justice-based solutions that are fair and have the interest of the individuals involved in mind.

INITIAL APPEARANCE The stage of criminal case processing in which defendants are brought before the court, informed of the formal charges against them, advised of their rights, possibly granted pretrial release, and made aware of the upcoming steps in their case.

INMATE CODE The norms and values developed and stressed in prison; it encourages toughness, insensitivity, disdain of and manipulation of fellow inmates and the prison staff. The code generally varies among institutions, as does inmate commitment to the code.

INSTITUTIONAL DISCRIMINATION The type of discrimination built into the structure of society.

INTERNATIONAL CRIMINAL COURT A permanent international court that investigates, prosecutes, and tries individuals accused of committing the most serious crimes that are of concern to the international community.

INTERNMENT A process by which the U.S. government required Japanese Americans and immigrants to be detained in refugee camps for the duration of the American involvement in World War II. This occurred despite the fact that most of the detainees were American citizens.

INVOLUNTARY MIGRATION The practice of bringing individuals to a new land against their will.

ISLAMIC LEGAL TRADITION A justice system approach that is based on the Qur'an and Sunna, as well as the doctrine of consensus and reasoning by analogy.

JAIL Facilities that hold detainees awaiting trial and those sentenced to incarceration for less than a year. In most states jails are operated by county-level officials, typically sheriff's departments.

JIM CROW An individual whose name is now associated with the label for the social, political, and legal separation of Whites and Blacks in all aspects of society.

JOCKER Also known as the wolf, this type of inmate is viewed by his fellow inmates as a "man." To remain a "man" and still engage in homosexual acts, the individual has to present an image of exaggerated toughness.

JURY NULLIFICATION The practice of jurors acquitting particular defendants despite strong evidence suggesting guilt.

JUST DESERTS A philosophy which argues that every person is equally responsible for their actions and should be punished according to what they have done.

JUVENILE DELINQUENCY Behaviors that violate the criminal code and are committed by youth who have not reached a specified age.

JUVENILE DELINQUENCY PREVENTION AND CONTROL ACT Recommended that children charged with noncriminal (status) offenses be handled outside the court system.

JUVENILE JUSTICE AND DELINQUENCY PREVENTION ACT OF 1974 Prohibited states from incarcerating status offenders and required them to detain juvenile offenders in separate facilities from adult offenders.

KINESICS Body language, including gestures, facial expressions, eye behavior, and body movements.

LATINO A term that refers to people and cultures of Latin America.

LONDON METROPOLITAN POLICE ACT Passed in 1829, this act led to the first formal police department, the London Metropolitan Police, led by Sir Robert Peel.

LOS BRACEROS Contracted workers who were allowed to enter the U.S. from Mexico due to the need for Mexican laborers.

MANDATORY MINIMUM SENTENCING A sentencing structure in which offenders convicted of certain offenses are to be sentenced to prison for no less than a specified term of years, and non-prison sentences (e.g., probation) are not an option. Mandatory minimum sentences are typically imposed on violent offenders.

MANDATORY RELEASE A policy in which inmates earn time off of their prison sentence through various incentives. Inmates are to be released when they've served the number of days they've been sentenced less good time.

MANNER Tells the audience what sort of role the performer expects to play in the situation.

MARIELITOS A term which refers to individuals who were herded on to boats by Cuban authorities in Mariel, the fishing port west of Havana.

MARITAL RAPE The raping of an individual by his or her spouse.

MARKET SEGMENTATION Marketing practices that target a subset of potential candidates to identify those who will likely provide the greatest return for the efforts.

MATERIAL CULTURE Objects that are real to the senses (e.g., a baton, handcuffs, a judge's gavel) and contribute to cultural identity.

MCJOBS Jobs in the lowest paying sectors of the market, including many minimum wage jobs.

MELTING POT A society that blends together a variety of backgrounds and cultures into a cohesive whole.

METROPOLITAN POLICE ACT Passed in 1829, this act led to England's first formal police department, the Metropolitan Police, led by Sir Robert Peel.

MODEL MINORITY MYTH The belief that Asian Americans constitute an ideal minority because they have endured political, economic, and social obstacles.

MULTICULTURALISM The embracing of cultural diversity.

NATIONAL ADVISORY COMMISSION ON CIVIL DISORDERS Also known as the Kerner Commission, this group was created to study the causes behind the 1960s rioting. The Commission identified a series of issues that contributed to the collective violence, including unequal justice, institutional racism, unemployment, and discrimination.

NATIONAL COUNCIL OF LA RAZA The largest Hispanic civil rights organization in the United States.

NATION OF ISLAM A religious, social, and political group that seeks to resurrect the mental, social, economic, and spiritual condition of Blacks.

NEGATIVE ATTRIBUTION African Americans developing a negative view of Whites that attributes evil motives and traits, due to the history of how Blacks have been treated.

NEOCOLONIALISM A type of dependence that arises when a country remains dependent on their dominators long after they separated from them politically.

NEORICANS Puerto Ricans who return to the island after spending time away, typically in New York.

NIMBY An acronym that stands for "not in my backyard," and relates to citizen concerns about the siting of something unpleasant or potentially dangerous in their vicinity.

NINETEENTH AMENDMENT Ratified by Congress in 1920, it gave women the right to vote.

NOLO CONTENDERE Also known as "no contest," this plea has the legal effect of a guilty plea. Defendants may choose to enter a plea of *nolo contendere* instead of admitting guilt in attempt to cooperate with the court although they do not wish to directly admit guilt.

NONMATERIAL CULTURE Shared beliefs and values which contribute to cultural identity; the social expectations individuals have for one another.

OPERATIONALIZATION The process of researchers defining terms and variables for the purpose of analysis.

ORGANIZATIONAL CULTURE Shared beliefs, values, and assumptions that influence how individuals behave in organizations.

ORPHAN TRAINS Trains used to transport city youths to rural farms, where families assumed custody of and responsibility for them as apprentices.

OVERPOLICING The oppressive and extensive use of formal social control against minority groups.

OVERSTAYERS Individuals admitted to a country on temporary visas who either stay beyond the expiration of their visas or otherwise violate their terms of admission.

PARDON A type of clemency which involves the restoration of a former inmate's rights and privileges.

PARENS PATRIAE Latin for "parent of the nation." It refers to the power of the state to intervene and act as the parent of any child or individual who is in need of protection.

PAROLE Offender supervision in the community following a period of incarceration.

PATRONAGE The practice of politicians rewarding friends and/or acquaintances.

PERCEPTION The act of becoming aware or apprehending something via the senses.

PEREMPTORY CHALLENGE A motion through which attorneys can eliminate seemingly unfit or inappropriate members of the jury pool. Attorneys typically do not need to justify using a peremptory challenge, although they are limited in the number of peremptory challenges they can use.

PERSONAL FRONT Items of equipment that an audience identifies with performers and expects them to carry with them into the setting.

PLEA BARGAINING An exchange between the prosecution and defense designed toe ncourage a guilty plea in exchange for a benefit for the defendant.

POLICE DISCRETION Officer decision-making; it is evident in all aspects of police practices. It is necessary in policing as officers are consistently faced with difficult situations involving multiple variables.

POLICE OFFICERS STANDARDS AND TRAINING COMMISSIONS (POSTs) State organizations that establish minimum standards for policing, typically provide training criteria for police officers, and seek means to improve police training practices.

POLICE SUBCULTURE A distinct culture within policing; it promotes a particular working personality that encourages solidarity, authoritarianism, and sometimes the exclusion of females and minority officers.

POLICY Decisions or actions that address particular issues or problems.

POLITICAL ERA OF POLICING This era of policing (1840–1930) is characterized by police officers seeking an intimate relationship with the community and politics heavily influencing police departments and police practices.

POVERTY LINE The income level at which people are entitled to public assistance such as welfare.

PREDICTIONS Projections of expected future developments based on instinctual feelings (or "gut feelings") that lack scientific validity.

PREJUDICE A negative attitude toward certain people based solely on their membership in a particular group.

PREJUDICED DISCRIMINATOR An individual who has negative feelings toward a particular group or groups and translates these sentiments into unequal and negative treatment of people in that group.

PREJUDICED NON-DISCRIMINATOR An individual who might be called a closet bigot; someone who is prejudiced against members of some groups but does not translate these attitudes into discriminatory practices.

PRELIMINARY HEARING A stage in criminal case processing in which a prosecutor demonstrates to a judge why charges have been filed and justifies continued processing.

PRE-SERVICE TRAINING Training which occurs prior to one's formal participation on the job. It typically begins at an accredited academy for police and corrections officers.

PRESIDENT'S COMMISSION ON LAW ENFORCEMENT AND ADMINISTRATION OF JUSTICE Also known as the President's Crime Commission, this group focused on enhancing professionalization of policing and police officers. It suggested hiring more members of minority groups and encouraging departments to become more community-oriented.

PRESSURE PUNKS Inmates who submit to homosexual behavior because they have been threatened or raped by other prisoners.

PRETRIAL MOTIONS Motions offered in court prior to the trial in which an attorney seeks an order of the court. These motions are presented to a judge and can be a determining factor in the outcome of a case.

PRETRIAL RELEASE Releasing defendants prior to trial. Release can be secured monetarily, as in the case of bail, or non-financially, such as release on recognizance.

PRISON Correctional facilities that incarcerate inmates serving sentences of one year or more.

PRISONIZATION Inmate adaptation to prison culture. A social and physical transformation of the individual in an effort to compensate for the pains of imprisonment.

PRISON PLAY-FAMILIES An aspect of the social structure of prisons in which inmates assume the roles of different family members. Play-families are more common in female prisons than in male institutions.

PRISON RAPE ELIMINATION ACT An act passed in 2003 that was designed to address prison rape through developing standards to prevent incidents of sexual violence in prison, including a zero tolerance policy and emphasizing research and information gathering.

PROBATION Offender supervision in the community in lieu of incarceration.

PROBLEM-ORIENTED POLICING A four-step approach to addressing specific crimes in the community. The steps include scanning communities to identify a problem, analyzing the nature and extent of the problem, responding to the problem, and assessing whether or not the problem is properly addressed.

PROHIBITION The period (1919–1933) in which the sale, transport, or manufacturing of alcohol was criminalized.

PROXEMICS The space between the communicator and his or her audience.

PUBLIC DEFENDERS Attorneys who work in offices that exist solely to provide indigent representation. They face many challenges, including responsibility for large caseloads and limited resources.

PUBLIC POLICY Decisions or actions that address particular issues or problems and are supported by public resources and enforced by the legal system.

PUNK A homosexual inmate with one of the lowest statuses in the institution. They are despised by inmates who see homosexual behavior as the result of either weakness in the face of pressure or a willingness to sacrifice his manhood to obtain goods and services.

QUALITATIVE APPROACHES Consideration of non-numerical trends and patterns in attempt to anticipate future developments and changes.

QUANTITATIVE ANALYSES The use of statistics and trends to anticipate changes in society.

QUEEN A male inmate who prefers male sexual partners.

RACIAL PROFILING Recognizing individuals as suspects based merely upon race.

RECIDIVISM RATE The rate related to which individuals commit an undesirable act after one has been treated, or experienced a negative consequence for that behavior. It is also known as the re-offending rate.

RECONSTRUCTION A new social, political, and economic portrait of the South created after slavery was abolished.

RECONSTRUCTION ACT OF 1867 As act that required compliance with Reconstruction. According to the act, each Southern state was controlled by a military governor until a new state constitution could be written.

RED-LIGHT DISTRICT Area of a city frequented by prostitutes.

RED POWER MOVEMENT A movement that was similar to the Black Power movement for African Americans in that it attempted to gain economic, social, and political equality for Native Americans.

REENTRY An inmate's return to society.

REFORM ERA OF POLICING Also known as the progressive era, it was a time (1930–1980) characterized by police-community relations suffering and police becoming increasingly reliant on technology and overly concerned with efficiency.

REHABILITATION Attempts to "cure" or "fix" the ills leading to an offender's behavior.

REINTEGRATION Offenders reintegrating, or readjusting to life outside prison.

REPATRIATION A government-sponsored deportation program to send Chicanos back to Mexico.

REPRIEVE A type of clemency which involves the postponement of a sentence. It is typically associated with delaying an execution.

RESTRICTIVE COVENANTS A private contract between neighborhood property owners which stipulated that property could not be sold or rented to certain minority groups, thus ensuring minorities could not live in the area.

RETRIBUTION Punishment, or the "eye for an eye" approach.

REVERSE DISCRIMINATION The belief that efforts to remedy past mistakes in the treatment of minority groups are biased against members of the majority.

ROLE The behavior that is expected of an individual who maintains a particular status.

SANCTUARY LAWS Laws that prohibit police officers from inquiring about a suspect's immigration status.

SCENARIOS A method of forecasting the future in which narratives are used to describe anticipated future events and developments.

"SCHOOL-TO-PRISON PIPELINE" A term which refers to the increasing patterns of students having contact with the justice system as a result of more punitive approaches to addressing school-related problems.

SECESSION The process in which minority groups willingly depart from their country, perhaps for an opportunity to create their own society.

SEGREGATION The dominant group coexisting with the minority group, however, efforts are made to limit contact between the dominant group and minority members.

SENTENCING GUIDELINES Guidelines used by some jurisdictions to provide consistency and parity in sentencing decisions. They involve a risk assessment of the offender based on current offense and past history.

SETOFFS Deductions from the money due equal to the cost of federal services provided to a tribe.

SETTING The physical scene that ordinarily must exist if the actors are to perform.

SEX The biological characteristics that distinguish males and females.

SEXUAL ORIENTATION A term used to describe a sexual attraction toward people either of the same sex, the opposite sex, or both.

SHOWING ONLY THE END PRODUCT Nondisclosure of all that precedes a particular performance.

SITUATIONAL HOMOSEXUALITY Instances in which homosexual behavior occurs between two otherwise heterosexuals.

SLAVE CODES Laws regulating slave behavior.

SLAVE PATROLS Considered by some as the first American police departments, slave patrols were established as early as the 1740s. The patrols were tasked with preventing slave revolts and apprehending runaway slaves.

SNAKEHEADS Chinese human smugglers who lead illegal immigrants across borders.

SOCIAL CONSTRUCTION OF RACE The concept in which every culture must determine which physical features are used to define membership in certain races.

SOCIAL CONSTRUCTION OF REALITY The process through which people mentally construct ideas about phenomena and thus create a reality.

SOCIAL GROUPS Two or more individuals regularly interacting and feeling a sense of solidarity or common identity. Social groups typically share some norms and values while working to achieve common goals.

SOCIAL INTERACTION The process through which individuals act and react in relation to other individuals.

SOCIAL JUSTICE A perspective of justice that considers how a society provides for the needs of its members and whether or not it treats its subgroups equally.

STATUS The social position maintained by an individual.

STATUS OFFENDERS Youth who violate the law by engaging in acts that are prohibited for people younger than a certain age, such as truancy, running away, or underage drinking.

SUBCULTURE The meanings, values, and behavior patterns unique to a particular group in a given society.

SUMMONS A document informing individuals of their call to jury duty.

SWEAT LODGES Small huts in which Native American ceremonies are held to cleanse spirits in a religious rite of purification and penance.

SYMBOLIC ASSAILANT Particular individuals who are perceived by police officers to be a potential source of violence or as an enemy to be reckoned with.

SYMBOLIC REPRESENTATION Making our courts more representative of all racial/ethnic groups.

SYMBOLS Items used to represent something else.

TECHNICAL VIOLATION Misbehavior by a probationer or parolee that is not by itself a criminal offense and generally does not result in arrest. Serious technical violations or continuous misbehavior, however, while on probation or parole can result in re-incarceration.

TERMINATION ACT An act passed by Congress in 1953 which led to the termination of thirteen tribes between 1945 and 1962. The act also meant that certain tribes would lose tax-exempt status for their lands.

"THREE STRIKES AND YOU'RE OUT" SENTENCING A sentencing structure targeted toward repeat offenders. "Three strikes" legislation demonstrates the public's disdain for crime and an attempt to target those who seem undeterred by criminal law and punishment. Three strikes laws vary among the states that use them, with offenders in certain jurisdictions facing life sentences following a third felony.

TOKENS Individuals from underrepresented groups who are being hired, or received their position, solely because of affirmative action policies, regardless of their ability to perform the job.

TRAINING SCHOOLS Facilities which replaced and supplemented houses of refuge. Compared to houses of refuge, training schools placed a greater emphasis on education and vocational training.

TRANSFER The relocation of a case from the jurisdictions of the juvenile court to an adult court.

TRIAD SUBCULTURE The customs, beliefs, and practices of triad societies, which were created by ousted Chinese officials and the alienated poor in the seventeenth century in efforts to overthrow the government.

TRIBAL COURTS Courts that allow tribes the authority to hear and decide cases relating to life on the reservation without interference of traditional U.S. courts.

ULTRAMASCULINITY A primary concern for many prison inmates. The inmate subculture emphasizes being strong.

UNDERPOLICING Actions not taken by the police to protect members of minority groups.

UNPREJUDICED DISCRIMINATOR A person who treats members of some groups unequally not because they have any personal animosity towards them but because it is simply advantageous to do so.

UNPREJUDICED NON-DISCRIMINATOR An individual who accepts other racial or ethnic groups both in belief and practice. They embrace the idea of difference, of cultural diversity as a healthy concept, and do not try to impose their own cultural and social ideas on to others.

UPWARD SOCIAL MOBILITY Moving up a level in social status.

U.S. PAROLE COMMISSION The group which oversees federal parolees.

U.S. PROBATION AND PRETRIAL SERVICES SYSTEM The group responsible for, among other things, assisting the federal courts with pretrial practices and supervising federal probationers.

VENIRE A jury pool from which prospective jurors are selected and questioned.

VICARIOUS HASSLING Hassling individuals without cause.

VOCALICS Also known as paralanguage, it refers to vocal characteristics such as inflection, tone, accent, rate, pitch, volume, and vocal interrupters.

VOIR DIRE The process of questioning potential jurors regarding their suitability to serve on a jury.

VOLUNTARY MIGRATION The process involving people who willingly immigrate to a new country looking for a better life.

VOLUNTARY PLACEMENTS Youths referred to detention facilities because either their parents turned them over to a social service agency, or the agency placed them because they committed delinquent acts but were not formally adjudicated.

VOTING RIGHTS ACT An act that encouraged Blacks about their role in the political process and prohibited discrimination with regard to voting rights.

WAIVE JURISDICTION The relocation of a case from the jurisdictions of the juvenile court to an adult court.

WOLF Also known as the jocker, this type of inmate is viewed by his fellow inmates as a "man." To remain a "man" and still engage in homosexual acts, the individual has to present an image of exaggerated toughness.

YAKUZA The Japanese version of organized crime.

YELLOW PERIL A fear-based "threat" that contributed to strict immigration laws and the imprisonment of American citizens.

CREDITS

INDEX

Note: Page numbers followed by 'f' and 'p' refers to figures and photos.